Media Worlds

Media Worlds

Anthropology on New Terrain

EDITED BY

Faye D. Ginsburg,

Lila Abu-Lughod,

and Brian Larkin

UNIVERSITY OF CALIFORNIA PRESS

Berkeley   Los Angeles   London

University of California Press
Berkeley and Los Angeles, California

University of California Press, Ltd.
London, England

© 2002 by the Regents of the University of California

Library of Congress Cataloging-in-Publication Data

Media worlds : anthropology on new terrain / edited by Faye D.
  Ginsburg, Lila Abu-Lughod, and Brian Larkin.
      p. cm.
  Includes bibliographical references and index.
     ISBN 0-520-22448-5 (Cloth : alk. paper)—
  ISBN 0-520-23231-3 (Paper : alk. paper)
     1. Mass media and culture. I. Ginsburg, Faye D.
  II. Abu-Lughod, Lila. III. Larkin, Brian.
  P94.6 .M426   2002
  302.23—dc21

                                    2002002312

Manufactured in the United States of America
11   10   09   08   07   06   05   04   03   02
10   9   8   7   6   5   4   3   2   1

For Annie, Sinéad, Adrian, Justine, and Samantha,
whose media worlds will be even fuller than ours.

It is often said that [media have] altered our world. In the same way, people often speak of a new world, a new society, a new phase of history, being created—"brought about"—by this or that new technology: the steam engine, the automobile, the atomic bomb. Most of us know what is generally implied when such things are said. But this may be the central difficulty: that we have got so used to statements of this general kind, in our most ordinary discussions, that we fail to realise their specific meanings. . . .

Yet all questions about cause and effect, as between technology and a society, are intensely practical. Until we have begun to answer them, we really do not know, in any particular sense, whether, for example, we are talking about a technology or about the uses of a technology; about necessary institutions or particular and changeable institutions; about a content or about a form. And this is not only a matter of intellectual uncertainty; it is a matter of social practice.

RAYMOND WILLIAMS
Television: Technology and Cultural Form

CONTENTS

ILLUSTRATIONS

PREFACE

This volume represents much of the exciting work being done in the emerging field of the anthropology of media. Although we tried to be comprehensive, we could not, of course, include all the fine work currently being done in this area, particularly by younger scholars and those working on related topics such as the Internet and new media, photography, journalism, and music. We also do not include classic studies that laid the groundwork for our own efforts because it was our intention to highlight current research, although we discuss much of that scholarship in the introduction. Any omissions are simply due to the constraints of space. And we look forward in the future to seeing the work of others join ours in print, knowing that the field is developing quickly.

As the volume editors, our major debts are, first, to the contributors to this volume for their innovative ideas and research, and second, to each other because this has been such a wonderfully collaborative enterprise. Although our initial paths to this work were varied (as we elaborate below), this volume came out of a larger project in which we all participated while at New York University: the Graduate Program in Culture and Media, a joint training program for students in Anthropology and Cinema Studies and the interdisciplinary Center for Media, Culture, and History. This institutional focus at NYU has enriched us with graduate students and colleagues (some of whose work is represented in this volume) who have stimulated us, shaped our thinking, and convinced us that this is indeed an important topic with the potential to transform anthropology and media studies.

Lila Abu-Lughod's interest in media developed in the 1980s while doing fieldwork in Egypt with the Awlad 'Ali Bedouin, where she observed that local popular song culture was being commercialized and that generational conflicts were emerging in national media forms such as radio soap operas.

These phenomena fueled her discomfort with her own earlier tendencies, within the conventions of anthropology, to represent other societies as not part of "modernity" and to treat culture and cultures as bounded. Her desire to think more about forms of national culture that traversed communities found encouragement in the project Arjun Appadurai and Carol Breckenridge were then initiating on transnational cultural studies—what became the journal *Public Culture.* Her focus on the cultural politics of the nation-state developed especially in relation to the project "Questions of Modernity" that she and Tim Mitchell pursued throughout the 1990s, which brought together scholars of the Middle East and South Asia and gave her an education in postcolonial studies. But her understanding of media theory and issues came directly from the rich intellectual stimulation provided by the faculty and students in the Anthropology Department at NYU, and especially those in the Culture and Media Program. Her debts to Faye Ginsburg, who profoundly shaped her thinking about media and other aspects of our social and political worlds, are deep. The interest in media at NYU is extensive, reaching many other parts of the university. Most relevant for Abu-Lughod were the film festivals organized through the Kevorkian Center for Near Eastern Studies, with help from Ella Shohat, Shiva Balaghi, Viola Shafik, Walter Armbrust, and others, and the students and faculty interested in South Asia, including Teja Ganti and Anupama Rao. Finally, as any teacher does, she learned from the remarkable graduate students at NYU as they wrote research proposals and dissertations and discussed books and ideas in courses ranging from "Culture and the Nation" to "Theories of Modernity." Her thanks go to all of them, especially Teja Ganti, Sherine Hamdy, Ayse Parla, Elizabeth Smith, and Jessica Winegar. Those who contributed more directly to her research on Egyptian television are legion and are thanked separately at the end of her chapter in this book and in other publications.

Faye Ginsburg's work in the ethnography of media was shaped by her long-standing interest in social movements and the place of media in them; her background in visual anthropology—still inspired by her studies with Jean Rouch and his theory and practice of "anthropologie partagée"; and her ongoing conversations with fellow travelers Elaine Charnov, Jean Paul Colleyn, Jeff Himpele, David and Judith MacDougall, George Marcus, Howard Morphy, Harald Prins, Jay Ruby, Lucien Taylor, Terry Turner, and Elizabeth Weatherford. When she was asked by the late Annette Weiner (then chair of the Anthropology Department) and Brian Winston (former chair of Cinema Studies) to create a program in visual anthropology in 1986 at NYU—what became the Graduate Program in Culture and Media—she chose to respond to critiques of the field by developing a program that included curriculum on how media were being taken up in communities that had traditionally been the objects of ethnographic representation. This work offered an exciting way to rethink some of the questions about reception, reflexivity, and the politics and poetics of representation that have been central to visual anthropology. Simultaneously, indigenous media opened up thinking about the role of media as a dimension of cultural activism in identity-based social movements and became a major preoccupation of her research and program building over the past decade. She has learned an enormous amount from the people in the field, some of whom have also been visitors at the Center for Media, Culture, and History, which she directs; and from discussions with NYU colleagues: Fred Myers, without whom none of this would be possible, Barbara Abrash, Manthia Diawara, Steve Feld, Meg McLagan, Toby Miller, Bob Stam, and George Stoney. And she found working with Lila Abu-Lughod and Brian Larkin exhilarating, as each brought different insights to the shaping of the book. Last but not least she is grateful for the continuing intellectual excitement provided by present and former students in the Program in Culture and Media at NYU, in particular Tom Bikales, Teja Ganti, Alison Griffiths, Alexandra Juhasz, Brian Larkin, Jerry Lombardi, Maureen Mahon, Erica Wortham, Pegi Vail, and Kirsten Wehner. They are always a reminder of why this work matters.

Brian Larkin came to the ethnography of media from a background in British cultural studies. His research on media and popular culture in Nigeria led him to examine the role of cinema in the elaboration of colonial and postcolonial modernity. This examination in turn led in different directions: from examining the alternative worlds cinema transports one to, to analyzing the social spaces that theaters create around them as part of the evolution of colonial urbanism. Drawing on work in early cinema, African popular culture, and media theory, he began to examine the materiality of media technologies and the dialectic between the disciplinary power of technology (in the context of colonialism and the postcolonial state) and the unexpected way technologies are reworked within local cultural logics. His ideas about media as well as on Indian film and Africa have emerged in close dialogue with others and with so much intellectual osmosis that it is difficult to know where the ideas originated. Meg McLagan in particular constantly provoked his investigation of how other social arenas such as politics and religion were intimately caught up with spectacular mediation; and the work of Teja Ganti, Alison Griffiths, Jon Haynes, and Birgit Meyer on Indian films, early cinema, and Nigerian and Ghanaian video films provided never-ending dialogue. As a student at NYU, Larkin profited immensely from the advice and ideas of T. O. Beidelman, Faye Ginsburg, Lila Abu-Lughod, Maureen Mahon, and Erica Wortham. His work in Nigeria was furthered greatly by the ideas, stimulation, and support of Rudi Gaudio, Abdullahi Mahadi (and the Arewa House Center for Historical Documentation), Conerly Casey and Auwalu Hamza (and the Kano State History and Culture Bureau), Phil Shea, Alaine Hutson, Haj. Fatimah Palmer, and Sean Stilwell.

Special thanks from all of us are due to Alyshia Galvez, who did an extraordinary job of preparing the artwork for this book, and Pegi Vail, who along with Lisa Stefanoff and Dimitra Doukas provided expert assistance in the final preparation of the manuscript. We are grateful to Naomi Schneider and Sue Heinemann, editors at the University of California Press, and assistants Ellie Hickerson and Kristina Kite for their support and enthusiasm, and to Jay Ruby, Lucien Taylor, Danny Miller, Ella Shohat, Bob Stam, and anonymous reviewers for their insightful comments. We also want to acknowledge Mary Murrell of Princeton University Press, who first encouraged us to organize this volume.

Tobias Wendl and Heike Behrend, our colleagues in Germany, were extremely generous in allowing us to use several images from their groundbreaking collection (and exhibition) on African popular photography, *Snap Me One! Studiofotografen in Afrika* (Munich: Prestel, 1998). And we are especially grateful to the Ghanaian studio photographer Philip Apagya, who kindly allowed us to use his image on our cover; to the renowned Australian cartoonist/philosopher Michael Leunig for use of his witty cartoon "The Consumers"; to Mary Peacock and the estate of Jules Backus for the use of his dystopic "TV Head" photograph; and to Preminda Jacob for her spectacular photo of Tamil political and film celebrity giant "cutouts."

Finally, we offer our ongoing gratitude to our partners, Fred Myers, Tim Mitchell, and Meg McLagan, who shared in our research, offered advice on our writing, and sacrificed their time to let us bring this book to fruition; and for their constant reminder of the central role of the imagination in social life, to our children, Samantha Myers, Adrian and Justine Mitchell, and Sinéad and Annie Larkin.

Media Worlds

"The Consumers," 1984, by Michael Leunig (Courtesy Michael Leunig)

Introduction

Faye D. Ginsburg, Lila Abu-Lughod, and Brian Larkin

The questions this book addresses about the place of media in the world are not new; Raymond Williams, among others, wrote about them over a quarter-century ago. But the questions feel more pressing now because the ubiquity of media worldwide means that anthropologists encounter it in the diverse places where we work. This empirically driven sense of urgency led Arjun Appadurai to invent the concept of "mediascapes" in an article whose subtitle—"Notes and Queries for a Transnational Anthropology" (1991)—deliberately recalls an earlier period of disciplinary self-definition in order to signal the centrality of mass media to life in the late twentieth century and the concomitant requirement that anthropology explore its analytic and practical significance. A decade later, this collection of essays by anthropologists suggests that we need no longer lament, as Debra Spitulnik did in her comprehensive review essay in the early 1990s, that "there is as yet no 'anthropology of mass media'" (1993: 293). We now recognize the sociocultural significance of film, television, video, and radio as part of everyday lives in nearly every part of the world, and we bring distinctive theoretical concerns and methodologies to our studies of these phenomena.

As we have recognized the place of media in a critical anthropological project that refuses reified boundaries of place and culture, so we have attempted to use anthropology to push media studies into new environments and examine diverse media practices that are only beginning to be mapped. Media reception occurs "beyond the living room" and media production "beyond the studio" not only because they occur in places like the Amazonian rainforest or the Australian outback but also because, as Roger Silverstone notes, regarding television watching, for example, they occur as part of "a set of daily practices and discourses . . . through which that complex act is itself constituted" (1994: 133). It is the anthropological commitment to a wider concept of ethnography that gives us purchase on the wider social fields within which media practices operate. Collectively, then, our work takes advantage of and pushes forward the theoretical insights and methodological sophistication of our own discipline as well as neighboring fields with which we engage.

Ethnography of media expands "what counts" in a variety of ways. Anthropologists, for example, track the social players involved when one "follows the thing" (Marcus 1995)—a film or television serial as it moves from elite directors to consumers (Abu-Lughod 1995, 1997; Dickey 1993; Mankekar 1993a, 1993b; Skuse 1999) or an object like a cassette recorder (Manuel 1993), a radio (Spitulnik, this volume), or even radio sound itself (Tacchi 1998) as it circulates through various milieux. Such strategies help us see not only how media are embedded in people's quotidian lives but also how consumers and producers are themselves imbricated in discursive universes, political situations, economic circumstances, national settings, historical moments, and transnational flows, to name only a few relevant contexts.

As anthropologists, we take for granted a "global" perspective on media. Cross-cultural work is fundamental to our project; indeed, some have expanded on the textual traditions of film studies to show how one might look at "a film's anthropology" (Caton 1999; Fischer 1995). The kind of alternative circuits that we routinely encounter in our work—the spread of illegal cable networks or the widespread presence of pirate videos as a means of media exhibition outside the West—are rarely counted in the statistics about the U.S. or global media industries on which many accounts of transnational media are based. Indeed it is one of our arguments that the construction of media theory in the West, with rare exceptions (e.g., Sinclair, Jacka, and Cunningham 1996; Sreberny-Mohammadi and Mohammadi 1994), has established a cultural grid of media theory with the effect of bringing into visibility only certain types of media technologies and practices. These lacunae are now being addressed from both within and outside media and cinema studies, and the work in this volume is aimed at remapping the diversity of media worldwide.

While anthropologists are always firmly grounded in the local, we recognize that certain sweeping technological and institutional changes have had irreversible consequences over the past decades. The strong historical link between broadcast television and twentieth-century nation-building, for example, relied on a capital-intensive terrestrial technology that could be controlled and tied to state interests with relative ease. Satellites and Internet technologies, however, have opened up other kinds of spaces that cross cultural and geopolitical borders more easily, have increased privatization of media ownership, and have created new markets. They have also facilitated new social configurations. This occurs through access determined by class distinctions or diasporic connections. New technologies have also exacerbated what Toby Miller has termed "the new international division of cultural labor"—exporting media labor to the Third World—that has accompanied "the shift from the spatial sensitivities of electrics to the spatial insensitivities of electronics" (1998: 377). These technologies have facilitated the creation of privatized media empires (Schiller 1969, 1991), and at the same time, research on video culture and other forms of decentralized "small media" suggests the emergence of a "new media era" that is more fragmented and diverse in its economic and social organization (Larkin 2000), more characteristic of the expansion of informal markets under neoliberalism and the fluidity of late capitalism than the older forms of mass media. Situating media as a social practice within these shifting political and cultural frames enables us to speak to the larger concerns we share with many of our colleagues in media studies: how media enable or challenge the workings of power and the potential of activism; the enforcement of inequality and the sources of imagination; and the impact of technologies on the production of individual and collective identities.

ANTHROPOLOGISTS AND MEDIA

For many years mass media were seen as almost a taboo topic for anthropology, too redolent of Western modernity for a field identified with tradition, the non-Western, and the vitality of the local. As a result, anthropologists came to the study of media a little later than colleagues in some other fields. Despite some singular efforts to study feature and propaganda films as cultural documents in the 1940s (Mead and Metraux 1953; Bateson 1943), the social relations of the film world of Hollywood in the 1950s and the impact of mass media in Africa (Powdermaker 1950, 1967), and Navajo filmmaking in the 1960s (Worth, Adair, and Chalfen [1972] 1997)—what Sol Worth called "the anthropology of visual communication" (1980)—it was not until the late 1980s that anthropologists began to turn systematic attention to media as a social practice.

The anthropology of media emerged from a particular historical and theoretical conjuncture: the ruptures in anthropological theory and methodology of the 1980s and 1990s, and the development of an "anthropology of the present" (Fox 1991) that engages and analyzes the transformations of the past half-century in which media play an increasingly prominent part. Alongside a growing acceptance of work in North America and Europe came more attention to the economic, political, and cultural traffic between urban and rural and "First" and "Third" Worlds. This relocation of geographic and theoretical focus meant that anthropologists were both working in societies where media were more central and confronting the fact that forms of electronic media were penetrating societies once seen as beyond their reach.

These shifts, in turn, catalyzed a critical rethinking of one of our most productive notions—culture—and the parameters of our key methodology: in-depth, intensive, and long-term ethnographic fieldwork (Abu-Lughod 1997; Gupta and Ferguson 1997a, 1997b; Marcus and Fischer 1986; Ortner 1999). Increasingly, our theory and practice are unbounded, multisited, traveling, or "itinerant" (as Schein proposes in this volume), a transformation that is particularly evident for those studying media.

Anthropologists doing research on and writing ethnographies of media have come to this work in different ways. The chapters in this book reflect diverse and often overlapping intellectual legacies from within the discipline and drawing from related fields. For many of us, our interest was first piqued by unexpected encounters with the popularity, power, or passion of media in particular locales (e.g., Fischer 1990; Kottak 1990; A. Lyons 1990; H. Lyons 1990). A number of the contributors to this volume (Ginsburg, Turner, and Prins) link their work to the rethinking of visual anthropology over the past couple of decades (see, e.g., Banks and Morphy 1997; Ginsburg 1994, 1998; MacDougall 1998; Ruby 2000; Taylor 1994). This critical revision of the field has been catalyzed by the increasing accessibility of media to people who traditionally had been in front of the lens, as well as by an intellectual shift that has expanded questions about the politics and poetics of documentary representation—how anthropological filmmakers represent others (e.g., Prins 1997; Ruby 1991, 1995)—to encompass issues of how media are being taken up and made meaningful in different societies and popularized in our own. This revisionist work in visual anthropology also draws on postcolonial studies (as well as film practices) addressing the complexities of cross-cultural representation (Marks 2000; Rony 1996; Russell 1999; Shohat and Stam 1994), as well as minority (Juhasz 1995; Downmunt 1993; Riggins 1992), diasporic (Cunningham and Sinclair 2000; Gillespie 1995; Kolar-Panov 1997; McLagan 1996; Schein, this volume; Naficy 1993), and small media practices (Manuel 1993; Sreberny-Mohammadi and Mohammadi 1994). For those whose emphasis is on the institutional sites for the production of media work, Pierre Bourdieu's (1993) framing of the field of cultural production—the system of relations (and struggles for power) among agents or institutions engaged in generating the value of works of art, while creating cultural capital for themselves—has been especially influential.

Others were influenced by the contemporaneous turn toward ethnography in cultural studies, which opened up a common intellectual and methodological space, especially for those interested in media (Gurevitch et al. 1982). British cultural studies explored mass media's centrality to contemporary projects of cultural hegemony, focusing on media consumption as one of a wide range of active forms of social engagement through which it is reproduced but also altered and resisted (Fiske 1987; Hall 1980, 1997). This work, in turn, laid the groundwork for a range of groundbreaking reception studies, such as Radway's influential study of women's interpretations of romance novels (1984), research on the responses of culturally diverse viewers of American exported television shows (Liebes and Katz 1990; Ang 1985), and ethnographies revealing the creativity of an appropriative and irreverent fan culture for television shows such as *Star Trek* (Bacon-Smith 1992; Penley 1997; Jenkins 1992). Equally influential were those who looked more broadly at the place of television in the construction of "the nation" (and other abstractions) in everyday life (Morley 1986, 1992; Silverstone 1994; Silverstone and Hirsch 1992), and the construction of the notion of audience on the part of media industries (Ang 1996), to mention only a few key works.[1]

Many anthropologists found media a rich site for research on cultural practices and circulation that took seriously the multiple levels of identification—regional, national, and transnational—within which societies and cultures produce subjects. The work of Benedict Anderson (1991) and Jürgen Habermas (1989) have been central to those concerned with studying and theorizing the cultural effects of flows of people, ideas, and objects, flows crucially mediated by communication technologies. Both Anderson and Habermas have had a considerable influence in anthropology because their supple concepts—"imagined communities" and "the public sphere" respectively—offered means of theorizing the formation of collectivities that cross ruptures of space and are outside formal definitions of "culture." In the case of Habermas, the well-known criticisms of his work (Calhoun 1992; Fraser 1993; Robbins 1993) have forced attention to the formation of alternative or counterpublic spheres (see Himpele, this volume; Baker 1994; Diawara 1994; Eickelman and Anderson 1999). A number of writers—in anthropology, cultural studies, and other fields—have also used these ideas to extend Lacan's psycholanalytic notion of the imaginary (1967) as a way to comprehend the construction of "national imaginaries," when media are harnessed by state and commercial interests as technologies of personhood.[2]

Appadurai's work on public culture and global cultural flows draws on Anderson and on Habermas, synthesizing these frameworks with contemporary anthropological concerns and methods as well as newer media forms. His influence for this volume is most felt in his insistence on the centrality of these media to the articulation of national and transnational with local processes and to the significance of "the imagination" in the production of culture and identity in the contemporary world (Appadurai 1991). Along with other recent work that rethinks material culture and exchange theory (Marcus and Myers 1995; Miller 1995; Thomas 1991), Appadurai's work draws on anthropology's longstanding theoretical interest in the complex subtleties of exchange—of objects, narratives, and technologies—and the implications of these processes for culture-making and personhood (Mauss 1967; A. Weiner 1992). Objects shift in meaning as they move through regimes and circuits of exchange. This argument, like that of active audience theorists, challenges the ontology of the text, arguing instead that the meaning of texts or objects is enacted through practices of reception. The usefulness of exchange theory to media studies can be seen clearly in the work of Daniel Miller (1992), whose study of American soap operas in Trinidad, part of a wider project on consumption under capitalism, reveals an active process of societal self-production through which people incorporate objects into their own social value systems.[3]

The anthropological studies of media presented in this book challenge stereotypes of media ethnography as narrowly empiricist versions of market research—querying television watchers in their living rooms about what they *really* think of certain programs, without placing them in wider structures or recognizing their complexity. The contributors, drawing on a range of scholarly traditions, take for granted the necessity of linking media production, circulation, and reception in broad and intersecting social and cultural fields: local, regional, national, transnational. They examine a range of phenomena in order to understand the social impact and cultural meaning of media in the everyday lives of those we study. Through grounded analyses of the practices, cultural worlds, and even fantasies of social actors as they interact with media in a variety of social spaces, we have begun to unbundle assumptions regarding the political economy and social relations shaping media production, circulation, and reception, and the impacts of media technologies themselves.

THE SOCIAL FIELDS OF MEDIA

Although the essays in this book reflect diverse intellectual legacies, they all bring to the study of media anthropology's capacious methodology. Many ethnographies of media strategically include both producers and audiences in the query, as well as intertextual sources through which meaning is constituted, as Sara Dickey did in her groundbreaking study of the significance for the urban poor of Tamil popular cinema, an industry that has a remarkable influence in the creation of political celebrity in South India, part of a "vast system of popular literature, greeting cards and posters, clothing, fashions, gossip, legends, memories, and activities supporting the stars" (1993: 41). Others have underscored the importance of the neglected area of distribution. Power and status are signified through spatial and temporal dimensions of exhibition, a central process through which media help constitute and reflect social and religious difference in nation-states (Himpele 1996; Rajagopal 2001). Others also point to the significance of exhibition sites—from the architecture of movie theaters as a diacritic of social class and modernity (or its lack), to the social space of cinema as an arena of social experimentation (Armbrust 1998; Hughes 2000; Larkin, this volume).

Film festivals are analyzed as loci for the consolidation of new cultural formations (Bikales 1997), professional subcultures (Lutkehaus 1995; Nichols
1994), and regional and national claims (Ganti 1998).

Although the authors all situate their work in particular historical moments and political economies, producing what Purnima Mankekar aptly calls
"conjunctural ethnography" (1999: 49), the different kinds of media practices represented in this volume can be placed on a sociopolitical continuum reflected in the different sections of the book. On one end are the more
classic formations of mass media produced through large governmental and
commercial institutions intent on constituting modern citizens and consumers. Anthropological research on these kinds of mediations, which include popular soap operas, telenovelas, and melodramatic serials focuses on
the complex ways in which national cinemas, television, advertising, and development media operate from production to distribution to consumption
(see Abu-Lughod, Dávila, Ganti, Hamilton, Mandel, Mankekar, Wilk, and
Yang, all this volume; Hamburger 1999). This work assumes some social segregation between producers and audiences and tracks the often unstable relation between intention and effects.

In the middle range are more reflexive processes in which practical and
imaginative encounters with cinematic or televisual images and narratives
may express and/or constitute a variety of subaltern social and cosmologi-
cal worlds. Such work is typical of diasporic and minoritized communities
as they are reframed under different regimes of power and in diverse cultural contexts through video, television shows, films, and even popular graphics (see Hobart, Morris, Pinney, Schein, and Yang, this volume).

On the other end of the continuum are more self-conscious practices, often linked to social movements, in which cultural material is used and strategically deployed as part of a broader project of political empowerment by
indigenous and other disenfranchised groups (Ginsburg, Himpele, Prins,
Turner, and McLagan, this volume). Such work can provide a "third space"
(Bhabha 1989) for the representation of their concerns. However, the negotiation of mass media forms for counterhegemonic purposes is not without compromises. While the authors in this section tend to stress the activism
of the people with whom they work, they also point out how media can facilitate the penetration of state power as well as consumer capital in local societies. In the remainder of this introductory essay, we introduce and discuss
key theoretical issues raised in the various sections of the collection.

CULTURAL ACTIVISM AND THE ACTIVIST IMAGINARY

Since the early 1980s, indigenous and minority peoples have begun to take
up a range of media in order to "talk back" to structures of power that have
erased or distorted their interests and realities. Faye Ginsburg has called this

kind of work "cultural activism," to underscore the sense of both political agency and cultural intervention that people bring to these efforts, part of a spectrum of practices of self-conscious mediation and mobilization of culture that took particular shape beginning in the late twentieth century (1993, 1997). Similarly, George Marcus has coined the term "the activist imaginary" to describe how subaltern groups turn to film, video, and other media not only to "pursue traditional goals of broad-based social change through a politics of identity and representation" but also out of a utopian desire for "emancipatory projects . . . raising fresh issues about citizenship and the shape of public spheres within the frame and terms of traditional discourse on polity and civil society" (1996: 6). The section focuses mainly on indigenous media as a key arena where these processes are being enacted but includes other processes of cultural objectification for strategic political purposes, as in McLagan's essay on Tibetan Buddhist activists and their supporters.

Indigenous media incorporate a distinctive form of cultural activism that has attracted scholarly attention (Asch 1991; Aufderheide 1995; Berger 1995; Carelli 1988; Fleming 1991; Ginsburg 1991; Leuthold 1998; Meadows and Molnar, 2001; Philipsen and Markussen 1995; Prins 1989; Roth 2002; Turner 1991a, 1991b, 1992, 1995; Vail 1997; Weatherford 1990; Wortham 2000).[4] It developed in response to the entry of mass media into the lives of First Nations people, primarily through the imposition of satellites and commercial television. In almost every instance they have struggled to turn that circumstance to their advantage, a point effectively made by activist researcher Eric Michaels in the Central Desert of Australia where, in the 1980s, he worked with Warlpiri people to develop their own low-power television as an alternative to the onslaught of commercial television.[5] Such formations seem particularly well suited for anthropological inquiry: small in scale and sustaining an alternative to the mass media industries that dominate late capitalist societies, they occupy a comfortable position of difference from dominant cultural assumptions about media aesthetics and practices. In addition, indigenous media projects have often been a site for activist participation on the part of anthropologists; they and native peoples alike have been quick to see the political promise and cultural possibilities of indigenously controlled media-making. In this volume, those working with Native Americans (Prins), Aboriginal Australians (Ginsburg), and Amazonian Kayapo (Turner) have helped to produce and/or promote as well as analyze the making of film and video as part of indigenous cultural projects of cultural revival, whether through recording traditional rituals or through the use of video, film, and media events as a persuasive tool for claims to political sovereignty.

Most indigenous media are produced and consumed primarily by people living in remote settlements, although the work circulates to other native communities as well as to nonaboriginal audiences via film festivals, human rights forums, court hearings, and broadcasts. The range of the work is wide, moving from small-scale community-based videos, to broadcast quality television, to major independent art films. Indigenous people who live in or closer to metropoles, such as the urban Australian Aboriginal filmmakers discussed by Ginsburg, participate in a wider world of media imagery production and circulation (e.g., national film and television industries), and feel their claim to an indigenous identity within a more cosmopolitan framework is sometimes regarded as inauthentic. Debates about such work reflect the changing status of "culture," which is increasingly objectified and mediated as it becomes a source of claims for political and human rights both nationally and on the world stage. As Terry Turner has shown regarding the work of Kayapo media-makers, cultural claims "can be converted into political assets, both internally as bases of group solidarity and mobilization, and externally as claims on the support of other social groups, governments and public opinion all over the globe" (1993: 424).

This activist objectification of culture encompasses not only indigenous work but also media being produced by other colonized and minority subjects who have become involved in creating their own representations as a counter to dominant systems, a framework that includes work being done by people with AIDS (Juhasz 1995); Palestinians in Israel's occupied territories (Kuttab 1993); the transnational Hmong refugee community (Schein, this volume), and African American musicians (Mahon 2000a). Appadurai suggests the word "culturalism" to denote the mobilization of identities in which mass media and the imagination play an increasingly significant role (1996).

Part of the attraction of media for these groups is the publicity they generate, a critical component of political and cultural activism in late modernity. Meg McLagan shows the tensions inherent in the Tibet Movement's efforts to publicize their positions in the United States by analyzing celebrity benefits, Buddhist spectacles, and cultural performances. Her analysis of the use of public relations specialists by Tibet activists reveals the contradictions involved in objectifying culture as a strategy for gaining access to media venues and projecting a political movement into national and international visibility (McLagan 1997; also this volume).

The broader question this raises—whether minority or dominated subjects can assimilate media to their own cultural and political concerns or are inevitably compromised by its presence—still haunts much of the research and debate on the topic of the cross-cultural spread of media. In the context of indigenous peoples, some anthropologists have expressed alarm at these developments (Faris 1992); they see these new practices as destructive of cultural difference and the study of such work as "ersatz anthropology" (J. Weiner 1997), echoing the concerns over the destructive effects of mass culture first articulated by intellectuals of the Frankfurt school.[6] Other scholars actively support indigenous media production while recognizing the dilemmas that it presents. Lorna Roth, for example, queries whether a state-supported Aboriginal People's Television Network in Canada is a break-through or a "media reservation" (Roth 2002). Ginsburg suggests that in-digenous media present a kind of Faustian contract with the technologies of modernity, enabling some degree of agency to control representation un-der less-than-ideal conditions (1991). However, the capacity to narrate sto-ries and retell histories from an indigenous point of view—what she calls "screen memories"—through media forms that can circulate beyond the lo-cal has been an important force for constituting claims for land and cultural rights, and for developing alliances with other communities (this volume). Harald Prins (this volume), who has catalyzed indigenous filmmaking for Native American claims to land and cultural rights, nonetheless points out "the paradox of primitivism" in which traditional imagery of indigenous people in documentaries about native rights, though effective (perhaps even essential) as a form of political agency, may distort the cultural processes that indigenous peoples are committed to preserving. Chris Pinney, in contrast, makes a compelling argument that despite the colonial origins of photog-raphy it is now so firmly inserted into everyday religious and secular prac-tice that it is best seen at the confluence of overlapping visual regimes rather than as the province of one (1997: 112).

Meanwhile, as anthropologists and media scholars debate the impact that media technologies might have on the communities with which they work, indigenous media-makers are busy using the technologies for their own pur-poses. Activists are documenting traditional activities with elders; creating works to teach young people literacy in their own languages; engaging with dominant circuits of mass media and projecting political struggles through mainstream as well as alternative arenas; communicating among dispersed kin and communities on a range of issues; using video as legal documents in negotiations with states; presenting videos on state television to assert their presence televisually within national imaginaries; and creating award-winning feature films.

Rather than casting aspersions on these efforts to use media as forms of expressive culture and political engagement, a number of us see in the grow-ing use of film and other mass media an increasing awareness and strategic objectification of culture. As Daniel Miller has argued regarding the grow-ing use of media more generally:

> These new technologies of objectification [such as film, video, and televi-sion] . . . create new possibilities of understanding at the same moment that they pose new threats of alienation and rupture. Yet our first concern is not to resolve these contradictions in theory but to observe how people sometimes resolve or more commonly live out these contradictions in local practice. (D. Miller 1995: 18)

Whatever the contradictions, as new technologies have been embraced as powerful forms of collective self-production, they have enabled cultural activists to assert their presence in the polities that encompass them and to more easily enter into much larger movements for social transformation for the recognition and redress of human and cultural rights, processes in which media play an increasingly important role (Castells 1997).

CULTURAL POLITICS OF NATION-STATES

Although many people consider themselves to belong to subnational or transnational communities, the nation is the primary context for the everyday lives and imaginations of most of the people who produce media and constitute its audiences. Even if nations are always in relations with other nations and transnational entities or ideas (and may be losing sovereignty and power, as Appadurai [1993] and Hannerz [1992] among others have argued), the nation is still a potent frame of reference, especially in the many countries where the state has been the prime actor in the creation and regulation of media networks.

If we accept Anderson's (1991) insight that nations are "imagined communities," we must recognize that media, from the novels and newspapers Anderson discussed to the television broadcasts and video cultures analyzed in this book, play crucial roles in producing nations and shaping national imaginaries. One can analyze, for example, the ways that radio helped create the postcolonial nation in Zambia by formalizing language hierarchies in a multilingual state, influencing speech styles, signifying modernity itself, and even embodying the state (Spitulnik 2001). Or one can, as Mankekar does in this volume, ask how certain popular television serials in India, in this case the televised *Ramayan*, "might have participated in reconfigurations of nation, culture, and community that overlapped with and reinforced Hindu nationalism" in the early 1990s (see also Mankekar 1999). As she argues, the serial was part of a sociohistorical conjuncture in which the discourse of Hindu nationalism was increasingly voluble, even though it was not the intent of the producers to foster communal violence, to create the exclusions felt by some viewers, or to conflate Indian with Hindu culture. Finally, the sense of belonging created in nationalist structures of feeling can also be commodified or produced for specific commercial imperatives, as Arlene Dávila's examination of the construction of "Latinidad" by the U.S. Hispanic advertising industry shows (Dávila, this volume).

Perhaps the most complex theoretical issues arise when we begin to consider the implications of the political uses of media by national or state apparatuses. Most radio and television has been state-controlled or in the hands of culture industry professionals who, as Stuart Hall (1980) has argued, tend to share the "dominant codes" of the nation-state. Censorship and anticipatory self-censorship are the norms. Whether to create loyalty, shape political understandings, foster national development, "modernize," promote family planning, teach privatization and the capitalist ethos, make good socialists, or innocuously entertain, media have been viewed as powerful tools for hegemony or social transformation.

The connections between media and politics can be quite direct, as when state media is controlled, as it is in Egypt, not by the minister of culture but by the minister of information. By contrast, media are often counterhegemonic to certain state interests, as when a Bolivian television host uses the Aymara audience for his program to create a new political party which he heads (see Himpele, this volume); or when Tibetans in exile seeking freedom from control by the Chinese state hire public relations consultants to manage their media campaign in the United States (McLagan, this volume); or when clerics used "small media" like audio cassettes in Iran to mobilize people for a religious revolution (Sreberny-Mohammadi and Mohammadi 1994); or when Palestinians use faxes and cell phones in the *intifada* to coordinate their resistance to Israeli rule.

Three key intellectual issues emerge from these links between media and national politics. First, what is the relationship between media professionals in the "culture industry" and the state? These producers are critical mediators, articulating and translating larger projects. However, it is important to remember that these producers of media are creative individuals, working with their own professional codes, their own career interests, and their own visions, sometimes oppositional because of training under earlier and different conditions or because they represent a new generation with other influences. They also work within organizations—such as the British Broadcasting Corporation (Born 1998), the U.S. Public Broadcast Service (Dornfeld 1998; and this volume), or the training program for would-be soap opera writers set up by the British Know How Fund in Kazakhstan (Mandel, this volume) that establish dynamics of knowledge and power that intersect with state projects in complicated ways. Early studies of cultural imperialism rightly stressed that cultural domination was exported through models of professionalism and professional standards instituted through Western training of non-Western media producers. What Mandel, Born, and other ethnographers of production show, however, is that frequently there is slippage between the standards insisted on by professionals and the way those standards are adopted and transformed in local settings.

Second, one must ask what happens to media when state interests are complex and contradictory. This is especially obvious in many of the countries in which anthropologists work today, places where neoliberalism or structural adjustment policies have been adopted or where socialism is being replaced by "reform" or "transition to the market." Ruth Mandel (this volume) tracks the complex crosscurrents at work, and the conflicts that arose, in making *Crossroads*, the first Kazakhstani soap opera. Initiated by the British Know How Fund to "teach capitalism to the communists," it brought BBC professionals trained in the genre of British realist drama to Kazakhstan to train writers, many of whom had worked in the tradition of Soviet socialist realism, to develop the program. The emerging nation-state tried hard to control the product while the commercial interests it welcomed and its citizen-audiences, newly enamored of American soap opera imports, made other demands. As Mayfair Yang (this volume) notes for post-Mao reform China, a reemergent pan-Chinese nation or alternative community that eludes the state has been encouraged by the introduction of new media forms and the access to films, popular music, and television from beyond the mainland, mostly from Taiwan and Hong Kong. Although eager to keep control over media, the state's cautious embrace of capitalism and encouragement of links (for investment) to overseas Chinese have led to the development of transnational subjectivities and desires that threaten to shake its authority.

Third, one must ask how effective state media products—or any media products, for that matter—are in achieving their goals of influencing audiences. The thorniest questions in media studies are those about reception; the history of attempts to assess the impact of media is discouraging. What anthropology is able to bring to these questions is an exploration of the multiple levels at which failures and successes occur by studying the social fields that structure these engagements and the actual ways that audiences engage with media. Anthropologists have revealed ironies such as the way commercial broadcasts uncontrolled by the state or not linked directly to state interests can have the unintended consequence of bolstering national identity or pride. This seems to have been the case with a popular television show in Puerto Rico that was a vehicle to promote Budweiser beer (Dávila 1999) or with the hookup to satellite that brought U.S. television directly to Belize (Wilk, this volume). But they have also examined the way programs have backfired. State-sponsored television soap operas intended to bolster national sympathies instead foster debate and dissent. In Syria, the debate focused on who has the right to control public representations of Syrian history (Salamandra 1998), while in China the dissent revolved around state repression of intellectuals' challenges to state power (Rofel 1994). Annette Hamilton (this volume) analyzes how the state used mass media to create a sense of the nation in Thailand via a distinctive set of programs aired on national television, alongside intense mass-mediated public spectacles of the royal family, while other media technologies, such as cable and videocassette recorders, were embraced to serve local social concerns.

The challenge is to trace both how and why media messages go awry and yet also how they shape lives, treating audiences neither as resistant heroes to be celebrated nor as duped victims to be pitied. In Thailand, Hamilton argues, the disjunction people perceived between the way national television represented the news and their knowledge of what was going on in the streets may have led them to join in democracy protests. In Egypt, Lila Abu-Lughod (this volume) traces how television melodramas produced by professionals with middle-class assumptions about modernity and the kinds of individuals appropriate to it help stage, and thus foster, the kinds of selves that make good citizens. But she also notes that even those viewers most involved with television participate in other social institutions and engage in other practices, most notably of contemporary religious groups, that powerfully reorient subjectivity. If the messages of state television "go wrong," they do so in patterned ways linked to the larger social fields that offer audiences other interpretive frameworks.

TRANSNATIONAL CIRCUITS

The capacity of mass media to circulate beyond national boundaries implicates it in most transnational processes, whether the borrowing by Australian Aboriginal activists of American songs like "We Shall Overcome" during the heyday of the U.S. civil rights movement (Ginsburg, this volume); or the more contemporary use of Western media for the representations of cultural differences meant to mobilize support for a political cause in another part of the world, as in the case of the Tibetans (McLagan, this volume). Unfortunately, the dominant frameworks for thinking about media's transnational reach have been either globalization or cultural imperialism, which tend to privilege media originating from or dominant in the West, with less attention to other circuits (but see Sinclair, Jacka, and Cunningham 1996).

One of our central concerns, then, is to develop a media theory that is genuinely transnational and helps remap the presence and circulation of specific media forms. From our perspective, media studies deploy a culturally specific cartography whereby only particular media forms and flows have been made visible and are considered sociologically significant. The category "Third World cinema," for instance, has had a somewhat ambiguous relationship to some popular forms.[7] Hindi cinema remains perhaps the most striking example of a non-Western media form with a deep history and wide global reach that has remained largely absent from debates on cultural imperialism and global media in the Western academy. In particular, the popularity of Indian films with Indian and non-Indian audiences in places as diverse as Egypt, Kenya (Fugelsang 1994), Japan, and Nigeria (Larkin 1997) underscores the significance of alternative circuits of media flows that operate outside the West.

A more recent example of media that are "off the map" are video films in Nigeria and Ghana.[8] These video films are commercial and rarely circulate on film festival circuits where the concept of "African cinema" is produced and maintained. Unlike many African films, they circulate locally and are extremely popular. In 1999 the Ghanaian film industry produced over fifty of these narrative dramas, which were shot on video, released at the cinema (through video projection), and sold in markets. This output is perhaps larger than the entire repertoire of Ghanaian feature films, but it pales in comparison with the over 500 films that were produced and released in Nigeria in 1999 alone (Ukah 2000). This staggering growth of an industry that was virtually nonexistent in 1990 is redrawing the media map of West Africa. Ghanaian directors have been overwhelmed by the success of these more violent Nigerian films and feel forced to conform to their narrative styles. The negative influence of Nigerian videos is much more pressing locally than the influence of films from the United States or Hong Kong.[9] Nigerian video films, the regional dominance of Egyptian media in the Arab world, the popularity of Hindi cinema, Aboriginal television productions, and Latin American telenovelas are all examples of alternative productions and circulations of media that are being brought into focus by an emergent transnational perspective in media studies.

Anthropological studies of media in "other" places can reveal the existence and power of circuits that do not include the West. Mayfair Yang and others are critical of the cultural imperialism framework that assumes Western hegemony. Yang's work on mass media and transnational subjectivity in Shanghai tracks a new phenomenon, what she calls a Chinese "traveling culture." Over the past century, media have played a part in transformations of the Chinese state, first in the development of a new national community, then in the creation of a powerful state subjectivity and its effects on the modernist project of the nation-state. In the case of post-Mao China, it is not Western domination but regional/ethnic Chinese capitalist modes of power that are contesting the power of the Chinese state. The result is a "transnational Chinese global media public," a subjectivity detached from the state and linked up, across imaginary space, with other far away Chinese subjectivities, created through the interaction of mainland people with popular culture from Hong Kong and Taiwan. All this is facilitated by satellite dishes, the introduction of new music and programs from other Chinese sites, and the availability of films and television shows that explore what it might mean to be Chinese abroad.

"Transnational subjectification" occurs, with the help of small media, in a different way for a diasporic group living within a nation but with links to distant homelands. Louisa Schein describes how the Hmong, who came to the United States after the end of the Vietnam War, have developed both a pop music world of their own and a thriving video industry. Through these media, Hmong not only create a community and shape its memories and desires, but mark it as transnational, beginning with efforts to show the crucial role played by Hmong who were recruited by the CIA during the Vietnam War. Among the most popular videos are documentaries about "homelands," particularly China, and feature films that involve stories about Hmong who go to these other places where Hmong are supposed to have originated. Some are nostalgic and picturesque representations of Asian homelands and brethren; others are about the relationships being forged between Miao (the Chinese counterparts of the Hmong) and U.S.-based Hmong, relationships that are fraught because of the inequalities apparent in the imbalance of camcorder ownership.

Because anthropologists often site themselves outside the West, even when they examine media circuits originating in the United States or Europe, they find that the local consequences of media flows are not so predictable. Mandel's work on the exportation of British "know-how" about media and capitalism to Kazakhstan shows both that cultural imperialism, built on a particular political and economic scaffolding, is alive and well and that imported formulas, ideas, expertise, and codes of professionalism enter into a local field whose historically specific dynamics of state power, class, ethnicity, consumption patterns, and access to other media products subvert and derail intentions. Richard Wilk, in contrast, shows that, ironically, the introduction in Belize of direct access to U.S. television through satellite hookup actually produced a new sense of coevalness that allowed people in Belize to stop seeing themselves as backward or lagging behind the metropole. Instead, they could come to understand themselves in terms of cultural difference, a process that reinforced a sense of nationhood. Mankekar (1999: 346) has analyzed the introduction of satellite television to India, noting how commercial success for transnational television channels like Star required "Indianization" of their programming and thus a "reterritorialization."

And finally, a key set of issues that anthropologists working with new media maps are well positioned to consider concerns the role of media in the emergence of alternative modernities (Martin-Barbero 1988; Gaonkar 1999; Morley and Robbins 1995; Sreberny-Mohammadi 1996). In his study of media in northern Nigeria, for example, Brian Larkin uses the trope of "parallel modernities" to describe the worlds of those who are not mobile but who nonetheless, through media, "participate in the imagined realities of other cultures as part of their daily lives" through media. Hausa youth can choose between "Hausa or Yoruba videos, Indian, Hong Kong or American films, or videos of Qur'anic *tafsir* (exegesis) by local preachers" (Larkin 1997: 409). He argues that the spectacle and plot of Indian films and their indigenization in a local genre of *soyyaya* books (love stories) as well as in locally produced videos (Larkin 2000; Haynes 2000) offer Hausa youth a medium through which to consider "what it means to be modern and what may be the place of Hausa society within that modernity" (Larkin 1997: 434). Similarly, in his study of youth in Kathmandu, Nepal, Mark Leichty argues that Bombay and Hollywood films, "teen" magazines, pirated cassettes, and interactive radio shows—the cultural economy of a transnational public sphere—provide the experience of modernity as a space of imagined possibilities contained within a commodified logic (1994: 194).

Clearly, any analysis of the subjective and imaginative must be linked to the economic and social. The transnational circuits of media that enable the circulation of ideas and images cannot be understood apart from the political economies that underwrite this circulation, not to mention the technologies. States everywhere attempt to control the mediation of their own representations, and that of others, through regulation, censorship, and control over the means of distribution. Yet as media are implicated in constructions of alternative modernities and local appropriations, they can also uncover the ways in which transnational media flows can decenter nations and produce transnational subjectivities, whether in geolinguistic regions or across long distances.

THE SOCIAL SITES OF PRODUCTION

If mass media presented a kind of forbidden object to anthropologists in non-Western settings, the final boundary (breached only by Powdermaker's prescient study of Hollywood in the 1950s) was fieldwork in the social worlds of media institutions where "dominant ideologies" are produced, in our own as well as other societies. Anthropologists are bringing new methods and insights to the territory already established by a small but significant body of work by sociologists of media who focused in particular on the production of "news" (Gitlin 1983; Pedelty 1995; Silverstone 1985) (a tradition that Bourdieu joined in his lectures and subsequent 1998 book on television).

The more recent work is bifocal, attending to both the institutional structures and the agency and circumstances of cultural producers (Faraday 2000; Mahon 2000b; Marcus 1997). The essays in this volume that focus on media producers cast a wide net, from American educational television, to the Hispanic advertising industry, to decision-making in Bombay's Bollywood, to a popular political talk show in Bolivia. In every case, they make clear the impossibility of separating ideas of the audience from the process of production. Some, such as Barry Dornfeld (1998), call for a radical rethinking of the very divide between production and reception. In his research on the production unit that created a seven-hour educational documentary series on childhood for American public television, he shows the complex negotiations through which a piece gets made. He demonstrates Ang's argument (1991, 1996) that in mass media, audiences not only are empirically "out there" but also are prefigured in nearly every dimension of the production process, as public television workers bring certain assumptions about the particular class fraction of "the American public" that they imagine (and hope) will watch their work.

Given the close institutional and ideological association between television programming and commercial capitalism, it is not surprising that stereotypical notions of audiences undergird operations in TV and in the advertising industry. But what happens when both advertisers and their markets are from the same minority ethnic group, as Dávila (this volume) asks in her study of advertisers, "creatives," and producers in charge of the commercial imagining and representation of "Hispanics" in the U.S. Latino advertising and marketing industry? Their mission is not only to sell products and help sustain a niche for this ethnically based market but also to challenge stereotypes and educate corporate clients about Hispanic languages and cultures. In the end, Dávila suggests, it is difficult for advertisers to untangle their imagery from U.S. racial and ethnic hierarchies, despite claims to be a "politically correct" alternative to mainstream advertising.

Like the work of Dávila and Dornfeld, Tejaswini Ganti's work on film production in the Bombay film industry shows how decisions are predicated upon an act of imagined consumption (Ganti 1999; and this volume). Her analysis, which joins a small but growing body of ethnographic studies of non-Western cinema industries (Sullivan 1993; Armbrust 1996, 2000), provides a critique of prevailing ideas about how media producers imagine audiences, as well as an incisive look at the actual routines whereby processes of cultural imperialism become internalized, enacted, and transformed. Ganti examines the remaking of Hollywood films by Hindi filmmakers, focusing on the decision-making processes whereby the "copy" is transformed to conform to conventions of Indian film narratives. This process makes the Hollywood original seem less like a hegemonic text than a resource to be strategically raided and incorporated into the bold intertexuality of Hindi cinema as a strategy for trying to manage the vagaries of box-office outcome.

Very different notions of a national audience—what Jeff Himpele calls the televisual public sphere—shape the production of *The Open Tribunal,* a popular television talk show in Bolivia that he studied as part of a broader research project on the circulation of media in Bolivia. The show, which features indigenous urban poor who describe their social problems and request (and sometimes receive) aid, also became the basis for a major political party led by the program's charismatic host. Himpele, along with the other authors in this section as well as other anthropologists who found themselves unwittingly cast on popular television (Gordon 1998), demonstrates how ethnographies of cultural production open up the "massness" of media to interrogation. They reveal how structures of power and notions of audience shape the actions of professionals as they traffic in the representations of culture.

THE SOCIAL LIFE OF TECHNOLOGY

The "ethnography of media," as a category of media studies, involved decentering the textual content of media technologies in favor of analyzing the social context of their reception. Refiguring the ethnography of media necessitates a further expansion by taking into consideration the physical and sensory properties of the technologies themselves and examining the materiality of communication across cultures. This scholarship draws on two main traditions. First, media technologies are not neutral. Each new medium imposes on society new relations to the body and to perception, time, and space, as theorists from McLuhan (1964) to Goody (1977), Ong (1991), Baudrillard (1984), and Kittler (1999) have argued. Those who highlight the materiality of communication insist on understanding this physicality of media and the form of its mediation, rather than any particular information being carried. The limiting of ethnography to content or its reception plays down the means by which technologies, through their very form, impose new social relations. The role of the subject in this tradition is submerged to the circuit of information, and focus is placed on the method of recording, storing, and transmitting data—what Poster has called the "mode of information" (Poster 1990; see also Kittler 1999). In this poststructuralist mode the subject of media has no autonomous existence outside of its enunciation as an address of the discursive operation of media flows.

Mapping the physical operations of media, as several essays in this volume do, avoids the mistake of presuming, rather than examining, the diverse ways that media technologies are manifest across different social spaces. The dropouts on pirate video images, the temperature of cinema halls, and the multiple shadows that appear on poor television reception all constitute what Russian formalists referred to as the "semiotics of interference," the process whereby the physical qualities of media create noise that threatens to overwhelm the message itself (see Tsivian 1994). These tactile physical qualities suggest a need to focus on media as technology.

Larkin's chapter on the introduction of cinema theaters in northern Nigeria, for instance, examines the ways in which cinema halls were part of the construction of public space under colonial rule. These new spaces—libraries, parks, theaters, and cinema halls—created new modes of racial, social, and sexual interaction that raised anxieties about social hierarchies and spatial segregation in Nigeria. What the cinema was allowed to be—who could attend, how it was built, where it was to be located—was the outcome of a specific project of colonial modernity. This subject is also taken up by Spitulnik in her examination of a few days in the social life of a radio set. By tracking the placing, possession, and circulation of radio sets in Zambia, she provides a clear example of the precise ways in which the material environment of technology determines its use and presence as an icon of status and modernity.

In an earlier paper on the introduction of radio sets as consumer items in Zambia, Spitulnik (1999a) unpacks the complex of meanings associated with the "radio listener." In her examination of advertisements for radio sets, Spitulnik describes how "listening to the radio" was constructed as a social act involving specific modes of dress, consumption, education, and family organization—in short, the production of the ideal colonial subject. This connection between the materiality of media technology (in this case as a consumer item) and colonialism is also brought out by Rudolf Mràzek in his examination of the rise of radio in the colonial Netherlands East Indies. He argues that as well as being a site for communication flows, the radio was also seen as a "shiny little furniture thing" and possession of it "became a tool to define a modern colonial space" and a significant organizing principle for the arrangement of the modern colonial home (Mràzek 1997: 10, 9). Mràzek and Spitulnik both point toward the double signification of media technologies, the fact that viewers and listeners are addressed by the content of media and at the same time interpellated by the technology itself, which often carries with it the larger ambitions of the colonial and postcolonial state. Electronic media in the colonial period, for instance, were part of the introduction of other forms of technology such as cars, electricity, factories, and railroads and thus part of the much larger discursive complex of science, rationality, time, personhood, and colonial rule. As technologies, media often carry the burden, prestige, and controversy of being made to speak for specific ideological projects. Zambians who circulate radio sets as icons of status and modernity (Spitulnik); Muslim Nigerians who oppose the construction of cinema halls as a "kafir," or un-Islamic activity (Larkin); and Thai spirits who refuse embodiment and media representation (Morris) all suggest ways in which technology mediates larger ideologies of modernity and postmodernity.

Several essays in this section examine the consequences of technological mediation for religious performance. In analyzing the production of Balinese plays in theater and on television, Mark Hobart insists on interrogating the precise circumstances and discursive traditions that create distinct acts of mediation. Hobart analyzes the difference between live theater performances and their televisual mediation, not to lament the replacement of an "authentic" cultural production with its televised other, but to see how both consist of dialogic productions, albeit rooted in different discursive regimes. In this, his concerns are shared by both Chris Pinney and Rosalind Morris. Pinney, for instance, critiques Benjamin's argument that mass reproduction destroys ritual and magical qualities of images. He argues instead for an understanding of the magical and spiritual power involved in mass images and interrogates this by looking at the "zone of mutuality" whereby filmic and chromolithographic images act upon viewers and vice versa. Icons of Hindi religious figures, for instance, demand a mode of viewing based on

Hindu concepts of *darshan*, the conferring of spiritual benefit through the act and presence of looking. According to Pinney, this direct spiritual benefit insists on the materiality of representations, especially their surface levels, and results in the sensation of the image acting upon its viewer in the moment that the viewer acts upon it (through looking). This tactile, embodied, engaged form of looking creates, for Pinney, a form of visuality that is radically different from the paradigm of the disinterested, exterior, and objectified gaze that marks the dominant mode of Western visuality, what Heidegger (1977) referred to as "the world as picture."[10]

The process of mediation is explored most provocatively by Morris through an examination of the absence, or refusal, of mediation. Thai spirits manifest themselves through embodiment in a spirit medium, the convulsing body, vomiting and jerky movements providing the outward signification of internal and invisible possession. Morris focuses on the story of a spirit who refused to become manifest and claimed to communicate without the need to materialize. Morris ties this event to the political economy of a modernist Thai state that has commodified spirit possession, repackaging it through its electronic mediation on video and television as an object of desire and longing. It was at the point when possession became an icon of alterity, of history and authenticity, that stories appeared of a spirit that refused mediation. Taken together these chapters invite us expand our concept of the ethnography of media to take into account the phenomenological experience of diverse forms of media technologies.

COMPLICITY AND ENGAGEMENT IN THE ETHNOGRAPHY OF MEDIA

Studying media is, for anthropologists, particularly useful in attempts to write against the grain of global inequalities because, as Abu-Lughod has argued, "it forces us to represent people in distant villages as part of the same cultural worlds we inhabit—worlds of mass media, consumption, and dispersed communities of the imagination" (1997: 128). Yet the social and geographic positioning of anthropologists working on media places them in complex relations to their objects of study: usually engaged, sometimes complicit, rarely neutral. More important, perhaps, for the kinds of political engagements our work on media entails, is the fact that anthropologists, like many of our informants, are mobile, moving back and forth from Native American reservations to U.S. law courts (Prins), from Amazonian communities in Brazil to protests at the national capital (Turner), or from Aboriginal outstations to international video festivals (Ginsburg). We circulate both geographically, as we move between "home" and "field," and socially, as we move up and down social hierarchies in our association with people often quite different from ourselves. This mobility gives us privileged knowledge of, and sometimes ability to intervene in, situations involving media, but it also can create dilemmas. Intervening in complex political arenas where the consequences for the local groups cannot be foreseen is tricky. As some have been quick to point out, participating in the processes of cultural objectification that media facilitates and the internal social and political jockeying that new media production inevitably occasions can place anthropologists in the position of potentially transforming, rather than observing, societies other than their own. What are the consequences? Finally, advocacy of subaltern groups makes criticism, public or otherwise, of any aspects of these groups' projects awkward.

Anthropologists' mobility across social hierarchies is just as crucial as geographic mobility for the kinds of engagements that mark their work on media. Often doing fieldwork among and thus sympathizing with dominated groups, anthropologists feel a responsibility to support projects by non-Western or postcolonial groups who are resisting the impositions of Western or global capitalist media; and to support media use by subaltern groups (e.g., women, peasants) or minorities within nation-states. The flip side of the coin is the sense of responsibility to critically analyze the instrumental use of media by the powerful, whether the state or transnational capitalist enterprises, or some combination. Thus Mankekar unveils the links between televised religious epics and the growth of religious nationalism and communal violence, while Abu-Lughod shows how Egyptian television melodramas and the projects of development and "modernization" both implicitly devalue the uneducated and carefully skirt the representation of Islam (1993b, 1997, 1998).

Yet the dilemmas entailed by a critical stance regarding the links between media and hegemonic projects are no less complex than those created by working actively with indigenous media-makers. Anthropologists' social mobility, for example, allows us access to both sides—the reception by subalterns and the production by the powerful, even in foreign countries. But our stance as intellectuals is what enables us to articulate and make public our critical analyses. When we do research in and write about countries other than our own, we may appeal to or consider ourselves to be joining with critics and intellectuals on the national scene. But it can be awkward for those living and working "outside," in the more powerful West, to criticize national projects and the professional elites who participate in them.

Most relevant is the fact that we are professionals and intellectuals like those who produce and analyze media anywhere. Media professionals are not only our peers; they are also often similarly engaged in processes of cross-cultural translation, as Pedelty's (1995) study of U.S. foreign correspondents and McLagan's analysis of a public relations strategist make clear. When we actually begin to study what they do, whether in our own backyards or on PBS (Dornfeld) or in the Hispanic advertising industry in the United States (Dávila), or elsewhere, such as Bollywood (Ganti), we find our positions unclear, and our ability to assert a privileged claim for cultural representation is sharply limited. Given our access to their work processes, we may find it difficult to see producers simply as tools of the state or commercial interests. We come to know the conflicts and compromises involved. How different are these from the conflicts raised by our own work as academics and professional representers of cultures, communities, and social issues?

In fact, the parallels between what we are doing as anthropologists studying media or analyzing and representing social and cultural life in general and what media professionals are doing are unsettling, as Himpele's analysis of his research on a Bolivian television program brings out clearly. He suggests that being suddenly invited to appear on the show and questioned in ways that served the host's intentions reversed the usual authority of anthropologist and subject. More problematic was what he called, following Taussig (1993), the "mimetic vertigo" he experienced when drawn into a rival, and parallel, arena of cultural production. What are the differences between himself as an anthropologist and Palenque, the show's host, in the elicitation and cutting off of participants' voices, in the appeal to lived experience to validate one's account, in advocacy for the marginalized, in the deployment of testimonials of suffering to mobilize popular sentiment, and in the construction of larger political analyses to frame individual accounts? Anthropologists now recognize that we are implicated in the representational practices of those we study; and we are engaged or complicit, as the case may be, in complex ways, with all those communities for whom media are important.

CONCLUSION: REMAPPING MEDIA

This book explores the dynamics of all these social processes of media consumption, production, circulation, and theorizing while making a strong case for the new kinds of knowledge to be gained from ethnographic work that studies practices in "out-of-the-way places" (Tsing 1994). Our work also underscores that oppositional logics are insufficient for grasping media practices; rather, our models must allow for the simultaneity of hegemonic and antihegemonic effects as we examine how "technologies of power" are created and contested within intimate institutional cultures, shaped by ideologies ranging from public service, to audience appeal, to aesthetics, to political empowerment.

While the media we study may be "off the map" of dominant media cartographies, they are no less crucial to the transformations of the twenty-first century and must be studied. Anthropologists seek to grasp the ways media are integrated into communities that are parts of nations and states, as well as transnational networks and circuits produced in the worlds of late capitalism and postcolonial cultural politics. We recognize the need for multisited research strategies to track the relevant social domains of contempo-

TV Head at ChuckBurger restaurant, San Leandro, California, 1988. (Photo: Jules
Backus, courtesy estate of Jules Backus)

rary life (Hannerz 1992; Gupta and Ferguson 1997a, 1997b; Marcus 1995).
Our relations with those we study are changing as our cultural worlds grow
closer in ways that push anthropology in salutary directions; it is difficult to
exoticize others or to maintain fictions of bounded or untouched communities of difference when one includes media in one's purview. Our work
crosses disciplinary boundaries as it intersects, overlaps, and sometimes dis-
places work not only in other social science disciplines such as sociology, with
which we share ancestors, but also in cultural studies, history, literary studies, and cinema and communication studies. Ethnographic studies of media
offer an interesting and important perspective on the arguments of Giddens
(and others) that one of the distinguishing characteristics of modernity is
"the lifting out of social relations from local contexts of interaction and their
restructuring across infinite spans of time-space" (Giddens 1990: 21; see also
Tomlinson 1999). Because anthropologists generally work "close to the
ground" and at the "margins," we can intervene in specific ways in academic
and wider debates about media and cultural imperialism or the dangers of
cultural homogenization represented by globalization. Our documentation
of local uses and meanings of media and of comparative political economies
of media production and consumption (including the constraints posed by
the unreliability of electricity and the vicissitudes of poverty) suggests the

persistence of difference and the importance of locality while highlighting the forms of inequality that continue to structure our world. Media practices are clearly central to these processes but not necessarily in the ways we might have expected. It is this unpredictability and often vitality of responses that anthropology helps us to understand, allowing us to better grasp how these "restructurings" are taking place.

NOTES

This essay draws on Faye Ginsburg's article "Shooting Back: From Ethnographic Film to the Ethnography of Media" (1999). Other comprehensive reviews of the current literature in the anthropology of media include Dickey 1998 and Spitulnik 1993.

1. For an overview of the influence of cultural studies on work in the anthropology of media, see Spitulnik 1993 and Traube 1992. The vitality of this tradition of media research influenced by cultural studies continues in two new journals, *Television and New Media*, launched in 2000 and edited by Toby Miller, and the *International Journal of Cultural Studies*, which began publication in 1997.

2. The use of the term "imaginary" as a dimension of national identity construction in which media play a central role became widespread in the 1990s. It appropriates Lacan's psychoanalytic use of the term as the mirror phase in human development when the child sees its own reflection as "other" (1967), and resignifies it through the work of Benedict Anderson (1991), Edward Said (1978), and others who have been central to our contemporary understanding of how nations are constituted as cultural collectives. Annette Hamilton, for example, in her seminal article on Aboriginals, Asians, and the national imaginary in Australia, writes: "Imaginary relations at the social, collective level can thus be seen as ourselves looking at ourselves while we think we are seeing others," citing such icons of Australian national culture as the film *Crocodile Dundee* (1990: 17). For a useful discussion of the concept of the imaginary, see Lilley 1993.

3. See, for example, the work of the Material Culture Group at University College London and the elaboration of this revisionist approach to this topic in the *Journal of Material Culture*.

4. Although indigenous can index a social formation "native" to a particular area (e.g., *I Love Lucy* is "indigenous" to America), we use it here in the strict sense of the term, as interchangeable with the neologism "First Peoples" to indicate the original inhabitants of areas later colonized by settler states (Australia, the United States, New Zealand, Canada, most of Latin America). These people, an estimated 5 percent of the world's population, are struggling to sustain their own identities and claims to culture and land, surviving as internal colonies within encompassing nation-states.

5. *Bad Aboriginal Art: Tradition, Media, and Technological Horizons,* a posthumous collection of Eric Michaels's writings based on his activist research in Australia, was published in 1994.

6. For this debate in the context of indigenous media, see the Spring 1997 issue of *Current Anthropology* (e.g., J. Weiner 1997) and the Spring 1998 issue of *Lingua Franca* (Palatella 1998).

7. For example, Solanas and Gettino in their famous 1971 essay "Towards a Third

Cinema," explicitly condemned both Hollywood (first) cinema and auteurist (second) cinema, favoring a militant documentary genre. Others called for a politicized auteurism that could incorporate popular culture (Rocha 1987). Thanks to Bob Stam and Ella Shohat for their comments on this.

8. For Nigeria see Haynes 2000; Ukah 2000. Knowledge of Ghanaian video production is based on Meyer 1999a, 1999b, and personal communication.

9. See Meyer 1999a; personal communication between Brian Larkin and the directors Willy Akuffo and Seth Ashong-Katai (thanks to Birgit Meyer for facilitating this conversation).

10. Drawing on Heidegger, J. Weiner (1997), for instance, makes the argument that visual technologies such as cameras are predicated on a culturally specific mode of vision—"the world as picture"—which is inherently Western and based on Western ideas of perspective, objectification, and surveillance. The cultural construction of the technology itself, Weiner thus argues, denies the possibility of appropriation by indigenous, subaltern, or even non-Western groups for whom use of the technology represents subjection to Western modes of visuality and subjectivity. Heidegger's concept of the modern roots of Western visuality remains intriguing, though many of the essays in this book make a powerful argument for media's often successful translation into other cultural fields.

REFERENCES

Abu-Lughod, Lila. 1993a. Editorial Comment: On Screening Politics in a World of Nations. *Public Culture* 5 (3): 465–69.

———. 1993b. Finding a Place for Islam: Egyptian Television Serials and the National Interest. *Public Culture* 5 (3): 493–514.

———. 1995. The Objects of Soap Opera: Egyptian Television and the Cultural Politics of Modernity. In *Worlds Apart: Modernity through the Prism of the Local,* edited by Daniel Miller, pp. 190–210. London: Routledge.

———. 1997. The Interpretation of Culture(s) after Television. *Representations* 59: 109–33.

———. 1998. Television and the Virtues of Education. In *Directions of Change in Rural Egypt,* edited by Nicholas Hopkins and Kirsten Westergaard, pp. 147–65. Cairo: American University in Cairo Press.

Allen, R. C., ed. 1995. *To Be Continued . . . Soap Operas around the World.* London: Routledge.

Anderson, Benedict. 1991. *Imagined Communities: Reflections on the Origins and Spread of Nationalism.* London: Verso.

Ang, Ien. 1985. *Watching Dallas: Soap Opera and the Melodramatic Imagination.* London: Methuen.

———. 1991. *Desperately Seeking the Audience.* London: Routledge.

———. 1996. *Living Room Wars: Rethinking Media Audiences for a Postmodern World.* London: Routledge.

Appadurai, Arjun. 1991. Global Ethnoscapes: Notes and Queries for a Transnational

Anthropology. In *Recapturing Anthropology,* edited by Richard Fox, pp. 191–210. Santa Fe: School of American Research Press.

———. 1993. Patriotism and Its Futures. *Public Culture* 5 (3): 411–30.

———. 1996. *Modernity at Large: Cultural Dimensions of Globalization.* Minneapolis: University of Minnesota Press.

Armbrust, Walter. 1996. *Mass Culture and Modernism in Egypt.* New York: Cambridge University Press.

———. 1998. When the Lights Go Down in Cairo: Cinema as Secular Ritual. *Visual Anthropology,* special issue, The Seen and the Unseeable: Visual Culture in the Middle East, 10 (2–4): 413–41.

———, ed. 2000. *Mass Mediations.* Berkeley: University of California Press.

Asch, Timothy. 1991. The Story We Now Want to Hear Is Not Ours to Tell—Relinquishing Control over Representation: Toward Sharing Visual Communication Skills with the Yanomamo. *Visual Anthropology Review* 7 (2): 102–6.

Aufderheide, Patricia. 1995. The Video in the Villages Project: Videomaking with and by Brazilian Indians. *Visual Anthropology Review* 11 (2): 83–93.

Bacon-Smith, Camille. 1992. *Enterprising Women: Television Fandom and the Creation of Popular Myth.* Philadelphia: University of Pennsylvania Press.

Baker Jr., Houston A. 1994. Critical Memory and the Black Public Sphere. *Public Culture,* special issue on the Black Public Sphere, 7 (1): 3–34.

Banks, Marcus, and Howard Morphy, eds. 1997. *Rethinking Visual Anthropology.* New Haven, Conn.: Yale University Press.

Bateson, Gregory. 1943. Cultural and Thematic Analysis of Fictional Films. In *Transactions of the New York Academy of Sciences,* pp. 72–78. New York: Academy of Sciences.

Baudrillard, Jean. 1984. The Precession of the Simulacra. In *Art after Modernism: Rethinking Representation,* edited by Brian Wallis, pp. 253–81. New York: New Museum of Contemporary Art.

Berger, Sally. 1995. Move Over Nanook. In *Wide Angle,* special issue on The Flaherty, 17 (1–4): 177–92.

Bhabha, Homi. 1989. The Commitment to Theory. In *Questions of Third Cinema,* edited by J. Pines and Paul Willemen, pp. 111–32. London: British Film Institute.

Bikales, Tom. 1997. From "Culture" to "Commercialization": The Production and Packaging of an African Cinema in Ougadougou, Burkina Faso. Ph.D. diss., Department of Anthropology, New York University.

Born, Georgina. 1998. Between Aesthetics, Ethics and Audit: Reflexivities and Disciplines in the BBC. Paper presented to Department of Anthropology, New York University, April.

Bourdieu, Pierre. 1993. *The Field of Cultural Production.* New York: Columbia University Press.

———. 1998. *On Television.* London: New Press.

Calhoun, Craig, ed. 1992. *Habermas and the Public Sphere.* Cambridge, Mass.: MIT Press.

Carelli, Vincent. 1988. Video in the Villages. *Commission on Visual Anthropology Bulletin,* May, pp. 10–15.

Castells, Manuel. 1997. *The Rise of the Network Society*. Oxford, England: Basil Blackwell.

Caton, Steven. 1999. *Lawrence of Arabia: A Film's Anthropology*. Berkeley: University of California Press.

Cunningham, Stuart, and John Sinclair, eds. 2000. *Floating Lives: The Media and Asian Diasporas*. St. Lucia, Queensland: University of Queensland Press.

Dávila, Arlene. 1999. El Kiosko Budweiser. *American Ethnologist* 25 (3): 452–70.

Diawara, Manthia. 1994. Malcolm X and the Black Public Sphere: Conversionists vs. Culturalists. *Public Culture*, special issue on the Black Public Sphere, 7 (1): 35–48.

Dickey, Sara. 1993. *Cinema and the Urban Poor in South India*. Cambridge, England: Cambridge University Press.

———. 1998. Anthropology and Its Contributions to Studies of Mass Media. *International Social Science Journal* 153: 413–27.

Dornfeld, Barry. 1998. *Producing Public Television*. Princeton: Princeton University Press.

Downmunt, Tony, ed. 1993. *Channels of Resistance: Global Television and Local Empowerment*. London: British Film Institute.

Eickelman, Dale F., and Jon Anderson, eds. 1999. *New Media in the Muslim World: The Emerging Public Sphere*. Bloomington: Indiana University Press.

Faraday, George. 2000. *Revolt of the Filmmakers: The Struggle for Artistic Autonomy and the Fall of the Soviet Film Industry*. State College: Pennsylvania State University Press.

Faris, James. 1992. Anthropological Transparency, Film, Representation and Politics. In *Film as Ethnography*, edited by P. Crawford and D. Turton, pp. 171–82. Manchester, England: University of Manchester Press.

Fienup-Riordan, Ann. 1990. Robert Redford, Apanuugpak, and the Invention of Tradition. In *Eskimo Essays: Yup'ik Lives and How We See Them*. New Brunswick, N.J.: Rutgers University Press.

Fischer, Michael. 1990. *Debating Muslims: Cultural Dialogues in Postmodernity and Tradition*. Madison: University of Wisconsin Press.

———. 1995. Film as Ethnography and as Cultural Critique in the Late Twentieth Century. In *Shared Differences: Multicultural Media and Practical Pedagogy*, edited by Diane Carson and Lester Friedman. Urbana: University of Illinois Press.

Fiske, John. 1987. *Television Culture*. London: Methuen.

Fleming, Kathleen. 1991. Zacharias Kunuk: Videomaker and Inuit Historian. *Inuit Art Quarterly* (Summer): 24–28.

Fox, Richard, ed. 1991. *Recapturing Anthropology: Working in the Present*. Santa Fe: School of American Research Press.

Fraser, Nancy. 1993. Rethinking the Public Sphere: A Contribution to the Critique of Actually Existing Democracy. In *The Phantom Public Sphere*, edited by B. Robbins, pp. 1–32. Minneapolis: University of Minnesota Press.

Fugelsang, Miniu. 1994. *Veils and Videos: Female Youth Culture on the Kenyan Coast*. Stockholm: Studies in Social Anthropology.

Ganti, Tejaswini. 1999. Centenary Commemorations or Centenary Contestations? Celebrating a Hundred Years of Cinema in Bombay. *Visual Anthropology*, special issue on Indian Cinema, 11 (4): 399–419.

Gaonkar, Dilip Parameshwar. 1999. On Alternative Modernities. *Public Culture*, special issue on Alter/Native Modernities, 11 (1): 1–18.

Giddens, Anthony. 1990. *The Consequences of Modernity*. Stanford, Calif.: Stanford University Press.

Gillespie, Marie. 1995. *Television, Ethnicity, and Cultural Change*. London: Routledge.

Ginsburg, Faye. 1991. Indigenous Media: Faustian Contract or Global Village? *Cultural Anthropology* 6 (1): 92–112.

———. 1993. Aboriginal Media and the Australian Imaginary. *Public Culture* 5 (3): 557–78.

———. 1994. Embedded Aesthetics: Creating a Discursive Space for Indigenous Media. *Cultural Anthropology* 9 (2): 365–82.

———. 1997. "From Little Things, Big Things Grow": Indigenous Media and Cultural Activism. In *Between Resistance and Revolution: Cultural Politics and Social Protest*, edited by R. Fox and O. Starn, pp. 118–44. London: Routledge.

———. 1998. Institutionalizing the Unruly: Charting a Future for Visual Anthroplogy. *Ethnos* 63 (2): 173–201.

———1999. Shooting Back: From Ethnographic Film to the Ethnography of Media. In *A Companion to Film Theory*, edited by Toby Miller and Robert Stam, pp. 295–322. London: Blackwell.

Gitlin, Todd. 1983. *Inside Prime Time*. New York: Pantheon.

Goody, Jack. 1977. *The Domestication of the Savage Mind*. Cambridge, England: Cambridge University Press.

Gordon, Joel. 1998. Becoming the Image: Words of Gold, Talk Television, and Ramadan Nights on the Little Screen. *Visual Anthropology*, special issue on Visual Culture in the Middle East, 10 (2–4): 247–64.

Gupta, Akhil, and James Ferguson, eds. 1997a. *Culture, Power, Place; Explorations in Critical Anthropology*. Durham, N.C.: Duke University Press.

———. 1997b. Discipline and Practice: "The Field" as Site, Method, and Location in Anthropology. In *Anthropological Locations*, edited by A. Gupta and J. Ferguson, pp. 1–46. Berkeley: University of California Press.

Gurevitch, Michael, Tony Bennett, James Curran, and Janet Woollacott, eds. 1982. *Culture, Society, and the Media*. London: Routledge.

Habermas, Jürgen. 1989. *The Structural Transformation of the Public Sphere*. Translated by Thomas Burger with Frederick Lawrence. Cambridge, Mass.: MIT Press.

Hall, Stuart. 1980. Encoding/Decoding. In *Culture, Media, Language*, edited by Stuart Hall, Dorothy Hobson, Andrew Lowe, and Paul Willis, pp. 128–38. London: Hutchinson.

———. 1992. Cultural Studies and Its Theoretical Legacies. In *Cultural Studies*, edited by L. Grossberg et al., pp. 277–94. New York: Routledge.

———. 1997. *Representation: Cultural Representations and Signifying Practices*. London: Sage.

Hamburger, Esther. 1999. Politics and Intimacy in Brazilian Telenovelas. Ph.D. diss., University of Chicago.

Hamilton, Annette. 1990. Fear and Desire: Aborigines, Asians, and the National Imaginary. *Australian Cultural History* 9: 14–35.

————. 1993. Video Crackdown, or the Sacrificial Pirate: Censorship and Cultural Consequences in Thailand. *Public Culture* 5 (3): 515–32.

Hannerz, Ulf. 1992. *Cultural Complexity: Studies in the Social Organization of Meaning.* New York: Columbia University Press.

————. 1996. *Transnational Connections.* New York: Routledge.

Harvey, David. 1989. *The Condition of Postmodernity.* Oxford, England: Basil Blackwell.

Haynes, Jonathan, ed. 2000. *Nigerian Video Film.* Revised and expanded. Athens, Ohio: The Ohio University Center for International Studies.

Heidegger, Martin. 1977. *The Question Concerning Technology and Other Essays.* New York: Harper Torchbooks.

Himpele, Jeff. 1996. Film Distribution as Media: Mapping Difference in the Bolivian Cinemascape. *Visual Anthropology Review* 12 (1): 47–66.

Hughes, Stephen P. 2000. Policing Silent Film Exhibition in South India. In *Making Meaning in Indian Cinema,* edited by Ravi Vasudevan. Delhi: Oxford University Press.

Jenkins, Henry. 1992. *Textual Poachers: Television Fans and Participatory Culture.* New York: Routledge.

Juhasz, Alexandra. 1995. *Aids TV: Identity, Community, and Alternative Video.* Durham, N.C.: Duke University Press.

Katz, Elihu. 1977. Can Authentic Cultures Survive New Media? *Journal of Communication* (Spring): 113–21.

Kittler, Friedrich A. 1999. *Gramophone, Film, Typewriter.* Translated and with introduction by Geoffrey Winthrop-Young and Michael Wurtz. Stanford, Calif.: Stanford University Press.

Kolar-Panov, Dona. 1997. *Video, War, and the Diasporic Imagination.* London: Routledge.

Kottak, Conrad. 1990. *Prime-Time Society: An Anthropological Analysis of Television and Culture.* Belmont, Calif.: Wadsworth Modern Anthropology Library.

Kuttab, Daoud. 1993. Grass Roots TV Production in the Occupied Territories. In *Channels of Resistance: Global Television and Local Empowerment,* edited by Tony Downmunt. London: British Film Institute.

Lacan, Jacques. [1967] 1982. *Ecrits.* Translated by Alan Sheridan. New York: Norton.

Larkin, Brian. 1997. Indian Films and Nigerian Lovers: Media and the Creation of Parallel Modernities. *Africa* 67 (3): 406–39.

————. 2000. Hausa Dramas and the Rise of Video Culture in Nigeria. In *Nigerian Video Films,* edited by Jonathan Haynes. Athens, Ohio: Ohio University Press.

Lerner, Daniel. 1964. *The Passing of Traditional Society.* Glencoe, Ill.: Free Press.

Leuthold, Steven. 1998. *Indigenous Aesthetics.* Seattle: University of Washington Press.

Liebes, Tamar, and Elihu Katz. 1990. *The Export of Meaning: Cross-Cultural Readings of "Dallas."* New York: Oxford University Press.

Liechty, Mark. 1994. Media, Markets and Modernization: Youth Identities and the Experience of Modernity in Kathmandu, Nepal. In *Youth Cultures: A Cross-Cultural*

Perspective, edited by Vered Amit-Talai and Helena Wulff, pp. 166–201. London: Routledge.

Lilley, Roseanne. 1993. Claiming Identity: Film and Television in Hong Kong. *History and Anthropology* 6 (2–3): 261–92.

Lutkehaus, Nancy. 1995. The Sundance Film Festival: Preliminary Notes towards an Ethnography of a Film Festival. *Visual Anthropology Review* 12 (1): 19–29.

Lyons, Andrew P. 1990. The Television and the Shrine: Towards a Theoretical Model for the Study of Mass Communications in Nigeria. *Visual Anthropology* 3 (4): 429–56.

Lyons, Harriet D. 1990. Television in Contemporary Urban Life: Benin City, Nigeria. *Visual Anthropology* 3 (4): 411–28.

MacDougall, David. 1997. The Visual in Anthropology. In *Rethinking Visual Anthropology,* edited by Marcus Banks and Howard Morphy. New Haven, Conn.: Yale University Press.

———. 1998. *Transcultural Cinema.* Princeton, N.J.: Princeton University Press.

Mahon, Maureen. 2000a. Black Like This: Race, Generation, and Rock in the Post–Civil Rights Era. *American Ethnologist* 27 (2): 283–311.

———. 2000b. The Visible Evidence of Cultural Producers. *Annual Review of Anthropology* 29: 467–92.

Mankekar, Purnima. 1993a. National Texts and Gendered Lives: An Ethnography of Television Viewers in a North Indian City. *American Ethnologist* 20 (3): 543–63.

———. 1993b. Television Tales and a Woman's Rage: A Nationalist Recasting of Draupadi's Disrobing. *Public Culture* 5 (3): 469–92.

———. 1999. *Screening Culture, Viewing Politics: An Ethnography of Television, Womanhood, and Nation in Postcolonial India.* Durham, N.C.: Duke University Press.

Manuel, Peter. 1993. *Cassette Culture: Popular Music and Technology in North India.* Chicago: University of Chicago Press.

Marcus, George. 1995. Ethnography in/of the World System: The Emergence of Multi-Sited Ethnography. *Annual Review of Anthropology* 24: 95–117.

———. 1996. Introduction to *Connected: Engagements with Media,* edited by G. Marcus, pp. 1–18. Late Editions 3. Chicago: University of Chicago Press.

———. 1998a. *Ethnography through Thick and Thin.* Princeton, N.J.: Princeton University Press.

———. 1998b. The Uses of Complicity in the Changing Mise-en-Scene of Anthropological Fieldwork. In *Ethnography through Thick and Thin,* pp. 105–31. Princeton, N.J.: Princeton University Press.

———, ed. 1997. *Cultural Producers in Perilous States.* Late Editions 4. Chicago: University of Chicago Press.

Marcus, George, and Michael Fischer. 1986. *Anthropology as Cultural Critique: An Experimental Moment in the Human Sciences.* Chicago: University of Chicago Press.

Marcus, George, and Fred Myers, eds. 1995. Introduction to *The Traffic in Culture: Refiguring Anthropology and Art,* pp. 1–51. Berkeley: University of California Press.

Marks, Laura. 2000. *The Skin of the Film: Intercultural Cinema, Embodiment, and the Senses.* Durham, N.C.: Duke University Press.

Martin-Barbero, J. 1988. Communication from Culture: The Crisis of the National and the Emergence of the Popular. *Media, Culture, and Society* 10: 447–65.

———. 1993. *Communication, Culture, and Hegemony: From the Media to Mediations.* London: Sage.

Mauss, Marcel. 1967. *The Gift: Forms and Functions of Exchange in Archaic Societies.* Translated by Ian Cunnison, with an introduction by E. E. Evans-Pritchard. New York: Norton.

McLagan, Meg. 1996. Computing for Tibet: Virtual Politics in the Post–Cold War Era. In *Connected: Engagements with Media,* edited by G. Marcus, pp. 159–94. Late Editions 3. Chicago: University of Chicago Press.

———. 1997. Mystical Visions in Manhattan: Deploying Culture in the Year of Tibet. In *Tibetan Culture in the Diaspora,* edited by F. Korom. Vienna: Austrian Academy of Sciences.

McLuhan, Marshall. 1964. *Understanding Media: The Extensions of Man.* New York: New American Library.

Mead, Margaret, and Rhoda Metraux. 1953. *The Study of Culture at a Distance.* Chicago: University of Chicago Press.

Meadows, Michael, and Helen Molnar. 2001. *Songlines to Satellites: Indigenous Communication in Australia, the South Pacific, and Canada.* Leichardt, Australia: Pluto Press.

Meyer, Birgit. 1999a. Popular Ghanaian Cinema and the African Heritage. Working Paper no. 7, WOTRO-Project "Globalization and the Construction of Communal Identities," The Hague.

———. 1999b. Blood Money. On the Attraction of Nigerian Movies in Ghana. Paper presented to the Workshop on Religion and Media in Nigeria, School of Oriental and African Studies, London. February.

Michaels, Eric. 1986. *The Aboriginal Invention of Television in Central Australia: 1982–1986.* Canberra: Australian Institute of Aboriginal Studies.

———. 1994. *Bad Aboriginal Art: Tradition, Media, and Technological Horizons.* Minneapolis: University of Minnesota Press.

Michaels, Eric (with Frances Jupurrurla Kelly). 1984. The Social Organization of an Aboriginal Video Workplace. *Australian Aboriginal Studies* 1: 26–34.

Miller, Daniel. 1992. The Young and the Restless in Trinidad: A Case of the Local and the Global in Mass Consumption. In *Consuming Technology,* edited by R. Silverstone and E. Hirsch. London: Routledge.

———. 1995. Introduction: Anthropology, Modernity, Consumption. In *Worlds Apart: Modernity through the Prism of the Local,* edited by D. Miller, pp. 1–23. London: Routledge.

Miller, Toby. 1998. Hollywood and the World. In *The Oxford Guide to Film Studies,* edited by J. Hill and P. C. Gibson, pp. 371–82. New York: Oxford University Press.

Miyoshi, Masao. 1993. A Borderless World? From Colonialism to Transnationalism and the Decline of the Nation-State. *Critical Inquiry* 19 (4): 726–51.

Morley, David. 1986. *Family Television: Cultural Power and Domestic Leisure*. London: Comedia.

———. 1992. *Television, Audiences, and Cultural Studies*. London: Routledge.

Morley, David, and Kevin Robins. 1995. *Spaces of Identity: Global Media, Electronic Landscapes, and Cultural Boundaries*. London: Routledge.

Mrázek, Rudolf. 1997. Let Us Become Radio Mechanics: Technology and National Identity in Late-Colonial Netherlands East Indies. *Comparative Studies in Society and History* 39 (1): 3–33.

Naficy, Hamid. 1993. *The Making of Exile Cultures: Iranian Television in Los Angeles*. Minneapolis: University of Minnesota Press.

Nichols, Bill. 1994. Discovering Form, Inferring Meaning: New Cinemas and the Film Festival Circuit. *Film Quarterly* 47 (3): 16–30.

Ong, Walter J. 1991. *Orality and Literacy: The Technologizing of the Word*. London: Routledge.

Ortner, Sherry, ed. 1999. *The Fate of "Culture": Geertz and Beyond*. Berkeley: University of California Press.

Palatella, John. 1998. Pictures of Us. *Lingua Franca* 8 (5): 50–57.

Pedelty, Mark. 1995. *War Stories: The Culture of Foreign Correspondents*. New York: Routledge.

Pendakur, Manjunath, and Radha Subramanyam. 1996. Indian Cinema beyond National Borders. In *New Patterns in Global Television: Peripheral Vision*, edited by J. Sinclair, E. Jacka, and S. Cunningham, pp. 69–82. London: Oxford University Press.

Penley, Constance. 1997. *Nasa/Trek: Popular Science and Sex in America*. New York: Verso Books.

Philipsen, Hans Henrik, and Birgitte Markussen, eds. 1995. *Advocacy and Indigenous Filmmaking*. Aarhaus, Denmark: Intervention Press.

Pinney, Chris. 1997. *Camera Indica: The Social Life of Indian Photographs*. Chicago: University of Chicago Press.

Poster, Mark. 1990. *The Mode of Information: Poststructuralism and Social Context*. Chicago: University of Chicago Press.

Powdermaker, Hortense. 1950. *Hollywood, the Dream Factory*. Boston: Grosset and Dunlap.

———. 1967. *Copper Town: Changing Africa; the Human Situation on the Rhodesian Copperbelt*. New York: Harper and Row.

Prins, Harold. 1989. American Indians and the Ethnocinematic Complex: From Native Participation to Production Control. In *Eyes across the Water*, edited by R. Boonzajer Flaes, pp. 80–90. Amsterdam: Het Spinhof.

———. 1997. The Paradox of Primitivism: Native Rights and the Problem of Imagery in Cultural Survival Films. *Visual Anthropology* 9 (3–4): 243–66.

Radway, Janice. 1984. *Reading the Romance*. Chapel Hill: University of North Carolina Press.

———. 1988. Reception Study: Ethnography and the Problems of Dispersed Audiences and Nomadic Subjects. *Cultural Studies* 2 (3): 359–76.

Rajagopal, Arvind. 2001. *Politics after Television: Hindu Nationalism and the Reshaping of the Public in India.* Cambridge, England: Cambridge University Press.

Riggins, Stephen Harold, ed. 1992. *Ethnic Minority Media: An International Perspective.* London: Sage.

Robbins, Bruce, ed. 1993. *The Phantom Public Sphere.* Minneapolis: University of Minnesota Press.

Rocha, Glauber. 1987. The Aesthetics of Hunger. In *Brazilian Cinema,* edited by Randal Johnson and Robert Stam, pp. 97–112. Austin: University of Texas Press.

Rofel, Lisa. 1994. Yearnings: Televisual Love and Melodramatic Politics in Contemporary China. *American Ethnologist* 21 (4): 700–22.

Rony, Fatima. 1996. *The Third Eye: Race, Cinema, and Ethnographic Spectacle.* Durham: Duke University Press.

Roth, Lorna. 2002. *Something New in the Air: Indigenous Television in Canada.* Montreal: McGill Queens University Press.

Royal Anthropological Institute of Great Britain and Ireland. 1951. *Notes and Queries on Anthropology.* London: Routledge and K. Paul.

Ruby, Jay. 1991. Speaking for, Speaking about, Speaking with, or Speaking alongside: An Anthropological and Documentary Dilemma. *Visual Anthropology Review* 7 (2): 50–67.

———. 1995. The Moral Burden of Authorship in Ethnographic Film. *Visual Anthropology Review* 11 (2): 83–93.

———. 2000. *Philosophical Toys: Explorations of Film and Anthropology.* Chicago: University of Chicago Press.

Russell, Catherine. 1999. *Experimental Ethnography: The Work of Film in the Age of Video.* Durham, N.C.: Duke University Press.

Said, Edward. 1978. *Orientalism.* New York: Pantheon.

Salamandra, Christa. 1998. Moustache Hairs Lost: Ramadan Television Serials and the Construction of Identity in Damascus, Syria. *Visual Anthropology,* special issue on Visual Culture in the Middle East, 10 (2–4): 227–46.

Schiller, Herbert. 1969. *Mass Communications and American Empire.* New York: Augustus Kelley.

———. 1991. Not Yet the Post-Imperialist Era. *Critical Studies in Mass Communication* 8: 13–28.

Sen, Krishna. 1994. *Indonesian Cinema: Framing the New Order.* London: Zed Books.

Shohat, Ella, and Robert Stam. 1994. *Unthinking Eurocentrism: Multiculturalism and the Media.* New York: Routledge.

Silj, Alessandro. 1988. *East of Dallas: The European Challenge to American Television.* London: British Film Institute.

Silverstone, Roger. 1985. *Framing Science: The Making of a BBC Documentary.* London: British Film Institute.

———. 1994. *Television and Everyday Life.* London: Routledge.

Silverstone, Roger, and Eric Hirsch, eds. 1992. *Consuming Technologies: Media and Information in Domestic Spaces.* London: Routledge.

Sinclair, John. 1996. Mexico, Brazil, and the Latin World. In *New Patterns in Global Television: Peripheral Vision,* edited by J. Sinclair, E. Jacka, and S. Cunningham, pp. 33–66. London: Oxford University Press.

Sinclair, John, Elizabeth Jacka, and Stuart Cunningham, eds. 1996. *New Patterns in Global Television: Peripheral Vision.* London: Oxford University Press.

Skuse, Andrew. 1999. *'Negotiated Outcomes': An Ethnography of the Production and Consumption of a BBC World Service Radio Soap Opera in Afghanistan.* Ph.D. diss., University College London, University of London.

Solanas, Fernando, and Octavio Gettina. 1971. Towards a Third Cinema. *Afterimage* 3 (summer): 16–35.

Spitulnik, Debra. 1993. Anthropology and the Mass Media. *Annual Review of Anthropology* 22. Palo Alto, Calif.: Annual Reviews.

———. 1999a. *Producing National Publics: Audience Constructions and the Electronic Media in Zambia.* Durham, N.C.: Duke University Press.

———. 1999b. Mediated Modernities: Encounters with the Electronic in Zambia. *Visual Anthropology Review* 14 (2): 63–84.

———. 2001. *Media Connections and Disconnections: Radio Culture and the Public Sphere in Gambia.* Durham, N.C.: Duke University Press.

Sreberny-Mohammadi, Annabelle. 1996. The Global in the Local in International Communications. In *Mass Media and Society,* (2d ed.), edited by J. Curran and M. Gurevitch, pp. 177–203. London: Edward Arnold.

Sreberny-Mohammadi, Annabelle, and Ali Mohammadi. 1994. *Small Media, Big Revolution: Communication, Culture, and the Iranian Revolution.* Minneapolis: University of Minneapolis Press.

Sreberny-Mohammadi, Annabelle, Dwayne Winseck, Jim McKenna, and Oliver Boyd-Barrett, eds. 1997. *Media in Global Context: A Reader.* London: Edward Arnold.

Sullivan, Nancy. 1993. Film and Television Production in Papua New Guinea: How Media Become the Message. *Public Culture* 5 (3): 533–56.

Tacchi, Jo. 1998. Radio Texture: Between Self and Others. In *Material Cultures: Why Some Things Matter,* edited by D. Miller. Chicago: University of Chicago Press.

Taussig, Michael. 1993. *Mimesis and Alterity—A Particular History of the Senses.* New York: Routledge.

Taylor, Lucien, ed. 1994. *Visualizing Theory: Selected Essays from V.A.R., 1990–1994.* New York: Routledge.

Thomas, Nicholas. 1991. *Entangled Objects: Exchange, Material Culture, and Colonialism in the Pacific.* Cambridge, Mass.: Harvard University Press.

Tomlinson, John. 1991. *Cultural Imperialism: A Critical Introduction.* London: Pinter.

———. 1999. *Globalization and Culture.* Chicago: University of Chicago Press.

Traube, Elizabeth. 1992. *Dreaming Identities: Class, Gender, and Generation in 1980s Hollywood Movies.* Boulder, Colo.: Westview.

Tsing, Anna. 1994. *In the Realm of the Diamond Queen.* Princeton, N.J.: Princeton University Press.

Tsivian, Yuri. 1994. *Early Cinema in Russia and Its Cultural Reception.* New York: Routledge.

Turner, Terence. 1991a. The Social Dynamics of Video Media in an Indigenous Society: The Cultural Meaning and the Personal Politics of Video-Making in Kayapo Communities. *Visual Anthropology Review* 7 (2): 68–76.

———. 1991b. Representing, Resisting, Rethinking: Historical Transformations of Kayapo Culture and Anthropological Consciousness. In *Colonial Situations*, edited by G. Stocking, pp. 285–313. Madison: University of Wisconsin Press.

———. 1992. Defiant Images: The Kayapo Appropriation of Video. *Anthropology Today* 8 (6): 5–16.

———. 1993. Anthropology and Multiculturalism: What Is Anthropology That Multiculturalists Should Be Mindful of It? *Cultural Anthropology* 8 (4): 411–29.

———. 1995. Representation, Collaboration, and Mediation in Contemporary Ethnographic and Indigenous Media. *Visual Anthropology Review* 11 (2): 102–6.

Ukah, A. F-K A. S. 2000. Advertising God: Nigerian Christian Video Films and the Power of Consumer Culture. Paper presented to "Consultation on Media, Religion and Culture in Africa," GIMPA, Ghana, May.

Vail, Pegi. 1997. Producing America: The Native American Producer's Alliance. Master's thesis, New York University.

Weatherford, Elizabeth. 1990. Native Visions: The Growth of Indigenous Media. *Aperture* 13 (5): 58–61.

Weiner, Annette. 1992. *Inalienable Possessions: The Paradox of Keeping-While-Giving.* Berkeley: University of California Press.

Weiner, James. 1997. Televisualist Anthropology: Representation, Aesthetics, Politics. *Current Anthropology* 38 (2): 197–236.

Wilk, Richard. 1994. Colonial Time and TV Time: Television and Temporality in Belize. *Visual Anthropology Review* 10 (1): 94–102.

Williams, Raymond. 1974. *Television: Technology and Cultural Form.* New York: Schocken.

Worth, Sol. 1980. Margaret Mead and the Shift from "Visual Anthropology" to "The Anthropology of Visual Communication." *Studies in Visual Communication* 6: 15–22.

Worth, Sol, John Adair, and Richard Chalfen. [1972] 1997. *Through Navajo Eyes,* with a new introduction, afterword, and notes by R. Chalfen. Albuquerque: University of New Mexico Press.

Wortham, Erica Cusi. 2000. News from the Mountains: Redefining the Televisual Borders of Oaxaca. In *Sphere 2000.* New York: World Studio Foundation.

Yang, Mayfair Mei-hui. 1994. Film Discussion Groups in China: State Hegemony or a Plebian Public Sphere? *Visual Anthropology Review* 10 (1): 47–60.

I

Cultural Activism
and Minority Claims

Beastie Boys at the Tibetan Freedom Concert, 1998, Washington, D.C. Between 1996 and 1999, spectacles such as this one organized by the Beastie Boys attracted thousands of people, the majority of whom had little or no prior knowledge about the situation in Tibet, and extended the processes of mass mediation of the Tibet issue to new heights. (Photo: Sonam Zoksang)

1

Screen Memories

Resignifying the Traditional in Indigenous Media

Faye D. Ginsburg

ENTANGLED TECHNOLOGIES

In a familiar moment in the history of ethnographic film, a well-known scene in Robert Flaherty's 1922 classic *Nanook of the North,* the character identified on the intertitle as "Nanook, Chief of the Ikivimuits" (played by Flaherty's friend and guide, Allakariallak) is shown being amazed by a gramophone.[1] He laughs and feels the record three times with his mouth, as if tasting it. We now recognize the scene as a performance rather than documentation of first contact, an image that contradicts Flaherty's journals describing the Inuit's sophisticated response to these new recording technologies, as well as their technical expertise with them by the time the scene was filmed (Rotha 1980). Like the gramophone scene, the film itself obscures the engagement with the cinematic process by Allakariallak and others who worked on the production of Flaherty's film in various ways as technicians, camera operators, film developers, and production consultants (as we might call them today). Not long after the character of Nanook achieved fame in the United States and Europe, Allakariallak died of starvation in the Arctic. Although he never passed on his knowledge of the camera and filmmaking directly to other Inuit, the unacknowledged help he gave Flaherty haunts Inuit producers today as a paradigmatic moment in a history of unequal "looking relations" (Gaines 1988). Their legendary facility with the camera—from imagining and setting up scenes, to helping develop rushes, to fixing the Aggie, as they called the camera—foreshadows their later entanglement with media-making on their own terms.

The Nanook case reminds us that the current impact of media's rapidly increasing presence and circulation in people's lives and the globalization of media that it is part of—whether one excoriates or embraces it—are not simply phenomena of the past two decades.[2] The sense of its contemporary

Photogravure of Allakariallak, who played the character Nanook, listening to a gramophone at Port Harrison Post, ca. 1920. (Photo: Robert Flaherty, property, Museum of Modern Art)

novelty is in part the product of the deliberate erasure of indigenous ethnographic subjects as actual or potential participants in their own screen representations in the past century. These tensions between the past erasure and the current visibility of indigenous participation in film and video are central to the work of the aboriginal media-makers who are engaged in making what I call screen memories. Here I invert the sense in which Freud used this term to describe how people protect themselves from their traumatic past through layers of obfuscating memory (Freud [1901] 1965: 247).[3] By contrast, indigenous people are using screen media not to mask but to recuperate their own collective stories and histories—some of them traumatic—that have been erased in the national narratives of the dominant culture and are in danger of being forgotten within local worlds as well. Of course, retelling stories for the media of film, video, and television often requires reshaping them, not only within new aesthetic structures but also in negotiation with the political economy of state-controlled as well as commercial media, as the following case makes clear.

THE DEVELOPMENT OF INUIT TELEVISION

In the 1970s, half a century after Nanook was made, the Inuit Tapirisat, a pan-Inuit activist organization, began agitating for a license from the Canadian government to establish their own Arctic satellite television service, the Inuit Broadcast Corporation (IBC), which was eventually licensed in 1981 (Marks 1994). The Tapirisat's actions were a response to the launching over their remote lands of the world's first geostationary satellite to broadcast to northern Canada, Anik B (David 1998). The small-scale encounter with Flaherty's film apparatus was nothing in comparison with CBC television programming's invasion of Inuit lives and homes: the government placed Telsat receiving dishes in nearly every northern community, with no thought to or provision for aboriginal content or local broadcast (Lucas 1987: 15). The Inuit Tapirisat fought this imposition and eventually succeeded in gaining a part of the spectrum for their own use. The creation of the IBC—a production center for Inuit programming of all sorts—became an important development in the lives of contemporary Canadian Arctic people, as well as a model for the repurposing of communications technologies for indigenous people worldwide.

By 1983 it became apparent that although IBC programming was remarkably successful, distribution was still problematic because Inuit work was slotted into the temporal margins of the Canadian Broadcast Corporation (CBC) late-night schedules. In 1991, after considerable effort, a satellite-delivered northern aboriginal distribution system, TV Northern Canada (TVNC), went to air, the first unified effort to serve almost 100 northern communities in English, French, and twelve aboriginal languages (Meadows 1996; Roth 1994).[4] By 1997, TVNC, seeking ways to hook up with aboriginal producers in southern Canada, responded to a government call for proposals for a third national cable-based network that would expand beyond northern communities to reach all of Canada. The group was awarded the license and formed the Aboriginal Peoples Television Network (APTN). This publicly supported and indigenously controlled national aboriginal television network, the first of its kind in the world, officially went to air in September 1999 (David 1998: 39; Roth 2000).[5]

Rather than destroying Inuit cultures as some predicted would happen,[6] these technologies of representation—beginning with the satellite television transmission to Inuit communities of their own small-scale video productions—have played a dynamic and even revitalizing role for Inuit and other First Nations people, as a self-conscious means of cultural preservation and production and a form of political mobilization. Repurposing satellite signals for teleconferencing also provides long-distance communication across vast Arctic spaces for a range of community needs: everything from staying in touch with children attending regional high schools to the delivery of health care information (Brisebois 1990; Marks 1994).

Prominent among those producing work for these new aboriginal television networks is Inuit director and producer Sak Kunuk, a carver and former Inuit Broadcast Corporation producer. He has developed a community-based production group in Igloolik, the remote Arctic settlement where he lives, through a process that, ironically, evokes the method used by Robert Flaherty in *Nanook*. Kunuk works collaboratively with the people of Igloolik, in particular elders, to create dramatic stories about life in the area around Igloolik in the 1930s before settlement. Along with his partners, cultural director and lead actor Paloussie Quilitalik (a monolingual community elder) and technical director Norman Cohn, a Brooklynite relocated to Nunavut, who together make up the production group Igloolik Isuma, Kunuk has produced tapes such as *Qaggiq* (*Gathering Place;* 1989, 58 min.), depicting a gathering of four families in a late-winter Inuit camp in the 1930s; and *Nunavut* (*Our Land;* 1993–95), a thirteen-part series of half-hour dramas recreating the lives of five fictional families (played by Igloolik residents) through a year of traditional life in 1945, when the outside world was at war, and a decade before government settlements changed that way of life forever.[7]

These screen memories of Inuit life are beloved locally and in other Inuit communities. They also have been admired in art and independent film circles in metropolitan centers for their beauty, ethnographic sensibility, humor, intimacy, and innovative improvisational method.[8] While reinforcing Inuktitut language and skills for younger members of the community, at a more practical and quotidian level, the project provides interest and employment for people in Igloolik (Berger 1995a, 1995b; Fleming and Hendrick 1991, 1996; Marks 1994). For Inuit participants and viewers, Igloolik Isuma serves as a dynamic effort to resignify cultural memory on their own terms. Their work not only provides a record of a heretofore undocumented legacy at a time when the generation still versed in traditional knowledge is rapidly passing; by also involving young people in the process, the production of these historical dramas requires that they learn Inuktitut and a range of other skills tied to their cultural legacies, thus helping to mitigate a crisis in the social and cultural reproduction of Inuit life. In the words of an Igloolik elder posted on their website: "We strongly believe this film has helped in keeping our traditional way of life alive and to our future generations it will make them see how our ancestors used to live."[9] In December 2000, they premiered *Atanarjuat (The Fast Runner)*, a film based on a traditional Igloolik legend and set in sixteenth-century Igloolik. It was the world's first feature-length dramatic film written, produced, and acted by Inuit. By summer 2001, it had picked up awards all over the world, including the prestigious *Camera D'or* at the Cannes Film Festival, awarded to the best feature.

Igloolik Isuma Productions Executive Committee, 1990, Baffin Island. (Photo:
© Igloolik Isuma Productions, www.isuma.ca)

There are those who argue that television of any sort is inherently destructive to Inuit (and other indigenous) lives and cultural practices. They
claim this despite the fact that many of those participating in media projects
had themselves been critical of the potential deleterious effects of media and
had sought ways to engage with media that would have a positive effect on
local life. The participants are also acutely aware of the necessity of such work
in a wider context in which native minorities in Canada are struggling for
self-determination. For them, these media practices are part of a broader
project of constituting a cultural future in which their traditions and contemporary technologies are combined in ways that can give new vitality to
Inuit life. This benefit is apparent not only in the narrative constructions of
Inuit history on their own terms, but in the social practice of making the
work, and in seeing it integrated with Canadian modernity, embodied in the
flow of television. One outside observer, after spending time in the Arctic in
the 1980s in settlements where Inuit were making community-based videos
about their lives for the IBC, concluded that:

> The most significant aspect of the IBC's progammes is that they are conceived
> and produced by the Inuit themselves. . . . and it brings a new authority to the
> old oral culture. . . . When IBC producers first approached elders in order to
> record songs and stories from their childhood, they took a lot of persuading

because many believed that these activities had been officially banned by missionaries. But now, as old crafts and skills have appeared on the IBC screens, so they have proliferated in the settlements. Watching the fabric of their everyday lives, organized into adequate if not glossy TV packages introduced by titles set in Inuktitut syllabics, has helped to weaken for the Inuit the idea that only the whites, with the unrelenting authority of the literate and educated south, can make the final decisions on the value of the Inuit lifestyle. (Lucas 1987: 17)

This effort to turn the tables on the historical trajectory of the power relations embedded in research monographs, photography, and ethnographic practice is intentional, a deeply felt response to the impact of such representational practices on Inuit society and culture. Thus, it is not only that the *activity* of media-making has helped to revive relations between generations and skills that had nearly been abandoned. The *fact* of their appearance on television on *Inuit* terms, inverts the usual hierarchy of values attached to the dominant culture's technology, conferring new prestige to Inuit "culture-making."

CLAIMS TO THE NATION:
ABORIGINAL MEDIA IN AUSTRALIA

A decade after the Inuit postwar encounter with televisual media, indigenous Australians faced a similar crossroads. In part because of their early consultation with Inuit producers and activists, they too decided to "invent" their own Aboriginal television (Michaels 1986) initially by making video images and narratives about and for themselves, shown locally via illegal low-power outback television similar to the Inuit projects described above. By the late 1990s, Aboriginal media production had expanded from very local television in remote settlements to feature films made by urban filmmakers that have premiered at the Cannes Film Festival. Today, the people who are engaged in media work across many divisions within Aboriginal life, which are themselves influenced by the shifting structures of the Australian polity that have provided resources and ideological frameworks for the development of indigenous media.[10]

The embrace of media—film, video, television—as a form of indigenous expression coincided with an increasing sense of empowerment for Aboriginal people that has accelerated since the 1960s. Until the 1996 elections that brought in the conservative government headed by John Howard, Australian social policy under Labour Party leadership had made a commitment to social justice for indigenous Australians, establishing in 1990 an indigenous body, the Aboriginal and Torres Straits Islanders Commission (ATSIC)—a complex and sometimes controversial Aboriginal bureaucracy—to govern the affairs of Aboriginal people.[11] In these kinds of formations, media played an increasingly important role in dramatizing Aboriginal claims on the nation. By the 1980s, as part of their demands, both remote living and urban activists increasingly insisted on Aboriginal control over media representations of their lives and communities, which quickly escalated into explicit interest in gaining access to production. At the same time, Aboriginal culture was becoming critical to a distinctive Australian national imaginary linked to its land and oriented away from its European origins.

The evident and often conflicting interests of both Aboriginal Australians and the Australian state in media as a site for the production of local identity and sociality as well as claims to a presence in the national imaginary is apparent in the extraordinary development of indigenous media over the past two decades.[12] Questions about the impact of mass media on Aboriginal lives first received widespread public attention in the mid-1980s with plans for the launching of Australia's first communications satellite over Central Australia. As in the Inuit case, its launch generated considerable debate among Aboriginal people, policy makers, and academics about the impact of "dumping" mainstream television signals into traditional indigenous communities in this remote desert area (Ginsburg 1991, 1993; Michaels 1986). To preempt the impact of the satellite, the Warlpiri speaking Aboriginal community of Yuendumu, with the help of American adviser and researcher Eric Michaels, developed its own video production and low-power television station, enabling it to make and show its own productions as an alternative to mainstream Australian television received via satellite. The government used that station as a model for some not very effective schemes to bring indigenously governed small media to other Aboriginal outback settlements.[13] Through Michaels's writing, other scholars took the example of Warlpiri low-power television as exemplary of the possibilities of alternative TV production, distribution, and reception, though few seem concerned with the considerable changes to both the Warlpiri Media Association and Aboriginal media more generally since the late 1980s.

Since its inception in 1983, the Warlpiri Media Association (WMA) has had an unpredictable life according to the presence or absence of certain key players in the community such as Michaels, as well as the variable reliability of white advisers whose crucial impact on these operations—both negative and positive—has been neglected in the analysis of these projects. Frances Jupurrurla Kelly, the Warlpiri man with whom Eric Michaels worked very closely (1994), carried on the work of WMA for a number of years after Michael's death in 1988, but increasingly acquired other responsibilities in his community that made it difficult for him to sustain the same level of activity and interest. It was only in the late 1990s that WMA was reactivated with the presence for a few years of an energetic and entrepreneurial young white adviser and the renewed interest of community members, and especially women, in using video to record their efforts to solve some of their community problems. Most recently, radio has become a focus of community interest.

Since the late 1990s, with the growth of the indigenous media sector across Australia, WMA has been involved intermittently with co-productions. In 1997, WMA worked with two other groups—a regional as well as a national indigenous media association—to produce a piece for a new initiative, the National Indigenous Documentary Series[14] meant to reflect media being produced in Aboriginal communities throughout Australia and broadcast in late 1997 on the ABC, Australia's prestigious state-sponsored channel. Such efforts are much applauded for supporting cooperation between remote and urban Aboriginal people. However, some attention to the production process reveals some of the tensions inherent in trying to bring remote Aboriginal media, produced at its own pace for members of the Warlpiri community, into the domain of broadcast television's relentless, industrially-driven programming schedules and the imperative to attract mass audiences.

In this case, WMA decided to create a piece about the activities of some of the senior women at Yuendumu who had organized what they had called *Munga Wardingki Partu (Night Patrol)* to control drinking, abuse, and petrol sniffing at Yuendumu.[15] For a community used to producing video on its own terms and in its own time frame, outside the industrial logics of dominant television practice, the need to have a work on schedule for the anticipated national air date on the ABC, and that could be understood by diverse television audiences, created considerable tension during the production process. Indeed, between the time the proposal was submitted to the ATSIC bureaucracy and when the project was approved and funded, the Night Patrol had become relatively inactive (in part because of its success), although it managed to reconstitute itself for the documentary. Still, WMA was having difficulty meeting the broadcast deadlines.

Eventually Rachel Perkins, a Sydney-based Aboriginal filmmaker (whose work I discuss below) and executive producer of the series, called in Pat Fiske, an experienced and sympathetic white documentary filmmaker, to help WMA complete the piece on schedule, in only three weeks and on a small budget. The working style required by such constraints was a source of friction; what in the dominant culture is regarded as a normal production schedule under such circumstances—twelve hours a day—was not appropriate to the pace of life at Yuendumu. To complicate things further, every senior woman who had served on the Night Patrol insisted on being interviewed (and paid), although it was not possible to include all of them in the half-hour show. Decisions also had to be made about to how to show some of the violent scenes; it was finally agreed to stylize them in a way that obscured the identity of the people involved. In the end, it is one of the few works of indigenous media that addresses these kinds of community-based problems positively by focusing on efforts to solve them internally. Despite the difficulties in making it, people at Yuendumu now proudly claim *Munga Wardingki Partu* as their own.[16] It was considered one of the more innovative pieces in the national series and has translated successfully to non-Aboriginal audiences abroad as well.[17]

ABORIGINALITY AND NATIONAL NARRATIVES

In the Australian mediascape, Aboriginal participation and visibility have developed not only on video in remote areas but also on national television; most recently, they are a presence in Australia's lively independent film culture, the products of which are among the nation's most visible exports. The concern to be included in that dimension of Australia's culture industries is not simply about equal access to the professional opportunities; it also reflects a recognition that distortion and/or invisibility of Aboriginal realities for the wider Australian public and even international audiences can have potentially powerful effects on political culture. Aboriginal activists from urban areas were particularly vocal in demanding a positive and creative presence on state-run national television such as Australia's ABC and its alternative multicultural channel, the Special Broadcast Service (SBS). The indigenous units that were established out of that moment became an important base for a small and talented group of young urban Aboriginal cultural activists— many of them children of the leaders of the Aboriginal civil rights movement— to forge a cohort and gain the professional experience that is placing them and their work onto national and international stages.

The twenty or so urban Aboriginal people who have entered into film-making recognize the potential of their work to change how Aboriginal realities are understood for the wider Australian public and even international audiences. As a case in point, I want to briefly track the career of Rachel Perkins. The daughter of the late Charles Perkins, a well-known Aboriginal activist/politician and former sports hero, she exemplifies those most active in the indigenous media scene today, a generation of cultural activists who came of age when the struggle for Aboriginal civil rights was already a social fact, due in large measure to the efforts of their parents. She grew up with new political possibilities in place but a recognition that the world of representations and the cultural spaces available for them were not so easily changed. For example, when she was born in 1970, just after citizenship was granted to Aboriginal Australians in 1967, blacks and whites were still segregated in cinemas in some parts of Australia.

In 1988, at the age of 18, hoping to gain some skills in media and make some contact with Arrernte people, from which her family was descended, Rachel began her training at a regional Aboriginal media association that serves both remote communities and the small towns and cities that dot Australia's Northern Territory.[18] Once there, she worked her way up to produce and direct language and current affairs programs. In 1991, Rachel went to Sydney to head the indigenous unit of the SBS, Australia's state-run multicultural television station.[19] While there, she commissioned and produced *Blood Brothers* (1992), a series of four one-hour documentaries about different aspects of Aboriginal history and culture told through the personal lives of four prominent Aboriginal men. Her agenda was, in a sense, to create "screen memories" for the majority of Australians—black and white—who knew virtually nothing of the role of Aboriginal people in the formation of modern Australia. The first was about her father, Charles Perkins, a national soccer champion who then became the first Aboriginal student at Sydney University. In 1965 he worked with other student activists to organize "freedom rides" to challenge the racist conditions in which rural Aboriginal people lived at that time. The documentary retraces the history of this initial stage of the Aboriginal civil rights movement through retrospective accounts by Perkins and his fellow protesters, both black and white, as they revisit the places where they had carried out civil disobedience more than twenty-five years earlier.

Rachel Perkins and other indigenous producers who have worked for Australian state television carry a specific burden of representation: they must create an Aboriginal presence on national mass media in settings where they are subject to large Euro-Australian television bureaucracies. For them, questions of cultural accountability are worked out quite differently than they are in remote areas where the primary audience is from the producer's own community. Rachel, for instance, had to make compromises with SBS editors because of what they felt would draw non-Aboriginal audiences. As she explained to me:

> I scripted to include the massacres which happened in the area in the early 1800s right up to 1985 where a guy was gunned down in the street. But the script editor was just saying, "Look, you're not making an epic film here, . . . you've got to concentrate on the guts of the story which is the freedom ride." So all of those sort of really bloody relations couldn't be part of the film. . . . I wanted to make it entertaining and personal and humorous so that people would watch it, you know, and become more involved in it. There was a lot of violence that happened within that period though that I didn't show, and that's also because people didn't necessarily want to talk about it. . . . But you don't have to measure racial inequality by the amount of people that are killed. In Australia it's more of a psychological warfare with people, growing up under that regime, that was the thrust of what I was trying to get across.

In reaching out to a mixed but still predominantly non-Aboriginal national audience, *Freedom Ride* spoke directly and deliberately to their relationship to the struggle for Aboriginal civil rights, serving as a reminder of the possibility of white activism on behalf of that cause nearly thirty years earlier, at a contemporary moment when political separatism too often serves as an excuse for apathy. Using a mixture of archival footage, recreations of historical scenes, oral histories, and contemporary verité footage, the documentary is powerful testimony to how political consciousness was created in everyday experiences of discrimination and transformed through direct action, much of it inspired by knowledge of the American civil rights movement gained in part through the mass media. In a particularly poignant moment that also reveals the key role of such mediations in creating transnational links among activists, Charles Perkins recollects a solidarity visit from an African American delegation and how unexpectedly moved the Australians were when the visitors sang "We Shall Overcome," which they had heard many times on records, radio, and television. This example of the role that such media played historically in creating contact between social movements in different parts of the world point to a broader frame: the documentary itself is embedded in a context of social action in which its presence on national television is yet another level of assertion and insertion of a rarely visible Aboriginal presence and perspective on Australian history.

In the 1960s, Rachel Perkins's father was inspired to become an activist in part by his knowledge of African American civil rights leaders. Thirty years later, Rachel named as models a new generation of African American cultural activists such as Spike Lee, whose feature films, based on his own cultural experience, still speak to many audiences:

> We don't see making only Aboriginal stuff as being ghettoized; we see it as leading to a really dynamic area of the industry which is black film-making. . . .
> There's a huge perception that Aboriginal stuff is only interesting to Aboriginal people, and that it's boring. Yet *Blood Brothers* was one of the highest rating doco [documentary] series that has ever been on SBS. Until *Once Were Warriors* [the 1994 feature film made by Maori director Lee Tamahori], all I'd heard was that indigenous films will never get an audience, people aren't interested in indigenous characters, that audiences are racist.

In 1993, frustrated by a lack of funds and compromises she had to make, Rachel left the SBS.[20] Eventually she formed her own production company, Blackfella Films, in order to complete her first feature film, *Radiance* (1997). Adapted from a work by Euro-Australian playwright Louis Nowra, the story unfolds as unspoken complex secrets are revealed about the relationships among three Aboriginal sisters who reunite after the death of their mother, each of whom embodies a different relationship to her cultural identity. The film was a major success in Australia, and in the summer of 1997 it was screened at the Cannes Film Festival in France.

Rachel Perkins's work as filmmaker, producer, and activist is exemplary of a young Aboriginal cultural elite engaged in constituting a vital Aboriginal modernity through a variety of media, including music, visual arts, film, and drama. These forms provide vehicles for new narrations of the place of Aboriginality in the nation—*Freedom Ride, Night Patrol,* and *Radiance* are but three examples—that are not tied to traditional practices. This work has helped to establish and enlarge a counterpublic sphere in which Aboriginality is central and emergent, especially in the changed circumstances signified by the 1993 Australian High Court decision granting native title to Australia's indigenous people—that is, recognizing their prior ownership of so-called Crown Land. It stemmed from the landmark Murray (Mer) Island Land Case (1992), commonly known as the Mabo land rights case after one of the plaintiffs, the late Eddie Mabo, a Torres Straits Islander man. In an article written in 1994, in the post-Mabo euphoria, cultural critic Stephen Muecke argued that these transformations would mobilize "new ways of positioning Aboriginal history identity and culture . . . in which Aboriginal Australians occupy a very different and very crucial site from which new postnational subjectivities can be constituted, in which new stories enable new 'structures of feeling' and of agency that in turn translate into a new politics of nation" (1994: 254).

His optimistic claims clearly were written before the 1996 elections of the politically conservative government of John Howard. Nonetheless, in the indigenous media sector, these concerns—to broaden the representation of national narratives to include Aboriginal lifeworlds past and present—are still the issues engaging the cohort of media-makers of which Rachel Perkins is a part. The notion of nationhood that helped establish Aboriginal media's emergence in the 1980s embraced Australia's own regional and cultural diversity, underscoring a sense of national identity that is decentered, flexible, and inclusive of indigenous cultures. The work has continued under the Howard regime that has mobilized right-wing and racist backlash among some white Australians against what they see as undue cultural and political gains by Aboriginal people and other claims to multiculturalism as a legitimate frame for the Australian nation. Thus, at the beginning of the twenty-first century, Aboriginal media-makers are engaged in a broader war of position over the question of Australian national identity in which the visibility of Aboriginal lives and histories play a key role.

Central to that process are efforts to reverse and resignify the history of colonial looking relations in which film and photography became the visible evidence of an indigenous world that was expected to disappear but instead persists. Part of the evidence for rights to land on Mer Island (north of Australia) was some of the first footage ever made of indigenous people: English anthropologist Alfred Court Haddon's film documenting Mer (Murray) islanders performing dances in 1898 that are still in use today, proving continuity of tradition. There is some irony in this resignification, since Haddon, in the tradition of his day, was interested in capturing images of these people before they disappeared from the face of the earth (Holgate 1994). Instead, the Haddon footage provided the visible evidence—the screen memories—that proved the opposite: that they are still very much alive and continue to occupy the land that has been part of their cultural legacy. The use of this ethnographic footage for the purpose of a land claim reversed its status as a late nineteenth-century sign of the imagined extinction of Aboriginal culture. It turned the footage instead into an index of their cultural persistence and a basis for indigenous claims to their land and cultural rights in the present. This reversal stands, metaphorically, for the ways in which indigenous people have been using the inscription of their screen memories in media to "talk back" to structures of power and state that have denied their rights, subjectivity, and citizenship for over two hundred years.

ALTERNATIVE ACCOUNTINGS

Film, video, and television—as technologies of objectification as well as reflection—contain within them a double set of possibilities. They can be seductive conduits for imposing the values and language of the dominant culture on minoritized people, what some indigenous activists have called a potential cultural "neutron bomb," the kind that kills people and leaves inanimate structures intact (Kuptana, cited in David 1998: 36). These technologies—unlike most others—also offer possibilities for "talking back" to and through the categories that have been created to contain indigenous people. It is not the technologies themselves, of course, that produce the latter possibility, but the timing and social location of their arrival. Despite his facility with the camera, Allakariallak's participation in Flaherty's film was not acknowledged; nor were the structures in place that would have enabled him to really make use of "the Aggie." For Inuit fifty years later, politically mobilized and subject to the regimes of the state in their lives, access to a satellite has been crucial, linking communities across the Arctic (and Canada) in ways that are culturally and politically powerful.

Similarly, after a long history as objects of photographic representation, media were first embraced by Aboriginal people at a particular historical conjuncture in Australia. In the 1980s, progressive state policy, indigenous activists, an independent and alternative film culture, and remote and urban Aboriginal people all became interested—sometimes for different reasons—in how these media could be indigenized formally and substantively to give objective form to efforts for the expression of cultural identity, the preservation of language and ritual, and the telling of indigenous histories. Socially, they are creating new arenas for meaningful cultural production for people living in both remote and urban-based communities. In cosmopolitan centers like Sydney, groups such as the Indigenous Programmes Unit at the ABC serve as a critical node in a mixed-race network of filmmakers, musicians, activists, artists, and writers who make up an elite stratum of Australia's equivalent of a post–civil rights generation. And increasingly, new bureaucratic structures of state-mediated Aboriginal modernity are emerging, such as the National Indigenous Media Association of Australia and the Indigenous Branch of the Australian Film Commission. In 1997 the Indigenous Branch launched a new initiative to train Aboriginal people in drama and feature-film production, marking a significant shift from the usual consignment of indigenous media to either the extreme localism of outback television that marked its emergence in the mid 1980s or the genre-defined limits of documentary that shaped its presence on national television after 1988.

Tracking these emergent media practices, one can see how they have developed in relation to Aboriginal concerns and national policies. In the 1980s the experimental efforts of people in remote communities to document their lives, cultures, and histories were spurred by an initial protectionist desire to block the penetration of Western television while also working out the formal, social, and cultural protocols for indigenizing media—what media scholar and activist Eric Michaels called *The Aboriginal Invention of Television in Central Australia* (1986). By the late 1980s, spurred by the moment of national redefinition constituted around Australia's Bicentenary, Aboriginal interest in media expanded to the urban sector and the creation of an indigenous presence on state television. In that context, producers focused initially on the presentation to national audiences—indigenous and otherwise—of what they called positive imagery of their lives and of Australian history from an Aboriginal point of view. This was intended to counter both the absence and the unremitting negativity of their representation in the media more generally, from the celebratory history of *Freedom Ride* to the efforts to combat problems such as alcoholism and violence against women through local forms of self-determination exemplified in *Night Patrol*.

By the mid 1990s, when a new cohort started to leave the confines of documentary and work in dramatic genres, they found yet another mode of expressive possibility. These more recent fictional works offer self-conscious, alternative, and multiple accountings of Aboriginal lifeworlds, as in the complex gendered, cultural landscape given almost surreal shape in feature films such as Rachel Perkins's *Radiance*. They are testimony to the range of experience and practice contained within the category "indigenous"; their vitality speaks to the importance of the recuperation of "screen memories" for contemporary generations of Aboriginal Australians. Positioned somewhere between the phenomenological lifeworlds of their everyday lives and the colonial categories through which they have been constituted, the making of these media is part of a broader set of practices through which First Nations people in Australia and Canada are reflecting on and transforming the conditions of their lives.

NOTES

An early version of this essay was given as the 1998 Daryl Forde Lecture, Anthropology Department, University College, London. Thanks to Danny Miller, Howard Morphy, and Anna Grimshaw for their comments at that event; to Lila Abu-Lughod, Brian Larkin, Fred Myers, Barbara Abrash, and Jay Ruby for their helpful readings of later versions; and to the many people engaged in indigenous media in Australia and Canada who generously shared their time and insights with me while I was there, including: Brian Arley, Philip Batty, Norman Cohn, Brenda Croft, Graham Dash, Jennifer Deger, Francoise Dussart, Pat Fiske, Melinda Hinkson, David Jowsey, Tom Kantor, Frances Jupurrurla Kelley, Sak Kunuk, Brett Leavy, Marcia Langton, Mary Laughren, Michael Leigh, Rachel Perkins, Frances Peters, Catriona McKenzie, Michael Meadows, Helen Molnar, Nicki McCoy, Michael Riley, Sally Riley, Lorna Roth, Walter Saunders, and many others. Support for travel for my research was provided in part by Guggenheim and MacArthur Fellowships.

1. *Nanook* is discussed in nearly every book written on documentary, as well as in much of the revisionist scholarship on the genre. For other discussions of the gramophone scene, see Rony 1996; Ruby 2001; Taussig 1994.

2. In the case of *Nanook,* for example, in terms of the broader political economy, the film bears traces of the end of the global fur trade that fueled much of the settlement of North America. *Nanook* was sponsored by Revillon Frères, the French fur company that owned the trading post in the film, and was completed in 1922 at a historical moment when the fur of Arctic foxes, which Nanook hunts in the film and brings to the post, graced many a Parisian shoulder. These global trading processes underwrote and set the stage for the initial engagement of Allakariallak and others with the technologies of cinematic objectification (Rotha 1980).

3. Through processes of displacement and condensation, Freud writes: "What is important is replaced in memory by something else which appears unimportant" ([1901] 1965: 248). For a fuller discussion of his concept of screen memory, see chap. 5 in *The Psychopathology of Everyday Life.*

4. A 1986 report by the Federal Task Force on Broadcasting Policy, in its support of aboriginal broadcasting as an integral part of the Canadian broadcasting system, called for a separate satellite distribution system to carry aboriginal language programming (David 1998).

5. The APTN is a unique TV experiment in many ways. The Canadian government has ordered cable systems to carry it as part of their basic package, a mandate that has met with some opposition from the Canadian Cable Television Association. Although there is some concern that this might be perceived as a "guilt tax," others have been more enthusiastic. For further information on all this, see the APTN website at www.aptn.ca.

6. Jerry Mander (1991), for example, argues that video and television technologies are irredeemably destructive to native life. His argument, as Laura Marks pointed out in her overview of Inuit media, "equates tradition with rigidity, rather than understand adaptability itself as a longstanding value" (1994: 6) and also fails to account for what kind of media are actually being made. A more recent example is anthropologist James Weiner's 1997 polemic, "Televisualist Anthropology," directed against indigenous media (which he calls "ersatz culture") and those who study it,

including myself. We argue that far from being subsumed by contact with mass cultural forms, as these critics have argued, indigenous media-makers have taken on Western media technologies to defend themselves against what they see as the culturally destructive effects of mass media, producing work about their own lives, a strategy some have called "innovative traditionalism." A more poetic phrasing, "Starting Fire with Gunpowder," used for the title of a film about the IBC (Poisey and Hansen 1991), captures the sense of turning a potentially destructive Western form into something useful to the lives of indigenous people.

7. Their works are produced in the Inuktitut language and syllabics (for titling) and are subtitled in English and French. For those interested in finding out more about the work of this extraordinary group, I recommend their website, www.isuma.ca.

8. Produced with the support of the Canada Council, the National Film Board, and the government of the Northwest Territories, the work of Igloolik Isuma has been seen on TVNC and in screenings at many institutions, including the National Gallery of Canada, the Museum of Modern Art in New York, the American Film Institute, the Museé d'Art Moderne in Paris, and the Museum of Northern Peoples in Hokkaido, Japan. Reviews in mainstream papers have been appreciative to laudatory.

9. See comments by T. Nasook at www.isuma.ca.

10. Elsewhere, I situate the work within more global developments, from the marketing of satellites and small media technologies, to the growth of transnational political networks supporting the rights of indigenous peoples. In addition, more specialized cultural arenas such as international indigenous film festivals have become important sites for constituting linkages among indigenous media-makers worldwide (Ginsburg 1993).

11. These state policies and bureaucracies must be understood in part as an outgrowth of modern movements for Aboriginal rights. The expansion of indigenous political and cultural activism—inspired in part by the civil rights and Black Power movements in the United States—helped to catalyze constitutional changes that granted Aboriginal Australian voting rights in 1962 and Australian citizenship in 1967 and set the stage for the developing recognition of Aboriginal claims for land rights and cultural autonomy beginning in the 1970s.

12. In 1980 only a few radio shows existed. In a 1994 survey of indigenous involvement in media (not including the growth in radio), remote communities had 150 local media associations, eighty small-scale television stations, and two satellite television services with indigenous programming (Molnar 1995: 170). By 1993 a representative body, the National Indigenous Media Association of Australia (NIMAA), had been formed to advocate for and help link the hundreds of indigenous broadcasters working in radio, video, and television throughout Australia. In addition, the creation of Indigenous Program Units at the state-sponsored television stations, the Australian Broadcasting Corporation (ABC), and the Special Broadcast Service (SBS) in 1989 helped create a base for a strong urban cohort of media-makers that came into their own a decade later.

13. For scholars alarmed by the "wasteland" of TV, the Yuendumu experiment acquired the aura of a plucky outback David whose tiny satellite dishes and culturally distinctive video productions served as a kind of well-targeted epistemological slingshot against globalizing satellites and mass media programming (see, e.g., Hebdige 1994). This valorization of circumstances in which indigenous people are rep-

resented as existing comfortably with both their own traditions and Western technologies is embodied in state policy, a particular embrace of Aboriginal modernity that elsewhere I have called hi-tech primitivism (Ginsburg 1993: 562).

14. WMA has worked with the regional group CAAMA (the Central Australian Aboriginal Media Association) based in Alice Springs, as well as the national indigenous advocacy organization, NIMAA (National Indigenous Media Association of Australia), which sponsored the series with support from the Aboriginal bureaucracy ATSIC, as well as the ABC and the Olympic Arts Festival.

15. The video project about the night patrol was directed by a Warlpiri woman, Valerie Martin, who worked with the help of WMA's white adviser, the late Tom Kantor.

16. Some of this was going on while I was in central Australia in 1997. I am also grateful to Pat Fiske and Tom Kantor for providing me with their views of the situation.

17. For example, it was one of two works from the series selected for the Margaret Mead Film Festival in New York City and was warmly received at the screenings I attended there.

18. The station she trained at was the Central Australian Aboriginal Media Association (CAAMA) in Alice Springs. For an account of the formation of this station, see Ginsburg 1991. Rachel's knowledge of work from remote communities and regional media associations was influential in bringing that work into urban Aboriginal settings; she has continued to play a key role in programming work from both remote and urban Aboriginal communities on national television.

19. With a small budget and few resources, she created work at SBS but also brought in material from regional and local Aboriginal media associations through her links to CAAMA and more remote groups in its orbit, such as the Warlpiri Media Association (WMA) at Yuendumu.

20. The next year she was recruited to head up the Indigenous Programmes Unit at the ABC where, in addition to continuing their Aboriginal cultural affairs show, *Blackout,* she produced a series on Aboriginal music, *Songlines,* and negotiated the agreement with NIMAA to act as executive producer for the eight works for the National Indigenous Documentary Series—*Night Patrol* was one—made in 1997 and screened on the ABC later that year. During that period, Rachel took a temporary leave from the ABC in order to complete *Radiance* with her partner, Euro-Australian filmmaker Ned Lander.

REFERENCES

Berger, Sally. 1995a. Move Over Nanook. In *Wide Angle,* special issue on The Flaherty, 17 (1–4): 177–92.

———. 1995b. Time Travellers. *Felix: A Journal of Media Arts and Communication* 2 (1): 102–12.

Brisebois, Deborah. 1990. *Whiteout Warning: Courtesy of the Federal Government.* Inuit Broadcasting Corporation. October.

David, Jennifer. 1998. Seeing Ourselves, Being Ourselves: Broadcasting Aboriginal Television in Canada. *Cultural Survival Quarterly* 22 (2): 36–39.

Fleming, Kathleen, and Stephen Hendrick. 1991. Zacharias Kunuk: Video Maker and Inuit Historian. *Inuit Art Quarterly* 6 (3): 24–28.

———. 1996. Igloolik Video: An Organic Response from a Culturally Sound Community. *Inuit Art* 11 (2): 30–38.

Freud, Sigmund. [1901] 1965. *The Psychopathology of Everyday Life.* New York: Norton.

———. 1975. *Abstracts of the Standard Edition of the Complete Psychological Works of Sigmund Freud.* Edited by Carrie Lee Rothgeb. Rockville, Md.: NIMH.

Gaines, Jane. 1988. White Privilege and Looking Relations: Race and Gender in Feminist Film Theory. *Screen* 29 (4): 12–27.

Ginsburg, Faye. 1991. Indigenous Media: Faustian Contract or Global Village? *Cultural Anthropology* 6 (1): 92–112.

———. 1993. Aboriginal Media and the Australian Imaginary. *Public Culture* special issue, Screening Politics in a World of Nations, 5 (3): 557–78.

———. 1994. Culture/Media: A (Mild) Polemic. *Anthropology Today* 10 (2): 5–15.

Hebdige, Dick. 1994. Foreword to *Bad Aboriginal Art: Tradition, Media, and Technological Horizons* by Eric Michaels. Minneapolis: University of Minnesota Press.

Holgate, Ben. 1994. Now for a Celluloid Dreaming. *Sydney Morning Herald,* November 23.

Lucas, Martin. 1987. TV on Ice. *New Society* 9: 15–17.

Mander, Jerry. 1991. *In the Absence of the Sacred: The Failure of Technology and the Survival of the Indian Nations.* San Francisco: Sierra Club Books.

Marks, Laura. 1994. Reconfigured Nationhood: A Partisan History of the Inuit Broadcasting Corporation. *Afterimage* (March): 4–8.

Meadows, Michael. 1996. Indigenous Cultural Diversity: Television Northern Canada. *Culture and Policy* 7 (1): 25–44.

Michaels, Eric. 1986. *The Aboriginal Invention of Television in Central Australia: 1982–1986.* Canberra: Australian Institute of Aboriginal Studies.

———. 1994. *Bad Aboriginal Art: Tradition, Media, and Technological Horizons.* Minneapolis: University of Minnesota Press.

Miller, Toby. 1995. Exporting Truth from Aboriginal Australia: 'Portions of Our Past Become Present Again, Where Only the Melancholy Light of Origin Shines.' *Media Information Australia* 76: 7–17.

Molnar, Helen. 1995. Indigenous Media Development in Australia: A Product of Struggle and Opposition. *Cultural Studies* 9 (1): 169–90.

Muecke, Stephen. 1994. Narrative and Intervention: Aboriginal Filmmaking and Policy. *Continuum* 8 (2): 248–57.

Poisey, David, and William Hansen. 1991. *Starting Fire with Gunpowder.* Video by Tamarack Productions, Edmonton, Canada.

Rony, Fatima. 1996. *The Third Eye: Race, Cinema, and Ethnographic Spectacle.* Durham, N.C.: Duke University Press.

Roth, Lorna. 1994. *Northern Voices and Mediating Structures: The Emergence and Development of First Peoples' Television Broadcasting in the Canadian North.* Ph.D. diss., Concordia University, Montreal, Quebec, Canada.

————. 2000. The Crossing of Borders and the Building of Bridges: Steps in the Construction of the APTN in Canada. In *International Journal of Communication Studies*, special issue on Canadian communications, 62 (3–4): 251–69.

Roth, Lorna, and Gail Valaskakis. 1989. Aboriginal Broadcasting in Canada: A Case Study in Democratization. In *Communication for and against Democracy*, edited by Marc Raboy and Peter Bruck, pp. 221–34. Montreal: Black Rose Books.

Rotha, Paul, with Basil Wright. 1980. Nanook and the North. *Studies in Visual Communication* 6 (2): 33–60.

Ruby, Jay. 1980. Introduction: Nanook and the North. *Studies in Visual Communication* 6 (2).

————. 2001. *Philosophical Toys: Explorations of Film and Anthropology*. Chicago: University of Chicago Press.

Taussig, Michael. 1994. *Mimesis and Alterity*. New York: Routledge.

Weiner, James. 1997. Televisualist Anthropology: Representation, Aesthetics, Politics. *Current Anthropology* 38 (2): 197–236.

2

Visual Media
and the Primitivist Perplex

Colonial Fantasies, Indigenous Imagination,
and Advocacy in North America

Harald E. L. Prins

Striking images of tawny humans collaged with soaring eagles or some other form of wildlife, aesthetically photographed against a backdrop of pristine wilderness—such imagery is standard fare in visual representations of indigenous peoples. Based largely on the European primitivist stereotype of the "noble savage" as child of nature, this time-tested construct has long allowed the instant wrapping of the indigenous "other."

Beginning with Carpenter (1973), several anthropologists have recognized the destructive potential of such media "myths" on tribal communities (see also Biesele and Hitchcock 1999; Marshall 1993; Tomaselli 1996). More recently, some scholars have started to focus on the currency of such ideologically charged ideas in counterhegemonic strategies of indigenous self-representation (Conklin 1997; Ginsburg 1991, 1993; Prins 1989, 1997b; Turner 1992). On both fronts, too little attention has been given to the question of why indigenous peoples frequently collaborate with outsiders in the production of such myths.

In this essay about indigenous peoples and the politics of exotic imagery, I argue not only that indigenous peoples may recognize the primitivist formula, but also that some actively draw on it as a cross-cultural "structure of comprehension and imperatives for action" (Wolf 1999: 200). Having become a key element in their rhetoric of self-fashioning, it shows up in their "visual performatives" (ibid.: 56) and thus may serve as a persuasive device in their collective quest for biological and cultural survival. In previous writing I have referred to this dialectical complex as "the paradox of primitivism."

My own interest in the concept of primitivism relative to indigenous peoples is more than theoretical. As an anthropologist also trained in filmmaking, I have long operated in the craggy corridor between action anthropology, indigenous political advocacy, and visual media production. My activism began in 1981 when an Indian organization hired me as its director of research and development. This led to a decade of native rights work on behalf of a Mi'kmaq community, resulting in a land-claim settlement and federal recognition of their tribal status (Prins 1994a). Their success was due in part to a film about them, which I coproduced and they sponsored. Since then, I have been involved in several other film projects with and about North American Indians.

INDIGENOUS RIGHTS, THE POLITICS OF DOMINANCE AND PRIMITIVISM

"Indigenous peoples" is a widely used term embracing an enormous diversity of tribal and semitribal groups. It includes those "people living in countries which have populations composed of different ethnic or racial groups who are descendants of the earliest populations which survive in the area, and who do not, as a group, control the national government of the countries within which they live" (pamphlet by World Council of Indigenous Peoples, n.d.). In the United States, 558 indigenous groups are formally recognized by the federal government—223 "Native Villages" in Alaska and some 335 "tribes" in the lower forty-eight states. Hundreds more have no official status. In Canada, indigenous peoples are officially organized in almost 600 native bands, now also called First Nations. Allowed to endure as quasi-sovereign communities in both countries, most of the federally recognized native groups have tracts of land reserved for their exclusive use. However, less than half of all people identified as indigenous reside in these enclaves. Today there are 278 Indian reservations (also called pueblos or rancherias) in the United States, and Canada counts a total of 2,283 (mostly small and isolated) "reserves."

Because they survive largely at the mercy of the encapsulating polities, indigenous peoples often must appeal to foreign or international institutions in order to secure (or regain) their vested interests, including their right to govern themselves and determine their own affairs. These native or aboriginal rights form part of an ill-defined jural bundle that takes on different forms in the ever-changing context of domination and resistance. Whatever its complexity, there is a direct moral link between native rights and internationally recognized principles of human rights. Especially significant for indigenous peoples are the International Human Rights Covenants (passed in 1966 and enforced as treaties ten years later). For instance, the Covenant on Civil and Political Rights insists that "in those states in which ethnic, religious or linguistic minorities exist, persons belonging to such minorities shall not be denied the right . . . to enjoy their own culture, to profess and practice their own religion, or to use their own language" (Human Rights 1978, article 27, p. 12). Yet while Canada and the United States, like most other sovereign states, endorse the principles of human rights, they do not support indigenous quests for full self-determination or sovereignty.

Indigenous peoples may base their defense in part on the idea of "natural" law and its essential freedoms, but hand in hand they use the construct of primitivism in their political efforts to stir outsiders into action on their behalf. Primitivism facilitates a quick wrapping of the "other," and it has long been a defining device in European portrayals of indigenous peoples. Its stereotypic imagery represents an obvious message: a modern Moloch is about to devour a pristine wilderness where free humans still embrace ancient traditions of natural beauty and purity (see Berkhofer 1973; Lemaire 1986).

In North America, where memories of vicious encounters between invaders and defenders are sometimes too offensive to recall, much frontier history has been repressed, cleansed, and collapsed into popular myth, elaborately illustrated by the imagery of romantic exoticism. A pivotal moment in this mythopoeia took place in the early 1770s, when Euro-American colonists began to separate themselves ideologically from Britain and turned the primitivist construct of the "Indian" as noble savage into a political symbol of "natural" freedom in the New World (Prins 1986, 2001a). In search of a new national identity after the American Revolution, the newly independent "patriots" positioned themselves as the ideological heirs of America's original inhabitants and developed the "Indian" into a national icon. As born-again "Indians," American whites declared the continent's indigenous peoples unfit for civilization and cast them into a yet another mythic role—the Vanishing Indian. Turning into an enduring national neurosis, the new American veneration of the surrogate Indian led to a mortification of the authentic one. This obsession, in the form of romantic nationalism, swept the Atlantic seaboard and found abundant expression in poetry, literature, drama, painting, and pageantry. Especially from about 1830 onward, the idea of the vanishing Indian became highly popular with the American white public. Sometimes represented in contradictory terms as racially inferior or naturally vigorous, it was the image of the doomed Indian hero that most appealed to the white public.

Meanwhile, American Indian communities were reduced as internal colonies. Encapsulated, they survived on reservations but became sharply limited in their cultural practices. White dominant society then began to subvert indigenous understandings of themselves and the world around them. Acting out their own colonial fantasies, whites superimposed the invented "Indian" of their own imaginations on the captive indigenous nations. In this hegemonic configuration, North American Indians became subjects of internal colonialism in a double sense—both politically and psychologically. We might think of this as the "primitivist perplex." In the ongoing (com)modification of Indian identities, visual media played an ambiguous role.

INDIAN IMAGES ON FILM: IMAGINATION OR DOCUMENTATION?

The cross-cultural activity of taking pictures of indigenous peoples has always been politically charged, involving complex power relations. White photographers began visiting Indian reservations in the 1850s. Some of the tribes referred to them as shadow catchers—an apt name on more than one level because they were creating a romanticized pictorial record of exotic peoples white society presumed were about to vanish. In the 1890s, Edward S. Curtis, the most famous shadow catcher, embarked on a massive salvage project in visual anthropology. Viewing his 40,000 Indian photographs as deathbed shots, taken primarily for posterity, he tried to eliminate evidence of Western civilization in his images.

At the turn of the century, the emerging motion picture industry discovered American Indians as popular entertainment. Recently herded onto reservations, doomed to languish in boredom and abject poverty, large numbers of Plains Indians signed on to play "Indians" in the movies. The genre became so popular so quickly that between 1910 and 1914 studios released some 900 Indian features. While some Native Americans made a modest living as actors, others made early public protests about the way their people were portrayed in the new media (Friar and Friar 1972: 89–111, 250).

Ethnographic films and documentaries, which became increasingly common after the 1920s, are more difficult to assess in terms of truth and reality than feature films, which are always staged and usually based on fiction. Here, it suffices to note that ethnographic films concern the description and explanation of human cultures. Historically associated with a discipline that specialized in the cross-cultural study of scriptless, non-Western ("primitive") peoples, this genre still routinely concentrates on indigenous peoples and their traditional lifeways. It has become instrumental in the salvage ethnography of numerous indigenous cultures.

Documentaries, in contrast, typically promote an explicit social agenda such as community betterment, or they involve political advocacy on behalf of the disenfranchised. This genre quickly developed into a powerful instrument of political persuasion. Initially documentary filmmakers focused on the downtrodden within modern Western society. However, in the 1960s, in the wake of Third World decolonization movements, they began to train their cameras also on the native rights struggles of indigenous people, giving birth to the ethnographic documentary (see also Loizos 1993: 171).

INDIGENOUS MEDIA, ROMANTIC EXOTICISM, AND CULTURAL SURVIVAL

Although it is true that indigenous peoples have long been portrayed along lines of dominant society's primitivist ideology, evidence suggests that tribespeople who willingly posed or performed for strangers had their own perceptions about the politics of visual representation. Ironically, the pictorial genre of romantic exoticism provided them with an effective means of communicating the message that they, as the continent's indigenous peoples, represented a way of life utterly distinct from that of their white opponents. Without these pictures, there would be very little to remind future generations of what they had tried to preserve as guardians of their own ancestral heritage.

Especially the "Vanishing Indian" trope has spawned countless romantic portrayals of "authentic" precontact Indian culture—a remarkable collection of visual images intended to exclude any indication of the presence and influence of white society. These images took on new significance in the 1960s. The ideological crisis that occurred within Western civilization during that decade fueled counterculture fascination with primitivism and provided a unique opportunity for indigenous activists to create a new discursive space for cultural revitalization in their depressed communities.

Challenging mainstream society's repressive policies, radicalized Indians proclaimed Red Power and sought to end long-standing forced assimilation programs on their reservations. Searching for information about missing traditions, some could still find knowledgeable tribal elders. Many more, however, discovered their ancestral cultures through the works of outside ethnographers and visual media-makers. Paintings, photographs, and films, along with descriptive texts, became treasure troves—especially those that masked the presence of white civilization. "Born-again primitives" (Means 1995: 146–51) reclaimed these visual records as important pieces of their cultural heritage and dismissed criticisms that many of these romantic images are fabrications—yet another patronizing effort by white outsiders to degrade their ancestral legacy. Asserting their own signifying privileges, they have resolved for themselves what these visual records really mean—reconnection to tradition and inspiration to reclaim and build upon what was lost (see also Horse Capture 1993: 14–15).

In the wake of the Red Power movement, many American Indian activists have become involved in visual media production on both sides of the camera—as subjects, directors, producers, and distributors. Beyond advocacy, they recognize the value of modern visual media as a means to make a coherent record of their cultural heritage for future generations. Indigenous groups now embrace film, and especially video, as tools for educating their own communities and encouraging self-reflection and discussions about tribal identity. These tools also provide a venue to inform and link up with other indigenous communities and the rest of the world.

Since the early 1970s, indigenous film- and video-makers in North America have produced numerous documentaries. Often sharing a commitment to the cause of indigenous justice and freedom, they typically employ modern visual media to further public awareness of treaty rights, land claims, hunting and fishing rights, religious freedom, language preservation, repatriation of artifacts, and reburial of ancestral remains. Among the better-known indigenous media-makers are Sherman Alexie (Spokane), George Burdeau (Blackfeet), Shirley Cheechoo (Cree), Chris Eyre (Cheyenne/Arapaho), Hanay Geiogamah (Kiowa-Delaware), Doug George (Mohawk), Alexie Isaac (Yup'ik), Phil Lucas (Choctaw), Catherine Martin (Mi'kmaq), Victor Masayesva (Hopi), Alanis Obomsawin (Odanak Abenaki), Sandra Osawa (Makah/Hilohitsa), Anna Romero (Winnebago), Chris Spotted Eagle (Houma), and Loretta Todd (Cree), to mention a few.

Native American Public Telecommunications (NAPT), originally founded as the Native American Public Broadcasting Consortium in 1976, has gained notable influence over the way indigenous peoples in North America are represented. Funded largely by the Corporation for Public Broadcasting, this nonprofit organization's headquarters are at the Nebraska Educational TV and Radio Center in Lincoln. With a majority-Indian board, it aims to be "the authoritative national resource for authentic, culturally educational and entertaining programming by and about Native Americans."

Thanks largely to NAPT, the 1990s witnessed tremendous growth in telecommunications services by, for, and about North American Indians. In 1992, together with Nebraska Educational Television, NAPT joined the American Indian Higher Education Consortium and now assists in a video telecommunications satellite network for tribally controlled Indian community colleges throughout the country. Also, NAPT has provided support for five national Public Broadcasting Service (PBS) program series and commissioned several dozen independent films and videos for public television. Moreover, it has created its own indigenous media company, Vision Maker Video, which claims to have the largest collection of "culturally authentic Native American videos" in the United States, most of them produced, co-produced, or written by Indians.

Whatever the technological means of cross-cultural communication, and however great the measure of media control, tribal groups and media-makers must confront a vexing question rooted in primitivist ideology and internal colonialism: What is "culturally authentic" in contemporary indigenous communities? Negotiating this problem of the primitivist perplex is vital in the quest for full emancipation and decolonization. With this in mind, I turn now to two examples from my own work on film projects concerning indigenous cultural survival and native rights.

DILEMMA OF PRIMITIVISM 1: THE MI'KMAQ FILM PROJECT

Our Lives in Our Hands (1986) is an example of film as political agency. The idea for this cultural survival documentary about a band of Mi'kmaq Indians emerged in 1981, shortly after I hired on as director of research and development for the Association of Aroostook Indians (AAI) in Houlton, Maine. Established in 1970, AAI served off-reservation Mi'kmaqs and Maliseets, Algonquian-speaking tribal communities living in the state's northernmost county of Aroostook. Many of these Indian families lived in shacks and suffered poor health. Most survived on welfare or eked out an existence as seasonal farm laborers or loggers. Some supplemented their income with craft production, especially basketry. (Local farmers used their sturdy ash-splint baskets for the potato harvest.) As a small and powerless minority in a rural region, they faced poverty, cultural repression, and stinging racial prejudice.

During the 1970s, AAI helped Mi'kmaqs and Maliseets challenge discrimination and gain access to funding and special services to improve their dismal living conditions. Meanwhile, Maine's other two tribes, the Passamaquoddy and Penobscot, filed a massive land claim, resolved by the 1980 Maine Indian Claims Settlement Act (MICSA). In the eleventh hour, Maliseets were included in the settlement. Each of the three tribes won federal recognition and shared $81.5 million, earmarked in part to purchase enormous tracts of tribal land.

Lacking the ethnohistorical data needed to substantiate their inclusion in MICSA, Aroostook Mi'kmaqs (pop. 600) failed to benefit from the settlement. In fact, MICSA extinguished their aboriginal title in Maine, along with recently gained benefits and services. On top of this, a sharp decline in farm acreage in Aroostook, coupled with an increase in mechanical harvesting, all but eliminated demand for potato baskets.

When I arrived on the scene in 1981, the community was depressed and depressing. In 1982, AAI dissolved, and I branched off with the newly formed Aroostook Micmac Council (AMC), which established headquarters in nearby Presque Isle. After MICSA, federal and state politicians, as well as the general public, erroneously believed that Maine's entire "Indian problem" had been resolved. Few had ever heard of the hapless Mi'kmaqs in the northern hinterlands, and those who had usually thought they were Canadian Indians. (Aroostook Mi'kmaqs form part of a large cross-border tribe, the Mi'kmaq Nationimow—pop. 25,000—made up of twenty-nine bands, all but one situated in Canada; see Prins 1996: 1–5.) Aiming to tackle these problems, AMC leaders and I worked with legal specialists to devise a native rights strategy based on local community-building, ethnohistorical documentation, legal research, political support, and last but not least, public relations. Without these interlocking elements, a land claim settlement and federal recognition of their Indian status would be impossible.

Recognizing the importance of informing the public, politicians, and government agencies about the band's cultural identity and tribulations, I agreed to help the Mi'kmaqs make a documentary about themselves. We quickly discovered the political ambiguity of visual self-representation. In seeking political support, the powerless Mi'kmaq were wary of provoking or offending their neighbors by sharply exposing the discrimination and injustices inflicted on them. They hoped to debunk negative stereotypes and avoid the romantic exoticism of Hollywood stereotypes, while presenting themselves in a positive light and showing how they actually made their living. As tribal leader Donald Sanipass later explained, "We wanted a film in which our voices can be heard and in which we show how we live, how we work, and where we have chosen to continue the life of our forefathers and mothers." Working closely with the community (AMC sponsored the film), we marked out three objectives: to document and preserve traditional Mi'kmaq arts and crafts, in particular basketry; to strengthen their own cultural identity through collaboration on a collective project of self-representation; and to inform the public of their existence and (indirectly) their legitimate struggle for native rights in Maine.

At the time, fewer than a dozen families still practiced basketry, but until recently it had been a common livelihood for generations of Mi'kmaqs. Finding, felling, and hauling brown ash trees deep in Maine's forests, pounding the trunks into splints, and weaving the strands into the sturdy baskets is no romantic endeavor, but it gave them some autonomy in a white-dominated world (McBride 1990). Because it represents a stubborn desire for self-determination, we chose to focus on traditional basketry as emblematic of Mi'kmaq identity and cultural survival.

Trained in 16 mm filmmaking, I served as project director and wrote the basic treatment. In 1983, having secured start-up funding, I invited filmmaker-friend Karen Carter (who has some Nanticoke Indian ancestry) to be co-producer. Working with a small camera crew, we used an Arriflex 16BL camera and a Nagra 4.2 audio recorder. In addition to documenting Mi'kmaqs making baskets, we filmed them working on white-owned potato farms and shot footage of large modern harvesting machines that were replacing hand-pickers (I only recently recognized the latter as a hint of the familiar theme of primitivism). After producing a five-minute pilot film titled *Earning Our Keep,* we won major funding to complete the project and did a second shoot in late 1984. It included footage of Mi'kmaq day laborers working in potato houses, basketmakers venturing into the forest to cut ash trees, the pounding of wood into splints, and the weaving and selling of the baskets.

Completed in December 1985, the film—retitled *Our Lives in Our Hands*— featured a soundtrack assembled from interviews with Mi'kmaqs and a musical score by Stuart Diamond, based on a seventeenth-century Mi'kmaq melody. A week later, it premiered at the Native American Film Festival in New York City, introduced by Sanipass, one of the featured basketmakers. Early in 1986 it debuted in Presque Isle and soon had several airings on Maine Public Television. Many other public screenings followed, not only throughout the state but also at numerous national and international film festivals.

To rally political support for their native rights cause, tribal spokespeople (including myself) almost always accompanied the film at live showings.

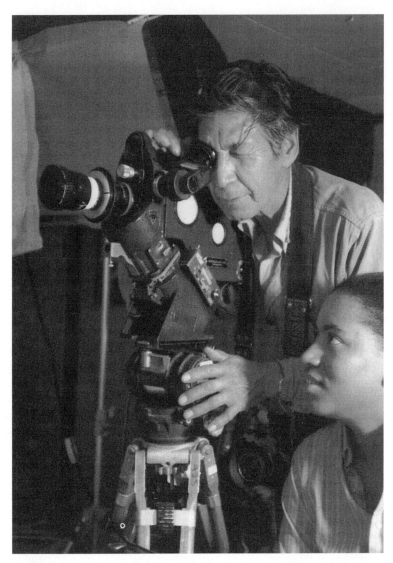

Production still from the making of *Our Lives in Our Hands,* a documentary crucial to the Aroostook band of Micmacs' successful federal recognition and land claims effort. Tribal leader Donald Sanipass checks a scene filmed at his family compound in Maine through the lens of a large Arriflex camera, with the film's coproducer, Karen Carter, at his side. (Photo: Harald E. L. Prins)

The effort paid off: in 1990 Maine's congressional delegation in Washington, D.C., introduced a special bill to acknowledge the tribal status of the Aroostook Band of Micmacs and settle its land claim. When formal hearings were held in the U.S. Senate (where I testified as the tribe's expert witness), Donald Sanipass's son David recorded the event with his new video camera. A year later the tribe gained federal recognition and $900,000 to purchase a small reservation.

Ostensibly just a documentary about Mi'kmaq Indian basketry and seasonal work, *Our Lives in Our Hands* succeeded as political advocacy film without being framed in primitivist terms (Turnbaugh and Turnbaugh 1988). As a visual performative, it could only do so because of the larger roadshow in which Mi'kmaq cultural activists made direct personal appeals for political and moral support. The film played a key role in reshaping the political landscape in northern Maine and helped the region's Mi'kmaqs to dramatically improve their own place in it. Revisiting the community in 1999, I experienced a peculiar form of culture shock: With an annual budget of several million dollars, Aroostook Mi'kmaqs now run their own affairs from a new administration building located on recently purchased reservation land near Presque Isle. Several dozen Mi'kmaq families have relocated there, within easy reach of a new tribal health clinic. Last but not least, the community has rekindled some long-neglected Mi'kmaq cultural practices. As could have been predicted, the group has also adopted various pan-Indian neotraditions that echo the primitivist formula (see also Prins 1994b, 1996: 213–14, 1999: 301–2).

DILEMMA OF PRIMITIVISM 2: THE PLAINS APACHE FILM PROJECT

In contrast to the native rights challenge behind *Our Lives in Our Hands,* the Plains Apache film project is about an indigenous dilemma of self-representation, in which a tribe's decision to document certain cultural practices is at odds with their own conventions of keeping such traditions under wraps. My association with this group began in 1993. By that time they had initiated a tribal project to preserve their endangered ancestral heritage and planned to use film or video to document their traditions. The following background information explains the unique circumstances of this project.

Referring to themselves as Naishan Dene (Our People), the Plains Apaches are the northernmost of some fifteen Apache bands. Historically, they ranged the Great Plains as mounted buffalo hunters. In the nineteenth century the U.S. government forced them to settle on a southwestern Oklahoma reservation shared with Comanches and Kiowas. Today, having lost that reservation, some 1,400 Plains Apache live quite dispersed, surrounded not only by the more numerous Comanche and Kiowa, but—more uncomfortably— by a dominant majority of non-Indians (see Davis 1994; Meadows 1999).

In recent years Plains Apaches have become increasingly concerned that their traditional culture could be lost forever. At this writing in 2001, just three elders still speak the ancestral tongue fluently. Several dozen tribal members understand it but cannot speak it well. Describing his people's condition as "desperate," Alonzo Chalepah, a tribesman in his mid-forties, noted that "young Apaches had always relied on their older generations to preserve all history and culture," but now the old ones are too few in number to keep traditions alive. In 1991 a group of Apache conservatives took action. They formed a special culture committee, initiated a language preservation project, and began documenting hundreds of words and phrases on tape. They also discussed the importance of documenting other aspects of their culture, such as ancient ceremonial customs, arts, rituals, dances, songs, stories, and other tribal lore. Here, they hit a snag: the need for help from outsiders. This was delicate, for Plains Apaches traditionally view their history in terms of hermetic learning—inside information that is taught only to special initiates and cannot be released into the public domain. In Alonzo's words, "Our custom was never to reveal anything of our people to strangers. . . . Those who are responsible for keeping history [usually medicine men, chiefs, and calendar keepers] . . . regarded this a highly sacred and religious meaning. Annually, in the beginning of spring, the history of the people was revealed to a few men who in turn would expose this to other members of the tribe for the importance of all to know who we are and where we come from." One such keeper of historical knowledge is Alonzo's father, Alfred Chalepah ("Old Man Tipi Pole"). Born in 1910, Alfred has long been a highly respected ceremonial chief and spearheads the Plains Apache cultural preservation effort.

Struggling to reconcile their hermetic ethos with the need to make a record of their traditional culture, the Apache finally decided to enlist outside scholars, first a linguist and then an ethnohistorian. In 1993 they determined that the time had come to make a visual record. Having heard of my involvement in other Indian film projects, Alonzo asked if I might help them document ceremonies, dances, and oral traditions—some of which had never been shared with or performed in the presence of outsiders. With the understanding that the Apache elders would be in charge of the project, I agreed. During our first year of collaboration, no filming happened, but we occasionally discussed the project by phone or letter, exchanging ideas about form and content.

In the spring of 1994 I visited the Apache headquarters in Anadarko, Oklahoma, and met with the elders on the culture committee. During our discussion, old Alfred Chalepah explained why it was time to make a record: "We better do this now while I'm still here. There's lots to talk about. I wished one day something like this would come about. When I'm gone, everything will be gone. I would like to see many of our ways to continue on down the road."

The committee concluded that there should be two components to their film project. First they wanted a filmic record for the tribal archives. Second, they desired a documentary for public viewing, based in part on selected film footage. Commenting on part two of the project, Apache elder Irene Chalepah Poolaw noted: "Many tribes have told their history. It's time for us to tell our story. We want a true and accurate explanation of our people. There are a lot of people who don't know who we are."

My first visit with the committee gave us an opportunity to develop a measure of mutual understanding, identify sensitive issues, and discuss how to avoid problems. Afterward, I attended a tribal gathering that featured dances by the Manatidie (Blackfeet Dancing Society). Then, quite unexpectedly, I was invited to accompany Alonzo for a peyote ceremony. Some twenty Apaches, Cheyennes, and I gathered around the fire and "sand moon" (altar) in a large canvas tipi for the all-night ritual. Eugene Blackbear, a Cheyenne, served as "roadman" (chief of the meeting) and sat just behind the altar. His tribespeople sat along the side of the tipi to his left. Alonzo, as chief drummer, sat to his right, followed by me and a row of Apaches. At some point after midnight, Blackbear signaled Alonzo, who asked me to stand and then flicked my body with a bright feather fan while praying softly for blessings for the film project. I cannot fully relate what happened during this unanticipated ritual, but it was a stirring experience. Certainly, it reinforced the idea of my responsibility toward the Apache elders who had decided to entrust me with precious information.

Back home, I stayed in regular touch with the culture committee, and in August 1994 I returned to Apache country with two student assistants, Bruce Broce and Chad Buehler. This time we documented three days of tribal celebrations at the ceremonial dance ground immediately west of Fort Cobb. Using a video camera (JVC KY 411, S-VHS format) we filmed drumming, chanting, tribal dances (including Manatidie dances by members of the Redbone Society), and long interviews of tribal elders talking about Apache history. Later I sent copies of all videotapes to the Apache committee for analysis and commentary.

In June 1996, I went back for more filming. Newly equipped with a lightweight Hi-8 mm video camera (Handycam CCD-TR700), I documented a series of tribal ceremonies in the Tonkawa Hills based on discussions with my Apache hosts and their general directions about what and where to film. Since then, the community has invited me regularly to film during celebrations such as Alfred Chalepah's birthday, always a good occasion for a special feast. Typically, a religious peyote meeting is held the night before. On the day itself, various traditional ceremonies take place, in particular the Naishan Manatidie performed by the Chalepah Apache Blackfeet Society, followed by an evening meal and then an all-gourd dance program until midnight.

More recently, I have focused on making a visual record of several lengthy interviews with Chalepah, now the tribe's oldest living member. His grandfather, Gon-kon ("Man Over His Camp"), raised him. Called "Apache John" by white newcomers, this chief was a traditional doctor, whipman (dance leader in the Manatidie), Peyote Roadman, and keeper of one of the sacred medicine bundles. After Gon-kon's death, Chalepah inherited the traditional leadership positions of whipman and bundle keeper. He also inherited Gon-kon's Peyote Road and concomitant paraphernalia. In the mid-1970s, Chalepah was elected tribal chairman. Recently he passed some of his ceremonial responsibilities on to his son, Alonzo, but he is still keeper of the medicine bundle. Considering his advanced age, his family has discussed filming the ritual of the medicine bundle. But for now, this vital aspect of their traditional culture remains too sensitive for such record-making.

Since its inception, the culture committee has steadily increased its documentary holdings, all stored in the tribal archives. The Apache project is especially remarkable because its authentic cultural imagery appeals to the romanticism of primitivist imagination. (After all, the Hollywood Indian was modeled after such former horse warriors and buffalo hunters ranging the Great Plains.) As they continue to record their culture for themselves and contemplate how to present part of their heritage to the wider public, the Plains Apache look over their shoulders. They feel the threat of modern mass media ready to further commodify their traditions and turn them into tourist attractions.

INDIGENOUS PEOPLES IN CYBERIA

Although indigenous peoples committed to cultural survival have increasingly staked claims on their rights not only of self-determination but also of self-representation, those who have acquired modern media to produce their own visual documents have rarely controlled the means to distribute the information beyond their own communities. This is changing. Now that much of the globe is being wrapped together with fiber-optic cables, radar, and communication satellites, even some of the most remote tribal communities are becoming interconnected. And since the emergence of the World Wide Web in 1992, tribal nations have gained a powerful new media tool. Overall, the Fourth World remains relatively underrepresented in cyberspace (for obvious reasons such as economic poverty, technological unfamiliarity, linguistic isolation, cultural resistance, and political repression), but many groups—especially in North America's Indian Country—are investing in cybertechnology. An immense medium, the World Wide Web is a multifunctional communication venue that facilitates engagement in local and global information exchange, social networking, economic marketing, political advocacy, and even cultural preservation. It enables tribal communities and individuals to represent themselves and to do so largely on their own terms and according to their own aesthetic preferences (Hill and Hughes 1998).

The first indigenous website was posted by the Oneida Indian Nation in New York back in 1994 (even before the U.S. White House had one). Just one year later, the Blackfeet Confederacy in Alberta became the first tribal group in Canada to post a site. Since then, many hundreds of other indigenous groups have followed suit. Some tribes, such as the Seminole, now run their own indigenous webrings, connecting dozens of Indian and Indian-related sites. Among the Mi'kmaq, a few heavily trafficked tribal sites offer detailed textual and visual information about traditional culture and current affairs, with hyperlinks to most of the twenty-nine officially recognized Mi'kmaq bands. The Miawpukek Band in Newfoundland has even become an Internet server (Prins 2001b).

Indigenous websites are usually designed to publicly articulate the particular cultural identities of their owners. Typically, they feature primitivist images. For instance, the homepage of Ojibway activist and American Indian Movement leader Dennis Banks is illustrated with a sepia (Curtis-style) photograph of himself, appearing below a buffalo skull flanked by eagle feathers. But there are also more culture-specific motifs. For instance, quite a few Mi'kmaq sites are marked by the eight-pointed star, or kagwet, well known from traditional porcupine quillwork designs. To distinguish official tribal websites from those that have been created and are maintained by indigenous (and other) individuals, Fourth World governments often mark their sites with a tribal seal, flag, or some other official insignia (Prins 2001a).

As the Internet creates new political space for indigenous peoples, encapsulating polities and corporate media will find it difficult to be the designated gatekeepers of information. But virtual power is no panacea, as I recently discovered in a courtroom. In February 1999 I served as expert witness in a fishing rights case on behalf of the Mi'kmaq community of Miawpukek in the Provincial Court of Newfoundland, Canada. During cross-examination, the prosecutor representing the federal government or "Crown" questioned me about the historic evidence for Mi'kmaq aboriginal claims. The Crown contends that the tribe migrated to Newfoundland well after European colonization and thus does not possess aboriginal title to its ancestral lands there. In his argument, the prosecutor noted a Mi'kmaq website featuring a map that did not include Newfoundland as part of traditional Mi'kmaq territory. He demanded an explanation. I dismissed the significance of his finding, saying that someone had simply found a map, posted it, and put it up for all to see, apparently not noticing or not knowing that it contained misinformation (Provincial Court of Newfoundland 1999: 112–15). But my response did not alter the fact that a Mi'kmaq stepped into Cyberia and posted a piece of misinformation that could be exploited by an adversary.

Clearly, the Internet provides indigenous peoples powerful new means of self-representation, but as its use expands and intensifies, so does the "overseeing gaze" of encapsulating polities and transnational corporations. This given, the current relief from visual imperialism afforded to indigenous peoples by the web may be phantasmagoric, and the "virtual performative" alone will not overturn their subaltern positions in the political arena.

CONCLUSION: A FAUSTIAN DEAL

European expansionism set into motion a dialectical process, which I have outlined here in terms of the politics of dominance and the ideology of primitivism. In particular, I have shown how American Indians became subjects of a dual internal colonialism—both political and psychological. This created what I have referred to here as the primitivist perplex, an identity puzzle promulgated by visual media. Paradoxically, romantic exoticism, as embedded in white ideology, meshed quite well with indigenous concepts of self-understanding.

In the cultural revitalization movement now going on in the Fourth World, including Indian Country in North America, modern media technology plays a crucial and fast-growing role. Through the World Wide Web, cross-cultural communication has become global and instant. Linked together in Cyberia, even the most remote and isolated indigenous communities can make common cause, confront the dominating polities, and perhaps begin to transform the global landscape.

As I have argued here, the primitivist formula appears to have worldwide appeal and relevance in the indigenous decolonization movement. Used as a counterhegemonic construct, it operates on several related levels. First, because romantic exoticism still resonates powerfully within North America's white dominant society and parts of the Western world, it serves as a ready-made device to successfully promote native rights. Second, because romantic exoticism has long reflected indigenous self-understanding as victims of technologically more advanced powers, it provides contemporary tribal nations worldwide with an attractive image of self-fashioning.

Finally, in their global outreach, indigenous peoples have marked out a collective identity, and they are employing the countercivilizational formula to unite and strengthen their own culturally heterogeneous force known as the Fourth World. Indigenous visual media, especially as articulated in Cyberia, play an important role in the propagation of this political formation. Because indigenous use of the primitivist formula is a "Faustian contract" (Ginsburg 1991), its global agency remains to be explored and critically evaluated.

NOTE

This text is a revised and updated version based on Prins 1997b. The author thanks Bunny McBride for her feedback and editorial input.

REFERENCES

Berkhofer, Robert F. 1973. *The White Man's Indian: Images of the American Indian from Columbus to the Present.* New York: Vintage Books.

Biesele, Megan, and Robert K. Hitchcock. 1999. 'Two Kinds of Bioscope': Practical Community Concerns and Ethnographic Film in Namibia. *Visual Anthropology* 12: 137–51.

Carpenter, Edmund. 1973. *Oh, What a Blow That Phantom Game Me!* New York: Holt, Rinehart and Winston.

Conklin, Beth A. 1997. Body Paint, Feathers, and VCRs: Aesthetics and Authenticity in Amazonian Activism. *American Ethnologist* 24 (4): 711–37.

Davis, Michael G. 1994. Plains Apache. In *Native America in the Twentieth Century: An Encyclopedia,* edited by Mary B. Davis, pp. 456–57. New York: Garland.

Friar, Ralph, and Natasha Friar. 1972. *The Only Good Indian. . . . The Hollywood Gospel.* New York: Drama Books Specialists.

Ginsburg, Faye. 1991. Indigenous Media: Faustian Contract or Global Village? *Cultural Anthropology* 6: 92–112.

———. 1993. Aboriginal Media and the Australian Imaginary. *Public Culture* 5 (3): 557–78.

———. 1995. Mediating Culture: Indigenous Media, Ethnographic Film, and the Production of Identity. In *Fields of Vision: Essays in Film Studies, Visual Anthropology, and Photography,* edited by Leslie Devereaux and Roger Hillman, pp. 256–91. Berkeley: University of California Press.

Hill, Kevin A., and John E. Hughes, 1998. *Cyberpolitics: Citizen Activism in the Age of the Internet.* Lanham, Md.: Rowman and Littlefield.

Hitchcock, Robert K. 1998. Genocide of Indigenous Peoples. In *Encyclopedia of Genocide,* vol. II, pp. 349–54. Santa Barbara, Calif.: ABC-CLIO.

Horse Capture, George. 1993. Foreword to *Native Nations: First Americans as Seen by Edward S. Curtis,* edited by C. Cardoso, pp. 12–17. Boston: Bullfinch Press.

Human Rights: A Compilation of International Instruments. 1978. New York: United Nations.

Lemaire, Ton. 1986. *De Indiaan in ons Bewustzijn: De Ontmoeting van de Oude met de Nieuwe Wereld.* Baarn, Netherlands: AMBO.

Loizos, Peter. 1993. *Innovation in Ethnographic Film: From Innocence to Self-Consciousness, 1955–1985.* Chicago: University of Chicago Press.

Marshall, John. 1993. Filming and Learning. In *The Cinema of John Marshall,* edited by Jay Ruby, pp. 1–133. Chur, Switzerland: Harwood Academic Publishers.

McBride, Bunny. 1990. *Our Lives in Our Hands: Micmac Indian Basketmakers.* Gardiner, Maine: Tilbury House.

Meadows, William C. 1999. *Kiowa, Apache, and Comanche Military Societies.* Austin: University of Texas Press.

Means, Russell, with Marvin J. Wolf. 1995. *Where White Men Fear to Tread: The Autobiography of Russell Means*. New York: St. Martin's.

Prins, Harald E. L. 1986. Mohock the Tories: Political Symbolism at the Boston Tea Party in 1773. Paper read at the First Interdisciplinary Conference on New England Culture and History (1699–1830), University of Massachusetts, Boston.

———. 1989. American Indians and the Ethnocinematic Complex: From Native Participation to Production Control. In *Eyes across the Water*, edited by Boonzajer Flaes, pp. 80–90. Amsterdam: Het Spinhof.

———. 1994a. Micmac. In *Native America in the Twentieth Century: An Encyclopedia*, edited by Mary B. Davis, pp. 339–40. New York: Garland.

———. 1994b. Neo-Traditions in Native Communities: Sweat Lodge and Sun Dance among the Micmac Today. In *Proceedings of the 25th Algonquian Conference*, edited by W. Cowan, pp. 383–94. Ottawa: Carleton University Press.

———. 1996. *The Mi'kmaq: Resistance, Accommodation, and Cultural Survival*. Fort Worth, Tex.: Harcourt Brace.

———. 1997a. Visual or Virtual Anthropology: In the Wilderness of a Troubled Genre. *Reviews in Anthropology* 26: 279–94.

———. 1997b. The Paradox of Primitivism: Native Rights and the Problem of Imagery in *Cultural Survival*. *Visual Anthropology* 9: 243–66.

———. 1999. Federal Recognition for Native Americans. In *Cultural Anthropology*, by W. Haviland, 9th ed., pp. 301–2. Fort Worth, Tex.: Harcourt College Publishers.

———. 2001a. Digital Revolution: Indigenous Peoples in Cyberia. In *Cultural Anthropology*, by W. Haviland, 10th ed., pp. 306–8. Fort Worth, Tex.: Harcourt College Publishers.

———. 2001b. Resolving a Native American Tribal Membership Dispute. In *Cultural Anthropology*, by W. Haviland, 10th ed., pp. 283–85. Fort Worth, Tex.: Harcourt College Publishers.

Provincial Court of Newfoundland. 1999. Trial Proceedings in the Provincial Court of Newfoundland, R. versus A. W. John and J. R. John, Section 78(a) of the Fisheries Act. Gander, Newfoundland, transcript.

Tomaselli, Keyan G. 1996. *Appropriating Images: The Semiotics of Visual Representation*. Hojbjerg, Denmark: Intervention Press.

Turnbaugh, William, and Sarah Peabody Turnbaugh. 1988. Film review of *Our Lives in Our Hands*. *American Anthropologist* 90 (1): 234–35.

Turner, Terence S. 1992. Defiant Images: The Kayapo Appropriation of Video. *Anthropology Today* 8 (6): 5–16.

United Nations Draft Declaration on the Rights of Indigenous Peoples. 1993. *Cultural Survival Quarterly* 19 (1): 65–68.

Weatherford, Elizabeth. 1993. Film and Video. In *Native America in the Twentieth Century: An Encyclopedia*, edited by Mary B. Davis, pp. 197–202. New York: Garland.

Wolf, Eric R. 1999. *Envisioning Power: Ideologies of Dominance and Crisis*. Berkeley: University of California Press.

3

Representation, Politics, and Cultural Imagination in Indigenous Video

General Points and Kayapo Examples

Terence Turner

Right! All over the world people are looking at these videos we are making of ourselves. So I am glad to have come today to this place where videos are made. This had not yet appeared when I was a youth. Now that we are becoming more like the whites, however, we are going to need to watch these videos we are making of ourselves.

It is not whites who are doing this work, but I, a Kayapo, who am doing it, as all of you can see.

These videos will be seen in all countries. Tell your children and grandchildren, don't be deaf to my words, this [work] is to support our future generations, all our people. This is what I want to say to you today.

I am a Kayapo doing this work. All of you in all countries who see the pictures I make can thereby come to know our culture, my culture of which I tell you today.

MOKUKA, KAYAPO LEADER AND VIDEOMAKER, *explaining the significance of his work in a video he made at the Centro de Trabalho Indigenista, São Paulo, August 1991 (translated from Kayapo by Terence Turner)*

INTRODUCTION: KAYAPO VIDEO
IN THE CONTEXT OF "INDIGENOUS MEDIA"

The global expansion of telecommunications, coupled with the availability of new and cheap forms of audiovisual media, above all video recording, has given rise within the past two decades to an unprecedented phenomenon: the appropriation and use of the new technologies by indigenous peoples for their own ends. This essay discusses a series of general issues related to the politics of representation, cultural "authenticity," and the reimagination of social identity by indigenous peoples in contexts of interaction with state and global systems, with particular attention to the role of indigenous uses of video. The peoples most involved in this development have been among those most culturally and technologically distant from the West: Australian Aborigines, Canadian Inuit, and Amazonian Indians. Among the latter, the

Kayapo of central Brazil provide one of the most striking and varied examples of the indigenous use of video.

The use of video and other visual media like television broadcasting by indigenous peoples differs in a number of ways from the making of ethnographic films or videos by anthropologists and other nonindigenous persons. Only since the 1980s has it begun to receive attention in its own right from anthropologists and media theorists, and there are as yet only a few ethnographic studies or descriptive accounts of specific cases of indigenous media use: of these, the work of Eric Michaels on Central Desert Aboriginal Television laid key theoretical groundwork (Michaels 1984, 1986, 1991a, 1991b; Prins, this volume; Ruby 1991). Michaels's and the other existing studies deal almost entirely with the Australian and Canadian cases, in which state-subsidized indigenous TV broadcasting via communications satellite is the principal medium in question. These cases present special problems of their own (e.g., the sometimes insidious effects of dependence on government subsidies, or the fact that the satellite-TV connection also serves as a conduit for Western TV programming, which is then directly received by Aboriginal, Inuit, and Indian viewers) (Kuptana 1988; Murin 1988; Ginsburg 1991). These factors are absent in the Amazonian cases, where video recorders and generator- or solar panel–powered VCR decks and monitors comprise the limits of communications technology and there is no question of government financial subsidy. The state agency for indigenous affairs, FUNAI (Fundação Nacional do Indio), neither supports nor takes any interest in videomaking by members of the communities over which it presides. To the limited extent that indigenous-made videos circulate among communities, it is the result of individual acts, either by nonindigenous video-makers or anthropologists or indigenous leaders or video-makers who happen to travel from village to village or meet one another in a Brazilian town. Moreover, although many Kayapo communities possess monitors and even satellite antennas, most still lack VCRs. Most viewing of videos by Kayapo takes place in Brazilian towns like Tucuman or Redencao, where chiefs or leaders may maintain town houses with video viewing equipment and show videos to visiting Kayapo from other communities. The relatively small world of indigenous media thus nevertheless contains important differences: hence the need for more empirical studies of different cases and greater theoretical attention to the significance of the differences. This account of the Kayapo case represents an effort in this direction.

Faye Ginsburg has noted that the appropriation of visual media by indigenous peoples typically occurs in the context of movements for self-determination and resistance, and that their use of video cameras tends to be "both assertive and conservative of identity," focusing both on the documentation of conflicts with or claims against the national society and the recording of traditional culture (1991, 1995a, 1996). She makes the important point that indigenous cultural self-documentation tends to focus not on the retrieval of an idealized vision of precontact culture, but on "processes of identity construction" in the cultural present (1995a, 1995b). Her essential point is that cultural media form part of social projects of communication of cultural knowledge for political and social ends. This implies shifting the focus of the term "media" from the denotation of technologies of representation, or the representations themselves, to the social processes of mediation in which they are used:

> In order to open a new "discursive space" for indigenous media that respects and understands it on its own terms, it is important to attend to the processes of production and reception. Analysis needs to focus less on the formal qualities of film/video as text, and more on the cultural mediations that occur through film and video works. (Ginsburg 1995a: 259)

Much indigenous video tends to focus on aspects of the life of contemporary indigenous communities that are most directly continuous with the indigenous cultural past. It is often undertaken by indigenous video-makers for the purpose of documenting that past to preserve it for future generations of their own peoples. A mere emphasis on the continuity of indigenous culture or "tradition," however, runs the risk of slipping into uncritical cultural essentialism. It tends to ignore or obscure the extent to which the production of representations is both an individually creative and a socially contested process, involving the conjunction of differing voices, perspectives, and values of different groups and individuals within indigenous communities. The production of social and political reality, as well as the representations through which it is mediated by and to its producers, is a multivocal process in which the participants draw in different ways upon their common cultural stock of ideas, symbols, tropes, and values. In the process, they may alter to varying degrees the form and content of their stock of representations. Even when indigenous actors employ a reified, homogeneous representation of their own "culture" to present a common ideological front against assimilative pressures from nonindigenous social or political-economic agents, close examination of the social process of creating and asserting such representations of common "culture" may reveal the complexity and conflict among the structural perspectives, views, and objectives of the actors involved. This point has been cogently made by Wright in a recent comment on Kayapo political use of representations of their own "culture" (Wright 1998).

SOCIAL EFFECTS OF INDIGENOUS MEDIA IN INDIGENOUS COMMUNITIES

The emphasis on processes of production and reception and on media as "mediation" provides a useful point of departure for my discussion of Kayapo video. "Mediation," however, is a Protean notion that can subsume many specific meanings. As most though not all anthropologists working with indigenous media have recognized, there are fundamental differences between the sorts of mediation going on in indigenous media and those involved in ethnographic film and video or in the circulation of mass-culture images and ideas by television (see, e.g., Ginsburg 1997; Hamilton 1997; Turner 1995, 1997; cf. Wiener 1997).

One major difference concerns the act of video-making itself. As video takes on political and social importance in an indigenous community, which member of the community assumes the role of video cameraperson and who makes the prestigious journey to the alien city where the editing facilities may be located become issues fraught with social and political significance, and consequently, social and political conflicts. These may seem petty issues with no connection to the grander issues of theory and politics normally addressed in the anthropological and media literature; but they are often the channels through which an indigenous community translates the wider political, cultural, and aesthetic meanings of media such as video into its own local personal and social terms. They can have cumulatively important effects on the internal politics of a community and the careers of individuals. It is especially important for nonindigenous people working in the field to attend to the specific effects their projects or support may have in the communities where they work.

An outsider attempting to facilitate the use of video by a community, for either political or research purposes, by donating a camera or arranging access to editing facilities, in other words, does not escape the invidious implications and responsibilities of "intervention" simply through handing over the camera to "them." To whom it is handed can become a very touchy issue, and may involve consequences for which the researcher bears inescapable responsibility. On several occasions when I brought video cameras to villages and attempted to arrive at understandings with the members of the community that would guarantee open access to their use while enabling experienced camerapersons to use and maintain them, I stumbled into long-standing rivalries and personal animosities that I was unable to reconcile or mediate to the satisfaction of all parties. In one case the jealousy that I inadvertently stirred up led to the temporary exile of a cameraman who had been my closest collaborator from his community (I describe this and other personally fraught cases in detail in Turner 1991).

Returning, then, to the theme of "mediation," the act of video-making itself, when done by an indigenous person or member of a local community, begins to "mediate" a variety of social and political relationships within the indigenous community in a way that has no exact parallel when the video maker is an outsider, as is the usual case in documentary and anthropological film and video-making. Among the Kayapo, for example, becoming a video cameraperson, and even more important, a video editor, has meant combining a prestigious role within the community with a culturally and politically important form of mediation of relations with Western society, two of the prerequisites for political leadership in contemporary Kayapo communities. Several of the younger chiefs acted as video camerapersons during their rise to chieftainship, and a number of the more ambitious younger men have taken up video at least in part in the hope of following in their footsteps.

KAYAPO CONSCIOUSNESS OF THE USES OF VIDEO: CULTURAL FACILITATION, CREATION, OR DISTORTION?

The idea of editing a video—cutting, selecting, and recombining sections of raw video (rushes) so as to construct a condensed and reordered representation of the activities and events covered in the raw original—was originally introduced to the first group of Kayapo video camerapersons trained by the three Brazilian media specialists who brought the Kayapo their first video camera in 1985 (their collaborative project was called *MenKaron Opoi Djoi*). The first Kayapo-edited video was produced in that year by a Kayapo cameraman whom one member of the project brought to Rio to take a course in video-making at the Museum of Modern Art (about which, he has assured me, he understood very little beyond elementary techniques of camera work and editing).

The *MenKaron Opoi Djoi* project ran out of funds in the same year, without being able to provide more video cameras or editing facilities accessible to the Kayapo villages. The videotapes shot by Kayapo camerapersons rapidly deteriorated in the villages because the Kayapo had no way of copying or storing them in a safe place. In 1990, to supply these needs, I started the Kayapo Video Project with a grant from the Spencer Foundation. In this I had from the beginning the cooperation of the Centro de Trabalho Indigenista (CTI) of São Paulo. The CTI's "Video in the Villages" project, directed by Vincent Carelli, made available its well-equipped editing studio and technicians to train Kayapo in editing, and its video storage space for a Kayapo video archive for original videos and edited masters.

In the Kayapo Video Project, CTI personnel and I have sought to limit training both in camera work and in editing to the essential minimum, to allow the maximum room for Kayapo camerapersons to develop their own culturally and individually specific styles. Some critics have suggested that introducing Kayapo camerapersons to elementary techniques of camera use and editing is tantamount to indoctrinating them in Western cultural conventions, thus aborting their potential ability to develop spontaneous, culturally specific, and "authentic" modes of visual organization (Ruby, personal communication; Faris 1992; Wiener 1997; cf. Turner 1997). This surprisingly widespread view seems to me to be rooted in an inability to credit indigenous persons with a capacity for creativity and aesthetic judgment on a par with their Western counterparts, and an analogous denial to indigenous cultures of the ability to make use of borrowed elements and techniques without becoming "lost" or inauthentic upon the slightest pollution by Western techniques and ideas. Thus even the simplest directions for using a video camera or editing a videotape are viewed as the cultural equivalent of a poison pill, too much for "their" culture to withstand, while "we" remain robustly impervious (and indifferent) to all forms of cultural contact with "them." This appears to me to be an unselfconsciously ironic variant of the ethnocentric conviction of the evolutionistic superiority of Western culture associated with the ideology of Western imperialism.

This view is manifestly contradicted by the record of indigenous appropriations of video, not to mention the historical and ethnographic record of intercultural exchanges in general. Indigenous societies that have learned to use video and other electronic media of representation have not collapsed or suffered the eclipse of their own categories of space-time, agency, or power. On the contrary, many have been able to employ video representations, *and specifically the processes of producing them,* to strengthen their sense of cultural identity and the continuity of cultural traditions. The Kayapo discussed in this essay are a case in point. The experience of the Kayapo Video Project has shown that indigenous video makers, drawing upon their own social and cultural categories, have developed culturally idiosyncratic forms of representation once they have mastered a basic vocabulary of elementary techniques. From the early work of Worth and Adair with the Navajo, through the Australian Aboriginal work discussed by Michaels, Hamilton, and Ginsburg, to the Kayapo Video Project, the consistent lesson of indigenous video production has been that indigenous film and video makers tend to draw upon deeply embedded cultural categories and social schemas organizing forms for the complex visual representations they create and produce. The real issues are not the preservation of "culture," non-Western or Western, but the empowerment of social actors, whatever their degree of cultural "purity" as defined by whatever standard, to produce their own cultural mediations. In the process, cultural forms, together with the capacity and motivation of social actors to produce them, are reinforced, rearticulated, and transformed in various ways through the use of new techniques of representation and new social forms of utilizing and circulating them.

The fundamental ethical and political issue involved in such processes is the empowerment of social subjects to use and transform their stock of social and cultural forms in ways that empower them to produce social relations, values, and identities for themselves under existing and future conditions. New techniques of representation, such as, in the case in question, videotaping and editing, may potentially be among such empowering tools.

Mokuka, a Kayapo leader and video maker, expressed similar ideas in a speech, delivered in Kayapo to his intended audience of fellow Kayapo but also directed toward a wider, nonindigenous audience, which he incorporated into a video he was editing at the CTI studio in São Paulo in 1991. The speech is intended as an explanation of why his video work is important to the Kayapo people as a whole (the first part of the speech is printed as the epigraph to this essay).

> I am a Kayapo doing this work. All of you in all countries who see the pictures I make can thereby come to know our culture, my culture of which I tell you today. Look at these videos, stored here in this place where I work—it's not just my workplace, any one of you [Kayapo] can come for the asking, it's all of ours, for any one of us with enough understanding to come here to look at these videos of ourselves.
>
> Look, everybody, at all these videotapes of us here. See! They're all about us. This row of tapes are all pictures of us Kayapo. These in the next section are of other indigenous people, our relatives. These tapes aren't just left here idly. From here our videos of ourselves are sent far away to the lands of the whites, so our [white] relatives can see how we truly are. This is what I want to explain to you today, what this editing studio and these videotapes are all about, so you will understand.
>
> Do whites alone have the understanding to be able to operate this equipment? Not at all! We Kayapo, all of us, have the intelligence. We all have the hands, the eyes, the heads that it takes to do this work. I am not doing this work for my own selfish advantage. I have learned this skill to work for our common good. That's what I am doing here. This is what I am doing and telling you about.
>
> This is a picture from another group of our people, from Catete [holds up photograph]. This picture here. Is there someone somewhere who has learned something about them too from having looked at this? Our young people can learn about our kindred peoples from different places by looking at pictures like this. We should do the same for ourselves by making pictures of ourselves with which to teach and learn about ourselves.
>
> With this, my speech to you is ended.

CULTURAL SCHEMAS AND THE PRODUCTION OF THE IMAGE

An indigenous video maker operates with the same set of cultural categories, notions of representation, principles of mimesis, aesthetic values, and notions of what is socially and politically important as those whose actions he or she is recording. Worth and Adair, in their early project on Navajo filmmaking, were of course the first to realize the potential significance of indigenous filmmaking in this respect. As schemas guiding the making of the video, cultural categories serve as forms of activity rather than as static textual structures or tropes. What Calderola (1988) has called "the imaging process" can therefore be a rich object of ethnographic inquiry.

Most Kayapo videos thus far have been of cultural performances such as rituals or political meetings that form natural narrative units, with self-defined boundaries and sequential order. In such cases, the social and cultural forms of the events tend to become the schemas used by the camerapersons and editors to guide their construction of the video image. Fundamental social attitudes and values also assert themselves as formative components of the imaging process. Both in camera work and editing, Kayapo have spontaneously tended to use technically simple long shots, slow cuts, and alternating panoramics and middle-range close-ups of collective activities such as ceremonial performances and political meetings, while avoiding extreme close-ups of individual faces.

The indigenous video maker draws upon his or her own cultural categories and forms to guide the camera work and editing process. For the indigenous video maker, in other words, the process of video production itself mediates the indigenous categories and cultural forms that simultaneously inform and constitute its subject matter. The indigenous product, and above all its process of production, thus has an ethnographic and theoretical value lacking in nonindigenous work. Keeping the shot record for Kayapo editors, which has been my main practical role in the work of the Video Project, affords an excellent vantage point for studying this process, while allowing me to make myself useful in a relatively unintrusive way. It also enables the systematic compilation of ethnographically significant details in the visual record, which can be discussed with informants to elucidate their cultural meanings.

These methods can provide a unique perspective for observing the construction of representations and analyzing the interaction of received cultural categories and new experiential content and representational techniques, as I illustrate with the following examples.

VIDEOS OF CEREMONIES

The Kayapo have used their video cameras primarily to record their own ceremonies (in itself an ethnographic datum of cultural significance). Consider the example of a video of a men's naming ceremony, the Mebiok, performed in the village of Kubenkakre. The cameraman and editor was Tamok, then aged about 17, a native of the village where the ceremony was performed. The ceremony has the form of successive performances of the same suite of dance steps, each with its own song. The video shows the three successive performances that constitute the framework of the sequential order of the ceremony.

The initial performance, which marks the beginning of the ceremony, is held at a spot in the forest far from the village. Everyone is doing the same step, singing the same song. The video, using pan shots of the line of dancers, shows the uniformity of movement; the audio track relays the singing in unison. The second performance marks the temporal halfway point of the ceremony. The performers have also come halfway in their spatial trajectory from forest to central village plaza, where the final performance will be held. Although the song, gestures, and steps are the same, the dancers now wear decorations, and women—the paternal aunts or grandmothers of the little boys who will be named—have joined the dancing line, some carrying the boys. The spectacular final performance takes place in the central village plaza, with everyone performing the same songs and steps, but now wearing complete ritual regalia, including the gorgeous feather capes that are the most valued items of Kayapo ceremonial finery. Through successive replications the performance has become simultaneously complete (all its parts being present in the proper order) and fully socialized (moved into the center of the village), or in other words, fully reproduced as a social form.

In Kayapo thought, replication of originally "natural" forms (such as ceremonial songs and dances themselves, thought to be originally taught to shamans by birds, animals, or fish) through concerted social action is the essence of the production of human society. It is what specifically human behavior ("culture") consists of. The perfection of such socialized forms through repeated performance embodies the supreme Kayapo value, at once social, moral, and aesthetic, of "beauty." "Beauty," in this sense, comprises a principle of sequential organization: successive repetitions of the same pattern, with each performance increasing in social value as it integrates additional elements and achieves more stylistic finesse, thus approaching more closely the ideal of completeness-and-perfection that defines "beauty."

This is what Tamok's video of the ceremony also does. He faithfully shows every repetition of every performance, each with its successive increments of regalia and participants. His video replicates, in its own structure, the replicative structure of the ceremony itself, and thus itself creates "beauty" in the Kayapo sense. The master categories of social production and cultural value, replication and beauty, thus become the master schemas guiding Tamok's editing: his construction of his representation of the ceremony.

The same principle applies to his editing and to his camera technique. For example, in his video of the women's version of the same naming ceremony, he has a long pan shot at semi-close-up so that it frames only the feather capes of the dancers moving by. The capes thus appear as a succession of identical objects, replications of the same cultural form, in abstraction from their human wearers. Tamok thus creates a frame that embodies the quintessence of the cultural value of replication as beauty.

THE KAYAPO REPRESENTATION OF REPRESENTATION:
RITUAL DRAMA AS PERFORMATIVE MIMESIS

Kayapo notions of mimesis and representation are evident in dramatic skits performed as integral parts of rituals dealing with their social and political interaction with Western society. They are faithfully brought out in Kayapo video representations of these ritual dramas. In the ceremony for war, performed before the departure of the raiding party, a skit is enacted in which Kayapo actors take the parts of the intended Brazilian victims of the forthcoming raid. At the end of the skit, they flee in feigned terror from the successful attack of other Kayapo warriors, playing themselves. Mokuka's video of such a performance in his village, A'ukre, shows the actors representing Brazilians, mimetically evoking the essence of Brazilianness through the imitation of typical Brazilian ways of eating, dancing, playing music, and other daily activities. Their comedic exaggeration of imitated qualities has a quasi-performative function: the satirically diminished intended victims are easily defeated when Kayapo warriors, acting the role of themselves, attack the "Brazilians'" camp. Life is supposed to imitate art.

This example helps to bring out the close relationships between Kayapo notions of mimesis or representation as imitation on the one hand and replication as the essential form of social and cultural production on the other. The two notions are in fact continuous, drawing on the same notions of imitative or replicated action as an effective mode of constructing reality, and they are culturally elaborated through the same complex ritual forms. These same fundamental categories of Kayapo culture emerge as the master tropes of Kayapo video camera work and editing. Representation, far from being an exclusively Western project foisted on the Kayapo through the influence of Western media, is as Kayapo as manioc meat pie.

VIDEO, SELF-REPRESENTATION, AND GETTING REPRESENTED BY OTHERS

Although the Kayapo are accomplished in their own cultural modes of representation, an extraordinary feat of creative mimesis has undoubtedly been their enactment of themselves in their self-presentations to Brazilians and other Westerners, from environmentalists to World Bank executives. These self-representations have played a central role in their successful political actions over the past decade.

The Kayapo quickly made the transition from seeing video simply as a means of recording events to understanding it as an event to be recorded in its own right. There has been a complex feedback relationship between Kayapo self-dramatization in their political encounters with Brazilians, many of which have taken on the aspect of guerrilla theater, and the Kayapo use of video media. On the one hand, Kayapo leaders have planned politi-

Kayapo activists and Granada Television crew document a 1989 demonstration in Altamira, Brazil, against World Bank funding of dams that threatened to flood indigenous lands. (Photo: Alex King, courtesy Terence Turner)

cal actions like the 1989 Altamira rally against a government project to build a huge hydroelectric dam that would have flooded Indian land, partly with a view to how they would look on TV (or video). On the other hand, for the Kayapo the act of shooting with a video camera can become an even more important mediator of their relations with the dominant Western culture than the video document itself. One of the most successful aspects of their dramatic and effective political demonstrations against Brazilians and other representatives of the Western world system such as the World Bank has been their ostentatious use of their own video cameras to record the same events being filmed by representatives of the national and international media. This has had the effect of making their camerapersons a major subject of filming by the other crews, as is attested by the number of pictures of Kayapo pointing video cameras that have appeared in international print and electronic media.

In sum, the reflexive objectification of Kayapo consciousness of their own culture in the contemporary interethnic context has not been merely the effect of Western media or cultural influences; it has drawn upon powerful native cultural traditions of representation and mimetic objectification and has at the same time extended and strengthened those traditional forms.

KAYAPO USES OF VIDEO AS A SOCIAL AND POLITICAL DOCUMENT

From the moment they acquired video cameras of their own, the Kayapo have made a point of making video records of their major political confrontations with the national society, as well as of more exotic encounters such as tours to Quebec to support the Cree Indians in their resistance to a giant hydroelectric dam scheme that would have flooded aboriginal lands in Canada. They have also employed video to document internal political events such as meetings of leaders from different communities to settle disputes or the foundation of new communities. In these efforts, the Kayapo have not been purists, demanding that only their own camerapersons represent them. On some occasions, they have asked for the collaboration of trusted nonindigenous video makers, making clear the general outlines of what they wanted the video to show but leaving the detailed shooting and editing decisions to the collaborators.

An example of the latter strategy may illustrate the general point. In December 1991, a young leader from the large village of Gorotire, who was about to lead some sixty followers to found a new village at one of the frontier posts the Kayapo have established along the boundaries of their reserves, telephoned me in Chicago from a Brazilian town near Gorotire to ask me to come down and video the group's establishment of the new village. "Hurry, we're leaving Saturday," he said (it was then Tuesday). There were no Kayapo video cameras or camerapersons available, and the leader of the group was intent on having a video documentary made of the foundation of the new community under his leadership. He wanted the public record of his first major chiefly act of leadership and authority to help him establish his claim to chiefly status. He also hoped that the video document would help to lend social facticity to the new community itself, which as it turned out needed all the reality reinforcement it could get.

Although I was unable to go myself on such short notice, I was able to arrange for a Brazilian videomaker who had previously worked with the Kayapo and two colleagues to go to the new village and videotape the first month of its existence. The Brazilian video crew arrived at the new site a few days after the Kayapo settlers. The Kayapo, however, insisted on having a video document that would record the whole story of the establishment of the new village, including their initial arrival at the site. Calling upon their mimetic traditions, they therefore reenacted their original journey and arrival, to serve as the beginning of the video documentary of the founding of their new community. They continued to enact for the camera all the aspects of village life they considered essential to a good community, from ceremonies to home-building to soccer games. By creating a representation of themselves as a fully established, normal community, they were helping to create the social reality they were representing. Here, then, is an instance of spontaneous reflexive mimesis: the Kayapo acting themselves, for themselves.

This case illustrates several points about the purposes served by Kayapo videos as social documents. The Kayapo do not regard video documentation merely as a passive recording or reflection of existing facts, but rather as helping to establish the reality it records. Representation, in other words, has a performative function. The representation of transient events in a medium such as video, with its capacity to fix the image of an event and to store it permanently in a form that can circulate in the public domain, objectively accessible to all in exactly the same way, can seem to confer upon private and contingent acts the character of established public facts. The properties of the medium itself may thus be felt to confer a different kind of social reality on events than they would otherwise possess. For the Kayapo, in other words, the medium mediates its own properties as a permanent, objective, publicly circulating representation to the consciousness of social reality.

Political acts and projects, such as a young leader's claims to chiefly authority, that in the normal run of Kayapo political life would remain relatively contingent and reversible, can be represented by video in ways that help to establish them as objective public realities. This, of course, does not by itself make them objective realities, as the leader in question found to his dismay. I returned to Brazil seven months after the shooting of the video to edit the rushes and take the edited video back to the new community and the leader who had commissioned it. As it happened, I was too late. The new settlement had fallen apart as the result of internal squabbles provoked by the young would-be chief's wife when he was away at the 1992 UN Conference on Environment and Development in Rio, only a month before my return with the edited videotape that was to confirm the establishment of his new settlement as an objectified social fact.

The Kayapo penchant for using video to document not only historic encounters with Brazilian state power but internal political events as well, such as meetings of chiefs or the founding of a new village, may thus be understood in part as an attempt to infuse these events with the more potent facticity and verisimilitude of audiovisual images. The notion of an objectively determined social reality, permanently fixed by public documents, which many nonliterate societies first acquire through the medium of writing, has come to the Kayapo and some other contemporary nonliterate peoples through the medium of film and video. To this extent, it seems fair to say

that video has contributed to a transformation of Kayapo social consciousness, both by promoting a more objectified notion of social reality and by
heightening their sense of control over the process of objectification itself,
through the instrumentality of the video camera.

NOTE

This paper is derived, with many deletions, additions, and other changes, from my
Forman Lecture at the 1992 R.A.I. Festival of Ethnographic Film and Video in Manchester, England. The text of the lecture was published in *Anthropology Today* (Turner
1992).

REFERENCES

Calderola, Victor J. 1988. Imaging Process as Ethnographic Inquiry. *Visual Anthropology* 1 (4): 433–51.

Faris, James C. 1992. Anthropological Transparency: Film, Representation and Politics. In *Film as Ethnography*, edited by Peter Ian Crawford and David Turton, pp.
171–82. Manchester, England: Manchester University Press.

———. 1993. A Response to Terence Turner. *Anthropology Today* 9 (1): 12–13.

Ginsburg, Faye. 1991. Indigenous Media: Faustian Contract or Global Village? *Cultural Anthropology* 6 (1): 92–112.

———. 1995a. Mediating Culture: Indigenous Media, Ethnographic Film, and the
Production of Identity. In *Fields of Vision: Essays in Film Studies, Visual Anthropology,
and Photography*, edited by Leslie Devereaux and Roger Hillman. Berkeley: University of California Press.

———. 1995b. The Parallax Effect: The Impact of Aboriginal Media on Ethnographic
Film. *Visual Anthropology Review* 11 (2): 64–76.

———. 1996. "From Little Things, Big Things Grow": Indigenous Media and Cultural Activism. In *Between Resistance and Revolution: Cultural Politics and Social Protest*,
edited by Richard Fox and Orin Starn, pp. 118–44. New Brunswick, N.J.: Rutgers
University Press.

———. 1997. Comment on J. Weiner, "Televisualist Anthropology." *Current Anthropology* 38 (2): 213–16.

Hall, Stuart. 1990. Cultural Identity and Diaspora. In *Identity: Community, Culture, Difference*, edited by J. Rutherford, pp. 222–37. London: Lawrence and Wishart.

———. 1992. Cultural Studies and Its Theoretical Legacies. In *Cultural Studies*, edited
by L. Grossberg, C. Nelson, and P. Treichler, pp. 277–94. New York: Routledge.

Hamilton, Annette. 1997. Comment on J. Weiner, "Televisualist Anthropology." *Current Anthropology* 38 (2): 216–19.

Kuptana, Rosemarie. 1988. Inuit Broadcasting Corporation. *Commission on Visual Anthropology Newsletter* (May): 39–41.

Michaels, Eric. 1984. The Social Organization of an Aboriginal Video Workplace. *Australian Aboriginal Studies* 1: 26–34.

―――. 1986. *The Aboriginal Invention of Television: Central Australia 1982–1986.* Canberra: Institute for Aboriginal Studies.

―――. 1991a. Aboriginal Content: Who's Got It—Who Needs It? *Visual Anthropology* 4 (3–4): 277–300.

―――. 1991b. A Model of Teleported Texts (with Reference to Aboriginal Television). *Visual Anthropology* 4 (3–4): 301–24.

Murin, Deborah Lee. 1988. *Northern Native Broadcasting.* Canada: Runge Press.

Ruby, Jay. 1991. Eric Michaels: An Appreciation. *Visual Anthropology* 4 (3–4): 325–44.

Turner, Terence. 1990. Visual Media, Cultural Politics and Anthropological Practice: Some Implications of Recent Uses of Film and Video among the Kayapo of Brazil. *CVA Review* (Commission on Visual Anthropology, Montreal) (Spring): 8–13.

―――. 1991. The Social Dynamics and Personal Politics of Video Making in an Indigenous Community. *Visual Anthropology Review* 7 (2): 68–76.

―――. 1992. Defiant Images: The Kayapo Appropriation of Video. *Anthropology Today* 8 (6): 5–16.

―――. 1995. Representation, Collaboration and Mediation in Contemporary Ethnographic and Indigenous Media. In *Visual Anthropology Review* 11 (2): 102–6.

―――. 1997. Comment on J. Weiner, "Televisualist Anthropology." *Current Anthropology* 38 (2): 226–32.

Weiner, James F. 1997. Televisualist Anthropology: Representation, Aesthetics, Politics. *Current Anthropology* 38 (2): 197–211.

Worth, Sol, and John Adair. 1972. *Through Navajo Eyes.* Bloomington: Indiana University.

Wright, Susan. 1998. The Politicization of 'Culture.' *Anthropology Today* 14 (1): 7–15.

4

Spectacles of Difference

Cultural Activism and the Mass Mediation of Tibet

Meg McLagan

Recently a friend of mine gave me a photograph taken in the Sixty-sixth Street subway station on the West Side of Manhattan. Someone had spray-painted "Free Derry" and below it "Free Tibet" on the wall, graphically linking these two modern-day anticolonial liberation struggles on different sides of the globe. At the same time, I remembered an advertisement I had seen around the city publicizing FreePhone.com's "free long-distance calling over the Internet," which contained the phrase "Free Tibet" in large white letters against a black background and the suggestion, "Call your best friend in Lhasa for free while he still has the oxygen to talk." Above this, a cartoon of a multiply pierced hipster mouthing the word "Yak." These two images reveal a movement pinned between two opposing, and at times complementary, processes—politicization and commodification.

The debates among and between Tibet activists and the public relations experts hired to help them illustrate some of the ways in which contemporary intercultural social movements have tried to negotiate a path between these two poles of mass-mediated activism. As the Tibet issue has expanded and become part of a much wider political imagination, this kind of symbolic work has become central to the Movement's existence, but not without some concern about what effect the objectification of Tibetan culture in the mass media might have. To better understand how this problematic relationship to media is negotiated in social practice this essay examines some of the dilemmas that emerged around the participation and public presentation of "Tibet celebrities" (the Dalai Lama and Richard Gere, among others) during the "Year of Tibet," a transnational political campaign mounted by activists in 1991–92.

The Tibet case rests on a century-long process in which democratic politics have been transformed by the emergence of mass communication, beginning with newspapers, then radio, and eventually television in the 1950s, which deepened and accelerated this trend. Since then, the political arena has been made over in light of the techniques and imperatives of this new medium, with images and spectacle becoming central to the definitions and meanings of legitimacy in politics, a fact well documented by a wide range of scholars (e.g., Boorstin 1961; Altschull 1995; Meyrowitz 1985; Marshall 1997). Although tactical image-making and political spectacle are nothing new (see, e.g., Burke 1992; Foucault 1979), the extent to which promotion has penetrated the heart of the political process in the West over the past four decades is unprecedented. As communicative strategies and public relations expertise have migrated from the entertainment industries to the organization of politics, boundaries between the domains of popular culture and political culture have become blurred (Marshall 1997). The result has been a widening of the spaces in which politics can be conceived and performed.

From the point of view of intercultural human rights concerns, this shift has intersected with another important development: the late twentieth-century rise of culturalist movements or "postnational" social formations (Appadurai 1996), which are based on the deliberate, strategic, and populist mobilization of "cultural material" in their struggle with states. Such movements signal the emergence of a "metacultural" framework in which culture becomes a necessary and favored idiom of political mobilization (Turner 1993: 423; see also Alvarez, Dagnino, and Escobar 1998; Fox and Starn 1997). The convergence of these two historical processes has led to the production of a form of political activism that trades heavily on the mass-mediated performance of cultural difference. It is a mode of mobilization that combines cultural spectacle, celebrity, and media to powerful effect, one that has become an increasingly significant means through which diasporic, indigenous, and other marginalized groups make political claims and construct their collective identities in the post–cold war era (e.g., see McLagan 1996; Turner, this volume; Conklin 1995; and Myers 1994).

The strategic objectification of culture for political purposes in the mass media is not without contradiction. Reliance on essentialized images of difference taps into a discourse of "otherness" that can deny social actors their historical agency and contemporaneity. Nowhere is the dilemma this contradiction poses for activists more clearly illustrated than in the case of the Tibet Movement, which over the past decade has depended heavily on "New Age Orientalist" representations of Tibet as Shangri-la in order to transform popular fascination with Tibetan Buddhism into grassroots political support (see Lopez 1994).

Tibet's emergence as a fashionable cause in the United States and Europe is largely due to the skillful staging of spectacles of Tibetan cultural and religious difference epitomized by the Year of Tibet campaign. Although spectacle is often a part of mobilization in any society, whether religious or political, the meanings of such spectacles become destabilized when they are mobilized cross-culturally.[1] The Year of Tibet events that took place in New York City in October 1991 entailed the production of a variety of spectacles— from an eight-day tantric initiation given by the Dalai Lama in Madison Square Garden's Paramount Theater to a huge exhibition of Buddhist art (including a VIP opening night attended by the Dalai Lama) to cultural performances by dancing, chanting, sand mandala–making monks in venues around the city. In mounting these kinds of spectacles, activists evoked a whole domain of cross-cultural knowledge, the meaning of which had to be managed for the media as well as the largely non-Tibetan, non-Buddhist public to whom Year of Tibet events were advertised.

Recent social movement theory emphasizes that movements are always actively engaged in the production and management of meaning—for participants, for antagonists, for observers. That is, movements self-consciously struggle to fashion meaningful accounts of themselves and the issues in order to motivate and legitimate their efforts, everyday symbolic work that political scientists call "framing."[2] Most of the research on framing, however, focuses on formal modes of representation—speeches and writings of activists—rather than on social process such as the internal debates through which particular "frames" are produced.

I address this gap in this chapter, focusing on the Kalachakra initiation given by the Dalai Lama and the debates behind the scenes among activists (both Tibetan and non-Tibetan) and public relations experts over how to frame it. These meetings, which constitute the ethnographic core of this essay, point toward a central problematic inherent in this form of activism, generated by the tension between the hard political goals of Tibetans in exile and the means by which they have been projected in the mainstream American public sphere. While the conflation of cultural spectacle, celebrity, and media has succeeded in garnering a lot of public attention for the Tibet issue, Barnett and others have argued that it has also evacuated the issue of its political content and contributed to its banalization (see Barnett 1998). My analysis of internal discussions of the management of the Kalachakra challenges this conclusion by attending to how Tibetan activists themselves construct the efficacy of such spectacles and the media coverage they generate.

Managing meaning across boundaries of cultural difference is a complex social process, made more difficult by the fact that social formations are inherently unstable.[3] To compound that, activists rarely agree on strategies, methods, or even ultimate goals because heterogeneous social movements may be and are based on different principles than those that prevail in the West—for example, those organized around Buddhism or Islam that do not readily conform to mainstream American media frames that attempt to separate religious and political domains.

Contemporary theorizing about mass media tends to be ethnocentric in that it usually focuses on mainstream political topics in Western liberal democratic societies such as the role of advertising and spin doctors in electoral campaigns.[4] Little ethnographic work has been done that explores how cross-cultural political actors acquire their knowledge of mass media in the course of their activism—how they learn to insert themselves into the North American representation machinery and the translations entailed in this process. I argue that this is an important aspect of the social process that constitutes contemporary social movements and one that deserves serious analytic attention. My aim in foregrounding the discordant dimensions of the debates around the Dalai Lama's participation in the Kalachakra event, however, is not to emphasize the radical otherness of the Tibetan leader or diasporic Tibetans, but instead to understand how cultural difference is doing "new kinds of work" in the creation of alternative modes of publicity and political subjectivity in American activist and media contexts (Ortner 1997: 9).

CELEBRITIES, MONKS, AND THE MASS MEDIATION OF TIBET

The Tibet issue has not always enjoyed the widespread visibility it does at the moment. When the Dalai Lama fled Tibet in 1959, he was met at the Indian border by a crowd of international journalists eager to get a glimpse of the mysterious "god king" from the land of snows. Accounts of his escape appeared in newspapers and magazines around the world, stoking interest in the Tibetan situation, especially among anticommunists in the West. Despite this initial support, however, the issue remained a marginal one in diplomatic circles for more than two decades. A combination of factors conspired to keep Tibet off the international agenda, including cold war politics of the 1960s and later China's acceptance into the United Nations and America's rapprochement with the People's Republic of China in 1972 (see Knaus 1999).[5] During this period, the United States consistently refused to issue the Dalai Lama a visa, further limiting the American public's exposure to the Tibet issue (this despite the fact that the CIA actively supported the Tibetan guerrilla movement in the 1950s and 1960s).[6]

In the decade between the Dalai Lama's first trip to the United States in 1979 and his trip to Oslo to receive the Nobel Peace Prize in 1989, the Tibet issue was transformed from a struggle of a tiny handful of exiles and their devoted Western friends into a transnational political movement. As I argue elsewhere, this change took place for several reasons, the most important of which was a decision by the Tibetan government-in-exile, based in Dharamsala, India, to wage a vigorous campaign for international support (McLagan 1996). The decision was made in consultation with a small circle of very well connected foreigners that had gradually coalesced around the Dalai Lama since 1979 and who had the political and financial means to make this happen (Goldstein 1997: 75–76; Shakya 1999: 412). Demonstrations in Lhasa, Tibet, in 1987 and 1988, which were violently repressed by Chinese forces and witnessed by Western tourists, provided Tibetan exiles with media-friendly images and stories that helped galvanize support in the U.S. Congress and various European parliaments.[7]

It is celebrity interest in Tibetan Buddhism and the Dalai Lama specifically, however, that propelled the Tibet issue into public consciousness in the 1990s to a degree that far exceeded anything activists could have dreamed of ten years earlier. When actor Richard Gere stood up at the Academy Award ceremonies in 1993 and urged China to negotiate with the Tibetan leader, he reached an estimated television audience of 1 billion people; when the Beastie Boys brought together the cream of alternative rock to perform in the Tibetan Freedom Concerts in 1996, 1997, 1998, and 1999, they informed tens of thousands of concert-goers (and millions of MTV viewers) about human rights abuses in Tibet; when it was announced that action film star Steven Seagal had been recognized as a *tulku* (reincarnated lama), the Tibet issue was projected into the imagination of mainstream America in a very powerful way.

Richard Gere has been at the heart of celebrity interest in Tibet, as the first and most dedicated entertainment personality; his commitment had a snowball effect, attracting other celebrities and making Tibet one of the most fashionable issues in Hollywood in the 1990s.[8] In many ways, Gere as a figure embodies the tension between the ends and means of this form of activism described in the introduction. Gere is well known in the United States as the star of blockbuster films (e.g., *Pretty Woman, An Officer and a Gentleman*) and was once married to supermodel Cindy Crawford. In Tibetan circles, at least initially, Gere was known as a long-time Buddhist practitioner and student of the Dalai Lama who was also a big patron. When I visited Dharamsala in 1990 to attend a Movement conference, Gere was there. Many Tibetans remarked that they had had no idea who he was when he first approached the Dalai Lama and began donating money in the 1980s. In other words, Gere's influence within the Movement and with high Buddhist leaders (at least at the outset) came not from his celebrity status but from his recognized position as a powerful patron of the exile community to whom he had donated hundreds of thousands of dollars over the years, a fact that placed him in the important Tibetan cultural category of *sbyin-bdag,* a traditional patron-client social relation in which spiritual guidance is exchanged for material support.

Over time, however, Gere's celebrity became an important factor in his patronage of Tibetans. In 1987, Gere cofounded Tibet House, an organization dedicated to promoting Tibetan Buddhist culture in the West. Following successful tours of Tibetan monks in 1988–89 sponsored by Tibet House, Gere decided to organize a year-long series of similar kinds of performances in sites around the world. His success in realizing his vision for the Year of Tibet both reveals his dedication to the Tibet issue and suggests how much power celebrities can wield in activist contexts. For instance, Gere managed to bring together the spiritual heads of the different Buddhist and Bon lineages to give a total of fifteen days of teachings and initiations in Madison Square Garden's Paramount Theater (the Dalai Lama is the head of the Gelugpa lineage; the others include Nyingma, Kagyu, and Sakya; all of them are based in India). It was a remarkable and unprecedented feat in Tibetan history that required equal amounts of political and religious finesse.

His aim with the International Year of Tibet, as it came to be known, was to "blitz the planet with Tibetan spiritual energy." Gere outlined his "mystical vision" at a Tibet Movement conference in 1990:

> We want to create a context to make Tibet extraordinary news politically, culturally, and spiritually. We want to make Tibet cross-over. . . . Almost all of us are dharma people, tantric people, we are talking about a new universe, a new order. We plan to hold a Kalachakra [Buddhist ceremony] in New York City in October 1991, and a museum show called Wisdom and Compassion . . . we plan to bombard New York, which is the political and media capital of the world. (Field notes)

Gere described a series of programs that would run throughout the year, stressing the "in-your-face" quality for which he was aiming: "We are selling Tibet . . . what is important about the Year of Tibet is its PR aspect, the awareness it raises."

Gere's dream of "blitzing" Manhattan with "Tibetan spiritual energy" came true in October 1991 with the arrival of the Dalai Lama and the aforementioned high lamas from India to give teachings and initiations. In addition, a Tibetan Buddhist art exhibition opened at the IBM Gallery, and monks made an accompanying sand mandala in full view of the street traffic on Madison Avenue. Other major events included a public talk by the Dalai Lama, an interfaith concert at the Cathedral of St. John the Divine, a symposium on Tibet at the Asia Society, and a "sunrise meditation for world peace" in Central Park, as well as film festivals, photographic exhibitions, television documentaries, and screenings on the SONY Jumbotron in Times Square—all dedicated to Tibet. Dance, chanting, and butter sculpture "performances" by monks from different lineages in venues around the city rounded out the month's activities.

From the outset, Gere conceived of the Year of Tibet as a spectacle in the service of politics. His aim, and the project of Tibet House as a whole, was to stage cultural and religious events and in so doing to transform audiences interested in Buddhism into political supporters. As one employee at Tibet House put it:

The way I see Tibet House is, it's like a gameboard, we pull everyone in and then educate them and then we send them off to do the real work, which is in the Office of Tibet and the Campaign for Tibet, that's the real work. . . . Tibet House is the point of entry for . . . broadening the grassroots base of support here and perhaps internationally as well. The easiest door of entry for the regular American with money is the culture, is to fall in love with Tibet through seeing the beauty of Tibet's culture. (Field notes)

The discourse of cultural survival that underpins this mode of mobilization is a far cry from that of the 1960s and 1970s when the Dalai Lama was barred from entering the United States and the Tibet issue was framed in terms of anticolonialism and independence by exile leaders and intellectuals based in India. It is a much "softer" discourse that has had unintended and contradictory consequences for the activists who have deployed it. Yet it is important to note that Tibetans themselves have long viewed their Buddhist culture as an asset and a potentially important resource in international politics. Indeed, the use of Buddhism to secure the protection of outsiders has deep historical roots, having been a central means through which the Tibetan state established and maintained relations with its more powerful neighbors for three centuries. The use of Buddhism in contemporary times to engage both Western individuals and publics, as illustrated in the Year of Tibet, is simply an extension of this practice (McLagan 1996). This point highlights Tibetans' complicity in their own objectification. It also underscores the fact that Tibetans themselves do not necessarily view the circulation of Buddhism in the West as commodification in the same way that Western critics of the phenomenon appear to. For religiously minded leaders like the Dalai Lama who stress the importance of "saving" Tibetan culture not only for Tibetans but for all humanity, the need to embed their nationalist claims within a more universalistic framework in accordance with basic tenets of Mahayana Buddhism has compelled them to self-consciously adopt a narrative of Tibetanness which—as it has been embraced by activists like Richard Gere—unfortunately has tended to reinforce and perpetuate Western stereotypes and fantasies of Tibetans rather than provide representations of them as historical actors with serious and legitimate political claims. This point was brought home to me by an incident during my fieldwork.

One afternoon in October 1991, I was sitting in the Manhattan office of Tibet House. The office was abuzz with anticipation because Richard Gere was scheduled to arrive soon to do an interview and photo session with a reporter from *Women's Wear Daily* (*WWD*) about the Year of Tibet. When he arrived, Gere was shown into an office on the second floor of the brownstone that housed Tibet House and several Tibetan-run nongovernmental organizations. The reporter from *WWD* interviewed the actor, and at the end of the interview, when it came time for a photograph to be taken, Gere asked that it be taken with a monk. Unsurprisingly, there were no monks working in the "Tibet building," and Gere had to settle for the highest-status layperson around, who happened to be the Dalai Lama's representative in North America. After Gere left the building, one of the Tibetan women with whom I worked came upstairs and exclaimed with great annoyance to the non-Tibetans sitting around the room, "We're not all monks you know!!"

In the context of a political campaign, Gere's commitment to Buddhism and his sense of what would signify Tibetanness for the magazine's readers— i.e., a monk—demonstrates the contradictions inherent in this form of activism. On the one hand, the celebrity component of the Year of Tibet enabled activists to engage with the image-based, publicity-driven discursive structures of American mass-mediated politics by connecting them with a category of social actors who have a huge amount of cultural capital (Bourdieu 1993), and who are intimately involved with processes of producing spectacle and managing media on a daily basis. It brought the Tibet issue to the attention of a wider range of the American public—such as *Women's Wear Daily's* readers—than ever before and set the trend for the cultural extravaganzas that followed and became the Movement's main mode of activism in the 1990s.[9]

On the other hand, celebrity involvement has allowed the Tibet issue to be defined by its religiosity, given that most celebrities, like Gere, are drawn to the struggle through their interest in Buddhism rather than by its political content. This has annoyed many activists, especially young lay Tibetans in exile who, despite their willing participation in the objectification of Tibetan culture, find the privileging of Buddhism at the expense of other identities Tibetans carry to be profoundly constraining.

As more and more celebrities have embraced the Tibetan cause, the issue has received a lot of publicity, though not necessarily targeted media coverage, that might lead to a meaningful political outcome (see Barnett 1998 for a discussion of this point). This is because Tibet-related events attended by celebrities have tended to be framed in terms of the celebrities' stardom, rather than the issue at hand. For example, Gere's stardom tends to overwhelm his own real political interest in Tibet; the narratives that circulate about him make interesting fodder for entertainment stories but get in the way of the political communication that activists, including Gere himself, ultimately seek. One consequence of this is that as the mainstream American public sphere has been increasingly saturated with stories and images of glamorous celebrity-oriented Tibet events, the desire to dismiss the issue *because* of the famous people with whom it is associated has grown and at times even made the issue an object of parody.

There are many examples of how overexposure of the Tibet issue has led to a kind of cultural backlash in the United States. For example, the announcement in 1997 that the action film star Steven Seagal was recognized by a high lama in India as a *tulku* generated a wave of cynicism in the press.[10] Overexposure has become a problem for the Dalai Lama as well. Another observer, lamenting the Dalai Lama's appearance on CNN's *Larry King Live!* New Year's Eve show on December 31, 1999, argued that the Tibetan leader is overexposed in the West, this despite the fact that he was asked by King what he, "as a leading Muslim," thought of the millennium celebrations. Claiming this blooper as evidence of the danger popular overexposure poses to the Tibetan leader's moral stature, a Canadian newspaper columnist opined: "The message of the Dalai Lama may be sound, but the medium is en route to perversion. You simply can't plop down a monk in the midst of the gilded cultural establishment without the ironies colliding. The kitsch factor becomes too hard to ignore. The charisma starts to crumble from Too Much Information" (Govani 2000).

MANAGING THE DALAI LAMA

The Dalai Lama's willingness to participate in the various cultural spectacles that have been mounted since 1989 in the United States, cemented by his relationship to his student Richard Gere, has been crucial to efforts by activists to focus public attention on the Tibet issue. As the number of his visits to the United States has multiplied, his presence in the popular imagination has grown, and he has been transformed into a pop icon of sorts. He has been embraced by movie stars, rock musicians, and other public personalities; his life has been depicted in Hollywood films such as Martin Scorsese's *Kundun* and the Brad Pitt star vehicle *Seven Years in Tibet,* both released in 1997; his image has appeared on billboards and in magazines; and his face has adorned posters in bookstore windows as his latest books, the *Art of Happiness* (1998), *Ethics for a New Millennium* (1999), and *The Path to Tranquillity* (1999), shot to the top of the *New York Times* bestseller list. He has even become a screen saver.[11]

Despite this ubiquity, popular understanding of the Dalai Lama and Tibet's recent political history remains simplistic, as the all-too-common reference to the Tibetan leader as a "god-king" in the press reveals. The complex nature of the Dalai Lama's personage and the Tibetan political system he embodies pose all sorts of problems of translation, particularly for the diverse actors who constitute the Tibet Movement who must work collectively to render political discourse meaningful across cultural frameworks in order to make the Movement politically visible. He is the head of both a transnational political movement and a government-in-exile as well as an emanation of Avalokitesvara (Skt.), the Buddha of compassion and the protector deity of Tibet. It is difficult to communicate his dual status as a living Buddha and worldly political leader to audiences unfamiliar with him, especially to members of the Western media who are generally ignorant about the intertwining of religion and politics that defines the Tibetan system and challenges their own fundamental cultural categories.

Before 1991, Tibetan political leaders based in the United States had been wary of the American media (despite their generally positive treatment by the press); they worked with a Washington-based media consultant on an ad hoc basis when the Dalai Lama was in town but otherwise resisted advice that they hire a full-time consultant. But the decision to hold the Year of Tibet raised concerns about how the Dalai Lama would be handled and what effect such publicity would have on the Movement's political goals. To allay these fears expressed by Tibetan political leaders based in the United States as well as the Dalai Lama's American advisers, Gere decided to hire Jane Kelly (a pseudonym), a respected media consultant with a long history of media-related human rights advocacy and a reputation for intelligence and sensitivity.

Although the management of meaning is a fundamental aspect of the political process in all societies, in liberal democratic countries media managers, political consultants, and other PR experts have become highly specialized players in the political sphere over the past few decades. They provide the symbols and frameworks through which political action is constituted and legitimized in the mass media. As Marshall (1997: 206) argues, in the process of legitimation, these frameworks use affect to turn politicians into public personalities, or celebrities, through their intense focus on the personal, the intimate, and the individual qualities of leadership. This particularly American narrative of political leadership (which media consultants such as James Carville are increasingly exporting to other countries) is based on a certain instrumental notion of political efficacy, one that assumes a self-interested and calculated motivation behind all action (see Nagourney 1999).

The cultural specificity of the narratives of leadership preferred by Western media consultants was highlighted vividly in discussions among activists in strategy meetings about the Dalai Lama's public actions and whether they would be construed as political during the Year of Tibet. In these discussions, different understandings of how political power is constructed emerged, with Kelly representing the Western media point of view and certain activists—both Tibetan and non-Tibetan—representing a more "traditional" Tibetan perspective. Western assumptions about political efficacy involve seeing people act. The Dalai Lama and the political system he personifies exemplify a different discourse of power that has a long history and is not organized around the seemingly transparent exercise of power. In the Tibetan system, certain people are believed to have extraordinary powers; they can see and even act in realms normally concealed from view. The individuals raised under this system, as the Dalai Lama was, believe the world is populated by invisible forces. Thus, for instance, in addition to making decisions based on instrumental political concerns, the Tibetan leader acts based on consultations with oracles, dreams, and "certain feelings," as one activist put it. Decisions based on "feelings" are inexplicable according to the logic that prevails in Western political discourse, which is designed to augment the authority and legitimacy of the political leader.

This point was made clear in an anecdote told by one of the Dalai Lama's representatives at a post–Year of Tibet strategy meeting. In response to Kelly's assertion that media coverage would have improved if activists had "packaged" the Tibetan leader better, the Tibetan representative pointed out that the Dalai Lama had a "distinctive" way of doing things:

> Like for instance, when he was invited to Washington, he also accepted an invitation from a small college in Findlay, Ohio. The people in Findlay, they were shocked to find out His Holiness is visiting here, a small town, and someone from Findlay called me to say—why is His Holiness choosing Findlay as part of his visit? . . . He visits Washington, Boston, New York, not a really small town in Ohio. What does he want to accomplish by visiting a small town?

The group of activists sitting around the table laughed heartily as he continued:

> I'm telling you, His Holiness does not judge what he can accomplish by coming to a place; of course we do have several invitations, and out of several, he just picks one. And he thinks that perhaps by visiting this particular university he can benefit those who have invited him. Of course, we try to make recommendations, but then he doesn't go through the recommendations; he has his own choices. (Field notes)

According to his representatives, the Dalai Lama justifies his choices in terms of his Buddhist conviction that his primary purpose is to provide spiritual benefit to those with whom he comes into contact. His deep commitment and unconventional ways were further underscored by the representative's second anecdote:

> When the Nobel Peace Prize was announced . . . we were in Newport Beach, California. And we had calls from all the media networks, including Diane Sawyer, who wanted to interview His Holiness. We went to His Holiness and said that we have a lot of demand for the interview. Then he said there is no time. Just bring the schedule. And we got the schedule and there were some unimportant meetings and then we suggested that we could cancel a few of them. He said, look, no matter whether these are important or not, we have committed to meet these people three months back. Now how could I say that I have more important work to do and cancel these and give an interview? I can't do that. He said that if there is any time left over after the meeting, we are free to schedule. But of course after meeting these people there was no time.

These anecdotes reveal how, as the embodiment of different principles, the Dalai Lama presents a complicated, even at times unruly, figure who sometimes does not follow his own script, not to mention those of his handlers.

Moreover, they suggest why the Tibetan leader has been perceived in the West as having a kind of moral authority that other politicians lack; his apparent lack of political calculation in seeking media coverage (at least in 1991) and his unrehearsed, often awkward off-the-cuff performances in broken English when he does appear in the news media (along with his consistent message of nonviolence) is taken as a sign of the Dalai Lama's authenticity, which in turn gives him a legitimacy in the eyes of many of his followers.

FRAMING THE KALACHAKRA

The Kalachakra was by far the biggest and most visible event that took place in New York during the Year of Tibet. Eight days long, it was attended by some four thousand people, including Gere and his then-wife, Cindy Crawford, and many other members of the New York social elite.

The Kalachakra is a tantric initiation, a complex ritual that represents in many ways the pinnacle of Buddhist esotericism (Sopa, Jackson, and Newman 1985: 91). Buddhist empowerments into particular tantras occur through an initiation that involves extensive visualizations, prayers, offerings, and the use of ritual implements and substances. In order for the guru, in this case the Dalai Lama, to conduct such an empowerment, he must take on the qualities of the deity himself or herself. Then through a series of consecrations, he transfers his power and blessing or *chin lab* to the student. During the empowerment, the Dalai Lama sits on a large colorful throne surrounded by monks and nuns (who sit at the outer perimeter of the stage); three enormous *thangkas* (painted scrolls) hang behind him and a brightly painted "mandala house" sits stage left. The audience wears red cloth blindfolds, and at various times throughout the ritual the Dalai Lama puts on and takes off a fringed yellow hat. To Tibetans and non-Tibetans alike, it is a fantastic spectacle, a locus of religious communitas, a social occasion.

The Dalai Lama's decision to participate in such an event threw diverse members of the Movement into conflict. For the activists who were Buddhists, the Dalai Lama's stature as a political leader rests entirely on his moral authority as a Buddhist teacher, and thus his participation in a tantric ritual posed no interpretive problem whatsoever. It was simply the Dalai Lama doing what he does best. Others, however, including media consultant Kelly and the political advisers who had been working since 1987 to help the Tibetan leader create a political presence on the world stage, believed that the publicity generated by holding such an event in the "political and media capital of the world," as Gere put it, would be a liability rather than an advantage. These individuals feared that having the Dalai Lama sitting on an elaborate throne with a fringed yellow hat and talking an audience through a series of esoteric visualizations for eight days in the heart of New York City would merely create images of the Tibetan leader that would reinforce exotic stereotypes about Tibetans, confuse his political supporters, and produce feature stories about the celebrity Buddhists in attendance instead of generating hard news coverage of the Tibetan situation.

Tension among members of the Movement became clear during the Year of Tibet, especially in the weeks preceding the Kalachakra while I was working as a volunteer at Tibet House, the nerve center of the Year of Tibet campaign. Upon hearing that a Kalachakra initiation was scheduled to take place in October in Manhattan, several unofficial advisers to the Tibetan government-in-exile, all of them Westerners, attempted to pressure organizers into canceling the event. In an interview, one of the organizers of the Kalachakra named Jean recalled that "their main argument was that he [the Dalai Lama] would be too visible, that it is not in His Holiness's interests to be seen as a spiritual leader, as a religious person, that it would jeopardize his credibility as a political leader on the world stage, and couldn't we do this somewhere out in the country someplace?" This effect might be further exaggerated, the advisers argued, by the fact that the initiation was scheduled to coincide with the opening of the UN General Assembly. Comparing the Tibetan leader to Archbishop Desmond Tutu, they told the organizers: "Although Desmond Tutu is a religious figure, you would never see him doing a religious service. His basic persona is political. You never see him in a weird hat or carrying a staff or doing anything strange."

These comments reveal some of the debates that emerged around how to represent the Dalai Lama in order to render him a more transparent figure legible within the context of Western political representation. These debates, which divided participants along Buddhist/non-Buddhist lines rather than Tibetan/non-Tibetan lines, became a powerful undercurrent during the planning and actual staging of the Kalachakra.

It is interesting to note that discussions of Tibetan legibility centered on visual imagery. Many theorists, from Lippmann ([1922] 1954) to Barthes (1977, 1981) to Mitchell (1994) to Virilio (1991), have commented on the modern tendency to picture or visualize existence. Thus it is not surprising that visuality is a medium in which politics are conducted in a public sphere that is mainly constituted by forms of mass spectacle and the mediatization of experience. As Mirzoeff (1999: 12) argues, "Visuality does not replace discourse but makes it more comprehensible, quicker, and more effective."

Some have argued that the visual is dangerous—that it is too open to misinterpretation.[12] Photographs contain too many meanings, their sensual immediacy is too engaging, and there is much excess meaning that is not easily controlled, a fact clearly recognized by activists who worried over how images of the Dalai Lama conducting a Buddhist ritual would be read. I heard Kelly herself make the point over and over to activists that "media do not understand through explanation; they understand through pictures." Indeed, she worked extremely hard to contain press access to the initiation, limiting the number of photographers and making sure they took photos at specified times, in part out of respect for the solemnity of the occasion, but also out of a desire to curtail the production of images of the Dalai Lama "wearing funny hats."

Once plans to hold the Kalachakra initiation were finalized, organizers had to decide how to frame the event in the overall context of the Year of Tibet. In the past, Kalachakra initiations in the United States (in 1981 in Madison, Wisconsin; in 1989 in Santa Monica, California) had been advertised only within American Buddhist and Tibetan circles, where presumably people understood what they meant. In this instance, however, the tantric initiation was intended for a primarily non-Buddhist audience. The job of managing the media coverage of the event initially fell to Jane Kelly. Part of her job entailed reconciling competing interests and opinions among activists. To do this, Kelly frequently brought the Dalai Lama's representative to North America together with representatives from Tibet support organizations such as Tibet House, the Tibet Center, the Tibet Fund, and the International Campaign for Tibet. Through regular consultations, Kelly decided on a media strategy that would attempt to tie Tibetan culture, politics, and religion together. However, Kelly's job became more complicated when, only three weeks before the Kalachakra initiation, Richard Gere hired a public relations firm, Livet Reichart, to handle it as a separate event. When I asked Tibet House's executive director why Gere had decided to hire Livet Reichart so late in the day, she explained:

> At one point Richard panicked. He put in a hell of a lot of money and they'd only sold one third of the seats and he said, we need more pre-event publicity. Jane Kelly isn't getting it, I need somebody who is going to go to the *Post,* to the shitty newspapers, and get publicity. So he brought in Livet Reichart, who, of course, thought they were going to be able to monopolize everything. . . . Jane had begun all the processes, it was all ready to happen, but Richard didn't have the patience to wait.

In the early 1990s, Livet Reichart was a firm well known for its celebrity clients and art-world connections. Unlike Jane Kelly, whose approach represented PR in the service of politics, Livet Reichart epitomized PR in the service of spectacle. That is, their main goal was to generate as much short-term media coverage of the Kalachakra as possible, regardless of its political consequences or implications.

If Tibet House wanted to attract average Americans to the Tibet issue through relatively apolitical cultural spectacles, Livet Reichart explicitly attempted to attract people to the initiation through the Dalai Lama's association with Richard Gere. The firm began planting stories and photographs linking Richard Gere to the Dalai Lama in newspapers and magazines. For

Richard Gere speaking at the March for Tibet rally, Washington, D.C., July 1, 2000.
(Photo: Sonam Zoksang)

example, in the October 10, 1991, "Chronicle" column of the *New York Times,*
Nadine Brozan wrote a piece titled: "Richard Gere Follows the Dalai Lama."
The story quoted Gere as saying, "I have been planning this for four years . . .
it took years to get Tibet House going and the last year to crank up for the
Year of Tibet, and now it's a 20-hour-a-day gig." On that same day, William
Norwich (1991) wrote a piece about the Dalai Lama in the *New York Post,*
noting, "Where goes the Dalai Lama these days so goes Richard Gere . . .
and the actor's significant other, Cindy Crawford." Stressing the celebrity appeal of the Dalai Lama, the article named a number of famous artists and
society figures who planned to attend Year of Tibet events in New York.
Around the same time, an article appeared in another newspaper gossip column about the legal feud between John Avedon (son of photographer
Richard Avedon) and his former wife, Elizabeth, who had left her husband
for Richard Gere a few years earlier. The article mentioned that all three
were followers of the Dalai Lama and were involved with Tibet House. Deeply
offended, one Tibetan complained: "To put the Dalai Lama in the center
of that story is disgusting." Other Livet Reichart–generated stories included:
"Dalai High: Richard Gere's Intoxicant of Choice Is Tibet" in *Women's Wear
Daily* (Ryan 1991); "Gere-ing Up for the Guru" in *New York Live* (Hays 1991);
and "Tibet Festival in High Gere" (Farolino 1991).

In the end, Livet Reichart's success in selling out the Kalachakra event undermined the overall media strategy for the Year of Tibet. As Tibet House then-executive director recalled: "Jane [Kelly] thought that the media should focus on different aspects, not on Richard and how he loves Tibet and his career and so on, which is obviously the way we were going to get more press, but Jane thought it was the wrong type of press." Kelly had decided previously not to advertise the Kalachakra in the newspaper, preferring instead to highlight the Tibetan leaders' less esoteric programs, including an ecumenical service at the Cathedral of St. John the Divine. She felt the advertisements worked against the impression she was trying to create of the Tibetan leader as a world spiritual leader and statesman; by inviting non-Buddhists to attend, she felt the Tibetan leader might appear to be proseletyzing and that this would send a conflicting message to the media.

Many Tibetans in New York objected to the publicists' attempts to link the Tibetan leader with Gere. The ones I interviewed, mainly young exiles, worried that such an association would diminish their revered leader's status and detract from Americans' recognition of his sincere motivation and spiritual accomplishments. At the time, rumors about Gere's supposed sexual proclivities were circulating in the American tabloids, a fact that only added to my informants' anxieties.

Other Tibetans complained that the ads for the Kalachakra made it appear to be a sort of "show" starring the Dalai Lama. As one young man complained to me in an interview:

> The teachings are not a show, and while the Dalai Lama has to operate within this environment, here it's something that is taken out of a cultural context and put in something totally alien. . . . For Tibetans in India or Tibet, if a lama gives a teaching, that teaching is viewed in the same way as the teacher views the teaching, which is something very religious, it's not just something Hollywood. Some Americans think the Dalai Lama comes and for them it is a show, and the Dalai Lama is nothing other than a Hollywood actor doing his piece and leaving the stage. But for a Tibetan he's not an actor, he's trying to help you attain enlightenment.

My friend's observation exemplifies the sorts of concerns about the loss of control over their representation that many Tibetans experience once they decide to objectify themselves through mass culture circuits (McLagan 1997), concerns that tend to focus on the Dalai Lama, whose presumed divinity makes him the object of intense feelings of devotion from his people. Ironically, as his stature as a global guru has grown, the Dalai Lama indeed has crossed over and become a celebrity in American terms in much the same way that he is in the Tibetan world. Yet I would argue that instead of transforming the Dalai Lama into a commodity and evacuating him of any meaning, the mass mediation of the Dalai Lama, if anything, has "re-auraticized" him, a fact attested to by his current popularity as a spiritual teacher in the West.

CONCLUSION

In recent years, social movement theorists have argued that in the contemporary era social movements must be seen as cultural struggles in a fundamental sense, as struggles over meanings as much as over political or economic conditions (see, e.g., Alvarez, Dagnino, and Escobar 1998; Fox and Starn 1997; Touraine 1988). These struggles involve symbolic processes that are mediated in ever more complex ways. How does cultural difference play into this mediation process, and what difference does it make, after all? As I have described, if they want to achieve visibility, activists must fit themselves into Western media frames, which require certain kinds of performances in order for the action to be read as politically meaningful in Western terms. I take the social practices involved in managing this difference through media forms that cross cultural boundaries to be a vital form of cultural production that remains little understood outside of media circles. By paying ethnographic attention to the mechanics by which stories are put into circulation, via press conferences, press releases, publicity tours, and quiet words with journalists, as well as the backstage negotiations through which these stories are formulated in the first place, one can defamiliarize what for many are apparently familiar yet unexamined cultural practices. In so doing, one emphasizes the mediating role that such social practices play in the way media and "culture" are deployed in the production of contemporary politics.

At the same time, we must ask, from what position do Tibetans manipulate and rescript Western media-political practices to serve their own political ends? From what experiential or cultural reserves do Tibetan political practices and historical consciousness in the diaspora emerge? In the case of the Tibet Movement, I want to argue, contrary to many observers, that immersion into First World media technologies and publicity circuits does not automatically imply co-optation of Tibetans or the Tibet issue, as my discussion of the Dalai Lama reveals (see also McLagan 1996).

To be sure, there is a high cost for this form of mediated activism, as scholars such as Turner and Prins (this volume) have documented in the case of indigenous peoples, and Barnett (1998) has argued in relation to the Tibet issue. But media effects are notoriously hard to trace; research has largely failed to demonstrate that media have any kind of direct or predictable effects on people.[13] Thus, for instance, it is hard to know exactly how contemporary Tibetan activism has affected American foreign policy toward Tibet and China. One thing is clear, though: we need to think about the mobilization of cultural difference differently. We should not think about the strategic objectification of culture solely in terms of commodification and consumption; rather we need to inflect our analysis with a more complicated understanding of what it means to the various actors involved and what is at stake for them.

This point is most evident in the case of the Kalachakra, which, as a mass-mediated cultural spectacle, had a certain efficacy that the media consultants, public relations experts, and political advisers failed to address or understand. For Tibetans and other Buddhists, rituals such as the Kalachakra achieve their efficacy through audience participation; they are not passively received but are understood in an active sense to bring blessings, if not spiritual insight, to participants. In other words, being in the presence of the lama, seeing the lama, and being seen by the lama is a transformative experience, a belief that parallels the concept of *darshan* in Hindu worship.[14] At the root of the issue, then, are the very different understandings that Tibetan Buddhists and non-Buddhists have of the efficacy of visual spectacle. Similarly, from the Dalai Lama's point of view, participation in the Kalachakra could be construed as a spiritual benefit—for those in attendance at the event as well as for humanity at large—a fact linked to this particular tantra's eschatology as having a "special connection with all the people of this planet" (see McLagan 1996). By teasing out these differences and their specific meanings in social context, we can better understand the persistence of alternative forms of publicity and political subjectivity in Western mass-mediated contexts as well as the sites where they might productively intersect with others' agendas.

NOTES

The field research on which this paper is based was funded by the Wenner Gren Foundation for Anthropological Research. The Bunting Institute at Radcliffe College provided crucial time and support for writing. Many thanks for the stimulating comments on the substance of my argument from my fellow "sisters" at the Bunting (1998–99), especially Neta Crawford, and from my colleagues in the Tibetan studies world, Robbie Barnett and Georges Dreyfus. Thanks also to Sonam Zoksang, New York–based Tibet activist and photographer, for the use of his photographs and to Leo Hsu, who helped in their preparation for publication. Finally, I am indebted to my editors Faye Ginsburg and Lila Abu-Lughod for their patience and insightful feedback, and especially to Brian Larkin, who soldiered through many versions of this essay, graciously taking precious time away from his own work to offer invaluable intellectual criticism and support.

1. Debord (1967) analyzes the penetration of the commodity form into mass communication, which he argues results in the spectacle. There is a long tradition of work in political science on political spectacle; see, e.g., Edelman 1988; or more recently Wedeen's work on spectacle in Syria (1999).

2. McAdam (1996) reminds us that mobilization and ongoing collective action are social accomplishments. He argues that the concept of framing draws attention toward the everyday signifying activity of activism that has been largely overlooked in social movement theory.

3. For other interesting case studies of intercultural activism, see Stoll 1997 and Landsman and Krasniewicz 1990.

4. Among the more colorful popular books written recently on political communication in the United States and England are Jones 1995; Michie 1998; Morris 1996; Routledge 1999; Tye 1998; and Stephanopoulos 1999. Some of the more discerning academic work on the subject of political communication includes McNair 1998, 1999; Ewen 1996; Maltese 1994; and Kahana 1999.

5. For an analysis of the historical events before and after 1959, see Shakya 1999.

6. See Knaus 1999 and the documentary film *The Shadow Circus* by Tenzing Sonam and Ritu Sarin (1998) for accounts of covert American involvement with the Tibetan resistance movement.

7. For descriptions and analyses of these events, see Barnett and Akiner 1994 and Schwartz 1994.

8. Richard Gere has a long-standing interest in humanitarian and human rights issues, which he supports through the Gere Foundation. Over time, Gere has given large sums of money to the Dalai Lama's exile government and Tibetan organizations in India and the United States. In the spring of 1999, Gere was reported to have visited refugee camps in Macedonia, where he met with Kosovar Albanian refugees. See "www.tibetcenter.org/gere.html" for more information on the foundation's work.

9. See Crosby and Bender 2000 for a personal history of musical activism from the 1960s to the present.

10. Seagal, a longtime Buddhist practitioner, was recognized by a high Nyingma lama based in India as a reincarnated lama. See 1997 interview in the Buddhist newspaper *Shambhala Sun*: http://www.maavwik.simplenet.com/seagal/nov97interview.html.

11. When asked what he thought about this development, the Dalai Lama is reported by the Associated Press to have said, "I don't mind. People can use me as they want. My main practice is to serve human beings." Quoted in *World Tibet Network News*, August 29, 1999.

12. There is a vast literature on the photographic image, including Sontag 1989 and Barthes 1972, 1977, and 1981.

13. See, for example, David Gauntlett's (1998) critique of the "effects model" in media studies.

14. See Eck 1981 for a discussion of the concept of *darshan*.

REFERENCES

Altschull, J. Herbert. 1995. *Agents of Power: The Role of the News Media in Human Affairs*. New York: Longman.

Alvarez, Sonia, Eva Dagnino, and Arturo Escobar, eds. 1998. *Culture of Politics, Politics of Cultures: Revisioning Latin American Social Movements*. Boulder, Colo.: Westview Press.

Appadurai, Arjun. 1996. *Modernity at Large: The Cultural Dimensions of Globalization*. Minneapolis: University of Minnesota Press.

Barnett, Robert. 1998. Essay. In *The Tibetans*, edited by Steve Lehman. New York: Umbrage Editions.

Barnett, Robert, and Shirin Akiner, eds. 1994. *Resistance and Reform in Tibet*. London: Hurst.

Barthes, Roland. 1972. *Mythologies*. New York: Hill and Wang.

———. 1977. *Image, Music, Text*. Translated by Stephen Heath. New York: Hill and Wang.

———. 1981. *Camera Lucida*. Translated by Richard Howard. New York: Noonday Press.

Boorstin, Daniel J. 1961. *The Image: A Guide to Pseudo-events in America*. New York: Atheneum.

Bourdieu, Pierre. 1993. *The Field of Cultural Production*. New York: Columbia University Press.

Burke, Peter. 1992. *The Fabrication of Louis XIV*. New Haven, Conn.: Yale University Press.

Conklin, Beth. 1995. Body Paint, Feathers, and VCRs: Aesthetics and Authenticity in Amazonian Activism. *American Ethnologist* 24 (4): 711–47.

Crosby, David, and David Bender. 2000. *Stand and Be Counted: Making Music, Making History*. San Francisco: HarperSanFrancisco.

Debord, Guy. 1967. *The Society of the Spectacle*. Detroit: Black and Red.

Eck, Diana. [1981] 1998. *Darshan: Seeing the Divine Image in India*. New York: Columbia University Press.

Edelman, Murray. 1988. *Constructing the Political Spectacle*. Chicago: University of Chicago Press.

Ewen, Stuart. 1996. *P.R.! A Social History of Spin*. 2d ed. New York: Basic Books.

Farolino, Audrey. 1991. Tibet Festival in High Gere. *New York Post*, October 11.

Foucault, Michel. 1979. *Discipline and Punish: The Birth of the Prison*. New York: Vintage Books.

Fox, Richard, and Orin Starn, eds. 1997. *Between Resistance and Revolution: Cultural Politics and Social Protest*. New Brunswick, N.J.: Rutgers University Press.

Gauntlett, David. 1998. Ten Things Wrong with the "Effects Model." In *Approaches to Audiences: A Reader*, edited by Roger Dickinson, Ramaswani Harindranath, and Olga Linne. London: Arnold.

Goldstein, Melvyn. 1997. *The Dragon and the Snow Lion: China, Tibet, and the Dalai Lama*. Berkeley: University of California Press.

Govani, Shirin. 2000. Revere the Dalai Lama as If He Were Royalty. *National Post* (Canada), January 5. Reprinted in *World Tibet News*, January 7, 2000.

Gyatso, Tenzin. 1998. *The Art of Happiness*. New York: Riverhead Books.

———. 1999a. *Ethics for a New Millennium*. New York: Riverhead Books.

———. 1999b. *The Path to Tranquillity*. New York: Viking.

Hays, Charlotte. 1991. Gere-ing Up for the Guru. *New York Live*, October 13, p. 15.

Jones, Nicholas. 1995. *Soundbites and Spin Doctors: How Politicians Manipulate the Media and Vice Versa*. London: Indigo Press.

Kahana, Jonathan. 1999. The Reception of Politics: Publicity and Its Parasites. *Social Text* 58 (17): 93–109.

Knaus, Kenneth. 1999. *Orphans of the Cold War: America and the Tibetan Struggle for Survival.* New York: Public Affair Books.

Landsman, Gail, and Louise Krasniewicz. 1990. "A Native Man Is Still a Man": A Case Study of Intercultural Participation in Social Movements. *Anthropology and Humanism Quarterly* 15 (1): 11–19.

Lippmann, Walter. [1922] 1954. *Public Opinion.* New York: Macmillan.

Lopez, Donald. 1994. "New Age Orientalism: The Case of Tibet." *Tibetan Review* (May): 16–20.

———. 1998. *Prisoners of Shangri-la: Tibetan Buddhism and the West.* Chicago: University of Chicago Press.

Maltese, John. 1994. *Spin Control: The White House Office of Communications and the Management of Presidential News.* Chapel Hill: University of North Carolina Press.

Marshall, P. David. 1997. *Celebrity and Power: Fame in Contemporary Culture.* Minneapolis: University of Minnesota Press.

McAdam, Douglas. 1996. The Framing Function of Movement Tactics: Strategic Dramaturgy in the American Civil Rights Movement. In *Comparative Perspectives on Social Movements,* edited by Douglas McAdam, John McCarthy, and Mayer Zald. Cambridge, England: Cambridge University Press.

McLagan, Meg. 1996. Mobilizing for Tibet: Transnational Politics and Diaspora Culture in the Post–Cold War Era. Ph.D. diss., Department of Anthropology, New York University.

———. 1997. Mystical Visions in Manhattan: Deploying Culture in the Year of Tibet. In *Tibetan Culture in the Diaspora,* edited by Frank Korom. Vienna: Austrian Academy of Sciences.

McNair, Brian. 1998. *Introduction to the Sociology of Journalism.* London: Edward Arnold.

———. 1999. *Introduction to Political Communication.* 2d ed. London: Routledge.

Meyrowitz, Joshua. 1985. *No Sense of Place: The Impact of Electronic Media on Social Behavior.* New York: Oxford University Press.

Michie, David. 1998. *The Invisible Persuaders: How Britain's Spin Doctors Manipulate the Media.* London: Bantam Press.

Mirzoeff, Nicholas. 1999. *An Introduction to Visual Culture.* New York: Routledge.

Mitchell, W. J. T. 1994. *Picture Theory.* Chicago: University of Chicago Press.

Morris, Dick. 1996. *Behind the Oval Office.* New York: Random House.

Myers, Fred. 1994. Culture Making: Performing Aboriginality at the Asia Society Gallery. *American Ethnologist* 21 (4): 679–99.

Nagourney, Adam. 1999. Have Attack Ad, Will Travel. *New York Times Magazine,* April 25: 42–48, 61, 70.

Norwich, William. 1991. Column. *New York Post,* October 10.

Ortner, Sherry. 1997. Introduction. *Representations,* special issue on Clifford Geertz, 59: 1–13.

Routledge, Paul. 1999. *Mandy: The Unauthorized Biography of Peter Mandelson.* London: Simon and Schuster.

Ryan, Kimberley. 1991. Dalai High: Richard Gere's Intoxicant of Choice Is Tibet. *Women's Wear Daily,* October 25–November 4: 7–8.

Schwartz, Ronald. 1994. *Circle of Protest: Political Ritual in the Tibetan Uprising.* New York: Columbia University Press.

Shakya, Tsering. 1999. *Dragon in the Land of Snows.* London: Pimlico Press.

Sontag, Susan. 1989. *On Photography.* New York: Anchor Books.

Sopa, Geshe Lhundub, Roger Jackson, and John Newman. 1985. *The Wheel of Time: The Kalachakra in Context.* Madison, Wisc.: Deer Park Books.

Stephanopoulos, George. 1999. *All Too Human: A Political Education.* New York: Little, Brown.

Stoll, David. 1997. To Whom Should We Listen? Human Rights Activism in Two Guatemalan Land Disputes. In *Human Rights: Culture and Context,* edited by Richard Wilson. London: Pluto Press.

Touraine, Alain. 1988. *Return of the Actor: Social Theory in Postindustrial Society.* Minneapolis: University of Minnesota Press.

Turner, Terence. 1993. Anthropology and Multiculturalism: What Is Anthropology That Multiculturalists Should Be Mindful Of? *Cultural Anthropology* 8 (4): 411–29.

Tye, Larry. 1998. *The Father of Spin: Edward L. Bernays and the Birth of Public Relations.* New York: Crown.

Virilio, Paul. 1991. *The Aesthetics of Disappearance.* Translated by Philip Beitchman. New York: Semiotext(e).

Wedeen, Lisa. 1999. *Ambiguities of Domination: Politics, Rhetoric, and Symbols in Contemporary Syria.* Chicago: University of Chicago Press.

II

The Cultural Politics
of Nation-States

(Previous page) Giant cutouts hand-painted on plywood by the Sakti Arts banner company made for a 1990 political rally in Anna Salai, Chennai (Madras). Featured here are: the chief minister of Tamilnadu state, Mu. Karunanidhi (also a popular screenplay writer); the former prime minister of India, V. P. Singh; and the late chief minister of Andhra Pradesh, N. T. Rama Rao (also a popular film actor). (Photo: © Preminda Jacob)

5

Egyptian Melodrama—Technology of the Modern Subject?

Lila Abu-Lughod

MELODRAMA AND MODERNITY

Melodrama has been the subject of a great deal of literary and media theory. The touchstone is Peter Brooks's *The Melodramatic Imagination,* which makes a powerful case for the significance of melodrama as a literary/theatrical genre associated with the upheavals of the French Revolution and the onset of the crisis of "modernity." Brooks (1976: 15, 21) argues persuasively for a particular definition and understanding of the melodramatic imagination—as concerned with the revelation of the moral order in the everyday in a "post-sacred era." Most intriguing is his claim that melodrama is "the central fact of the modern sensibility."

Brooks is concerned with theater and novels in nineteenth-century Europe. In the twentieth century, melodrama is more closely associated with forms of mass media such as radio, film, and television. In Egypt, as in other postcolonial contexts, cultural forms such as television melodrama, projected by national television industries, are seen by state officials and middle-class professional producers as particularly effective instruments of social development, national consolidation, and "modernization" (Abu-Lughod 1995; Das 1995; Karthigasu 1988). This raises the question of what sorts of "modern sensibilities" television melodrama might mark in a place such as contemporary Egypt, where those who make melodrama see themselves as trying to produce modern citizens and subjects. This question is particularly intriguing given that these television producers work in a secular idiom in a social context where religious practices and identity are important to many of their viewers.

There remains a good deal of confusion—or at least an enormous range of possibility—in the use of the term "melodrama" in literary, film, and television studies today (see Gledhill 1994) and some justification for questioning whether the term actually designates a single genre at all (see Merritt 1983). But it is useful to keep the term "melodrama" for Egyptian television serials to remind us of a few shared features. These serials that draw on modernist traditions of literature, film, and radio are mostly about the everyday and involve ordinary people. Their characters are not the universally known heroes of epic poetry or folktales, but representations of the common citizen. Like Latin American telenovelas and unlike British, Australian, and American soap operas, the Egyptian serials are finite, generally running between fifteen and thirty episodes. Like melodrama, therefore, they come to a resolution, something Robert Allen considers crucial to ideological clarity (1995: 21). Egyptian serials are generally more forthright in their moral lessons and more emotional than contemporary Euro-American television dramas, thus doubly deserving of the popular label of melodrama.[1]

In this essay I explore whether portraying the quality of emotionality may be one way in which Egyptian television serials attempt to create a "modern sensibility." But I also explore the difference it makes when a "modern sensibility" is being crafted in a society for which notions of national development remain strong as part of a political legacy, where the embeddedness of individuals in kin and family remains an ideal, and where secularism has been only ambivalently constructed as essential to modernity.[2]

Television serials in Egypt work with modernist projects at two levels: intentionally, through disseminating in their story lines moral messages inflected by local and national political ideologies, thus attempting to set the terms of social and political debate; but also more subtly, through popularizing a distinctive configuration of narrative, emotion, and subjectivity.[3] It is in this latter way, as a genre with certain conventions, that television melodrama in Egypt might be understood most directly as a technology for the production of new kinds of selves (Foucault 1988, 1993). By staging interiorities (through heightened emotionalism) these melodramas construct and encourage the individuality of ordinary people. One can see how this works in the life stories of a domestic servant in Cairo.

Yet I also want to show that this technology is put to work in local social and political contexts that differ in many ways from the contexts of soap opera production and viewing in Europe or the United States, particularly in the overt projects to produce national citizens in a society in which kinship remains important and other forms of community and morality—most notably religious—exist.[4] The growing relevance of religious identity and the practices of self-monitoring being encouraged in the mosques place the genre of television melodrama, though popular, in a field with other technologies of modern self-making, some pulling in the same direction, some not. These trends suggest that we should be wary of telling any unilineal stories about modernity, melodrama, and individualism.

MELODRAMATIC EMOTION

In keeping with media ideologies in postcolonial nations, television drama is viewed by most of its producers in Egypt not simply as entertainment but as a means to mold the national community. Viewers, whether ordinary television watchers or critics, recognize to varying degrees the ideologies informing these melodramas and react to them—either sympathetically or with hostility, depending on their own situations and political visions (Abu-Lughod 1993, 1995, 1997, 1998). Yet what viewers may be less conscious of—and thus less able to resist—is another aspect of televised melodramas that is widely shared: its placing of strong emotion in the everyday interpersonal world. This is a generic convention that cuts across content, that has its source in the genre itself (as adapted and developed over thirty years in Egypt) but is underwritten by the educated middle-class assumptions about personhood of those who produce television. This aspect of melodrama may be even more important to the projects of modernity than are the conscious political messages of the serials, because of the way it stages, and perhaps shapes, selfhood.

This is not the place to discuss general debates about reception and the effects of media, among the thorniest problems in the ethnography of media. I think it is abundantly clear that melodramatic texts can work on viewers in multiple ways. One cannot simply analyze the overt messages of plot and character, just as one should not limit oneself to the study of reception, as this volume amply demonstrates. What I want to explore in this essay, however, is how the representation of characters' emotions in Egyptian melodrama might provide a model for a new kind of individuated subject.[5]

By attaching strong sentiments to everyday life, melodramas fashion ordinary characters whose personhood is defined by what seems a rich inner life and an intense individuality. This focus on the emotionally laden interpersonal domestic world, what in the United States and Europe is thought of as the women's world, is what has made feminist media scholars take soap opera so seriously.[6] Yet the significance of sentiment in the sphere of interpersonal relations has gone almost unremarked upon, perhaps because it is taken for granted in our society where women and emotion are so ideologically conjoined (Lutz 1986). Modleski (1982) comes closest to noting what I would like to consider in more detail. In her analysis of the link between daytime television and women's work, she argues that the narrative structures and close-up shots so favored by soap operas exercise women viewers' abilities to read how intimates are feeling. Their viewing experiences thus replicate their primary emotional work in the family—anticipating the needs and desires of others.

These ideas about emotions and personhood can be linked to Raymond

Williams's (1989) hypothesis that the unprecedented exposure to drama that television has allowed has led to a "dramatization of consciousness." By this he means that television has led us to see our own daily lives as dramas. Although I would caution against some aspects of this analysis, citing the methodological impossibility of gaining access to people's "consciousness" and a discomfort with the humanist assumptions of an unproblematic inner life such a term suggests, I think Williams's great insight is to suggest that something novel happens to viewers' subjectivity as a result of watching television drama: in Egypt we might call this the "melodramatization" of consciousness.

In other words, the question is whether the growing cultural hegemony of television melodrama (following along lines laid down by radio serials and films) might be engendering new modes of subjectivity and new discourses on personhood, ones that we could recognize as "modern" in their emphasis on the individual. The main features of the modern subject as it has been understood in the West—autonomous, bounded, self-activating, verbalizing him/herself—have been delineated in the philosophical and historical literature, with Foucault offering us the most interesting theories of the development of the technologies of the modern (bourgeois) self and their links to new forms of power (see also Chakrabarty 2000). In the introduction to the second volume of *The History of Sexuality*, he suggested that the discourse on sexuality has been crucial to the development of the modern self; one becomes the subject of one's sexuality. In some later works (1988, 1993) he speculated on the relationship between the confession in Christianity and the modern forms of hermeneutics of the self. Psychologizing, buttressed by the whole discourse of psychoanalysis with its vivid conjuring of a self at the center of the narrated drama of family dynamics, a self with a rich and conflictual inner world, is also instrumental in constructing modern subjects. And the discourse of feelings and emotion—the very stuff of melodrama— is essential to the psychological (Abu-Lughod 1990).

What is interesting about Modleski's argument that television soap opera helps to train women for interpersonal work is the assumptions it makes about selves and emotion. It presumes women who live in modern bourgeois families and have a vocabulary of sentiment that is attached to gesture and expressive of the inner feelings and personal truths of others. This set of assumptions about emotion and personhood must be recognized as historically and culturally specific. As Cvetkovich notes, nineteenth-century mass and popular culture played an important role in constructing the discourse of affect crucial to establishing the middle-class hegemony of a "gendered division between public and private spheres and the assignment of women to the affective tasks of the household" (1992: 6).

The untheorized corollary, however, of the discourse of affect is the discourse of the individual, the subject of these sentiments, who is being highlighted in the heightening of emotionality in Egyptian melodrama. The serials are directed not only at women but at men as well. And though they mark men and the upper classes as, on the whole, less emotional than women and the lower classes, all characters are more emotional than might be thought appropriate by a bourgeois European or American self.

In part, the extreme staging of melodramatic selves may seem necessary for those whose goal is to "modernize" a society whose dominant social form is still the family and kin network and whose cultural forms until quite recently (and even contemporaneously in some regions) could be understood to work in different ways and with differing constructions of personhood. So I first want to contrast the melodramatic "structures of feeling" with those of some other popular Arab cultural forms that might previously have provided materials for constructing or conceptualizing selves. One goal is to reveal the particularity of the relationship between modernity and melodrama in the formation of subjectivity. I further want to suggest that the forms of melodrama in Egypt, like the structures of the social and economic worlds in which people there find themselves, differ in crucial ways from their Western counterparts. In the final section of the essay, I turn to the sensibilities and the life stories of a woman who was extraordinarily enmeshed in the world of television and radio serials in order to suggest how we might trace the influence of distinctive affective and narrative forms of melodrama on forms of personal subjectivity in Egypt. I also show, however, how other aspects of Egyptian modernity—in particular the practices of the Islamic revival—bolster, or undermine, the work of television melodrama.

DISTINCTIVE SUBJECTIVITIES

Whatever its inter-references with or roots in other forms of cultural expression, Egyptian television melodrama is distinct in its structure and sentiment. The serials are created by people versed in modern literature, theater, and film—Egyptian, Arab, and European—which are concerned with the themes of modernism (Armbrust 1996). Although occasionally drawing on what they would consider "folk" traditions for local color or regional identification, or to invoke the authentic (as when they have "simple" protagonists reciting proverbs), the primarily urban, middle-class producers of melodrama distinguish their work unambiguously from "traditional" Egyptian and Arab forms of cultural expression that were, until the introduction of mass media, the popular and familiar forms in rural areas and among the uneducated. And the differences between the emotional styles and imaginaries created by these narrative and poetic traditions and those of television melodrama are striking.

This difference can be seen especially clearly in the adaptations to television of local folk forms. This happened in 1997 with the serialized dramatization during the month of Ramadan of the epic of Abu Zayd al-Hilali, considered by many the most magnificent work of Arab oral narrative poetry. The epic, which in its entirety runs to thousands of verses, follows the adventures across North Africa of the Bani Hilal, a Bedouin tribe driven by drought from their home in the Arabian Peninsula. As described by Slyomovics (1986) for Upper Egypt and Reynolds for Lower Egypt (1995), it is recited professionally by socially marginal poets with astonishing verbal talents, not to mention prodigious memories.

The television drama shared with the printed versions (on which the scriptwriter most likely relied) a chronological development and decreasing attention to linguistic play, and indeed to the verbal itself (Slyomovics 1987). It further transformed the epic by turning it into a melodrama about interpersonal relationships and individual longings and passions, many set in the domestic. The best illustration of these transformations—and thus the genre conventions of serialized melodramas—is how the serial dramatized the birth of the hero Abu Zayd, the son of Rizq of the Hilali Bedouin tribe, and Khadra Sharifa, the daughter of the Sharif of Mecca, a descendent of the Prophet. The birth itself constituted the first and crucial week of the television serial when viewers need to be drawn in. The show establishes that Khadra has been barren for many years. Despite their happiness with each other, husband and wife are miserable because of the absence of a son. Finally, Khadra is taken to a pool to supplicate. She sees a powerful black bird driving away the other birds and prays for a son as strong and ferocious as this bird. Miraculously, she bears Abu Zayd, a black child who becomes the hero of the epic. In the version performed for Slyomovics by an Upper Egyptian poet, the pregnancy and birth are described quickly, the love scene after Khadra's visit to the pool being slightly more elaborate (Slyomovics 1997). In a version recorded by Reynolds (forthcoming), the narrative is more elaborate and dramatic, but the focus is on the reactions of others to the black infant and the anger and accusations of Rizq. Neither version dwells on the emotions of the protagonists just before the birth.

In the televised episode of the birth, covered in the Upper Egyptian performance in just the last six lines, we see Khadra going into labor, the anxious father just outside her door awaiting the birth, a desperate fight in the streets over the midwife (who is needed in three places at once), more agonies of labor, the husband praying to God, and later, when he hears the child has been born, falling to his knees, tears in his eyes, and raising his arms to praise and thank God. Then we see hushed arguments in Khadra's room between the midwife and the attendant women, the midwife refusing to give the father the news. What's wrong? The midwife points and says "Look." They carefully lift the cover off the baby. In close-up, with dramatic music playing, we see a black baby. The mother is sleeping, beatific. When she sits up and is confronted with this, she holds the baby lovingly, innocently saying, "The boy is our son, mine and Rizq's. Whether light or dark, he is a gift from God whom we accept." But then she too becomes alarmed. It dawns on her that the others are worried that she will be accused of adultery.

It is not that the television drama is emotional and the performed epic not. The performed epic too describes feelings, in the conventional formulas for such things. In an earlier segment, for example, Rizq and his wife, Khadra, cry in pain over their inability to have a son. But the televised drama focuses on the relationships among characters and the shifting emotions of a set of characters who often stare off into space while music evokes their inner feelings. Instead of formulaic phrases about tears and their plenitude, what could be thought of as the phenomenology of emotion, television drama tries to produce, mimetically, the inner states of beings who feel these emotions through close-ups of facial expressions and melodramatic acting. Moreover, the serial brings the mythic heroes down to earth and makes them ordinary people in line with the process of "descending" individualization, which Foucault has described as so characteristic of modern disciplinary regimes.[7] This is reinforced by the overwhelming visual presence of interior worlds and domestic spaces (always the case, of course, with soap operas, whose budgets rarely allow for the expense of location shooting).[8]

In contrast, and like all "folk" traditions, the oral epic's main intent is not the development of the inner life of characters. Most of the epic, like folktales told all over Egypt, consists of what characters did and said and includes little "emotion language" or the gestures and music that substitute for it in melodrama. This is not to say that one cannot find in the cultural traditions the elaboration of sentiment. The poetic rather than the narrative genres are the place to look for this. Yet I would argue for a fundamental difference in the localization of the emotions in melodrama and poetry. For example, the *ghinnaawas* or little songs of the Awlad 'Ali Bedouin that I have written about, are short expressions of sentiment (Abu-Lughod 1986). Although people recite them as part of stories, to express the sentiments of particular characters, and otherwise in the contexts of intimates to express their own sentiments about particular life events, they are conventional and formulaic. They are thus, in a sense, depersonalized. They are repeated and appropriated by others and thus are also disembodied. Furthermore, much of the appreciation of these poems—like the performed Hilali epic—comes from the poetry of their language.

Ritual lamentation of the dead in Egypt, as in other parts of the Arab and circum-Mediterranean world, is another highly developed poetic art that is quintessentially emotional. However, as Wickett has shown for Upper Egypt, laments are "ritual texts performed in an emotional arena" (1993: 166) and therefore, I would argue, differ significantly from melodrama in being limited in context and sentiment. They are specific to the ritualized context of the funeral. In contrast, the emotions of melodrama cover a wide range and are attached to individuals and embedded in the everyday, the ordinary, and the domestic.

By establishing these contrasts, I am not trying to assert the existence of a rigid distinction between modernity and tradition, the "folk" art inhabiting (and defining) the traditional past and the melodrama the contemporary present. All sorts of cross-referencing and transformations occur, especially as "traditional" forms aggressively enter the mass media world contemporaneous with the melodrama. Rather, I argue that television melodramas offer distinctive constructions of the world and images of persons, especially within a context defined by "traditional" forms and "traditional ways of life" from which modernist writers and directors are distancing themselves. Their specificity is in the emotionalization of the quotidian world, which in turn works to enforce a sense of the importance of the individual subject—the locus and source of all these strong feelings.

HEROINE OF HER OWN MELODRAMA

To illustrate how television melodrama may have come to inform individual lives, I want to discuss the person I knew in Egypt who was most deeply involved with television and radio melodramas: an unmarried domestic servant in Cairo I call Amira.[9] My fieldwork on television reception was with domestic workers in Cairo and with women in a village in Upper Egypt, both socially marginal groups. Many of the domestic workers shared aspects of Amira's hard situation, but, like the village women busy with families, they were less wedded to television. Amira, in contrast, listened to her transistor radio while she cooked for her employers. When she could, she stopped to watch the noon serial on television. She always watched the evening serials when she got home. She was knowledgeable about the actors and actresses; she had watched not only most serials but also most of the popular Egyptian films that are screened on television. Intelligent and articulate, she could summarize plots easily and remember most. She rarely watched foreign imports.

Unmarried and with no children, she was both freer to follow television and more dependent on it for companionship and emotional-social involvement than most women I worked with in Egypt. She was somewhat isolated socially because she lived on her own. Her mother and brothers still lived in the countryside. Her main contacts in Cairo were an unmarried sister, with whom, however, she had frequent conflicts, and one friend, a single woman who also had come to Cairo from the countryside and worked as a domestic servant. With both, she watched television.

Amira was both more sentimental and more volatile than many women I have come to know. She was often moved by the serials she watched. When we watched television together, her explanations of particular characters carried moral and emotional valences. But her sentimentality extended to other areas. Once when we turned on the television in 1990 and saw a clip of people in Iran crying after an earthquake, this triggered her memory of having wept "for an hour" after the Egyptian soccer team lost the World Cup match. She had kept herself awake until the early hours of the morning to watch the game on television. She was upset because "they worked so hard and got so tired and then God didn't reward them." She had wept when they lost, and then wept again when she saw the Egyptian players crying. "It really hurt." Amira's emotional style extended beyond the world of television. She was often embroiled in conflicts and arguments—with her sister, her employers, and her neighbors.

Although I cannot argue for a direct causal link between her involvement with television serials and her emotionality, I suspect there is one. There is, however, a more obvious link between television melodrama and the ways she constructed herself as a subject. This link is through the ways she made herself the subject of her own life stories. I found it striking that of all the women whose life stories I have heard, Amira was the one whose tales most clearly took the form of melodrama. Hers was a Manichean world with good kind people who helped her and were generous, and greedy, stingy, or cruel people who victimized her.

One can see this in the way she constructed her story of coming to Cairo to find a better life. Amira came from a poor family and had worked on construction sites, hauling dirt and sand, for a daily wage. She wanted to go to Cairo because she saw her sisters, who had gone there to find work, coming home dressed well and wearing gold. At the age of nineteen she finally went. But she lasted only a month in the first job. The family mistreated her. They woke her up at six in the morning, did not feed her, kept the food locked up, and paid her only 6 L.E. per month (about $9 at that time). She cried and cried and finally persuaded her sister to call and say that she was needed at home to tend a sick relative. She found another employer and another. Each time, she found some excuse to go home to her village. Eventually she found a job with a good family as a cook and stayed with them for eight years. The themes repeat: exploited and mistreated, the innocent victim escapes until fate deals her some kind people.

It is when she talks about her brief marriage, however, that all the elements of drama crystallize. At the time of one of our conversations, at age 37, she declared that she was too old to hope for marriage. "Who would want to marry me?" But someone had wanted to, in 1985, when she was about 30. The ease with which she told the story suggested it was a well-rehearsed one. When a plumber who saw her at work asked about the possibility of marriage, she sent him to discuss it with her brother-in-law. They were engaged for four months, but she never went anywhere with him. When she suggested

it, he refused. She claims it was because he did not want her to know what
he was like or to know anything about him.

Once they were married he began beating her. He wanted her to hand
over her wages. She refused, saying she had a loan to pay off and then planned
to stay at home. A man, she explained, is supposed to support his wife. He
locked her in the house. All she wanted was to be rid of him, and so she got
her brother-in-law—whom she held responsible because he was supposed to
have looked into the man's background—to pay the man a thousand pounds
(approximately $700) to divorce her. It turned out he was a tough from a
poor quarter. Amira is convinced that he wanted to kill her to take her apartment. In the end, the marriage lasted twenty-nine days.

Bitterly she added, Egyptian men are no good. Lots of men have asked
to marry her—men on the streets, men she meets at work. But they all want
her money, and when they discover that she has an apartment and furniture
they know they will only have to contribute inexpensive things as a dowry.
Her husband, for example, had provided the living room furniture, but she
already had the bedroom furniture and the apartment. (With the severe
shortage of housing, the exorbitant "key money" that must be paid to get a
rental unit, and the expenses of furnishing the apartment, considered the
responsibility of the groom, many young men find it difficult to marry.)

We must ask, as have Ruth Behar (1990) and Laurel Kendall (1988), about
the narrative qualities of life stories. If Behar's Mexican informant's life story
was shaped by the Christian model of suffering and redemption, Amira's con-
forms more closely to the model of melodrama. Like the television dramas,
the themes of her story are money, with the villain trying to cheat her out
of hers, and the secret, with the truth about her sinister husband discovered
too late. The melodramatic heroine, innocent and good, is wronged and victimized. Seeking a better life, symbolized by her sisters' good clothes and
gold, she leaves the village and home to find herself overworked, underpaid,
and hungry in a house where the food is locked up. Seeking love, companionship, or respectability—whatever it is that marriage is supposed to bring—
she finds herself betrayed.

What I think is most significant about this way of telling her life stories,
however, is that through it Amira makes herself the subject, the melodramatic heroine of her own life. Perhaps inspired in part by her love of television melodrama, she has been encouraged to see herself as the subject of
the emotions that sweep her, and thus as more of an individual. This view of
herself puts her in a better position to be a modern citizen, something the
television producers want from their melodramas. For Amira, this position
is reinforced by the structures of her life: her migrant status and separation
from her family, her reliance on her own labor for survival, her private apartment with its own electricity and water bills, and her subjection to the law
and to taxation as an individual.

POSTCOLONIAL DIFFERENCES

Yet Amira's story and her life present certain complications for a straightforward narrative of coming to modern individual subjecthood as we might tell it along familiar Western lines. First, Amira's tragic story is marked by critical absences and failures. The most specific is the failure of her brother-in-law to take seriously his family responsibility of protecting her from a bad marriage. More generally, she suggests that her vulnerability is caused by the absence of a strong family that could have supported her and kept her from having to work as a maid. Her emptiness is related to her failure to marry and have a family of her own, as most women do. In all the life stories of domestic servants I have recorded, it is always a rupture to the ideal of women's embeddedness in family and marriage that accounts for their positions doing work that is both hard and not respectable, and for their not being, in a sense, full persons. Amira's story, though told mostly in terms of herself as an individual moving through life, evokes the ideal she cannot have—the ideal of being a subject fulfilled and defined by kinship and family.

To note that kinship remains crucial for Amira is not to deny television melodrama's effectiveness. Although the genre conventions may encourage individuality and the political messages promote citizenship and national belonging, television serials do not overtly challenge the ideal of family so taken for granted in Egypt. In keeping with the urban middle-class ideals of the scriptwriters, the nuclear family gets more play than the extended family. But almost all characters, male and female, are still placed within families and, in line with increasing moral restrictions on media, there is little place for plotlines about such things as extramarital relationships between men and women.

However, there is something else of great importance in Amira's day-to-day life that does not derive from television melodrama and that in some, but not all, ways undermines the processes television encourages. In part because she is cut out of family life and cannot rely on kin to provide community, purpose, and social respectability, Amira is attracted to the new path to individual expression and respectability opened up to women in the past two decades by the movement to make Islam more central to everyday life and politics. This fact, along with the continuing centrality of kinship and the ways that Egyptian melodramas embed morality in the social, reminds us that this modern form of drama and the forms of selfhood it encourages are being produced in a postcolonial nation with its own specific history and forms of modernity (see similar arguments by Appadurai 1996 and Chakrabarty 1997).

Religious practice organizes Amira's schedule, informs her sense of self, and colors her understanding of her world as much as work and watching

Family watching television in an Upper Egyptian village, 1993. (Photo: Lila Abu-Lughod)

television do. Since the mid-1980s mosques have flourished, and it has become much more accepted that lower- and middle-class urban women should pray in them and attend religious lessons. The same structural features that make Amira more dependent on television and free to follow it—living alone as an unmarried woman without children—also enable her to pray more regularly, go to mosque on Fridays and sometimes even after work, and participate in the special mosque prayers of Ramadan, the month of special devotion and fasting as well as heavy television watching. That she wears the *higab,* the modest head covering that has become a fashionable sign of piety and middle-class respectability in the towns and cities, is not unusual. But Amira's regular participation in lessons at the mosque has intensified her identity as a Muslim and given meaning to the wearing of this item of clothing. As a result of her involvement in these religious practices and identifications, Amira is pulled into a community, and not the national community to which individual citizens are, according to television scriptwriters, supposed to relate themselves (Abu-Lughod 1993, 1995, 1996, 1998).

Yet many of Amira's religious observances are self-oriented and thus might be thought of as running along the same tracks as the individualizing and interiorizing of television melodrama (even though many religious authorities preach against television). This is especially true with the discipline of fasting, which she takes very seriously. She fasts all the days of Ramadan, like most Egyptian Muslims, making up later the days lost because of menstruation. But she also fasts all the other possible and recommended days of the Muslim calendar. One can also see this concern with the self and bodily discipline in the way she constantly asks others to forgive her for the smallest things—such as angering someone or even helping herself to a piece of cake from an employer's larder. Her references to her sinfulness and the need to cleanse it with fasting, prayer, and asking forgiveness, were especially striking to me because her life was so moral and proper. This obsessive concern with the self is, it seems, strongly encouraged by the rhetoric of the lessons at the mosque (Mahmood 1998).

Like television everywhere, Egyptian television seems to be changing to accommodate (not to mention appropriate for its own legitimacy) the concerns of its viewers, in this case the new intensity of religious practice and identity. There have long been religious television serials, historical costume dramas about the early history of Islam. These were often aired late at night and were not particularly popular. Like all religious programming, they were segregated from the popular evening serials, as if to compartmentalize religion. But in the past few years, major actors participated in the big-budget religious/historical serials broadcast during Ramadan, and major writers and directors were called upon to produce them. These serials were, it turned out, so popular that the head of television production appointed in 1997 announced a plan to do many more serials about "our Arab Islamic heritage," as he gingerly put it, over the next few years.

The serialization of the Hilali epic broadcast during Ramadan in the early slot that children are sure to be watching is part of this effort. Although not strictly speaking a religious serial, it gave a prominent place to discourse about God, as does the oral performed epic traditionally recited by and for people for whom being Muslim is an important part of identity. Yet there is a striking difference in the forms religiosity takes in the television version and the oral epic as performed by traditional poets. This suggests how television religion, much like Amira's, may be part of a new individualizing of religion.

In the epic as performed in Egypt, God's power is a constant theme. All great deeds and miraculous happenings, like the birth of the hero, Abu Zayd, are attributed to it. Poets always open their performances with a praise poem to the Prophet. This praise poetry introduces the themes of the segments to be recited but also has the rhetorical effect of praising the poet himself by linking his poetic abilities and his status to that of the Prophet, whose divine words were miraculous, and praising the audience for being part of the community of Muslims (Slyomovics, forthcoming).

The television serial also represented God's miraculous power: in computer-generated special effects like the strong bird whose likeness Khadra prays for in a son. But for the most part, religion figures as the origin of the emotionalized attitudes of characters—their supplication, their awe, and their gratitude. We see this clearly when Rizq, the hero's father, waits anxiously while his wife is in labor. There is a cut to a scene (perhaps at sunrise of the same day) of him standing by his horse watching the sun, his hands held up in the position of prayer. Back home, his hands are clasped and he asks God to keep his wife safe. When he is told the news that he has a son, he repeats again and again, "A thousand praises and thanks to you O Lord." He faces different parts of the room, arms up toward Heaven, thanking bountiful God for having generously given him a son after all these years, and for ending his sorrows and enabling him to face the men and know that his name would remain. He then drops to his knees, thanking God again. Later his wife will say she accepts her son as a gift from God. In these scenes, it is the personal faith, rather than the power of God, that is stressed. Piety has been made into a characteristic of the self.

SOCIAL CONTEXTS AND NATIONAL INFLECTIONS

Some years ago, while I was in the midst of my research on television in Egypt, there appeared in a popular Egyptian women's magazine an article by Muna Hilmi, daughter of Nawal El-Saadawi, an Egyptian feminist writer well known in the West. She praised the American daytime soap opera *The Bold and the Beautiful,* then being broadcast on Egyptian television (and widely condemned by the Egyptian intelligentsia). She contrasted it with Egyptian serials, which she disparaged for their remorseless attention to social and political problems. She lauded the American soap opera for its feminism (it had strong women characters who were determined to achieve what they wanted in their careers and their lives), but most of all for its subtle exploration of the human psyche.

What I have tried to show here, though, is that the emotionality and domesticity that characterize Egyptian melodramas, genre conventions developed by educated professionals (not unlike Muna Hilmi) in the context of Egyptian genres and social circumstances, may be part of an effort to construct individuals with vivid interior lives and encourage the development of those human psyches she extols. But there is a difference. The human psyches in an American soap opera like *The Bold and the Beautiful* lack any obvious political context, a trait that initially rendered the serial harmless in the eyes of the Egyptian censors. In contrast, producers working in the government-controlled medium of television and imbued with an ideology of national development and the legacy of Arab socialist ideals, insist on placing their characters squarely within the social and moral national nexus. And because of the increasing hegemony of an assertive religious identity in a society in which most people had never accepted the principle that religious practice and morality were not part of modern everyday life—something Muna Hilmi and the class fraction she represents most likely disapprove of—the vectors of modernity crisscross. Melodrama, and to some extent what I would argue to be a new focus on the self in religious practice, may be encouraging the kinds of individuated subjectivities a sophisticated modernist secularist like Hilmi wants. Yet this new focus on the self, entangled with similar processes associated with current religious practices, is counterbalanced by the enduring ties of kinship and the very appealing, and modern, politics of religious identity that pull such selves away from individualism and into communities with their own authorities and disciplines.

Mass media have made the melodramatic genre a part of everyday life for most Egyptians. This development may have led to a melodramatization of consciousness, to return to my adaptation of Raymond Williams's phrase, by offering up models for subjectivity and narratives of the self in the characters whose quotidian lives are emotionalized. This melodramatization may indeed be tied to what Brooks called "modern sensibilities," encouraging individuated subjects appropriate for citizenship and perhaps consumerism.

It is clear, however, that there are national inflections of common genres and that the social contexts of reception deeply affect, and potentially undermine, the impact of the projects of television. In Egypt, serials are both more tied to political context and more concerned with social issues than are serials produced in some other countries today. They are also quite varied in their political message and moral stance, depending on the writers and directors who make them. This should give us pause regarding any generalizations about melodrama based on studies of French novels or American daytime soap operas.

More significant for an understanding of media as situated is the way that the specific social context of Egypt in the 1990s shapes reception. State television and those who produce for it can try to reflect certain social transformations, to gain popularity, just as they have made efforts for years, in line with ideologies of development, to shape or mold their audiences and bring them into a national modernity. Yet they cannot control the experiences people seek outside of television-watching or the everyday social worlds in which people live their lives. In the increasingly popular fields of religious practice, some of the individualizing encouraged by melodrama (evident in serials with both secular and religious themes) may be reinforced by the current practices of cultivating moral selves. But as with the ties of kinship that continue to be important in new contexts, religious identities in this supposedly "post-sacred era" draw individuals into community, emphasizing their ties to others and to God, not the distinction of the self. Such experiences are surely another dimension of "modern sensibilities" in Egypt, intersecting with those of television melodrama.

NOTES

This chapter was adapted from "Modern Subjects: Egyptian Melodrama and Post-colonial Difference," in *Questions of Modernity*, edited by Timothy Mitchell (© 2000 The Regents of the University of Minnesota), and is used here with permission from the University of Minnesota Press. For diverse contributions, I am grateful to Talal Asad, Nick Dirks, Faye Ginsburg, Tim Mitchell, Samira Mohammad, Gyan Prakash, Dwight Reynolds, Reem Saad, Omnia Shakry, Susan Slyomovics, Ted Swedenburg, and Lisa Wideen. Fieldwork in Egypt was supported by the American Research Center in Egypt, the ACLS/SSRC Near and Middle East Committee, the National Endowment for the Humanities, and New York University.

1. Lopez notes that the Mexican telenovelas are stereotypically more weepy (1995: 261). Clearly the Egyptian serials are less sophisticated, glossy, and sexually charged than the Brazilian telenovelas, but even these have something in common: in Egypt as in Brazil, many television writers are serious and progressive (Guillermoprieto 1993).

2. See Asad 1993 for the argument that secularism, and the notion of religion it implies, is a concept that developed as part of the history of Christianity in the West.

3. For more on the ideologies, see Abu-Lughod 1993, 1995.

4. See T. Miller 1993 for an analysis that links modern forms of subjectivity—the individual as consumer and as citizen—to mass-mediated cultural forms.

5. Although Ang (1990) notes that melodrama may be characterized by its "tragic structure of feeling" and the sense that characters are "victims of forces that lie beyond their control"—favorite themes in the many Egyptian television dramas that treat the tribulations of good families facing the problems created by the shortage of housing, a Kafkaesque bureaucracy, or the forces of corruption—the most appealing dramas display a range of emotions.

6. Feminist critics have done for television soap opera what Brooks did for literary melodrama: they have forced a reevaluation of a genre dismissed as pap, as well as developing some critical ideas about female pleasure through its serious analysis. The feminist literature on soap opera is extensive and much of it quite good. Some key texts are Allen 1985; Ang 1985, 1990; Brunsdon 1995; Feuer 1984; Geraghty 1991; Joyrich 1992; Modleski 1982; Mulvey 1986; Mumford 1995; Seiter et al. 1989.

7. "The disciplines mark the moment when the reversal of the political axis of individualization—as one might call it—takes place. In certain societies . . . it may be said that individualization is greatest where sovereignty is exercised and in the highest echelons of power. The more one possesses power or privilege, the more one is marked as an individual, by rituals, written accounts or visual reproductions. The 'name' and the genealogy that situate one within a kinship group, the performance of deeds that demonstrate superior strength and which are immortalized in literary accounts . . . all these are procedures of an 'ascending' individualization. In a disciplinary regime, on the other hand, individualization is 'descending': as power becomes more anonymous and more functional, those on whom it is exercised tend to be more strongly individualized." (Foucault 1978: 192–93)

8. It could be argued that the interiority of the domestic scenes of soap opera are metaphors for the inner life of the persons around which their plots revolve. Elsaesser, in his classic article on cinematic melodrama, has suggested in fact that "the

space of the home" does relate "to the inside space of human interiority, emotions, and the unconscious" (cited in Mulvey 1986: 95).

9. Since 1990 I have conducted my fieldwork in Egypt in two sites: Cairo, where I have interviewed producers of television and worked with domestic servants as television viewers; and a village in Upper Egypt. For rural responses to television, see Abu-Lughod 1997, 1998.

REFERENCES

Abu-Lughod, Lila. 1986. *Veiled Sentiments.* Berkeley: University of California Press.

———. 1990. Shifting Politics of Bedouin Love Poetry. In *Language and the Politics of Emotion,* edited by Catherine Lutz and Lila Abu-Lughod, pp. 24–25. New York: Cambridge University Press.

———. 1993. Finding a Place for Islam. *Public Culture* 5 (3): 493–513.

———. 1995. The Objects of Soap Opera. In *Worlds Apart: Modernity through the Prism of the Local,* edited by Daniel Miller, pp. 190–210. London: Routledge.

———. 1996. Dramatic Reversals. In *Political Islam,* edited by Joe Stork and Joey Beinin, pp. 269–82. Berkeley: University of California Press.

———. 1997. The Interpretation of Culture(s) after Television. *Representations* 59: 109–34.

———. 1998. Television and the Virtues of Education: Upper Egyptian Encounters with State Culture. In *Directions of Change in Rural Egypt,* edited by Nicholas Hopkins and Kirsten Westergaard, pp. 147–65. Cairo: American University in Cairo Press.

Allen, Robert C. 1985. *Speaking of Soap Opera.* Chapel Hill: University of North Carolina Press.

———, ed. 1995. *To Be Continued . . . :Soap Operas around the World.* London: Routledge.

Ang, Ien. 1985. *Watching Dallas: Soap Opera and the Melodramatic Imagination.* London: Methuen.

———. 1990. Melodramatic Identifications: Television Fiction and Women's Fantasy. In *Television and Women's Culture,* edited by Mary Ellen Brown, pp. 75–88. London: Sage.

Appadurai, Arjun. 1996. *Modernity at Large.* Minneapolis: University of Minnesota Press.

Armbrust, Walter. 1996. *Mass Culture and Modernism in Egypt.* Cambridge, England: Cambridge University Press.

Asad, Talal. 1993. *Genealogies of Religion.* Baltimore: Johns Hopkins University Press.

Behar, Ruth. 1990. Rage and Redemption: Reading the Life Story of a Mexican Marketing Woman. *Feminist Studies* 16: 223–58.

Brooks, Peter. 1976. *The Melodramatic Imagination.* New Haven, Conn.: Yale University Press.

Brown, Mary Ellen, ed. 1990. *Television and Women's Culture.* London: Sage.

Brunsdon, Charlotte. 1995. The Role of Soap Opera in the Development of Feminist Television Scholarship. In *To Be Continued. . . .* , edited by Robert C. Allen, pp. 49–55. London: Routledge.

Chakrabarty, Dipesh. 1997. The Difference-Deferral of a Colonial Modernity. In *Tensions of Empire*, edited by Frederick Cooper and Ann Stoler, pp. 373–405. Berkeley: University of California Press.

———. 2000. Witness to Suffering: Domestic Cruelty and the Birth of the Modern Subject in Bengal. In *Questions of Modernity*, edited by Timothy Mitchell, pp. 49–86. Minneapolis: University of Minnesota Press.

Cvetkovich, Ann. 1992. *Mixed Feelings: Feminism, Mass Culture, and Victorian Sensationalism.* New Brunswick, N.J.: Rutgers University Press.

Das, Veena. 1995. Soap Opera: What Kind of Object Is It? In *Worlds Apart*, edited by Daniel Miller, pp. 169–89. London: Routledge.

Feuer, Jane. 1984. Melodrama, Serial Form and Television Today. *Screen* 25: 4–16.

Foucault, Michel. 1978. *Discipline and Punish.* Translated by Alan Sheridan. New York: Random House.

———. 1985. *The Use of Pleasure.* New York: Random House.

———. 1988. Technologies of the Self. In *Technologies of the Self*, edited by L. Martin, H. Gutman, and P. Hutton, pp. 16–49. Amherst: University of Massachusetts Press.

———. 1993. About the Beginning of the Hermeneutics of the Self. *Political Theory* 21 (2): 198–227.

Geraghty, Christine. 1991. *Women and Soap Opera: A Study of Prime-Time Soaps.* Cambridge, England: Polity Press.

Gledhill, Christine, ed. 1994. *Melodrama: Stage, Picture, Screen.* London: British Film Institute.

Guillermoprieto, Alma. 1993. Letter from Brazil: Obsessed in Rio. *New Yorker*, August 16, pp. 44–55.

Hilmi, Muna. 1993. *The Bold and the Beautiful:* A Serial without Male Complexes [in Arabic]. *Sabah al-Khayr*, February 11, p. 59.

Joyrich, Lynne. 1992. All That Television Allows: TV Melodrama, Postmodernism, and Consumer Culture. In *Private Screenings*, edited by Lynn Spiegel and Denise Mann, pp. 227–51. Minneapolis: University of Minnesota Press.

Karthigasu, Ranggasamy. 1988. Television as a Tool for Nation-Building in the Third World. In *Television and Its Audience*, edited by P. Drummond and R. Paterson, pp. 306–26. London: British Film Institute.

Kendall, Laurel. 1988. *The Life and Hard Times of a Korean Shaman.* Honolulu: University of Hawaii Press.

Lopez, Ana. 1995. Our Welcomed Guests: Telenovelas in Latin America. In *To Be Continued . . .* , edited by Robert C. Allen. London: Routledge.

Lutz, Catherine. 1986. Emotion, Thought, and Estrangement: Emotion as a Cultural Category. *Cultural Anthropology* 1 (4): 405–36.

Mahmood, Saba. 1998. Women's Piety and Embodied Discipline: The Islamic Resurgence in Contemporary Egypt. Ph.D. diss., Stanford University.

Mankekar, Purnima. 1993a. National Texts and Gendered Lives. *American Ethnologist* 20 (3): 543–63.

———. 1993b. Television Tales and a Woman's Rage. *Public Culture* 5 (3): 469–92.

Merritt, Russell. 1983. Melodrama: Postmortem for a Phantom Genre. *Wide Angle* 5 (3): 25–31.

Miller, Toby. 1993. *The Well-Tempered Self.* Baltimore: Johns Hopkins University Press.

Mitchell, Timothy, ed. 2000. *Questions of Modernity.* Minneapolis: University of Minnesota Press.

Modleski, Tanya. 1982. *Loving with a Vengeance: Mass Produced Fantasies for Women.* Hamden, Conn.: Archon Books.

Mulvey, Laura. 1986. Melodrama in and out of the Home. In *High Theory/Low Culture,* edited by Colin McCabe, pp. 80–100. Manchester: Manchester University Press.

Mumford, Laura Stempel. 1995. *Love and Ideology in the Afternoon.* Bloomington: Indiana University Press.

Reynolds, Dwight. 1995. *Heroic Poets, Poetic Heroes: The Ethnography of Performance in an Arabic Oral Epic Tradition.* Ithaca, N.Y.: Cornell University Press.

———, trans. Forthcoming. *The Epic of the Bani Hilal.*

Seiter, Ellen et al., eds. 1989. *Remote Control: Television, Audiences, and Cultural Power.* London: Routledge.

Slyomovics, Susan. 1986. *The Merchant of Art.* Berkeley: University of California Press.

———. 1987. The Death-Song of 'Amir Khafaji: Puns in an Oral and Printed Episode of *Sirat Bani Hilal. Journal of Arabic Literature* 18: 62–78.

———.1997. The Epic of the Bani Hilal: The Birth of Abu Zayd I (Southern Egypt). In *Oral Epics from Africa: Vibrant Voices from a Vast Continent,* edited by John William Johnson, Thomas A. Hale, and Stephen Belcher, pp. 240–51. Bloomington: Indiana University Press.

———. Forthcoming. Praise of God, Praise of Self, Praise of the Islamic People: Arab Epic Narrative in Performance. In *Classical and Popular Medieval Arabic Literature: A Marriage of Convenience,* edited by Jareer Abu-Haidar and Farida Abu-Haidar. London: Curzon Press.

Wickett, Elizabeth. 1993. "For Our Destinies": The Funerary Lament of Upper Egypt. Ph.D. diss., University of Pennsylvania.

Williams, Raymond. 1989. Drama in a Dramatised Society. In *Raymond Williams and Television,* edited by A. O'Connor, pp. 3–13. London: Routledge.

6

Epic Contests

Television and Religious Identity in India

Purnima Mankekar

On January 25, 1987, the first episode of the *Ramayan*, a serial based on an important Hindu epic, was shown on state-controlled Indian television. Spanning seventy-eight weekly episodes and produced and directed by a successful Hindi film producer and director, the *Ramayan* received unprecedented ratings. Three years after its telecast, tensions between Hindus and Muslims, which had been exacerbated by Hindu nationalists' attempts to "reclaim" the site of the Babri Mosque as the birthplace of the Hindu god Ram, exploded into a series of riots all over the nation. In December 1992, Hindu nationalists stormed the mosque, precipitating one of the most widespread outbreaks of violence since the partition of the South Asian subcontinent.

Clearly there is no simple connection between the televising of the *Ramayan* and the outbreaks of communal violence that have ravaged the Indian subcontinent since the early 1990s;[1] my objective in this essay is to examine how this television serial might have participated in reconfigurations of nation, culture, and community that overlapped with and reinforced Hindu nationalism. The *Ramayan* was telecast at a moment when Hindu nationalists were attempting to seize upon civil society to redefine the Indian nation as a Hindu nation.[2] Indeed, the larger historical conjuncture, in the late 1980s and early 1990s, has been deemed a crucial period in postcolonial Indian history, when constructions of nation were rearticulated and religious identities renegotiated.[3] That conjuncture witnessed a fundamental shift in the meaning of Indian nationhood: the slippage between Hindu and Indian nationalisms was consolidated so that Hindu nationalism acquired unprecedented hegemony.[4] In this chapter, I develop an anthropological framework that combines ethnographic examples of viewers' interpretations with textual analysis to examine how the *Ramayan* may have helped reshape common-sense conceptions of Indian culture, community, and identity in an unfolding war of position. Why was this television serial so popular among the men and women I met during my fieldwork in New Delhi? Why did this narrative "work" as a hegemonic text, to whom did it speak, and whom did it exclude?

THE *RAMAYANA*

The extraordinary cultural import of this particular religious epic may be gleaned from the fact that millions of Hindus in the South Asian subcontinent (and in several regions of Southeast Asia) turn to the *Ramayana*[5] as a moral and cultural resource for their everyday practices, decisions, and relationships. The core narrative[6] of the television *Ramayan* is as follows: King Dashrath of Ayodhya has four sons from three wives. His eldest son, Ram, is the hero of the epic and is one of the most important gods of the North Indian Hindu pantheon.[7] Soon after Ram attains adulthood and is married, he is exiled to fourteen years in the forest because of a vow his father had made many years earlier to his favorite wife. Ram's wife, Sita, and younger brother, the loyal and passionate Lakshman, insist upon accompanying him into exile. In the forest, Sita is abducted by the powerful king of Lanka, Ravan. Ram and his brother defeat Ravan and his family in a battle and rescue Sita. Years later, after they return to Ayodhya, Ram banishes a pregnant Sita because of rumors that she became unchaste while a captive of Ravan's. Sita finds shelter with a sage in the forest and gives birth to twins. When the twins become teenagers, they vindicate her honor and the family is reunited. But Sita refuses to return to Ayodhya with Ram: the earth splits and she is swallowed by it.

THE *RAMAYAN* AND ITS RECEPTION

The *Ramayan* was telecast on Sunday from 9 A.M. to 10 A.M. on Doordarshan, the state-controlled television station; it was watched by between 80 and 100 million viewers and achieved unprecedented ratings. My analysis of the reception of the *Ramayan* is based on fieldwork in two neighborhoods in New Delhi, Vikas Nagar and Basti, both of which were fairly homogeneous in terms of their class composition. Vikas Nagar was a lower-middle-class neighborhood built by the government to house the lowest level of the bureaucracy: most of its inhabitants were junior clerks, typists, and stenographers. Although those who worked for the state had relatively secure jobs, their incomes were so low that many families needed at least two wage earners to make ends meet. The people I worked with in Basti faced even more difficult financial conditions. Yet there were some signs of upward mobility: most of the older generation had been domestic servants or casual laborers on construction sites, but many of their children now worked as assembly-line laborers in garment factories, and their grandchildren had at least a couple of years of schooling. About two-thirds of the men and women I worked with were Hindu; the remainder were about equally divided between Muslims and Sikhs.

Why was the *Ramayan* so popular with viewers? In what follows, I complicate the notion of "the popular" by analyzing how viewers of different religions responded to the serial.[8] For most Hindus, the serial's fascination appears to have resided not so much in its plot—that is, in "what happened"—but in how the story was told. Furthermore, unlike Sikh and Muslim viewers, many Hindus claimed that the story contained important lessons about morality, politics, and ideal manhood and womanhood.

THE POLITICS OF THE POPULAR

The *Ramayan* is about gods, about Lord Rama, yes. But why is he a god? Because he is an ideal man, an ideal king, an ideal son. And Sita is an ideal woman. The serial was . . . about how to behave with everybody, with [one's] father, mother. With [one's] wife, with [one's] brothers. It is about family life. It is about husband and wife. It is about government. There is something for everybody. It is about how to lead a good life.

Sukumaran leaned forward as he spoke, his soft voice rising in his earnestness to explain to me why he had watched the *Ramayan* so regularly. He was a brahmin from South India and had been in New Delhi all his adult life. A stenographer in a government office, he lived with his family in a tiny eight-by-ten-foot flat in Vikas Nagar. Viewers in South India had protested that the serial was based on a North Indian version of the story (Mankekar 1999). Although Sukumaran agreed in part with this objection, he enjoyed the *Ramayan* because it provided him with an easily comprehensible version of Hinduism that he could incorporate into his everyday life. Equally important, the *Ramayan* seemed to present him with moral guidelines about various aspects of the world: about ideal governance, ideal masculinity and femininity, duty toward one's family. As Sukumaran noted, "It is about Hindu *dharma* [code of conduct], a religious story, yes. But it is also about living in the world."

Although Sukumaran's views on the *Ramayan* were echoed in different ways by many Hindu viewers I worked with, they were drawn to it for various reasons. To comprehend the serial's popularity with these viewers, we need to combine ethnographic analyses of its reception with an investigation of its representational strategies. With its opulent sets and brightly colored costumes and in the facial expressions and postures of its main characters, the *Ramayan* drew heavily upon the iconography of religious calendar and poster art (Smith 1995; Pinney, this volume). It is thus not surprising that for many Hindu viewers watching the *Ramayan* was like engaging in a religious ritual (Gillespie 1995). Many of them recounted to me that they bathed and purified themselves before the epic came on; some lit incense sticks. They spoke of sitting in front of the TV set with their hands folded and heads bowed. A personal relationship of surrender and absolute devotion between a devotee and the subject of her worship, what many Hindus term *bhakti,* was an important form of engagement for many of them. The fact that their *bhakti* was electronically mediated did not diminish its authenticity.

In fact, for many Hindu viewers, the televisual medium seemed to encourage an intense form of devotion or *bhakti* through the visual process of seeing or *darshan.*[9] *Darshan* entails seeing, and being beheld by, the deity (Eck 1985: 3). *Darshan,* therefore, is not a passive act of seeing; it encompasses an interaction, a relationship, a profound engagement with the sacred. Seeing Lord Rama on television became a form of *darshan* for them.[10] From news reports, I determined that this response was far from unusual.

Let me give an example of how some Hindu viewers responded to the iconography of the *Ramayan.* Poonam Sharma was a young college student whose father was a junior clerk in a government department. She and her family lived in Vikas Nagar. I quote from one of many long discussions we had about the serial: "What was amazing about the *Ramayan* serial was that Ram and Sita looked exactly like I had imagined. Sita [had a] peaceful expression. Ram also [looked] peaceful. Lakshman [Ram's younger brother] [looked] angry. Ravan [looked] frightening. It was just as I had always imagined. How did the actors manage it?"

Her mother, Shakuntala, agreed and said that the actor playing Ram had "Ramji's form." In calendar art and other popular iconography, Ram is often depicted in "the peaceful form" *(shaant mudra)* with his eyes half-closed, his right hand raised in benediction, a faint smile playing around his lips. My conversations with several of my Hindu informants revealed that some of the power of the *Ramayan* rested precisely in the iconicity of its portrayals of Ram, Lakshman, and Sita.[11] The iconicity of these images was heightened by the use of close-up and medium-range shots, which enhanced *darshan* of the gods and goddesses.[12]

However, this serial was popular with Hindus not only because of its religious content but also because it drew upon a range of narrative traditions and representational strategies. In addition to using the iconography of popular calendar art, the *Ramayan* combined the cinematic techniques of popular Hindi film with the performative traditions and choreography of folk genres like *nautanki,* popular musical traditions, and computer-simulated special effects.[13] The welding of different narrative strategies in the mass mediation of religious epics is not a new phenomenon. Several of the first few Indian films were "mythologicals" (Barnouw and Krishnaswamy 1980) and also depended on the iconography of calendar art (Rajyadhaksha 1986), local performative traditions and, of course, cinematic techniques newly imported from Europe at the turn of the century. Several mythologicals were also produced in southern India. After the introduction of sound in 1931, the popularity of religious epics waned; it resurfaced in 1975 with the enormous box office success of the film *Jai Santoshi Ma* about a lesser-known goddess of northern India. All these films combined the representational strategies of popular cinema with local performative traditions. Thus by the time the *Ramayan* was telecast on Doordarshan, a majority of its viewers were likely to have acquired the semiotic skills to derive pleasure from its televisual narration.[14]

As in many folk theatrical traditions and in popular film, music played a crucial role in the *Ramayan*'s ability to create specific structures of feeling and modes of viewing. Many episodes began with prologues consisting of hymns, which aimed to produce a devotional structure of feeling in Hindu viewers. As in some folk plays and Hindi films, background music was deployed to induce a particular mood or to emphasize a character's emotional state (for instance, Sita's fear when she is abducted by Ravan). Computer-simulated special effects were used to depict the divinity of gods and goddesses (for example, early in the serial, Ravan is portrayed as larger-than-life as he tramples on a [very modern] image of a revolving globe).

What did viewers from different religious communities, for whom it neither contained lessons on morality nor commanded the same iconic power, make of this serial? For some of the Sikh and Muslim women I worked with, the *Ramayan*'s appeal lay in its portrayal of the relationship between Ram and his wife, Sita. Sita's story resonated with some women whose life experiences drew them to the serial. Although the same was true of some Hindu women, it was the Sikh and Muslim women who spoke most often of the trials of Sita. Sometimes they appropriated Sita's story to talk about the difficulties they faced in their own lives.

I became particularly close to Harbhajan Kaur, a young Sikh widow. Her husband had died two years earlier and left her, a young woman of 32, with two small children and huge debt. Harbhajan worked very hard to make ends meet: she sewed clothes for women of the middle-class neighborhood adjacent to Basti and, when the opportunity arose, did assembly-line work in garment factories. Harbhajan told me that she watched the *Ramayan* regularly because it depicted the trials of "a good woman who was always misunderstood by her family." She added that the *Ramayan* provided important insights into the negotiation of family conflicts.

For Harbhajan, it was not faith in Lord Ram that made her such a fan of the *Ramayan*. Its appeal to her was that it was the story of a woman who had been betrayed by her husband and mistreated by her in-laws and her community, as she had been. She was very bitter that her husband's family, who lived across the street from her, did nothing to help her. Instead, whenever she worked outside the home, her husband's uncle reprimanded her. Her husband's family seemed to keep a close watch on her activities; they went so far as to gossip about her "lack of modesty" to me, a relative stranger. The comparison she suggested between her life and Sita's was significant. For one, her words poignantly underscore her acute sense of being marginalized (and "misunderstood") by her family. Second, and perhaps more pertinent to the argument at hand, for her Sita was neither an ideal woman nor a goddess but a woman whose experiences were all too human; like Harbhajan herself, Sita was a woman wronged.

VIEWERS' DISCOURSES OF SELF AND OTHER

The *Ramayan*'s conflation of Hindu and Indian identity rested on its "othering" of non-Hindu identities.[15] The politics of gender, community, and nation converged powerfully in the serial's construction of the other as sexual predator, revealing the co-implication of Hindu nationalism and discourses of sexuality.[16] In both the *Ramayan* and the *Mahabharat,* the second Hindu epic serialized on television, episodes depicting the sexual dishonor of Sita and Draupadi are particularly significant (Mankekar 1999). In both serials, they provide the turning point of the narrative: wars are fought over the honor of women, which in turn is conflated with and subsumed by the honor of the patriarchal clan. The humiliation of women is avenged by men who interpret it as an assault on their masculinity.

However, there are crucial differences in the two serials' portrayal of sexual dishonor. Unlike Draupadi, who is disrobed by her own brother-in-law (that is, by a member of her husband's clan), Sita is abducted by Ravan, the embodiment of the demonized other. As pointed out by Sheldon Pollock, the *Ramayan* contrasts sharply with the *Mahabharat* in being "profoundly and fundamentally a text of 'othering'" (1993: 282–83). This is clearest in its depiction of women's sexuality as a site for contests between self and other. When Ravan first sees Sita he can barely conceal his lust for her. The political significance of representations of demonized others who steal or dishonor "our" women becomes clearer when we place them in the context of communal discourses on sexuality, according to which women must be protected from the other because their sexual purity is metonymic of the honor of communities. Therefore, "true men" must protect their women and avenge any assaults on them. As pointed out by several observers, communalists constantly raise the specter of the "violation of our sisters and mothers" and exhort men to "take revenge" and prove their manhood (Chhachhi 1989: 577) as a means of policing the boundaries of the community (Butalia 1995).

In addition, the *Ramayan* deployed essentialist notions of culture that encouraged viewers to equate Hindu culture with Indian culture. Renuka Sengupta was an upper-caste Bengali Hindu woman who had grown up in New

Delhi. As one of the first generation in her family to get a postsecondary education, she was lower middle class with aspirations to upward mobility. We had several conversations about the *Ramayan*. One stands out in my memory. It was late afternoon; we were sitting in her living room talking about one of her favorite TV serials. Our conversation was frequently interrupted by a jeep on the street outside the house advertising a Hindu-nationalist public meeting on a loudspeaker. Renuka said that she wanted to attend the rally because she thought that it was important for Hindus to claim their "cultural rights." She felt that "the government" allowed Muslims to have four wives and made the Hindus feel like "guests in their own homes." Then she went on to say: "The *Ramayan* has taught us a lot about Hinduism." She claimed that, until recently, many of her friends had felt ashamed of exhibiting their Hindu identity but most of them now felt it was "all right to be traditional . . . *Ramayan* has taught us to be proud of our heritage." When I pressed her to explain how a Hindu epic could teach Indian values, she clicked her tongue impatiently and exclaimed: "But Indian culture is based on Hindu culture!" For her, tradition and heritage were embodied in the representations of Hindu culture in the *Ramayan*.

Renuka constructed the alien-ness of Muslims in discourses of sexuality, hygiene, and their alleged loyalty to the Pakistani cricket team (and therefore their presumed lack of loyalty to India). According to her, Muslims were alien because "they have four wives, they can divorce easily . . . all they have to say is *talaaq, talaaq, talaaq* [here Renuka snapped her fingers], and they can get rid of one wife and acquire another," and because "they do not bathe everyday and are unclean." Further, she claimed, during cricket matches between India and Pakistan, Muslims always cheered for the Pakistani team. Agitated, she said, "Tell me, how can we trust them?"[17]

The Hindu men and women I worked with tended to have two kinds of discourses about Muslims, both of which were based on essentialist notions of culture.[18] Some insisted that although Muslims were "originally" Hindus who had converted to Islam, they had "basically" the same culture, implying an essential Hindu culture overlaid by Islam. In conceptions of their own (Hindu) identity, Hindus conflated religion with culture; in their representations of Muslims, however, they conceived of Islam as an alien layer superimposed on an immutable Hindu culture: these conceptions of culture reinforced the authenticity of an original Hindu culture and the inauthenticity of Islam. Other viewers claimed that Muslims were intrinsically different and that everything about them—their family life, their habits, and their political allegiances—was "alien" or "foreign." The alleged difference of Muslims was also constructed on the basis of and in opposition to essentialist notions of a monolithic Hindu/Indian culture. An overwhelming majority of the Hindu viewers I worked with appropriated the *Ramayan*'s conflation of Indian/Hindu culture. For instance, even those Hindus who criticized the performative styles of the serial mentioned that it represented "our" culture and, occasionally, "our" history. The fact that this serial was telecast on state-owned Doordarshan reinforced the perceived authenticity of these narratives of Hindu/Indian culture and history.

Indeed, the discourses of culture, self, and other constructed in the *Ramayan* seemed to have enabled most Hindu viewers I interviewed to consolidate their Hindu identity and, further, to naturalize the slippage between Hindu culture and Indian culture. Predictably, none of the Sikh or Muslim viewers I interviewed ever mentioned the term "history" or "culture" in their discussions of the *Ramayan*. They were even less likely to claim the *Ramayan* as their own culture or history. As Parmindar Kaur, a 25-year-old Sikh school teacher who lived in Basti, said:

> We are Sikhs. We were not likely to ever read the *Ramayan*. But from watching it we learned a little about Hindus. The Aunty [living] opposite is Hindu. When we were children she used to tell us stories. But we had forgotten most of them. When we saw the *Ramayan* we remembered some of them. Some new stories also we learnt. . . . The troubles Lakshman and Sita had to face when they went into exile. We had never read it. We weren't ever likely to read it. So it was entertaining for us. We used to enjoy watching it. But naturally we don't know how authentic it was. We liked the way they showed it.

Parmindar added that she watched the *Ramayan* because she liked its story: even though she was familiar with it, she found the way it was televised "entertaining." Her words are important because, for one, they remind us that minority communities were hardly isolated from the narratives constructed by the dominant community: it is not surprising that Parmindar had heard tales from the *Ramayan* from Hindu friends and neighbors as a child and was familiar with them. Nonetheless, it is significant that she repeatedly claimed that Sikh viewers like herself had not read the epic and, more pertinent, that they were not likely to ever read it because it was a Hindu text. These repeated assertions underscore her sense of difference and marginalization from a majority community that, at this historical moment, was attempting to impose hegemonic narratives of the past, nationhood, and culture. At the same time, like many Sikhs, Parmindar explained her avid viewing of the *Ramayan* by claiming that she found it "entertaining."

The Muslim viewers I worked with gave both more varied and more critical responses to the serial than the Hindu viewers. For instance, although Hindu women commented on Sita's misfortune, they tended to dwell on her devotion to her husband and his lineage; most Muslim women, however, focused almost exclusively on Sita's sorrows and how she had had to "suffer all her life." Some interpreted the *Ramayan* as an interesting (if quaint) story about an ancient Hindu king and his family (see also van der Veer 1994: 177). Perhaps alluding to the dominant community's allegations of "Muslim promiscuity" indexed by the "privilege" of having more than one wife, several Muslim women repeatedly commented to me that Ram's father, the noble Dashrath, had had three wives. Most important, none of these viewers ever described the *Ramayan* as representative of Indian culture.

At least two Muslim women told me that they had refused to watch the *Ramayan*. Rasoolan Bi was a 49-year-old widow who lived with her son, daughter-in-law, and 5-year-old granddaughter. I had been visiting the family for about a month, and after being received with courteous, but distant, curiosity at the beginning, I began to feel I was being treated with a little less formality; nonetheless, my Hindu identity frequently shattered any complacency I might have felt about a rapport with them. When I asked Rasoolan Bi and Shahida if they had watched the *Ramayan,* they replied that they had refused to watch it. When I asked why, Shahida hotly retorted, "Why should we? What does it have to do with us?" Her mother-in-law, Rasoolan, stared coldly at her for a moment. She then turned to me and said, in a calm and matter-of-fact tone, that they had simply not been interested *(hamein koi dilchaspi nahin thi).* I knew that they often watched programs regardless of how interesting they found them. I sensed that they had refused to watch the serial because this was their way of claiming indifference to what it represented. Shahida's outburst, in particular, indicated their sense of exclusion from the *Ramayan* and its construction of culture and nationhood. When I tried to push them further, they evaded my questions by saying that it was too "boring" to watch and even more "boring" to talk about. It was obvious that they did not want to openly express their hostility because I was Hindu.[19] At the same time, they clearly wanted to register their antagonism to the serial by claiming to be indifferent to it. Rasoolan Bi and Shahida's response thus contrasted with the opinions of the Hindu viewers who had perceived the *Ramayan* as representing the heritage not just of Hindus but of the entire nation.

THE *RAMAYAN* AND HINDU NATIONALISM

As noted above, some of the power of the *Ramayan* lay in the fact that it was telecast on state-run television as part of its prime-time National Programme. The National Programme, telecast from New Delhi and relayed by satellite to low-power transmitters in different parts of the country, aimed to create a national audience.[20] The *Ramayan* represents a milestone in the history of commercial sponsorship on Doordarshan. Once it became clear that it had caught the attention of viewers, advertisers lined up to compete for airtime.[21] Its advertisers ranged from large Indian companies to multinationals, all of whom were eager to capitalize on the huge marketing potential of a nationwide audience of lower-middle-class and middle-class viewers. The *Ramayan*'s commercial success can be gauged from the enormous advertising revenues it generated.[22]

It is problematic to characterize the state's decision to telecast the *Ramayan* as part of a larger project of Hindu nationalism. In fact, the regime that sanctioned its telecast was the ostensibly secular Congress Party (not the Hindu nationalist Bhartiya Janata Party or BJP; in fact, the BJP was facing several electoral defeats at the time),[23] and the bureaucrat responsible for pushing the project through was S. S. Gill, a Sikh. Gill encountered considerable resistance from other bureaucrats when he first suggested telecasting the *Ramayan*, but he persuaded them by outlining a larger plan to telecast epics from different religious traditions.[24] He believed that by introducing Indian viewers to the "best of all faiths," Doordarshan would make them "proud of the unity in the diversity of India" and would also strengthen national integration.[25] Furthermore, the *Ramayan* was produced by an enormously successful Hindi film producer and director, Ramanand Sagar. Although he assumed a pious persona about halfway through the telecast of the serial, he was hardly a Hindu nationalist ideologue. Similarly, even though the actress who played Sita became a BJP member of parliament after the telecast of the *Ramayan*, her political career was brief and uneventful: having cashed in on her popular appeal following the telecast, she married a businessman and retired from politics.

Yet there is no question that the *Ramayan* provided "a language of mythopolitics" that represented cultural others as ineluctably alien (Pollock 1993: 264). In fact, many Hindu-nationalist activists credited the serial with contributing to their cause. As Balbir Singh, a spokesperson for one of the most powerful Hindu-nationalist organizations, the Rashtriya Swayamsevak Sangh (RSS), said: "[the television] *Ramayan* created an awakening. People who were sleeping were forced to wake up" (from Philipose 1990: 13). But how and why could a television serial, dismissed by many elites and scholars as irrelevant kitsch, participate in the reconfiguration of community and nation occurring in late twentieth-century India? After all, given the popularity of mythologicals in Indian cinema, this was not the first time that religious epics had been circulated on a mass scale. Rather than attribute its influence to the intentions of state officials or the creators of the *Ramayan*, it is essential to examine the conjunctural context of the *Ramayan*. The text neither transparently reflected nor produced shifts in dominant discourses of nation and identity; rather, it was part of the same sociohistorical conjuncture as the Hindu nationalist discourses becoming increasingly voluble at the time. In this section, I focus on one aspect of this conjuncture, the intertextual field in which the *Ramayan* was telecast and received.

The larger discursive formation was marked by struggles over the meaning of Indian culture and nationhood resulting from the resurgence of Hindu nationalism. Originally formulated by upper-caste ideologues as a form of cultural resistance to British colonialism (Fox 1990: 65; see also Chatterjee 1986, 1993; Sarkar 1994; and Pandey 1990), early leaders drew on Hindu revivalist discourses such as the notion of Mother India, a transformation of the Hindu concept of the Mother Goddess (Bagchi 1990). Further, many strands of Indian nationalism shared with Hindu nationalism the essentialist belief in an innate difference between the "materialist West" and the "spiritual East": to this extent, both nationalisms drew on Orientalist scholarship on Indian culture. The perception of Muslims as "the enemy within" grew after the 1920s with the rise of the Hindu Mahasabha and the RSS (Anderson and Damle 1987). Hindu nationalist organizations, with their primarily urban, lower-middle-class membership, became increasingly militant just before independence, but temporarily lost legitimacy after the assassination of Gandhi by a Hindu nationalist.

Though not absent in previous conjunctures, after the 1970s Hindu nationalism grew in popularity as a result of complex changes in caste and class relations in urban India (Fox 1990; Rajagopal 2001). Its strongest support came from urban, lower-middle-class Hindus (not coincidentally, those occupying the same socioeconomic positions as many of the people with whom I did fieldwork). The political ascendancy of Hindu militancy was facilitated by its seizure of the public sphere through the organization of several mass rituals, politico-religious marches, and mass pilgrimages to sacred Hindu sites. The differences between Hindu nationalism and mainstream Indian nationalism were further blurred in the early 1980s when, in a major strategic shift, the Hindu-nationalist political party, the Bharatiya Janata Party, appropriated some elements of Gandhian nationalism and acquired public symbols of authority (Fox 1990). Thereafter, from being one of several contending nationalisms, Hindu nationalism grew into one of the dominant forms.

The televised *Ramayan* shared some of the discursive features of Hindu nationalism. First, as in the case of Hindu nationalism, the serial was replete with the demonization of cultural others (Pollock 1993). Second, Hindu nationalism draws its potency from constructions of an ancient past in which Hindus existed as a clearly defined, unified community: the Hindu nationalist Ram Rajya (the kingdom of Lord Ram) is the exemplar of the utopian traditional community. The *Ramayan* overlapped with Hindu nationalist idealizations of Ram Rajya by evoking a strong nostalgia for a glorious Hindu past in which the state was benevolent and the rulers just and honest. Hindu viewers of the serial often appropriated its representations of Ram Rajya to critique the current political regime (see also Rajagopal 2001). For instance, praising Ram's ability to relinquish his claim to the throne, upper-caste and lower-middle-class Jayanthi Chandran commented to me: "That was the way things were in that era [*zamana*]. These days everyone clings to their chair."

Third, Hindu nationalism is based on the belief that Hindu culture, or Hindutva, is the substratum, the essential culture underlying the influences of Islam, Buddhism, or Christianity. The serial portrayed Hindu culture as national culture and hence converged with the attempts of Hindu nationalists to construct a hegemonic Hindu/national culture: it constructed a prehistory of the Hindu nation sought by Hindu nationalists. Further, the television version produced a hegemonic notion of Hindu/Indian culture by homogenizing the more heterogeneous oral traditions of the epic and excluded folk traditions and critical, heterodox interpretations (Thapar 1990; Krishnan 1990; cf. Lutgendorf 1990). The Hindu epic was represented as a cornerstone of Indian culture. Every episode began with a claim that its narrative was collated from several regional versions.[26] This claim, in fact, imposed a master narrative of a unified Hindu community by emphasizing the commonalities among the different versions of the Ram rather than their differences.

In some cases, this version of Hinduism converged with the discourses of Hindu/Indian culture formulated by Hindu nationalists. Middle-class and English-educated Bina Vaswani praised the television *Ramayan* for making "young people aware of our culture . . . [It] has instilled a pride in them." Bina's response illustrates the discursive overlap between the *Ramayan* and Hindu nationalism and demonstrates the growing hegemony of Hindu nationalism among Westernized middle- and upper-class Hindus in late twentieth-century India. The collective self implicit here, the "our" she referred to, consisted of upper-caste Hindus like herself who represented the normative voice in which the narrative was performed. Further, and more significant, her words echoed the war cry used by Hindu nationalist organizations to mobilize potential supporters: "Proclaim with pride that we are Hindu" *(Garv se kaho ham Hindu hain)*.

CONCLUSION

Since the early 1990s, Hindu nationalists have appropriated the *Ramayan*'s depiction of Ram Rajya as part of a hegemonic narrative of an ancient Hindu/Indian past that has to be recuperated from the alleged suppression of India during Islamic invasions and British colonial rule. In recent years, Hindu nationalism has become entrenched as a part of mainstream Indian nationalism. In 1999 the Hindu nationalist Bhartiya Janata Party obtained control of the government: it appears as if Hindu nationalists have been able not only to seize the state but also to consolidate the slippage between the Hindu nation and the Indian nation.

In the current context of satellite television and the accelerated circulation of transnational cultural texts, serials based on religious epics have not become obsolete. The *Ramayan* and the *Mahabharat* were given a new lease on life when they were rerun by Doordarshan in its (successful) attempt to compete with transnational satellite networks for the loyalty of viewers.

Hence, rather than assume a fundamental discursive shift resulting from the introduction of transnational satellite television,[27] it seems more appropriate to examine how the *Ramayan* and the *Mahabharat* may have prepared the ground for the telecast of other Hindu mythologicals. Other "tele-mythologies" followed in their wake (for example, *Sri Krishna, Mahabharat Katha,* and *Om Namah Shivay*). Despite (or perhaps because of) the presence of transnational television programs, these telemythologies received very high ratings (*Om Namah Shivay* obtained a TRP rating of 45 percent within a few weeks of its launch; reruns of *Sri Krishna* drew a 68 percent TRP rating).[28] Several scholars have argued that, far from becoming irrelevant, the hegemony of Hindu nationalist constructions of Indian culture have been reinforced and stretched to accommodate transnational discourses of consumerism and progress (see, for instance, Rajagopal 1999; Sunder Rajan 1993; Tharu and Niranjana 1996; and Mankekar 1999). In New Delhi, I found that at the same time that they were interpellated by transnational desires of consumerism and cosmopolitanism, several Hindu lower-middle-class and lower-class viewers expressed an anxiety that imported television programs would "contaminate" Indian culture. They asserted that, now more than ever, they appreciated serials based on Hindu epics, which they believed would provide crucial "reminders" and "lessons" about the glory of ancient Hindu civilization.[29]

My objective in this essay has been to examine how the *Ramayan* may have participated in reconfigurations of nation, community, and culture that overlapped with and reinforced Hindu nationalism. In so doing, I hope to have demonstrated the usefulness of ethnographic research on mass media. An anthropological analysis that synthesizes viewers' responses to the *Ramayan* with an examination of its representational strategies enables us to trace the complex factors underlying the popularity of the serial. This approach takes seriously the pleasures viewers derive from it and, at the same time, helps to complicate and politicize our understanding of "the popular." Thus, although the serial was indeed watched by viewers of different religious communities, their reasons for watching it and the pleasures they derived from it were anything but homogeneous. It was popular with some Hindu viewers because it contained important moral lessons that would guide them in their everyday lives and relationships; for others, the familiar iconicity of the serials' images enabled a particularly powerful form of *darshan*. However, as exemplified by Harbhajan Kaur, some non-Hindu viewers were avid viewers of the *Ramayan* because its portrayal of family politics and marital relationships resonated with the difficulties they were facing in their own lives. Other non-Hindu viewers found the story "entertaining," if somewhat quaint. Finally, the words of Shahida and Rasoolan Bi, two Muslim women who asserted that they had refused to watch it, remind us of the exclusionary implications of some popular narratives, hence further problematizing assumptions of "the popular" as monolithic.

At different historical moments *Ramayana* tellings have been appropriated to demonize cultural Others (Pollock 1993); however, it seems problematic to decontextualize those tellings from their respective historical and political contexts. A conjunctural ethnography of the *Ramayan* enables us to situate it in the broader discursive formation of Hindu nationalism at a moment when notions of nationhood, identity, and belonging were becoming increasingly exclusionary. Finally, an anthropological analysis of the intertextual field in which the *Ramayan* was received foregrounds the participation of mass-mediated texts in realigning community and nation, and in bringing culture to the center of conflicts over identity and belonging in the modern world.

NOTES

An earlier version of this essay appeared in *Screening Culture, Viewing Politics* (Duke University Press, 1999) and appears courtesy of the publisher.

The research for this chapter was funded by a Fulbright-Hays Dissertation Fellowship (1990–91) and an American Institute for Indian Studies Doctoral Dissertation Award (1992). I would like to thank the editors of this volume, Lila Abu-Lughod, Faye Ginsburg, and Brian Larkin, for their careful reading of this chapter. I am especially grateful to Akhil Gupta, Linda Hess, and Saba Mahmood for their comments on earlier versions. Finally, I am grateful, as always, to the members of the communities with whom I did fieldwork for generously sharing their thoughts and lives with me.

1. Communalism draws from the "belief that because a group of people follow a particular religion, they have as a result, a common social, political and economic interest" (Chandra 1984, quoted in Chhachhi 1989: 568). See Pandey 1990 for an analysis of the colonial construction of communalism.

2. For the transnational aspects of Hindu nationalism, see van der Veer 1994: 108 and Rai 1995.

3. This essay is in dialogue with analyses of the *Ramayan* serial by Gillespie (1995); Krishnan (1990); Lutgendorf (1990); Ninan (1995); Pollock (1993); Rajagopal (1994, 2001); Richman (1991, 1995); Thapar (1990); and van der Veer (1994).

4. It was during this period that the attempts by Hindu nationalists to redefine the Indian nation became particularly voluble and acquired a "mass" character. See Agrawal 1994; Bagchi 1990; Chatterjee 1986, 1993; Fox 1990; van der Veer 1994; Pandey 1990; Rajagopal 1994, 2001; Sarkar 1994; and Simeon 1994 for detailed discussions of overlaps and tensions between Hindu nationalism and (anticolonial and postcolonial) Indian nationalism. For an analysis of the relationship between the reception of the *Ramayan* and the "crisis of secularism" that allegedly occurred in India during the late 1980s and early 1990s, see Mankekar 1999. A genealogy of Hindu nationalism and its relationship with anticolonial Indian nationalism is outside the scope of this essay.

5. I refer to the larger narrative traditions of the epic as the *Ramayana;* in keeping with its Hindustani title, I refer to the television serial as the *Ramayan.*

6. Ramanujan has argued that, far from there being a single "ur-text" of the *Ramayana,* there are "hundreds of tellings"; he therefore prefers the word "tellings" (1991: 24–25). Further, as pointed out by Richman, "the story" of the *Ramayana* is "inseparable from the different forms it takes, forms which reflect differences in religious affiliation, linguistic allegiance, and social location" (1991: 5). Nonetheless, here I provide a skeletal version of the Rama story for readers unfamiliar with it.

7. I follow the pronunciation used in the serial and use the colloquial Hindustani spelling for the names of the *Ramayan*'s characters.

8. For a detailed analysis of the role of class and gender in mediating viewers' responses to the *Ramayan,* see Mankekar 1999.

9. Cf. Hawley on the "potency" of the experience of *darshan* in Hinduism (1981: 42). See also Appaswamy 1970; Babb and Wadley 1995; Babb 1981; and Smith 1995.

10. This response to the serial was not unprecedented. Cf. Lutgendorf 1990: 129.

11. According to Hawley, "Much of Hindu *bhakti* is specifically iconic" (1981). See Daniel 1984; Peirce 1982; and Silverman 1983 on the iconicity of signs.

12. See Agrawal 1994 for a trenchant critique of the conflation of *bhakti* with Hindu nationalism.

13. *Nautanki* is a performative tradition popular in small towns and rural communities in North India.

14. However, because the *Ramayan* was telecast on state-controlled television and broadcast during prime time it was able to reach, and indeed create, a mass audience unprecedented in its scale. I return to the political implications of the telecast in the next section.

15. I thank the editors of this volume for this succinct formulation.

16. Cf. van der Veer's discussion of female sexuality in Muslim communalism (1994: 98–104).

17. Cricket matches between India and Pakistan are always surrounded by a high degree of tension, which has led in some cases to Hindu-Muslim riots in India (Appadurai 1996). Indeed, one of the stereotypes perpetuated by Hindu nationalists is that Muslim spectators at these cricket matches betray their "true" loyalty to Pakistan (and therefore their lack of loyalty to India) by allegedly cheering for the Pakistani team.

18. For an analysis of the portrayal of Muslims in popular culture, see Zutshi 1993.

19. See Mankekar 1999 for a discussion of the place of subterfuge, elisions, and silences in feminist ethnography.

20. I analyze the political agendas and negotiations underlying the production of the National Programme in Mankekar 1999.

21. Interview with R. Srinivasan, January 17, 1992.

22. A few months after the commencement of its telecast, advertisers were lining up to pay up to Rs.40,000 (approximately $1,000) per ten-second slot. In the next nine months, the *Ramayan* outgrossed all other serials, yielding an estimated weekly income of Rs.2,800,000–3,000,000 ($700,000–750,000) for the network (Lutgendorf 1990: 136; see also Rajagopal 1994).

23. This is not to characterize Congress Party politics in the 1980s as even remotely secular or nonpartisan, but simply to point out that Hindu nationalism was not an overt part of its manifesto. To this extent, the Congress contrasted with the BJP, which mobilized voters on the basis of its explicit aim to build a Hindu nation.

24. Interview with S. S. Gill, January 23, 1992.

25. The only non-Hindu epic to be telecast was *Bible ki Kahaniyan (Stories from the Bible)* in 1992. It neither evoked public controversy nor achieved a following among Indian viewers (including Christians). By foregrounding contradiction and overdetermination, the Althusserian notion of conjuncture problematizes notions of intentionality. In hindsight, Gill's original plan to telecast epics from different religious traditions seems particularly ironic and underscores both the politically contingent nature of state policies and the disjuncture between the objectives of policies and their material consequences.

26. Lutgendorf argues that even though it occasionally draws upon the Avdhi Valmiki and the Tamil Kampan, Sagar's narrative chiefly follows Tulsidas's *Ramcharitamanas* (1990: 147).

27. See Mankekar 1999 and Ninan 1995 for a critique of such assumptions.

28. Jain 1997: 70–73.

29. I explore these issues in greater detail in Mankekar, n.d.

REFERENCES

Agrawal, Purushottom. 1994. Kan Kan Mein Vyape Hein Ram: The Slogan as a Metaphor of Cultural Interrogation. *Oxford Literary Review* 16 (1–2): 245–64.

Althusser, Louis. 1970. *For Marx.* Translated by Ben Brewster. New York: Vintage Books.

Anderson, Walter K., and Sridhar Damle. 1987. *The Brotherhood in Saffron: The RSS and Hindu Revivalism.* Delhi: Vistaar Publications.

Appadurai, Arjun. 1996. *Modernity at Large: Cultural Dimensions of Globalization.* Minneapolis: University of Minnesota Press.

Appaswamy, A. J. 1970. *The Theology of Hindu Bhakti.* Bangalore: Christian Literature Society.

Babb, Lawrence. 1981. Glancing: Visual Interaction in Hinduism. *Journal of Anthropological Research* 37 (4): 378–410.

Babb, Lawrence A., and Susan S. Wadley, eds. 1995. *Media and the Transformation of Religion in South Asia.* Philadelphia: University of Pennsylvania Press.

Bagchi, Jasodhara. 1990. Representing Nationalism: Ideology of Motherhood in Colonial Bengal. *Economic and Political Weekly* 25 (42–43): 65–71.

Barnouw, Eric, and S. Krishnaswamy. 1980. *Indian Film.* New York: Oxford University Press.

Butalia, Urvashi. 1995. Muslims and Hindus, Men and Women: Communal Stereotypes and the Partition of India. In *Women and the Hindu Right: A Collection of Essays,* edited by Tanika Sarkar and Urvashi Butalia, pp. 58–81. New Delhi: Kali for Women.

Chandra, Bipan. 1984. *Communalism in Modern India.* Delhi: Vikas Books.

Chatterjee, Partha. 1986. *Nationalist Thought and the Colonial World: A Derivative Discourse.* Minneapolis: University of Minnesota Press.

———. 1993. *The Nation and Its Fragments.* Princeton, N.J.: Princeton University Press.

Chhachhi, Amrita. 1989. The State, Religious Fundamentalism, and Women: Trends in South Asia. *Economic and Political Weekly* 24: 567–78.

Daniel, E. Valentine. 1984. *Fluid Signs: Being a Person the Tamil Way.* Berkeley: University of California Press.

Eck, Diana. 1985. *Darsan: Seeing the Divine Image in India.* Chambersberg, Penn.: Anima Books.

Fox, Richard. 1990. Hindu Nationalism in the Making, or the Rise of the Hindian. In *Nationalist Ideologies and the Production of National Cultures,* edited by Richard Fox. Washington, D.C.: American Anthropological Association.

Giddens, Anthony. 1979. *Central Problems in Social Theory: Action, Structure, and Contradiction in Social Analysis.* Berkeley: University of California Press.

———. 1981. *A Contemporary Critique of Historical Materialism.* Stanford, Calif.: Stanford University Press.

———. 1984. *The Constitution of Society: Outline of a Theory of Structuration.* Berkeley: University of California Press.

Gillespie, Marie. 1995. *Television, Ethnicity, and Cultural Change.* London: Routledge.

Hawley, John Stratton. 1981. Krishna in Black and White: *Darsan* in the Butter Thief Poems of the Early Sur Sagar. In *Tradition and Modernity in Bhakti Movements,* edited by Jayant Lele, pp. 43–58. Leiden: E. J. Brill.

Jain, Madhu. 1997. The God Factory. *India Today,* May 31, pp. 70–73.

Krishnan, Prabha. 1990. In the Idiom of Loss: Ideology of Motherhood in Television Serials. *Economic and Political Weekly* 25 (42–43): 103–16.

Lutgendorf, Philip. 1990. *Ramayan:* The Video. *The Drama Review* 34 (2): 127–76.

Mankekar, Purnima. 1999. *Screening Culture, Viewing Politics: An Ethnography of Television, Womanhood, and Nation in Postcolonial India.* Durham, N.C.: Duke University Press.

———. N.d. Transnational Terrains: Television, Globalization, and "National Culture" in India.

Ninan, Sevanti. 1995. *Through the Magic Window.* New Delhi: Penguin Books.

Pandey, Gyanendra. 1990. *The Construction of Communalism in Colonial North India.* Delhi: Oxford University Press.

Peirce, Charles Sanders. 1982. *Writings of Charles S. Peirce: A Chronological Edition.* Vol. 1: *1857–1866.* Bloomington: Indiana University Press.

Philipose, Pamela. 1990. An Epic Mistake? *Observer,* November, p. 13.

Pollock, Sheldon. 1993. *Ramayana* and Political Imagination in India. *Journal of Asian Studies* 52 (2): 261–97.

Pritchett, Frances W. 1995. The World of Amar Chitra Katha. In *Media and the Transformation of Religion in South Asia,* edited by Lawrence A. Babb and Susan S. Wadley, pp. 76–106. Philadelphia: University of Pennsylvania Press.

Rai, Amit. 1995. India On-Line: Electronic Bulletin Boards and the Construction of a Diasporic Hindu Identity. *Diaspora* (Spring): 31–57.

Rajagopal, Arvind. 1994. Ram Janambhoomi, Consumer Identity and Image-Based Politics. *Economic and Political Weekly,* July 2, pp. 1659–68.

————. 1999. Thinking about the New Indian Middle Class: Gender, Advertising and Politics in an Age of Globalisation. In *Signposts: Gender Issues in Post- Independence India,* edited by Rajeshwari Sunder Rajan, pp. 57–100. New Delhi: Kali.

————. 2001. *Politics after Television: Religious Nationalism and the Reshaping of the Indian Public.* Cambridge, England: Cambridge University Press.

Rajyadhaksha, Ashish. 1986. Neo-Traditionalism: Film as Popular Art in India. *Framework* (32–33): 21–67.

Ramanujan, A. K. 1991. Three Hundred *Ramayanas*: Five Examples and Three Thoughts on Translation. In *Many Ramayanas: The Diversity of a Narrative Tradition in South Asia,* edited by Paula Richman, pp. 22–49. Berkeley: University of California Press.

Richman, Paula. 1991. Introduction: The Diversity of the *Ramayana* Tradition. In *Many Ramayanas: The Diversity of a Narrative Tradition in South Asia,* edited by Paula Richman, pp. 3–21. Berkeley: University of California Press.

————. 1995. Epic and State: Contesting Interpretations of the *Ramayana. Public Culture* 7 (3): 631–54.

Sahlins, Marshall. 1985. *Islands of History.* Chicago: University of Chicago Press.

Sarkar, Tanika. 1994. Bankimchandra and the Incompatibility of a Political Agenda. *Oxford Literary Review* 16 (1–2): 177–204.

Silverman, Kaja. 1983. *The Subject of Semiotics.* New York: Oxford University Press.

Simeon, Dilip. 1994. Tremors of Intent: Perceptions of the Nation and Community in Contemporary India. *Oxford Literary Review* 16 (1–2): 225–44.

Smith, H. Daniel. 1995. Impact of "God Posters" on Hindus and Their Devotional Traditions. In *Media and the Transformation of Religion in South Asia,* edited by Lawrence A. Babb and Susan S. Wadley, pp. 24–50. Philadelphia: University of Pennsylvania Press.

Sunder Rajan, Rajeshwari. 1993. *Real and Imagined Women: Gender, Culture, and Postcolonialism.* London: Routledge.

Thapar, Romila. 1989. Imagined Religious Communities? Ancient History and the Modern Search for a Hindu Identity. *Modern Asian Studies* 23 (2): 209–31.

————. 1990. The *Ramayana* Syndrome. *India Magazine* 10: 30–43.

Tharu, Susie, and Tejaswini Niranjana. 1996. Problems for a Contemporary Theory of Gender. In *Subaltern Studies IX,* edited by Shahid Amin and Dipesh Chakravarty, pp. 232–260. Delhi: Oxford University Press.

Van der Veer, Peter. 1994. *Religious Nationalism: Hindus and Muslims in India.* Berkeley: University of California Press.

Zutshi, Somnath. 1993. Woman, Nation, and the Outsider in Contemporary Hindi Cinema. In *Interrogating Modernity: Culture and Colonialism in India,* edited by Tejaswini Niranjana, P. Sudhir, and Vivek Dhareshwar, pp. 83–112. Calcutta: Seagull Books.

7

The National Picture

Thai Media and Cultural Identity

Annette Hamilton

I view locality as primarily relational and contextual rather than as scalar or spatial. I see it as a complex phenomenological quality, constituted by a series of links between the sense of social immediacy, the technologies of interactivity, and the relativity of contexts.

ARJUN APPADURAI *(1996: 178)*

Although Thailand was among the first of the Asian nations to embrace new media—first film and radio, then television—as integral aspects of national development, this was not registered in anthropological research, most of which focused on "traditional" aspects of Thai society, especially "the village," and ethnic minorities.[1] In the 1970s a new focus on the role of the state was evident (see Anderson 1978). Following his influential book *Imagined Communities* (1983), Benedict Anderson edited a volume concerned with literature and politics in Siam (Thailand) (Anderson and Mendiones 1985). Even so, the broader implications of the spread of new media in Thailand seemed to interest few outside the fields of media and communication studies. It was in order to remedy this omission that I began my research on media and culture in Thailand in 1985.[2]

Since that time the rapidly expanding field of media anthropology (or "an anthropology of media"; see editors' introduction to this volume) has traversed many of the questions that prompted this research, and in some respects has overtaken it. The theoretical underpinnings of the present project arose from the idea of "imagined communities" in the emergent world of screening, rather than reading, and from questions about cultural imperialism, the constitution of a public sphere, and the role of media in the struggle for a civil society in the only nation in Asia that had not been subjected to formal colonial control. Works by others published during the course of the research addressed a number of my central interests, in particular those by John Tomlinson (1991) and Arjun Appadurai (1996). Lila Abu-Lughod's explorations of television melodramas and of media as a social technology through which a modern subjectivity is partially produced were also particularly stimulating (Abu-Lughod 1993, 1995).

The present essay focuses on the relation between locality and nation and suggests that local, national, and international imaginaries are uneasily co-implicated in the emergent formal and informal media spheres. Elsewhere I address the role of informal electronic media in the construction of sub-jectivities and the recent effects of satellite broadcasting on Thai diasporic communities outside the country.[3] Here I suggest that in Thailand the re-lationship between locality and nation can be understood only through a close examination of the way the "nation" has posed itself to the population it attempts to enfold. I describe the emergence of a national broadcast me-dia sphere that, in the name of national identity, excludes both local con-tent and social criticism. This national cultural identity has emerged over a long period as an assertion of distinctiveness in relation to a powerful ex-ternal world of "others," notably white Westerners *(khon farang),* against whom Thai culture and identity are posed by various agencies of the state.[4] Simultaneously, the sense of distinctive locality expressed through many tra-ditional narratives and practices in many neighborhoods has been suppressed and does not find expression in the array of nationally sanctioned repre-sentations. Broadcast television entered an existing relationship between people and nation at a time when social transformation was occurring more rapidly than ever before. Since the early 1980s people's sense of commit-ment to a neighborhood space (the village, the town) has diminished. The emergence of broader movements of identity in conjunction with internal and international labor migration and exposure to new forms of subjectiv-ity was prompted in part by the national media themselves. Nevertheless, a sense of locality has been sustained in many respects, and new media have in turn had a role in preserving it.

In Thailand the creation of an "official" national cultural identity has been an explicit project of the Kingdom for at least the past ninety years, and the mass media have been central to that project, which includes the extension of a single public education system (cf. Keyes 1991) and mass literacy in spo-ken and written Central Thai as the national language.[5] This official version of national identity is promulgated throughout the free-to-air media, along-side methods such as compulsory public broadcasting systems installed in most small towns and many villages.[6] In these ways, "Thailand" becomes imag-ined as a distinctive space with which "its" people are required to identify, invited to see their own uniqueness and distinctiveness against an outside world depicted as unstable, ambiguous, and uncertain in its effects. The re-cent intensive globalization and social transformation in Thailand have ac-centuated these effects, with an intensification in national self-representa-tion at the same time that new social practices, values, and attitudes are being promoted in line with the goal of achieving "modernity." Through media, both print and broadcast, people in Thailand have been "trained" to participate in nonindigenous rituals of consumption. In late 1988, for instance, I documented a series of television broadcasts and advertisements in national newspapers showing people what kinds of gifts were appropriate for Christmas and New Year, how to wrap such gifts and present them correctly, and what kinds of domestic spaces were appropriate for decoration. These of course are Western celebrations, which the Thai have now added to their own calendrical rituals. Also from the late 1980s, and with increasing elaboration into the 1990s, spectacular public rites have been staged, almost all nationally televised.

During the spectacular funeral ceremony in Bangkok in 1996 for the present King's mother, all television channels screened nothing else for the entire day. The half-million mourners dressed in black were "joined" by the rest of the nation as co-participants in a rite that effectively recovered and restaged Royal funerary rites of the distant past. Official participants were dressed in versions of costumes of earlier dynasties, and some were mounted on elephants that passed slowly through the streets. The television cameras were present throughout the ritual and able to provide both panopticon views of the entire space as well as intimate close-ups, such as the image of the King's face as he personally lit the funeral pyre. Many commented that television meant people viewing in the far provinces had a much better view than did those at the actual event. The monarchy's revival of various elements of "ancient Thai rites" has been part of an assertion of distinctive identity. Another is the promotion of various acceptably modified rituals from more distant parts of the nation, revised as a kind of folklore particularly attractive to both internal and international tourism (see Rhum 1996).

To understand the importance of locality and the problems of its expression in Thailand, it is necessary to grasp the colonizing projects of the Thai Kingdom as it developed from the mid-nineteenth century. Recent reconsideration of Thai history has pointed overwhelmingly to the view that Thailand as a nation in effect colonized itself (Grabowsky 1995). The premodern polities of the region were composed of culturally and linguistically distinctive groupings placed at various levels of subordination to the central power of the reigning dynasty. Many of these were "Tai," but others were non-Tai, especially in the more distant regions, most notably in the far South. As well, there were many distinctive ethnic and cultural groups, populations that had been relocated to provide labor for the Kingdom. Before the mid-nineteenth century, the expansion of Siamese power had incorporated vast regions, establishing vassal-like relations in which rural populations were subject to corvée labor and debt-slavery. Slavery remained legal until the early twentieth century. The impact of Western colonialism in the region resulted in a new concern with boundaries and the control of specific spaces, especially after the forced cession of territories to France in the Northeast and

Britain in the South and the subsequent drawing up of strict spatial borders (see Thongchai 1994 for the classic account of this process and its effects). The administrative reforms during the reign of King Chulalongkorn (1868–1910) were explicitly modeled on the colonial practices of the Dutch in the "East Indies" and to a lesser extent those of the British in India, Malaya, and Burma. These were followed by a period of nation creation both in ideology and in practice. During the next reign (King Vajiravudh, 1910–25) an explicit demand by the Kingdom for recognition by Western nations as an equal resulted in the promulgation of a distinct idea of Thai national identity, one that was consolidated further after the overthrow of the absolute monarchy during subsequent military-dominated regimes. Ethnic and regional differences were progressively obscured, and a distinctive model of a homogeneous national culture developed and found numerous forms of expression, especially in public political and religious rituals, in the mass media, and in increasingly rigid educational and bureaucratic practices. In recent decades, however, and especially as the impact of national and international tourism on the economy has expanded, some forms of diversity became increasingly acceptable, appropriated in turn as part of a distinctive Thai culture. Local festivals and dance forms, rituals, foodstuffs, plants and flowers, and sites of pilgrimage and natural beauty were identified as legitimate expressions of the national culture at local levels. Diversity could thus exist, but only within carefully delimited boundaries (see Rhum 1996).

In places where conformity to the emergent concept of "the nation" was most in question, the anxiety of state agencies was most acute, especially near borders where outright subversion and rebellion occurred repeatedly, most notably among the Muslims of the far South (Che Man 1990). However, until recent times a sense of constant surveillance has been the dominant experience of Thai people, especially in the provinces. The state has determined the appropriate form and expression of Thai public culture and has given no "space" to those who do not conform to it. Thus the public sphere has been subject to direction from above and has not emerged out of organic or gemeinschaft-like processes. At the same time, powerful forces of transformation have been unleashed by the development processes since the 1970s, and in the years of the boom (1987–97) resulted in the articulation of new demands by a rising middle class for forms of democracy and grassroots participation, identified by the term "civil society," of the kind imagined to exist in the West (see Pasuk and Baker 1998).[7]

Even in areas where people are far from being rebels and troublemakers, elements of a distinctive local culture with deep roots in historically recognized practices can be identified. The recognition and circulation of distinctive narratives and practices provides the bedrock for this sense of "the local," which is further evoked by reference to signifying spaces such as shrines, sacred sites, and physical land forms with associated mythological accounts (see Gesick 1995, for an example from the South). Founding stories of villages and tales of the founding ancestors are common in many areas, with statues and memorials to the founding "mother" and "father" of the place commonly found in temple grounds and on hills overlooking the area in question. Tales of shipwrecks and pirates are common along the sea coasts, and the presence of Chinese traders and merchants is marked by Chinese temples and shrines. Buddhist temples act as repositories for the material objects from the past that are often imbued with mystical powers and are placed on display in small museums. More important, some temples are associated with famous popular monks, whose charisma and beneficence is believed to spread into the districts where their supporters live. Today such individuals and their temples have become increasingly identified with the national level, in another form of appropriation of the local (see Jackson 1999). Local spaces and identities remain important even where residents are widely scattered as a result of labor migration; people's commitment to their home areas is reconfirmed annually at festivals when people return to them en masse to join their relatives in celebrations such as weddings and funerals, and especially at Thai New Year in April.

The following discussion describes how Thai national television, during the 1980s and early 1990s, provided the elements of a nationally accepted "public culture" that increasingly conflicted with the aspirations and emerging values of a changing society. These observations are largely based on a lengthy period of fieldwork in Hua Hin, a small town some four hours south by road from Bangkok, as well as many discussions with others living in Bangkok, including academics and intellectuals. The practices and preferences of Hua Hin residents can be taken as fairly typical of a Thai town experiencing the effects of the new globalizing economy. The spread of new media and the tourist boom drew this town and its hinterland rapidly into the expanding economy. Television entered a collective public sphere in the small-town context and provided an ambiguous space for both challenge and identification.[8]

The old part of town consisted of a maze of interconnecting lanes and streets, where many families operated small businesses from the lower floor of their houses, which opened directly onto the street. Down by the seaside, fishing families lived in wooden houses on piers that extended out above the high-water line, with their fishing boats pulled up underneath or beside their houses. Up on the main road was the more modern commercial heart of the town, where shops and stalls sold every variety of goods, from bulk rice to audio- and videocassettes. Almost every shop and many stalls inside the enclosed day market had a television set turned on throughout the day. In the night market, stall holders also provided television sets, which shoppers and diners could spend some time viewing and chatting about before passing on. On the beachfront was the famous Railway Hotel, a faded colonial-style masterpiece that had provided elegant accommodation for Thai elites since the 1920s. In 1985 this beachside area began to become popular with non-Thai tourists, and new restaurants opened there. Whether catering to Thais or non-Thais, restaurants always had a television turned on in the evenings. The families running these establishments changed the channels according to their own viewing preferences. Family members often prepared food, chopping vegetables and mixing sauces, at a table in the restaurant itself while children did their homework and visitors dropped in. The boundary between public and private was very unclear.

By the mid-1980s the videocassette recorder had become an item of status consumption and very quickly entered the local viewing environment, in significant competition with broadcast television. One of my informants in Hua Hin, a member of an influential local family, said he had paid around 30,000 baht ($1,200) for the first VCR he purchased in 1983. Prices began to fall rapidly thereafter as cheap Korean and Taiwanese brands entered the market in competition with the products of the Japanese giants such as Sony. Many fewer households had VCRs than television sets, but the boom in international tourism resulted in a new and powerful presence of the VCR in town. Whereas Hua Hin had been a famous resort for Thai people for decades, after 1987, Thailand's Year of Tourism, an increasing number of foreigners flooded into the town. Apart from the old Railway Hotel and a couple of very ordinary Chinese hotels near the Highway, accommodation was very limited, especially near the beach. As the number of foreign visitors increased, local people realized they could cash in on the influx and began to open their houses to "guests," providing simply furnished rooms for low prices (100–200 baht per night, $4–8) and opening "restaurants" downstairs. The tourists were both young and old; there were some backpackers but many more curious couples and lonely singles of all ages. They loved the laid-back atmosphere of Hua Hin and the fabulous fresh seafood; but there was singularly little to do at night. At that time there was no nightlife in the town—no bars or discos and just a few restaurants featuring "nightclub singers," patronized by local Thais. There were no bar-girls or prostitutes catering to foreigners, and only one flea-bitten old cinema screened almost unviewable Chinese and Thai films. Lonely and disoriented, uncertain why they had come to this hot, strange land where almost no one spoke English, the tourists wandered about the Night Market and went home early to their lodgings. Soon enough the locals realized they could keep the tourists in their restaurants eating and drinking expensive beer, for hours on end, by screening foreign videos. Almost overnight, the food shops and restaurants, all of them open to the street and the balmy tropical air, placed large television monitors and VCRs on their premises. A continuous flood of tourists sat in this small Thai town drinking beer, transfixed by American movies: Schwarzenegger action thrillers, blockbusters, recent releases. This created a strange kind of public—a displaced public, people far from their homes, seeking an exotic experience in a foreign environment, drawn together momentarily, their sense of estrangement assuaged by visions of the Western world: New York, Los Angeles, Moscow, Paris, anywhere, everywhere, via Hollywood. And of course the Thais who lived and worked among these new tourist facilities were watching too—learning to enjoy the foreign style of film and learning English, the key to affluence in this new tourist-oriented development of the town and the language of modernity.

But many preferred Thai and Chinese films, and many entrepreneurial locals realized another potential for the VCR. In several of the old wooden houses open to the street, householders purchased VCRs and invited neighbors, friends, and anybody else who cared to come to watch videos for a modest entry price—10–20 baht was average ($ .50–1.00). Viewers could make special requests for an additional fee. Householders sold a variety of local snack foods to the viewers: sweets, cakes, dried squid, crisps, and soft drinks with ice in plastic bags. Mobile vendors set up their carts nearby and offered noodle soups and other savory dishes, the diners sitting on stools in the laneway and watching the program from a distance. Video viewing thus became another occasion for neighborhood sociality, along with other more traditional events such as spirit-medium seances, performances of various kinds of dance-drama, and even funeral gatherings; these might be held in or adjacent to public thoroughfares in the older parts of town, often at the same time. Further, the choice offered met local preferences more satisfactorily than most of the material on broadcast television. However it was dependent on the availability of suitable films provided by the many new video rental businesses that sprang up around town.

Video viewing thus became part of an immediate experience of neighborhood. For a period of several weeks, a mini film festival took place in one house, with Bruce Lee and Jackie Chan movies creating excitement and sometimes inciting hilarity. In another house, women gathered to view Thai movies around themes of desire, family, and the law on Saturday afternoons. Video viewing thus constituted one aspect of a local "public," where preferences arising from gender, age, and personal concerns could be met. Films provided a source for conversations, narratives, jokes, and observations, often pertaining to matters of personal or national concern that otherwise found little opportunity for expression.

It was into this context of a local viewing culture that cable television emerged. Cable arrived in Bangkok in the late 1980s for the big-city audience. However in Hua Hin and many other provincial towns local cable services sprang up independent from the national developments. There were no laws governing businesses of this kind—government regulators had never thought of establishing them. Operating out of a small shopfront in the older part of town, the Hua Hin Cable Service was founded by a young local man

who had been trained in television production in Bangkok. He strung cables manually from roof to roof across the town; subscribers paid 250 baht
a month ($10), coming to his shop to make the payments or paying one of
his assistants who collected door to door. He had a powerful aerial and signal booster system through which he could download programs such as the
national news from Bangkok and Thai boxing. However, he interspersed
these programs with other programs and shows, including films on video.
In addition, he began taping important local events for cable broadcast, including formal occasions such as the local high school graduation ceremonies, the competition for floral plaques held in honor of King Chulalongkorn's birthday each October, performances of traditional *lakhon chatri*
(dance-dramas for the spirits), special promotions at the local market, and
monks blessing new businesses. On several occasions a famous wandering
monk temporarily residing in a local monastery was invited to give a *dhamma*
preaching for the cable service. This event was coupled with a request for
donations for a new Buddha image and temple repairs. Management of the
cable service was complicated and it was run on a shoestring, but it provided
an immensely popular service in the town, bringing together national, local, and regional events of special interest to the provincial audience. At the
end of 1989 there were over 2,000 subscribers (in a town of 50,000 people)
producing a revenue of around $5,000 per week.

People began to request purpose-recorded videos of family and "private"
events such as weddings and funerals. Most people could not afford to purchase video cameras; moreover certain aesthetic and production values common in Thai movies and TV shows were more highly valued than amateur-
ish tapes produced by individuals. When a local woman, daughter of a
well-known local Sino-Thai family, began to incarnate the spirits of two famous beings, one a local *chao por* (male deity of the region) and one the Chinese Goddess of Mercy *(Chao Mae Kwan Im)*, she arranged for the cable operator, who lived on the same street, to videotape her possession and healing
ceremonies. Initially the intention was to play some of this on the local cable, and indeed a couple of extracts were shown under the heading "local
news." However, after a particularly important period, during which she
arranged for a group of young girls to perform a "trance dance" in the street
outside her house, she herself delivered powerful oracular messages, all of
which were taped. Realizing that the tapes themselves were sacred and su-
pernaturally endowed, she placed them on an altar in her shopfront. Her
fame as a spirit medium spread, and she received requests for the tapes from
people all over the country. Members of her extended family living elsewhere
asked for copies. Once the tapes had been suitably blessed and packaged,
she authorized their wider distribution and thus further increased her fame
and repute.

Other events of spiritistic significance began to circulate on video. The

A video store in Mahboonkrong Mall in Bangkok, 1988. The aesthetics of display, particularly the use of Western film material, created a context in which "foreign" film material came to signify "glamour" while local film and television appeared, by contrast, "authentically Thai" on the one hand, and "dull and banal" on the other. (Photo: Annette Hamilton)

annual "Vegetarian Festival" in Phuket, an occasion when hundreds of entranced mediums carry the gods through the streets with faces and bodies pierced by halberds, metal poles, and a variety of other items, became a matter of intense interest in Hua Hin. The national news broadcasts covered it briefly in 1987, and a longer piece was broadcast on local cable. Tapes of the event, each of three hours' duration, were eagerly snapped up in video stores. These tapes were edited, with a voice-over in standard Thai commentary style, and soon began to be sold in local photo shops and through the cable operator.

Through these developments, broadcast television began to be challenged by another form of screening, one much more accommodating to local preferences and reflective of local issues. During the same period, national television broadcasting, which failed to accommodate the local level, was also failing to reflect the increasingly significant political and social events emerging at the national level.

The practices and attitudes of people in a small provincial town such as this are not the same as those of the emergent Bangkok middle class, but the sense of disjunction between everyday reality and the world on television was beginning to take on increasing significance for both. Although many educated people disparaged much of the programming popular among rural and provincial people, television still provided a common framework from which a more critical perspective on the nature of the Thai public world could be articulated. At the same time, local people were increasingly aware of the distinctions between themselves and Bangkokians. In a town like Hua Hin, longtime residents found their livelihoods and local practices increasingly threatened by the economic changes and their social reflections. Whole blocks of housing were bought up, rent-paying residents were evicted, and new townhouses, hotels, and tourist facilities replaced them. The new middle class expressed its "distinction" with its Mercedes-Benz cars and new condominiums; local people were for the most part unable to participate but were bidden to join the new consumerist frenzy, at least on television. The demands for democracy, civil society, and freedom of expression arising in Bangkok also had resonances for many rural groups, and various ad hoc alliances were formed throughout the country to press for fair treatment of farmers and other local people. Grievances concerning developments in Hua Hin prompted numerous local meetings and petitions to the Municipal Council, which brought together high-status long-standing residents and lower-class working people such as food vendors, who protested the negative impacts of new tourist developments for the benefit of Bangkokians and foreigners, for example.

This sense of disjunction between the world on-screen and the world of the everyday must be understood as a result of the mass media's long-standing role in endorsing a particular form of public culture. Although television was introduced in the capital in the 1950s, it was not until the late 1970s that people throughout the country began to purchase black-and-white television sets, after electrification had spread broadly throughout the Kingdom as a part of national development policy. As the affluent 1980s emerged, color sets and then videocassette recorders became increasingly common. In one way or another, all five national channels were controlled by agencies of the state, including the army, the Education Ministry, and the Ministry of the Interior. All broadcast material and programs came from Bangkok. There were no local or regional stations, and when local content was included it was first sent to Bangkok for approval. One small segment of the news programs, once a week, included stories from the "regions," defined as the North, the Northeast, the Central Plains, and the South. These were recorded in advance and voice-over commentaries were provided at the central station. Interviews with local people *(chao baan)* were sometimes included, but only within accepted conventions of the national interest. Thus conflicts over development policies and programs, especially over dams, forestry, and land use, seldom appeared, and when they did it was from a reassuring perspective of official concern and an emergent consensus.

In Hua Hin television was notably inserted into public life. "Viewing" did not become a major factor in domestic life, but it nonetheless offered certain important "moments" through which people could participate in a collective experience. Television news was the most widely watched segment on a daily basis, and one channel (Channel 7) was preferred over others. The news was broadcast at the same time in the evening on all channels, usually for an hour and a half. It began with the station logo and a familiar sound track, then focused on an image of the nation, its boundaries clearly defined and the principal regional cities appearing as stars or links. The conceptual outline of the nation was graphed for the viewers as a unified entity, made to appear as an island in a sea of nothingness rather than as a space contiguous with similar spaces and peoples. In the late 1980s the news broadcasts were usually anchored by three presenters: a man at the center flanked by two women, who shared the introduction and reportage of the various visual items. Viewers joked that they were his two wives, comparing their clothes, hairstyles, and makeup. Big international news stories were followed by national news, during which people continued to chat, eat, or carry out household tasks. However, the most eagerly watched segment was the Royal News, which lasted as long as half an hour and showed the activities of the Royal Family and sometimes of high government officials. For example, the King might be shown visiting an agricultural station, the Crown Princess opening a center for craft production, the second Princess attending a scientific congress in Europe, or the Crown Prince conferring degrees. The demeanor of viewers changed during the Royal News; they stopped their other activities and fell silent. This behavior was consistent with other practices expected when ordinary people are brought into conjunction with Royalty. Until the mid-nineteenth century, commoners were not permitted to see the King at all. Only in the twentieth century was it possible for people to see his face, most notably when King Chulalongkorn introduced his own image on Thai coinage. Even today when Royal motorcades pass through the city the police close off all streets to other vehicles, and pedestrians stand in hushed silence until the Royal personage passes by. However the mass media have opened up an entirely new relationship between people and the Royal Family. With television, the personage of the King can be looked upon every day, and at times his face and eyes meet those of the viewers and his voice speaks directly to them. Strict laws of lèse-majesté are still enforced, comments about the Royal Family are carefully regulated, and the media are never permitted to include material that disparages or questions the activities of Royalty.[9] Hence the silence and absorption commonly displayed in both public and private spaces can be seen as part of a constituent set of bodily practices intended to express respect and reverence. The presence of the monarchy looms over and behind matters in a way that renders the "imagined community" much more resonant with premodern social formations. The media have operated to maintain the idea of a national community with the King at its center. The possibility of "difference" then is modulated by the commonality of subordination and subjecthood. The media affirm the King as Master-Signifier, quite beyond any local, bureaucratic, or elected leadership (Zizek 1991: 235–37).

The people's reception of the Royal News can be interpreted in another way as well. One of the most significant issues in Thailand concerns the destiny of the Chakri dynasty and the dynamics of power relations within the Royal Family itself. These are fascinating and anxiety-provoking matters, which everyone recognizes as having profound implications for the future of the country. Because such matters cannot be directly addressed in public, indirect references to them are often made through discussion of material shown during non-news programs, especially melodramas and Chinese mytho-historical series.

Viewers in Hua Hin had only a limited program choice until the early 1990s, and the great majority of the programming was Thai in origin. Any non-Thai material was dubbed into Thai.[10] International sporting events such as boxing matches and Japanese women's wrestling were provided with Thai voice-overs using the same stylized commentary form used for local productions. These included a regular diet of melodramas, multipart narratives structured around family, romance, treachery, mistaken identities, and other plotlines familiar to the viewers of classic Western "soaps." However, these always have distinctive Thai themes, notably the problems of the "minor wife" or the virtuous girl who loses her high position and is forced to become a servant or a prostitute.[11] Locally produced Thai movies in the 1980s were closely related to the television melodramas, and one was often based on or developed from another using the same stars. The movie industry was flourishing at this time, with a wide variety of films presenting a distinctively Thai viewpoint, some of high quality but mostly low-cost, quickly produced material in stylized genres of the melodrama, action movie, ghost story/thriller, and young people's film (Boonrak 1992; Hamilton 1993a). Many Thai movies were shown on television on weekends and became increasingly popular in the 1980s.

The only foreign programming widely watched and popular were Chinese drama series, mostly ghost stories and mytho-historical sagas made in Hong Kong. All national channels screened at least one or more, dubbed into Thai. Set in a generic past, featuring magical powers, martial arts, and mystical themes embedded in struggles over family, dynasty, and power, these series touched on themes with strong local overtones—struggles between good and bad Royal houses, siblings, fathers and sons, and mothers and daughters-in-law. These series became increasingly popular in the 1990s, with one in particular, *Pau Puu Chiin,* gluing people to their televisions throughout Thailand, week after week. Thai producers began to imitate these programs with increasingly complex scripts involving flashbacks to a Thai past where reincarnated heroes and heroines moved between modern times in Bangkok and past lives in the ancient capital of Ayutthaya.

Other very popular programs included beauty contests. Every Thai town and region has its own beauty contest in which young women dress in traditional Thai style and win substantial prizes, culminating in a street parade. On television national and international beauty contests enhance this interest. When a Thai woman, Bui, won the Miss Universe contest in 1988, the country went into a delirium of self-congratulation, and Bui was used to promote a wide variety of beauty products in television advertisements, such as brands of shampoo from abroad, just then widely entering the local market. In late 1989 the International Mother-Daughter Beauty Contest, staged in a lavish resort on an American Micronesian island, gained peak viewing; many people taped the show and watched it over and over. These programs brought into dramatic visual form the emergence of a new world order of femininity: the mothers in the contest spoke in their national languages, and the daughters spoke in English. They competed in a variety of costumes, most of the mothers wearing national dress and the daughters wearing Western clothes; the finalists appeared first in ball gowns and then in bathing suits. During the late 1980s the Thai viewing audience was being exposed as never before to the idea of its place in an international environment, both in time and space, and to the forms of behavior and consumption appropriate to that new identity.

Finally, the popularity of Thai boxing (Muay Thai) needs to be mentioned. Thai boxing has a long and complex history; it possesses a special place in Thai popular culture and is overlaid with complex myth and symbolism (see Vail 1998). A popular feature of local festivals and events, Thai boxing is brought via television to local and regional populations as another of the integral aspects of local identity through which people can experience themselves as Thai and as superior to others. When Thai boxing is screened on Saturday afternoon entire townships and villages come to a standstill. *Samlor* drivers drop their cycles, and every shop is full of viewers cheering, commenting, and engaging in illegal betting on the outcome of matches. When Thais are matched against foreigners, the excitement is most intense.

The spread of Thai broadcast television to all parts of the country has thus brought into focus a series of themes and practices through which people are engaged in constructing their subjectivity as modern Thai citizens. At one level, this process clearly provides pleasure and results in enthusiastic responses. At another, however, the Thai viewer sees through this image and is engaged in a different perception of the real world than that shown on television. In particular, it is recognized that the sources of power and influence that operate behind the scenes are not the same as those depicted in the blandness of the television news. These sources of power are difficult to discern and even more difficult to influence. In part they derive from the world of knowable human action, both legal and illegal, and in part from the mystical world of supernatural influence that lies behind the perceptible external world. The popular print media, for instance, depict a very different condition of life and causality. Popular newspapers, magazines, and cheap paperbacks show a world of violence, secret dealings, collusion, magical appearances, hideous murders and tortures, and suspicious activities by the high and mighty. Everyone knows that secret deals and evil deeds are being done, that politicians become unusually wealthy, that police act arbitrarily and judges take bribes, and that the powerful have a thousand ways of becoming more so. Worse, Buddhist monks grow wealthy on the donations of the faithful and lead private lives that are far from blameless.

In the late 1980s there was no legitimate space for public discussion of such matters, no forum at which people might express their views openly or hear others do so. Although newspapers were able to print what they liked, any direct mention of individuals or groups was likely to result in a hand grenade thrown through the bedroom window of an editor or a journalist. On television there were no investigative shows or commentary, on radio no call-in shows. The restriction and circumspection resulted in the creation of a para-discourse, where something could be discussed only by referring to something else—notably, television and film stories. Narratives could be interpreted as being "about" something else—for example, a wealthy eldest son in a current Chinese drama who was having marital troubles could be coded as a subject for conversation about the Crown Prince. Current events and television and film narratives could take their place within a vast signifying chain of Thai history and destiny, meaning much more than they would seem to do at a literal level. This interpretive relationship between national events and the mass media formed a significant element in the emergent consciousness of Thai society as the boom years of the 1990s got under way, constituting a shared consciousness of what it meant to be Thai in both positive and negative terms.

The emergent disjunction in the representation of the world on Thai television no doubt played a significant role in the huge public protests that culminated in the street demonstrations and subsequent slaughter of civilians in May 1992. The collapse in the relationship between the official world on television and the reality in the streets became starkly apparent. The national broadcast television news bulletins showed nothing but preparations for the 1992 Miss World contest in Bangkok at the same time that the streets were running with the blood of murdered demonstrators and fax machines and mobile phones were spreading word of the events both nationally and internationally. All of this took place during the period of Thailand's most intensive exposure to incorporation into the globalized and transnationalized economy. (See Ubonrat 1996 for a masterly discussion of the relationship between television and civil society in Thailand.)

In part the Thai case allows us to consider how a carefully controlled and constructed national media environment, operating through indigenous rather than imported programming, can itself produce a certain kind of locality. The meaningful world produced through national broadcasting is a shared and distinctive one. Its component elements (melodramas, the Chinese series, Thai boxing, the news and Royal News, to mention the most obvious) provide a central sense of shared national identity to people all over the Kingdom, irrespective of their local histories and differences. To be Thai is to know and understand the significance of certain kinds of narratives and to be able to interpret them in meaningful ways that are incomprehensible to outsiders. The Thai state, by promulgating a national television policy that rests on local production, has successfully created a distinctive sense of identity that poses "Thai people" against "foreign others," even while assimilating many stylistic aspects of the cultural forms of those others. This distinctive sense of Thai-ness intersects with certain identities and at the immediate level of everyday life in villages, towns, and regions, but this locality finds its expression also in a wide variety of local practices, rituals, places, and shared histories that seldom if ever appear on television. (Meanwhile other forms of cultural production such as film have been allowed to wither.)

Since the early 1990s many changes have occurred in the Thai media environment. New regulations concerning videocassette circulation resulted in the virtual eclipse of Thai (and many Chinese) films on video (see Hamilton 1993a). The government closed down local cable channels, claiming they represented a threat to national security. Satellite television and national cable broadcasting have penetrated all parts of the country. In the aftermath of the 1992 protests, some liberalization has occurred in the acceptable broadcast television programming, which now includes commentary shows and call-in programs (see Ubonrat 1996).

Nevertheless, the official public culture of Thailand has remained extraordinarily resilient in the sense that neither the realities of local cultural expression nor the aspirations of emergent sections of the national elite have been accommodated. In response, in both urban and rural sectors, and particularly since the economic crash of 1997, a powerful new expression of public culture has emerged, no longer controlled by the officially sanctioned media expressions of Thai national identity. Modernity was promised as the way forward by the government, based on a concept of national public culture promulgated through an unchallengeable monopoly of communicative power. Against this, at the end of the 1990s, a different collective culture emerged, one preoccupied with mystical forces, meditation cults, and the intercession of spirit mediums and other transcendental specialists. These movements are being brokered largely through the new electronic media in the informal sphere, especially through the circulation of video- and audiocassettes originally developed as means of expression of locally important significations that otherwise were unable to obtain general circulation. Economic forces, media, and the state now stand in a relationship of dynamic unpredictability. Every Tuesday night, thousands gather in Bangkok at the memorial shrine to King Chulalongkorn, the patron of modernity. There people respond to the bizarre consequences of late global modernity by placing their faith in spirit mediums who are seen on videocassettes performing remarkable feats of endurance. These provide visible evidence of the powers that underlie the merely superficial world of power so forcibly expressed for decades in the official Thai media.

NOTES

Research for this study was supported by Macquarie University research grants and the Australian Research Council. Thanks are due to many individuals and institutions in Thailand, especially colleagues from the Faculty of Communication Arts, Chulalongkorn University, Bangkok.

1. There is still no comprehensive historical account of the development of modern media in Thailand. Ubonrat (1989) has discussed the development of radio broadcasting, and numerous studies touch on various aspects of the subject or provide a summary outline; see, e.g., Hamilton 1987.

2. The project has developed in several phases; first, through the study of popular Thai media genres and narratives in film and television, and some production and reception issues (see Hamilton 1992, 1993a, 1993b); second, in the study of a town and its hinterland, focusing on the relation between locality and nation, to which this essay is a contribution and which will be completed shortly as a monograph; finally, in multisited research in the southern border region where ethnicity, identity, and media are co-implicated in a complex politics of space and culture.

3. The rapid spread of privately produced videocassettes, especially those concerned with ritual and cult practices, and the availability of national broadcast television via satellite to Thais living abroad (e.g., in Sydney from approximately mid-1999), clearly have important implications for these issues, which I will address in subsequent publications.

4. The problem of the *farang* and of Thailand's relation to the West generally is too complex to discuss further here. China and Japan are also important to the national imaginary, but in different ways.

5. Thai is part of the Tai language family but is not (other than in diasporic communities) used outside a limited area of Southeast Asia. It is not comprehensible by speakers of Burmese, Khmer, Chinese, Vietnamese, or Indonesian/Malay or any of their variants. Strictly speaking, the national language is Standard Thai, but many rural Thai speakers do not speak Standard Thai in everyday life, or at all (see Diller 1991). Standard Thai is the ideal language of writing and speaking and the actual language of relevant elites. Smalley divides Thai into four major regional languages

and many marginal regional languages, as well as enclave, town and city, and displaced Thai dialects (Smalley 1994: 27, 69). Thais generally do not learn a second language, although the recent boom in tourism has encouraged the spread of "hospitality English." Many educated Thais have only limited facility with any language other than Thai, and some consider this a merit because it excludes foreign and "alien" elements from the nation. At the same time it is thought to facilitate control over the circulation of ideas and enhance the sense of distinctiveness so strongly stressed as a marker of self-respect in Thai public culture.

6. Many Bangkokians are amazed to discover that most small towns are subjected to a daily period of exhortation, which generally begins at 7:00 A.M. and includes information about important local events, road closures, aid appeals, the activities of the local council, and so on. After an hour or so, it terminates with the broadcast of the national anthem, at which time everyone is expected to cease their activities and stand completely still until it is completed. Loudspeakers are set up at intervals throughout the town such that no household can avoid hearing the broadcasts and all people going about their morning business will be likewise exposed to them. This very direct method of the "official world" communicating with "local people" seems to have been present for decades, although I have been unable to establish exactly when it began.

7. The Seventh International Thai Studies Conference in Amsterdam in July 1999 was organized around the theme of "Thailand as a civil society." It became clear that there was little consensus on exactly what that would be in the Thai case and what effects the development of a civil society would have on the maintenance of "authentic Thai culture," which is also of great concern to contemporary Thai intellectuals.

8. Elsewhere I show how people of the district responded by incorporating the new media technologies in distinctive ways that do not replicate the forms of "audience" understood as normative in Western media studies. Locality was able to achieve expression through the appropriation of cable technology, which permitted a distinctive mix of local and national broadcasting in close accord with the viewing preferences of the townspeople. This material is currently being prepared for publication as a book that will include the Hua Hin regional media study.

9. See Streckfuss 1998. These laws apply as much to foreigners as they do to Thais. For example, in 1987 a British restaurateur in Hua Hin was overheard criticizing the physical appearance of one of the Princesses (in English) to his friends with whom he was drinking in his restaurant. A prominent Hua Hin local reported this to local police, who immediately arrested him and threw him in jail. He was obliged to pay a large fine and leave the country on the next train.

10. Dubbing was a highly organized profession in Thailand, and the same individuals were used to provide voice-overs for many programs, thus producing a strange "flattening out" of spoken text and some interesting transformations of meaning. Most foreign movies in the commercial cinemas were dubbed in Thai, though some in Bangkok had Thai subtitles. The implications of dubbing and subtitles for a globalized screen culture would be a valuable topic of analysis.

11. Polygamy was common and legal in Thailand until the reforms of the early twentieth century. Most wealthy and successful men continue to maintain one or more "minor wives," although this position is no longer legally recognized and the status of the offspring from these marriages depends on the goodwill of the father. This circumstance sets up a series of complex family dynamics that provide an excellent ba-

sis for dramatic scenarios and confrontations. The prostitution theme is encountered in a modified form—for example, where a respectable girl is herself forced to become a minor wife in order to pay off her father's gambling debts. The actual facts of life as a prostitute in Thailand are never depicted openly on screen. (But see Berry, Hamilton, and Jayamanne 1994 for a discussion of the responses to Dennis O'Rourke's film *The Good Woman of Bangkok*, which depicted a real-life Thai prostitute on screen, to the horror of the Thai viewing audience.)

REFERENCES

Abu-Lughod, Lila. 1993. Finding a Place for Islam: Egyptian Television Serials and the National Interest. *Public Culture* 5 (3): 493–513.

———. 1995. The Objects of Soap-Opera: Egyptian Television and the Cultural Politics of Modernity. In *Worlds Apart: Modernity through the Prism of the Local*, edited by Daniel Miller. London: Routledge.

Anderson, Benedict. 1978. Studies of the Thai State: The State of Thai Studies. In *The Study of Thailand*, edited by Eliezer B. Ayal, pp. 193–247. Athens, Ohio: Ohio Centre for International Studies.

———. 1983. *Imagined Communities: Reflections on the Origins and Spread of Nationalism*. London: Verso.

Anderson, Benedict, and Ruchira Mendiones, eds. and trans. 1985. *In the Mirror: Literature and Politics in Siam in the American Era*. Bangkok: Editions Duang Kamol.

Appadurai, Arjun. 1996. *Modernity at Large: Cultural Dimensions of Globalization*. Minneapolis: University of Minnesota Press.

Berry, Chris, Annette Hamilton, and Laleen Jayamanne. 1994. *The Filmmaker and the Prostitute: Dennis O'Rourke's 'The Good Woman of Bangkok.'* Sydney: Power Institute.

Boonrak Boonyaketmala. 1992. The Rise and Fall of the Film Industry in Thailand, 1897–1992. *East-West Film Journal* 6: 62–98.

Che Man, K. 1990. *Muslim Separatism: The Moros of Southern Philippines and the Malays of Southern Thailand*. Singapore: Oxford University Press.

Diller, Anthony. 1991. What Makes Central Thai a National Language? In *National Identity and Its Defenders, Thailand 1939–1989*, edited by Craig Reynolds. Chiang Mai: Silkworm Books.

Gesick, Lorraine. 1995. *In the Land of Lady White Blood: Southern Thailand and the Meaning of History*. Ithaca, N.Y.: Cornell University Press.

Grabowsky, Volker, ed. 1995. *Regions and National Integration in Thailand, 1892–1992*. Wiesbaden, Germany: Harrassowitz Verlag.

Hamilton, Annette, 1987. *Mass Media and Development in Thailand*. Proceedings of the Third International Conference on Thai Studies. Vol. 2, pp. 45–55. Canberra: Australian National University.

———. 1992. Family Dramas: Film and Modernity in Thailand. *Screen* 33: 259–73.

———. 1993a. Cinema and Nation: Dilemmas of Representation in Thailand. *East-West Film Journal* 7: 81–105.

————. 1993b. Video Crackdown, or the Sacrificial Pirate. *Public Culture* 11: 515–32.

Jackson, Peter. 1999. The Enchanting Spirit of Thai Capitalism: The Cult of Luang Phor Khoon and the Postmodernisation of Thai Buddhism. *Southeast Asian Research* 7: 5–60.

Kanchana Kaewthep. 1994. "East" Meets "West": The Confrontation of Different Cultures in Thai TV Dramas and Films. In *Gender and Culture in Literature and Film, East and West: Issues in Perception and Interpretation,* edited by Nitaya Masavisut, George Simson, and Larry E. Smith, pp. 180–96. Honolulu: University of Hawaii Press.

Keyes, Charles F. 1991. The Proposed World of the School: Thai Villagers' Entry into a Bureaucratic State System. In *Reshaping Local Worlds,* edited by Charles F. Keyes. New Haven, Conn.: Yale University Southeast Asian Studies.

Pasuk Pongpaichit and Chris Baker. 1998. *Thailand's Boom and Bust.* Seattle: University of Washington Press.

Rhum, Michael R. 1996. "Modernity" and "Tradition" in Thailand. *Modern Asian Studies* 30: 325–55.

Smalley, William A. 1994. *Linguistic Diversity and National Unity.* Chicago: University of Chicago Press.

Streckfuss, David. 1998. The Poetics of Subversion: Civil Liberty and Lèse-Majesté in the Modern Thai State. Ph.D. diss., University of Wisconsin-Madison.

Thongchai Winichakul. 1994. *Siam Mapped: A History of the Geo-Body of a Nation.* Honolulu: University of Hawaii Press.

Tomlinson, John. 1991. *Cultural Imperialism.* London: Routledge.

Ubonrat Siriyuvasak. 1989. Radio in a Transitional Society: The Case of Modern Thailand. Ph.D. diss., Leicester University.

————.1996. Television and the Emergence of "Civil Society" in Thailand. In *Contemporary Television: Eastern Perspectives,* edited by David French and Michael Richards. Thousand Oaks, Calif.: Sage.

Vail, Peter. 1998. Violence and Control: Social and Cultural Dimensions of Boxing in Thailand. Ph.D. diss., Cornell University.

Zizek, Slavoj. 1991. *For They Know Not What They Do.* London: Verso.

8

Television, Time, and
the National Imaginary in Belize

Richard R. Wilk

Commercial broadcast television invites us constantly to think about the content of programs; this is part of the way we become an audience. Often, this is the way scholars approach television as well, by viewing programs and thinking or talking about the characters, formats, conventions, and plots presented. It is no surprise that the vast majority of television scholarship is concerned with content and genre, the way it is produced, financed, and transmitted, and its real or imagined effects on the audience (see, e.g., Schiller 1976; Burton and Franco 1978; Lee 1989).

By studying the advent of television in the developing world, anthropologists gain something that has largely been lost in the parts of the world where television is now a taken-for-granted social fact. That is the opportunity to think beyond programming and content to the form of the medium itself, to the way television constitutes a new form of cosmology and creates new social worlds. An earlier generation of media theorists in the West, particularly Raymond Williams and Marshall McLuhan, made fascinating and sometimes prescient predictions about how the form of the new medium would change the world. With hindsight it is now possible to reflect on some of their insights, drawing on studies of the expansion of television to new parts of the planet. Of course, the medium has also changed as it has expanded, and we can now see some effects on and consequences for television that earlier scholars did not predict.

This essay is based on my experience living and working in the Caribbean and Central American country of Belize in the early 1980s, when television was first introduced. In 1989 and 1990 I returned to conduct fieldwork on consumer culture, much of which involved studying the impacts of television. Others have studied the ways that television viewing changes family life, daily routines, values, and attitudes when it enters new places (e.g., Kottak 1990; Lull 1988). Here I focus instead on two different but related issues. The first is the way people talk about and debate television. I suggest that the discourse about television is itself one of the impacts of the medium. In Belize, discourse about television has focused attention on national character and cultural difference and has helped realign political alliances. The second is the way advanced television technology—in particular the direct access to the metropole provided by satellite broadcast—changes people's perception of time. Time, I argue, is linked to geography and power in colonial and neocolonial contexts. The coevalness between the periphery and the metropole in what I call "TV time" breaks the links between geographic distance and cultural lag. Instead of seeing themselves as backward or stuck in the past, Belizeans have come to understand their difference from the metropole in cultural and political terms. In the process, the Belizean elite has lost much of its role as the conduit of progress and the transmission of fashion. Neither effect, both of which involve new forms of national consciousness, is related to the content or message of television programming.

THE TELEVISION INVASION

Belize, once called British Honduras, is a tiny country 280 kilometers long and 109 kilometers wide with a population of about 200,000. Independent from Britain since 1981, it rests uneasily alongside its Central American neighbors. Through a long history as a British colony it developed close cultural ties with the islands of the Caribbean, but its ethnic composition changed dramatically in the last quarter of the twentieth century because of Latin immigration from Central America and Afro-European ("Creole") emigration to the United States. Today the official ethnic composition is about 30 percent Creole, 44 percent Hispanic, 11 percent Mayan, 7 percent Garifuna (Afro-Amerindian), and the remainder of five other national origins.

The colonial government tightly controlled the kinds of films and printed matter available in Belize through the period of internal self-rule in the 1960s. The government continued to control the single national radio station through the 1980s, though many were able to receive commercial broadcasts from California and Texas on clear nights (and as a result a whole generation became Dodgers fans and lovers of country and western music). In the 1970s many of the richest Belizeans bought TV sets and VCRs, which they used to screen films privately; some also had friends and family in the United States tape network programming for them. The East Indian and Chinese communities were pioneers, importing tapes in their native languages that were often played publicly in shops and restaurants. In this form television aroused very little public interest or alarm.

It was only when private entrepreneurs began to rebroadcast pirated satellite signals in December of 1981 that the newspapers and magazines announced the beginnings of "Television Mania" and "The Video Invasion." (Anon. 1981). Commenting on the euphoric feeling of freedom that swept the capital, one local writer said, "The 'tube' has hit Belize like a heady wine" (Ewens ca. 1982).

Controversy followed, as Belizeans debated both the cultural and political ramifications of the new medium. The government first turned a blind eye, then cautiously tried to regulate the new industry (under pressure from the United States, where the signals originated). With the approach of the 1984 elections the government took stronger steps to control television and began to raise alarms about its cultural impacts. The minister of education (who was elected prime minister in 1998) proclaimed that television was more dangerous than an invading army of ten thousand soldiers.[1] The perception that the government was going to clamp down on television broadcasting was one of the issues that led to the crushing electoral defeat of the ruling party. Subsequent governments have only gingerly regulated the new medium, and by 1994 there were at least six cable networks and nine transmitters, mostly providing U.S. programming from satellites. The northern part of the country gets some TV broadcasts from Mexico, and the South receives transmissions from Guatemala and Honduras. Other areas of the country receive some Spanish-language broadcasts from American networks that in turn use Mexican and South American programming. There is some local programming now, particularly news, religion, and sports, though the vast majority is still fed, legally and illegally, from U.S. satellites.

Every settlement with more than a thousand inhabitants now has a cable system linked directly to satellite downlinks. From my own 1990 survey, I estimated that about 35 percent of urban residents had access to cable, and most of the rest received rebroadcasts; 95 percent of the urban population had daily access to TV, and more than half of the adults surveyed stated that they watch television at least several times a week. In 1996 a Belize City station opened rebroadcast facilities that covered almost the entire country, bringing access to direct U.S. programming to virtually the entire population.

Shortly after the television invasion, another invasion began, this time of foreign scholars and journalists attracted by the drama of TV's sudden arrival. Most of their work followed a diffusionary paradigm, portraying Belize as a victim of cultural imperialism or the neocolonial world information order. They studied the impact of the new medium on politics, social organization, psychology, consumption patterns, and migration (Barry 1984; Bolland 1987; Everitt 1987; Lent 1989; Oliveira 1986; Petch 1987, 1988; Roser, Snyder, and Chaffee 1986; Snyder, Roser, and Chaffee 1991; Westlake 1982). With the exception of Bolland, few demonstrated much knowledge of local history or culture. On my return to Belize in 1989, much of the initial furor had died down, and the media scholars had moved on to newer pastures.

But the local debate about television continued; everyone I spoke with had an opinion about television.

TELEVISION DISCOURSE

Watching television is a social activity. While many media scholars were focused on the production and reception of the television text, an early generation of ethnographers looked primarily at the social context of television viewing (Kottak 1990: 127–28, 140–42; Michaels 1988; Kent 1985). Their premise was that the information that comes through television is directly mediated through a social process of debate, discussion, and public discourse. There is also a growing, more ethnographic literature on the ways that people understand, contest, and mediate the messages provided by imported mass media, in the process renegotiating the positions and meanings of local and global cultures (e.g., Abu-Lughod 1993; Ginsburg 1993). From this we learn that watching television and talking about television are inseparable parts of a single process. Accordingly, the viewing experience should be seen as active and socially negotiated, and the content of messages is a matter of dispute and contention rather than being simply given. Here I want to focus not on the intimate domestic social mediation of television but on the broader arena of public and political debate (see also Ossman 1994).

In general, television has imbued Belize's political debate with a new moral content and has secularized issues that were traditionally the terrain of the church. In the process it moves many issues that were once seen as Belizean, local, and even familial into a global context. The problems of youth, social welfare, ethnicity, and gender roles, for example, are now cast in a global context of "our way" or "our Belizean traditions" as opposed to "those seen on television." Now that television has presented Belizeans with an objectified "other," the problem of defining the self has a new dimension. Differences between Belizeans seem to fade away when confronted with the light from the box. There is now more common language for the discussion of otherness and sameness, and a visible standard of comparison. In the past, images of foreign culture were received indirectly, with the colonial elite acting as selective agents, the gatekeepers to the outside world.

Some of those differences actually have faded away. Belize is still a multiethnic and multilingual country with great disparities in wealth and education. But television has proven a uniting force in two ways. First, at the level of content, all Belizeans with television now share access to some of the same sources of news and entertainment, even if those sources are CNN and Tom Brokaw. Now all Belizeans have a common conversation about NBA basketball, network sitcoms, and the *Cosby* show. Second, television has engaged Belizeans in a common debate about the impact of television on the country, and in the process has made everyone aware of "the local and the global" as a matter of concern. If we liken Belizeans to voyeurs watching North America through an electronic peephole, we find they are united both by their common knowledge of what goes on in the United States and by their shared experience of voyeurism. So while Belizeans may make different moral judgments about what is good and bad on television, they share a common language when they debate those moral issues (Wilk 1995).

I do not want to overemphasize this unity. The country remains highly factionalized and divided by politics, ethnicity, and class. But television discourse and debate have changed existing social divisions and the alignment of factions. For example, religious organizations that used to have a very close relationship with political conservatives now find themselves sharing important common ground with the left. Both are concerned about the danger of foreign television. The Baptist minister and the nationalist student have a shared agenda, the control of foreign influence. The old nationalist program of building local cultural institutions now finds a much broader constituency, and Belizean cultural production of all kinds (music, art, literature) receives broad support.

Another important effect of television discourse among these new coalitions is that it changes the terms of the debate about local and foreign. Instead of being about political and economic independence from the British, or about local economic development, now debate is carried out in cultural terms. In Belize since the advent of television, people talk about "culture" constantly, in ways that were not possible before. Television has made Belizeans focus on the autonomy of local culture—on music, cooking, dance, and language—rather than political or economic autonomy. New notions of the relationship between distance and time have come into play.

TELEVISION AND THE REORDERING OF TIME

The idea that culture orders time is a venerable one in anthropology (see, e.g., Evans-Pritchard 1940: 94–138). If timekeeping is a process of control, a way of imposing order, distance, or power on nature and culture, then we need to pay close attention to the cultural instruments that keep and mark time. Although in a technological society clocks order the everyday consumption of time, temporality is also instituted and constructed by things as diverse as museums and calendars, houses, schoolbooks, births, closets full of shoes, family photographs, and journal articles about other cultures (see Ossman 1994).

When looking at the global political economy of time, at the temporal relations between north and south, two instruments stand out. The first is the techno-scientific discourse of development and progress, transmitted by thousands of institutions, government codes, consultancies, and classrooms. The "denial of coevalness" found by Fabian (1983) is much more obvious and fundamental in the rhetoric of economic growth and development than it has ever been in anthropology. The second important instrument of global time is the global mass media, most of all television. I argue here that television can challenge the temporal basis of the legitimacy of the political and economic order in neocolonies (see also Gillespie 1995).

Others have noted a close connection among communications media, the cultural sense of the passage of time, and human consciousness. Carey, for example, discusses how the telegraph led, for the first time, to a separation of notions of communication and transportation. News could precede goods. In the hands of commerce, the telegraph equalized the distribution of knowledge over space, thereby shifting the focus of commercial activity from the manipulation of space to the management of time. For the populace at large, however, the most conspicuous effect of the telegraph was the regularization of standard time, as when each American town's clocks were brought into synchrony in 1883 through the efforts of the railroads (see Carey 1989: 213–19). For Carey and others who have written on the industrial regulation of time, temporality is part of modern state and industry efforts to control the lives of citizens, a foundation of the Fordist revolution (see also Thompson 1967; Hareven 1982).

A similar theme in media studies is that modern communications media have tended toward "widening the range of reception while narrowing the range of distribution" (Carey 1989: 136; see also Williams 1974: 29–31). With each new medium, the production of information is more and more concentrated, channeled, and controlled, and the audience has less input about what it receives. With the goal of profit, television producers manipulate, control, and sell time, serializing the flow of experience (Browne 1984; Williams 1974; Ossman 1994: 60). As with the manipulation of temporality, control of content enforces the crushing dominance and centralized hegemony of mass-produced northern capitalist consumer culture (Belk and Zhou 1987; Nordenstreng and Varis 1974).

The counterarguments to these dire predictions usually take the form of arguments for reappropriation of content, or for the possibility that the new media may be culturally "hijacked" and used for resistant local or subnational purposes. There is something satisfying in the notion that the tools of global capitalism may be grasped by their supposed victims and turned on their creators. Here I am suggesting something quite different and more subtle: that something fundamental about the structure of some of the new media undercuts one of the central ideological foundations of colonialism and neocolonialism.

COLONIAL TIME

I find the best starting place to approach these issues is the time before any kind of television arrived in Belize—the 1960s. The temporal world of the country was dominated then by what I call colonial time: a system that merges time with physical distance and cultural difference (much like the anthropological discourse discussed by Fabian [1983]). The three dimensions of difference are treated as aspects of the same phenomenon. In the systematics of colonial time, time, geographic distance, and culture are almost interchangeable concepts in explaining and justifying the differences between the colony and the metropole. In colonial time the colony is described using metaphors that combine the connotative meanings of time, distance, and cultural development. Primitive, backward, and underdeveloped are blends; other words draw more directly on temporal, cultural, or spatial meanings (e.g., simple, uncultured, isolated, natural, savage, barbaric, degenerate, primordial, wild, rude, marginal, peripheral, uncivilized).

The ultimate effect of colonial time is to objectify the concept of tradition, of a kind of culture that is rooted in a distant time and remote place (as in the pages of *National Geographic* magazine, analyzed by Lutz and Collins [1993]). The colony is backward because it is dominated by unchanging tradition, timeless, isolated, and pervasive. The flow of time in this context is the product of the colonial agents themselves, the administrators, officials, leaders, intelligentsia, and technocrats who collectively represent themselves as agents of "progress," a term opposed to "tradition" that also merges time, distance, and culture. Progress implies movement in time from the unchanging past to the dynamic future, in space from the isolated hinterland to the bustling city, and in culture from static tradition to fashionable modernity. In colonial culture, time is a blueprint for social and political change; it carries the burden of an entire cultural plan.

If colonial time is at the heart of colonial cosmology, style and fashion are its outward concrete symbols. The gap in fashionable clothes, furnishings, housing styles, language, and customs between the colony and the metropole is seen by participants in the colonial system as the concrete measure of the lag in colonial time between the traditional backwardness of the colony and the modernity of the metropole. The flow of consumer goods and intellectual goods between the metropole and the colony is a form of cultural timekeeping; the objects and ideas are clocks marking off colonial time. The units might be called "years behind."

In Belize in the 1960s the fashions seen on the street lagged four or five years behind those of New York (and many New York fashions were filtered out of the flow and never made it to Belize at all). In colonial time this put Belize many "years behind" New York, at an equal age/distance and on an equal cultural footing as say, Tegucigalpa or Barbados, but still far "ahead" of rural Belize or San Pedro Sula (a city in neighboring Honduras) or the small Caribbean island of Antigua. The irony of colonial time is that though it is premised on the promise of progress, there is really no catching up (Sangari 1987). The lag can become smaller or larger, but the clock is set in the metropole; ground zero is New York or London or Paris, and the colonies will always be in another time zone. The flow of fashion requires the colonies to keep running faster to catch up. They may be able to cut the distance in half each year, but like Zeno's rabbit, they will never reach their destination.

It is this very lag that makes it possible for the metropolitan consumer to savor the archaism of an African mask, an experience that emphasizes the time gap even if the wood of the mask is still green. The middle-class colonial avoided such evidence of backwardness like the plague, and preferred to decorate the house with modern Western goods.

Although it may seem an elaborate form of bondage, colonial time served the social and political interests of both the colonial elites and the metropolitan powers. On the macroeconomic level the demand for metropolitan status goods such as clothes, appliances, and even houses will always be there; even when the colonials are starving, the answer is still progress, and progress is still measured by colonial time (Chakrabarty 1992). Colonial time lends weight and authority to the ideas, policies, and goals of metropolitan politicians, allowing them to set the terms of debate even when their policies counter the interests of the colony or the colonial elite. On the global scale, colonial time affirms the political dependency of the undeveloped and developing on the developed and keeps the colonial elite in a permanently subordinate position.

On the local level, however, the counting of events and processes in colonial time is a potent tool for the colonial elite, for it makes them the timekeepers. Colonial time runs through narrow channels. The merging of distance, culture, and time means the local elite, who can travel to the metropole and come back with new styles and fashions, are the conduit through which time flows and progress occurs. The metaphors of colonial time allow this process of cultural flow and bridging of physical distance to be recast as "progress." Only "change agents" break the timeless stasis of tradition because of their contact with the outside world. The local elite can be these agents, as long as they accept the premise that their home is a backward place.

TV TIME AND THE SATELLITE CONNECTION

There is nothing inherent in the medium of television that necessarily changes the colonial conception of time. Watching ten-year-old reruns of *I Dream of Genie* in a Mexico City hotel in 1978 did nothing but reinforce my feeling that Mexico was "behind" the United States, in some ways parallel but lagging. The kind of TV programming offered in many Third World countries—budget local programs interspersed with well-produced but outdated metropolitan productions—seems designed as an object lesson in colonial time. The viewer is hard pressed to tell whether the differences between their own experience and those depicted in *Father Knows Best* are the result of the passage of time, the geographic distance between their country and the United States, or real cultural differences between themselves and Americans. The three distinctions are obscured and collapsed into each other. When news and current events are presented in local programs with low production values, their quality and content prove that the present in the ex-colony is "years behind the present" in the metropole.

In this kind of TV the local broadcasting authorities, government regulators, and advertisers still stand between the viewing public and the metropolitan producers of entertainment and news. The local purveyors of foreign media have national cultural and political agendas of their own (Mahan 1990). The manual trade of videotapes seems to parallel the other colonial fashion trades. Television can simply become another fashion item, another good on the endless conveyer belt from the metropole to the ex-colonies.

What makes a real difference in Belize is satellite broadcast technology, which changes the fundamental relationship between time and distance (as predicted by Raymond Williams [1974: 143–45]. For a good part of the day Belize television consumers can watch real-time broadcast television from the United States. The most popular types of programs in 1990 were, in decreasing order, sports, soap operas, news, and situation comedy; but the most popular single program was the *Cosby* show.

One of the most popular rebroadcasts was WGN from Chicago, at the time the only "local" station available on the satellite. Many Belizeans quickly became avid Chicago Cubs fans, and since the arrival of satellite TV the popularity of soccer and cricket have declined, while baseball and basketball have soared. When the Cubs made it into the league playoffs in 1983 the country came to a standstill for days, and shops closed during the games. One leftist politician told me that the baseball brainwashing of Belizean children had gone so far that he had heard them singing "The Star Spangled Banner" before starting their games![2] This pattern is not unique to Belize—all over the Americas access to satellites enables direct, up-to-the-minute programming from the metropole, some of it in Spanish. Similar satellite networks have spread rapidly in the eastern hemisphere.

Why does direct broadcast transmission make such a difference? Because the programs, especially the sports and news broadcasts, are immediate. There is no lag. Not only can the Belizean family in their rickety house in a swamp on the edge of Belize City watch the same programs as their counterparts in urban North America; far more important, they can watch them at the same time. What the Belizeans watch is being broadcast at the same time they are watching it.

Satellite television has thereby removed an essential element from the equation of colonial time. Distance between the metropole and the colony can no longer be reckoned in terms of time. The immediacy of contact makes it abundantly clear that only distance and culture set Belize apart from the United States, not time. TV time is now a single clock ticking away a single rhythm in every place it reaches, a continuous cycle of news, advertising, entertainment, and special events. TV time is alarming and strange at first: it is the direct experience of a flow of events that was once far away, safely filtered, and dimly and indirectly perceived. Things seem to be moving more quickly, almost out of control.

TV TIME, CULTURE, AND POLITICS

For the political and cultural elite, TV time is out of control. The old conduits of power have been largely circumvented. Fashion is no longer channeled solely through the local elite because information flows directly from television to the masses. Ten years ago when someone returned to Belize from a trip to New York or Miami he strutted around in his new clothes for weeks, tried out new words at parties, and displayed the latest bit of technology in his home. Now the consumer goods of the Belize elite are revealed as frauds or shallow imitations; though the elite presume to sit on top of the local heap, their consumption styles cannot come close to matching the materialism that everyone can see on *Falcon Crest*, in the advertisements, on the news. The local elite are no longer the only ones to emulate or envy, for they are no longer the source of new things, the local agents and representatives of the metropole. They no longer sit ahead of everyone else on the time line. In this light the laments about television that pour from Belize's educated elite acquire a new meaning. The statements from the local elites reflect the diminished value of their role as retailers of metropolitan cultural capital and cultural dependency. In fact, television allows Belizeans to perceive the culture of their nation in ways that were not available before. Colonial time served the purpose of the metropole by making the distance between the colony and the metropole uncrossable. It clouded and obscured the causes and symptoms of dominance. Colonial time rationalized exploitation, poverty, and domination by submerging them in the terms of backwardness, underdevelopment, and primitivism.

TV time has therefore removed one of the ideological props of the colonial and postcolonial world order. Those who watch a Lakers-Knicks playoff game on a TV in Belize City have an immediacy of experience, an emotional involvement in the present on an equal basis with viewers in Los Angeles and New York. Their reception is not poorer, and they are not seeing a game that happened last week; they are in the here and now. And when the game is over, both the stink of garbage and the aroma of home cooking are in the here and now too; there is no escape. To steal Conrad's metaphor from *Heart of Darkness,* the journey upriver is no longer a journey back in time. It is just a trip upriver that takes some time. The lack of speed is a problem, not a metaphor, and it can be overcome by applying a bit of technology. If things are different upriver it is not because of some kind of time lag. We cannot just sit back and expect that problems will be solved when Belize "catches up." Between Belize and the United States the time lag is gone; the distance is closing. What remains are cultural, economic, and political differences that require new explanations, or new rationalizations.

By changing temporality, TV time must also alter local systems of control and power. The tragedy is not so much that local culture will disappear. There is some objectively measurable increase in the "Americanization" of Belizean institutions, customs, and language, but it is paralleled by a decline in British influence (Wilk 1990). The lasting tragedy is instead that important kinds of power have now moved entirely out of the country to the metropole. Whereas colonial time left something for a local elite, TV time is established in the metropolitan centers; as consumers of information and programming the Belizeans have no power to affect what they see, except to turn it on and off (Martin-Barbero 1988). The control of time cannot be regained. The rhythms of life now move in accord with the cycles of sport (baseball season, basketball season, Superbowl Sunday), the cycles of weekly programming (Thursday night, *Cosby*), and the daily schedules of soaps. In 1990 my fieldwork in a rural community came to a halt every afternoon at 4:30 when people turned on televisions powered by car batteries to watch *Another World*. And for many the new rhythm of life includes periodic flights to Chicago, Miami, or Los Angeles, where they know what to expect, having seen it on the television.

The change in temporality is clearly reflected in Belizean music and artistic production. In the 1950s and 1960s there were primarily three kinds of music performed in Belize. The first was classical: the "enlightening" music of bourgeois Europe taught in the best schools and played in churches and at elite cultural events. Visiting artists sponsored by the British government occasionally performed classical music; otherwise teachers and clergy were the agents who brought it to Belize. The second genre was the local version of American, English, and to some extent Caribbean popular music, including country and western, rock and roll, rhythm and blues, calypso, and reggae. The local newspapers published the "top ten" lists from New York and London, but it often took weeks or months for a limited selection of the actual recordings to arrive in Belizean record shops. (It was especially hard to find a good selection of Caribbean music.) Local groups competed to be the first to "cover" popular foreign songs at dances and parties. Third, there were several kinds of folk or ethnic music in Belize, including Garifuna drumming, Creole boom and chime, Mayan harp, and marimba. None of these genres was considered "real" music by the middle class ("horrible primitive scratching and howling" as one elderly informant put it), and they were performed mainly at rural festivities and street gatherings. Many Belizeans were embarrassed by folk music, which was widely thought to be a holdover from the distant past.

All three genres were tangled up in colonial time; each kind of music stuck in the past in ways that also expressed cultural distance (classical music, folk music), and geographic distance and poor communication (copied popular music). Performing or listening to any kind of music in colonial Belize could never break down that distance. No amount of virtuosity ever made the local copy equal to the foreign original. The Belizeans were forever latecomers to both classical and popular music, and the music that could be their own was stigmatized as primitive and undeveloped.

MTV arrived along with the satellite feed in the 1980s, and the Belizean music scene changed almost immediately. There was no longer a lag between the popular music played in New York, London, and Los Angeles and that played in Belize or Orange Walk; the same bands and the same songs were everywhere at once. Local bands still copy foreign music; consumers still tend to think that foreign music is better; and local bands still gain status by leaving Belize to record and perform in the United States. But many people recognize that the problem is that Belize is a small place with limited markets, talent, and resources. And local music is no longer stuck in a time trap either. People are not ashamed of local folk music any more, as it is transformed from a vestige into a heritage. Once it was freed from its chains, some of the local genres further creolized and hybridized it, producing "Punta Rock," among other forms. By 1990 Punta Rock was "Belize's contribution to World Music," through which Belize asserts its equality in a global pageant of different musical styles (Wilk 1995).

CONCLUSION

Although Belize as a nation has lost a measure of control over TV time, the outcome may not be such a bad bargain. Certainly a better understanding of cultural, spatial, and temporal distance has resulted. Fashions and products from outside the country have lost some of their magic—they are no longer gifts from the future that carry the message of inevitability. Local products are seeing something of a resurgence because they are no longer pale imitations of the real thing, mimics stuck "behind the times." Now they may be inferior or superior, dear or a bargain, but they can be assessed qualitatively without the extra burden of acting as symbols of time and history. They are no longer things out of date in the metropole (the despised aspect of colonial goods) but can now be presented as objects that exist with their own distinct (usually national) identity in the legitimate present. This is an enormous change in a country that has been exporting raw materials and importing everything else for 350 years. Sandwiched in the two-minute gaps between episodes of *The Jeffersons,* advertisements for local products, churches, and politicians now have a powerful implicit message.

TV time is a key factor in understanding the process of making and expressing history in ex-colonies. In colonial time, the present was history, dripping with inferences of archaism and tradition, "rooted in the past." TV time allows for explicit historical references by separating the present from the past. For example, a box of Belizean matches is undesirable in colonial time because the object is archaic. The design of the box and the poor-quality wooden sticks are the products of an outdated technology. This kind of artifact has been around for a long time, and it has long been replaced by better products in the metropolitan countries. Similarly, local foods are "traditional," reflecting the inability to procure foreign foods and a background in the backward "bushy" parts of the country where people are not even familiar with modern foods.

But TV time helps sever these items from their temporal, historical baggage. The box of matches can now become merely "old-fashioned"; local food can become national cuisine, "roots" food, or ethnic cooking. Historical items can now represent the familiarity, security, and continuity of the past rather than the uncertainty and shame of being backward. Local customs are becoming symbols of identity and pride, of resistance and opposition, rather than badges of ignorance and isolation (Friedman 1995).

As many anthropologists have suggested, history is itself a cultural construction, and Western linear history is a particularly Western product that grew along with the colonial world system. The expansion that turned the rest of the world into "peoples without history" (Wolf 1982) gave the colonies a master narrative of progress and left the colonial subject with a historical clock that could only count cultural difference (Chakrabarty 1992: 59). But TV time seems to have the power to unfreeze clocks by extracting the present from the past and objectifying both. It allows time and events to be separated from each other and ordered into sequences that do not all lead inevitably in the same direction—toward the metropole. TV time frees the past from its colonial bondage and makes it fertile ground for political dispute in the present. A growing political awareness is one possible result.

But of course, satellite television is no informational panacea; behind its illusion of chaotic open choice are some very narrow channels of capital and control. Caldarola (1992) argues that satellite television coverage of the Gulf War deliberately manipulated the temporality of the medium, distorting the relationship between temporality and distance to further the war agenda. The immediacy of the medium, in his view, denied history, submerged the real in a fictional narrative, and reinforced the cultural and temporal distance between the global viewing audience and the country being bombed.

I do not think it is a coincidence that with the arrival of satellite television history has reemerged as an important topic of public interest and political debate in Belize. Each year since the early 1980s the September holiday commemorating the Battle of St. George's Cay in 1797 has been marked by intense and often acrimonious publications and speeches contesting the importance of the event. One party condemns the holiday as a colonial leftover of British imperialism, arguing that it celebrates a nonevent that gave legitimacy to the slaveholding aristocracy. The other party reveres the battle as an event that marked the beginnings of Belizean national identity, in the mutual solidarity of slave and master in bravely resisting a Spanish invasion. The historical details and their meaning are a common topic of public and private debate and conversation, and they became an important political issue in the 1984 elections, the same elections determined partially by the television issue. As it happened, the party of the revisionist and anticolonial version of the famous battle lost the election, and the traditional version of the story was officially reinstated (Judd 1989). But of course it has a new meaning now, a meaning extracted from the web of colonial time.

Most important, television affects Belizean ideas about time and cultural distance. This new medium has created a temporal watershed, a dramatic change in the nation that allows for new interpretations of the past. The beam from satellites provides a new image of the foreign "other" that furthers an emerging consensus about the content and identity of Belizean culture. Paradoxically, television imperialism may do more to create a national culture and national consciousness in Belize than forty years of nationalist politics and nine years of independence.

NOTES

This chapter is a revision of two previously published papers (Wilk 1993, 1994). Though the text has been substantially rearranged, little new material and few new references have been added, so it only partially reflects the substantial and exciting developments in the anthropology of television that emerged in the 1990s.

1. This remark has been widely quoted and misquoted since 1984. The opposition claimed it was an elitist position, an attempt to deny access to the media to the poor majority. It must be noted that at the time there was a serious danger that an army of more than ten thousand Guatemalan soldiers really would invade at any moment.

2. One editorial observed that a local football match was called off when a number of players stayed home to watch a Chicago Bulls basketball playoff game.

REFERENCES

Abu-Lughod, Lila. 1993. Finding a Place for Islam: Egyptian Television Serials and the National Interest. *Public Culture* 5 (3): 493–514.

Anonymous. 1981. The Video Invasion. *Brukdown Magazine* 5 (6): 15–21.

Barry, Jessica. 1984. The Belize Dilemma. *Media in Education and Development* (March): 11–13.

Belk, Russell, and Nan Zhou. 1987. Learning to Want Things. *Advances in Consumer Research* 14: 478–81.

Bolland, Nigel. 1987. United States Cultural Influence on Belize: Television and Education as "Vehicles of Import." *Caribbean Quarterly* 33 (3–4): 60–74.

Browne, Nick. 1984. The Political Economy of the Television (Super) Text. *Quarterly Review of Film Studies* (Summer): 174–82.

Burton, Jullianne, and Jean Franco. 1978. Culture and Imperialism. *Latin American Perspectives* 1: 2–12.

Caldarola, Victor. 1992. Time and the Television War. *Public Culture* 4 (2): 127–36.

Carey, James. 1989. *Communication as Culture: Essays on Media and Society*. Boston: Unwin Hyman.

Chakrabarty, Dipesh. 1992. The Death of History? Historical Consciousness and the Culture of Late Capitalism. *Public Culture* 4 (2): 47–66.

Evans-Pritchard, E. E. 1940. *The Nuer*. New York: Oxford University Press.

Everitt, J. C. 1987. The Torch Is Passed: Neocolonialism in Belize. *Caribbean Quarterly* 33 (3–4): 42–59.

Ewens, Debbe. ca. 1982. Television Hits Belize. *Focus*. Belize City: Caribbean Publishers.

Fabian, Johannes. 1983. *Time and the Other*. New York: Columbia University Press.

Friedman, Jonathan. 1995. *Cultural Identity and Global Process*. London: Sage.

Gillespie, Marie. 1995. *Television, Ethnicity, and Cultural Change*. London: Routledge.

Ginsburg, Faye. 1993. Aboriginal Media and the Australian Imaginary. *Public Culture* 5 (3): 557–78.

Hareven, Tamara. 1982. *Family Time and Industrial Time*. Cambridge, England: Cambridge University Press.

Judd, Karen. 1989. Who Will Define Us? Creole History and Identity in Belize. Paper presented at the annual meeting of the American Anthropological Association, Washington, D.C.

Kent, Susan. 1985. The Effects of Television Viewing: A Cross-Cultural Perspective. *Current Anthropology* 26 (1): 121–26.

Kottak, Conrad. 1990. *Prime Time Society*. Belmont, Calif.: Wadsworth.

Lee, Wei-Na. 1989. The Mass-Mediated Realities of Three Cultural Groups. *Advances in Consumer Research* 16: 771–78.

Lent, John. 1989. Country of No Return: Belize since Television. *Belizean Studies* 17 (1): 14–36.

Lull, James, ed. 1988. *World Families Watch Television*. Beverly Hills, Calif.: Sage.

Lutz, Catherine, and Jane Collins. 1993. *Reading National Geographic*. Chicago: University of Chicago Press.

Mahan, Elizabeth. 1990. Communications, Culture and the State in Latin America. *Journal of Interamerican Studies and World Affairs* 32: 146–54.

Martin-Barbero, Jesus. 1988. Communication from Culture: The Crisis of the National and the Emergence of the Popular. *Media, Culture and Society* 10: 447–65.

Michaels, Eric. 1988. Hollywood Iconography: A Warlpiri Reading. In *Television and*

Its Audience: International Research Perspectives, edited by Phillip Drummond and Richard Patterson, pp. 109–24. London: British Film Institute.

Nordenstreng, K., and T. Varis. 1974. *Television Traffic: A One-way Street?* Paris: UNESCO.

Oliveira, Omar. 1986. Satellite Television and Dependency: An Empirical Approach. *Gazette* 38: 127–45.

Ossman, Susan. 1994. *Picturing Casablanca: Portraits of Power in a Modern City.* Berkeley: University of California Press.

Petch, T. 1987. Television and Video Ownership in Belize. *Belizean Studies* 15 (1): 12–14.

———. 1988. Belize. In *Video World-Wide,* edited by Manuel Alvarado, pp. 311–21. London: John Libbey and UNESCO.

Roser, Connie, Leslie Snyder, and Steven Chaffee. 1986. Belize Release Me Go: The Impact of U.S. Mass Media on Emigration in Belize. *Belizean Studies* 14 (3): 1–30.

Sangari, Kumkum. 1987. The Politics of the Possible. *Cultural Critique* (Fall): 157–86.

Schiller, Herbert. 1976. *Communication and Cultural Domination.* New York: International Arts and Sciences Press.

Snyder, Leslie, Connie Roser, and Steven Chaffee. 1991. Foreign Media and the Desire to Emigrate from Belize. *Journal of Communication* 41 (1): 117–32.

Thompson, E. P. 1967. Time, Work-Discipline, and Industrial Capitalism. *Past and Present* 38: 56–68.

Westlake, Donald. 1982. The Box Rebellion. *Harper's* (July): 22–26.

Wilk, Richard. 1990. Consumer Goods as Dialogue about Development. *Culture and History* 7: 79–100.

———. 1993. "It's Destroying a Whole Generation": Television and Moral Discourse in Belize. *Visual Anthropology* 5: 229–44.

———. 1994. Colonial Time and TV Time. *Visual Anthropology Review* 10 (1): 94–105.

———. 1995. Learning to Be Local in Belize: Global Systems of Common Difference. In *Worlds Apart: Modernity through the Prism of the Local,* edited by Daniel Miller, pp. 110–33. New York: Routledge.

Williams, Raymond. 1974. *Television: Technology and Cultural Form.* New York: Schocken.

Wolf, Eric. 1982. *Europe and the People without History.* Berkeley: University of California Press.

III

Transnational Circuits

Photomontage with Indian film star, 1980, by Omar Said Bakor, Lamu, Kenya. (Courtesy Omar Said Bakor. From the collection of Heike Behrend. Originally published in *Snap Me One!: Studiofotografen in Afrika* [1998], edited by Tobias Wendl and Heike Behrend [Munich: Prestel]).

9

Mass Media and Transnational Subjectivity in Shanghai

Notes on (Re)Cosmopolitanism in a Chinese Metropolis

Mayfair Mei-hui Yang

In thinking about the history of the Roman Empire, Marshall McLuhan noted that writing and paved roads brought about "the alteration of social groupings, and the formation of new communities" (McLuhan 1994: 90). They enabled the formation of an empire that broke down the old Greek city-states and feudal realms in favor of centralized control at a distance. A similar process can be seen in the history of the Chinese empire, where writing enabled the bureaucracy to hold together diverse ethnic and linguistic groupings. However, it is with modernity and its new mass media that local and kinship identities come to be radically dissolved by a more powerful national space of identity. Anthony Giddens has noted that an important feature of modernity is the "disembedding of social systems" or the "'lifting out' of social relations from local contexts of interaction and their restructuring across infinite spans of time-space" (1990: 21). In twentieth-century China, the mass media's "disembedding" operations have constituted, first, a new national community, and then a powerful state subjectivity. This essay is an initial inquiry into a *third* disembedding process: the reemergence of a transnational Chinese global media public.

The mass media are vehicles for imagining not only the nation, as elaborated by Benedict Anderson (1991), but also the larger space beyond the national borders.[1] Increasing transnational electronic linkages "all presage a delocalized, potentially nomadic future" (Friedland 1994: 15), which can offer postmodern challenges to state modernity (M. M. Yang 1999a). In post-Mao China, what can be discerned is a process in which the modern mass media, which had been (and continue to be) a central constitutive force for state projects of modernity and the nation-state, have now also begun to construct a Chinese transnational imaginary world order.

Because media provide ways for audiences to traverse great distances without physically moving from local sites, they are crucial components of transnationalism. In China in the 1980s and 1990s, the media increasingly enabled national subjects to inhabit transspatial and transtemporal imaginaries that dissolve the fixity and boundedness of historical nationhood and state territoriality. What is occurring via the mass media in China today is no longer the simple picture of a Third World culture "locked in a life-and-death struggle with first-world cultural imperialism" (Jameson 1987: 68), but a more complex variegated process of eager accommodation, appropriation, and resistance to foreign cultures. This is now a culture more confidently and creatively constructing a "third space" (Bhabha 1994) of transnational Chinese identity through interaction with Hong Kong and Taiwanese mass culture. From a nationalist anticolonial culture, what is now being created is a Chinese "traveling culture" that reaches out around the globe (Clifford 1992). Not only are Chinese migrating to faraway lands and experiencing cultural dislocations in new places, but back in the homeland they are experiencing a similar displacement. People in imaginary travel increasingly look outward and participate via mass media in what is going on with their fellow nationals in other parts of the world. This essay documents another reaction to colonialism besides nationalism, the increasing cosmopolitanism of the homeland.[2]

THE SPATIALIZATION OF NATIONAL AND STATE SUBJECTS

Too often in Western academic discourse, scholars use "nation" and "state" interchangeably. Two exceptions are Arjun Appadurai (1990, 1996), who argues that diaspora populations around the world comprise emerging "postnations" that deterritorialize states, and Katherine Verdery (1994), who has shown that after the collapse of a super-state such as the Soviet Union, (re)emergent ethnic nationalist imaginaries (whose subjects are dispersed among the eastern European states) seek to define and bolster themselves territorially with new and separate state apparatuses. My own effort to distinguish between nation and state stems from a different historical situation and a different set of political and theoretical concerns. Rather than thinking of China as a nation in search of a state, I believe that we need to examine how the powerful Chinese state apparatus of the twentieth century came to "overcode" itself onto the nation (Deleuze and Guattari 1983), and how a reemergent nation or alternative community has now begun to "decode" or elude the state.

In China's transition from a traditional dynastic order to a modern nation-state, the centripetal and hierarchical social realm, whose borders were hazy and indistinct, was "flattened" into a novel social space that is defined by horizontal linkages of comradeship inside and by distinct outer borders (Anderson 1991: 15; Foster 1991: 253; Chun 1994). In the first three decades of the twentieth century, through the print medium, the urban reading public was exposed to the literature and culture of the West and Japan (Chow 1960) and came to share a growing alarm at China's comparative poverty, "ignorance," and "backwardness." At the same time, print also fanned the growing nationalist outrage at the imperialism of these same countries. The task of "saving the nation" (*jiuguo*) in the Darwinian struggle for existence between nations became a rallying cry that interpellated patriotic subjects into the project of making the Chinese nation "prosperous and strong" (*fuqiang*) (Althusser 1971). There is a historical significance to the fact that China's opening to the world was forced and its entrance into the world of nations was not on equal terms. China's encounter with global forces was disastrous for the country's cultural self-esteem, and out of this was born nationalism. The violations of the empire's territorial space, first by Western powers in the Opium Wars and Treaty Port systems of the mid-nineteenth century, and then in the Japanese seizure of Shandong in 1914, the annexation of Manchuria, and the invasion of eastern China in 1937, induced this traumatized new nation-state to close its doors for the first three decades after the Communist Revolution of 1949. There followed the tight sealing of state borders. Outside contact was limited to government exchanges with the Soviet bloc until 1960 and with the nonaligned Third World. Foreign visitors and returning overseas Chinese were relatively rare, as were Chinese emigrants. Few foreign films were shown; reading foreign literature was also frowned upon as a submission to bourgeois culture; even the exchange of letters with people in foreign countries was severely curtailed. During the Cultural Revolution it was politically dangerous to have overseas connections (*haiwai guanxi*) in one's family or personal past, and those who tried to flee across the borders in southern China were often executed as traitors (*pantu*).

By the mid-1950s, all private publishing firms, newspaper companies, radio stations, and film companies had come under centralized state administration, so all the paths and networks of print and electronic media led to Beijing. The Central People's Broadcasting Station was established in Beijing in December 1949. All provincial, municipal, and local radio stations were required to transmit news, commentary, and political programs in the national language, Mandarin (Chang 1989: 155). Film in the Maoist era can be described in Walter Benjamin's terms as both the politicization of art and the aestheticization of politics (1969: 242), but the former was more dominant than the latter because aesthetic standards were often deemphasized (Clark 1984). During the Cultural Revolution, audiences across the country were restricted to a repertoire of nine revolutionary operas (*yangbanxi*). In Maoist China, the mass media helped create a homogeneity of culture that played down regional identities, promoted the voice of the central government in Beijing in Mandarin, and reiterated the same state messages in all media, whether radio, newspapers, or film.

Thus, along with the centralization of all media in the Maoist era, the national identity that was first constructed by print capitalism in the early twentieth century came to coincide with the contours and logic of the state.

MASS MEDIA DEVELOPMENT IN POST-MAO SHANGHAI

In the post-Mao era there has been an explosion in the development of mass media. If the Maoist period can be described as a period in which the mass media sought to level and homogenize the Chinese public, the post-Mao period can be said to have brought about the pluralization, differentiation, and stratification of media publics according to class, educational level, region, locality, gender, occupation, and leisure interests, fragmenting the state's mass public.

These developments are well illustrated in Shanghai, a former media capital whose cosmopolitan and commercial culture was severely curtailed by the Revolution and Maoist policies.[3] In Shanghai, radio culture was transformed with the establishment of the new Eastern Broadcast Station (*Dongfang Guangbotai,* DFBS) in January 1993, which quickly drew listeners away from the more official *(guanfang)* Shanghai Broadcast Station. When I first heard this station's broadcasts in June 1993, I could not believe that I was in China. The Chinese media culture I was familiar with in the 1980s and elsewhere in the country still featured broadcasters with solemn voices speaking standard Mandarin dialect about portentous affairs of state. On DFBS, in contrast, the voice and style were soft, fast-paced, and chatty, resembling those of the Taiwan media culture. Programming had switched from covering only Beijing news to market news and international and Shanghai local news; there were interviews with Taiwanese, Hong Kong, and domestic stars of the film and popular music scene; and several times a day the stock market quotes were read. In addition, all DFBS programming was live, and the station solicited call-in comments and opinions from its listeners. All day long, the voices of ordinary people talking about their everyday problems and dreams, in Shanghainese accents, filled the air (Bao 1993). When I visited someone's home or got into a taxi, eight times out of ten this station was playing in the background. A further novelty was that several late-night programs brought issues from the private sphere—marriage and romance, and the hitherto unmentionable topic of sexual life—to the public arena of radio.

At the Shanghai Film Studio, the career of Xie Jin, its most well known and successful director, is also emblematic of the change. His films had always followed the changing Communist Party policies and adapted to the political vicissitudes of the country. But in 1987, in *The Last Aristocracy (Zuihou de guizu),* Xie departed from politics for the first time and took on the new theme of personal identity and cultural displacement in a foreign land. The film expresses both the territorial restlessness and the longing for home experienced by a cosmopolitan Chinese woman whose identity is unmoored from her homeland. She flees war-torn Shanghai to study in the United States. Prevented from returning home because of the Communist victory, she is cast adrift in that foreign land to lead a lonely and alienated life. Nostalgia for Old Shanghai is evident not only in the 1940s setting, but also in the fact that the story is based on a novel of the same title by the Taiwanese ex-mainlander Kenneth Pai (Bai Xianyong), who now resides in Santa Barbara. The film was shot on location in the United States and Venice, Italy, exemplifying the growing transnational forays of Chinese media production. This combination of reconnecting with Old Shanghai, with Taiwan, and with the overseas world encapsulates the transformation of the imaginary taking place in Shanghai today.

NEW TECHNOLOGICAL MEDIA AND PUBLICS

Two significant social changes have accompanied the widespread adoption of new media forms in the post-Mao era such as audiotapes, telephone, television, VHS videotapes, audio compact discs (CDs), video compact discs (VCDs), digital video discs (DVDs) and the Internet. First, in their use and reception they have greatly expanded the private, personal, and familial spheres. In the Maoist era, telephones were found mainly in work units, to be used in a public context for public business. By 1995, of the 39 million telephones in China (up from 6.26 million in 1985), 70 percent were in residences (*China News Digest*, May 17, 1995). Urban neighborhood phone stands and booths multiplied in the early 1990s, making it easy to transact personal business and weave *guanxi* or personal networks independent of state administrative organizations. By 2000, cell phones *(dageda)* had become a ubiquitous personal accessory on the streets of Shanghai, and the Ministry of Information announced that, at the current growth rate of 20 percent a year, the Chinese telecommunication network would become the second largest in the world in two years and the largest by 2005 (*China News Digest*, December 7, 2000).

Whereas in the Maoist era information usually came from a centralized source (official newspapers and editorials, state documents [*wenjian*], or the radio), new media technologies such as the telephone, cassette recorder, CDs, videotapes and VCRs, and VCDs tend to decentralize information sources. Information flows through personal relationships as these media are loaned and circulated via *guanxi* networks. In the Maoist era, state directives and didactic art were usually received in collective contexts: state pronouncements were transmitted and newspaper editorials were often read in political study group sessions at the work unit; film-going was often organized as a work unit outing by labor unions; revolutionary operas were viewed by the whole community in local theaters. Television viewing now, however, takes place in the private sphere of family, neighbors, and friends. Whereas in the public state-monitored context one had to show one's acceptance of what was received from the state, in the private context of reception one could also debate, mock, or reject the messages with one's family and friends, thus reducing the capacity for state media to sustain state subjects.

Another significance of these new media is that they have brought about increasing transnational connections for ordinary people. In the late 1970s and early 1980s when cassette recorders and tapes first became widespread, they were primarily used to listen to music and to practice a foreign language such as English. Anyone wishing to listen to the sweet crooning of Taiwan's popular female singer Deng Lijun had to have access to a cassette recorder because her songs were not played on the official radio stations (Gold 1993: 909). Now that telephone service has been established with virtually all countries of the world, those with relatives and friends abroad can be constantly connected with life overseas.

The television documentary *Their Home Is in Shanghai (Jia zai Shanghai)* illustrates well the role of the media in keeping people connected to their kin or fellow Chinese nationals in foreign lands. When it first aired in early 1994, its gripping portrayal of the lives of Shanghai migrants in Tokyo emptied the streets in Shanghai as viewers gathered in front of televisions (Guo 1994: 48). Shot on location in Tokyo by a Shanghai Television Station crew led by a woman filmmaker, Wang Xiaoping, mainly in Shanghainese dialect, it made documentary more vivid and fascinating than fiction. Part III includes a poignant interview with a Shanghainese man who lives by himself in a cramped apartment and works three jobs a day to send money to his family back in Shanghai. He sits on the floor watching his daughter (whom he has not seen for four years) on a videotape the camera crew has brought from Shanghai. He tells the interviewer that he calls home once a week.

Beginning around 1995, VHS videotapes were quickly replaced by video compact discs as the medium of choice for viewing foreign, Hong Kong—Taiwan *(Gangtai)*, and 1930s Chinese feature films. Borrowing from Japanese technology, several Chinese manufacturers soon produced VCD players that cost only about 1,000 yuan ($120) in 1998, making them widely affordable for middle-class Shanghai families. An illegal industry producing VCDs of pirated foreign films was spawned in Guangdong Province in the mid-1990s, and in big cities such as Shanghai pirated VCDs costing only 8–12 yuan ($1.00) each were commonly available on certain side streets.[4] Thus VCD technology greatly increased the availability and widened the selection of foreign films and old pre- and early revolutionary films for Shanghai residents.

The final form of connection is the Internet. Whereas in China in 1996 there were only an estimated 150,000 Internet users (Barme and Sang 1997: 140), at a press conference in December 2000 the Ministry of Information estimated that there were 16.9 million Internet subscribers (*China News Digest,* December 7, 2000). According to Scott Savitt, editor of *Beijing Scene,* and China scholar Geremie Barme (personal communication), this figure is conservative, because many e-mail accounts are shared by several users to cut subscription costs, and many local telephone companies in urban areas offer free Internet service. On Sina.com, a popular national web browser, news about the protracted U.S. presidential elections of 2000 was amazingly detailed and up-to-date.

THE POST-MAO TRANSNATIONAL DISEMBEDDING OF CULTURE

The post-Mao era can be seen as a period in which a decoupling of nation from state is taking place and Chinese identity is becoming defined culturally rather than in terms of the state. Although capitalism has brought back many disturbing tendencies to a state socialist society, such as wide income disparities, prostitution and child labor, and government corruption, it has also started the transnationalization of Chinese identity out of the confines of the state. What has been developing in urban China, and especially in cities along the eastern seaboard such as Shanghai, is a fascination with and hunger to learn about the world outside the state borders. The new mass media both cater to and create this interest and longing for the outside world, especially through the media's linkages with the global market economy. The new Oriental Television Station (*Dongfang dianshitai*) in Shanghai is an example of this change: its revenues come from advertising, and it caters more to popular taste than the official government station does. No longer relying on state subsidies, the media are becoming increasingly independent of the state and dependent on the market.

In this process of the commodification of state media, we can see the clash of two often incompatible logics. The Maoist state logic of power was a form of control that worked through a state monopoly of distribution and the fixing of people, goods, and information in a strictly defined space. Whereas information in Maoist society was dispersed according to rank and degree of political reliability (and level of state secrecy), once information becomes a commodity, it has to reach as many people as possible in order to produce profits. Whereas the Maoist state prohibited or constrained spatial movement, capitalism is a deterritorializing culture whose power depends on inciting encounters such as that between "flows of convertible wealth owned by capitalists and a flow of workers possessing nothing more than their labor capacity" (Deleuze and Guattari 1983: 140)—flows of desire that are unleashed by a consumer economy and capitalist media. At this juncture, moments of conflict between these two logics are evident because capitalist and state logic have not yet been melded into a fully shared common logic of *controlled flows* or a system of *flowing controls.*

There are countless examples of this tension between state and capital in the cultural realm. Until 1995 the state limited the number of foreign (including Hong Kong and Taiwan) films imported into the country to sixty films per year chosen by the state film distribution bureaucracy. In the early 1990s there developed a widespread craving for American Oscar-winning films, which were seldom shown in Chinese theaters. Video technology solved the problem through the illegal private circulation of videotapes, most of which were smuggled in from Hong Kong or by Chinese returning from overseas. Although it was illegal to bring in videotaped programs from abroad, airport customs inspections were often lax. Often the smuggled videos were barely viewable, being second- and third-generation copies that had already been viewed countless times before. College students were perhaps the biggest audience for American films, and student entrepreneurs acquired videos and laser discs through various means and showed them in campus theaters on large video screens for four yuan a person. Sometimes there were no subtitles, only a translator at the front of the theater. Some of the films were shot on video directly in a Hong Kong cinema: the sound quality was bad, and once in a while one could even see the heads of the Hong Kong audience on the screen or hear their laughter.

Television brought the greatest exposure to the outside world and to the "culture industries" of Asia, the West, and other places. Given that the Chinese urban television audience was formed only in the first half of the 1980s and the rural audience in the second half (Zhang 1992), the growth of the television industry since then is astounding. Already in 1986, 95 percent of all urban families owned at least one television set (Lull 1991: 23). Television programs were imported from Taiwan, Hong Kong, the United States, and Japan (in that order in the mid-1990s); those programs, broadcasts of transnational sports and competitions, and guided television tours of foreign cities all respond to a keen appetite on the part of the Chinese audience. In the mid-1990s, many people told me that when a domestically produced show *(guochanpian)* comes on screen, they or their children immediately change the channel or turn off the television without bothering to find out what it is about. Zhou Yigong, a division head at one of the two Shanghai TV stations informed me that the station often receives directives from the Municipal Party Propaganda Department to decrease its advertising for songs and TV shows from Hong Kong and Taiwan and to avoid showing them during prime time *(huangjing shijian)*.

The Shanghai audience's interest in the world outside China finds economic expression and allies in the growing advertising industry and in the business interests that it represents, both at home and abroad. In addition to pressures from the government, Zhou's television station must respond to those who buy commercial time on its shows. In the mid-1990s businesses refused to buy ad time on domestically produced shows. "They don't even bother to check out the show to see if it's any good, they just don't want to have anything to with it," he said. Perhaps domestic films were not welcome by most viewers because people no longer wished to plug themselves into the state imaginary; instead they wished to cast their imagination outward. Other reasons people gave me were the poor quality of the technical production, the plot and narrative structure, and the stilted acting.

In pursuit of advertising patrons, the station has ignored a long-standing state regulation limiting imported TV series to two per year. It actually shows about twenty per year, Zhou said. The authorities usually do not make an issue of this. Thus advertising has exerted a powerful influence on television programming, decreasing officially sanctioned, domestically produced didactic and political drama in favor of foreign and overseas Chinese products, as well as a new generation of innovative domestic dramas and soap operas. These latter shows constitute an exception to advertisers' usual reluctance to buy commercial time on domestic programs. Popular among viewers are shows made by Wang Shuo, a prolific writer who appeals to intellectuals and mass audiences alike, and by TV director Feng Xiaogang at the Beijing Television Production Center, which produced the very popular *Yearning* (*Ke Wang*, 1990), China's first television soap opera to be shot indoors on a studio set (Zha 1995; Rofel 1994). *Stories from the Editing Department* (*Bianjibu de gushi*, 1992) and *A Beijing Native in New York* (*Beijingren zai Niuyue*, 1993) were subsequent successes by the same producers.

Another point of contention between the public and the state was the issue of personal satellite television dishes. These receive programs from Hong Kong, Taiwan, and Japan, and on more powerful receivers from the United States, Russia, and Europe (Yang 2001). Although state regulations prohibited personal satellite dishes, in the early 1990s many private Shanghai homes were equipped with them, most of them made in China by rural factories. Only work units with extensive international business were allowed to install the dishes (Anonymous 1993). The Public Security mounted periodic raids in Shanghai to confiscate private dishes, but the dishes always went back up and the police then chose to ignore them.

SUBJECTIVE MOBILITY: IDENTIFYING WITH OVERSEAS CHINESE OTHERS

Through the mass media of a growing consumer culture, the space of the state is becoming disembedded by transnational spaces of orientation. At least two mechanisms of subjective spatial mobility can be discerned operating in the mass media that can construct a transnational Chinese imaginary. First, there is the mainland identification with roles played by Taiwan and Hong Kong stars in films, TV shows, and popular songs. In the Maoist era, the "absent others" were the voice of the state and its symbolic leaders in Beijing. In the current commercialized period, party leaders are being replaced in popular culture by new icons of identification: pop singers and film stars often located outside the national borders in Taiwan, Hong Kong, and beyond. Second, there is the transnational Chinese imaginary at play in the identification of the audience with a mainland character who goes to foreign lands.

Popular Music and a Pan-Chinese Identity

Just as most of the capital flowing into China in the past two decades is overseas Chinese, not American, so the impact of American media cannot compare with the influence of Hong Kong and Taiwan popular culture. One most vivid indication of this cultural invasion can be found in the pop songs that young people croon to and the popularity of karaoke singing. Hong Kong and Taiwan popular cultures have gained a firm foothold on the mainland: visiting singers present concerts to packed halls filled with adoring fans who pay high prices for their tickets (Zhen 1992; Gold 1993); 16- and 17-year-old girls want to embrace and kneel in the footsteps of such male idols as Tong Ange and Tang Yongling. The longing to be a star oneself can be temporarily satisfied using the imported karaoke audiovisual systems now found in work units, schools, restaurants, and karaoke bars. Music stores sell this music on cassettes and CDs. Hong Kong songs are sung in Cantonese by young Shanghainese whose point of comparison in their urban imaginaries these days is not Beijing but Hong Kong.

A radio program host in his thirties who introduces Anglo-American rock music explained to me the appeal of Hong Kong–Taiwan pop music in Shanghai: "It represents the modern for young people, and that is why it has replaced folk music [*mingge*]," which dominated the airwaves during most of the 1980s. Chinese folk music is also about love between man and woman, and the lyrics also depict scenes of nature, but "there is something old-fashioned about it, it's for middle-aged and old people, it feels rural and quaint now. In contrast, Hong Kong and Taiwan pop feel new, advanced, and urban." It represents what young people aspire to, a faster-paced, more prosperous and sophisticated life they think exists outside the borders of the mainland.

In watching Hong Kong and Taiwan shows, in listening to and singing their songs, the mainland mass media audience is undergoing four processes simultaneously: (1) identification with Hong Kong and Taiwan people; (2) internalization of another kind of Chinese culture not so tied in with a statist imaginary; (3) differentiation of gender in identification and performance; and (4) insertion into a discourse of love and sexuality. In these four processes, karaoke singing has a deep impact because it involves the active performance and oral and bodily enactment of a different way to be Chinese, where state identity diminishes in importance and female and male genders become salient categories. It is through repeated performances that gender and national identity are constructed and reconstructed. To be sure, karaoke singing in China may be putting into place a new regime of normalized heterosexual male and female objects of imitation, but it is also instituting different ways of being Chinese. The subjectivities produced by karaoke singing and those produced by the Maoist loyalty dance are vastly different. Whereas Maoist subjectivity sought to merge the self with the body of the state and its embodiment, Mao's body, karaoke places the subject in a narcissistic dynamic between self and the love object through which it learns to desire, and whose desire it needs, to fulfill and strengthen the fragile self (see M. M. Yang 1994c). This other through which the self yearns to be completed is no longer the larger and powerful collective "I" of the nation, but a Chinese cultural other of Taiwan or Hong Kong who has a gender.

The longing to be reunited with or merged with the Chinese other outside the borders of the Chinese state is given full expression in a popular song of the 1990s, "My 1997 Hong Kong," written and sung by Ai Jing, a young mainland female singer who is also popular in Taiwan and Hong Kong. I translate some excerpts:

> The year I was 17, I left my hometown Shenyang,
> Because I felt that the place didn't fulfill my dreams, . . .
> I sang from Beijing to Shanghai,
> And from Shanghai I sang to the South that I had dreamed of.
> My stay in Guangzhou was rather long,
> Because my "other," he is in Hong Kong.
> When will we have Hong Kong?
> When will we know what Hong Kong people are like?
> My boyfriend can come to visit Shenyang,
> But I can't go to Hong Kong.
> Hong Kong, oh that Hong Kong!
> I should have gone out into the world to broaden myself when
>   I was young, . . .
> Let me go to that dazzling world,
> Give me that big red official seal of approval to go abroad.
> 1997! May that year arrive quickly! . . .
> Then I can go with him to the night markets.
> 1997! May that year arrive quickly! . . .
> Then I can go to Hong Kong! . . .
>   (AI JING *1993*)

This song often made Hong Kong Chinese anxious because it reminded them that in 1997 China would become Hong Kong's new master. However, mainland Chinese were impatient for the day when Hong Kong's dazzle, wealth, and cosmopolitanism would become accessible to them. In contrast with mainland official discourse about 1997, which stressed Hong Kong's "return to the embrace of the Motherland" *(huidao zuguo de huaibao),* the song expresses a yearning to break free from the Motherland, to cross the state borders that forbid another way of being Chinese, although this alternative is to become a consuming Chinese. Along with the strengthening of the desiring "I," what emerges is a culture of desiring, consuming individuals yearning to be fulfilled.

The incursions of Hong Kong–Taiwan popular culture, called *gangtai wenhua* (Gold 1993), into mainland state culture also show that it is no longer adequate for critical theory to identify capitalism only as a Western force. What post-Mao China is encountering is mainly the regional or transnational ethnic capitalism of overseas Chinese in Hong Kong, Taiwan, and Southeast Asia.[5] Increasingly the West is no longer the only, or the primary, outside influence in local cultures, as Leo Ching's (1994) work on the importance of Japanese mass culture in Taiwan, and Brian Larkin's (1997) study of Indian and Hong Kong film popularity in Nigeria both show. China is being drawn into a regional or ethnic Chinese capitalist mode of power with its media culture of hybridized consumer modernity. At the beginning of the twenty-first century, China is mainly a receiver or "victim" of this overseas Chinese cultural imperialism; however, as the century continues these roles and cultural flows will likely be reversed.[6]

Following Mobile Chinese Subjects in Other Lands

The second mechanism for constructing a new transnational identity is the imagining of a mobile Chinese identity moving through foreign lands. This is where the media audience follows mainland Chinese characters experiencing life in an alien culture. The "leave the country fever" *(chuguore)* reached a peak after the Tiananmen tragedy of 1989. The phenomenon of urban Chinese going abroad to live, whether as students and scholars, emigrés, laborers, or entrepreneurs, has been satirically called "joining a brigade overseas" *(yang chadui)*. This expression conjures up the image of city people in the Cultural Revolution going down to the harsh life of physical labor on a production brigade in the countryside. Like their predecessors in the Cultural Revolution, today's Chinese are going to alien lands where they must struggle to survive through their own labor and wits. In the popular television documentary *Their Home Is in Shanghai* discussed earlier, the Shanghai audience heard the Shanghainese laborer express his longing for home, which the interviewers and program hosts interpreted as a nationalist sentiment. However, the Shanghainese dialect he spoke foregrounded his Shanghainese identity over his national identity. In a more subtle way, they also portrayed his displacement from the confines and strictures of the Chinese nation-state and the contradictory experience of being at once subject to the pressures of work in a competitive capitalist society like Japan and also free from the habitus of state subjects.

In recent years bookstores in Chinese cities have been selling a new genre of semiautobiographical and semifictional writing: people's accounts and stories about the experience of living in the United States and Japan. Theater, film, and television productions have also taken up these themes: a popular 1999 release shot in Los Angeles and Monterey Park, *Be There or Be Square (Bujian busan)*, is about a Beijing man and woman who try out various schemes in their effort to make a living in the United States.

One of the best-known books in this genre was *A Beijing Native in New York*, written by Cao Weilin, which was made into the first television drama series shot entirely on location in New York City. This popular show aired in China in October of 1993 and was made by the Beijing Television Production Center. It tells the story of Wang Qiming, a cello player in the Beijing Symphony who goes with his wife, Guo Yan, to New York City. There they do not receive the help of their relatives and have to start life at the bottom of American society, he as a Chinese restaurant dishwasher, she as a seamstress in a sweatshop owned by an ambitious American named David McCarthy. In his uphill climb to become a wealthy sweatshop owner himself, Wang Qiming employs some ruthless tactics, loses his wife to McCarthy, and joins up with his employer, A Chun, an astute, independent, single businesswoman from Taiwan.

On three trips to Shanghai in 1991–93, I conducted fieldwork among informal discussion groups called "film criticism among the masses" *(qunzhong yinping)*. These informal groups were set up in state work units (factories, offices, schools, etc.) in the 1950s with a view to fostering mass participation in public culture. Whereas in the 1950s through the 1970s "participation" was mainly understood by the organizers as a way to help the masses digest the state didactic messages encoded in Chinese films, by the 1980s and 1990s discussions took on a more lively character and critical ethos, expressing the increasing nonstate outlooks available in society (see also M. M. Yang 1994a). The twenty members of the Shanghai Textile Bureau Workers' Film Criticism Group with whom I discussed this series convey how this show has engendered multiple effects, including: transnationalizing the audience; tapping into feelings of unease and suspicion with capitalism; giving vent to yearnings for a better life in the United States; disseminating a new model of independent womanhood that is sensual and hard-edged at the same time; and providing a forum to critique state policies.

Everyone in the film discussion group agreed this was a popular series, and people were very interested in seeing what American streets and building interiors looked like. They were curious about the life of Chinese abroad, especially because many of them had relatives or friends abroad. Five themes emerged in the discussion. First, a middle-aged man said that a feature of this film is international exchange. For him, America is a place that is not xenophobic *(paiwai)*, where everyone is treated equally, and where different races and cultures are engaged in competition. The lives of Chinese in

America are not ones of luxury, he said, for they must work hard in order to get anywhere. Just as he was learning about America, he thought Americans could also learn about life in China from watching a hypothetical show called "An American in Beijing" or "An American in Shanghai." What can be detected in this man's statement is a subjectivity traversing great distances and a resulting change of perspective. Through television, this man could imagine himself in another land observing people there; he could even reverse the process and imagine himself as an American coming to China. Indeed, in a popular magazine discussion of the program, one reviewer quoted the old Chinese adage, "Not knowing the real nature of Mt. Lushan is due to one's living in its midst" *(bushi Lushan zheng mianmu, zhi yuan shen zai cishan zhong)*, to say that the show enabled Chinese to come to a new understanding of their own country by seeing it from a new vantage point (R. Yang 1993:12).

A second theme was that of losing one's status, privileges, and support network, things that give one an identity and a social role at home, and being propelled into a different status in America where everyone starts out equal and only some rise to the top through their own efforts. One man said that the show smashed not only the Chinese fantasy that one could pick up gold on the streets in America, but also the fantasy that one could rely on one's relatives abroad. Viewers of the show see the stripping away of familiar ways of being Chinese, such as relying on prescribed social status and relatives. Through imagining these different ways of being Chinese abroad, the possibility is opened up for a reconstructing of both subject and society at home. So, for example, one man said that Chinese should learn to be more self-sufficient and called for a different way to raise children so that they would not rely on their parents.

A third theme was the ferociousness of capitalism and its cutthroat competition in which "big fish eat little fish." A middle-aged man repeated a refrain from the program's theme song: "America is neither heaven nor hell, it is a battleground." Several people commented on the intense competitiveness of American society. One factory worker in his thirties sympathized with Wang, the protagonist. "He won the economic battle, but lost his personal integrity. He became dehumanized in the struggle; his human nature became twisted *[niuqu]*." This showed how deeply Western culture has penetrated Chinese culture, he thought. Why did Wang, a person from a culture over 2,000 years old, lose himself to a culture only 300 years old? Because he was shocked at finding out about the West's economic might. Sun consoled himself by projecting that the Chinese market economy would not be as twisted and dehumanizing as the United States. What was perhaps being worked out here among these viewers was the anxiety and ambivalence of plunging into capitalism and the global society that it represents. There was the fear of being corrupted by alien outside forces, of losing one's self and identity. At the same time there was the feeling that this was the only way to go, that it was necessary to overcome one's scruples and hesitations and make the leap.

A fourth theme in the discussion concerned the female characters in the show. A Chun, the Taiwanese lover, and Guo Yan, the mainland wife, were compared by the discussion group. A Chun won the admiration of both men and women for her economic astuteness and her knowledge of the market and Western culture. As a soft-spoken traditional woman who could endure hardships, Guo Yan won the approbation of the male discussants, who thought she represented "Eastern beauty and virtue" *(dongfang meide)*. They considered A Chun to be very Americanized, and some believed that she had been like Guo Yan when she first arrived in the United States. The men thought that astute businesswomen like A Chun were good to have in a market economy, but they did not want her for a wife. Sun said that in China it is not common to find a woman like A Chun who is so successful in the market. He confessed that his worldview had still not completely turned around to fully accept her, although he admired her. "It's as though we have to tear off a layer of skin before we can completely turn around," he said. It would seem that the disturbing thing about capitalism is not only the cutthroat competition, but also the new kind of independent women like A Chun it demanded.

In separate discussions with women, I found that women generally liked the character of A Chun. They admired her independence, her no-nonsense toughness, and the way she managed to separate her economic relationship with Wang from their romantic relationship. However, one of the women said that she did not want to challenge the men openly about their preference for Guo Yan, the traditional wife, at a public forum, and that even though men and women are now equal, it was still not easy for women to speak out in public.

Finally, this television series also provided an opportunity for these film discussants to question the wisdom of past state policies that have caused so many people to want to leave China in the hopes of finding a better future. Referring to a well-known phenomenon, one man declared, "There is something deeply wrong when some Shanghai women want to escape abroad so much that they are even willing to become prostitutes in someone else's country in order to survive."

This discussion of *A Beijing Native in New York* may seem to many in the United States, both Americans and Chinese who have seen the show, to be discrepant with the pervasive allegory of big state rivalry and capitalist competition between China and the United States, personified by the characters Wang Qiming and David McCarthy. However, as Stuart Hall has shown, an audience's decoding of media messages often "does not constitute an 'immediate identity'" with the process of authorial encoding of the messages, for there is a "relative autonomy" in decoding due to "the structural differences of relation and position between broadcasters and audiences" (1980: 131). As recent audience reception studies show, textual criticism of media products does not get at the full range of their social effects because audiences selectively misread or read past the intentions of the producers (de Certeau 1984; Radway 1988; Ang 1990; M. M. Yang 1994a). What I discerned from this film discussion group in 1993 was not so much a tendency to identify with the Chinese state against the United States, but more an interest in exploring the possibilities of transnational mobility and displacement.

A Deterritorialized Chinese Subjectivity

We can detect in these two examples of a pop song and a television series a deterritorialized Chinese subjectivity that cannot be contained by the state apparatuses of either mainland China or Taiwan. What Homi Bhabha calls a "third space" of cultural hybridity has begun to spill out over the constrictive molds of a fixed-state spatialized Chinese identity and homogeneous national culture. This "third space" is the "intervention of the 'beyond' . . . [which] captures something of the estranging sense of the relocation of the home and the world—the unhomeliness—that is the condition of extra-territorial and cross-cultural initiations" (Bhabha 1994: 9). Whereas only a tiny proportion of people in Shanghai have been able to physically cross state boundaries and venture into the outside world, it is through the proliferating media that the masses now also occupy a "third space" of transnational encounters.[7] In this space, the lines between home and world, one's own nation-state and another country, Chinese and foreign, and socialism and capitalism get blurred through traveling identities.

For several years songs like "My 1997 Hong Kong" were heard on the airwaves of cities in the mainland, Taiwan, and Hong Kong; in addition, Chinese audiences are viewing an increasingly common set of programs, although they are separated by state boundaries. Even without satellites, this sharing of a common set of media products is developing across a large portion of the globe and creating a linked Chinese community of media audiences stretching from Shanghai and other parts of China to overseas Chinese in Southeast Asia and the United States.[8] These increasing overlaps and commonalities in programming being viewed by Chinese of various places make for the emergence of a transnational (read transstate) Chinese-language imagined community in the twenty-first century (Nonini 1995: 16; Lee 1993).

Because the media are caught up with the commercial promotion and celebration of material consumption, their detaching of subjects from the state is often at the price of what has been called the "distraction" of these liberated subjects from serious social reflection and critique (see Benjamin 1969: 240). However, in the present historical moment, despite the commercialism, there is something implicitly oppositional about the new media. Most intellectuals I spoke with in Shanghai adopted a pained expression when asked about the influx of overseas popular culture. They were disturbed by the sudden shift to the vulgar, the shallow, and the commercial. Lan Tian, a college professor, had his own explanation: "Mainland Chinese are like children who have been shut up at home for years. When finally you let them out, everything outside is good in their eyes." However, he also saw the potential in this imported culture for a challenge to state culture. This wave of another type of Chinese culture is a relief from the "linguistic violence" or "rape" *(yuyan qiangbao)* that people were subjected to before, he thought. Popular culture threatens both "official discursive power" *(guanfang huayu quanli)* and "central core culture" *(zhongxin wenhua)*; "money knows no center," he said, with some sarcasm.

Zhang Daoming, a writer in his late thirties, was even more affirming of Hong Kong–Taiwan popular culture. He wanted larger doses of it: "Let's have more of this 'cultural garbage' *[wenhua laji]*, so that it becomes a flood and disaster, then people will get sick of it. It will make people feel isolated and displaced so that they can throw off this great monolithic unity [of the nation] *[da yi tong]*." Zhang was much more willing for people to be trodden down by economics than by politics: "At least in karaoke pop songs, people are singing their individual hearts, not that of the state."

CONCLUSION

The recosmopolitanism of Shanghai is part of a countermovement of transnational cultural identity that deflects state messages to wander imaginatively across the globe. Transnational media have enabled the detaching of Chinese subjectivity from the state and its mobilization across imaginary space to link up with alternative Chinese subjectivities far away. Through the new mass media, those who have stayed in the country have started to undergo a change in subjectivity perhaps just as dramatic as those who have traveled abroad. However, even while transnational Chinese subjects have begun to displace state subjects, they immediately face the danger of getting trapped in new and different tentacles of power. In the transnational mass media "liberation" from state subjectivity we should not forget what Foucault (1980) realized about the early twentieth-century discourse of sexual liberation: that liberation is always a prelude to a new insertion into another mode of power.

NOTES

I wish to thank Lila Abu-Lughod, Aihwa Ong, Faye Ginsburg, Roger Rouse, and Everett Zhang for insightful suggestions on this essay. Thanks also to Don Nonini for his helpful comments and the idea for the title. This essay was first presented at a conference at Singapore National University in 1994, as well as at the Chicago Humanities Institute, University of Chicago, in 1996. It is reprinted: copyright 1997 from *Ungrounded Empires*, edited by Aihwa Ong and Don Nonini. Reproduced by permission of Routledge, Inc., part of The Taylor & Francis Group.

1. Anderson's work has also had an impact on studies of electronic media and national identity, such as recent works by feminist anthropologists who show how television and other electronic media are important means of constituting national identity through gender (see Mankekar 1993; Rofel 1994; Abu-Lughod 1993; Brownell 1999; M. M. Yang 1999a, 1999b).

2. I conducted fieldwork and interviews on recent developments in mass media and media publics in the post-Mao market economy during five and a half months in Shanghai in 1991–93 and 1998, among mass media professionals and intellectuals and among working-class "film and television criticism groups" (see M. M. Yang 1994a).

3. In the 1920s and 1930s, Shanghai was the most urban, industrial, and cosmopolitan city in all of Asia (Bergere 1981). This bustling metropolis saw the birth of a modern urban, commercial, and mass media culture that, despite its foreign influences, was nevertheless Chinese. Shanghai was home to China's main publishing companies, newspapers, and magazines. The city was also the cradle of a dynamic Chinese film industry in the 1920s and 1930s and had China's largest moviegoing audiences (Leyda 1972). Virtually all of the major film companies in the country were established there, and Shanghai films were distributed to other regions of the country and in Southeast Asia.

4. Lu Wei, filmmaker, Xian Film Studio, "The Social Effects of Copyright Piracy in CD's and VCD's in China," lecture in Chinese presented at University of California, Santa Barbara, November 19, 1998.

5. Since the 1980s, overseas Chinese economic investment in the mainland has increased dramatically (Harding 1993; Ong 1997; Ash and Kueh 1993). In 1990 Hong Kong surpassed Japan and the United States as the largest investor in China, and Taiwan became the second largest investor (Hsiao and So 1994: 2).

6. See Shih 1995 on the reception of mainland rock music in Taiwan.

7. Mike Featherstone's notion of "third cultures" is more narrowly defined, referring to the world of transnational professionals in architecture, advertising, film, global financial markets, international law, and other international agencies (1990: 6–8, 1992: 146). I include the transnational mass cultures created by mass media as well.

8. In the 1990s in the United States there were three Chinese-language satellite television stations: North American TV, a station airing programs from Taiwan and some mainland programs; Jade Channel/TVB, a Hong Kong channel; and the new Eastern Satellite TV, founded by mainland Chinese in Chicago and airing mainland shows (Qiu 1993; Sheng 1995; Hamilton 1995).

REFERENCES

Abu-Lughod, Lila. 1993. Finding a Place for Islam: Egyptian Television Serials and the National Interest. *Public Culture* 5 (3): 493–513.

Ai Jing. 1993. "Wode yijiujiuqi Xianggang" (My 1997 Hong Kong) (song distributed on cassette tape by Beijing Film Academy Sound Production and Distribution).

Althusser, Louis. 1971. Ideology and Ideological State Apparatuses. In *Lenin and Philosophy, and Other Essays*, pp. 123–73. Translated by Ben Brewster. London: New Left Books.

Anderson, Benedict. 1991. *Imagined Communities: Reflections on the Origins and Spread of Nationalism*. New York: Verso.

Ang, Ien. 1990. Culture and Communication: Towards an Ethnographic Critique of Media Consumption in the Transnational Media System. *European Journal of Communication* 5 (2–3): 239–60.

Anonymous. 1993. Guanyu weixin dianshi dimian jieshou wenti (On the Question of on-the-Ground Satellite Reception). *Mei zhou guangbo dianshi (Radio and Television Weekly)*, November 1–7.

Appadurai, Arjun. 1990. Disjuncture and Difference in the Global Cultural Economy. *Public Culture* 2 (2): 1–24.

———. 1996. Patriotism and Its Futures. In *Modernity at Large*, pp. 158–77. Minneapolis: University of Minnesota Press.

Ash, Robert, and Y. Y. Kueh. 1993. Economic Integration within Greater China: Trade and Investment Flows between China, Hong Kong and Taiwan. *China Quarterly* 136 (December): 711–45.

Bao, Ming. 1993. Shanghai shiting dazhan (The Great Wars of Television and Radio in Shanghai). *Zhongguo shibao (China Times)*, April 4–10.

Barme, Geremie, and Sang Ye. 1997. The Great Firewall of China. *Wired,* June.

Benjamin, Walter. 1969. The Work of Art in the Age of Mechanical Reproduction. In *Illuminations,* edited by Hannah Arendt, pp. 219–53. New York: Schocken Books.

Bergere, Marie-Claire. 1981. 'The Other China': Shanghai from 1919 to 1949. In *Shanghai: Revolution and Development in an Asian Metropolis,* edited by Christopher Howe. Cambridge, England: Cambridge University Press.

Bhabha, Homi K. 1994. *The Location of Culture*. London: Routledge.

Brownell, Susan. 1999. Strong Women and Impotent Men: Sports, Gender and Nationalism in Chinese Public Culture. In *Spaces of Their Own: Women's Public Sphere in Transnational China,* edited by Mayfair Mei-hui Yang, pp. 207–31. Minneapolis: University of Minnesota Press.

Chang, Won Ho. 1989. *Mass Media in China: The History and the Future*. Ames: Iowa State University Press.

Ching, Leo. 1994. Imaginings in the Empires of the Sun: Japanese Mass Culture in Asia. *Boundary* 2 21 (1): 198–219.

Chow, Ts'e-ts'ung. 1960. *The May Fourth Movement*. Cambridge, Mass.: Harvard University Press.

Chun, Allen. 1994. Discourses of Identity in the Politics of the Modern Nation-State: Spaces of Public Culture in Taiwan, Hong Kong and Singapore. *Culture and Policy* 5 (March).

Clark, Paul. 1984. The Film Industry in the 1970s. In *Popular Chinese Literature and Performing Arts in the People's Republic of China, 1949–79*, edited by Bonnie McDougall. Berkeley: University of California Press.

Clifford, James. 1992. Traveling Cultures. In *Cultural Studies*, edited by Lawrence Grossberg et al., pp. 96–116. New York: Routledge.

Dai, Jinhua. 1995. Invisible Women: Women's Films in Contemporary Chinese Cinema. Translated by Mayfair Yang. *Positions* 3 (1): 255–80.

de Certeau, Michel. 1984. *The Practice of Everyday Life*. Translated by Steven F. Rendall. Berkeley: University of California Press.

Deleuze, Gilles, and Felix Guattari. 1983. *Anti-Oedipus: Capitalism and Schizophrenia*. Minneapolis: University of Minnesota Press.

Ding, Yi. 1994. Shanghai shiluo 50 nian? (Has Shanghai Fallen Behind by 50 Years?). *Zhongshi zhoukan (China Weekly)*, November 13–19.

Featherstone, Mike. 1990. Global Culture: An Introduction. In *Global Culture: Nationalism, Globalization, and Modernity*, edited by Mike Featherstone, pp. 1–14. London: Sage.

———. 1992. *Consumer Culture and Postmodernism*. London: Sage.

Foster, Robert J. 1991. Making National Cultures in the Global Ecumene. *Annual Review of Anthropology* 20: 235–60.

Foucault, Michel. 1980. *The History of Sexuality*. Vol. 1. Translated by Robert Hurley. New York: Random House.

Friedland, Roger. 1994. NowHere: An Introduction to Space, Time, and Modernity. In *NowHere: Space, Time and Modernity*, edited by Roger Friedland and Deirdre Boden, pp. 1–60. Berkeley: University of California Press.

Giddens, Anthony. 1990. *The Consequences of Modernity*. Stanford, Calif.: Stanford University Press.

Gold, Thomas. 1993. Go with Your Feelings: Hong Kong and Taiwan Popular Culture in Greater China. *China Quarterly*, 136 (December): 907–25.

Guo, Ke. 1994. "Jilupian bianjishi" zhendong Shanghaitan ("Documentary Editing Room" Shakes Shanghai). *Zhongshi zhoukan (China Weekly)* August 14, pp. 48–49.

Hall, Stuart. 1980. Encoding/Decoding. In *Culture, Media, Language*, edited by Stuart Hall, D. Hobson, A. Lowe, and P. Willis, pp. 128–38. London: Hutchinson and Center for Contemporary Cultural Studies, University of Birmingham.

Hamilton, Denise. 1995. Providing a Space Link to Homeland: Chinese-Language Satellite TV Gets a Good Reception among Immigrants in U.S. *Los Angeles Times*, August 2.

Harding, Harry. 1993. The Concept of "Greater China": Themes, Variations and Reservations. *China Quarterly* 136 (December): 660–86.

Hsiao, Hsin-Huang Michael, and Alvin Y. So. 1994. Taiwan-Mainland Economic Nexus: Socio-Political Origins, State-Society Impacts, and Future Prospects. Hong Kong Institute of Asia-Pacific Studies. Chinese Occasional Paper no. 37, University of Hong Kong, August.

Jameson, Fredric. 1987. Third-World Literature in the Era of Multinational Capitalism. *Social Text* 15: 65–88.

Larkin, Brian. 1997. Indian Films and Nigerian Lovers: Media and the Creation of Parallel Modernities. *Africa* 67 (3): 406–40.

Lee, Benjamin. 1993. Going Public. *Public Culture* 5 (2): 165–78.

Leyda, Jay. 1972. *Dianying: An Account of Films and the Film Audience in China.* Cambridge, Mass.: MIT Press.

Lull, James. 1991. *China Turned On: Television, Reform, and Resistance.* New York: Routledge.

Mankekar, Purnima. 1993. Television Tales and a Woman's Rage: A Nationalist Recasting of Draupadi's "Disrobing." *Public Culture* 5 (3): 469–92.

McLuhan, Marshall. 1994. *Understanding Media: The Extensions of Man.* Cambridge, Mass.: MIT Press.

Nonini, Donald. 1995. The Chinese Public Sphere and the Cultural Boundaries of the Malaysian Nation-State. Paper presented at the annual meeting of the American Ethnological Society, Austin, Texas.

Ong, Aihwa. 1993. On the Edge of Empires: Flexible Citizenship among Chinese in Diaspora. *Positions* 1 (3): 745–78.

———. 1997. Chinese Modernities: Narratives of Nation and of Capitalism. In *Ungrounded Empires: The Cultural Politics of Modern Chinese Transnationalism,* edited by Aihwa Ong and Donald Nonini, pp. 171–202. New York: Routledge.

Qiu, Xiuwen. 1993. Heima chuangjing beimei huayu dianshi shichang (A Black Horse Charges into the N. American Chinese-language Television Market). *Zhongguo shibao (China Times),* September 12–18.

Radway, Janice. 1988. Reception Study: Ethnography and the Problems of Dispersed Audiences and Nomadic Subjects. *Cultural Studies* 2 (3): 359–76.

Rayns, Tony. 1991. Breakthroughs and Setbacks: The Origins of the New Chinese Cinema. In *Perspectives on Chinese Cinema,* edited by Chris Berry, pp. 104–13. London: British Film Institute.

Rofel, Lisa. 1994. Yearnings: Televisual Love and Melodramatic Politics in Contemporary China. *American Ethnologist* 21 (4): 700–22.

Sheng, Feng. 1995. Beimei shangkong de Zhongwen dianshi dazhan (Chinese Language Television Wars in North American Outer Space). Huaxia wenzhai (Chinese electronic news service), April 15.

Shih, Shu-mei. 1995. The Trope of "Mainland China" in Taiwan's Media. *Positions* 3 (1): 149–83.

Verdery, Katherine. 1994. Beyond the Nation in Eastern Europe. *Social Text* 38: 1–19.

Yang, Mayfair Mei-hui. 1993. Of Gender, State Censorship and Overseas Capital: An Interview with Chinese Director Zhang Yimou. *Public Culture* 5 (2): 1–17.

———. 1994a. State Discourse or a Plebeian Public Sphere? Film Discussion Groups in China. *Visual Anthropology* 10 (1): 47–60.

————. 1994b. *Gifts, Favors, and Banquets: The Art of Social Relationships in China.* Ithaca, N.Y.: Cornell University Press.

————. 1994c. A Sweep of Red: State Subjects and the Cult of Mao. In *Gifts, Favors, and Banquets: The Art of Social Relationships in China,* pp. 245–86. Ithaca, N.Y.: Cornell University Press.

————. 1996. Tradition, Traveling Anthropology, and the Discourse of Modernity in China. In *The Changing Nature of Anthropological Knowledge,* edited by Henrietta Moore, pp. 93–114. London: Routledge.

————. 1999a. Introduction. In *Spaces of Their Own: Women's Public Sphere in Transnational China,* edited by Mayfair Yang, pp. 1–31. Minneapolis: University of Minnesota Press.

————. 1999b. From Gender Erasure to Gender Difference: State Feminism, Consumer Sexuality, and a Women's Public Sphere in China. In *Spaces of Their Own: Women's Public Sphere in Transnational China,* edited by Mayfair Yang, pp. 35–67. Minneapolis: University of Minnesota Press.

————. 2001. Goddess across the Taiwan Straits: Ritual Space, Nation-State Territoriality, and Satellite Television Footprints. Paper presented at the Institute for Advanced Study, Princeton University, and the conference Media, Nationalism, and Globalization: The Case of China, University of Minnesota, Minneapolis.

Yang, Rujie. 1993. Jingcai yu wunai—Cong 'Beijingren zai Neuyue' tan dongxifang wenhua chongji (Gripping and Frustrating: On East-West Collisions in "A Beijing Native in New York") *Dianying wenxue (Film Literature)* 12.

Zha, Jianying. 1995. *China Pop: How Soap Operas, Tabloids, and Bestsellers Are Transforming a Culture.* New York: New Press.

Zhang, Hong. 1992. TV, TV, fangcun shijie de jingcai yu wunai (TV, TV, the Brilliance and Frustration of That Square World). *Shehui (Society)* 92.

Zhen, Hanliang. 1992. Wo liaojie sandi de Zhongguoren: zhuanfang Luo Dayou (What I Understand of the Chinese in the Three Chinas: An Interview with Luo Dayou). *Zhongguo shibao (China Times),* August 23.

10

A Marshall Plan of the Mind

The Political Economy of a Kazakh Soap Opera

Ruth Mandel

THE SHAME AND SIGNS OF A SOAP OPERA

"I am no longer ashamed to say that I write for a soap opera," exclaimed a beaming Leyla Akhinjanova, the author of episode one of *Crossroads*, the brand new Kazakhstani soap opera. It was 1995, and Leyla was speaking to a camera crew filming her, part of a BBC documentary recording the process of bringing British-style social realist soap opera to Central Asia.[1] *Crossroads* was no ordinary soap opera but an initiative of the British government's overseas development plan designed to promote transition to a free-market economy. Behind Leyla's statement lies a history of conflict and controversy between competing national visions of the soap's trajectory and content. The discussion that follows examines, first, the sociocultural and political-economic field into which the British soap opera consultants entered; next, the often discordant conjunction of the Kazakhstani and British visions; and finally, the consequences of this British development sojourn, after the British consultants' departure. I argue that this particular set of interactions and cultural productions is indicative of the cultural politics of post-Soviet transition.

Crossroads occupies the site of the articulation of several worlds along with specific historical and global processes. It is the site of the confrontation between Second World postsocialist realism and First World postindustrial social realism, all the while influenced by ubiquitous globalizing influences. This clash is situated in a unique space delineated by postcolonial British emissaries sent to bring the ideological tools and techniques of capitalism to ambivalent (at best), quondam Second Worlders who are realizing a Fourth World inflection for themselves. Kazakhstan emerged as an independent country following the collapse of the Soviet Union. Its titular nationals, the Kazakhs, comprise a plurality though not quite a majority of its population. They increasingly see themselves as a Fourth World nation, hith-

Map of familial relationships among soap opera characters in the TV series
Crossroads, Kazakhstan. (Photo: Ruth Mandel)

erto colonized, whose autonomy and expressions of culture and identity were
severely circumscribed and repressed over the previous seventy years by the
hegemonic Russian/Soviet "Second World" state apparatus and ideology.[2]
Thus one unusual aspect of this project is that it is the site of these particular convergences.

The making of *Crossroads* was informed by the assumption that the
medium of television is an appropriate tool to further the logical and inevitable transition to a capitalist free-market economy, transforming the national imagination in the process.[3] However, the project from its inception
has been the site of multiple contestations, including competing and growing nationalisms of both international and nonstate varieties, as well as numerous states' interventions.

Following from this, I examine the roles of two states, Great Britain and
Kazakhstan, along with their occasionally unwitting representatives, in their
attempts to control the signs and signals (sometimes literally) of the soap
opera. Ideological dominion of this teleserial has been understood by locals
and foreigners alike to have serious political potential for the control of and
influence over the viewing public.[4] A particularly sensitive issue during this
precarious period of post-Soviet state formation and consolidation, the soap

opera has been appropriated by the Kazakhstani state in trying to forge a new type of citizen amid tremendous internal and external pressures and unprecedented official and business corruption. Some of the troubles in the making of *Crossroads* stemmed from the shift from Soviet socialist realism to British-style social realism. The British confronted local resistance to their own vision, particularly given the recent saturation of regional television programming by U.S. soap operas and Latin American telenovelas. Following is a discussion of this and multiple other lines of resistance to the British Foreign Office's initial agenda, from both British and Kazakhstani quarters as they interacted with each other and came to question the project's original mission. Now, turning to this agenda, I look at *Crossroads*' primary donor/sponsor, the British government's foreign aid program and its mission.

MARSHALL PLAN OF THE MIND—MARGARET THATCHER'S
ANSWER TO EMERGING MARKETS AND TRANSITOLOGY

Crossroads began life as a project of the British Know How Fund, an agency envisioned as a unique creation conjoining two separate British institutions: the Overseas Development Administration (ODA) and the Foreign and Commonwealth Office.[5] It was conceived during the Thatcher government with the specific brief to aid in the transition from command-driven socialist societies to free-market economies.[6] Know How Fund projects were to be foreign development aid with a new spin: teaching capitalism to the communists. Such a brief demanded creative solutions, and it was determined that the mass media would be the appropriate vehicle to spread the word. Marshall Plan of the Mind (MPM) was created in November 1992 as just this vehicle. From the chairman of Marshall Plan of the Mind came this statement:

> BBC-MPM is an educational, charitable trust . . . to transfer skills and knowledge of democratic principles and market economies via national radio and television to assist the transition process. It is the most significant project dedicated to mass knowledge transfer within the Former Soviet Union. (Letter from John Tusa, chairman, BBC Marshall Plan of the Mind Trust, June 14, 1996)

With this agenda dozens of programs, including several soap operas, have sprung to life. *Crossroads* was conceived as an elaboration of an MPM radio soap opera in Russia, *Dom Sem' Pod' ezd Chetyre (Apartment 7, Entrance 4)*. Based on an *Archers* format, *Dom Sem'* has met with enormous success.[7] Kazakhstan's program, *Crossroads*, was to be slightly different, however: rather than a daily radio program it would be a weekly television serial.

Unlike the Know How Fund's MPM-BBC collaboration, *Crossroads* was produced by a private London-based production company, Portobello Media. It was to be modeled on *EastEnders,* the long-running, extremely successful

British social realist TV soap set in London's working class east end. *Cross-roads* aimed to teach economic literacy to the Kazakhstani population, incorporating issues such as privatization, banking, entrepreneurship, and market reform into the story lines. In addition to the transmission of these ideological messages, issues of ethnic pluralism and technology transfer also have been important components of the project. One aspect of the technology transfer effort was teaching the fine art of attracting corporate funding, because the project was committed to raising matching private sector funds. Thus British American Tobacco products (in the incarnations of Kent and Lucky Strike), Wrigley's gum, and Smirnoff vodka all found their way into the episodes via product placement from an early stage in the series.

In a discussion, one Know How Fund official admitted that the assistance came loaded with "unashamedly political objectives." He described the project "to support changes we want; the transition to a market economy will be better for them, and for us, for politics, trade, etc. There are real political objectives rather than simply humanitarian assistance."

PRODUCING TECHNOLOGIES

Even before the project began, a public relations blitz shot through Kazakhstan's capital, Almaty, a city of 1.5 million. For the Kazakhstani media, it was the biggest, practically the only, game in town.[8] Un- or under-employed actors, writers and artists aspired to be part of the project, which promised cash dollars and prestige.

When the British arrived they set about assembling teams of Kazakhstanis to be trained. Close to two hundred people had been involved in the realization of the momentous first episode, the one after which Leyla Akhinjanova declared that she no longer was embarrassed by the product of her labors. For several months she and numerous trainees had been learning the ways and means of television serial production—British-style. Builders, painters, carpenters, and designers, under the tutelage of experienced British set builders and designers, had learned new techniques, including the method of building weighted movable "flats," standard set-construction in the West but unheard of in the Soviet film industry, where scenery was normally nailed to the floor and therefore difficult to strike.

The British trainers also made it their mission to teach good work habits: punctuality, no absenteeism, and no turning up to work hungover.[9] Kazakhstanis were trained in costumes, makeup, props, sound, production, lighting, directing, film editing, acting, assisting, and cost accounting. A team of about twenty-five local writers worked intensively in small groups with several British soap opera writers and editors. They were introduced to concepts such as cliff-hanger, story-lining, narrative, open-endedness, and other key elements of the British genre.

Initially the British supplied the writers with ideational structures, implicitly meant to determine the didacticism of the venture. Thus if most of the scenes were to be shot in privately owned enterprises—a cafe, a kiosk, a hotel lobby, an outdoor market with privately owned stalls, a private medical clinic—then the idea was that naturally emerging stories would revolve around the business of the businesses. The set became a mini free-enterprise zone, allowing free markets free reign as writers struggled to fill in the explicitly delimited blanks. The scripts were to describe these new Kazakhstanis and their unprecedented lives and problems, revolving around bank accounts, business plans, small enterprises, marketing, mafia extortionism, interior design, a private employment bureau, and customer service—all alien concepts until quite recently. In addition, Islam has been written into the story line in the character of long-suffering, upright Sherxan, who goes on the hajj (Ro'i 1997).

After several months of training the local writers, the British faced the inevitable process of choosing the best ones to retain. A few had proved to be able and quick learners. Others, some of whom had been famous, even decorated State Artists during the Soviet period, were let go. Those who did not make the cut were inevitably resentful. At least one fought back with his pen and wrote a scathing article in a popular daily paper alleging corruption and incompetence at *Crossroads*.

Actors also found fault with the British-imposed structure and story line. One lead actor took me aside to give me tickets to see him perform at the prestigious Lermontov Theater; "That is real theater—this is only money," he explained scornfully. In addition, the actors disliked being kept in the dark about future story lines; in their previous work they had always been presented with a complete script—a beginning, a middle, and an end. The uncertainty built into soap opera proved irksome. On one occasion they staged a mini-revolt. Unused to the "open" nature of the genre, they essentially demanded to know "the ending" to a structurally potentially endless story (see Allen 1995a).

Many of the central conflicts of the group of scriptwriters and editors paralleled the larger issues and tensions within Kazakhstani society, particularly on ethnic matters (in local terms, the "nationalities question"). Controversial discussions took place among the writers about which characters should be Russian and which Kazakh. Some of the Kazakhs were bothered that the evil character was Kazakh, not Russian: the ubiquitous mafia is personified by Timur, played by a Kazakh actor.[10] They were equally dismayed when the sole indigent unmarried mother who abandons her baby was to be a Kazakh woman. It was decided—by the British—that the story line would revolve around two extended families, one Kazakh and one Russian. The Kazakh Umarovs were joined to the Russian Platonovs through the marriage of the former's daughter to the latter's son. The younger couple would operate one of the new private enterprises, a cafe where many scenes take place. Some of the Kazakh writers grumbled at the disparities represented by the two ethnic groups—the Platonov husband and wife were both upstanding doctors, part of the prestigious intelligentsia now struggling to find a role in a transformed society. They were meant to represent respectability; they were admirable characters with high moral values. A displeased Kazakh writer remarked that Dr. Platonov was "like our big Russian brother." Mixing irony with bitterness, she referred to Russia's hegemonic role during the Soviet period. Her statement reflected a socialist realist sensibility, where characters were meant to stand for things, to represent ideals.[11] In sharp contrast to the intellectual Platonovs (the name derived from Plato), the star of the Umarov family is Gulbibi, an earthy outspoken grandmother with village origins, the matriarch of an extended family with whom she lives in a small flat along with her unsophisticated, irascible husband. The elderly couple freely punctuate their speech with Kazakh expressions.

The tensions that plagued the project reflect the strains in Kazakhstani society: they have been played out in striking parallel both before the cameras and behind the scenes. The British arranged several other intermarriages, which also displeased some of the Kazakh writers. The interethnic issue comes across in the early episodes, particularly when a mixed couple attempts to adopt the abandoned Kazakh baby, only to be discouraged by the authorities. Some Kazakh writers privately discussed killing off many of the Russians. In the years after the departure of the British advisers, the Kazakh writers were able not only to fire most of their non-Kazakh colleagues, but also to ensure that the mixed couples experienced extensive marital problems. Two years into the story line, all of these intermarriages terminated in divorce. When asked about this, the Kazakh writers defended themselves, claiming they were "being realistic and responding to audience reactions." A year after the original British sponsors had left, the story line editor explained to me some of the recent changes in personnel. When discussing Shamil, the good cop–detective, she added, "You know, the British wouldn't let us have a detective. We explained to them that every soap opera had a detective—*Santa Barbara* has one, others do. But they said no. So we kept quiet, since they were paying us $200 a month. Then, after they left, we wrote in our detective."

REALISMS: FROM SOCIALIST TO SOCIAL

Imparting a British social realist sensibility did not prove to be straightforward.[12] Instead it was resisted, producing tensions between the two sets of writers. The local writers shared some of Leyla's initial sense of shame at writing for what they considered a lowly vernacular; after all, they felt they had been accustomed to writing in a *Hoch Kultur* tradition. Oblivious to the brief of social realism, many felt demeaned by this task, overcompensating with "creativity."[13] Some attempted to write into their scripts improbably marginal characters, one of whom, for example, recited Nietzsche while standing on his head. In another case, the sole wealthy scriptwriter had the "novyi Kazakh" mafia character cross-dress, parading in his wife's clothing; she assured her astounded colleagues that this was characteristic behavior of the local nouveau riche.

The British trainers were left baffled by such writing attempts and by their own inability to convey realism British-style. This sort of realism they described as creating believable characters and showing their everyday activities and surroundings—though selectively. One trainer explained to the group, "You should write your script using the sort of behavior and language you hear around you every day. You do not need to show them performing mundane activities—like writing checks—but instead you should write the most dramatic moments of their everyday lives."[14] They also stressed an ontological difference between the social-realist drama of British soaps and the melodrama characteristic of American soaps. One trainer explained, "Drama is where the emotional content comes out of the story, through the characters; melodrama is where the emotion simply comes out of the actors, with no substance to the scene."

Implementing this British vision of realism proved confusing for the student writers, many of whom were former members of the cosseted Soviet intelligentsia who had come of age in an era of socialist realism. Socialist realism, a product of the Soviet state, sought to transform the consciousness of the masses through carefully crafted works of art. Lenin declared that "all literature must become Party literature. Every newspaper, journal, publishing house, etc., must be integrated into one Party organisation" (James 1973: 106). In 1921 the People's Commissar of Enlightenment proclaimed that "Agitation and propaganda acquire special edge and efficacy when decked in the attractive and powerful forms of art" (quoted in James 1973: vii).

In this respect socialist realism, almost the polar opposite of social realism, had little to do with the quotidian lives of the people. Boym writes, "The 'realism' part of socialist realism has virtually nothing to do with the everyday existence of Soviet citizens; it does not even attempt to mime or imitate it. The point is to visualize the mythical and utopian world and thus bring it into existence." Socialist realism, a "total—and potentially totalizing—vision," rejected art as "an autonomous domain of the beautiful in favor of the idea of art as a 'road to life'" (Boym 1994: 318).[15]

Throughout the seventy years of the USSR's existence what was considered approved and permitted art shifted,[16] but the basic tenets of socialist realism continued; they were part and parcel of the Soviet project of modernity. Soon after Stalin's death, the party's message to the Second Writers' Congress of 1954 stated:

Soviet writers receive their inspiration from the great ideals of the struggle for Communism . . . To the false and hypocritical bourgeois slogan of the "independence" of literature from society, and the false concept of "art for art's sake," our writers proudly contrast their noble ideological stance of service in the interests of the masses, of the people. (James 1973: 98)

What social and socialist realisms share is an orientation toward shaping their respective popular audiences through didactic means. The most popular and long-running social-realist soap opera in the UK, *The Archers,* was meant to teach modern techniques of agriculture and animal husbandry. Other British social-realist soap operas have raised provocative issues such as incest and domestic violence, offering telephone hotline services at the end of controversial episodes. Though the didacticism of socialist realism was less oriented toward social services than informed by a monolithic Communist Party, it shared with the British model a tacit assumption that television (and other arts) could raise both consciousness and practice, directing hearts and minds of the *narod,* the people. Another arguable point of convergence is the rejection of "art for art's sake." They diverged radically, however, in the mode, means, and mission of representation. Whereas social realism strove for transparency, socialist realism constructed a prescriptive prism; while social realism attempted to strip away accretions, socialist realism concerned itself with ideological expansion.

Though it might be questioned whether the North and South American soap operas represent art for art's sake, they have nevertheless had an important influence on the local writers. As in the example of the detective cited above, other aspects of these foreign imports have excited the imaginations of the writers as well as the rest of the production crew. What one of the British trainers called the "*Santa Barbara* fallacy" was evident in the sorts of spending sprees the crew enjoyed. One day at the studio the British production adviser ranted and raved because the set designers had just spent three thousand dollars to furnish the one-room set of the living room of the mafia boss, Timur. They argued that they had bought the very sort of furniture Timur's real life counterpart might have purchased. The adviser was not assuaged and failed to see the "realist" irony in this. She exploded, "Why did they have to shop at the most expensive furniture store in the city? Why couldn't they have first tried one of the second-hand stores? They have glitz and glamour in their minds—*Santa Barbara,* not *EastEnders.*" She also was angered by the wastefulness—for they had purchased a costly and useless glass coffee table for the set, the reflection of which would cause shooting difficulties. She was peeved as well at some of the actresses, prima donnas demanding to be dressed and coifed far beyond the means either of the costume budget or of their particular characters.

On more technical grounds, the British writing consultants found the

Kazakhstanis' lack of attention to certain sorts of detail bewildering and frustrating. One frustrated trainer remarked, "In their writing they are supposed to follow the story line, but they take it upon themselves to make the story do this or that, irrelevant to where it's meant to be leading . . . we tell them what the rules are, but they just break them." Geraghty has discussed the attention this is paid in British soaps: "Some viewers . . . remember a serial's past very clearly and expect any references to it to be accurate, down to the last detail. . . . The *Coronation Street* production team includes a programme historian who ensures that any references to the past are correct" (1981: 16).

The British trainers felt a lack of attention to historical consistency within the story line was due to laziness and lack of discipline on the part of the Kazakhstani writers. When questioned about the less plausible turns taken by the story line the writers dismissed it, explaining, "The audience will never notice."[17] This attitude may stem from Soviet times, when their professional experience entailed neither ratings nor commercial or corporate sponsorship.[18] The state, the only possible producer and sponsor, dictated the subtexts and themes.[19]

Once it became a more purely Kazakhstani production after the British funding ceased, in a shift that would certainly dismay the British trainers, *Crossroads* entered what Peter Brooks has called the "moral occult," the typical melodramatic characteristic whereby the improbable meets the unlikely (1985; cited in Allen 1995a: 23). Thus Shamil, the honest detective, learns that his half-brother is his sworn enemy, Timur, the mafia boss; a previously unknown girl (with an identical twin) appears in the story line as suddenly as a long-lost brother returns from America, and a female character is killed off following a brief illness. This last event happened after the writers persuaded the producer that she ruined their lines with her wooden acting.

In some respects, the mission animating the British social-realist project was beset by internal contradictions, which paradoxically lay only a step removed from the socialist-realist world it was displacing. Though the trainers' methodological brief was to impart the techniques of the social-realist genre, paradoxically their ideological brief resonated more with certain tenets of socialist realism. The emphasis on teaching the techniques of the market economy meant that characters needed to be iconically representative; in the Umarov family one son represents progress, Kazakhstan's future, and the potential of small entrepreneurs, while another son reacts retrogressively to the vulgar taint of money. These typologies mimic the mythic proletarian paragons of an earlier day, the heroic miner or tractor driver, who shared the similar paradigmatic burden of representing ideal types.

Dissidence was evident among the British writing consultants, who nearly unanimously objected to their terms of reference. None wished to feel like a Thatcherite Tory puppet, bringing capitalism to the vanquished. Instead, some of them subtly taught their students routines of resistance. They stressed quality above all, and the "natural," the realistic. "No one can tell you what to write; you must decide what is natural in the scene. If social or economic issues arise naturally, fine, but they must not be forced," lectured one of the teachers; "this is not propaganda; the point is to show the new system working." Another British consultant told me that he simply was un-interested in, even disdainful of, any Foreign Office or Know How Fund agen-das concerning privatization and the market; his only concern was teaching the local writers techniques and quality. Another instructor is shown in the BBC documentary *East of EastEnders* warning the trainee writers that they could expect to be approached to insert other's messages into their story lines. He tells them to be strong, uncompromising, and firm and that uni-formly high quality should be their guide.

The three competing narrative styles discussed—socialist realism, social realism, and American melodrama—represent distinct genres, each with its own ideology and history. It is in the conjunction and subsequent disjunc-tion that a novel textual bricolage has emerged, a distinct aesthetic expres-sion of the political economy of postsocialist transition.[20]

GLOBAL PRODUCTION, LOCAL CONSUMPTION

The mid-1990s witnessed a critical transitional moment as people began to change their intellectual, consumption, and commodity allegiances and ori-entations from Moscow and Russia to Europe and North America. At this time an unprecedented cascade of foreign commodities (including phar-maceuticals) began to flow in, from Korea, China, Turkey, India, the United Arab Emirates, eastern and western Europe, and the United States. Kazakh-stanis became savvy consumers who learned how to "read" the foreignness of these imported products. The often expired sell-by dates were scrutinized, and the computer-generated bar codes assumed a new significance. The mi-crographic digits indicated that a product came from Turkey, Hungary, or Germany, and the consumers quickly established a hierarchy, aware of which venues were more likely to produce high- or low-quality products flogged in Central Asia.

Bearing in mind these changes in consumption practices, analogous changes in the discourse about the soap opera began to emerge. Those who initially had compared *Crossroads* unfavorably with *Santa Barbara* and other foreign imported soaps began to revise their opinions. Originally they had criticized *Crossroads* for being "too close to our own miserable lives," ex-pressing the view that "our lives are already so difficult and grim; when we turn on the television we want some relief, to see other places, beautiful people, and houses—in *Crossroads* we just see our own reflection and get more depressed."

After about a year, some of these skeptical viewers had been converted.

Those who had been disdainful about local native products began to talk of the program with pride: "People who look, act, and speak like us are on television!" The shift reflected a growing national confidence and pride, increased Kazakh nationalism and indigenization of many spheres of life—*Kazakhifikatsia,* or Kazakhification. In the end, they liked it for precisely the same reasons they had disliked it initially: because it was a local product.

Crossroads also came to represent style. In the post-Soviet era, for those who can afford it, the cultivation of style has risen to paramount importance.[21] Here soap operas enter the discussion, as they provide a template for receptive viewers keen to mimic what they see as "true" style, defined by the much emulated "modern" West—the diametric antithesis of what passed as Soviet modernity. In Kazakhstan those who are inclined and able use the public presentation of self (hair, makeup, jewelry, clothing) and the decor of their home interiors to identify themselves, to define who they are both to themselves and to the outside world. The counterpoint of this heightened, even hyper-, awareness of Western style is, of course, the recent Soviet past, where too flagrant oppositional desire and behavior—including sartorial practice—could land one in a gulag. Antistate opposition thus often was expressed through dress, through dissident dressing in what was imagined to be Western style—e.g., the blue jeans craze of the 1970s. Though most Soviets were unsure what exactly Western taste and style consisted of, many nevertheless were sure that it was superior. Their own culture of shortages, including sausages, apartments, and quality fabrics, the inevitable consequence of a corrupted command economy, made them more keenly aware of what they were missing. The absence of commodities led to the determination to overcompensate in whatever way possible (see Boym 1994 for a discussion of Soviet domestic taste and kitsch). Some examples:

One artist/designer/decorator in Almaty, whose main source of income derived from commissions from the nouveau riche "novyi Russkii/ Kazakhii" segment of the population, complained that he was awakened late at night by telephone calls from clients who insisted that he turn on the television. "Do you see that staircase (or wallpaper, color, sofa, etc.)?" he would be asked by the excited client. "That's what I want you to do in my home."

Young nouveau middle-class Almaty residents beg their foreign friends to bring them Western home interior and fashion magazines that are unavailable in Central Asia.

Local dressmakers who sew custom-made dresses for Almaty's wealthier women are instructed to copy the styles seen on foreign TV shows.[22]

For the first time the viewers are seeing Kazakhs who are meant to represent them, but living a newly cast modernity. Yet at the same time the characters being broadcast also represent a pastiche of projected Western tastes and styles, refashioned according to interpretations of the *Santa Barbaras* and the limits of Almaty's meager retail choices. *Crossroads* has influenced its viewers' expressions of taste and ideas of themselves. The hairstyles of two of the young beautiful Kazakh women characters have been widely copied throughout the country. It is said that the apartments of some wealthy mafia types have been decorated à la Timur's. *Crossroads,* then, provides a serious lesson for Kazakhstani students hungry for knowledge of foreign style and taste, predigested for a local clientele. It has been so successful partly because of the conjuncture of the foreign and global with the Kazakhstani local. Thus the fusion of global, foreign taste and style thus becomes not just palatable, but accessibly localized and indigenized.

CONCLUSION

My concerns echo those of Skuse, who studied a very differently oriented development soap opera, a BBC radio serial in Afghanistan. Similar to Skuse's study, this essay has attempted to address the "relatedness and disjuncture displayed between spheres of mass media production and audience consumption" (1999: 19). In addition, I have examined the ways producers and audiences create meaning "as product and appropriation—in distinctly different, but related ways" (ibid: 20). During its several years of broadcasting, *Crossroads* has represented a myriad of products and appropriations and has recreated itself numerous times. After the departure of the controlling British editorial gaze it underwent numerous transformations in its struggle for financial viability and political survival. These incarnations stemmed from competing agendas of changing private and public sponsorship, political pressures, and the changing personnel involved in different aspects of production. The cessation of direct British control and involvement also resulted in a structural change, as content and construct of the story line as well as the nature of the production took unforeseen forms and directions.

One direction in which the tenor of the program has tended to swing has been toward the influences of global satellite television, carrying North and South American soap operas as well as MTV. The other direction is toward state imperatives as government advisers and censors inform scriptwriters to stress issues like the virtues of a moderate Islam, the benefits of trading in Soviet passports in exchange for Kazakhstani ones, or the importance of moving the country's capital. By suggesting that *Crossroads* air stories about controversial issues, such as the nonpayment of pensions, the state increases the impression that it is more liberal than the previous regime while still offering party lines to its citizenry.

Looking back on the first three years of *Crossroads* sponsorship, an interesting pattern of repeated hijackings can be identified. First, the instantiation of the Know-How Fund's market-oriented agenda; next a scrambling for a hodge-podge of commercial sponsorship; then, a period of paid public service sponsorship along with the commercial; and all along, increasing control by the Kazakhstani government censors and policy makers. *Crossroads,* then, as the first postindependence and now indigenously produced teleserial, represents a highly contested site where past and present politics, genres, ideologies, and nationalism meet the melodramatic glamour of *Santa Barbara* and *Tropicana,* the two most popular imported soap operas.

Such a fusion of melodramatic sensibility blended with development messages produces no single message conveyed or consumed, no "unified whole" or "unitary viewer."[23] The intertextualities of the products broadcast as *Crossroads* are variously understood by producers, sponsors, and audiences to be vodka, information on a new tax law, or a fashion statement. Thus the social experience of this soap opera has been mobilized in unpredictable ways at each stage of its production and consumption (Fiske 1989: 58). The overdetermined nature of *Crossroads* has itself led to an indeterminate dissonance, as changes within the audience echo not only the shifting sponsorship but also transformations within the larger society.

The British, and later other international and Kazakhstani sponsors, were working implicitly with a simple model of how media work: an unproblematic message is delivered and duly received—in the shape in which it putatively was sent.[24] The discussion above of the audience's reactions and responses concurs with criticism by others who have shown that the model does not, ultimately, describe the much more heterogeneous and polysemic models of audience reception (e.g., Hall 1994; Abu-Lughod 1995; Dávila 1997; Mankekar 1993; Rofel 1995). Similarly on the production side, the evidence from Kazakhstan echoes Dornfeld's (1998) findings, in demonstrating the extremely complex sets of factors and contests competing for inclusion in the production.[25]

Equally problematic has been the consultants' role in assisting in the construction of a new national identity, an identity designed to compete with accelerating "popular imagery from abroad" in the shapes of Marlboro and the U.S. TV series *Dallas.* They were to write a new national narrative, ideologically and commercially driven, to replace the monopolistic Soviet one (Price 1995: 51).[26] Ironically, several years later, the lead *Crossroads* writer seems to be taking her cues from the imported popular imagery and its locally projected imaginary. Moreover, the soap operatic narrative proposed by the British, informed by a pluralist model of national identity and aimed at reinforcing a delicate multiculturalism, proved somewhat at odds with the essentialist model of new nationalist indigenization promoted implicitly by the Kazakhstani government and explicitly by the Kazakh writers.[27] In addition, different levels of resistance and subversion, among both trainers and trainees, at times undermined the project's original mission.

An irony of *Crossroads,* then, is the tale of how a Thatcherite propaganda tool for the teaching of privatization, market reform, and democracy to ex-Soviet citizens was repeatedly hijacked and transformed—even derailed—until ultimately it became, at least in part, the voice of a nationalized highly censored state-controlled media empire, not dissimilar from its Soviet predecessor. But complicating this process throughout has been the inevitable entanglement of diverse and competing messages sent and received, messages outside the domain of the state censors.[28]

Returning to the multiple worlds invoked earlier, I argue that this Kazakhstani example offers an intriguing instance in which a Second World society, now realizing itself as a Fourth World nation, is given a First World genred medium that it in turn transforms itself into an indigenized product. Numerous forces shaped these transformations as international development agencies' agendas were adapted to the Kazakhstani state's nationalizing project. Aesthetic struggles drawing on the past have had to accommodate the present in both foreign and local guises. As such this has been the story of the struggles for mastery of both the medium and its many messages.

NOTES

The research on which this essay is based took place in Almaty, Kazakhstan, between 1995 and 1998. It entailed participant-observation at KazakhFilm Studios—the production site—as well as interviews with approximately 100 viewers, the consumers. This essay benefited tremendously from the comments and suggestions of Lila Abu-Lughod, Victor Buchli, Faye Ginsburg, Brian Larkin, Danny Miller, Scott Newton, Susan Pattie, Dan Segal, and Patricia Spyer.

1. The documentary *East of EastEnders,* produced by independent filmmaker Jemma Jupp, was broadcast on BBC World and in the United Kingdom in July 1997 in its Omnibus series.

2. Kazakh refers to the titular nationals of Kazakhstan, the ethnic Kazakhs who make up close to 50 percent of the population. "Kazakhstani" is the term for the entire population of citizens of Kazakhstan, encompassing Russians (who make up approximately 35 percent of the population) and over 100 other groups.

3. Numerous soap operas are broadcast, often on radio, throughout the Third World; funded by development agencies, they are intended to educate about health, agriculture, nutrition, and other topics. See also Mandel 1998.

4. The genre of soap opera has received serious analytic attention from anthropology, sociology, and media and cultural studies. Miller (1995a), Abu-Lughod (1993a, 1995, 2000), and Das (1995) have written on the reception and ideological content of soap operas in Trinidad, Egypt, and India; Allen discusses the soap opera as commodity and commodifier. Soap operas also capture the imagination and interest of museum curators; an exhibition in Rotterdam's ethnographic museum, "SOAP," codified the genre cross-culturally.

5. The Know How Fund was established in 1989. The Overseas Development Ad-

ministration (ODA) has since been upgraded and renamed the Department for International Development (DFID); its minister at this writing is Clare Short. ODA/DFID is the functional equivalent of the United States Agency for International Development (USAID), though funded on a more modest scale.

6. "Transition" is a term begging to be problematized. Commonly used in the literature on post-Soviet societies, it presumes a unilinear trajectory from communism to capitalism. There has been some anthropological critique of the concept (e.g., Hann 1994; Kandiyoti and Mandel 1998; Berdahl et al. 2000).

7. *The Archers*, broadcast in Britain twice daily for half a century, may be the world's longest-running soap opera. Having begun life as a didactic serial aimed at helping farmers modernize in postwar Britain, it since has captured the imagination of much of the nation, appealing to the fantasy of a rural idyll.

8. In 1998 the capital of Kazakhstan officially moved from Almaty to the northern city of Astana, formerly known as Akmola, Tselinograd, and Akmolinsk.

9. This tactic was not unlike that of an earlier generation of British missionaries, who also devoted much energy to teaching time- and work-discipline. For more on this see Comaroff and Comaroff 1992.

10. Timur is Kazakh (and Turkic) for Tamerlane, a popular name among Turkic peoples. The historic person of Tamerlane, during the Soviet period considered a villainous monster, has since been rehabilitated in Central Asia.

11. Nathan Englander's story "The Twenty-Seventh Man" has a dialogue between two writer-prisoners awaiting execution on Stalin's orders the following day. Pinchas criticizes Korinsky, the latter having written odes to Stalin. The former tells the latter, "I'm no fan, sir . . . the core of all your work is flawed by a heavy-handed party message that has nothing to do with the people about whom you write." Korinsky shouts back, "The characters are only vehicles, fictions!" (1999: 14).

12. The very notion of realisms of all sorts as applied to soap operas has been questioned by O'Donnell (1999).

13. This attitude was evident among some viewers as well. In a dinner conversation with a group of Almaty artists there was near consensus that Kazakhstan's finest actors were demeaned by working on a soap opera.

14. The example of writing checks was particularly inapt because few Kazakhstanis were familiar with such things as checks and credit cards.

15. For a compelling discussion of the relationship between socialist realism and the Russian avant garde, see Boym 1994.

16. Once lauded official State Artists sometimes found themselves overnight labeled "enemies of the people" when ideologies and fashions changed.

17. Interestingly, in terms of the material culture of the program—the stuff of the sets—more care was shown. Olga, the prop woman, was given the task of taking Polaroid photos of the sets in order to achieve a modicum of consistency.

18. It is important to recall that the reception by the consumers of Soviet cultural production represented a wide range, from dissident, to cynical-critical, to fervent *partinii* believers. Soviets were sophisticated consumers, able to read skillfully between the lines. Producers represented a range as well, sometimes pushing the party envelope through irony, humor, or alternative visions; others reproduced the party ideology.

19. This attitude has been reproduced by the post-Soviet state. But there are dif-

ferences: first, the willingness of the population to react negatively and to criticize the government (albeit gingerly); and second, the alternative options. Those who can afford it now buy satellite dishes to access unjammed news—CNN, Russian, BBC—and programming (including soap operas) from around the world.

20. Thanks to Brian Larkin for his suggestions in this section.

21. Others have clung to alternate visions of consumption practices, reflecting an "antimateriality" creed, a facet of Soviet modernist ideology intensely at odds with the values and conspicuous display characterized by soap operas (Viktor Buchli, personal communication). On the effects of soap opera on the appropriation and indigenization of style in Trinidad, see Miller 1995a: 225.

22. Many young urban Kazakhstani women attempt to dress in a manner that imitates what they see on Western TV aired in Kazakhstan, from MTV to *Dallas*. Thus, Westerners often are startled by the somewhat risqué styles displayed on the streets of Almaty: stilettos, makeup befitting the stage, micro-skirts on a wide variety of bodies, diaphanous dresses without the benefit of underclothing, excessively dyed hair (but minus the irony of Western punk-dyed hair). All have become the norm for those trying to achieve an imagined version of Western modernity.

23. Fiske asserts the absence of a unitary viewer; the program or television text delivers different messages to a differentiated audience (1989: 56).

24. Several international development agencies sponsored episodes of *Crossroads* in exchange for having their messages inserted into the story line.

25. Questioning Allen's claim about the relationship between soaps with overt social messages and sponsors (1995a: 21), *Crossroads* has served as a vehicle for promoting as unlikely bedfellows free-market reform, tobacco products, chewing gum, birth control, presidential priorities, antismoking, and small enterprise, along with agendas from the United Nations High Commission for Refugees and USAID.

26. It could be argued, however, that the ideologically informed substitute has been equally monolithic and monopolistic, presenting the audience/population with a single worldview option, albeit an option that contrasted with the previous one.

27. For a discussion of these models see Price 1995: 41.

28. For much of its run the scripts were vetted by two members of the presidential apparat who met regularly with the producer.

REFERENCES

Abu-Lughod, Lila. 1993a. Finding a Place for Islam: Egyptian Televisions Serials and the National Interest. *Public Culture* 5 (3): 493–513.

———. 1993b. Introduction. *Public Culture* 5 (3): 465–67.

———. 1995. The Objects of Soap Opera. In *Worlds Apart: Modernity through the Prism of the Local*, edited by Daniel Miller, pp. 190–210. London: Routledge.

———. 2000. Modern Subjects: Egyptian Melodrama and Postcolonial Difference. In *Questions of Modernity*, edited by Timothy Mitchell. Minneapolis: University of Minnesota Press.

Allen, Robert. 1995a. Introduction. In *To Be Continued . . .*, edited by Robert Allen, pp. 1–26. London: Routledge.

———, ed. 1995b. *To Be Continued . . .* London: Routledge.

Baldwin, Kate. 1995. Montezuma's Revenge: Reading Los Ricos Tambien Lloran in Russia. In *To Be Continued . . .*, edited by Robert Allen, pp. 285–300. London: Routledge.

Berdahl, Daphne, Matti Bunzl, and Martha Lampland, eds. 2000. *Altering States: Ethnographies of Transition in Eastern Europe and the Former Soviet Union.* Ann Arbor: University of Michigan Press.

Boym, Svetlana. 1994. *Common Places: Mythologies of Everyday Life in Russia.* Cambridge, Mass.: Harvard University Press.

Brooks, Peter. 1985. *The Melodramatic Imagination: Balzac, Henry James, Melodrama and the Mode of Excess.* New York: Columbia University Press.

Comaroff, John and Jean Comaroff. 1992. *Ethnography and the Historical Imagination.* Boulder, Colo.: Westview.

Crofts, Stephen. 1995. Global Neighbours? In *To Be Continued . . .*, edited by Robert Allen, pp. 98–121. London: Routledge.

Das, Veena. 1995. Soap Opera: What Kind of Object Is It? In *Worlds Apart: Modernity through the Prism of the Local,* edited by Daniel Miller, pp. 169–89. London: Routledge.

Dávila, Arlene. 1997. *Sponsored Identities: Cultural Politics in Puerto Rico.* Philadelphia: Temple University Press.

Dornfeld, Barry. 1998. *Producing Public Television, Producing Public Culture.* Princeton, N.J.: Princeton University Press.

Englander, Nathan. 1999. *For the Relief of Unbearable Urges.* London: Faber and Faber.

Fiske, J. 1989. Moments of Television: Neither the Text nor the Audience. In *Remote Control: Television, Audiences and Cultural Power,* edited by Ellen Seiter et al., pp. 56–78. London: Routledge.

Geraghty, Christine. 1981. Coronation Street: "The Continuous Serial—a Definition." In *Coronation Street,* edited by Richard Dyer et al., pp. 9–26. London: British Film Institute.

———. 1991. *Women and Soap Opera: A Study of Prime Time Soaps.* Cambridge, England: Polity Press.

———. 1995. Social Issues and Realist Soaps. In *To Be Continued . . .*, edited by Robert Allen, pp. 66–80. London: Routledge.

Ginsburg, Faye. 1991. Indigenous Media: Faustian Contract or Global Village? *Cultural Anthropology* 6 (1): 92–112.

———. 1993. Aboriginal Media and the Australian Imaginary. *Public Culture* 5 (3): 557-78.

Hall, Stuart. 1994. Reflections on the Encoding/Decoding Model. In *Viewing, Reading, Listening: Audiences and Cultural Reception,* edited by J. Cruz and J. Lewis. Boulder, Colo.: Westview.

Hann, Chris. 1994. After Communism: Reflections on East European Anthropology and the 'Transition.' *Social Anthropology* 2 (3): 229–49.

James, C. V. 1973. *Soviet Socialist Realism: Origins and Theory.* London: Macmillan.

Kandiyoti, Deniz, and Ruth Mandel. 1998. Editors' preface. *Central Asian Survey* 17 (4): 533–37.

Katz, E., and T. Liebes. 1986. Mutual Aid in the Decoding of Dallas: Preliminary Notes from a Cross-Cultural Study. In *Television in Transition,* edited by P. Drummond and R. Patterson. London: British Film Institute.

Lull, J., ed. 1988. *World Families Watch Television.* Beverly Hills, Calif.: Sage.

Mandel, Ruth. 1998. Structural Adjustment and Soap Opera: A Case Study of a Development Project in Central Asia. *Central Asian Survey* 17 (4): 629–38.

Mankekar, P. 1993. National Texts and Gendered Lives: An Ethnography of Television Viewers in India. *American Ethnologist* 20 (3): 543–63.

Miller, Daniel. 1995a. The Consumption of Soap Opera: *The Young and the Restless* and Mass Consumption in Trinidad. In *To Be Continued . . . ,* edited by Robert Allen, pp. 213–33. London: Routledge.

———, ed. 1995b. *Worlds Apart: Modernity through the Prism of the Local.* London: Routledge.

O'Donnell, Hugh. 1999. *Good Times, Bad Times: Soap Operas and Society in Western Europe.* London: Leicester University Press.

Price, Monroe. 1995. *Television, the Public Sphere, and National Identity.* Oxford, England: Clarendon Press.

Radway, Janice. 1988. Reception Study: Ethnography and the Problems of Dispersed Audiences and Nomadic Subjects. *Cultural Studies* 2 (3): 359–76.

Rofel, Lisa. 1995. The Melodrama of National Identity in Post-Tiananmen China. In *To Be Continued . . . ,* edited by Robert Allen, pp. 301–20. London: Routledge.

Ro'i, Yaacov. 1997. Islam in Post-Soviet Central Asia. *The Royal Institute of International Affairs, Former Soviet South Project,* no. 12 (March).

Seiter, Ellen, et al., eds. 1989. *Remote Control: Television, Audiences and Cultural Power.* London: Routledge.

Skuse, Andrew. 1999. 'Negotiated Outcomes': An Ethnography of the Production and Consumption of a BBC World Service Radio Soap Opera in Afghanistan. Ph.D. diss., University College London.

Tauxe, Caroline S. 1993. The Spirit of Christmas: Television and Commodity Hunger in a Brazilian Election. *Public Culture* 5 (3): 593–604.

11

Mapping Hmong Media
in Diasporic Space

Louisa Schein

In this essay, I explore the contours of media production and consumption by Hmong refugees in the United States. I do so with an eye toward analytically situating these practices in transnational space. That Hmong Americans have migrated to the West only since 1975, and that they left their home country of Laos under involuntary conditions of political exile, means that they have continued to live out their lives and their identities in a diasporic space—one that involves travel back and forth to Asia for some, and participation in an imagined and highly media-constructed supranational community for many more. In the 1990s there was a boom in camcorder-toting, world-traveling Hmong Americans, who in turn involved many less mobile others in their privileged travel through the circulation of images garnered from their Asian voyages. Media practices, as we shall see, have become pivotal in securing, and even generating, Hmong transnationality.[1]

The range of Hmong media forms is broad, centering on music and video. In audio cassettes, compact disks (CDs), and performance video formats, Hmong create original pop and heavy electronic sounds with live bands and synthesizers. Hmong newspapers and magazines, usually in bilingual format, spring up around the country and sometimes achieve national circulation. Weekly television and radio talk shows are produced and aired in California and Minnesota. Still photography has burgeoned, reflecting a growing demand for glamour and traditional portraits, calendars, posters, and packaging for Hmong products. Hmong young people are also studying computer animation, theater, and film with myriad designs for ethnic creations.

Videos, the focus of this essay, are in the Hmong language and, like all Hmong media, are targeted exclusively for intraethnic consumption. Shrink-wrapped and usually copyrighted, videos sell for up to $30 a piece. Although usually produced for profit, they are not backed by corporate or other advertising interests. Among the many genres—love dramas; war adventures; historical reconstructions; martial arts thrillers; documentary accounts of festivals, beauty pageants, and other public events; and dubs of feature films from Asian countries—is a sizable selection concerning Asia, the site of a panoply of Hmong memories. There are those that portray Laos, birthplace of almost all Hmong Americans and scene of the Secret War orchestrated by the CIA in which Hmong fought as guerrillas in Vietnam. There are those set in Thailand, where Hmong sojourned in refugee camps before being granted permission to migrate to the West. And there are those that document a mythologized land of origins in the mountains of southwestern China.

DIASPORIC WEBS, ITINERANT TRACKS

The Hmong of Southeast Asia have origins in China, where they are officially referred to as "Miao." The umbrella term Miao refers to the fifth largest minority ethnic group in China, a group numbering 7.3 million scattered over seven southwestern provinces. One to two centuries ago, several hundred thousand of these people migrated into Vietnam, Laos, Thailand, and Burma after conflicts with the Qing state. By Southeast Asian and Western convention, they are referred to as "Hmong." Their relocation took place enough generations ago that direct kinship ties and living memories of the Miao in China have been almost completely lost.

There are now well over 120,000 Hmong in the United States and other large refugee populations in France, Canada, and Australia.[2] In different communities they have pursued different strategies for livelihood, including skilled and unskilled wage labor and reliance on social services and public assistance. The largest U.S. aggregations are in the California Central Valley and Minneapolis–St.Paul, where the presence of tens of thousands means that Hmong ethnic businesses thrive. Not surprisingly, these are the locations of much of the Hmong media production and the outlets for most direct sales.

An ethnographic study of Hmong media needs to take account of the synergistic relation between community formation and what I call transnational subjectification. The way people understand who they are and how they belong is never anterior to, indeed is inseparable from, the kinds of media they consume. Moreover, such understanding is not static but is subject to ongoing revision in the course of social and discursive life. This is what Stuart Hall had in mind when he advocated thinking of "identity as a 'production', which is never complete, always in process, and always constituted within, not outside, representation" (1990: 222).

In diasporic situations, physical dispersal and territorial uprooting regularly give rise, with the availability of cultural technologies, to reconstitutions of primal kinds of identity, often fused with manufacturings of a homeland remembered as more timeless and essential than the actual place that was left behind. Anchors in a turbulent sea of displacement, they offer "discursive and symbolic order and rigidity in the face of personal and social disorder and fluidity" (Naficy 1993: 118). In turn, communities are forged that are not limited to migrants' *imaginings* or to the semiotic terrain of media *contents*. Through various modalities, emergent translocal interchanges redraw the horizons of ethnic community, stretching the bounds of the national. The use of videos sent back by Tongan Americans to communicate with islanders at "home" can be seen as such an interchange (see Hammond 1988), an instance of what Faye Ginsburg noted as the potential for indigenous media to "mediate, literally, historically produced social ruptures and to help construct identities that link past and present in ways appropriate to contemporary conditions" (1991: 94).[3]

It is not an overstatement to say that Hmong media have changed the nature and quantity of people's linkages around the globe, as well as the way they are felt. Apprehending this process requires a polyfocal research method, one that incorporates media messages into a mapping of the ways in which they are produced, disseminated, and consumed. Not only because of the differences between Hmong communities, but also because of the quickening movement of people, goods, and images among globally dispersed Hmong, I employ a fieldwork modality I call "itinerant ethnography." Extending the "multisite" method (Marcus 1998), itinerant ethnography is in spirit *siteless,* a recognition of the deterritorialized character of the cultural politics that are under examination. In this strategy, some research encounters are ephemeral, constituted by transient aggregations of people, such as festivals or international meetings—or living rooms when the VCR is turned on (see Schein 1998, 1999). Others are mobile—such as those with videos, video producers, and returned migrants to homeland sites—and hence require the tracking of movements.

I use the image of "mapping" in the title of this essay to point to relationality of positions and places. The practices of media are not only structured by, but also participate in creating, the structures of social life both within the Hmong American scene and between national sites of Hmong residence. Here global geopolitics and asymmetrical economies are formative and ever in tension with the horizontal unities that are strived for in so much of transnational imagining. They demand that we complicate a more homogeneous sense of "indigenous" media in which actors play themselves to themselves (Turner, this volume), operate out of a more singular home territory, or use images as activist cultural self-portraits for others (Aufderheide 1995; Gallois and Carelli 1995; Prins, this volume). Polyfocal ethnography enables a sharper perspective on the politics of discrepant locations within a supralocal framework (see Himpele 1996: 48).

Steve Thao of the *Hmong Tribune* newspaper and the Minnesota Hmong
cable show interviews a traditionally dressed woman on camera at a Hmong
demonstration in Washington, D.C. (Photo: Louisa Schein)

BORDER-CROSSING AT THE FRONTIERS OF HMONG MEDIA:
A VIDEO PIONEER

ST Universal Video, the venture of the first Hmong American "media mo-
gul," Su Thao, illustrates the decidedly translocal character of video production. Based in the city of Fresno, the largest aggregation of Hmong in
the United States, the video company also has branches in St. Paul, Minnesota, and Sarabury province, Thailand, in the vicinity of Wat Thamkrabok,
a Buddhist temple that has sheltered 23,000 Hmong from Laos. The headquarters of ST Universal occupy the spacious corner unit of what appears at
first glance to be a generic American strip mall. Flanking the video company,
however, are not-so-generic Hmong-run businesses—a beauty parlor and a
grocery that sells Asian specialty foods and a selection of Hmong video- and
audiocassettes.

Inside the entrance to ST, a Hmong receptionist behind a large desk tosses
out a greeting in unaccented English, "May I help you?" Kay has long hair

and trendy clothes and has made three music albums of her own. "Ever since I was a little girl, I remember loving to sing," she explains. She has also acted in one of the video dramas. Two Hmong men are sitting on one side of the office, waiting to turn over a technical project to Su Thao. A video monitor in the corner plays scenes of a family reunion in Laos from a home video that is being copied for the returned travelers.

A bookshelf displays a selection of ST's latest movies. Kay produces a list "as of Spring 1998." It includes features from India, China, and Thailand that have been dubbed and titled in Hmong. The category "Documentary–Original Production" lists twenty-eight films that were conceived, shot, or edited by ST. There are original dramas and documentaries of the Hmong in Asia, covering Laos, Burma, Vietnam, and China. There are also music videos of popular Hmong performers and documentaries of Hmong New Year festivals in the United States.

The facilities at ST headquarters are spacious and technically state-of-the-art. Su Thao takes me through an editing room, where the company processes its own videos, and an insulated sound room that others can rent for making radio spots. A storeroom is shelved to the ceiling with the company's video- and audiocassette stock. A large back room houses equipment for shrink-wrapping and mail-order packaging. Thao flips with pride through a thick stack of invoices that reveal how widely distributed his products have become—and not only in the United States. He gets orders almost weekly from France and now has a salesperson there.

In Su Thao's office a framed diploma reveals that in 1994 he received certification from the Hollywood Film Institute as a cinema director and line producer and as a feature film producer. He tells me the story of his life, of his immigration to the United States, and of the development of his entrepreneurial ventures. Born in Xieng Khouang province, the heart of the Hmong highlands, he was privileged to have attended high school and attained the rank of lieutenant in the CIA-funded secret army. In 1976 he was resettled in the small Dutch community of Pella, Iowa. Thao went to work immediately and took night classes to improve his English. He was employed as a janitor, in manufacturing, and as a job counselor for the state. Then in 1981 a national Hmong association—Lao Family Community—engaged him as director of its Stockton, California, office. After two years, he was hired away by Iowa Beef Processors, the "largest meat industry in the world," where he worked in personnel recruitment.

In March of 1989 an old Cambodian friend from his Stockton days who had borrowed $40,000 to establish a studio for dubbing Asian films for sale in the Cambodian community, hired Thao as his general manager; that studio became the technical training ground for Thao's own venture. His friend's business did not last, but by then Thao was ready to start his own company dubbing films for the Hmong audience. By 1990 he had decided to produce his own videos and traveled to Laos with permission to film Hmong life in the countryside. Over the next eight years he had been to Laos thirteen times, Burma twice, Vietnam twice, China six times, and Thailand more times than he could count.

Some but not all of these trips resulted in "documentaries," realist expositions of faraway lands with Thao's informative voice-over narration offering facts and figures. In addition to showing the lifestyles and conditions of the Hmong across Asia, Thao recorded special events such as festivals and international conferences. Sometimes he enhanced the cultural productions that he wanted to document by donating money to Hmong festivals in Asia to make them more extensive and elaborate.

Instead of picturing his Asian coethnics as distant and objectified exotics, Thao's videos place encounters with Hmong Americans center stage. *China Part 3* (*Hmoob Nqaum Toj Paj Tawg Teb*, 1995), the third in a series of tapes that portrays the activities of Hmong delegates to the China homeland, is the account of a 1995 New Year's festival in Yunnan province. Accompanying opening scenes of a smorgasbord of festival activities is Su Thao's authorial voice: "Welcome everybody! ST Universal presents *China Part 3*. . . . This year's New Year is a fun one for we Hmong from America, France, and Thailand to join. They have bullfighting, dialogue singing, playing the bamboo reed pipe—but the most important thing is that Hmong Americans have come to teach them how to do the ball toss." The tape proceeds through a concatenation of scenes showing both Hmong Americans and the panorama that met their eyes as they participated as key dignitaries. In trenchcoats, parkas, and business suits they are shown posing and interacting with locals, especially ornately costumed women. Su Thao narrates: "These girls are here to get a look at real Hmong Americans. . . . There are about 50,000 people here—all to learn about Hmong from other countries. Upon hearing we'd be here, Hmong from all over the place wanted to come and shake our hands and learn about our lives." The action proceeds to the high point of the tape. On the stage erected especially for the event, overseas Hmong men confidently toss balls back and forth with maladroit local women, completing the circle that brings Hmong migrants back "home" to reconstruct cultural unity.

China Part 3 has been one of ST's best-selling videos, but the biggest blockbuster was *Koj Muaj Kuv Pluag* (*You're Rich, I'm Poor*, 1996), a tale of a Hmong boy in the old country, impoverished by his parents' use of opium, who courts a wealthy Hmong girl against the wishes of her parents. Also successful have been *Kev Hlub Tsis Paub Kawg (Love Has No End)*, an Indian love story dubbed from Hindi into Hmong, and *Ncu Txug Txaj Ntsij Hmoob* (*Hmong Recognition Awards*, 1995), an account of a 1995 ceremony in Colorado in which U.S. military officials formally recognized Hmong contributions during the Vietnam War. But Thao is especially proud of the historical reconstruction *Hanoi, Dien Bien Phu* (1994). "Hmong were very impressed!" Thao exclaims; "They

had always heard about Dien Bien Phu, but everybody loved to see for themselves how the French lost the war." Then speaking to the interconnection
between memories of Asia and current Asian travel he adds, "I was the first
Hmong to go to Hanoi. I even got footage of a B-52 getting shot down!"
Thao's most recent project was "a true one—about the retribution of the
Lao government after 1975, their treatment of us." He comments on the
emotional impact he hopes it will have: "If they don't cry," he says of his projected audience, "they are not Hmong."

HOME HOLLYWOOD: STARDOM, FANDOM, AND OTHER GLAMOUR

Su Thao's training in Hollywood gives him a rare degree of professionaliza-
tion within the Hmong American media domain. Indeed, he boasts that his
is the only company to have purchased $25,000 worth of Beta SP professional
equipment. And few of the dozens of companies in operation have actually
established offices; most operate in homes or with rented equipment. Most
of the videos that one sees on the stands at festivals and on the racks in
Hmong shops are amateur productions by people who take a video camera
with them when they travel, or develop a hobby by making a video drama
with local friends and relatives. Some of these amateurs, along with many
non-Hmong patrons, rent ST's space and equipment to do their editing.

Nonetheless, Hmong "home" video takes its place within a thriving Hol-
lywoodization of a Hmong American youth culture that has its epicenter in
the music scene. The scores of Hmong pop bands that have sprung up
around the country provide a focal activity for many young adults. These
bands began to be formed in the late 1970s when Hmong youth were first
resettling in the West and were looking for a way to engage with the dominant culture. Teenagers and twenty-something Hmong purchased rudi-
mentary electric instruments and amplifiers and churned out blaring sounds
in the homes where they lived with their parents and/or their own young
children. Once established, these groups were invited to perform at weddings, festivals, and other events. They were avidly appreciated by all generations. Whether in Hmong, Thai, or Lao, their lyrics are comprehensible to
elder Hmong, and the majority concern the time-honored themes of romance and heartbreak. Some songs are original, but most are adaptations
of existing melodies.

At the New Year and other Hmong festivals, youth activities feature parties at rented halls where attendees must pay a fee for admission. Formal or
evening wear is usually de rigueur and dancing is the focal activity, with one
or two popular bands showcased live. At an event I attended in Fresno in
1996, a mini Academy Award ceremony was staged in which trophies were
ceremonially bestowed upon stars of recent blockbuster Hmong videos. The
entire ritual—of announcing the winners, having them take the stage to a

roar of applause, and the winners giving speeches thanking all those who contributed to their success—was enacted with solemnity.

Musicians, especially lead singers, generate far more than just their music tapes. Image management is a huge corollary enterprise. In a quest for both monetary gain and fame within the Hmong scene, they place ads at the beginning of videos promoting their music videos and glossy posters. Cassette tapes and CDs entice with packaging featuring sexy women and dapper young men in trendy or formal wear. Photography for these cover inserts—highly resonant with the semiotic codes of fashion and women's magazines, as well as with television commercials for beauty products—is a labor of love, involving grooming and posing for the glamour look. There are carefully chosen accessories, painstakingly styled hair, and outlandish makeup. Parted lips, inviting smiles, and tilted heads are also regular features.

Popular bands, then, are at the heart of a proliferating pattern of Hmong publicity and fandom. What started as local operations with extended family support and audiences, have been transformed into an ever more canonized star system whose reach is national and even transnational, involving France, Australia, Canada, Thailand, and Laos. Lee Vang of Minnesota, for instance, made it big by writing and singing Hmong lyrics to Indian pop melodies. So popular was this unusual hybrid form that she was invited on concert tours in France and Canada and paid $2,000 a show.

Some singers in homeland countries have achieved their fame on the patronage of Hmong in the West. Su Thao, for instance, "created" several Hmong pop stars. On his early trips to Laos, with his canny eye for marketability, he located a Hmong woman with singing talent, Mai Moua, and sponsored and recorded her. She became a sensation in the U.S. Hmong music scene and her cassettes sold well, especially on the strength of her being in Laos. Thao also sponsored four Thai-based Hmong male pop stars who have produced enough songs to fill three well-received music videos. Much of the popularity of these overseas stars derives from the authenticity of their homeland location.

RECEIVING CULTURE

The dream of so many Hmong producers to canonize histories and capture living memories accords with the consumption desires of many older Hmong American viewers. It is as if both their sense of war-induced loss and their minoritization within the strictures of U.S. class and race politics have prompted a genealogical thirst, a longing to trace out their conflicts and engagements with more powerful groups in former times. The immediacy of the formative years of war in Laos, which were also the coming-of-age years for most older Hmong, is writ large as the story of centuries of war in which their politico-cultural identity congealed. As ethnographer Jo Ann Koltyk suggests: "By providing strategies for working through new meanings of space and place, and for continuity and belonging in the United States, the Hmong videos may very well be indicators of health and healing in the grieving process for a group having lost a homeland" (1998: 130).

Long Yang lives in an understated row house on the north side of Philadelphia. He is 51 years old and the father of five grown children, some of whom live with him. Yang was a radio technician in the Special Forces in Laos. He had done radio repair work during the war, commanded an operation of radio wave interception for strategic purposes, and survived the falling of a shell that blasted him out of his chair as he sat at the military base one day. Resettled outside Indianapolis in 1976, Yang insisted on working for wages from his first week as a refugee. Using his technical skills in radio and electronics, he progressed, in the space of less than two decades, from yard and janitorial work to managerial work in technology firms, where he earned as much as $70,000 a year; eventually he started his own business. But he developed a heart condition, and in 1995 he left work for a few years to restore his health. While his wife worked, he stayed home to care for his two-year-old granddaughter so that his son could go back to school. That situation left him plenty of idle time to use his VCR.

The consumption styles of Yang's multigenerational family reveal the particularities of Hmong media markets. When I visit Yang in 1999, two big crates of videos sit next to a large-screen television, the focal point of his living room. "This is my history collection," he tells me; "I am thinking of getting all my videos on DVD, and my tapes on CD, so I can keep them longer." As he places the first box on the floor for me to sort, the little granddaughter rushes over to do her own sorting. She extracts tape after tape, strewing them across the living room carpet, glancing with a discerning eye at each one she discards. Finally she finds the one of her choice. It is *China Part 3* by ST Universal Video. Wordlessly nudging her grandpa, pleading to him with her eyes, she insists that he play the tape. She plunks down in front of the television to watch a kaleidoscope of dancing, singing, and costumes with narration in her first language, which she is just beginning to understand.

Yang tells me that the toddler's favorite videos are the China dancing tapes and those of Hmong beauty contests. "All the Hmong babies like this kind of video," comments her 28-year-old dad, upon returning from his class. His younger sister, a 22-year-old Temple University student, has just told me that she enjoys every genre of videos, *except* the cultural documentaries. "I don't know . . . I wasn't born there," she demurs, defending her disinterest. Her brother concurs, emphasizing that the China tapes are simply not engaging. He watches his daughter sit riveted before the swinging skirts of dancing Miao girls, listening to the crooned melodies of old-time courtship songs, watching the virtuoso dancing of bamboo reed pipe players. He is not drawn to the screen but speaks directly to me, imputing a nascent ethnic identification to his daughter with a touch of incredulity: "It's the culture, I guess."

There are fifty-nine commercial tapes in Yang's two crates, but he tells me the family owns many more that are boxed away in closets. "I buy them when I go to Minnesota or California, or people send them to me," he explains. Over a third of Yang's collection fall into the category of traditional culture and homeland videos—documentaries about life in China, Laos, and Thailand, recordings of festivals and *kwv txhiaj* (Hmong singing), histories of the war, and dramatizations of old folk tales. Almost as many are love dramas and music videos, staples of the Hmong American cultural landscape. The remaining handful include dubbed Indian, Thai, and Chinese movies, a film of a Hmong beauty pageant, and an educational video designed to deter gang activity. Asked what kind are their favorite videos, Yang and his wife say they favor the documentaries and war histories over the fictional love dramas. People even older than they are, he explains, prefer enactments of old folktales, especially those with fine-grained evocations of daily life in rural Southeast Asia. Speaking to the way both social mobility and memory are lived through video consumption, Yang states: "Old people like to watch how poor people were."

THE VOICE OF DIASPORA

One of the hallmarks of Hmong American video is the mixing of genres. Some studies of diasporic video have emphasized a direct communicative function, with videos supplementing the media of the telephone and the audiocassette to convey messages between homeland and migrants (Hammond 1988; Kolar-Panov 1996). Here video is seen as a visual addition to what migrants and those at home want to tell each other about themselves. There are, to be sure, Hmong American videos used in this way, but the scope is severely limited by the conditions in Asian homeland villages where video capability, and even reliable electricity, is a rarity. Such videos as convey messages between Asia and the United States usually take the form of documentary with a sprinkling of direct address mixed in. The basic representational structure is not that of personal communication, in which the self is transmitted through images and words, but rather of an exploration of a faraway and almost out-of-reach place, one whose details and textures are only accessible through the power of vision. Such nostalgia tapes include an array of motifs that play to pastoral memories. They depict a simple existence, one structured by agriculture and physical labor. Both craggy mountains and slopes terraced with rice fields evoke a closeness to the land that is lost to migrants. Families labor together, not separated by the institutional structures that organize and segment urban lives.

Moments of more passive watching are occasionally interrupted by someone speaking directly to the camera, bridging the gulf across the Pacific and casting a voice right into migrants' living rooms. In one such video, a sumptuous dinner banquet constitutes the closing scene of an extended tour in which the viewer has been introduced to many aspects of the province of Yunnan. Guests and hosts are introduced to the camera. Eating and toasting is recorded, as is gift-giving. Then, at the very end, the hosts are invited to speak some words of greeting directly to the audience in America.

In *China Part 3,* an elderly Hmong leader in Chinese cadre uniform takes the stage to make the following speech with the knowledge that it will be "heard" worldwide:

> Welcome everyone to this event! Today is a great day for all Hmong to get together. Not only that, but we have Hmong from all over the world who we've been apart from for 200 years. I am as happy as I've ever been in my life. We hope you take our words and images back to your country. Tell them that you saw our people in China. We want to see you come back again. I hope that the heavens will help the Hmong, whether farming or working for a living, to survive throughout the world!

In another documentary-style piece, the roving tourist eye of the camera suddenly takes on a brokering function. After introducing the landscape, villages, and lifestyles of the local Miao people, it turns to a more instrumental function. Three rural young women are arrayed on a hilltop, colorfully dressed before a backdrop of panoramic scenery. The cameraman asks: "Will you sing a song for me to take back to America to find you a man?" And then: "Are you girls still young and unmarried?"

The girl who is apparently the eldest, but who appears to be no older than her mid-teens, "Yes, we don't have 'it' yet."

"Thank you very much," he replies. The camera hesitates, zooms in on the face of the speaker, then pans to the other two girls. They smile awkwardly, like would-be picture-brides, and smooth their skirts and aprons self-consciously. The cameraman, now self-appointed matchmaker, narrates: "These are three of our Hmong girls. They are going to sing and I'm going to record a couple songs to take back to our men in America." He chuckles audibly, then asks one of them a key question for the determination of potential marriage partners in the Hmong/Miao clan-exogamous social system:

"What clan are you?"

"Zhou clan," the eldest offers.

Then they proceed to sing, not knowing where to cast their eyes. They appear disoriented at the staging of what, in face-to-face courtship, would have been a dialogue, but now has been rendered as a one-way self-marketing opportunity about which their faces convey primarily ambivalence. Like catalogue-brides, they communicate, but only from a position of "rhetorical vulnerability" in which they are commandeered to present themselves in codes not of their own making to audiences not visible to them (Wilson 1988: 119). It could be argued, then, that while these moments appear to be instances of homelanders speaking, the voice at the level of representational control is decidedly that of the video's maker. As Ruby has suggested, the "native" we see in films about others or selves is ultimately the one behind the camera (1991: 62). The control of the technology is ultimately decisive, for the tapes will be taken home and processed to fit the consumption desires of Hmong refugees who listen to such songs and speeches in very particular ways.

THE TRANSNATIONAL AS TEXT

There is common recognition among Hmong I have talked to in many U.S. communities that, in 1999, the two-part drama *Yuav Tos Txog Hnub Twg*, colloquially referred to as *"Dr. Tom,"* was the "most popular" Hmong video. Shot in Thailand on the spur of the moment with a shoestring budget and an improvised script, the blockbuster is the creation of Ga Moua, who was formerly involved in the music scene and a frequent traveler to Asia. The story combines time-honored Hmong folklore motifs—including the tragic orphan boy and the exquisite torment of unconsummated love—with newfangled themes of transnational relationships gone wrong.[4]

Set in a refugee camp in Thailand, Part One tells the story of a beautiful young woman who is falling in love with a young man who has been raised as her stepbrother after the horrible murder of his parents by a predatory Thai gang as they crossed out of Laos. In jets "Tom," a Hmong American man, with slicked hair, sunglasses, a cowboy's swagger, a camcorder, and claims of being a highly paid doctor. He immediately begins wooing the girl's family with money and convinces them that it would be best for everyone's future if she married him. Despite her broken heart, the family gives her away, just in time for her new husband to run out of money and flee back to his vindictive first wife in the United States. His new bride is left behind to wait and waste her life indefinitely.

The more didactic Part Two reveals the gradual demise of the evil-doing Dr. Tom, who turns out to be nothing but a janitor in an American doctor's office. Lying to an uncle-in-law that he needs a loan to start a farm, he raises enough money to race back to Thailand, where he learns that his second wife has abandoned her marriage to him and returned to her original boyfriend. He tries in vain to impress many other women, all of whom let him know that they will not be duped by men from America. Humiliated, he returns home and violently vents his frustration on his wife, who reports him for domestic abuse. In a dramatic climax, he is arrested, handcuffed, and carted off to jail.

The *Dr. Tom* story, and its resounding reception within the Hmong American community, shows that ethnic media have a role not only in bringing the images of coethnics in distant Asia into Western living rooms for entertainment, but also of working through current issues in the ongoing development of Hmong transnationalism. Asked about *Dr. Tom,* most Hmong I spoke to chuckled or smiled, with a glimmer of irony. Why did they think it was so popular? "Because it's true," most of them said; "It's a real story." It is not that this particular story actually happened, they hastened to explain, but that this kind of thing happens all the time. One middle-aged man suggested a fantasy effect: "It's what many men want to do, but know that they can't." Others talked disapprovingly about the calculations of Hmong and Miao families, situated in the Third World and willing to offer their daughters to secure that transnational alliance that would magically transform their economic fortunes. What the text precipitates is a collective concern over emerging cleavages, a painful awareness that beyond horizontal solidarity, Hmong/Miao transnationality is fraught with pitfalls for identitarian aims— it is a minefield in which those from the West suspect those in Asia of economic opportunism, while those in Asia see those from the West as sexual predators. Read at the level of its barely veiled didacticism, *Dr. Tom* can be seen as a call for ethnic self-scrutiny in which the tragedies of internal exploitation can be brought to light and expelled.

THE TRANSNATIONALISM MADE BY MEDIA

Hmong American media-making is a polyglot enterprise that reveals itself to be a major force in Hmong social life, identity formation, and economic strategies. It emerges out of the historical moment of the camcorder revolution and the particularity of Hmong positioning within U.S. ethno-racial stratification. How do immigrants negotiate their cultural practice while undergoing U.S. minoritization? Viewed in the context of dominant media, and a culture of Americanism that disciplines immigrants as particular kinds of subordinated subjects, we might think of Lisa Lowe's tenet that "the subject that emerges out of Asian American cultural forms is one in excess of and in contradiction with the subjectivities proposed by national modern and postmodern modes of aesthetic representation," that "the current social formation entails a subject less narrated by the modern discourse of citizenship and more narrated by the histories of wars in Asia, immigration, and the dynamics of the current global economy" (1996: 32–33). In this light, Hmong could be seen to be making space for their very particularized narratives, ones that enunciate their own cultural memories, war genealogies, sentiments of loss, and struggles of resettlement. Not only in explicit texts such as war docudramas, but even in pop music formed out of the sojourn in Thailand, the traces of their specific pasts can be retained and processed. At the same time, they participate in the decentering of a "national culture [that] has become increasingly strained, fractured and demystified" (Buell 1994: 144).

I hold, however, that it is not the politics of the American site that is the primary shaper of Hmong media, and this is how it differs from case studies in specifically national contexts (Abu-Lughod 1995; Mankekar 1999; Rofel 1994). Fruitful anthropological work has been done on the transnational imaginings that are enabled through the consumption of media products from within particular localities (Appadurai 1996; Miller 1992; Schein 2001; Yang, this volume), but the peripatetic character of Hmong media demands more complex methodologies. Generated within webs of diasporic linkage, such media are produced in, circulate in, represent, and structure relations across national borders. Yet they are far from being generically cosmopolitan. Benedict Anderson has pointed out that, "Not least as a result of the ethnicization of political life in the wealthy, postindustrial states, what one can call long-distance nationalism is visibly emerging. This type of politics, directed mainly towards the former Second and Third Worlds, pries open the classical nation-state project from a different direction" (1998: 73).

For these reasons I emphasize the imbrication of media with transnational subjectification. It is not only that the relations precipitated by Hmong media—from the transfer of dollars, to the transfer of wives, to the movement of travelers back and forth across the Pacific—are materially consequential at the supranational scale. It is also that the specific meanings embedded in so many of the texts that are produced can be seen as interpellating Hmong consuming subjects into a kind of border-crossing sensibility, one that sites their identity in no one nation-culture, but only in the interstitial spaces they have carved out through millennia of wars and conflicts with dominant others. These events and processes and their meanings become the substance of Hmong collective memory, avidly imbibed in the form of polychrome homeland customs by video-happy toddlers and encountered through the oblique glance of Americanizing young adults as they pass through family living rooms. Not seduced by celebratory globalism, both texts and production relations struggle with internal fractures, figuring geopolitical differences into their narratives and practices as irrevocably constitutive of their diasporic condition.

NOTES

For research support I would like to thank the Committee on Scholarly Communications with the People's Republic of China, the Fulbright-Hays Doctoral Dissertation Research Abroad Program, the Samuel T. Arnold Fellowship Program of Brown University, the University of California at Berkeley, and the Rutgers Research Council, as well as numerous institutions and individuals in the United States, Thailand, and China who sponsored or otherwise facilitated my work. I am grateful to Nouzong Ly, Ly Chong Thong Jalao, and Long Yang for assistance with translations.

1. This essay represents part of a larger ongoing study of transnationality among Hmong Americans and their coethnics in Asia (Schein, n.d.). My field research, which

I have been conducting intermittently in the United States since 1979, has also included trips to urban and rural China in 1982, 1985, 1986, 1988, and 1993 and one trip to Thailand in 1982.

2. Estimates of Hmong populations in the diaspora in 1992 were: 120,000 in the United States, 13,000 in France (including 1,500 in French Guyana), 650 in Canada, and 650 in Australia (Yang 1993).

3. For other treatments of diasporic media and cultural interchange, see Kolar-Panov 1996; Fischer 1995; Gilroy 1993; and Hall 1990. For more general overviews of diaspora cultural politics see Clifford 1994; Safran 1991; and Tölölyan 1991.

4. Space does not permit discussion of Part Three, which had just been released at the time of this writing.

REFERENCES

Abu-Lughod, Lila. 1995. The Objects of Soap Opera: Egyptian Television and the Cultural Politics of Modernity. In *Worlds Apart: Modernity through the Prism of the Local*, edited by Daniel Miller, pp. 190–210. London: Routledge.

Anderson, Benedict. 1998. *The Spectre of Comparisons: Nationalism, Southeast Asia and the World*. London: Verso.

Appadurai, Arjun. 1996. *Modernity at Large: Cultural Dimensions of Globalization*. Minneapolis: University of Minnesota Press.

Aufderheide, Patricia. 1995. The Video in the Villages Project: Videomaking with and by Brazilian Indians. *Visual Anthropology Review* 11 (2): 83–93.

Buell, Frederick. 1994. *National Culture and the New Global System*. Baltimore: Johns Hopkins University Press.

Clifford, James. 1994. Diasporas. *Cultural Anthropology* 9 (3): 302–38.

Fischer, Michael M. J. 1995. Starting Over: How, What, and for Whom Does One Write about Refugees? The Poetics and Politics of Refugee Film as Ethnographic Access in a Media-Saturated World. In *Mistrusting Refugees*, edited by E. Valentine Daniel and John Chr. Knudsen, pp. 126–50. Berkeley: University of California Press.

Gallois, Dominique T., and Vincent Carelli. 1995. Video in the Villages: The Waiapi Experience. In *Advocacy and Indigenous Filmmaking*, edited by Hans Henrik Philipsen and Birgitte Markussen. Hojbjerg, Denmark: Intervention Press.

Gilroy, Paul. 1993. *The Black Atlantic: Modernity and Double Consciousness*. Cambridge, Mass.: Harvard University Press.

Ginsburg, Faye. 1991. Indigenous Media: Faustian Contract or Global Village? *Cultural Anthropology* 6 (1): 92–112.

Hall, Stuart. 1990. Cultural Identity and Diaspora. In *Identity: Community, Culture, Difference*, edited by Jonathan Rutherford, pp. 222–37. London: Lawrence and Wishart.

Hammond, Joyce D. 1988. Visualizing Themselves: Tongan Videography in Utah. *Visual Anthropology* 1: 379–400.

Himpele, Jeffrey D. 1996. Film Distribution as Media: Mapping Difference in the Bolivian Cinemascape. *Visual Anthropology Review* 12 (1): 47–66.

Kolar-Panov, Dona. 1996. Video and the Diasporic Imagination of Selfhood: A Case Study of the Croations in Australia. *Cultural Studies* 10 (2): 288–314.

Koltyk, Jo Ann. 1998. *New Pioneers in the Heartland: Hmong Life in Wisconsin.* Boston: Allyn and Bacon.

Lowe, Lisa. 1996. *Immigrant Acts: On Asian American Cultural Politics.* Durham, N.C.: Duke University Press.

Mankekar, Purnima. 1999. *Screening Culture, Viewing Politics: An Ethnography of Television, Womanhood, and Nation in Post-Colonial India.* Durham, N.C.: Duke University Press.

Marcus, George E. 1998. *Ethnography through Thick and Thin.* Princeton, N.J.: Princeton University Press.

Miller, Daniel. 1992. The Young and the Restless in Trinidad: A Case of the Local and the Global in Mass Consumption. In *Consuming Technologies: Media Information in Domestic Spaces,* edited by Roger Silverstone and Eric Hirsch, pp. 163–82. London: Routledge.

Naficy, Hamid. 1993. *The Making of Exile Cultures: Iranian Television in Los Angeles.* Minneapolis: University of Minnesota Press.

Rofel, Lisa. 1994. Yearnings: Televisual Love and Melodramatic Politics in Contemporary China. *American Ethnologist* 21 (4): 700–22.

Ruby, Jay. 1991. Speaking for, Speaking about, Speaking with or Speaking Alongside—An Anthropological and Documentary Dilemma. *Visual Anthropology Review* 7 (2): 50–67.

Safran, William. 1991. Diasporas in Modern Societies: Myths of Homeland and Return. *Diaspora* 1 (1): 83–99.

Schein, Louisa. 1998. Importing Miao Brethren to Hmong America: A Not So Stateless Transnationalism. In *Cosmopolitics: Thinking and Feeling beyond the Nation,* edited by Pheng Cheah and Bruce Robbins, pp. 163–91. Minneapolis: University of Minnesota Press.

———. 1999. Diaspora Politics, Homeland Erotics, and the Materializing of Memory. *Positions* 7 (3): 697–729.

———. 2001. Chinese Consumerism and the Politics of Envy: Cargo in the 1990s? In *Whither China: Intellectual Politics in the 1990s,* edited by Xudong Zhang. Minneapolis: University of Minnesota Press.

———. N.d. Identity Exchanges: Cultural Production in the Hmong/Miao Diaspora. Unpublished ms.

Tölölyan, Khachig. 1991. The Nation State and Its Others: In Lieu of a Preface. *Diaspora* 1 (1): 3–7.

Wilson, Ara. 1988. American Catalogues of Asian Brides. In *Anthropology for the Nineties,* edited by Johnnetta B. Cole, pp. 114–25. New York: Free Press.

Yang Dao. 1993. *Hmong at the Turning Point.* Minneapolis: Worldbridge Associates.

IV

The Social Sites of Production

Juliana Lopez, a Tzeltzal woman from Amatenango, Chiapas, Mexico, viewing herself on video making pottery, part of a collaborative video project made with craftswomen in her village. (Photo: Lyn Pentecost)

12

Putting American Public Television Documentary in Its Places

Barry Dornfeld

Ethnographies of media production practices present both significant challenges and substantial possibilities for engaging with the circulation of media forms in contemporary societies, inviting us to rethink both the ways in which we situate ethnographic research and how we theorize media. What gets broadcast on television are texts produced in multiple places, in the profilmic locations represented on camera and in the occupational settings where the pre- and postproduction work takes place. And it is stating the obvious to note that these are not the places, for the most part, where television is consumed. Media researchers might, by design or necessity, limit their focus to one or two of these three arenas, each of which, of course, can and often does involve multiple sites. However, to engage with media with any theoretical depth is to see the implications of at least more than one, if not many, of these spaces that a given work or genre traverses.

This chapter builds on an ethnography of the production unit that created the seven-hour educational series *Childhood*, which aired nationally on public television in the fall of 1991, in England in 1992, and in several other countries subsequently, and then entered educational distribution in several formats. Geoff Haines-Stiles, the executive producer of *Childhood*, collaborated with WNET-TV in New York, one of the major producing stations in the PBS system, to coproduce and present the series. They added British funding and partnership, as well as a team of production staff, freelance crew members, and esteemed academic researchers from the fields of child development, psychology, history, and anthropology, disciplines concerned with the life of children and families. *Childhood* juxtaposed the articulation of scholarly knowledge about child development from these disciplines with observational scenes depicting family life in diverse settings in Brazil, Russia, Cameroon, Japan, and the United States.

These representations of child development were crafted by a group of public television and media production professionals located in New York, London, and several other places around the world and academics at American and British universities. These media professionals and academics developed the series with particular groups of viewers in mind (primarily audiences for public broadcasting in the United States and England) and with particular orientations to the broad subject areas (biology, culture, and history). Given these social constraints, an examination of this series reveals a great deal both about the complex social practices of encoding these understandings in the contemporary form of public television documentary and about the complexities of studying media production as a form of public culture.

MEDIA ETHNOGRAPHY AS MULTISITED AND MULTITHEORIZED

To engage with the *Childhood* series through the various stages of its production—from proposal development, to fundraising, preproduction, and production, and through its circulation to various viewers—is to think through the importance of multiple locations, multiple networks of work (including several organizations and ad hoc professional teams), multiple mechanisms for distribution, and a variety of settings for reception. In this way, an ethnography of the series, like any work on media practices, would be enriched by being a multisited study in the vein articulated by George Marcus (1998), by focusing on the multiple sites in which these media texts intersect with the lives of those producing and consuming them. Methodologically, tracking this "object," this set of texts, across all these sites would be very difficult if not impossible. Yet broadening the territory in these directions offers a useful shift in perspective.

On the level of theory, also, this model of a multisited ethnography has something significant to offer media studies. I agree with Lila Abu-Lughod (1997) that the domain of media studies has been disappointingly thin from the perspective of ethnographic depth, but I would add that media studies' theoretical foundations have been constrained in scope as well. Media theory has grown up in three broad arenas linked to conventional stages of media practices: theories of production, theories of textuality, and more recently, theories of consumption. Scholars have tended to confine their work to one of these three areas, with little in the way of integration or holism.

I would illustrate these theoretical silos with a diagram that links stages of communication with a related theoretical framework:

PRODUCTION	TEXT	POSTPRODUCTION
Auteur theory	Textual poetics	Theories of reception
Theories of authorship	Genre theory	Audience theory
The production of culture	Thematic analyses	

Over a period of time, a number of authors, myself included, have argued for an integration of these theoretical domains (see Worth 1981; Tulloch 1990; Michaels 1991; Dornfeld 1998). According to one line of thinking, these theoretical debates are contained within the media industries' own categorical system, accepting the media industries' own models of orthodoxy. In other approaches, these domains have been integrated on the level of theory but rarely actualized. Yet a "unified" theoretical framework for looking at the media is necessary and useful because it both simplifies and grounds our understandings of media in the experiences and practices of the agents who both produce and consume these forms. This in turn enables us to understand how media become enmeshed in the social lives of people in various places and cultures. I want to build an argument here about how a more holistic theory of media practices can grow out of the multisited research imaginary that Marcus describes and construct this theoretical argument from the ethnographic material.

SITES OF TELEVISION TEXTUAL PRODUCTION:
THE SOCIAL SPACE OF PBS DOCUMENTARY PRODUCTION

I begin in this vein by tracing a description of the multiple locations within which *Childhood* took shape. An adequate media ethnography, however, requires not only that we track how the members of the production community created the final product but also that we elucidate carefully the multiple constraints within which they worked.

A collaboration between two independent producers, Geoff Haines-Stiles and David Loxton, gave birth to the *Childhood* series. Their careers had taken them through different trajectories intersecting with the public television system in the United States: Loxton was working inside WNET in New York City, one of the two largest producing stations in the American Public Broadcasting System; Haines-Stiles was located in Los Angeles and working in both public and commercial television but had coproduced a program with Loxton years before they conceived the idea for *Childhood*. A conversation between them led to a meeting in New York in 1985 and eventually to the development of a proposal for the series. After a typically long process of obtaining WNET's backing and funding from the Corporation for Public Broadcasting (CPB) and other sources, the *Childhood* project moved into its initial phases of production in 1989 just as Loxton was succumbing to cancer. Haines-Stiles pushed on, adding the British-based Peter Montagnon as a co-executive producer and beginning the complex process of documentary production within the PBS model.

We might place these media professionals and the academics they recruited for the team in what Abu-Lughod (1997: 122) termed a "transnational habitus" of upper-middle-class, mobile, cosmopolitan, educated knowledge

Shooting of the "Budding Babies" sequence for the PBS television series *Childhood* in a New York studio, 1990. (Photo: Barry Dornfeld)

workers. The producers were multisited characters themselves—occupationally nomadic as they moved from Los Angeles to London to New York in their sites of employ, and in the case of the field producers, from India to China to Tibet.

The institutional structure supporting the series invokes another set of translocal, even transnational, relationships—among a federally funded production support mechanism, the Corporation for Public Broadcasting; a local PBS station, WNET-NY, with a large impact on the national system through its production of national series for broadcast; a British production and distribution network, Channel Four in London; a British production company, Antelope Films; local crews and companies in the many locations in which the *Childhood* series was shot; and other organizations involved in the circulation of the series.

Even *Childhood's* aesthetic form, what the producers referred to as a "blockbuster PBS series," can be categorized as a transnational documentary format, cultivated as a hybrid out of British and American public service broadcasting programming and adapted for the American PBS context. Tracing the history of this genre intertwines counterinfluences from public television makers and academics moving between England and the United States, often sharing funding and distribution and sometimes engaging in forms of coproduction. That is, the public broadcasting series is a genre whose history is rooted in specific individuals and organizations working in specific sites but migrating and interacting across these sites. In studying the *Childhood* project, then, I was focusing on the arena of production for a group of professionals involved in the production of a socially influential, state-supported form of television.

Childhood's executive producers assembled a production staff with substantial documentary and public television production experience. The New York–based staff, housed on the tenth floor of WNET's building on West 58th Street in Manhattan, fluctuated in size between fifteen and twenty people. By design, the New York staff represented an unusually diverse set of cultural backgrounds and a balance in gender. Though organized and managed by two white male executive producers, under the oversight of mostly male, mostly white administrators at WNET, the series relied on key people of color, including an Asian (female) series producer and an Asian (female) and an African-American (male) as associate producers. As for cinematographers, usually a male bastion, the ranks included two women. In addition, a carefully chosen pool of freelance workers in production and postproduction contributed a significant amount of work to the series, making up much of the temporary community formed for the production.[1] Although most of the staff members were middle to upper middle class and college-educated, they had highly varied cultural backgrounds, advanced degrees, and types of production experience that influenced their work.

New York was the central locus for the series, the place where the segment producers worked, where script and planning meetings took place, and where editing eventually happened. While researching and shooting the series, producers traveled to field locations in the United States, Brazil, Japan, Russia, Italy, Ghana, and Guatemala and used footage from Baka communities in Cameroon. In the United States, producers used the freelancers from the pool they had recruited. Overseas, they worked with designated stringers, freelancers to whom previously established production contacts had led them. *Childhood's* academic advisers and on-camera hosts, called observers, formed a critical part of this community as well. They were chosen over the course of the project's development and early production. A brochure for fund-raising described them as "prominent experts in the many fields that touch on childhood."

It was through intense negotiations over the shape and approach to the series that the producers and advisers began to articulate and create an aesthetic approach to this documentary material and a shared perspective about what they wanted to say about childhood. The producers' positions within the social space of public television production oriented their frameworks for decision-making and the strategies and practices they employed. These positions could be demarcated by various factors: the relevant models for program production they value and incorporate, their own previous work and the work they hope to do in the future, their place within the institutional hierarchies and constraints of this territory of cultural production, and their lives within the social spaces they occupy outside their labor. We can also locate the *Childhood* series itself in a social and historical trajectory and look at the limitations and constraints imposed on the series by the social field within which it was produced. In this logic, we can look at choices made by the agents involved in producing the series from among what Bourdieu called "the space of possibles," a field of forces that orient specific strategies and struggles, defined by the present state of public television programming and these agents' places within that territory (Bourdieu 1983). By looking at the relationships between this cultural production and these broader social forces, we can raise larger questions about the consequences of the series as an example of contemporary public culture in the United States, thereby locating the series in social space.

For instance, conditions created by both public policy and the market at the time this series went into production affected public broadcasting as a whole and put in place broad parameters within which *Childhood's* producers worked. PBS's "need" to broaden its audience and strengthen certain demographic segments (including the age bracket of young parents), driven by the system's unstable financial and threatening political circumstances, contributed to the view of this series as an attractive opportunity. *Childhood's* subject matter resonated with the "family values" orientation popular with conservative social and political movements in the 1990s, and its populist subject matter offered the potential to tap into these underserved audiences. The system's "blockbuster mentality," its strategy for revitalizing its identity through high-profile national series on topics with broad appeal, which was propelled by the success of *The Civil War* series, presented the producers with a model to aspire to and some strategies for getting there. The ongoing political attacks on the system, attacks that carried potentially dire financial consequences, limited the kinds of risks that the institutions supporting the series were willing to take and contributed to the definitions of relevant ideas and formats to be presented in televisual form.

The social organization of television production, what we might call the "culture of documentary authorship," also influenced the course of production. The division of authorial responsibility resulting from a particular hierarchy of personnel combined with the necessity of creating a series that was coherent and consistent from episode to episode (requiring the sharing of footage and sequences). These forces led to a production style that discouraged authorial distinctiveness and viewed authorship as collegial and negotiated both among the production staff and between producers and advisers. The orientation of the series toward a broad public audience, including the funding it received, its high visibility as a major PBS series, and its eventual position on the PBS schedule, constrained the producers, who had to work in a style that would accommodate and make the material clear for a broad cross-section of audience segments. At the same time, the series had a more limited set of viewers to appeal to within internal and external institutions of power (public broadcasting organizations, funding agencies, institutions for social policy, and academia). The producers employed a format and style that attempted to balance broad audience engagement with the necessary criteria for "a discourse of sobriety," documentaries dedicated to disseminating information and knowledge (see Nichols 1991). The construction of these relevant audiences and their interests had a formative impact on the series from its inception through broadcast. Simultaneously, the genres of major documentary series that preceded *Childhood* presented the project with a range of thematic and stylistic strategies to choose from, while eliminating others.

On the broadest level, *Childhood* became the kind of series it did in large part because of the agitation and adjustment present in the public television system at the time and the life history of WNET, one of PBS's highest-profile stations. *Childhood* was a high-budget multipart series, one form of programming on the public television schedule that was undertaken when the system was searching for, or at least reconsidering, its identity in the ecology of broadcast television and grappling for a greater share of certain audiences. The system's support of these national series was described by one writer as "yielding to public television's equivalent of Hollywood's blockbuster mentality" (Schapiro 1991: 31), investing significant resources in several large projects, and avoiding risky topics. We need to see *Childhood's* existence within this context as part of the public television system's strategy for expanding its audience base. In this sense, we are locating the series in relation to policy struggles taking place in specific locales: in the Washington, D.C.–based offices of PBS and CPB; among program officers, WNET representatives, and *Childhood's* producers; and even to extend the multisited frame, on Capitol Hill and in other related places where funding for the public broadcasting system is at stake.

The programming and funding strategy supporting the series created three principal imperatives to frame the series. First, the system wanted to broaden its audience by developing and broadcasting more populist programs, material whose subject matter might appeal to a larger demographic proportion of the U.S. viewing audience than the more elitist programs for which the system was famous (or infamous). A series about family life seemed to fit that requirement rather easily. Second, the system looked for programs that would avoid offending conservative political sentiments—programs that were safe. Although I do not think that the series intentionally steered away from difficult political topics to avoid offending segments of viewers, the producers did consciously exclude an approach that would dwell on the poor conditions of children's lives internationally and historically, afraid to turn viewers away. The portrait of the families that evolved did not exclude domestic and social conflict, disease, and poverty, but set those negative dimensions as a background to a more positive view of the life of children.

This second strategy ties in with a third, the desire for a multicultural focus in public television programming. Just as *Childhood* began full-scale production, PBS appointed Jennifer Lawson as its executive vice president of programming and promotion; one approach she stressed in rethinking public television programming was multiculturalism, which she defined as "our commitment to cultural diversity."[2] In large part because of these broader forces, *Childhood's* orientation became populist, politically neutral, and multicultural. The way the individuals and institutions involved in its production constructed and constrained the framing of this material is intertwined with and reveals a great deal about the emergence of and tensions within contemporary American public culture: about how public television producers mediate the cultural worlds and bodies of information they represent, how public television conceives of and encodes scholarly and scientific knowledge in television documentary form, and who producers and administrators project their audiences to be.

MULTIPLE SITES OF RECEPTION: LOCATING THE PUBLIC BROADCASTING AUDIENCE IN THE UNITED STATES AND ABROAD

Given this multiply-sited production process and a documentary series that represents many places in the world, how do the social positions and locations of multiple audiences come into play? One way to address this is to ask who constitutes the public television audience in the United States and Great Britain, the principal sites for broadcast. We can answer this with some statistical profiles about typical PBS and Channel Four viewers in the United States and U.K., demographic and regional outlines of who watches, when, and how much. The portrait these profiles paint is of a viewership more demographically narrow than that of the mainstream broadcast audience, though not as narrow as public discourse in the United States assumes.[3]

We can also consider how the institutions of production create and assess these audiences and how the forms of television they produce address the particularity of these viewers. In this sense, the organizations and individuals involved in public broadcasting construct the very viewers they hope will watch (see Ang 1991). I was able to approach this question in the ethnographic framework I employed. As I observed and participated in the production process, it became clear that the series producers spent a great deal of time and energy predicting, invoking, and strategizing about how to hold the attention of the hoped-for audiences. The audience was not an academic construct to them but a more or less predictable and diffuse group of people. However, the producers did not project a unified location or social position for this imagined audience. They debated the possibilities of audience interpretation across national and social boundaries as well, especially comparing the likely reception by American and British viewers.

Locating the audience often involved predicting how a variety of viewers from a variety of places would react to sequences about other cultures and nations, about the exotic other. In an exchange that exemplifies the ways in which producers "prefigured" their audience, adviser Sandra Scarr, a well-known American psychology professor and researcher, expressed her concerns that footage acquired from a filmmaker who had shot material with the Baka, a small-scale, forest-dwelling society in Cameroon, might not be appropriate for the American audience:

> *Sandra Scarr:* I've got a question about the Baka material in general. My question is whether it's too exotic, that it's too different from the average viewer's knowledge or experience, and will just seem peculiar.

> *Haines-Stiles:* I think that that is not a problem that I'm aware of in somebody responding to the two films that have been made, the three films that have been made by Channel Four, and Gwynn [Pritchard], Brits are undoubtedly more insular even than Americans. I'm sorry, English people are even more insular than Americans, you can latch on to this and see how people responded in the U.K. But it's my sense that the particular uniqueness of this footage is that it does relate to what Levine would call the environment of evolutionary adaptiveness in a filmic way, and that you can see enough footage in which there is enough intimate behavior of a similar caliber to that which our cameramen got in Russia or in the U.S., that you can respond to these characters. . . . I profoundly believe that, and I would like to just ask maybe Gwynn to just blast that in any way.

> *Gwynn Pritchard:* . . . . I think, and speaking in generalizations in this company is always extremely dangerous, British society is probably less self-consciously racist than North American society. But if that series was going to fall into the trap that you've described, among audiences, that the audience research we did, but anyway the press to the series would have elicited and brought it out pretty obviously and quickly. And indeed, to my knowledge, the universal response in the papers, from the qualities through to the tabloids, was precisely this way, not exactly White Plains but that these are beautiful and charming people, and it was that particular family in the first series, actually con-

centrated on Ali as a little boy, it was a response actually wonderful. . . .

Urie Bronfenbrenner: It humanized them . . .

Robert Hinde: There is a certain sense in which the relation of the Baka to the other families is the same as the relation of your children on an aseptic table is to the other families, they're stripped of all the nonsense of civilization, and here are the same basic processes going on. And you see them more clearly. (Advisers' meeting, February 3, 1991)

These discussions among members of the production team were common and contributed significantly to the shaping of the series. Buried beneath these discussions are the diverse assumptions that various stakeholders bring to the series about their own "ideal" audiences. The producers were interested in total numbers of American viewers but also in the critical reception of the series by their colleagues within the PBS system and by influential players in the public sphere (such as newspaper critics and high-profile academics). The academic advisers, I would argue, had their scientific colleagues in mind when they thought about the reception of the series and were therefore concerned about the scientific legitimacy of much of the material. Freelance personnel brought their own ideal audiences with them, who included other producers who might look at their specific contributions and hire them for future work.

In a sector of the media industry increasingly forced to apply marketplace principles in its operation and a free-market rationale in defending its existence, techniques of measuring audience size and membership, and comparing these measurements with the demographics of commercial broadcasting, take on a sense of urgency. At the same time, the system's mandate, the mission of public broadcasting, is rooted in an argument about its educational value and the important niche it fills in a world dominated by commercial broadcasting. These discussions of reception take us to wider issues of circulation: *Childhood's* place, and the place of public television, in the spheres of cultural production and consumption in the United States. In the broadest sense, we enter here into national debates and conflicts over the mission of public broadcasting and its place in American public culture, a set of discourses touching on policy questions about the regulation of the media industry, the funding of cultural production, and the mission of public broadcasting. These issues connected to the day-to-day work of the series as the producers planned and executed the programs. Elsewhere I have characterized the producers' points of view as lodged in tensions between opposing tendencies or imperatives of education and entertainment, opposing pedagogical significance with audience engagement and social scientific relativism with what I termed "televisual humanism" (see Dornfeld 1998).

These tensions locate this series (and similar material on public television) between highbrow culture and something approximating middlebrow (or middle-to-lowbrow) culture. These very tensions reflect the crisis in mission and identity burdening the public broadcasting system, which the system's programming strategies help to perpetuate.

The PBS documentary format provides aesthetic strategies to manage these potentially conflictive goals, to work out approaches that make programs "work" on multiple levels, though as co-executive producer Peter Montagnon stated in an interview, "It's easy to think of the right arguments; it's very, very difficult to visualize it and to express it in such a way that it is truly illuminating on the screen" (Advisers' meeting, December 12, 1989). The intent to visualize ideas that are either expository or narrative, or both, is a struggle most documentary filmmakers share, and that they approach through different strategies of production and articulation. The producers constantly search for dramatic material to illustrate intellectual points or to stand on its own. In the end, tensions get played out, more or less successfully, between the "magic" of documentary realism and the edification of expository explanation, between the programs as engaging televisual experience and the programs as scholarly knowledge, both tendencies mediated by the producers' practical logic and the aesthetic ideologies of program production.

Of course, the popular sensibility American public television targets is not that of the mass audience (left to network and cable television), but of the educated, privileged layperson, the viewer interested in spending some "quality time," as a report on the future of public broadcasting was titled (Somerset-Ward 1993). But herein lies an irreconcilable tension, since members of most class and regional sectors in the United States treat the consumption of television primarily as a leisure activity and resist intellectual pursuits as part of this leisure. As Andrew Ross argued (1989), intellectuals and intellectual discourse have historically had a problematic and somewhat marginal place in American popular culture. Public television is a primary arena for what Ross described as the recruitment of intellectuals into public culture, an arena that gives "experts" a prominent televisual role.

On the aesthetic level, the tensions between information and drama, between expository and observational sequences, between hard data and soft illustrations, and between sobriety and engagement resurfaced repeatedly. For reasons that are both historical and institutionally reproduced, American public television documentary is propelled by an ideology for the encoding of knowledge into televisual form that borrows more from British models of cultural enlightenment through television than from the orientation of television in American culture. In fact, several programs that have become mainstays of public television in the United States, such as the science program *Nova,* explicitly borrowed from British program ideas. PBS imports other fare from England. There is some irony here, though, since the British explicitly designed their broadcasting system to avoid the commercialism present in American broadcasting. In the United States, the place of public broadcasting in national cultural life is much more tendentious and problematic than in other industrialized nations in Europe, Asia, and North America. In Great Britain, Canada, and Australia, vital policy discussion exists over the state funding of television, driven by the belief that the maintenance of a national cultural identity is at stake in these policy decisions. As Toby Miller described with regard to both Australia and Canada, "There is little doubt that this desire to form a national identity underlay much of the argument for state subvention of film and television" (Miller 1993: 128).

The thrust in these other national settings is to argue for both a moral and a pedagogical function for television, and to bolster this mandate with institutional supports in funding certain forms of programming (educational, public affairs) and restricting others (entertainment-based, imported). The situation is rather the opposite in the United States, where the public broadcasting system has been rhetorically attacked as contrary to the national economic ideology (anti–free market), or as destructive of the kind of value-based moral identity that political conservatives favor. Recent policy initiatives have even further eroded the place of the public interest in the media landscape and opened new arenas for market-based control. A conflict exists, then, between the liberal social imperatives behind the founding of the public broadcasting system as part of Johnson's Great Society government programs, essentially a social-welfare, antimarket ideology, and the more libertarian, free-market contemporary political/economic climate. We can trace much of the cultural and political conflict back to divisions of class and regionalism. Indeed, part of the popular resistance, hostility, criticism, and political contentiousness felt toward public television stems from the perception that it is a system designed by and for cultural elites and political liberals (mostly from the Northeast), a charge that the institutions devoted to the system's vitality simultaneously disavow and embrace.[4]

ELECTRONIC COMMUNITIES, PUBLIC SPHERES, AND NATIONALITIES: RETHINKING MEDIA AS PUBLIC CULTURE

Despite its anticipated success, *Childhood* did not win the viewership its producers expected, and the series received mixed press reviews. I believe that its lack of national success reflects the problematic place of public television in American public culture. Ultimately, I attribute the mixed reaction the series received to differences between class and regional fragments within American culture and related disagreements over what people think public television should be. It would be convenient if we could map the differences between reviews in the *New York Times* and more populist publications like

USA Today and the *Cleveland Plain Dealer* onto social differences between readerships, real or perceived, to understand reception in its multiple sites. However, frameworks for reception are not usually so easily categorized or linked to demographics or geographies. And though their writing styles classify them as they classify the texts they review, critics are too unpredictable and idiosyncratic to succumb to this simple pigeonholing process. Ultimately most of the critics understood and appreciated the intentions of the series, and from this we can conclude that *Childhood* was a typical PBS series. But the differences between critics' assessments of the worth of the series indicate more dissent than agreement over the value of public television documentaries like *Childhood,* and it is this lack of consensus that needs to be explicated. If we extrapolate this diversity of opinion and interest to some body of television viewers, we can see how the issue of consensus dissipates even further.

This line of thinking raises pertinent questions about the constitution of American public culture: Can we locate an abstraction such as "the public sphere" in any empirical basis in the United States? What is the place of public television within such a projection, given the highly commercial and corporate, technologically volatile, and socially fragmented nature of American public cultural life? The issue of nationality and the role that media forms play in the making of national cultures, central to the emerging work in the anthropology of media and other fields, challenges us with regard to the United States.[5] Theories of public culture or the public sphere that look at national media as reflective of some monolithic national identity do not do justice to the conflictive nature of these cultural forces in the United States and elide the ways these forces, based in tensions over class and culture, are embedded in the structures and process of cultural production. Unlike many other countries, developed and developing, with state-sponsored television systems, the United States has a unique situation in that the television network the government explicitly supports has a marginalized viewership; the network is only one choice along the expanding televisual landscape, and garners only a few percentage points of the average national television audience. I would suggest that rather than producing a shared national culture (as one might argue that the BBC has done with some success), programs like *Childhood* both reflect the tensions within American public cultures and, crucially, serve to reproduce or even foster them. The various cultural frames that producers, scholars, bureaucrats, critics, and viewers bring to the work of production and reception reflect a broader cultural fragmentation than our typical understandings of media acknowledge, and perhaps serve to produce this very fragmentation rather than construct some shared democratic forum or public sphere.

Commentators who favor the public television system, as well as those who are critical of it, tend to share the view of the system as a hybrid and conflictive conglomerate of national policy, borrowing from and loosely based on the British model but with a haphazard history that has led to its current state of confusion. It would therefore be problematic to speak of public television as reflective of a dominant national consciousness or political ideology, of a "national imaginary," particularly in light of the vehement and politically and regionally factionalized debates over what public television is and should be, without positing that national imaginary as a multiple and contested one, as some have done (see Ginsburg 1993; Appadurai 1990). At the same time, the portion of society that both watches and produces the programming, and that supports these institutions, includes a powerful segment of the cultural elite. That support gives public television an important role in the production of the public sphere and in cultural policy (as *Childhood's* producers were well aware). The "viewers like you" that the institution of public television is seeking, the audiences it needs to construct, become an imagined community on which it depends (Anderson 1991). Though this community aspires to some shared national participation, in the end it remains largely a community based in class and cultural exclusions, a community whose hybrid boundaries reflect the culture of production in which it is grounded.

To extend this community's influence to the level of the national would misapprehend the increasingly global "mediascapes" (Appadurai 1991) in which American media forms participate. The comparisons with state-dominated mediascapes like those we find in European countries reveal that corporate interests exert much more control over media flows in the United States than they do in other countries.[6] These differences are eroding, as industrialized countries give over ever more of their broadcast infrastructure to private control and interests (many of these global rather than national, such as Rupert Murdoch's expanding multinational media conglomerate). Corporate and market forces control our dominant national media and leave only a small, marginal space for public interest considerations. This situation has clear historical precedents: corporate interests have exerted control over broadcasting since the late 1920s, when "they began to sense the immense profitability of advertising-supported broadcasting" (McChesney 1995: 16). Since then, they have dominated policy debates and eclipsed attempts to limit their dominance of the airwaves, constraining public broadcasting in the process. The result, of course, has been a national media ecology dominated by corporate interests, hardly the public sphere that Habermas imagined and for which European scholars continue to advocate, or the electronic democracy touted by American pundits. Public broadcasting's marginal position in our national public culture determines the pressures the system feels.

Thinking about media production within the framework of multisited research transcends certain ongoing and naturalized theoretical frameworks and dualities. Analyzing media production through on-the-ground practices and against the background of institutional settings provides a different qualitative understanding of how media forms make meaning, one that forces us to confront both the symbolic and the material conditions and practices of production. The negotiations producers engage in with administrators, funders, scholars, crew members, subjects, programmers, promoters, critics, and ultimately viewers (though all the previous are important viewers as well) represent acts of mediation that result in a media text. The forms of mediation that result in the production of a television program are socially and historically situated in relation to other public cultural forms. In this sense, television is not just a media form but a format through which complex acts of cultural mediation take place, and through which, at least in the United States, a fragmented society produces and reproduces its differences, even while in search of some forms of commonality.

NOTES

1. The role of freelance crews in independent and public television production has not been given much scholarly attention but represents an important dimension of how creative labor is utilized in these domains of production. These crews constitute a kind of mobile community in this project-based enterprise. See DeFillippi and Arthur 1998 for a discussion of these labor forms from the perspective of management theory.

2. James Day (1995: 304–5) writes: "In a memorandum to her station constituency, she summed up her seven-point prescription for the newly named National Programming Service. Primary emphasis was to be placed upon 'the creation of a distinctive, culturally diverse variety service demonstrating leadership in children's programming and increasing the visibility of public television's public service and educational role.' The prescription's key word was *multiculturalism,* the fashionable term for the 1990's, which Lawson defined as 'our commitment to *cultural diversity'*— the wish to make certain that all PBS programs 'accurately reflect and serve our society in all its diversity.' If the goal had a ring of old coinage—cultural diversity has been a strong element in public television's programming for more than forty years—the emphasis was new: Lawson would have every show proposed for the National Program Service vetted for multicultural content." Lawson's comments come from a memorandum entitled "National Program Service 1991 Annual Report," January 17, 1992.

3. Based on October–November 1996 Nielsen data compiled by PBS. Posted on *Current* web page (www.current.org), revised Oct. 7, 1998. Current Publishing Committee, Washington, D.C.

4. See James Day's comments on this in his reflections on teaching about public television to an undergraduate body of working-class students at Brooklyn College (1995: 331–32).

5. See, for instance, the special section of essays in Abu-Lughod 1993; and also Price 1995.

6. See Avery 1993 for a series of essays comparing institutions of public service broadcasting across national boundaries.

REFERENCES

Abu-Lughod, Lila. 1997. The Interpretation of Culture(s) after Television. *Represen-tations* 59: 109–34.

———, guest ed. 1993. Special section of *Public Culture* 5 (3): 465–606.

Anderson, Benedict. [1983] 1991. *Imagined Communities: Reflections on the Origin and Spread of Nationalism.* London: Verso.

Ang, Ien. 1991. *Desperately Seeking the Audience.* London: Routledge.

Appadurai, Arjun. 1990. Disjuncture and Difference in the Global Cultural Econ-omy. *Public Culture* 2 (2): 1–24.

———. 1991. Global Ethnoscapes: Notes and Queries for a Transnational Anthro-pology. In *Recapturing Anthropology: Working in the Present,* edited by Richard G. Fox, pp. 191–210. Santa Fe, N.M.: School of American Research Press.

Avery, Robert, ed. 1993. *Public Service Broadcasting in a Multichannel Environment: The History and Survival of an Ideal.* White Plains, N.Y.: Longman.

Bourdieu, Pierre. 1983. The Field of Cultural Production, Or: The Economic World Reversed. *Poetics* 12: 311–56.

Day, James. 1995. *The Vanishing Vision: The Inside Story of Public Television.* Berkeley: University of California Press.

DeFillippi, Robert J., and Michael Arthur. 1998. Paradox in Project-Based Enterprise: The Case of Film Making. *California Management Review* 40 (2): 125–39.

Dornfeld, Barry. 1998. *Producing Public Television, Producing Public Culture.* Princeton, N.J.: Princeton University Press.

Fraser, Nancy. 1990. Rethinking the Public Sphere: A Contribution to the Critique of Actually Existing Democracy. *Social Text* 25/26: 56–80.

Friedland, Lewis. 1995. Public Television and the Crisis of Democracy: A Review Es-say. *Communication Review* 1 (1): 11–28.

Ginsburg, Faye. 1993. Aboriginal Media and the Australian Imaginary. *Public Culture* 5: 557–78.

Haines-Stiles, Geoffrey, Erna Akuginow, and Eugene Marner. 1991. Letter to the Ed-itor. *New York Times,* November 10, p. 4.

Jensen, Joli. 1984. An Interpretive Approach to Culture Production. In *Interpreting Television: Current Research Perspectives,* edited by Willard D. Rowland Jr. and Bruce Watkins, pp. 98–118. Beverly Hills, Calif.: Sage Publications.

Marcus, George. 1998. Imagining the Whole: Ethnography's Contemporary Efforts to Situate Itself. In *Ethnography through Thick and Thin.* Princeton, N.J.: Princeton University Press.

McChesney, Robert. 1995. America, I Do Mind Dying. *Current* (August 14): 16–19.

Michaels, Eric. 1991. A Model of Teleported Texts (with Reference to Aboriginal Television). *Visual Anthropology* 4: 301–23.

Miller, Toby. 1993 *The Well-Tempered Self: Citizenship, Culture, and the Postmodern Subject*. Baltimore: Johns Hopkins University Press.

Nichols, Bill. 1991. *Representing Reality: Issues and Concepts in Documentary*. Bloomington: Indiana University Press.

Price, Monroe. 1995. *Television, the Public Sphere, and National Identity*. New York: Oxford University Press.

Ross, Andrew. 1989. *No Respect: Intellectuals and Popular Culture*. New York: Routledge.

Rubenstein, Carin. 1991. A Tour of the Wonder Years: It's a Small, Small World. *New York Times*, October 13, section F, pp. 29, 33.

Schapiro, Mark. 1991. Public TV Takes Its Nose out of the Air. *New York Times*, November 3, pp. 31–32.

Somerset-Ward, Richard. 1993. *Quality Time: The Report of the Twentieth Century Task Force on the Future of Public Television*. New York: Twentieth Century Fund Press.

Tulloch, John. 1990. *Television Drama: Agency, Audience and Myth*. London: Routledge.

Worth, Sol. 1981. *Studying Visual Communication*, edited by Larry Gross. Philadelphia: University of Pennsylvania Press.

13

Culture in the Ad World

Producing the Latin Look

Arlene Dávila

Today 50% of all bookings at Radio City Music Hall are Hispanic artists. Salsa outsells ketchup in the Midwest. Nachos beat hot-dogs at movies. What's happening? Simple: A cultural and marketing phenomenon known as the U.S. Hispanic market.
BROMLEY AGUILAR & ASSOCIATES ADVERTISING, San Antonio, Texas, 1999

In recent years, Latinos have become one of the U.S. advertising industry's most coveted market segments. Fueled by the "salsa beats ketchup" phenomenon, they are increasingly targeted by culturally customized advertising generating powerful representations of and for Latinos. This chapter examines the Hispanic marketing industry and the images with which it constructs and imagines the diversity of populations of Latin American background in the United States as a generic and undifferentiated "Hispanic market." I explore this industry as a self-identified arena of Latino self-representation which, dominated by corporate intellectuals of Latin American background in the United States and directly tied to the structures of the U.S. economy, serves as a fruitful entry point for an analysis of the complex interests that coalesce in the commercial imagining and representation of this emerging identity. My goal is to bring attention to the local repercussions of the commodification and mass mediation of culture through a study of how culture-specific marketing affects public definitions of Latinidad and hence Latinos' place and sense of belonging within contemporary U.S. society.

My analysis draws from interviews with the staff of sixteen Hispanic advertising agencies and from the content of ads created for nationwide distribution in the Spanish language TV networks, Univision and Telemundo, which share the common goal of addressing Latinos as a unified and culturally specific market. It speaks to current anthropological research on the media's role in the construction and expression of identities through ethnographic analyses that expose the multiplicity of interests engaged in the production of these texts. With some exceptions, anthropologists have largely overlooked the U.S. media, and particularly commercial media, even though it constitutes the largest advertising and media market worldwide and hence a determinant influence in the global rendering of marketable identities.[1] Such an emphasis on foreign noncommercial media is not surprising considering that the dominance of Western media has historically fueled the widespread use of the media as a tool for asserting cultural and national identities, as well as the very growth of the anthropology of the media and of anthropologists' growing interest in its use as a tool of social activism and cultural assertion (Ginsburg 1991, 1999; Turner 1992). More and more, however, commercial representations play a pivotal role in the social imagining of populations; whether as exiles, citizens, permanent residents, or immigrants, individuals are consumers first and foremost. By focusing on one segment of the U.S. advertising industry—a division of ethnic and targeted marketing—my goal is therefore to explore this industry's imagining of U.S. Latinos in light of global trends in the advertising industry that increasingly affect not only the growing U.S. Latino community but also other segments of U.S. society, as well as global markets worldwide.

Specifically, Hispanic marketers are not unique in their intention to create a self-contained market but exemplify the local repercussions of global trends in advertising, particularly what Miller (1997) has called the "revolt of the local," involving the appeal to the supposed intrinsic differences of particular populations as individuals are turned into consumers and populations into markets (Burke 1996; Firat and Dholakia 1998). Such appeals to authenticity corroborate the ubiquity of particular racial and nationalist ideologies and even of global hierarchies of culture and place in the commercial imagining of populations, prompting us to analyze how they come to bear or are purposefully deployed by the many interests that coalesce in the marketing of difference. Anthropologists have long noted how nationalist ideologies are necessarily implicated in the production of a range of media texts (Mankekar 1993; Abu-Lughod 1993; Naficy 1993), yet I see advertising as additionally revealing of how discourses of identity, race, or nationality come to bear in these representations given their makers' dual and direct attachments with different interests and constituencies. These dual engagements, we shall see, make Hispanic "creatives" (the staff member who conceives the creative strategy for ads) and advertising professionals brokers and mediators of preexisting hierarchies of representation as they seek to shape definitions of "Hispanics" that meet both the expectations of their corporate clients and those of their prospective audience of consumers.

But first let me address briefly a contentious issue of terminology and definition. "Hispanic" and "Latino" are used interchangeably in this chapter, as is done by people in the marketing industry, although this industry is most commonly known as "Hispanic marketing." This is undoubtedly due to the industry's preference for the officially census-sanctioned category of "Hispanic" over "Latino." Although both terms are used to encompass a highly heterogeneous population—one that spans the recent immigrant from any part of Latin America to the U.S.-born Latino and that differs along lines of class, race, and historical background among other variables— "Latino" is not an officially sanctioned term but one of self-designation that is connected to past social struggles and activism (Noriega and López 1996). Hispanic is also more suitable to this industry's emphasis on the Spanish language as a source of commonality. Although both terms are used equally by this industry to sell, commodify, and market populations of Latin American background in the United States, it is the official "Hispanic" that agencies most often use to designate their work, themselves, and their target audience in their marketing presentations and printed materials. I use these terms throughout this chapter, but my intention is not to reify either "Hispanic" or "Latino/a" by treating these terms as unitary and unproblematized constructs, but to interrogate the inherent inclusions and exclusions that are involved in the commercial promotion of Latinidad as the essentialized encompassment of a highly heterogeneous population. I start by examining the industry and the composition of its staff and go on to analyze the dominant tropes for representing Latinos as a generic market. I conclude with a discussion of how this industry may shape and affect contemporary definitions of Latinidad and notions of belonging and citizenship in public life.

HISPANIC MARKETING AND THE PEOPLE BEHIND IT

Hispanic marketing is conducted by a network of over eighty advertising agencies in every U.S. city with a sizable Latino population. Yet only thirty years ago this industry consisted of little more than a couple of recently arrived Cuban expatriates who were intent on convincing a skeptical corporate America of the profitability and existence of a culturally specific market. What fueled this growth were three interdependent and parallel developments: the federal designation in the 1970s of any person of Spanish descent in this country as "Hispanic," the growing interest on the part of marketers in segmented and targeted campaigns,[2] and the immigration of Cuban media and advertising professionals to New York City shortly after the Cuban Revolution. Many of them had been active in transnational advertising agencies in Cuba and had the expertise and contacts to establish their own agencies in New York, Miami, and later Los Angeles. Today, however, it is not solely these early entrepreneurs that are marketing to Latino populations but hundreds of self-identified Latinos or Hispanics, many of whom are recent arrivals from Latin America attracted to the business opportunity offered by Hispanic marketing. Their commercial representations of and for this market, however, are never produced in a vacuum. They are always dependent on their clients' approval, most of whom are Anglos representing the local and transnational interests of corporate clients, adding to the interests screening and affecting the production of commercial representations of Latinos.

This constant interaction between Anglo and Latino personnel in the creation of ads has in turn led to an ethnic and linguistic division of labor in Hispanic marketing beyond the structural or departmental distinctions at play in the advertising industry at large. Accordingly, native Spanish speakers and less acculturated individuals, such as recent Latin American arrivals, are more likely found in creative departments, whose demand for "perfect" language skills bars most U.S. Latinos, while the latter are more common in production and client services departments, which require what was described to me as "more Americanized" skills to handle corporate clients and negotiate with other segments of the industry. Elsewhere I discuss how this division is affected by the political economy of the networks as well as some of the inequalities that are embedded within this ethnic and linguistic division of labor (Dávila 2001). Briefly, within the advertising industry at large, creative positions are far more prestigious than positions dealing with research, accounts, or clients. It is the creative individual who wins prizes and name recognition, earning what Dornfeld (1998) has called "career capital," in contrast to "financial capital," a distinction that stems from Bourdieu's (1993) discussion of the antieconomic logic that predominates, in various degrees, in different fields of cultural production.

What I would stress here, however, is that such ethnic and linguistic divisions in the Hispanic marketing industry are part and parcel of this industry's identity, guided by the premise that there are basic differences between Latinos and other consumers that need to be addressed through culture- and language-specific marketing, and that there is a continuous influx of Spanish-speaking populations who would otherwise not be reached by advertising were it not for this type of marketing. This emphasis on Spanish as the guarantor of Hispanics' authenticity has strengthened the role of the recently arrived Latin American "creative" and of the Spanish-dominant Latino who is more likely to be the recent arrival and hence not yet "tainted" with American culture, as the model Hispanic consumer. I purposefully emphasize the idea of not being contaminated by American culture because this industry is predicated on the view that Hispanics remain unassimilated relative to U.S. mainstream culture and thus dependent on culture- and language-specific ads. Notwithstanding the Spanish-dominant universe shared by creatives and their audience, however, the class, background, and education of most creatives are starkly at odds with those of the average U.S. Hispanic consumer. Thus whenever they need to establish the basis for their authority among clients and mainstream colleagues, they appeal to the one thing they do have in common with their audience—their shared ethnicity.

As one agency director stated, "What we have to convey to our clients is that only a Hispanic can really understand our culture, our way of being and feelings, to produce a truly compelling and relevant campaign. It is not a professional that a client gets when they hire us, but a *Hispanic* advertising professional" (his emphasis).

Hispanic ad professionals thus consistently implicate themselves with U.S. "othering" practices, ambiguously homogenizing themselves into the marginal category of "Hispanic" irrespective of their class or educational background or their actual identification with most Hispanics, while also becoming key "tropicalizers," that is, agents troping and imbuing Latinos with traits, images, and values derived mostly from dominant representations of Latinidad (Aparicio and Chávez-Silverman 1997: 8). In addition, as a general rule, the expertise of Hispanic advertising professionals is based less on their already mentioned putative commonality with the average U.S. Hispanic consumer than on conventions that are circulated in the industry as "knowledge" of this consumer. Modest budgets and hence lack of qualitative and quantitative research in this industry have led to heavy reliance on secondary research, particularly what Roberta Astroff (1997) has called popular para-ethnography, characterized by the reification of cultural characteristics legitimated in reference to the ethnic authenticity of its authors.[3] The preponderance of these cultural conventions is fueled by the market's definition on ethnic grounds, which compels ideas of cultural commonality with which to justify the development of new campaigns targeted to the "uniqueness" of the Hispanic consumer.

THE GENERIC PAN-HISPANIC

Primary among these ideas is the notion that U.S. Hispanics constitute a distinct "nation within a nation." In contrast to the territorially bounded nation, this ethnic "nation" would be conceived as a symbolic or "imagined community" (Anderson 1983) shaped and constructed through the media, which would vest it with its own idiosyncrasies and particularities. As stated by Peter Font, one of the first Cuban pioneers and founder of Fova advertising in New York, in order to become profitable, "this market had to be considered as a separate nation, as a country separate and apart from the U.S. with a totally different language and culture." The concept of a Hispanic nation is used mostly by the founders of this industry, not by its present practitioners, although they all shared an interest in promoting Latinos' cultural and identity boundaries and in presenting them as an inclusive and all-encompassing entity. In particular, they were all concerned with the construct of an ideal generic Hispanic and with defining and consolidating ideas about the most authentic or appropriate representation of him or her. These representations, however are always constructed under the specter of Latinos' minority and racialized status, which looms large in this industry where advertising staff consistently encounters Anglo-held beliefs that Hispanics are "suspects not prospects" and hence second-class consumers unworthy of a client's advertising money. Hispanic advertising staff are therefore additionally pressed to generate "positive" images—which, as we shall see, is tantamount to showing affluent and white Latino consumers—as a means of increasing the attractiveness to clients of Hispanics as potential consumers.

The contingent nature of these representations is evident when we consider that Latino/Hispanic identity would become crafted against or in opposition to a similarly stereotyped Anglo identity, which constitutes the dominant reference for defining what constitutes a "Hispanic." Specifically, in constructing such a bounded and recognizably distinct Hispanic, Latin American creatives have largely reproduced the same anti-imperialist dichotomies that Latin American intellectuals used to develop their nationalist ideologies after the turn of the twentieth century. In resistance to the growing ascendancy of the United States in the Americas, Latin American intellectuals developed theories of the greater worth of their own cultures in contrast to the presumed materialism, lack of culture, and greater technological advancement in the United States (Ramos 1989), although this time these dichotomous culturalist frameworks would function to construct an altogether new nation, within the confines of the United States. In this way, "culture" would become Hispanics' primary "domain of sovereignty" (Chatterjee 1986), through a preponderance of definitions and images drawing on a balance of superiorities between Anglos and Hispanics in which Hispanics are defined as more moral, virtuous, ethical, and spirited in relation to Anglos' superiorities in technology, material achievements, and progress, reproducing dominant definitions of Latinos as a "family-religion-and-tradition-bound people." As a Venezuelan creative noted when describing how best to target this market: "You have to touch the emotional buttons, the sentiments, and most of all the family. As different as we may be, we all care about the family; unlike the Anglo, we care about our people." These ideas inform the motto of different advertising agencies, such as that of New York–based Vidal Reynardus and Moya—"To get your message across to Hispanics you have to speak to their hearts"—as well as most advertising for this market. Hence the preponderance of the "family," which could well be considered the ultimate advertising "referent system" in this market—that is, a system of signs and meanings that are known and generalized and can be used to transfer and translate meaning to products (Williamson 1978). More than any other trope, theme, or image, the family has been implicated in and associated with the supposedly "intrinsic" Latin spirit and morality that are believed to characterize Hispanic consumers' collective rather than individualist orientation.[4]

Consider, for instance, the ads introduced in 1998 for Nicoret, a product designed to help people stop smoking. For the general (Anglo) market, this product was advertised through testimonials in which people discuss conquering the smoking habit as an act of individual achievement. For Hispanics, the tactic was different. As stated by a representative of Publicidad Advertising, "We realized that Hispanics are mostly influenced by their family, it is a personal decision but one that is taken in relation to others, thus we use the family, and a friend inducing people to quit." Their slogan captures the tactic succinctly: "Por tu Bien y el de los Tuyos" (for the well-being of you and yours). The 1997 advertisement for ITT Technical Schools provides another example of the family as the presumed arbiter of Hispanic values. Whereas most ads for community colleges and other types of postsecondary education for the general market draw on people's individual ambitions to succeed and improve themselves, this ad shows a thankful Hispanic character acknowledging the role his family, friends, and ITT Technical School played in helping him advance his dream of pleasing his parents and becoming a role model for his community. Interspersed in the narrative are images of his proud parents, images that would rarely be seen in an ad for the general market. In the same tenor, Fova Advertising's ad for Oil of Olay's in the Hispanic market features a woman explaining what "we [Hispanic] women want": details "like a touch, a caress, or a gentle word." As its creative explained, the execution for the ad was based on the view that, unlike Anglo women, Hispanic women beautify themselves not for "selfish, me-oriented purposes," but in order to please others and obtain their approval and praise. A milk ad for the Hispanic market is additionally revealing of the kind of images aimed at U.S. Latinos. While the general market campaign revolves around personalities wearing a milk mustache, the Hispanic version features a grandmother cooking traditional milk-based desserts with a caption that reads: "Have you given your loved ones enough milk today?" This was based on the fear that Hispanics would not understand the humor of the original ad and the belief that the Latin woman would be instinctively worried if she were not giving her family enough of such an important provision as milk.

Because such value-oriented ads present Hispanics in a positive light as loving and socially caring individuals, they are generally popular among consumers. I myself noticed the acceptance of these views after sharing marketing charts contrasting Anglo and Hispanic values with self-identified Hispanic consumers in New York City.[5] Most important, corporate clients see in the traditional and conservative Hispanic a brand-loyal and dependable consumer. Nonetheless, the question to ask here is: in relation to what, whom, and with what implications are these images positive? (see Stam and Shohat 1994). Specifically, it is worth calling attention to the fact that these types of representation would make little sense if they were not constructed within the aforementioned Anglo versus Hispanic behavioral dichotomy that has long patterned Hispanic stereotypes, in both the United States and Latin

America. As such, they are an extension of, rather than a departure from, dominant representations of Hispanics' "intrinsic" spirit and of the values and dispositions associated with Anglos and Latinos, the same ideas that, from the U.S. standpoint, have made Latin Americans appear ripe for and needy of U.S. colonization, modernization, or incorporation.[6] Are there no motivated and self-reliant Latinos?

It is the development of visual representations of generic Latinidad embodied in a look or in speech, however, that most directly evokes the predicaments of these representations. Traditionally, Hispanic marketers have adopted two main strategies for addressing Latinos: the customization of ads to different Latino nationalities, and the development of so-called generic ads. A good example of the first tactic are the Goya's Canilla rice ads produced in the mid-1980s, which were filmed and customized for Puerto Ricans, Dominicans, and Central Americans by showcasing scenes that would appeal to each nationality in a particular way. The Dominican version, filmed on the famous beach of Boca Chica, juxtaposed the image of a fisherman with that of a couple eating in a seaside restaurant and was accompanied by a jingle featuring a typically Dominican merengue beat. The Colombian/Central American ad showed a middle-class family scene with Andean/peasant music; and the Puerto Rican ad depicted countryside scenes aimed at recreating Puerto Rican landscapes with a melody of Puerto Rican *jíbaro* (peasant) music. Today, however, it is not customization but generic expositions that dominate the commercial representation of Latinos. In these ads, Hispanics are addressed as a nationwide constituency through generic nationwide executions featuring Latinos living in an imaginary Hispanic nation without any reference to the larger context in which they live and with few direct references to particular traditions, roots, or values. Goya's new campaign, for instance, features contemporary family scenes: in the ad for its cod-fish fritter mix, for example, a young man cooks dinner for his girlfriend and future mother-in-law, impressing them both thanks to Goya's ready-mix product. This does not mean that the industry has stopped targeting specific markets (most national TV campaigns are supplemented with a radio component that uses salsa musical backgrounds when advertising for East Coast audiences, *conjuntos* for the audiences in the West), but rather that customization has been reduced to the less costly and therefore more flexible realms of radio and print media, leaving TV as the exclusive realm of the generic pan-Hispanic.

I was given a number of explanations for these changes, from the increased heterogeneity of the Latino population since the 1980s as a result of a more diversified immigration from Latin America, which complicated the customization of ads, to the growing consolidation of a pan-Latino identity less dependent on overt signs and marks of Latin "traditions" or nationalistic appeals. What all advertising executives I talked to agreed on, however, was that the increase of generic representations was most affected not by the actual consolidation of Latinidad, but by the requirements of the corporate clients and their need for Latinos who could be easily marketed to. As one noted, "We were selling them the idea that all Hispanics are alike but then pitching them to do two or three different advertising executions. It got too complicated. We had to make it easy for them. They had to understand that advertising for Hispanics is like advertising for the general market. You just don't do an ad for Alabama and one for New York."

In this tenor, commercial TV and the world of advertising have generated new symbols and materials; but because they need to be persuasive to both their clients and consumers, these are necessarily more derivative than "new." Primary among these references is the so-called generic "Latin look" and "unaccented" Spanish, constructs that have become so common that their existence was taken for granted by almost everyone I talked to in the industry, from producers to creatives to casting directors. But who and what constitutes the generic Hispanic? A casting director explained, "You know what they want when they ask you for models; it's unspoken. What they want is the long straight hair, olive skin, just enough oliveness to the skin to make them not ambiguous. To make them Hispanic."

What makes anyone Hispanic in advertising, however, is more than olive skin. For one, the generic look is mediated by the look-demanding world of advertising, as well as by the aforementioned demands that this industry be representative of "Hispanics." Specifically, in contrast to advertising for Latin American or North American audiences, images for the U.S. Hispanic market have to be both aspirational (by showing beautiful, educated, or accomplished individuals) and representative. The blonde and Nordic types that are common in Latin American ads would not work for U.S. Hispanics who, as minorities, I was told, look at ads for representation and confirmation. However, despite the industry's emphasis on representative models, not solely beautiful and aspirational ones, content analysis of ads filmed in the early 1980s in comparison with those filmed today revealed just what I heard from experienced casting directors and model agents working in this market: namely, that the generic look has become whiter and thus less representative of the average Hispanic consumer. Early ads showed a greater percentage of darker Latinos, particularly among male models, who were never too dark yet dark enough to be recognized as ethnic Hispanics. This is what was described to me as the "dark, mustached, Mexican type" or the stereotypical Hispanic look of the past, that agencies had to rely on in order to convince clients of the authenticity of their ads, but that they have since been able to replace with a more modern and "representative" Latin look. The irony, however, is that in superseding this previous stereotype the industry has created yet another powerful one. They have fulfilled Vasconcelos's early twentieth-century dream of Latin American whitening by miscegenation, at least in the realm of the commercial imaginary, by showing whiter-looking and Mediterranean Hispanic types.[7] As one casting director explained: "What they want is a very conservative anglicized look, a Hispanic in an anglicized garb. It's very much what in the general market we used to call the 'P and G [Procter and Gamble] look,' the very clean cut, all-American, blonde and blue eyes, that was not representative of the U.S. That was changed a long time ago but has not been thrown out in the Hispanic market. It's been replicated. They are trying to make the squeaky clean perfect boxed Latino look, not too dark and not too light." And when in doubt, she continued, they would surely select the lighter over the darker Latino. Indeed, there are seldom indigenous or black models in Hispanic ads, unless they are minimally included in group shots or presented as signifiers of cultural authenticity; they are never included as representatives of beauty or generic appeal.

The bias in favor of whiter Latinos is often guided by Hispanic advertising professionals' penchant for images that portray this population in a positive light. This positive presentation is even taken as a mission by advertising professionals, most of whom are white, who repeatedly complained that corporate clients wanted to cast darker Latinos, which they saw as sign of their clients' racist stereotypes about Hispanics. An Argentinean creative noted: "We have to educate them because they think that all Latinos are dark, but I point to them that I am not and that there are millions of people like me who are Latino." He went on to point to his own whiteness as proof of the need to challenge the stereotype of the dark Latino, a gesture that represented more a challenge to his new debased status as Hispanic, and thus a member of an ethnic or racial minority, than an argument about the actual characteristics of the prospective audience. This response was not atypical in my conversations about race and the absence of dark Latinos in the ads. The ironic result is that challenging stereotypes becomes synonymous with defending the whiteness, affluence, and marketability of the Hispanic consumer. This is the profile of those involved in ad production.

The so-called generic Latin look has its linguistic match in what the industry calls "Walter Cronkite Spanish," the "unaccented," generic, or universal Spanish, supposedly devoid of regionalism or traceable accent and most of all devoid of English or Spanglish (or code-switching between the two). This construct is generally believed to be the most effective voice for campaigns designed to reach the entire market and is also the type of Spanish that most creatives and ad executives I spoke with were convinced they themselves have, serving to corroborate their authority to address this pan-ethnic market. Yet the existence of some type of generic Spanish is again implicated in the inequalities reproduced by such generic representations. Not only does this "standard Spanish" exclude the English-dominant and bilingual Latino from finding representation in the Hispanic TV networks, but it also veils the dissemination of a media register based mostly on upper-class Mexican Spanish as the embodiment of generic Hispanicity.

This dominance is, of course, directly related to the political economy of the Spanish-language TV networks, which have historically been tied to Latin American media empires and conglomerates. Univision, the top-rated Spanish network, for instance, is partly owned by Mexico's Azcarraga family, founders and owners of Mexico's Televisa, as well as by Venezuela's Cisneros family, owners of Venevision. These arrangements have virtually guaranteed a heavy reliance on Mexican programming and hindered the development of U.S.-based Latino producers and programs (Gutierrez 1984; Subervi 1994). Mexican mannerisms and accents (particularly upper-class Mexican Spanish) are therefore more likely to be accepted as "representative" of the market, whereas Caribbean Spanish is hardly ever heard in advertisements and is highly edited in the Hispanic networks' programming. In this way, generic constructions are predicated on particular exclusions, as Latinos are recast into sellable abstractions that become more bounded and defined but more distanced from the average consumer. In this case, behind the generic facade, an invidious ranking of Hispanic language varieties is engendered and sustained by the networks, while Spanglish and other everyday forms of speech are made invisible.

Ironically, these same ideas that have given cohesiveness to this ethnic niche market have simultaneously limited the ability of contemporary advertising professionals to tap into and therefore profit from its differences. The growing number of bilingual Latinos, both youth and the U.S.-born, remain elusive targets for this industry which, having naturalized the Spanish speaker and a conventional and traditional image of Latinos, faces great difficulty in convincing corporate clients to pay for alternative representations. A creative who shared some examples of the difficulties of challenging the standard image told me of two instances in which his attempt to show nonwhite Latinos either was met with resistance by Anglo clients, who saw it as possibly insulting to Latinos, or was stalled within the agency itself in anticipation of the censure of their client. In an ad for Kodak, in which a father, upon being asked by his son to define the word *patria*, is shown telling his son about his homeland (depicted as a nonspecific Latin American country), one of the scenes was supposed to include two black Puerto Rican child models eating *piraguas* (shaved-ice cones). Yet upon seeing the first shooting, the agency's account manager rejected the proposal on the grounds that the client believed it would be insulting to Latinos who, according to marketing studies, do not think of themselves as black. In the end, the models were replaced with two much lighter kids (one of them almost blonde), bypassing the creative's original selection.

Another example of the constraints on showing a broader range of rep-

Erase stereotypes...

Understand your target. Own the Hispanic market.

"Erase Stereotypes," a self-promotion ad by Zubi Advertising, Coral Gables, Florida, exemplifies the industry's self-presentation as a site of positive images for all Latinos, by uncovering the upscale, (white), and modern woman who lies beneath the stereotype and the Carmen Miranda headpiece. (Courtesy Zubi Advertising) resentations of Hispanics on the airwaves is provided by Robles Communications. That company's decision to include in a beer commercial music from the Puerto Rican group DLG, which mixes Latin music with urban black rhythms from hip hop to rap, was turned down by the corporate client in favor of a more "folkloric" and hence "authentically Latin" musical background with hints of Cumbia. Conflicts such as this are evidence of the difficulties faced by marketers when trying to overcome the same stereotypes that have made this market so profitable to begin with and that they themselves have helped develop.

Hispanic advertising professionals are, however, not oblivious to these processes of self-exotification and have tried to maneuver them to their advantage whenever possible. A market tour leader who sells outdoor ads in Latino neighborhoods, aware that his client could not tell a Mexican neighborhood from a Puerto Rican one, admitted that he has often presented the same mixed neighborhood as either Colombian-, Mexican-, or Puerto Rican-dominant according to the needs of his clients, a strategy that has allowed him to sell group-specific outdoor media, like signs and wall murals, targeting particular nationalities. But because attempts at complicating the representation of Latinos are consistently met with the fear that the market will lose its authenticity and hence its profitability, industry practitioners must necessarily be complicit with the stereotypes they claim to challenge.

PREDICAMENTS OF A "PACKAGED" CULTURE

I started this discussion by suggesting that the commercial representation of U.S. Hispanics has reduced what can be considered Hispanic in this country to a set of very specific conventions. Latinos are therefore increasingly codified around marketable tropes and images that have become more distanced from their everyday realities. After all, it is not the "Mediterranean Hispanic" who composes the majority of the U.S. Latino population, nor is it upscale "Mexican" Spanish that they speak. Moreover, although the ways in which these themes are represented have not remained static or unchanged, Hispanic advertising still responds to the social hierarchies that subordinate Latinos in this country and is still predicated on the need to project positive images, leading it to rely on the same clichés of the good, traditional, not-too-dark/not-too-light Latino who, against the always-present specter of Anglo culture, still dominates their commercial representation. Unfortunately these are the same clichés that, while making them safe and commercially viable for mass consumption, do little to subvert the dominant racial and ethnic hierarchies at play in U.S. society as well as among and across Latino subgroups, the same ones that make the lighter Latino the more marketable one, that favor the so-called standard Spanish over Spanglish, and that treat certain accents as more representative of La-tinidad than others.

The Hispanic marketing industry thus reveals how differences are ordered, contained, or partially indexed in the world of commercial representations. Far from being just shrewd fabrications, these images are produced through strategies of partial representation of the "Hispanic consumer," even when this is done through the erasure and reconstitution of differences into his or her very construction. This practice reminds us how the reconstitution of in-dividuals into consumers and of populations into markets is produced in con-versation and often in complicity with dominant hierarchies of race, culture, and nationality that circulate in the spaces—be they local, national, or global—in which these processes take place. As we saw, the production of Latinos as easily digestible and marketable within the larger structures of cor-porate America is predicated on notions of place, nation, and race that are at play in the United States and in Latin America, making the role of His-panic advertising professionals and creatives contingent on preexisting hi-erarchies of representation; as such they are brokers of old discourses of rep-resentation and only rarely generators of new ones. Yet media discourses are never produced in a vacuum; they are part and parcel of greater discourses of identity and identification. And the irony is that in constructing a Hispanic market that is easily marketable, remains authentic, and is ready for mass con-sumption, the industry helps erase the historical roots of Latinos in the United States, thus invalidating the political claims of Latino populations that they are an intrinsic rather than an external or recently incorporated segment of the U.S. population. This is the same view that feeds into the dominant im-age of Hispanics as immigrants and thus as foreign to U.S. society, politics, and culture, an image that is undoubtedly tied to recent U.S. immigration and social policy toward Latinos. This is the Hispanic that we can market to, but also expel or banish, who will remain in his or her place, within his or her culture: the "nation within the nation" that is never really part of the "Na-tion." One could then ask if the current interest in Hispanic marketing is di-rectly implicated in furthering this domesticated image and ponder the im-plications of this industry for contemporary cultural politics.

NOTES

I thank the editors of this volume, particularly Faye Ginsburg, for their constructive comments. Thanks are also due to Jerry Lombardi, who contributed comments and editorial help. Funding for this research was provided by the Wenner-Gren Founda-tion for Anthropological Research, the National Science Foundation, and the Ford Foundation.

   1. See for instance the works of Dornfeld (1998) and Lutz and Collins (1993).

Works by anthropologists on the commodification of U.S. culture, focusing in particular on how racial and ethnic differences are consumed in the U.S. media are few (see, for instance, Chin 2001) in relation to those by nonanthropologists (Gray 1995; Cashmore 1997). In a larger version of this work, I develop the importance of analyzing commercial media trends in the United States (Dávila 2001). For instance, I found that some of the insights developed in the United States to encompass Latinos as one common market are affecting attempts at globalizing Latin American cultures into yet another common market.

2. On this issue see Turow 1997.

3. I am not implying here that more quantitative or qualitative marketing research would dramatically change this situation, as Astroff (1997) seems to suggest. Though consumers have been increasingly incorporated into the making of ads through research, problems in the application of ethnographic methods in marketing research and in the interpretation of data make findings far from representative of consumers' views (Stern 1998). A case in point, discussed elsewhere (Dávila 2001), is the screening of Hispanic consumers for focus groups in ways that preselect the recent arrival and Spanish-dominant consumer, the one most likely to present the attitudes associated in the industry with the model Hispanic consumer.

4. The discussion in this section is based on analysis of the agency reels of the following agencies: Conill, Siboney, Fova, Bravo, and Vidal Reynardus and Moya, in New York; Mendoza Dillon (California); Acento (California); Bromley and Associates (San Antonio); Dieste (Dallas); Del Rivero Mesiano (Miami); Zubi Advertising (Miami); and AdAmericas (California). The historical material (ads shot in the early and late 1970s) is drawn from Bravo's historical reel and Univision's historical advertising reel produced as part of the network's anniversary. Univision's historical reel spans the early 1970s to the 1980s. It includes eighty-four ads, thirty-two of which showed or directly evoked the family. The most common image was that of the mother caring for and tending to her children.

5. Charts shared with consumers included "Broad Cultural Differences between Hispanic and the American Middle Class" and "Value Orientation Differences between Hispanics and the American Middle Class" printed in Valdes and Seoane 1995. More examples of these dichotomies are included in Roslow 1997.

6. On this point see Johnson 1980 for U.S. stereotypes and portrayal of Latin Americans and Takaki 1993 for the images of Mexicans that circulated during U.S. westward expansion and occupation of Mexico, all of which rationalized conquest on the basis of the inherent inferiority, indolence, or lack of discipline of Latin American populations.

7. Contrasting racial segregation in the United States, José Vasconcelos, first minister of education and a key figure of the cultural nationalism that accompanied the Mexican Revolution, saw racial mixing in Latin America as the key to the formation of a cosmic race, a new and improved civilization stemming from the harmonious integration of its racial components. Vasconcelos's ideas were developed as an anti-imperialist response to the dominant eugenic thought of the time that rejected mixing as deterioration. His argument was a simple one: unlike Anglo Americans, whose injustice and materialism had led them to exterminate or exclude indigenous populations, Latin Americans had kindly "mated" with them and assimilated them into a new culture where "inferior" and "lower" races could be improved and ameliorated

(yet another proof of Latin America's moral superiority to the barbaric United States) (Vasconcelos 1958).

REFERENCES

Abu-Lughod, Lila. 1993. Editorial Comment: On Screening Politics in a World of Nations. *Public Culture* 5 (3): 465–69.

Anderson, Benjamin. 1983. *Imagined Communities: Reflections on the Origins and Spread of Nationalism.* London: Verso.

Aparicio, Frances, and Susana Chávez-Silverman. 1997. *Tropicalizations: Transcultural Representations of Latinidad.* Hanover, N.H.: University Press of New England.

Astroff, Roberta. 1997. Capital's Cultural Study: Marketing Popular Ethnography of U.S. Latino Culture. In *Buy This Book: Studies in Advertising and Consumption,* edited by Mica Nava, Andres Blake, Iain MacRury, and Barry Richards. London: Routledge.

Bourdieu, Pierre. 1993. *The Field of Cultural Production.* New York: Columbia University Press.

Bromley Aguilar & Associates. 1999. Promotional Materials. San Antonio, Texas.

Burke, Timothy. 1996. *Lifebuoy Men, Lux Women: Commodification, Consumption and Cleanliness in Modern Zimbabwe.* Durham, N.C.: Duke University Press.

Cashmore, Ellis. 1997. *The Black Culture Industry.* London: Routledge.

Chatterjee, Partha. 1986. *Nationalist Thought and the Colonial World: A Derivative Discourse?* London: Zed Books.

Chin, Elizabeth. 2001. *Purchasing Power: Black Kids and American Consumer Culture.* Minneapolis: University of Minnesota Press.

Dávila, Arlene. 2001. *Latinos Inc.: The Marketing and Making of a People.* Berkeley: University of California Press.

Dornfeld, Barry. 1998. *Producing Public Television.* Princeton, N.J.: Princeton University Press.

Firat, A. Fuat, and Nikhilesh Dholakia. 1998. *Consuming People: From Politics to Theaters of Consumption.* New York: Routledge.

Ginsburg, Faye. 1991. Indigenous Media: Faustian Contract or Global Village? *Cultural Anthropology* 6 (1): 92–112.

———. 1999. ECU to Wide Angle: From Ethnographic Film to the Anthropology of Media. In *A Companion to Film Theory,* edited by Toby Miller and Robert Stam. London: Blackwell.

Gray, Herman. 1995. *Watching Race: Television and the Struggle for Blackness.* Minneapolis: University of Minnesota Press.

Gutierrez, Felix. 1984. Spanish International Network: The Flow of Television from Mexico to the United States. *Communication Research* 11 (2): 241–58.

Johnson, John. 1980. *Latin America in Caricature.* Austin: University of Texas Press.

Lutz, Catherine, and Jane Collins. 1993. *Reading National Geographic.* Chicago: University of Chicago Press.

Mankekar, Purnima. 1993. National Texts and Gendered Lives: An Ethnography of Television Viewers in a North Indian City. *American Ethnologist* 20 (3): 543–63.

Miller, Daniel. 1997. *Capitalism: An Ethnographic Approach.* London: Berg.

Naficy, Hamid. 1993. *The Making of Exile Cultures: Iranian Television in Los Angeles.* Minneapolis: University of Minnesota Press.

Noriega, Chon A., and Ana M. López, eds. 1996. *The Ethnic Eye: Latino Media Arts.* Minneapolis: University of Minnesota Press.

Ramos, Julio. 1989. *Desencuentros con la Modernidad.* Mexico City: Huracan.

Roslow, Peter. 1997. *A Guide to Market Dominance.* McLean, Va.: Association of Hispanic Advertising Agencies.

Stam, Robert, and Ella Shohat. 1994. *Unthinking Eurocentrism: Multiculturalism and the Media.* London: Routledge.

Stern, Barbara. 1998. *Representing Consumers: Voices, Views and Visions.* London: Routledge.

Subervi, Federico. 1994. Mass Communication and Hispanics. In *Handbook of Hispanic Cultures in the United States: Sociology,* edited by Félix Padilla. Houston, Tex.: Arte Público Press.

Takaki, Ronald. 1993. *A Different Mirror: A History of Multicultural America.* Boston: Little, Brown.

Turner, Terence. 1992. Defiant Images: The Kayapo Appropriation of Video. *Anthropology Today* 8 (6): 5–16.

Turow, Joseph. 1997. *Breaking Up America: Advertisers and the New Media World.* Chicago: University of Chicago Press.

Valdes, Isabel, and Marta Seoane. 1995. *Hispanic Market Handbook: The Definite Source for Reaching This Lucrative Segment of American Consumers.* Detroit: Gale Research Inc.

Vasconcelos, José. 1958. La Raza Cósmica. In *Obras Completas.* Vol. 2, pp. 903–42. Mexico, D.F.: Collección Laurel.

Williamson, Judith. 1978. *Decoding Advertisements: Ideology and Meaning in Advertising.* London: Boyars.

14

"And Yet My Heart Is Still Indian"

The Bombay Film Industry
and the (H)Indianization of Hollywood

Tejaswini Ganti

"FAILED ATTRACTION"

I got to Radhika's place around 7 o'clock. Everyone else had already arrived and assembled in her bedroom in front of the TV, some on the bed, some on the floor, and some on the treadmill. There were nine of us, two women and seven men, ranging in age from early twenties to early thirties. We had gathered to watch Fatal Attraction on laser disc because Radhika, who was an actress, and her friends—a director, a cinematographer, a screenwriter, an assistant director, and a few actors—were thinking about remaking it into a Hindi film. Although most of them had seen the film before, they were watching it that night to decide whether to remake it.

During a particularly passionate sex scene, Radhika asked Tarun, who would be directing the potential remake, "What will you do? Will you show a song here? How are you going to show them having great sex?"[1]

Tarun said, "I can do it."

"How can you?" pressed Radhika.

"I'll do it," assured Tarun.

"No, not like how you did in your last film, not with shadows and silhouettes and close shots. That's not going to do it."

When Tarun asserted, "Don't worry, I can do it," Radhika objected: "But wait, if you do it, I can't be seen doing that with someone I just met for the very first time! I can't do that!"

Tarun pointed out, "But you're not stable" [referring to the character, not to Radhika].

Radhika protested, "I don't want to be mentally unstable! It's quite unfashionable now; that's just not what's done!"

After the film was over, Tarun declared, "We can't make this film." Imran, who was a writer, concurred, "You're right. It doesn't work. It's really boring."[2]

In this essay, I examine why Tarun and his colleagues think *Fatal Attraction* cannot be remade into a Hindi film, to reveal how commercial film production is a practice imbued with a "difference-producing set of relations" (Gupta and Ferguson 1997: 46) between filmmakers and audiences. The Bombay film industry, one of the world's largest commercial film industries, which is increasingly referred to as "Bollywood" within and outside India, is a notoriously appropriative industry constantly on the lookout for new talent, faces, and stories. Although the driving force within the Bombay industry is commercial success, it is a difficult goal pursued by many and achieved by few. One of the strategies employed by Hindi filmmakers to reduce the chances of box-office failure is to remake or adapt Hollywood, Telugu, Tamil, and older Hindi films.[3] Bombay filmmakers regard box-office successes or "hits" in other Indian languages as attractive remake material because, having already succeeded with a set of audiences, such films are perceived as having a higher probability of succeeding with Hindi film audiences as well. Hollywood films, however, are not selected only on the basis of box-office outcome but are chosen for plots that seem novel and amenable to adaptation. Although remakes from other Indian languages resemble the original screenplay, adaptations of Hollywood films barely do because they have been transformed—or "Indianized," in industry parlance—to conform with the conventions of Hindi cinema.

I examine the process of "Indianization," drawing on first-hand observations of filmmakers watching Hollywood films, participation during the production of *Ghulam*—a film inspired by *On the Waterfront,* and conversations and interviews with members of the Bombay film industry.[4] Instead of comparing a Hindi film with the Hollywood "original" (Nayar 1997), I focus on the decisions, evaluations, and negotiations around Indianization in order to "turn from a project of juxtaposing pre-existing differences to one of exploring the construction of differences in historical process" (Gupta and Ferguson 1997: 46). Although Bombay filmmakers have been adapting Hollywood films for decades, the media landscape in which they operate has changed considerably since the entry of satellite and cable television in 1991, with the resulting increase in the number of television channels available locally, regionally, and nationally.[5] Filmmakers explain that because they are competing with television for audiences they must create a cinematic experience extraordinary enough to seduce audiences away from their television sets at home and into theaters, and Hindi film production since the mid-1990s has been marked by vastly improved production values, increased spectacle, foreign locales, slick marketing, and subsequently higher costs. The presence of satellite channels such as Star Movies and TNT that broadcast feature films also means that some portion of the audience has access to the Hollywood films that are the sources for adaptations.

Unlike recent work on cinematic remakes (Horton and McDougal 1998) and cross-cultural adaptations (Horton 1998; Aufderheide 1998; Nayar 1997), which are primarily concerned with questions of narrative, genre, and intertextuality, I examine Indianization, not as a relationship between texts but as a relationship between filmmakers and audiences. Much of the ethnographic research about the mass media has centered on television audiences and the moment of reception. However, as Ien Ang (1991) and Barry Dornfeld (1998) have argued, the idea of the audience must also be located in the production process. Whereas other scholars have examined Indianization with the purpose of delimiting what is uniquely "Indian" about the codes and conventions of mainstream Hindi cinema (Thomas 1985, 1995; Nayar 1997), I outline Indianization as a practice that allows one to see how Hindi filmmakers think about and construct their audiences.

Not every Hollywood film is capable of being "Indianized," however, and as the opening anecdote indicates, sometimes after watching a particular film closely the director decides that the film is unsuitable for adaptation. Unlike other methods, an ethnographic focus on media production provides access to these "negative" instances or episodes in which films get rejected in the conceptualization stage. Such moments of inchoate production reveal how Hindi filmmakers operate as cultural mediators, evaluating the appropriateness for their audiences of stories, characterizations, and themes from certain Hollywood films. I detail how Hindi filmmakers frequently elaborate the difference between their films and Hollywood films in a language of constraints and compulsions as mediated through the figure of "the audience." What becomes apparent during the processes of selection and adaptation is filmmakers' ambivalence toward their audiences, and I argue that rather than "indigenizing" or domesticating difference (Tobin 1992), Indianization is a practice of constituting difference—between India and the West, and more important, between filmmakers and audiences.

In thinking about the process of film production in terms of social relations, specifically the "relation of knowing" (Ohmann 1996) that producers exhibit toward their audiences, my goal is to bypass the dichotomies that have characterized the study of Hindi cinema and represent producers as an interpretive community. In much of this scholarship, depending on whether the focus is on films as texts or on the popularity of certain genres, producers are represented as isomorphic either with their films or with their audiences.[6] Rather than viewing the relationship between filmmakers and audiences according to an effects model or a reflectionist model, I see it as a "hermeneutic circle" in which there are multiple sites during the production, transmission, and reception of a media-text at which meaning can be constructed (Michaels 1990). By examining Indianization I reveal some of the "audience fictions" (Traube 1996) operating within the Hindi film industry and how such assumptions about reception affect filmmaking, thus illustrating the highly mediated nature of commercial film production.

SCREENING CULTURE: SELECTING A FILM FOR ADAPTATION

Tarun's statement that *Fatal Attraction* "can't be made" refers to the perceived lack of audience interest rather than any technical inability on the part of himself and his crew. Throughout the filmmaking process, Hindi filmmakers justify their narrative, dramatic, and aesthetic choices according to what they believe audiences will accept and reject. In the process of trying to produce a "hit," filmmakers theorize about audiences' motivations for seeing a film and how they derive pleasure from it. Rather than relying on any formal market research, their claims about audience tastes and preferences are based on a mix of intuition, observation of box-office successes and failures, and first-hand viewing of films in theaters with audiences. In this section, I examine how deciding which film is suitable for adaptation involves a complex amalgam of factors such as filmmakers' interpretations of films, their own film-viewing experiences, their assessment of a film's novelty, loyalty to the narrative conventions of Hindi cinema, and filmmakers' assumptions about their audiences.

After we had finished watching *Fatal Attraction,* Tarun, Imran, and Radhika engaged in a long discussion about the film. Tarun and Imran dissected the plot and screenplay, explaining to the rest of the room why the film was not appropriate for an Indian context. Their discussion centered on the audience. Because the goal of box-office success is articulated completely in terms of audience desire, taste, and satisfaction, their overwhelming concern was what would draw audiences to see this film. Since there had been a spate of Hindi films recently about obsession, the group was trying to figure out the "USP" (unique selling point) for this film that would make it stand out from the others. While Tarun and Radhika kept stating that they wanted to do something different from what had been done before, during their discussion it became apparent that they felt constrained by the issue of adultery and the characterizations of the male protagonist and the other woman.

What was particularly vexing to the group was the adaptation of Glenn Close's character of a lustful, obsessive other woman into an Indian context. The discussion kept trying to answer the question: Why would this woman have an affair with this man if she knew he were married? It is not that such a character could not exist in a Hindi film, but Tarun and Radhika's concern was to represent the other woman differently from a classic Hindi film "vamp." They hashed out a few scenarios in which the woman initially did not know that the man was married, but these were rejected because they felt that would render the man as extremely unsympathetic, which was also deemed undesirable. The question that kept arising in the discussion was whether audiences could "identify" with this film.

The term "identification" kept popping up in my conversations with filmmakers as the basic tenet of the relationship between viewers and a film in order for it to elicit pleasure and thus succeed commercially. As a concept, "identification" encompasses a range of meanings from literal similarities between audiences and the characters on screen to a familiarity with the circumstances, scenarios, and conflicts depicted in the film. Javed Akhtar, a highly successful screenwriter, lyricist, and poet, describes it: "Whatever is happening on the screen should make him laugh, should make him cry, he should be able to identify with it. He should be able to fantasize and at the same time, if it is too real, then he won't like it. If it has nothing to do with reality, then too he won't like it" (interview, 1996). From a Hindi filmmaker's point of view, identification is not dependent upon an aesthetic of social realism or even a realistic mise-en-scène (which could even impede pleasure according to Akhtar), but more dependent on whether the portrayal of the joys, sorrows, and dilemmas faced by the characters are able to resonate with—rather than replicate—audiences' own experiences.

Thus, according to filmmakers, the inability of viewers to "identify" with a film would lead to its failure at the box office—the most common explanation offered for the poor fate of Hollywood films in India. Since 1994, when *Jurassic Park* was released in India in its original and dubbed Hindi versions and was a huge box-office success, a small number of Hollywood films have been dubbed into Hindi and released annually.[7] However, none have been able to repeat *Jurassic Park*'s success, and in fact most do so poorly at the box office that the *Jurassic Park* experience is dismissed as an anomaly. As Rajat Barjatya, the marketing director for Rajshri Productions, asserts, "*Jurassic Park* is a very different film. People came for the curiosity: you know, what is a dinosaur? And how has a Hollywood film been dubbed first time in Hindi? There was a curiosity value attached to it—that's no longer the case" (interview, 1996).[8]

Hindi filmmakers do not perceive Hollywood as a threat to their business, citing the failure of most films as proof that audiences in India cannot relate to Hollywood films. Taran Adarsh, editor of *Trade Guide*, a trade weekly, asserts that audiences derive pleasure only from familiar stars and narratives:

I have asked a lot many people who have seen dubbed versions of English films and they say *ki*, "*bhai, yeh sab theek hai*" [This is all fine and good], they have the gloss, they have the glitter, everything, but "*yeh gore chamdi-waale, Hindi kaise bol sakte hain?*" [How can these white-skinned people speak Hindi?] It's like that. So the fact [is] that that identification is absolutely missing. . . . When I say Nana Patekar [an actor] is more popular, *kyon?* [Why?] *Kyon ki woh gaali deta hai.* [Because he curses.] *Pakad leta hai gale se, aur bolta hai, "Tu ne, tum log is country ko barbaad kar rahe ho!"* [He grabs you by the throat and says, "You, you people are destroying this country!"] *Phalana jo bhi ho* [Whatever it is], whatever he wants to say, and the guy sitting there, he somehow, feels as a person I am an impotent person, because there are certain things I cannot do. I cannot achieve in life, and when I see that guy doing it, he's doing the right thing. He's bashing up a criminal, which I can't. So that's where hero worship comes in, and that's where foreign films cannot be accepted because we just cannot, the identification is missing, the chemistry is missing absolutely. (Interview, 1996)

In Adarsh's view, the alien bodies, histories, and modes of address of Hollywood films are not capable of evoking in Indian audiences the psychological or emotional responses necessary for viewing pleasure. Identification can be understood as a type of cultural empathy, and in contemplating the adaptation of *Fatal Attraction* Tarun and Radhika were searching for ways to represent the characters so that they might evoke some form of empathy.

Although Hollywood films are characterized as unpleasurable for Hindi film audiences, they are not so for filmmakers who have access to them through laser discs and satellite television as well as trips abroad.[9] It is usually through such leisure viewing that a filmmaker stumbles across a film that he or she finds appealing and a potential candidate for adaptation. For example, *Ghulam*'s writer, Anjum Rajabali, explained that when he was approached by the director and producer to write a script with the only requirement that it be about two brothers, he happened to have just seen *On the Waterfront* at home and was very impressed by it. When Rajabali wrote out the screenplay exactly as it was, with merely the settings and characters changed for India, he realized, "It obviously didn't work! I said, *yeh to kya hai?* [What is this?] What am I doing? This doesn't work. *On the Waterfront* doesn't work in India" (interview, 1996). Because he liked the film immensely, he searched for what he had found so compelling about the film, which then helped him to construct the basic premise of *Ghulam*.

> *Chalo* [okay], but what did I like? I liked the relationship between the two brothers because it reminded me of my relationship with my brother at some stage and my relationship with my father. . . . That sentence, "You're my brother you should have looked after me," which Marlon Brando says to Rod Steiger, that for me became the starting point. Okay, that is my experience, and there I felt I had found the rib—Eve was made of the rib, no? I felt I had found the rib on which I could construct a human being, an entire story. I began with that and worked around. (Interview, 1996)

Rajabali's statements reveal how filmmakers themselves must be able to "identify" with a Hollywood film in order for it to be a candidate for adaptation. Later, when he reflected upon the experience, Rajabali remarked, "Perhaps unconsciously I realized that there was a universality in the story of *Waterfront* and that is why I am so impressed with it. I could interpret it in my own way, my own Indian way" (E-mail, April 9, 1998).

"Universality" is a very salient concept within the Bombay film industry as Hindi film makers aim for mass rather than niche audiences. "From 6 to 60" was a phrase I heard uttered frequently, describing how filmmakers strive to make films that appeal to everyone, regardless of age. A Hindi film is deemed an unqualified success only if it is a nationwide or an "all-India" hit, communicating to filmmakers that linguistically, regionally, and religiously diverse audiences have been able to "identify" with the film. Hollywood films that are perceived as having the potential to be adapted for an Indian context are described as having elements of "universal appeal"; those that are not are labeled "regional." Such a classification parallels the common discursive division of cinema in India into Hindi cinema or regional cinema by Bombay filmmakers: films in languages other than Hindi are referred to as "regional" films whose appeal is regarded as limited to specific geographic and linguistic constituencies. Vikram Bhatt, *Ghulam*'s director, explains how he judges whether a film is capable of being Indianized and what constitutes universal appeal:

> A Hollywood film has to have its relevance with our audiences. For me the film has to be that of a universal appeal, by which I mean that a film needs to be centered around a human emotion more then a set of circumstances. When I remade *Unlawful Entry*, it was because the film was about a villain's lust for a married woman. Lust is a universal emotion. People from all over the world regardless of the language understand it. *Ghulam,* though not a remake, was definitely inspired from *On the Waterfront,* which again is a story of two brothers against an oppressor, again, making it an understandable emotion. Every film need not be based on a universal emotion, but then it might have the portrayal of a very regional problem, making it difficult to adapt. Take, for example, films like *Mississippi Burning* or *Missing.* These are films that can't be made because their problems are relevant only to their regions. (E-mail, November 13, 1998)

Bhatt's comments illustrate how "emotion" refers to interpersonal relationships rather than an individual's internal state of being, a point that is elaborated later. Films that have been adapted in the recent past—*Sabrina, Kramer vs. Kramer, Mrs. Doubtfire, The Hard Way, Sleeping with the Enemy, French Kiss,* and *An Affair to Remember*—are all centered on relationships—romantic, marital, parental, filial, or friendship—allowing Hindi filmmakers to add new twists to narratives that are predominantly about romantic love, kinship, or the myriad levels of duty.

Although films that are centered on human relationships are thought to have wide appeal, *Fatal Attraction* was regarded as unsuitable by Tarun and his colleagues because they felt the manner in which marital infidelity was handled in the film would not be acceptable to audiences. In addition to the concept of identification, Hindi filmmakers exercise their discretionary judgment through the idea of "acceptance," by which they mean audience approval of a film's plot, theme, or characterizations, as signified by its fate at the box office. Filmmakers portray audiences in India as very sensitive, particularly about sexual mores, when discussing what they would and would not like to see, and represent audience sensibilities as a constraint upon the kind of narratives and characterizations available to them. Tarun explains why he was having such difficulty with the characterization of the male protagonist in *Fatal Attraction:*

> The audience does not understand protagonists with loose moral values. I don't mean drinking or anti-establishment or any thing like that. What I mean is more like a man willing to sell his wife for a night or a man who is willing to swap his wife with his neighbor for a night.[10] We have always placed our heroes on pedestals and sometimes it becomes very difficult. If you want to make films about normal people with their normal needs and normal drawbacks, then you have to really be very innovative so as not to hurt the audiences. The term used in story sittings is *yeh to* accept *nahin hoga* [This will not be accepted]. Loose moral values are only for the antagonist. (E-mail, March 7, 1999)

By explaining narrative and generic conventions as a consequence of audience sensibilities and desires, Tarun's statements reveal how filmmakers perceive their audiences as placing definite limits upon their filmmaking practices, which they may not follow otherwise. The paternalism expressed toward audiences also sets up a clear separation between filmmakers and audiences.

Filmmakers operate with a distinct sense of moral boundaries, usually pertaining to ideal kinship behavior, that cannot be transgressed when determining whether a Hollywood film is suitable for adaptation. Tarun abandoned the idea of adapting *Fatal Attraction* because he felt that audiences would not tolerate a protagonist who committed adultery simply out of boredom. He stated, "The audience will see him as a villain if he left a happy marriage just to go out and have a nice time. The concept of monotony in a marriage does not work here because most marriages are monotonous—the hero must have a bitch of a wife or something should be wrong in his marriage" (Internet chat, May 4, 1999). In addition to the generic convention in Hindi cinema in which a "hero" is someone who upholds the moral order, Tarun's decision is based on an assessment of social norms that to him renders the primary motivation for the plot incomprehensible to audiences. Tarun determines that marital monotony is not a meaningful concept to audiences — that is, they would be unable to identify with it and therefore would find it unacceptable—demonstrating how filmmakers' notions of identification and acceptance can operate to exclude certain themes. But Hollywood is characterized as free from all such compulsions. Screenwriter Sutanu Gupta states bluntly:

> There a widower can just meet a divorcee in a pub and they go to bed and then the story starts. We can't have that. We just can't have that. Though in a song you can suggest that, I think these days that is what is being suggested, but we still have not reached that permission where you can just, the two characters come and meet and get along in life and then the story starts about something. (Interview, 1996)

Gupta uses a series of what may be regarded as social taboos and symbols of deviance to contrast what he sees as the lack of a moral universe in a Hollywood film with the implicitly moral one of the Hindi film, as well as to posit a metonymic association between cinema and society. "There" refers to both Hollywood and the West, and "permission" refers to the sexual freedom that is not allowed by either Indian audiences or Indian society. Gupta's comment about songs, however, points to a space within the Hindi film form that may be able to accommodate a blurring of boundaries and indicates that acceptable representations may have more to do with *how* something is represented than with *what* is represented. Hindi films do not shy away from representing moral or social transgressions, an obvious example being the predominance of romantic love that frequently crosses boundaries of class, and sometimes caste, region, and religion. In fact, much of the dramatic and narrative tension in a Hindi film arises from threats to the moral or social order.

What must be stressed is that filmmakers' ideas about what constitutes acceptable representations are not fixed but fluid, and they are highly dependent upon commercial success or failure. Filmmakers' assessments of audiences are continually revised or reinforced based on how films perform at the box office. For every "rule" about narrative, plot, or characterization that filmmakers assert cannot be broken there are examples of mainstream Hindi films—based on original screenplays rather than adaptations—that have done so and enjoyed commercial success. The process of adapting a Hollywood film, however, generates a self-consciousness about social norms and moral codes that can make filmmakers more cautious than when they produce films from an original screenplay.[11] Because the practice of adaptation is motivated by a conscious desire to manage risk, Indianization tends to be a conservative process that precludes innovation in narrative and generic practices.

Although in Indianization the selection and encoding process of Hindi filmmaking is structured mainly through filmmakers' assumptions about their audiences, it also demonstrates how filmmakers themselves constitute an audience when they watch Hollywood films with an eye to adapting them in Hindi. With Rajabali's personal narrative about the inspiration for *Ghulam*, we can see how filmmakers react to films in ways that resonate with their own lives. The act of picking a Hollywood film to adapt is often based on personal cinematic preferences. Tarun and Radhika had initially been very enthusiastic about the possibility of remaking *Fatal Attraction* because they thought it was an interesting film, and Radhika was excited about the histrionic opportunities available in the character of the obsessive other woman.

Although the initial interest in a particular film may be based on personal tastes and preferences, once filmmakers embark upon the task of adaptation, they justify their choices according to what they believe audiences will

A song sequence rehearsal in Bombay's Mehboob Studios, 2000. (Photo: Tejaswini Ganti)

accept and reject. Determinations of which Hollywood films can or cannot be made demonstrate how Hindi filmmakers operate as cultural mediators with respect to their audiences' tastes and preferences. Through the concepts of identification and acceptance, we can see how filmmakers implicitly delineate a difference between their viewing habits and those of their audiences. This is especially clear in both Tarun's and Gupta's statements about how audiences cannot understand or cannot accept certain moral transgressions in films; the implication is that they have no such difficulties and can derive viewing pleasure from a greater diversity of plots, themes, and characterizations than their audiences.

CASTING CULTURE: THREE METHODS OF "INDIANIZING" A FILM

In the previous section, I discussed what sorts of plots, characterizations, and themes Bombay filmmakers feel they *cannot* use when aiming for wide-scale commercial success. This section focuses on what filmmakers feel they *must* do in order to adapt a Hollywood film appropriately so that it has the potential for box-office success. These include the addition of "emotions," the expansion of the narrative, and the inclusion of songs, which are explained by filmmakers in terms of audience expectations as well as cultural antecedents.

"Emotion"

At one point in the screening of *Fatal Attraction,* Imran declared, "We can't have the woman getting pregnant. That's so syrupy, but the Americans liked it because they're so starved of emotion," and everybody murmured assent. Along with identification and acceptance, "emotion" is another concept used in the Bombay film industry to underscore the alien nature of Hollywood. Hindi filmmakers frequently describe Hollywood films as "dry" or "lacking in emotion" and claim that in order to Indianize a film, one has to "add emotions." Anjum Rajabali explains:

> When you Indianize a subject, you add emotions. Lots of them. Feelings like love, hate, sacrifice, of revenge, pangs of separation. But, in a Hollywood film if a hero and heroine were to separate and you had five scenes underlining how they are suffering because they miss each other, people might find that soppy and corny too. Not here. Our mythology, our poetry, our literature is full of situations where lovers pine for each other. (E-mail, April 9, 1998)

Rajabali's statements illustrate the rich repository of meaning attributed to the word "emotion." He uses words that are transactional—love, hate, sacrifice—to define emotion, rather than those that denote states of being such as happiness, anger, or sadness. Revenge and pangs of separation may seem unusual in a list of emotions, but their inclusion demonstrates that for Hindi filmmakers emotions are not about an individual but about his or her relationship with others. Rather than referring to internal states, filmmakers are referring to social life in their discussions about emotion (Abu-Lughod and Lutz 1990), which has been described as a general feature of the discourse of emotion in India (Lynch 1990). Therefore, adding emotions to a film involves placing a character in a web of social relations of which kin are the most significant and common in Hindi films. The absence of kinship-related conflicts and dilemmas in Hollywood films, articulated as a lack of emotion, is offered as a reason for audiences' inability to identify with such films. Rajabali asserts: "That is why I think subjects like James Bond, detective stories, westerns and the like don't work as they are here. Who were James Bond's parents? Does Clint Eastwood of *Good, Bad, Ugly* love anyone? What about his brothers or sisters?" (Ibid.)

Rajabali illustrates the primacy of kinship relations in Hindi films by describing his impressions of a Hollywood film, *Murder in the First,* and how it would have been made in India.

> One brief flashback showed Kevin Bacon stealing bread for his sister and getting jailed, thus starting the whole story. In an Indian film, we'd have dwelt on that hugely, hugely. Really exploited that to underline the tragedy of the guy. Then, later [Christian] Slater brings Bacon's long-lost sister along to convince Bacon to testify or something. Bacon is very uncomfortable with her, behaves very awkwardly with her, turns away finally, and goes inside. After that scene,

the sister doesn't feature in the film at all. It works, in the context of this film. But, Jesus, here the first thing that Bacon would've asked of Slater was "Bring my sister to me," and she'd have been the moving force of the film. (Ibid.)

Adding emotions is also about making narratives more moral because being connected to others means that one's actions have consequences greater than oneself. Rajabali speculates that the greater concern with morality in Hindi films has to do with the continuing presence and relevance of older narrative traditions:

Our myths are full of them [emotions]. Take the *Mahabharat* and you'll see what I mean. Every situation has feelings—dilemmas, other kinds of conflicts, confrontations, sacrifices, moral issues coming up all the time. In a Hollywood film, James Bond kills on the job; here we need to justify it, because morality plays a more important part in our lives, because of our mythology, I suppose. (Ibid.)

While mythology is offered as an underlying reason for the moral universe of a Hindi film, when speaking about a specific film Rajabali invokes the need for audiences to feel sympathy for the protagonist, akin to the ideas of identification and acceptance:

Kiss before Dying was effectively remade as *Baazigar* [Gambler]. In the original, the hero's motive was to get rich by any means since he used to see the big company's train pass his house every day and that made him envious and ambitious enough to end up killing all those girls. That was enough—his plain ambition. But, in *Baazigar*, that wouldn't have worked. Guy killing for ambition? No sympathy for him at all. But, if the guy had a back-story, wherein his father was cheated by this company *wallah* [guy] and now the guy wants the company back as revenge and retribution for that. Okay, now he's my man. I can consider forgiving him all those killings. Not entirely of course, killing is killing, so he has to die himself in the end, but he will carry my sympathy with him. (Ibid.)

Narrative

During a scripting session for *Ghulam*, its director, Vikram Bhatt, quipped, "In *On The Waterfront*, they start right away. They have no pre-story. Everything in a Hollywood film just happens boom, boom, boom; here all the way up to the interval, there's all kinds of other things happening."[12] What Bhatt was referring to was how the incident at the very beginning of *Waterfront*—the heroine's brother being killed—takes place halfway through *Ghulam*. Sutanu Gupta compares the difficulty of writing a Hindi film with the straightforward narrative of a Hollywood film:

You see our films, it is more difficult to make, twenty times more difficult than the Hollywood film. A Hollywood film can interest their audiences with one track—you can have a bomb in a bus, a girl is driving the bus, and a man has to save the bus driver and the bus passengers.[13] This is the whole film! We can't do a film like that. It could be our climax, only one scene in the film. (Interview, 1996)

Hollywood films are frequently described as "single-track," and filmmakers express their amazement and envy at how films can be made on "one line"— a phrase conveying that a story's simple plot can be related in a sentence. However, such films are considered inadequate for audiences in India, as Gupta explains:

> When the audience comes to the theater, they have a very set belief, that the kind of entertainment, which is given in cinema, should be containing everything—they should see part of family life; they should see romance; they should have songs; everything they want! Which becomes very difficult. At the same time, they hate hodge-podge films. They want to know what is the emphasis— whether it's an action film or it's a thriller or it's a revenge or it's a ghost story or it's a love story. This is difficult to maintain. It's a massive kind of a balance to perform . . . so that's why we find it damn difficult to achieve very successful films always. (Ibid.)

Gupta's statements illustrate that filmmakers perceive their audiences as demanding and set in their ideas about the kinds of films they want to see. He presents audiences as providing him boundaries with which he has to juggle their demands. Yet at the same time the desire for complicated narratives and the fact that an entire Hollywood film could be a mere scene in a Hindi film bestows a sophistication and mastery to the audience usually not attributed to them in public discourses about cinema in India, which overwhelmingly characterizes audiences as the illiterate and unrefined "masses."

Thus adapting a Hollywood film involves enhancing the narrative in a variety of ways. Subplots or parallel "tracks"—romantic, comedic, dramatic— are seen as necessary additions. According to writers, the inclusion of "emotions" leads to greater narrative complexity because close family relationships provide moving stories of their own. In *Ghulam* a whole prehistory to the main narrative emerges through a flashback about the hero's childhood relationship with his father. The trauma of his father's suicide is presented as an underlying reason for the hero's petty hoodlum-like behavior. The first half of *Ghulam* is also taken up with situating the principal characters socially, developing the romance between the hero and heroine, establishing how the neighborhood is under the control of a crime boss, and portraying the interactions between the hero and the heroine's idealistic brother. Javed Akhtar likens a Hollywood screenplay to a short story and a Hindi film's to a saga and states that Indian audiences "want a story that will engulf generations and eras, a larger period of time, and incidents, big influences on a larger spectrum. . . . You see a short story will have a beginning and the end, but these sagas have to have a beginning, a middle, and the end" (interview, 1996).

Songs

The sheer ubiquity of diegetic music in Indian cinema is probably its most distinctive feature.[14] To those unfamiliar with popular Indian cinema, song sequences appear as ruptures in continuity and verisimilitude. However, rather than being an extraneous feature, music and song in popular cinema define and propel plot development, and many films would lose their narrative coherence if their songs were removed. Hindi filmmakers spend a great deal of time and energy crafting the song sequences, which play a variety of functions within a film's narrative and provide the main element of cinematic spectacle. One of the main functions according to screenwriters, who with the director determine the "song situations" within a screenplay, is to display emotion. Rajabali explains that every time he comes to a point of intense feelings in the screenplay he sees if a song will convey it better: "Where an emotion becomes intense, usually a song helps to underline it. It also cuts away the need for verbalization through dialogue and creates a mood that cues the viewer in to the state of mind of the characters or the narrator" (E-mail, April 9, 1998).

The most common emotion expressed musically in Hindi films is love, and in films like *Ghulam* where a love story is not the main focus of the plot, a "romantic track" is developed primarily through songs between the hero and the heroine. Even a love story focuses on the overcoming of obstacles to marriage rather than the process of falling in love, so songs provide a more efficient way to depict the romance developing between the hero and heroine than many scenes of dialogue. For example, the entire process of falling in love, from the initial attraction to the realization of being soulmates, can be established over the course of four or five songs, or about thirty minutes of screen time. Rajabali elaborates:

> When the first "thunderbolt" strikes either [the hero or the heroine], they express it through a song. When their love intensifies, usually the standard rain sequence, another song.[15] If there is a breach or a tragedy in the relationship because of which they separate, we deal with it musically. So, extreme happiness, extreme love, extreme sadness, all of these qualify as song situations. (Ibid.)

Songs are part of an elaborate system of allusions to, rather than explicit portrayals of, sexuality and physical intimacy in Hindi films as filmmakers navigate the perceived moral conservatism of their audiences, as well as the representational boundaries set by the Indian state through its censorship codes. Songs are the primary vehicles for representing fantasy, desire, and passion, so any form of sexual activity in a Hollywood film would most likely be transformed into a song sequence in a Hindi film, a point made explicit while watching *Fatal Attraction* when Radhika asked Tarun, "What will you do? Will you show a song here?" In addition to expressing intense emotion and signifying physical intimacy, songs are frequently used to facilitate the passage of time, evoke memories, aid in characterization, and operate as a mode of indirect address. Rajabali states, "See if you accept the dictum that songs are required almost invariably—all screenplays don't need them—then you keep that in mind while writing the screenplay. If you don't have enough situations for songs, then you have to create them" (ibid.).

However, some writers and directors, especially those who prefer to make genres other than love stories, view having to create song situations as burdensome, with the burden compounded when attempting to adapt a Hollywood film. I recall one director who was trying to adapt *Judgment Night*— a film that takes place in one night about an all-male group of friends who accidentally witness a murder and then have to flee—being utterly confounded about what kind of song situations would be plausible in such a film.[16] Most writers acknowledge that songs are not necessary to every film and can be awkward in certain genres, but come to terms with them in various ways. Rajabali rationalizes music in terms of tradition: "Once you really treat your own storytelling objectives and methods as part of a larger continuity of the storytelling traditions in India, integrating songs becomes more easy. In myths, legends, and their rendering in folk theater, etc., one finds lots of music" (ibid.).

Whereas Rajabali offers a culturalist justification, others point to the significant economic role played by music within the film industry. Tarun asserts, "Of course one would love to make a movie without songs, but the only really hampering factor is the economic and marketing aspect of songs" (Internet chat, May 4, 1999). Gupta resigns himself to their presence, citing the pressure of music companies: "My kind of film, the kind of stories that I write, the song situations are difficult to find. I guess the songs have to be there and there have to be enough gaps between the songs, at least five to six songs you require, because forty minutes recorded tape, the music companies want, that is the contract" (interview, 1996).

Music is absolutely essential to the marketing and financing of popular Hindi films. The sale of music rights has become a source of finance for filmmaking: audio companies vying for the top production companies in the industry are willing to pay sums that may amount to as much as 25 percent of a film's budget. There have only been a few examples of popular Hindi films without songs—so few that their most memorable feature is the absence of songs. Not having songs signifies that the film is outside the mainstream of the Bombay film industry, possibly even an "art film," which to most people in the industry means death at the box office. Songs are usually recorded before a film commences shooting, and a few of the song sequences are shot early in the production phase so that they can be used to sell a film to distributors. Songs have also become the most significant form of a film's publicity; Indian television has been packed with film-based programming, mostly around film music, since the onset of cable and satellite television in

1991. Even before a film has completed production, sometimes months in advance, its song sequences start airing on the numerous film-based programs on television or appear as commercials between other programs. There are plenty of rumors and stories in the industry about distributors and financiers pressuring filmmakers to add songs to films to increase their prospects at the box office.

Exhibitors and others in the film trade assert that songs give Hindi films a competitive edge over Hollywood films. In an article about Hollywood's presence in India in the English-language film magazine *Filmfare,* the publicity manager of 20th Century Fox in India states, "Though 20th Century Fox is linked with the STAR network (satellite channels), Hindi films still have an advantage. They have songs to draw the audience. We don't!" (Kumar 1995: 170). In the same article the joint manager of two movie theaters in Bombay, one devoted to foreign films and the other to Hindi, explains his significantly lower box-office collections at the former theater: "It's just that Hindi films have songs, dances . . . emotions. Indians want everything and they get the works only in Indian cinema" (ibid.). The overwhelming commercial significance of music can be frustrating according to Tarun: "You see it should be a choice for the director to use songs or not, it is the compulsion that really wears us down" (Internet chat, May 4, 1999).

Tarun's frustration arises partly from the altered media landscape since the late 1990s in which Hindi filmmakers not only have had to compete with cable and satellite television for audiences but also to contend with the presence of dubbed Hollywood films. The increased emphasis on songs, spectacle, and kinship-related conflicts in Hindi films made in the 1990s could be seen as a response to these changes in the media landscape. In Indianizing Hollywood films for Indian audiences, Bombay filmmakers feel more compelled to consciously heighten and intensify the differences between their films and the "originals." Tarun's frustration is the most explicit, but one can detect traces of frustration in some of the other filmmakers' statements presented in this section. Gupta's statements about Hindi films' narrative complexity and even Rajabali's thoughtful comments about songs belie a certain ambivalence toward these conventions.

CONCLUSION

The framework of commercial cinema production constructs a totalizing and tautological universe in which Bombay filmmakers' relationship to the abstract collectivity known as "Indian society" is mediated by box-office outcome. Through the concepts of identification and acceptance we can see how commercial success or failure is interpreted by filmmakers as a barometer of social attitudes and moral sensibilities, providing the basis for their knowledge about audiences. The practice of Indianization illustrates the ambivalent nature of filmmakers' relationship to their audiences. Although audiences in India are characterized as having very specific tastes that cannot be satisfied through Hollywood films, the same sensibilities that reject Hollywood and thus protect Hindi filmmakers from competition can also constrain them in their own filmmaking practices. They perceive their audiences as limiting the types of themes, plots, and characterizations available and therefore also limiting the kinds of films they can make.

While nearly all categories of social difference are elided in favor of presenting a monolithic Indian audience,[17] Indianization is also a site for Hindi filmmakers to elaborate differences between themselves and their audiences. When filmmakers describe audiences in India as unable to empathize with Hollywood films because of their alien themes and alien morality, the assumption running through such descriptions is that they, the filmmakers, have no such problems. Both film production and consumption become sites to imagine difference. The fact that Bombay filmmakers are able to enjoy and accept Hollywood films while their audiences cannot produces an opposition between traditional, conservative, and prudish audiences and modern, sophisticated, and worldly filmmakers. Whereas the process of Indianization operates as a commentary about the character and psyche of the vast filmgoing public in India, it also illustrates that "the 'distance' between the rich in Bombay and those in London may be much shorter than that between different classes in 'the same' city" (Gupta and Ferguson 1997: 50).

Rather than reflecting the essence of "Indian culture," I have tried to show how the highly reflexive and objectifying process of Indianization generates "culture effects" (Kondo 1992), signifying practices that produce the essence of "Indianness." Whether it is the generic convention of diegetic music, the thematic focus on kinship, or the imagining of audience response via concepts such as identification and acceptance, Hindi filmmakers are continuously elaborating the differences between their films and Hollywood films. The process of filmmaking predicated upon perceived cultural constraints leads to an image of shared collective norms. Whatever their ambivalence toward it, the process of Indianization becomes an arena for Hindi filmmakers to construct difference at the level of the nation—between an undifferentiated "Indianness" and its other, the West as represented by Hollywood.

NOTES

The phrase in the title, "And Yet My Heart Is Still Indian" *(Phir bhi dil hai Hindustani)*, will be recognized by all Hindi film viewers. It is from the well-known song "Mera Jootha Hai Japani" (My Shoes Are Japanese), which was heard in the 1955 movie *Sri 420* (Mr. 420). The phrase is also the title of a Hindi film released in January 2000.

I would like to thank Anjum Rajabali and Vikram Bhatt, for without their input this essay would not have been possible. I am grateful to Lila Abu-Lughod, Faye Ginsburg, Brian Larkin, Vipul Agrawal, Alice Apley, Ethel Brooks, Ayala Fader, Nitin Govil, Jeff Himpele, Jerry Lombardi, Ranjani Mazumdar, John McMurria, Toby Miller, Barbara Miller, Aradhana Sharma, and Christine Walley for their comments and suggestions on various drafts. Preliminary versions were presented at the University of Pennsylvania's 51st Annual South Asia Seminar Series in February 1999 and the 98th Annual AAA meetings in November 1999.

1. The presence of English as a language of production, apparent from the interviews and informal communication, may surprise some readers, but it is a testament to the cosmopolitan nature of the Bombay film industry, where people hail from nearly every linguistic region in India and are not necessarily native Hindi speakers. As a consequence, although the language of the films may be Hindi, the language of production is multilingual, encompassing all of the major Indian languages, of which English has become one. Some screenwriters even write their scripts in English and then have them translated into Hindi by others more proficient in the language—a practice that obviously warrants further attention but is beyond the scope of this essay.

2. I observed this incident on May 9, 1996, during fieldwork in Bombay funded by an American Institute of Indian Studies Junior Fellowship for dissertation research. Although many of my informants were celebrities and thus public figures, because the episodes and conversations occurred in private, informal settings and did not result in anything as public as a film, I have followed the standard anthropological practice of using pseudonyms and have avoided last names because they are markers of caste, religion, and/or region in India. When quoting from formal interviews, I have kept the original names of informants.

3. Telugu and Tamil are languages spoken in the southern Indian states of Andhra Pradesh and Tamil Nadu, both home to film industries equally and sometimes more prolific than Bombay's.

4. *Ghulam* literally means "vassal" but in the film's context refers to a person both psychologically and physically under someone's control. *Ghulam* started production in November 1996 and was released in June 1998, quickly becoming a commercial success. As an assistant to the director, I was involved with preproduction such as scripting, location hunting, and casting.

5. These changes are a consequence of the new regime in state economic policy—mandated by IMF structural adjustment policies in 1991—characterized as "liberalization," which has allowed multinational corporations greater access to various sectors of the Indian economy

6. For the most recent example of the former see Prasad 1998, and for the latter see Nandy 1998.

7. In 1999, a total of 154 Hindi films were released, out of which sixteen were dubbed Hollywood films.

8. Rajshri produced *Hum Aapke Hain Koun!* in 1994, the same year as *Jurassic Park*, which is reputed to be the most successful film in India to date, netting over 2 billion rupees according to trade experts (ticket prices at the time of its release ranged from 5 to 50 rupees).

9. Many Hindi films have song sequences shot in Europe, North America, or Australia. Stars frequently go abroad to perform in elaborate stage shows. Many filmmakers also vacation abroad.

10. This is an allusion to *Indecent Proposal.*

11. Readers familiar with Indian cinema may wonder why I have not discussed the Indian Censor Board. Though filmmaking in India is a private enterprise, all films for theatrical release have to be cleared and rated by the government's Central Board of Film Censors, a practice initiated by the British colonial authorities, who heavily censored any allusion to self-governance, the Indian nationalist movement, or Indian independence. During discussions of how to Indianize a film, the censors were rarely mentioned except as an obstacle to be overcome rather than as a constraint. Censors are viewed as capricious and nit-picking, and filmmakers have employed a variety of strategies to deal with them, such as leaving scenes longer than desired, knowing that the censors will ask for cuts. Film censorship in India is a very complex issue that is beyond the scope of this article.

12. All mainstream Indian films are presented in two halves, with an intermission referred to as the "interval" placed at a point of suspense or at a dramatic turn in the narrative.

13. This is an allusion to *Speed.*

14. In a narrative film, diegesis refers to the world of the film's story, and diegetic music is music presented as originating from a source within the film's world.

15. Rain, associated with fertility and rebirth, has always been invested with erotic, sensual significance in Hindu mythology, classical literature, and music. Indian classical music has many songs in which the anticipation of the monsoon rains is likened to a person's anticipation of his or her lover.

16. The film was abandoned for various reasons.

17. Audiences are portrayed as monolithic only in the case of Indianization; otherwise Hindi filmmakers classify audiences according to class, region, language, ethnicity, gender, and generation. See Ganti 2000 for a more detailed discussion of how Hindi filmmakers categorize and imagine their audiences.

REFERENCES

Abu-Lughod, Lila, and Catherine A. Lutz, eds. 1990. *Language and the Politics of Emotion.* Cambridge, England: Cambridge University Press.

Adarsh, Taran. 1996. Interview with author, September 29, Bombay.

Akhtar, Javed. 1996. Interview with author, November 25, Bombay.

Ang, Ien. 1991. *Desperately Seeking the Audience.* London: Routledge.

Aufderheide, Patricia. 1998. Made in Hong Kong: Translation and Transmutation. In *Play It Again Sam: Retakes on Remakes,* edited by Andrew Horton and Stuart Y. McDougal, pp. 191–99. Berkeley: University of California Press.

Barjatya, Rajat. 1996. Interview with author, April 29, Bombay.

Dornfeld, Barry. 1998. *Producing Public Television, Producing Public Culture.* Princeton, N.J.: Princeton University Press.

Ganti, Tejaswini. 2000. Casting Culture: The Social Life of Hindi Film Production in Contemporary India. Ph.D. diss., Department of Anthropology, New York University.

Gupta, Akhil, and James Ferguson. 1997. Beyond "Culture": Space, Identity, and the Politics of Difference. In *Culture, Power, Place: Explorations in Critical Anthropology*, edited by Akhil Gupta and James Ferguson, pp. 33–51. Durham, N.C.: Duke University Press.

Gupta, Sutanu. 1996. Interview with author, November 2, 18, Bombay.

Horton, Andrew. 1998. Cinematic Makeovers and Cultural Border Crossings: Kusturica's *Time of the Gypsies* and *Coppola's Godfather and Godfather II*. In *Play It Again Sam: Retakes on Remakes*, edited by Andrew Horton and Stuart Y. McDougal, pp. 172–90. Berkeley: University of California Press.

Horton, Andrew, and Stuart Y. McDougal, eds. 1998. *Play It Again Sam: Retakes on Remakes*. Berkeley: University of California Press.

Kondo, Dorinne. 1992. The Aesthetics and Politics of Japanese Identity in the Fashion Industry. In *Re-made in Japan: Everyday Life and Consumer Taste in a Changing Society*, edited by Joseph J. Tobin, pp. 176–203. New Haven, Conn.: Yale University Press.

Kumar, N. 1995. Born in the USA. *Filmfare* (November): 170–73.

Lynch, Owen M., ed., 1990. *Divine Passions: The Social Construction of Emotion in India*. Berkeley: University of California Press.

Michaels, Eric. 1990. A Model of Teleported Texts (with Reference to Aboriginal Television). *Continuum* 3 (2): 8–31.

Nandy, Ashis. 1998. Indian Popular Cinema as a Slum's Eye View of Politics. In *The Secret Politics of Our Desires: Innocence, Culpability and Indian Popular Cinema*, edited by Ashis Nandy, pp. 1–18. Delhi: Oxford University Press.

Nayar, Sheila J. 1997. The Values of Fantasy: Indian Popular Cinema through Western Scripts. *Journal of Popular Culture* 31 (1): 73–90.

Ohmann, Richard. 1996. Knowing/Creating Wants. In *Making and Selling Culture*, edited by Richard Ohmann, pp. 224–38. Hanover, N.H.: University Press of New England.

Prasad, Madhav. 1998. *Ideology of the Hindi Film: A Historical Construction*. Delhi: Oxford University Press.

Rajabali, Anjum. 1996. Interview with author, September 14, Bombay.

Thomas, Rosie. 1985. Indian Cinema, Pleasures and Popularity. *Screen* 26 (3–4): 116–31.

———. 1995. Melodrama and the Negotiation of Morality in Mainstream Hindi Film. In *Consuming Modernity: Public Culture in a South Asian World*, edited by Carol A. Breckenridge, pp. 157–82. Minneapolis: University of Minnesota Press.

Tobin, Joseph J., ed. 1992. *Re-made in Japan: Everyday Life and Consumer Taste in a Changing Society*. New Haven, Conn.: Yale University Press.

Traube, Elizabeth. 1996. Introduction. In *Making and Selling Culture*, edited by Richard Ohmann, pp. xi–xxiii. Hanover, N.H.: University Press of New England.

15

Arrival Scenes

Complicity and Media Ethnography in the Bolivian Public Sphere

Jeff D. Himpele

"We are definitely the best! Tonight, a North American anthropologist visits us to study The Open Tribunal, *a unique example of alternative communication across the entire world (fast music and announcer's voice over two-shot of Jeff Himpele and television cohost Adolfo Paco).*

(Close-up of Jeff speaking) ". . . a constant direct connection with the people that the Bolivian cinema does not yet have because . . ."

(Announcer's voice over wide-shot) "Tonight, after your soap opera Three Destinies."

(Radio Television Popular network logo and music fade in.)

I was certainly surprised to see this preview for the evening broadcast of *The Open Tribunal* following my first visit to its production earlier that day. Why feature me on a television program devoted to airing testimonials and resolving social problems for the more vulnerable people of La Paz? Whether I was aligned with these other participants seeking assistance from the Tribunal or whether my appearance privileged me to bestow its international significance, my image authenticated a rhetoric that had galvanized a neo-populist political party led by its host and network-owner Carlos Palenque. Seeing myself as an unwitting participant in that project and as a coming attraction made me apprehensive, if not suspicious, about the field relations this preview might be foreshadowing.[1]

I first interpreted this scene as an inversion of the classic model of ethnography. Instead of an ethnographer participating in, observing, and representing culture for those at home, local cultural observers were fixing upon me as a North American anthropologist, framing my image, and bringing me into people's homes. Yet if the producers and I are analogously committed to representing people in La Paz, then there is no reversal. If we are so alike, then what are the differences? And if *Tribunal* hosts respected my authority to speak about La Paz, did they also destabilize it by positioning

Still of anthropologist Jeff Himpele being interviewed by Carlos Palenque, host of the Bolivian populist TV talk show *The Open Tribunal*, La Paz. (From the collection of Jeff Himpele)

me to underscore theirs? Viewed as more than a reversal of ethnographic practice, the blurred positions now apparent in this preview do not establish ethnographic rapport, authenticity, or authority in the classic sense. Instead, they preview the larger scenario in which ethnography is entangled when practiced in the cosmopolitan public sphere. What affinities and tensions organize ethnography that takes place in, as, or through public spaces in which culture and society are already objects of representation that are self-consciously produced, scrutinized, strategized, and interpreted?

THE PARALLAX OF MEDIA ETHNOGRAPHY

This essay sorts through the images of my appearances on the *Tribunal* and calls for further reflection on how anthropologists, who are engaged in "inventing culture" themselves (Wagner 1981), are frequently recognized and drawn into the projects of other cultural producers. Reflexivity in media ethnography, however, has been concerned with the discursive imbalance toward scholars who select and classify their subjects and the stakes of depicting audiences' and producers' agency in processes of media signification. These concerns coincided with the anthropological critique of ethnographic discourse and representation that emerged in the 1980s around two key epistemological issues: (1) the relations of authority and political implications of representing the plurality and voices of ethnographic subjects (see, e.g., Clifford 1988); and (2) the need to write grounded ethnographies that trace power and culture across the world-system (Marcus 1995). If the textual analysis of ethnography revealed competing claims to represent culture and power in global contexts, then as the opening to this essay suggests, there is not only a continuing need to locate media and audiences in wider fields of power but also a need to situate the dynamics of field relations of ethnographers who negotiate positions in public alongside other cultural producers who also converge upon "culture."[2]

In a framework that theorizes this convergence between ethnographic filmmakers and indigenous media producers, Faye Ginsburg vividly draws the image of "a parallax effect" in which ethnographers and media producers are situated alongside one another while each produces similar representations of the same social phenomenon. By juxtaposing their perspectives on a continuum of practices of cultural representation that are enmeshed in wider historical processes and relations of inequality, Ginsburg provokes needed attention to the social engagements between them in sites of media production (1995: 65–66, 73). Similarly, Terry Turner (1992 and this volume) observes how the emergence of Kayapó ethnic consciousness through their video-making and his own analysis jointly produced politically valuable objectifications of "Kayapó culture." Turner demonstrates that these parallel positions can be allied in a form of complicity, but when the ethnographer is engaged with more powerful institutions of mass media this alliance may not always be as straightforward as it is in the Kayapó case. Barry Dornfeld's reflection on his ethnography of the making of a PBS documentary series reveals how his fieldwork in the public sphere entailed negotiating stances toward cultural producers who produce similar "ethnographic" representations themselves. Further, by shifting between positions as observer and participant, feelings of obligation and duplicity can emerge as one becomes part of social hierarchies created through media institutions (Dornfeld 1998: 21, 23–24).

The issue of how ethnographers handle diverse, rival, and even disagreeable ethnographic affiliations when shifting among locations is part of a wider recent reexamination of fieldwork traditions. This attention to field locations is coupled with the aspect of ethnographic practice involving the imagination and construction of field sites themselves as spatialized localities of social affiliation and experience (Gupta and Ferguson 1997). Arjun Appadurai calls this the "production of locality" in foregrounding how, in the same way, communities that anthropologists study also have defining locality as a primary objective and produce themselves through various local-izing practices (1996: 181–82). He urges us to recognize that because of this isomorphism, "Ethnography has been unwittingly complicit in this activity." In exploring the global conditions of ethnographic complicity, George Marcus (1997) argues that the deterritorialization of culture and power in the contemporary mise-en-scène of fieldwork shifts the basis of ethnographic knowledge and affinity away from the image of cultural "insidedness" suggested by "rapport" and "collaboration" and toward one of complicity that is entailed when both ethnographers and informants are anxiously interpreting and managing global forces originating from elsewhere. If complicity is a form of affinity that still marks ethnographers from "elsewhere" (Marcus 1997: 97), then ethnographers are subjects to be assimilated and managed as well as possible accomplices, as my preview shows.

This essay explores how *Tribunal* producers and I managed my arrival through a relationship of complicity that was constituted because our parallax positions on a continuum of practices of cultural representation, to adopt Ginsburg's phrasing, were broadcast live. The continuum on which ethnographers are situated alongside cultural producers is not only a socially uneven field of mutual intervention, I argue, but also a substantially public terrain where field relations such as complicity are shaped by the veiled strategies and unspoken tactics that lie in its hidden fissures and folds. Before exploring my assimilation in the Bolivian public sphere, I first describe the social and moral space of the *Tribunal* and the strategies of representation it embodied.

A CRISIS OF REPRESENTATION: OPENING THE PEOPLE'S TRIBUNAL IN THE PUBLIC SPHERE

Until his unexpected death in March 1997, *The Open Tribunal*'s host and owner of the Radio Television Popular network, Carlos Palenque, spoke for an hour each day on the air with the people of the urban indigenous majorities of La Paz about their social problems. Urban *cholos*, rural-born immigrant Aymaras, and their urban-born families who make up the city's "popular classes" converged each morning at Palenque's studios in the center of the city canyon hoping to resolve a variety of problems. They were there to seek medical assistance, to charge spouses with domestic violence, to obtain legal assistance, to call for lost children and family members, to warn people about scams, to denounce government policies, and of course, to thank the hosts for their previous assistance. After each brief interview, Palenque directed participants to his network's Social Wing of social workers, lawyers, medical counselors, and the Women's Commission who offered aid that the government was less and less inclined to provide.

Broadcast live on radio and videotaped for evening television, the *Tribunal* combined the testimonial realism of face-to-face communication between Palenque and his participant-viewers on a set decorated with Andean textiles while location footage from their cases was electronically inserted (or layered) over the interlocutors' voices. As a localizing practice, these images indexically connected the television studio with peripheral urban spaces coded as "popular." Interspersed with episodes from an international reality TV program *(Ocurrió Así)*, primetime on RTP interwove a cosmopolitan neighborhood of social discourse from a particularly "popular" angle. Palenque was accompanied by cohosts who included his wife, Monica Medina, and RTP directors Adolfo Paco and Remedios Loza; the two pairs evoked domesticity and represented different cultural identities and social statuses in La Paz. As a well-known former folklore musician and radio host, Carlos Palenque established his legitimacy by agreeing to relate to participants and audiences in the moral terms of *compadrazgo* (ritual co-parenthood) and the networks of reciprocal obligations it extends among co-parents. In these relationships people of higher economic or social status are obligated to sponsor children in weddings and baptisms, but the relationship can be deployed to acquire support for virtually anything. Palenque himself was usually referred to as "El Compadre" in a moral sphere of paternal social interaction that evoked familial solidarity while it tactically marked the unequal social hierarchy. Built on these micropractices of power in everyday and ritual life, the *Tribunal* broadcast this familial sphere into the public sphere and back into people's homes.

The Open Tribunal appeared on television in 1985 in the thick of Bolivia's worst social crisis. Seventeen years of military dictatorships, a jolting transition to an electoral government in the early 1980s, and a period of hyperinflation under a Leftist government were followed by the shocking overnight deflation of currency in 1985 and the implementation of bold neoliberal policies. As the members of impoverished, unemployed, and culturally marginalized Aymara *cholos* in the La Paz metropolitan area mushroomed, the sense of social crisis was exacerbated in two new public spheres of representation. On one hand, the popular classes were invisible on commercial television, which had just been authorized to operate under a neoliberal decree, and on the other, political parties continued to lose credibility and efficacy under the dismantling of the state. *The Open Tribunal* filled the airwaves with politically contentious denunciations as well as emotional and shocking images of the aftereffects of the new political economy as lived and told by people who suffered from it most severely. As if he were able to stem the social crisis, after the presentation of each case Palenque would take the participants' (often incoherent) testimonies and provide for them and viewers a soothing and therapeutically coherent framework of understanding. Though Palenque frequently conferred centrality and voice to his participants, thereby highlighting the *Tribunal's* terms of representation in the public sphere, his hypnotically musical voice and competence in masterfully framing cases within larger social processes also secured his potent authority to speak on their behalf. Using testimonials of the poor and the myriad problems brought to him as evidence, he frequently indicted government neoliberalism and corruption and then ardently demanded social justice.

When the government closed *The Open Tribunal* for almost a year in 1988–89 following Palenque's telephone interview with a drug trafficker, the familial social bonds constituted by the *Tribunal* were quickly assembled to convert the *Tribunal* from television to neopopulist politics. The program had amassed support among people for whom it promised social relief as well as others seeking alternative avenues in the new political landscape. These groups propelled the well-connected political outsider Palenque to create and lead the political party Condepa (Conscience of the Fatherland). With contradictory and uplifting discourses that evoked nostalgia for the 1952 popular-nationalist revolution, Condepa's electoral successes in local and national elections vented popular complaints and neutralized popular opposition during the social crisis (Mayorga 1995).[3]

At first glance it would be easy to see Palenque as having exploited the city's downtrodden for his own political and economic gains. Addressing the negotiation of hegemony between powerful media institutions and diverse audiences, I argue that the meetings of *Tribunal* hosts (as producers) and participants (as audiences) in the RTP production studio are crucial moments of social negotiation where prestige is advanced to Palenque in exchange for aid and visibility. Rather than being equipotent, emancipatory, or coercive, this implicit yet morally loaded cultural strategy of mutual obligation between ritual co-parents diffuses media and historical agency among them while it reproduces their unequal social status. As I describe next, it is this cultural strategy that organized my own entry into the *Tribunal* and Bolivian popular politics.

MY ARRIVAL SEEN: MIMETIC VERTIGO IN THE PUBLIC SPHERE

Drawn to the *Tribunal* while conducting other research on cinema and popular culture in La Paz, I saw its mass-mediated politics as uniquely occupying ideological space between neopopulism and revolutionism on the one hand, and grassroots cultural politics, social action, and protest on the other (Fox and Starn 1997). My eventual visit to the *Tribunal* was preceded by ethnographic work wherein I was aligned with viewers in the popular sectors. They held pragmatically positive ideas about the program's mission yet were ambivalent about its politics of representation. As I approached the unmarked RTP building hoping to gain access and do fieldwork there, I was sensitive to how the terms of my access might unfold. How should I address Palenque? Although I sought assistance from his *Tribunal*, were he and I "compadres" if I was not native to this social field? My wife, Nelly, who is Bolivian, offered to accompany me on my first visit since, as she put it, "There would already be a relationship between us," which could facilitate my entry. Though our own relationship would become a point of interest on the program because her family is from the same urban popular classes as most *Tribunal* viewers (with whom marriages with North Americans is uncommon), Nelly's mediation was not the only key to my field relations there.

As instructed by the receptionist the day before, Nelly and I arrived at 11:30; about fifty people were already lined up to be interviewed by the program coordinator and a social worker who selected the cases for television. Others were sent to the Social Wing for help. We entered the lobby and stood awkwardly outside the line, unsure where exactly to stand until the program's coordinator, Arturo Ruiz, approached me and accepted my request to observe his work and walk around freely. About a half-hour after *The Open Tribunal* began taping upstairs, Arturo returned and invited me to talk to "the Compadre" on the program. Reluctantly, I glanced around the lobby and said that I would not want to take time away from the people who needed time on the program more than I did. "Don't worry," he said; "it is normal that observers also participate in the *Tribunal.* Just for a minute. Both of you." Clearly this obligatory public introduction would be key to performing research here, and hesitation might appear aggressive. So I complied.

It turned out that instead of Palenque, cohost Adolfo Paco was conducting the program that day. We greeted him as "Señor Paco," and he first asked about my project and for my opinion of the *Tribunal.* I explained that I was interested in the direct relationships between the program and the people, and Paco wondered if there was a similar program in the United States. Instead of making an overdrawn analogy, I underscored the uniqueness of the social aid offered by the *Tribunal.*

"Aha. Because here we deal with cases, let's say, even personal cases, like the gentlemen we had on earlier, who tell us they had trouble with their community and, of course, we have lawyers who can support them, call the authorities, go to the authorities. We have complete follow-ups on social problems, on the personal conflicts. Isn't it true?"

Their social aid was among the things I wanted to investigate further, but Paco enclosed my research agenda with the answer he implied. I could only politely affirm the unique public image of the *Tribunal* as a source of immediate social aid, which coincided with my own interest in its particularity and my sense of its locality. "Yes."

Paco invited Nelly to speak, "So you are his wife? And you are a Bolivian? How did you meet?" Paco searched for melodramatic tension as he and Palenque often do. He asked us how our families felt about our marrying foreigners. After we had spoken positively and failed to supply him with a conflict to make our segment more interesting, he ended the interview with an invitation to continue visiting. As we walked off camera, Paco turned to viewers, "Well, in the *Tribunal* we have everything. We have said that before, and now we have talked with this nice *gringuito* about many things, Bolivian as well as American topics." Our story fit in among others with which the *Tribunal* frequently constructs its cosmopolitan appearance by hybridizing the national, the popular, and the global (Himpele 1999).

As the last participants and the crew spilled out into the street after the taping, a small family that also had been on the program approached us. The oldest son introduced himself and explained that their father had been killed in a rural town near Cochabamba, a city about seven hours away. They were urgently trying to raise money by selling a piece of rural land there and petitioned us to buy it. When I told them that we could not buy it ourselves, they asked if we knew another U.S. anthropologist who would buy their land right away. I did not know of any, I told them, and took down their address so that we could pass on the information if we did meet anyone working in that area.

The next day I began my solo work at the *Tribunal*. As I was talking with a cameraman near the rear of the studio, Palenque briskly walked in, with Arturo and cohost Remedios Loza a half-step behind him. Beginning the daily routine, the lights and folklore music faded up and under Palenque's voice as he began his opening commentary. After a commercial break, Palenque resumed, "Last night on the *Tribunal* we saw a North American interested in *The Open Tribunal*. An anthropologist married to a Bolivian who captured him. (A camera spun around to show me taking notes.) He is here again at the *Tribunal*; you are looking at him on the screen. He is here to make observations and take notes to bring to the United States. I saw him last night in the broadcast of *The Open Tribunal* to present his work about our program. I am going to speak a few words with him to see how he feels here. He is charmed by Bolivia and his heart has been split in two, one half is in the United States and the other half is in Bolivia; and he plans to be in both Bolivia and the United States. We are proud to know that, like him, there are many professionals who are interested in the form of communication here on the *Tribunal*." The screen returned to Palenque's deliberate speech as he reflexively highlighted the social reversals that are staged on the *Tribunal*. "Because the speaker—because the listener is converted into the speaker, because here problems are presented, solutions are sought, and here institutional issues as well as personal issues are taken on with absolute openness, and yes, the people can tell the truth." He went on to describe his recent trip to the United States to meet with politicians there. "With the anthropologist, I will chat in a few minutes. Until then, there are telephone calls. Hello? Good afternoon."

By the time I met with Palenque on the air, I was over the surprise that Palenque had been watching me and the slight indignation that he publicly obligated me to reappear without advance notice. I sensed that I was not only being used to enhance the program as an anthropologist, with both of us fixing on the *Tribunal*'s unique practice of offering social aid, but that I was also being subtly instructed to know which of us directs social representation at RTP. Palenque reintroduced me to the television audience, greeted me with a smile, and asked about the results of my work thus far. I first thought it a strange question for the second day of field research, but realized that he was asking me to provide a favorably sweeping judgment. Perhaps he was checking to see where else I had been and how my other fieldwork might have already shaped my views. In this precarious public exchange, however, I could not make critical judgments about how he channels individual crises into the totalizing narratives of his own project, but I also wanted to avoid endorsing his political agenda.

"Well, anthropological work is a bit . . . it takes a long time and one cannot make conclusions very quickly because one has to be very sensitive . . ."

"Of course. Of course," he broke in approvingly. At that moment, I became more aware of his technique, how he cuts off people in order to redefine their problems.

" . . . to all of the details. For the anthropologist it is in the details where the conclusions lie, so for now . . ." I continued, tactically evading the question while staying within its frame.

He pushed, "But right now, in general, taking a first glance at things, what results do you have up until now?"

"What I see now is, for example, that *The Open Tribunal* has had an important impact in La Paz, and that the people feel a direct connection with the *Tribunal* and that they can come directly to the studios to participate."

"And they can express themselves with absolute freedom."

"That's what they say, yes. Exactly."

Having co-opted me to reflect on and reiterate the *Tribunal*'s mode of representation, Palenque identified anthropology's project of producing knowledge based on experience and then asked me to compare and comment on social behavior in the United States. I made the argument that, like La Paz, the United States was too heterogeneous to allow a broad and unitary characterization. He was asking me to display a professional authority to make cogent generalizations, which seemed analogous to his own role. As is typical, he switched to a more personal topic and sought another generalization by delving into my experience: "What are the differences between the Bolivian woman, her personality, and the North American woman?"[4]

"Well, again Sr. Palenque, I can't draw a frame that is going to include all . . ."

He had to settle for an admiring depiction of Nelly and ended the dialogue. "Fine. Welcome to Bolivia. I hope all goes well. You are in your home. Very well," he concluded. I politely thanked him for the opportunity to visit the *Tribunal* and walked off camera.

Viewing the broadcast on television later that evening, I watched Palenque maneuver and encircle my authority in order to establish his own. Carefully navigating the engagement, I offered comments that were safe, honest, and nothing new to him, yet I was surprised to hear myself again repeating the *Tribunal*'s own discourse about its unique openness and accessibility to the urban poor. If I was speaking the public discourse and reinforcing the configuration of authority of the program, this same ventriloquism was a delicate contradiction for ethnographers who all edit and reframe their texts in subtly powerful ways. I watched him do so as I walked off camera, "He has his position. He is taking notes and is closely analyzing *The Open Tribunal* from his angle as a professional anthropologist." I felt that this comment was intended to contain, if not diminish, my particularistic approach and mark me from "elsewhere." Avoiding his demands for generalization, my answers drew connections between our common localizing practices instead. It seemed the more I struggled to separate my project of social representation from his, the more they appeared to converge. Palenque seemed to have already recognized our parallax positions, now evoked by the on-screen image of us standing beside each other and facing the public's gaze (see photo).

Watching the refracted image of myself alongside Palenque, I thought of the family I met from Cochabamba a day earlier who had petitioned me to buy land from them. Did I raise their hopes about possibly selling the land and then defer any help I might give them, as RTP often did? They had situated me alongside Palenque and RTP as a potential source of social aid rather than as one of them—a coparticipant. Would this be my relationship with the participants? "Was I a Palenque?" In a flash of recognition, the similarities and differences in our representational practices blurred and plunged me into a moment of "mimetic vertigo."[5] Michael Taussig's term describes a dizzy spell provoked by "the West as mirrored in the handiwork of its Others" that subversively dissolves the boundaries between self and other that structure colonial subordination as well as anthropology (1993: 236–49). In mimetic vertigo, he writes, "the self enters into the alter against which the self is defined and sustained" (236). Thus if for an instant I saw myself as Palenque, he was an embodiment of the repressed anthropological other constituted by critiques of the singularly controlling voice.

Recognizing myself in the same moral sphere of social engagement with the people I was studying and who were also watching me,[6] I began to ask myself if my ethnographic solicitation of and editing of informants' voices were different from Palenque's elicitation and cutting off of participants' voices while he praises their protagonism. What of anthropology's advocacy and concern for marginalized cultural processes, material inequalities, and social transformation? Do we appropriate images of suffering and testimonial narratives as our cultural capital to mobilize popular sentiment and solidarity (Kleinman and Kleinman 1997: 1)? What of Palenque's political totalizations that order social crises into narratives of global magnitude for people watching at home? This too seemed to be close to the heart of the anthropological project: In our attempts to provide a cross-cultural frame we too employ people's lives in narratives of varying scales that are meaningful for our own audiences at "home." Rather than simply turning the tables on and inverting ethnographic power, I felt this episode of mimetic vertigo rupture it.

I desperately sought to remind myself that anthropology's goals are not to commercialize and dramatize suffering in brief meetings, but to produce sustained analyses of social processes that look beyond rather than stay constrained by given frames of reference. I also thought of my aim to understand the construction of social agency rather than to naturalize it. If the convergence of our parallax lines of sight onto television screens among the public parodied any sense of ethnographic mastery embedded in my work, then it was appropriated to enhance the *Tribunal's* too. Faced with this image of complicity in the *Tribunal's* project, I felt charged to sharply distinguish a divergent ethnographic gaze, despite the fact that it might never disengage itself from this mimetic blur.

COMPLICITY AS A MODE OF PRODUCTION AND AS PUBLIC SECRET

In the public images disseminated from the studios in the center of the city, we were accomplices in producing the national and moral space of *compadres* and *comadres* constituted through ritual exchanges. I was implicitly obligated to take part in an open-ended transaction in which I would maintain prestige for them in return for the assistance I wanted in doing research there. From one angle, I was positioned as an outside authority bringing global attention to the *Tribunal.* From another angle, I was a subordinate participant; yet unlike others hoping to have direct access to Palenque and aid, I was welcome to visit and speak with almost whomever I wished at RTP. Like them, however, I complied with *Tribunal* producers, who held the upper hand in the dialogue and who framed our conversations through their process of interrogation. Yet if my ethnography could conversely portray the *Tribunal* favorably or not, this asymmetry did not last long as the terms of our relation took on the moral logic of the *Tribunal's* mode of production and I managed the delicate politics of doing ethnography on television. As people had noted with respect to the city's downtrodden, for example, Palenque only spoke with me "when a camera was on." Hosts often politely asked me to observe the studio, perhaps to keep me in their view and to keep themselves in mine. They were aware of the antagonistic readings of the *Tribunal* found in other social locations around the city.

Tracing the production process beyond the televisual frame, I accompanied *Tribunal* production staff and social workers, who come from the popular sectors of La Paz, on their routines and listened to their approval of Palenque's authority and the *Tribunal's* social mission. I also heard occasional cracks in the *Tribunal's* coherent discourse about itself: the morality of patron-client relations was subverted by employees' discussions of low salaries and inadequate resources at the Social Wing. Behind the scenes, these employees were also positioned alongside the participants and viewers they were ostensibly helping. Like the participants, they had a stake in Palenque's economic and political prosperity and tactically complied in the televisual production of the image of Palenque's social authority as seen within the TV frame.

If complicity was the mode of production on *The Open Tribunal,* then the appearance of hegemony was its product. It became clearer from further research that Palenque's social authority was not achieved by obtaining uncritical moral consent directly, but through cultural strategies involving cross-class alliances, deferential images, and moral obligations that structured and were structured by social inequality.[7] As my interviewers drafted me to reaffirm the unrestricted access, realism, and social aid provided by the *Tribunal,* I learned the public secret of complicity that participants, workers, and viewers had already known. Arguably then, the basis of Palenque's social authority was his framing of what could be said and done as well as what must be unsaid, but deployed nevertheless, in public. Twisting "the violence of ethnography" (Clifford 1988: 67), *Tribunal* hosts appeared to interrogate me as an informant for hidden truths but maneuvered me to enunciate the prefigured fictions of their power. Yet I also delved into *The Open Tribunal* for its secrets, which could only be learned by conferring to Palenque the prestige and authority to interrogate me and have the last word.

ON HAVING THE LAST WORD

During my fieldwork I envisioned the time when I would write about the *Tribunal.* Would or should my interviews and my ethnography appear as an "open tribunal" for underpaid RTP workers and viewers? I decided then that my implicit obligation to depict the *Tribunal* favorably would have to be kept; for as long as they were employed there I would conceal much of what they told me. If dissenting comments were linked to anyone specifically, then he or she would likely be dismissed under Palenque's tight control. Had he not died in 1997, it seemed the best ethical writing strategy would have been to continue colluding with his public image.[8]

As my project has shifted toward writing, what of my authority and tactics for framing and containing agency and experience? The question is too linear, given my moment of vertigo, and it exaggerates the difference between here and there and between fieldwork and writing. Should I perpetuate the mimetic vertigo and adopt a controlling voice on Palenque and the *Tribunal* to ape them? Indeed, if Palenque's political success was obtained through his framing strategies, the situation calls for a writing strategy that would embody his irresistible voice for readers to evaluate. Yet in order to avoid inadvertently defending uneven political projects like Condepa, the strategy would also carefully interpose alternative frames. As authorship is shifted in my direction and I now inevitably decide what texts and histories to include and exclude and how to frame them—for example, my prior account of the impact of sudden neoliberal political economic shifts as historical context for the *Tribunal*—my writings seem to echo some of Palenque's explanations of the causes of the contemporary social crisis. Given the similarities of our representational practices and the public mediation of my fieldwork, there is no escaping that the moral and public terms of the *Tribunal* intervene in my writing.

As an account of the way *Tribunal* producers and I negotiated our performances with each other on television, this essay demonstrates how complicity occupies the space between parallel projects of cultural representation. It poses the challenge that there is no neat separation between media ethnographers and media producers on the terrain of cultural representation. As an anthropologist working with people from the popular classes, I establish, delineate, portray, and link multiple sites of face-to-face conversation in the translocal televisual public sphere in La Paz. Indeed, these localizing practices closely resemble the *Tribunal*'s televisual production of multilayered and interwoven global and local images and spaces. Further, if Bolivian popular politics vie to forge a prevailing definition of locality through highly personalized and sometimes unanticipated alliances (Albro 1998), then I was a competitor from one angle, yet from another I was drawn in to appear as an accomplice of the *Tribunal*'s political project. In the spectrum of culturally available positions between collaboration and contention, self and other, and here and there, this complicity was not just the best tactic I could deploy for the sake of my work; nor was it only the outcome of epistemological problems of rendering locality within global fields of power. Complicity was the historically preexisting mode of representation couched tacitly in the contours of the public sphere and was jointly deployed precisely because our field relations were mediated in the public glare.

Such anthropological complicity also may be concentrated in public spaces like tourism, art, social movements, museums, and archaeological sites, where representations of culture and locality are self-consciously produced, objectified, and debated.[9] The ethnographic self-awareness that emerges from being compounded into the multiple layers of representation, being co-opted into the political projects, and articulating unspoken cultural strategies of such public spaces may be an aspect of modernity itself. Its primary significance to anthropology, however, may not only be as a form of confession or even self-monitoring. Moreover, it is available as an analytic and critical angle, blurred as it is from a parallax position, from which to grasp the competing and convergent configurations of power and authority with which we and others produce and represent culture in public.

NOTES

I am grateful to audiences, RTP producers, participants, and staff in La Paz who facilitated my research with them. I also thank the Alvarado family in Bolivia for all of their support, and especially Nelly Alvarado, who graciously and gracefully consented to join this project through our appearance. This essay also benefited from the presentation of an earlier version to the Department of Anthropology at New York University in January 1998, as well as from the insightful readings and comments of this volume's editors and two reviewers. Any exaggerations or errors are my own.

1. This essay focuses on the start of my fieldwork at the RTP studios in 1996 as part of a larger project on the *Tribunal* and the public sphere in La Paz. Fieldwork for this project was also done in 1994 and in 1998 sponsored by grants from Princeton University and California State University, Fullerton.

2. For a statement concerning media ethnography along these two lines, see the essay by David Morely in the collection edited by Crawford and Hafsteinsson (1996), which generally pursues a critique of media ethnography along the same epistemological lines raised by textual critiques. Allison Griffiths's piece in the book perhaps goes furthest in turning toward her own field relations.

3. In the elections of May 1989, Condepa shocked political analysts when it obtained enough popular votes (13 percent nationally and 28.15 percent in La Paz) to put Palenque into the negotiations with the second- and third-place winners to decide Bolivia's president. In the pact, Condepa obtained seats in the Bolivian Congress, and Palenque appointed his Aymara cohost Remedios Loza to one of them. Other subsequent Condepa candidates included Palenque's wife, Monica Medina, who was elected mayor of La Paz in 1994 and served until 1996.

4. Many viewers in La Paz interpreted this line of questioning for me by relating it to the developing rumor that Palenque's wife was having an affair with a top Condepa official. They suggested that he intended my characterizations to demonstrate to his wife, who viewers assumed was watching, how a Bolivian woman should behave properly as a spouse.

5. Many thanks to Faye Ginsburg for suggesting this important connection.

6. Subsequent fieldwork at the Social Wing drove this point home: I was sometimes positioned by social workers as a source of aid for participants; at other times I waited hours to speak to social workers along with other petitioners.

7. As I argue elsewhere, the *Tribunal* is part of a historical cultural strategy of compliance and resistance also described by Andean scholars in which indigenous peasantries and urban poor have sometimes surprisingly shaped their own access to social resources and autonomy through strategic alliances with political elites and institutions connected with the state.

8. In August 1998, eighteen months after Palenque's death, workers were more reluctant to speak about higher-ups at RTP because of the increased job uncertainty

for them that accompanied the battles between camps to control the station and Condepa.

9. Alternatively, as James Clifford writes of Marcel Griaule, ethnographers may see "culture itself as a performance or a spectacle." For Griaule, who felt monitored by the gazes of subjects, ethnography was a negotiated settlement in a struggle for control. Furthermore, the reflexive issues I raise in this essay share much with the wider set of circumstances for fieldwork in formal institutions of modernity, where ethnographers may be situated in various sympathetic and disagreeable affiliations with subjects at once, and where they converge upon and confront the preexisting representations practiced and produced by subjects themselves (as discussed, for example, in Marcus 1999). In this essay, my aim is to situate reflection on the circumstances for ethnography when it is performed and mediated by the cultural contours and strategies embodied by publicness itself.

REFERENCES

Albó, Javier. 1987. From MNRistas to Kataristas to Katari. In *Resistance, Rebellion, and Consciousness in the Andean Peasant World, 18th to 20th Centuries*, edited by S. J. Stern, pp. 379–419. Madison: University of Wisconsin Press.

———. 1993. . . . *Y de Kataristas a MNRistas?* La Paz: CEDOIN and UNITAS.

Albro, Robert. 1998. A New Time and Space for Bolivian Popular Politics, Introduction to theme issue. *Ethnology* 37 (2): 99–115.

Appadurai, Arjun. 1996. The Production of Locality. In *Modernity at Large: Cultural Dimensions of Globalization*, pp. 178–99. Minneapolis: University of Minnesota Press.

Clifford, James. 1988. *The Predicament of Culture: Twentieth-Century Ethnography, Literature, and Art*. Cambridge, Mass.: Harvard University Press.

Crawford, Peter I., and Sigurjon Baldur Hafsteinsson, eds. 1996. *The Construction of the Viewer: Media Ethnography and the Anthropology of Audiences*. Hojbjerg, Denmark: Intervention Press.

Dornfeld, Barry. 1998. *Producing Public Television, Producing Public Culture*. Princeton, N.J.: Princeton University Press.

Fox, Richard G., and Orin Starn, eds. 1997. *Between Resistance and Revolution: Cultural Politics and Social Protest*. New Brunswick, N.J.: Rutgers University Press.

Ginsburg, Faye. 1995. The Parallax Effect: The Impact of Aboriginal Media on Ethnographic Film. *Visual Anthropology Review* 11 (2): 64–76.

Gupta, Akhil, and James Ferguson, eds. 1997. *Anthropological Locations: Boundaries and Grounds of a Field Science*. Berkeley: University of California Press.

Himpele, Jeffrey D. 1996. Film Distribution as Media: Mapping Difference in the Bolivian Cinemascape. *Visual Anthropology Review* 12 (1): 47–66.

———. 1999. Reality Affects: Media Agency and Popular Politics in the Bolivian Public Sphere. Manuscript.

Kleinman, Arthur, and Joan Kleinman. 1997. The Appeal of Experience; The Dismay of Images: Cultural Appropriation of Suffering in Our Times. In *Social Suffering*, edited by A. Kleinman, V. Das et al., pp. 1–23. Berkeley: University of California Press.

Marcus, George. 1995. Ethnography in/of the World System. *Annual Review of Anthropology* 24: 95–117.

———. 1997. The Uses of Complicity in the Changing Mise-en-Scène of Anthropological Fieldwork. *Representations* 59 (Summer): 85–108.

———. 1999. *Critical Anthropology Now: Unexpected Contexts, Shifting Constituencies, Changing Agendas.* Santa Fe, N.M.: School of American Research Press.

Mayorga, René Antonio. 1995. *Antipolítica y Neopopulismo.* La Paz: CEBEM.

Platt, Tristan. 1982. *Estado Boliviano y Ayllu Andino: Tierra y Tributo en El Norte de Potosí.* Lima: Instituto de Estudios Peruanos.

Taussig, Michael. 1993. *Mimesis and Alterity: A Particular History of the Senses.* New York: Routledge.

Turner, Terence. 1992. Representing, Resisting, Rethinking: Historical Transformations of Kayapo Culture and Consciousness. In *Colonial Situations: Essays on the Contextualization of Ethnographic Knowledge,* edited by George W. Stocking Jr., pp. 285–313. Madison: University of Wisconsin Press.

Wagner, Roy. 1981. *The Invention of Culture.* Chicago: University of Chicago Press.

V

The Social Life of Technology

Photomontage, 1975, by Omar Said Bakor, Lamu, Kenya. (Courtesy Omar Said Bakor. From the collection of Heike Behrend. Originally published in *Snap Me One!: Studiofotografen in Afrika* [1998], edited by Tobias Wendl and Heike Behrend [Munich: Prestel].)

16

The Materiality of Cinema Theaters in Northern Nigeria

Brian Larkin

"Drop me at the Plaza." "Meet me at the El Dorado." These casual directions highlight the role of cinema theaters as built spaces in the urban geography of Kano, Northern Nigeria. Large, hulking buildings punctuate Kano urban topography. There, buses stop, taxis load up, motorbikes deliver people in the daily circumambulation from home to work to market and back again. Most of these travelers have little interest in films or the theater but have internalized the demarcation of public space marked out by cinema theaters, mosques, the post office, the emir's palace, and other institutions of the post-colony. Outside the theaters merchants, idlers, mechanics, and film fans depend on the particular social space created by cinema for their livelihood and leisure. Around the back and on the sides boys play football against the large dark walls. Men squat and piss against a wall painted with large letters "AN HANA FISARA A NAN" (Don't piss here).

This chapter is an examination of the fact of cinema in its materiality. It is about the fantasy space of cinema, but by this I do not mean the magical worlds to which cinema transports viewers. Rather, I view fantasy as the energy stored in the concreteness of objects, especially the commodified elements of every-day life (see Benjamin 1978). These objects are not just the products people buy but constitute the total sensory experience of urban living. In other words, this essay is about the material culture of cinema theaters as public institutions. I read the architectonics of cinema theaters and their location on the urban landscape as concrete allegories of the imposition of colonial urbanization and the experience of modernity in colonial life.

In Kano, the introduction of cinema theaters inaugurated a series of controversies over the siting of theaters on the urban landscape, the diabolical nature of cinema as a signifying technology, and the regulation of who was allowed to attend. Cinema theaters created new modes of sociability that challenged existing relations of space, gender, and social hierarchy. The controversies over cinema are moments of struggle in the reterritorialization of urban space, the attempt to define and rebuild Hausa moral space in the face of an encroaching colonial modernity. Cinema is a technology whose place in Hausa social life had to be defined. Its mass, the stories and rumors about cinema, and the words used to refer to the technology all contain traces of the history of colonialism and the urban experience. They tell us about the way that cinema as technology entered into Hausa space and took hold in the Hausa imagination.

In African postcolonies like Nigeria, a trip to the cinema has always been translocal, a stepping outside of Africa to places elsewhere.[1] To step from the foyer into the dark night of the cinema hall was to be magically transported into a universe where American realities, Indian emotions, and Hong Kong choreography have long occupied the fantasy space of Nigerian cinema screens. But cinema theaters are peculiar kind of social spaces marked by a duality of presence and absence, rootedness and transport, what Lynne Kirby (1997) refers to as the paradox of travel without movement. Cinema is seen as distinctively modern because of this ability to destabilize and make mobile people, ideas, and commodities. Onrushing images that raise the specter of cultural colonization threaten the local construction of space. This process of cinematic transportation is both ambivalent and multivalent. It erodes "the cultural distinctiveness of place" (Watts 1996: 64) by facilitating transnational cultural flows. But it can also reaffirm and intensify forms of belonging by providing a cultural foil against which local religious, ethnic, and national identities may be hardened. Finally, through Islamic or Hindu revitalization it can promote the rise of alternative forms of modernity that react against Westernization by providing their own modes of transforming space and people.

Elsewhere I have approached what I term the social space of media in this way, analyzing the fantasy worlds cinema transports one to by examining the ways Hausa viewers engage with Indian films as a secure third space from which they can imagine alternatives to Western modernity and Hausa tradition (see Larkin 1997). But while most often seen as engines of mobility, cinema theaters are also deeply parochial, intimate parts of urban topography that draw around them congeries of social practices that make cinemagoing an event that always exceeds (and sometimes has little to do with) the films that are shown on the screen. This aspect of the social space of media focuses on the spaces cinema theaters produce through their material qualities and their place on the urban landscape. My focus here is on the "materiality of specific domains" that directs attention to the "sensual and material qualities of the object" through which "we are able to unpick the more subtle connections with cultural lives and values" (Miller 1997: 9). The space of cinema is often rendered neutral by scholars in the attention given to cinemagoing as a perceptual practice. Though Hollywood and Bollywood and other national cinemas have indeed devoted great energy to regularizing relations of textual address in the attempt to create a homogeneous viewing audience, in practice the experience of cinema is still profoundly local. Cinema theaters, while commodified, do not offer up material objects we can take home with us but an emotional experience based on a sensory environment regulated by specific relations of lighting, vision, movement, and sociality.[2] By analyzing the built space of cinema theaters and the struggle over where they were sited on the Kano landscape I wish to shift the study of cinema toward the social practices the theaters create. I examine how specific cinematic environments are produced and use this to explore the nature of colonial urbanism.

CINEMA, THE PHENOMENOLOGY OF THE SURFACE, AND COLONIAL MODERNITY

Walter Benjamin built a powerful hermeneutics around the interrogation of objects, once swollen with the force of history, whose significance had ebbed with transformations in social and economic structure. His famous analysis of the Paris arcades, for instance, was not based on their newness but on the fact they were once new and that their historical moment had passed. According to his friend Adorno, Benjamin created a "petrified . . . or obsolete inventory of cultural fragments" that provided concrete embodiments of historical process or "manifestations of culture" (cited in Buck-Morss 1989: 58). Benjamin shared this evocative theorizing of material culture with Siegfried Kracauer, who also pioneered the historico-philosophical interrogation of the marginal, the momentary, and the concrete. Like Benjamin, Kracauer was interested in surface phenomena and argued that their marginal, mass-produced nature was revelatory of the social order. "The position that an epoch occupies in the historical process can be determined . . . from an analysis of its unconscious surface-level expressions," he wrote in his essay "The Mass Ornament," arguing that these "expressions . . . by virtue of their unconscious nature, provide unmediated access to the fundamental substance of the state of things" (Kracauer 1995: 75).

For Kracauer and Benjamin, the quotidian landscapes of life—posters on the walls, shop signs, dancing girls, bestsellers, panoramas, the shape, style, and circulation of city buses—are all surface representations of the fantasy energy by which the collective perceives the social order. This structure creates an interpenetrated analysis of urban culture in modernity, one in which strikingly different phenomena are structurally linked. Benjamin is, of course, best known for his analysis of the perceptual and psychological effects of mechanical reproduction, which has fed the analytic tradition in cinema studies concerned with vision, perception, and apparatus. Kracauer's and Benjamin's works are appealing to anthropologists because of their focus on the everyday, and by theorizing the workings of mass culture as part of a wider phenomenon of urban materiality they provide a sociologically rich means of linking critical urbanism and cinema studies with historical and ethnographic work in African studies and anthropology.[3]

I use the location of theaters on the urban landscape and the architectonics of theater construction as means of interrogating the nature of colonial modernity. The stained concrete, the open-air screens, and the proximity to markets reveal "knowledge of the state of things" (Kracauer 1995: 75), of both the structural conditions of colonial capitalism and the Hausa response. Cinema theaters were introduced to Kano as part of a much wider transformation of the colonial public sphere. Like beer parlors, theaters, public gardens, libraries, and commercial streets that preceded them, theaters created new modes of association that challenged existing social and sexual hierarchies regulating public space. The cinema theater thus created new modes of sociability that had to be regulated—officially by the colonial administration and unofficially within local Hausa norms—in a process of coming to be. Cinema theaters were not just involved in the creation of new modes of public; they also reaffirmed new modes of spatially ordering that public (Mitchell 1991; Thompson 2000).

I analyze the rise of cinema theaters as part of the much wider phenomenon of a transformative urban modernity that is deeply disruptive of relations of gender, class, and individuality. Because of this potential for disruption, how cinema theaters actually evolved and the social relations that surrounded them as technological and leisure practices cannot be taken for granted; they were a negotiation among built space, the apparatus itself. and local social relations. The formal and informal regulation of cinema— where it was to be located, who could attend, and what films could be shown—was a contested practice whereby a transnational phenomenon was constituted within local social, ethnic, and gender norms. This is true for the emergence of theaters in New York, Bombay, London, and Kano, but the particular relations of colonial rule make the trajectory of what cinema is strikingly different in the colonial arena. The rise of cinema in the United States, for instance, is famously rooted in the leisure practices of working-class immigrants. One of the most powerful stories about the origin of American cinema involves the way in which entrepreneurs actively tried to transform cinema into a bourgeois entertainment.[4] In the colonial context the trajectory is just the opposite: in most cases cinema was introduced as a specifically foreign colonial form of entertainment for European and native elites, and only after it became popular were auditoriums constructed (or opened) for the masses. Instead of being a marked lower-class activity it was often identified as an elite, racially coded, leisure practice. Despite this, in most places cinemagoing quickly became a local, indigenous activity (and in the case of India most notably, filmmaking itself became an indigenous phenomenon).

THE ARCHITECTONICS OF CINEMA THEATERS

In its materiality, its reproducibility over space and time, and its ubiquitous presence on metropolitan landscapes, the cinema theater appears reassuringly familiar, a self-effacing transnational technology that seemingly belongs to no particular country. The ontological security of theaters comes from the formal solidity of an auditorium that places audiences in a familiar spatial configuration: arranged in rows sitting beneath the ethereal spectacle of light and dark unfolding on the screen. In most parts of the world the theater has become second nature; we no longer query its existence or imagine a time when it could be queried, when its innovation brought with it a powerful transformative capacity. But this second nature is illusory and masks the process by which physical, public space becomes social: the forgetting of history in the creation of myth (Barthes 1986). The taken-for-grantedness of cinema theaters masks the historical conditions of colonial rule that made the technology possible.

The erection of cinema theaters in colonial cities created new social spaces of sexual, ethnic, religious, and racial intermixing, making them ambivalent institutions that often threatened existing hierarchies and boundaries about the public use of space. This ambivalence is seen very simply in the diverse ways colonies attempted to regulate the transformative capacity of these new institutions and reconstitute them within existing gender hierarchies. In India, for instance, separate entrances were built so that women could enter and exit without sharing the same social space as male cinemagoers (Arora 1995). In Damascus, by contrast, the same concern over female mobility and the threat of sexual intermixing was limited by reserving afternoon performances for women only (Thompson 2000). The same threat was contained in Lamu, Kenya, by making one night a week "ladies' night" (Fugelsang 1994), and in Northern Nigeria the immoral connotations of sexual intermixing were so intense that cinema theaters never became socially acceptable for women. This variety of structural and social regulations points to the necessity of interrogating the social space of the cinema theater, neither taking it for granted nor seeing it simply as a colonizing technology. Rather, cinema theaters are produced, and in the struggle over that production tensions over colonial urbanization are foregrounded.

In October 1937 the British colonial administration received an application from a Lebanese businessman for the construction of the Rex cinema, what was to become the first purpose-built cinema in Kano. The Rex was built as an open-air cinema, what was known as a "garden cinema," and consisted of two rooms as well as a bar, which the businessman proposed "to build quite decently and with stones."[5] This exhibition was modified, and two years later J. Green Mbadiwe, a hotel owner in Kaduna, the capital of Northern Nigeria, applied for a license to build a more formal and elaborate hotel and cinema complex in Kano. It was to include "all the latest amenities usually associated with first-class Hotels and Cinemas in the Aristocratic Countries of the world."[6] His application was denied, but his proposal gives witness to the conceptual construct of what constituted a cinema space in Nigeria at this time. In the proud insistence on the quality of construction material and the boast that Kano cinemas would be like "first-class" cinemas in the West, the applications signify the elite European clientele that the owners intended to attract. The emphasis on first-class quality found in "the Aristocratic nations of the world" promised reassuring familiarity for Europeans and created a spectacle of grandeur for local Hausa filmgoers. And the inclusion of a bar would have offered recreation other than the cinematic event itself, intended for Europeans only who could "come out and enjoy the cool air and evening." The design and social function of these early theaters was intimately associated with another public space of colonial modernity: the hotel. Like the hotel, the cinema is a public space of anonymity, a transient coming together of people unconnected by relations of kin, religion, or ethnicity. Making the cinema like a hotel means that the experience was not organized solely around watching a film but was part of wider complex of leisure activities that emerged for expatriate recreation.

As a product of a colonial ideology of transformation, the architectonics of the cinema theater expressed the particular historical conditions of colonial rule. Cinema as a social space helped create a new public, "the imagining of human beings as, in principle, an indefinitely extensible horizon of anonymous and interchangeable members" (Barber 1997: 349). Kracauer referred to this public as a "mass," arguing that the spatial organization of the audience at "mass ornament" events, arranged in patterns of "tier upon ordered tier," contributed to the spectacle itself (1995: 76). Through the disciplinary process of attendance the individuality of the audience member became subordinate to the totality of the mass, and space became the "aesthetic reflex of the rationality to which the prevailing economic system aspires" (1995: 79). The arrangement of seating in cinemas reflected the new bodily configurations of colonial rule, though of course could never be contained by them. The attempt at constructing an abstract and equivalent public was often frustrated by colonial and Hausa practices of hierarchy and distinction that were embedded in the conception of cinematic space.

In the highly stratified colonial world one immediate problem of common public space was the potential of racial mixing. What were the possible consequences of mixed-race audiences? In response to people's fears the Lebanese owners of the Rex originally intended their cinema for European

Crowds outside the Marhaba Cinema, Kano, Nigeria. Watercolor by Abdulhamid
Yusuf Jigawa. (From the collection of Brian Larkin.)

use and finally divided the exhibition schedule so that two nights a week were
reserved for Europeans and Arabs and two for African audiences. This segregation was intentional but informal and was regulated mainly through the
pricing of seats.[7] J. Green Mbadiwe went further, proposing to divide his auditorium into two discrete compartments, one for Europeans and one for
Africans, which would be approached through separate entrances. The only
connection was a fire door, but this, he assured the authorities, "will be always locked." This attempt at encoding practices of racial segregation into
the architectonics of the theater space reveals how the solid materiality of
the cinema theater expresses local ideologies of (in this case) racial hierarchy. The secretary of the northern provinces who wrote to the chief secretary in Lagos with a response to fire safety regulations reveals stunningly how
the physical space of cinema can be the outcome of a specifically colonial
situation of racial prejudice:

> As regards seating: In view of the natural tendency of some Africans when in
> a crowd to be seized by panic at the mere rumour of danger it is thought that
> in Cinema halls in Nigeria much wider spaces should be allowed between fixed
> seats, wider alleyways and more and wider means of exit than as obligatory in
> England.[8]

In Kano, the British imperial presence was reflected in the naming of theaters themselves. The first cinema in Kano following the Rex was the Palace, and later came the Queens Theater. These names encoded imperial splendor into the spectacle promised by the experience of cinema. Other theater names such as El Dorado (long part of the imperialist imaginary as the lost city of fabulous wealth waiting to be "discovered"), Plaza, and Orion connote travel and movement and are titular embodiments of the promise of transportation, of removal from the local and the mundane, which is the hallmark of cinematic escapism. Only one cinema in Kano has an identifiably local connection, Wapa (named after the area where the cinema is located).

THE MORAL AURA OF CINEMATIC SPACE

From their inception, cinema theaters were mapped onto a moral topography of Kano City from which they borrowed (and to which they were to contribute) a strongly immoral aura. Most significant in this mapping was Sabon Gari, the area that grew up after the Kano-Lagos railroad began to import large numbers of southern Nigerians to work in the North. Sabon Gari (literally, "New Town") was marked, in the words of one British Resident, as "an enclave of disrepute" that was full of "dissolute characters."[9] This was the area in which the new colonially constructed spaces of churches and schools, beer parlors and dance halls, brothels and theaters were built, creating new forms of sexual and ethnic intermixing that were deeply disruptive of Hausa moral practices. For Hausa living in the old city, the Sabon Gari (and Waje as a whole)[10] became the antithesis of Hausa moral space and known as the site of *bariki* culture, an immoral complex of alcohol, prostitution, dancing (and later cinema), named after the barracks that were constructed to house migrant workers to the north. One Hausa scholar summed up the difference between the restrictions of the old city and Waje, indicating the depth of this symbolic cleavage for Hausa:

> In the waje . . . life was permissive. The southerners, who were predominantly Christians, had built churches and Western schools there. There were beer parlours and brothels full of prostitutes and their pimps. There were also shops full of imported European goods. . . . To the majority of Kanawa, birni (the Old City) was home, and one only ventured to waje out of necessity. Its life was an evil which was tolerated because one had no choice. (Barkindo 1993: 94)[11]

The first film screenings took place in Sabon Gari, in dance halls like the Elsiepat, where film-watching became part of the emergence of a new public world of leisure defined by alcohol, commodification, and mixed-sex activities, which for Hausa was stigmatized as ethnically foreign, or southern Nigerian.[12] By 1934, however, cinema had become popular among poor Hausa youth, though it was still stigmatized as an illicit activity. The Kano

British Resident's annual report announced that films were being shown "with considerable frequency" at these irregular venues,[13] and within three years the first purpose-built cinema, the Rex, was opened on the edge of Sabon Gari market on the ethnic borderlands between the Kano commercial district, Sabon Gari, and Fagge (an area for Muslims outside the old city).

The Rex was situated on the edge of Sabon Gari, placing it in a liminal position for Hausa Muslims for whom Sabon Gari was culturally out of bounds. Cinema quickly established a reputation as an illicit, immoral arena, and cinemagoing was stereotyped as a cheap, poor man's entertainment, to be avoided by people in positions of respect. "The local outlook is as follows," wrote one colonial official in the early 1950s: "The intelligent and educated malams (religious teachers) simply do not go. . . . They disapprove of the sort of low-type Hausa that revels in the cinema."[14] The low-class, mixed-sex nature of the cinema theater meant that it became socially unacceptable for most Hausa women. Those who did attend were seen as *karuwai* (independent women/prostitutes), and their presence added significantly to the illicit nature of the arena. Sexual availability and sexual activity within the cinema meant that pleasure and desire were to be found both on and off the screen, the erotic pleasures of one context feeding off of the other.

Cinemagoing became established as a social activity, an experience that was always much more than the viewing of the film itself. "Among a large youthful class of Kano City, Fagge and Sabon Gari," the Kano Resident Featherstone remarked in 1948, "it has become quite the thing to go to the Cinema quite regardless of whether they understand what they see or hear or not." Featherstone's paternalistic disapproval of Hausa audiences misses the importance of cinemagoing as a social, as well as a visual, event. One viewer told Featherstone that although he did not always understand the films being shown, "he went regularly to the cinema to be seen and to see his friends."[15] This social activity was taking place in a particular social space that drew its moral aura from its social and moral place on an urban landscape in the process of transformation. One educated Hausa man who went regularly to the cinema in the late 1940s told me that cinemagoing involved leaving the safe confines of the old city and crossing from a moral to an immoral space (the Sabon Gari). For him this was an intentional act that involved a radical attitude toward Hausa authority and Islamic orthodoxy. Defined as undesirable by the values of orthodox Hausa Islam, the pleasure of going to the cinema was thus highly local, an intimate experience of illicitness that framed the spectacle of watching the film and that derived from the peculiar nature of Hausa colonial urbanization.

Religious questions about the ontology of the cinematic apparatus itself contributed to the wariness with which this colonial technology was greeted in mainstream Hausa society. Since the early days of British conquest, part of what Barkindo (1993) has termed the "passive resistance" of conservative

Islamic teachers to colonial rule had taken the form of intense resistance to the new commodities introduced by colonialists. Hiskett (1984) relates that elderly Muslim moralists condemned to hell-fire Muslims who used hurricane lamps, battery flashlights, or starched or wore buttons on their shirts. Nasiru Kabara, a prominent Kano sheikh who served on the first colonial censorship board, similarly told me that "local *malams*" (by which he meant poorly educated, neighborhood Islamic teachers) condemned cinema because they were unsure whether the images on screen were true or false. According to their logic, if someone was killed in a film they thought he might actually be dead. If not, then film was magic, and because Islam was against magic then film was *haram* (forbidden).[16] Many also believed that cinematic representation contravened the Islamic prohibition on the creation of images and idols.[17]

For Kabara this religious insistence on the blasphemous, magical nature of the rational technology of cinema was a mark of ignorance of both the world at large and Islam in particular. But the early Hausa names for cinema—*majigi*, derived from the word magic,[18] and *dodon bango*, literally, "evil spirits on the wall"[19]—reveal how popular the sense of the enchantment of cinema was. It reveals powerfully the symbolic layers that saturated cinema so that it could only be experienced through its associations with Christianity, paganism, and colonial rule.

THE PALACE, EL DUNIYA, AND THE MAINTENANCE OF HAUSA MORAL SPACE

Colonial rule in Northern Nigeria incorporated a non-Islamic, economically aggressive metropolitan space into Kano City but kept it outside of local Muslim control. Although the British promised to preserve Hausa cultural and religious practices in return for acceptance of their political rule, the consequence of this was to emphasize the distinction (for both Hausa and the British) between a traditional, Hausa Muslim old city and a modernizing, multiethnic, and liberal modern sector. The old city remained under the Islamic legal and political authority of the emir and was the repository of traditional Muslim Hausa values. It was the area where female seclusion *(kulle)* and the strict segregation of the sexes was maintained; where prostitution and the sale of alcohol were forbidden; and where children were educated at Islamic rather than Western schools. Waje, by contrast, was un-Islamic. It was particularly associated with the rise of new forms of public space—beer parlors and dance halls, workers' barracks and brothels, gentlemen's clubs and European shops, churches and Western schools—that created new modes of sociability and leisure.

The introduction of cinema theaters in Kano intervened in an ongoing conflict over the moral definition of urban space under colonialism.[20] How cinema theaters were to be built, what they were to show, and whether they could sell alcohol were all issues of formal regulation by which the transformative spatial and social ideologies of colonialism were embodied and enacted. Conflicts within the Hausa community over where theaters were to be located and who could attend them are best seen as attempts at the moral reterritorialization of an urban space that was rapidly expanding outside of Hausa control. Appadurai (1996) has referred to this process as the "production of locality," which, he argues, involves the assertion of socially organized power over places that are potentially chaotic. The mediation of cinema as a moral space was an attempt to reassert the Muslim basis of Hausa life in opposition to the encroachment of non-Muslim (both European and southern Nigerian) cultural and religious values. Cinema theaters became markers of neighborhoods, embodying the moral qualities that allowed those neighborhoods to exist. For urban Hausa the cinematic experience was (and is) thus embedded in the history of ongoing debate over the nature and regulation of urban public space.

In 1949 a Lebanese cinema distributor wrote the Resident, Kano emirate, asking for permission to build a cinema, the Palace, within the old city, in Jakara quarters, next to Kurmi market. When the application for the Palace was received, cinemagoing was well established in Kano; many Hausa regularly left the old city to travel to one of two cinemas located outside in Waje. The uniqueness of this application was that the Palace was to be the first cinema theater constructed within the confines of the old city. I can date the application and the opening of the Palace from the colonial archives in Kaduna, which contain copies of the application file. However the story of the Palace I engage with rests on rumors and prejudice, stories and memories that do not provide an objective history of the Palace as much as they reveal the social place that it and other cinemas occupy in the social imagination. Rumors about cinemas, stories that have come down from parent to child, are a form of local hermeneutics. They are quasi-religious allegories by which people divine the "real" motives underlying phenomenal events.

The emir's decision to allow the construction of the Palace cinema provoked a strong backlash in different sections of the Hausa community. Kano *ulama* (religious leaders) were outraged by the penetration of this disruptive sexual arena into the Islamic space of the old city. The more conservative among them issued a *fatwa* (religious teaching) forbidding the showing of films and citing the religious injunction on the creation of images as evidence that the technology itself was *kafirai* (pagan). According to a story I was told, this *fatwa* was overruled when it came before the emirate council despite the fact that the Kano emir at the time, Abdullahi, was widely known to be socially conservative. Abdullahi's decision then sparked its own set of rumors, including one that Abdullahi was forced into the decision as a result of pressure from the British Resident.[21]

In 1951, while the controversy over the Palace was raging but before the cinema was actually open, matters were brought to a symbolic head when the El Duniya cinema burned down, killing 331 people in an audience of 600.[22] The government enquiry that followed established that the cause of the fire was flammable nitrate films that caught fire in the projection room and spread along the ceiling. Hausa complicity in the tragedy was reinforced by the fact that 82 percent of the cinema audience during the afternoon performance were Hausa, not southern Nigerian or European. The youngest was only nine years old.

The rational, functional explanation of the colonial state for why the disaster occurred was accepted by Hausa as explaining how but not why the disaster occurred. In the context of the growing controversy over the Palace, it was widely believed by many that the fire was direct divine retribution for Hausa participation in illicit and immoral activity. The tragedy became seen as a judgment about the growing Westernization of Hausa society, and a series of rumors emerged to explain the tragedy. Most common, and still widely believed, was the accusation that the film being screened that night in the El Duniya contained the image of the Prophet Mohammed, the colonial technology of representation being harnessed for blasphemous ends. Others believed that during construction of the theater people passing every day cursed (tsine) the theater and the theater was engulfed not just by flames but by the combined magical force of these curses.[23]

In a religious society such as Kano, where God's divine intervention in the material world is an everyday occurrence, rumors and stories become part of a critical discourse in which everyday events are interrogated. Stories about the El Duniya represent conflict and ambivalence about the Western cultural arena that was infiltrating the Hausa moral world. They underscore the profane nature of cinematic representation, making it guilty of the heresy of representing Mohammed. These rumors grew so strong that the colonial government was forced to take official notice and counter them over the radio. Twice daily for two days in four different languages, the Radio Diffusion Service announced there was no truth to the stories that the people handling the bodies of El Duniya victims died, or that Native Authority Warders who helped in the tragedy had all gone mad, or that prisoners from Kano prison (who helped in handling the corpses) could not eat for days afterward.[24] Stories about the El Duniya became part of the informal moral economy that regulated the evolution of cinema in Kano.

On July 2, 1952, a year after the El Duniya burned down, the Palace finally opened after months of controversy. When the opposition to the cinema turned violent, the emir was forced to call in the police to arrest youths who were demonstrating against the opening.[25] Three months later, the British superintendent of police reported that ever since the Palace opened youths outside the open-air theater had been regularly stoning patrons inside. What was worse, he complained, was that the *alkali* (Muslim judge) to whom the cases were being reported was letting the youths go free and that it was difficult for the police to ensure "good order" during cinema performances.[26] Ironically, or perhaps inevitably, the Palace became the immoral social space that its opponents feared. It became a notorious place where, as one friend said to me, men would go to drink alcohol, take drugs, and engage in sex with women and other men ("There! There! Right there in the seat next to you!"). In the early 1980s the governor of Kano State, Sabo Bakin Zuwo, who came from Kano's old city and who was a veteran of the anti-Palace campaign, closed down the cinema and in a grand populist gesture converted it into a hospital clinic. Since that time no cinema theater has been opened in the old city,[27] and to this day hundreds of Hausa youths travel nightly through the mud gates marking the city's boundaries to cinemas that lie outside in Sabon Gari, Fagge, and Nassarawa.

CONCLUSION

The controversy over the Palace and the rumors that surrounded the El Duniya tragedy emerged from and helped to define the symbolic layers that gave cinema its particular moral aura in Hausa society. Cinema theaters in Kano were not discrete buildings but integrated nodes in an urban environment from which they drew their significance. As the site for screening fantastic texts of love and adventure, cinema theaters projected Hausa audiences into the imagined realities of American, Indian, and British culture (see Larkin 1997). Here my focus has been on the place of theaters as part of a wider urban materiality produced by, and thus expressive of, transformations in colonial modernity. Their social significance cannot be divorced from the other technologies and public spaces produced under colonial rule. Cinema theaters in Kano came into being only twenty years after the construction of the Kano-Lagos railroad. They were built in the areas created for the masses of male migrants uprooted and brought into Kano by the railroad's annihilation of space and time (Schivelbusch 1986); they were sited alongside the new colonially constructed markets marking out the borders and moral qualities of the new colonially constructed metropolis; and they formed part of the construction of new modes of sexual and ethnic interaction produced by the transformation in urban public space. Encoded in the physical mass of the theater, in the dirty bricks and broken lights, in the walls that divide the arena, and in the absences where divisions did not occur are traces of history of colonial rule and colonial urbanism. My aim has been to move away from the taken-for-granted quality that so often makes the cinema theater seem like second nature, an accepted and already understood site that disappears from analytic view as the lights are turned down and the films are projected. Instead, I analyze the materiality of the theater itself, theorizing its significance for an anthropology of the media that situates technologies in the wider social realms in which they take on significance.

The conflict over the Palace, the rumors that spread following the El Duniya tragedy, and the religious wariness of the cinematic apparatus are all attempts by Hausa to reestablish the moral and spatial equilibrium of urban Kano society in the face of the threat posed by colonial rule. The attempt to control the physical position and social place of cinema on the urban landscape by keeping cinema theaters outside of Muslim Hausa areas is thus a moment of reterritorialization, an attempt to recuperate potentially uncontrollable transnational technologies within local social frameworks. It reveals how cinema as a social as well as a physical institution is produced, often within the context of local political struggles.

NOTES

This essay is an abridged version of "Theaters of the Profane: Cinema and Colonial Urbanism" (Larkin 1999b), published as part of a special symposium I edited, and is reprinted by permission of the American Anthropological Association from *Visual Anthropology Review* 14 (2): 46–62. Not for sale or further reproduction.

Research for this essay was funded by the Wenner-Gren Foundation for Anthropological Research and a Research Grant from New York University. My research in Nigeria was dependent on the generous institutional support of the Kano State History and Culture Bureau and Arewa House Centre for Historical Documentation in Kaduna. The essay was revised in response to comments by Meg McLagan, Faye Ginsburg, T. O. Beidelman, Lila Abu-Lughod, Brian Edwards, and the anonymous reviewers of *Visual Anthropology Review*.

1. From the 1930s to the 1950s Kano cinemas were dominated by British and American films. By the mid-1960s Indian films had emerged as probably the most popular film genre (in northern Nigeria at least), and by the 1970s Hong Kong films began to gain in popularity. When I conducted my research in the 1990s, Indian films were shown five nights a week at cinemas, with one night for Hong Kong films and one night for American films.

2. The Russian film historian Yuri Tsivian (1994) provides an elegant account of cinemagoing as a sensory activity, paying attention to the temperature of the auditorium, the placing of the projector, the quality of light, and the nature of aural and visual interference.

3. For an introduction to early cinema in cinema studies, see Allen 1983; Bowser 1990; Chanan [1982] 1996; Friedberg 1993; Hansen 1991; Koszarski 1990; Kuhn 1988; Musser 1990; Petro 1989; Tsivian 1994. On the site of cinema theaters outside the West, see Armbrust 1998; Himpele 1996; Hughes 1999; Thompson 2000. Though only marginally interested in cinema, Martin (1995) provides a powerful account of the rise of new leisure practices in colonial Brazzaville.

4. This was accomplished in a number of ways: by attracting a female audience; by using bourgeois cultural forms such as the novel and plays as the basis of narra-

tive form and content; and through the construction of elegant "palaces" for exhibition in nonimmigrant areas (Sklar 1975; Hansen 1991).

5. Nigerian National Archives, Kaduna (NAK), Kano Prof. 2600, The West Africa Picture Co. (1) Application for C. of O. (2) General Correspondence.

6. NAK, Kano Prof. 4430, Mr. J. Green Mbadiwe, application for permission to erect a hotel and cinema at Kano.

7. "It is probably true to say that if an African sought admission on one of these [European] nights and was prepared to pay 3/6d he would not be refused admission but the number of Africans who would wish to pay 3/6d admission when they can attend exactly the same performance on another night for 2/-, or 1/- or 6d is very small" (NAK, Kano Prof. 2600). Informal segregation by pricing was a common practice in South India also (Stephen Hughes, personal communication). This raises the question of whether the practice was an empire-wide means of keeping races separate while avoiding the negative ideological connotations of hard-line racial segregation.

8. NAK, M.I.A. Kaduna 2d collection vol. 2, R.1493, Cinematograph Audience 1932–1952, Letter no. 16497.10A, Secretary, Northern Provinces to Chief Secretary Lagos, June 2, 1932.

9. This phrase, which may well sum up the entire symbolic value of Sabon Gari in the eyes of Kano Hausa, was coined by Resident Alexander of Kano in a speech to the Conference of Residents in 1926 (cited in Allyn 1976: 138).

10. Waje (literally "outside) was the name given to African areas of Kano that lay outside the Muslim heart of the old city.

11. Tahir describes Sabon Gari in much the same terms. Sabon Gari is, he wrote, "the home of strangers, on their way to assimilation, Nigerian and foreign Christians, the European Christian, *Nasara* or Nazarene, the urban drifter, the wage worker, the prostitute and the pimp. It contains churches, beer houses and dance halls, hotels and brothels. There deviant conduct prevails and custom does not have a stronghold" (1975: 110).

12. This mode of exhibition mimics the history of film in the United States and Britain, where the first films were often shown as part of a wider program of burlesque (see Hansen 1991) or vaudeville (see Chanan [1982] 1996).

13. NAK, Kano Prof. 1391, Kano Township Annual Report 1934.

14. Minute by M. H. (?), October 20, 1954, in response to a letter from the Director of Education, Northern Region, September 15, 1954, requesting an assessment of censorship, Kano State History and Culture Bureau (HCB), Simple list of files removed from cabinet, R.918, Films and Film Censorship.

15. Letter, from E. K. Featherstone, Resident, Kano, to The Secretary, Northern Provinces, January 9, 1948, HCB, Simple list of files removed from cabinet, R918, Films and Film Censorship.

16. Interview, Sheikh Nasiru Kabara, November 1995.

17. Although the Qur'an itself does not explicitly forbid the making of representations, the hadiths (the sayings and deeds of the Prophets) are explicitly negative about the status of artists (see Grabar 1973).

18. Later the name began to be applied mainly to the British government's mobile cinemas that traveled the cities and rural areas screening educational and propaganda films.

19. Both terms were later replaced by the more neutral *sinima* or *silima*.

20. In using "moral," I refer to two things. Cinema in Kano is defined as an immoral, sexualized space, one that (unlike in the United States) never achieved social legitimation. On another, underlying level, I follow Beidelman's (1993) concept of morality as the set of images and practices through which people both comprehend their world and act within it in ways that conform and subvert their moral understanding. Space, for Beidelman, is a "moral metaphor," a social product that encodes the imagined order of society and personhood and reveals basic ideas about, and conflicts between, the individual and society. Beidelman's assertion of the active presence of the imagination in moral space has the advantage of foregrounding the concept of space as formed by human action, as something *produced*.

21. Interview with Alhaji Adamu, April 1996.

22. See Report of the Commissioner appointed by His Excellency the Governor to enquire into the circumstances in which a fire caused loss of life at, and destroyed, the El-Dunia Cinema, Kano, on the 13th day of May 1951, Justice Percy E. Hubbard, NAK, Zaria Prof. vol. 2, EDU, 5 Cinema Cinematographs, Cinema Office, (2) Mobile Cinema Routine Correspondence. See also NAK, Kano Prof. 7564, El Dunia Disaster, Colonial Office (CO)583/317/8, Cinema Disaster at Kano, 1951.

23. The power to curse is a powerful magical attribute in Hausa society, as it is elsewhere in Africa. Certain people are believed to be have the magical power to make their curses come true, though if they are not evil people they may have this ability and not realize it. One person explained the rumor to me by saying that so many people were cursing the construction of the El Duniya that the combined weight of all these curses brought the theater down.

24. NAK, MOI, 55, Broadcasting, Radio Diffusion Service and BBC.

25. Interview, Alhaji Adamu, April 1995.

26. NAK, Kano Prof. 6945, Jakarta Palace Cinema, Letter to S.D.O.K. from Senior Superintendent of Police, Kano N.A., P. G. F. Sewall, June 9, 1952.

27. In Sani Mainagge, the Kano State History and Culture Bureau (HCB) operates an open-air theater that it uses for cultural performances such as plays and dances by the famous Koroso dance troupe. When it is not being used by the HCB, videos of Hausa dramas and Indian and Hong Kong films are screened there through a projection unit, making it something like a cinema but with the patina and authority of a government institution.

REFERENCES

Allen, Robert C. 1983. Motion Picture Exhibition in Manhattan, 1906–1912: Beyond the Nickelodeon. In *Film before Griffith*, edited by John Fell, pp. 162–75. Berkeley: University of California Press.

Allyn, David Edley. 1976. The Sabon Gari System in Northern Nigeria. Ph.D. diss., University of California, Los Angeles.

Appadurai, Arjun. 1996. The Production of Locality. In *Modernity at Large*, pp. 178–99. Minneapolis: University of Minnesota Press.

Armbrust, Walter. 1998. When the Lights Go Down in Cairo: Cinema as Secular Ritual. *Visual Anthropology* 10: 413–42.

Arora, Poonam. 1995. "Imperilling the Prestige of the White Woman": Colonial Anxiety and Film Censorship in British India. *Visual Anthropology Review* 1 (2): 36–49.

Barber, Karin. 1997. Preliminary Notes on the Audience in Africa. *Africa* 67 (3): 349–62.

Barkindo, Bawuro M. 1993. Growing Islamism in Kano City since 1970: Causes, Forms and Implications. In *Muslim Identity and Social Change in Sub-Saharan Africa*, edited by Louis Brenner, pp. 91–105. Bloomington: Indiana University Press.

Barthes, Roland. 1986. *Mythologies*. London: Paladin Books.

Beidelman, T. O. 1993. *Moral Imagination in Kaguru Modes of Thought*. Washington: Smithsonian Press.

Benjamin, Walter. 1978. The Work of Art in the Age of Mechanical Reproduction. In *Illuminations*, pp. 217–51. New York: Schocken Books.

———. 1979. Paris, Capital of the Nineteenth Century. In *Reflections: Essays, Aphorisms, Autobiographical Writings*. New York: Harcourt Brace Jovanovich.

Bowser, Eileen. 1990. *The Transformation of Cinema, 1907–1915*. New York: Scribner's.

Buck-Morss, Susan. 1989. *The Dialectics of Seeing: Walter Benjamin and the Arcades Project*. Cambridge, Mass.: Massachusetts Institute of Technology Press.

Chanan, Michael. [1982] 1996. *The Dream That Kicks: The Prehistory and Early Years of Cinema Entertainment in Britain*. London: Routledge.

Friedberg, Anne. 1993. *Window Shopping: Cinema and the Postmodern*. Berkeley: University of California Press.

Fugelsang, Minou. 1994. *Veils and Videos: Female Youth Culture on the Kenyan Coast*. Stockholm: Stockholm Studies in Social Anthropology.

Grabar, Oleg. 1973. *The Formation of Islamic Art*. New Haven, Conn.: Yale University Press.

Hansen, Miriam. 1991. *Babel and Beyond: Spectatorship in Early Silent Film*. Cambridge, Mass.: Harvard University Press.

Himpele, Jeffrey D. 1996. Film Distribution as Media: Mapping Difference in the Bolivian Cinemascape. *Visual Anthropology Review* 12 (1): 47–66.

Hiskett, Mervyn. 1984. *The Development of Islam in West Africa*. London: Longman.

Hughes, Stephen P. 1999. Policing Silent Film Exhibition in South India. In *Making Meaning in Indian Cinema*, edited by Ravi Vasudevan. Delhi: Oxford University Press.

Kirby, Lynne. 1997. *Parallel Tracks: The Railroad and Silent Cinema*. Durham, N.C.: Duke University Press.

Koszarski, Richard. 1990. *An Evening's Entertainment: The Age of the Silent Feature Picture, 1915–1928*. New York: Scribner's.

Kracauer, Siegfried. 1995. *The Mass Ornament: Weimar Essays*. Cambridge, Mass.: Harvard University Press.

Kuhn, Annette. 1988. *Cinema, Censorship and Sexuality 1909–1925*. London: Routledge.

Larkin, Brian. 1997. Indian Films, Nigerian Lovers: Media and the Creation of Parallel Modernities. *Africa* 67 (3): 406–40.

————. 1999a. Introduction to Media Technologies and the Design for Modern Living. *Visual Anthropology Review* 14 (2): 11–13.

————. 1999b. Theaters of the Profane: Cinema and Colonial Urbanism. *Visual Anthropology Review* 14 (2): 46–62.

Martin, Phyllis. 1995. *Leisure and Society in Colonial Brazzaville*. Cambridge, England: Cambridge University Press.

Miller, Daniel. 1997. Why Some Things Matter. In *Material Cultures: Why Some Things Matter,* edited by Daniel Miller. Chicago: University of Chicago Press.

Mitchell, Timothy. 1991. *Colonising Egypt*. Berkeley: University of California Press.

Musser, Charles. 1990. *The Emergence of Cinema: The American Screen to 1907*. Berkeley: University of California Press.

Petro, Patrice. 1989. *Joyless Streets: Women and Melodramatic Imagination in Weimar Germany*. Princeton, N.J.: Princeton University Press.

Schivelbusch, Wolfgang. 1986. *The Railway Journey: The Industrialization of Time and Space in the 19th Century*. Berkeley: University of California Press.

Sklar, Robert. 1975. *Movie-Made America: A Cultural History of American Movies*. New York: Vintage Books.

Tahir, Ibrahim. 1975. Scholars, Saints, and Capitalists in Kano 1904–1974: The Pattern of Bourgeois Revolution in an Islamic Society. Ph.D. diss., Cambridge University.

Thompson, Elizabeth. 2000. *Colonial Citizens: Republican Rights, Paternal Privilege, and Gender in French Syria and Lebanon*. New York: Columbia University Press.

Tsivian, Yuri. 1994. *Early Cinema in Russia and Its Cultural Reception*. New York: Routledge.

Watts, Michael. 1996. Place, Space and Community in an African City. In *The Geography of Identity,* edited by Patricia Yeager, pp. 59–97. Ann Arbor: University of Michigan Press.

17

Mobile Machines
and Fluid Audiences

Rethinking Reception
through Zambian Radio Culture

Debra Spitulnik

The very force and impact . . . of any medium changes significantly as it is moved from one context to another (a bar, a theater, the living room, the bedroom, the beach, a rock concert . . .). Each medium is then a mobile term, taking shape as it situates itself—almost always comfortably—within the different roadside rests of our lives. That is, the text is located, not only intertextually, but in a range of apparatuses as well, defined technologically but also by other social relations and activities. One rarely just listens to the radio, watches TV, or even goes to the movies—one is studying, dating, driving somewhere else, partying, etc.

LAWRENCE GROSSBERG, *"The In-Difference of Television"*

WIDENING THE FRAME OF RECEPTION STUDIES

Over the past decade there has been a serious rethinking of the concepts of "audience" and "reception" within media studies.[1] Most significantly, this work has rejected the familiar assumption that "the audience" is a unified aggregate that receives a fixed message. Scholars have increasingly shifted their attention to the fact that people *use* mass media and thus are not passive receivers but *active participants* in ongoing communication processes. In supplanting a simple picture of the function of media as one-way message transmission from sender to receiver, such revisionist research has moved into a "post-content" or "post-text" era (as suggested by Lawrence Grossberg's words above) and toward more ethnographic accounts of people's on-the-ground engagements with media. It is crucial to recognize, however, that interest in active media users and diverse interpretive practices are not entirely new concerns. Such issues have been central problems in empirical media research for well over fifty years (see Curran 1996; Spitulnik 1993). Thus many of the developments in the "new revisionism" or "new audience studies" have been critiqued for "reinventing" earlier models, creating mislead-

337

ing and oversimplified mythologies of what is a long and rich history of media research, and self-congratulatory assertions of a purportedly new intellectual direction (Curran 1996; Evans 1990).

What is new in this research, however, is a greater puzzling over how to *theorize* reception and audiences. What structures reception? What structures culturally specific ways of being a media consumer or a media addressee? What are we left with if "the audience" is de-essentialized? As Janice Radway (1988) and others have argued, it is important to deconstruct and particularize any notion of "audience" within an ethnographic study of media use, paying particular attention to the diversity of ways in which people actively construct themselves as media users, consumers, and owners (see Abu-Lughod 1997; Ang 1996; Ginsburg 1999; Mankekar 1999).

I propose here that, in addition to being attentive to such active processes, we also need to focus on two other factors. First, there is the question of how features of the *media technology* itself enable or inhibit certain kinds of audience engagements. And second, there is the possibility that *social context* is just as much a determinant of people's active reception and use than is any kind of individual interpretative process. Indeed, one of the greatest hazards of conventional reception studies—with their origin in literary criticism, printed texts, the single interpreting reader, and assumptions of a Western type of subjectivity—is that they entail a kind of egocentric (or subject-centric) rather than a *sociocentric* account of reception practices. From an ethnographic and a theoretical standpoint we need to be aware that the *individual interpretive moment* of "decoding" a media message or "moving" from a subject position may not be the only—or the most significant—aspect of what media "mean" in a given sociocultural context.

Grossberg's insightful comments help us to move in this direction, with the more phenomenological observation that the impact of a media technology changes with the context and the accompanying activities. This forcefully suggests that media both create and are created by social spaces. This observation also draws our attention to the more general question of how communication technologies as *technologies*—that is, devices with distinctive physical and perceptual qualities—are integrated with and influence social practices. Such questions are increasingly the focus of ethnographic studies of people's engagements with media technologies as technologies.[2]

Taken together, these lines of research point toward ways of widening the frame of reception studies. We need to understand "media reception" as a constellation of processes that includes: direct responses to media content; decodings of media messages; phenomenological comportment toward media technologies and appliances; social relations among groups of media users; and the material, economic, and cultural conditions of media ownership and use. It is possible to produce different kinds of ethnographies of media audiences, depending on which aspect of this reception constellation one chooses to focuses on. In addition, it is possible to de-essentialize "the audience" not only from the perspective of message interpretation but also from the perspective of styles of use and phenomenological attunement to the medium.

De-essentializing the audience does not mean, however, that analysis devolves into a running inventory of multiple particulars—that is, a series of disparate and unconnected accounts of reception practices. Although ethnographic details may chip away at notions of the generic homogeneous audience, it is crucial not to discard questions about how larger cultural patterns, genre-based constraints, economic determinants, technological properties, and shared forms of social organization shape the horizons of meaning for people's reception practices (see Corner 1991; Dickey 1993; Mankekar 1999; Morley 1997). In other words, I am arguing that reception studies should be more ethnographic in the anthropological sense of that term. Within the domain of media research, the question "Does culture (or place) matter?" is especially salient because we live in a context where the prevailing ideas about media too often hold them to be the same everywhere at all times for all people.

This essay contributes as a corrective to the unwitting ethnocentrism of media imperialism and globalization paradigms because it documents the different locally driven engagements that Zambians have with radio technologies. My focus here is specifically on the material aspects of radio technology and its relation to the domestic arena and beyond. I argue that the social place of radio as a technology depends on the ways in which the technology itself embodies ideologies of status and modernity (see Larkin 1999; Miller 1998; Silverstone and Hirsch 1992; Spitulnik 1998/99). I also show how the circulation of radios in communities rests on other cultural processes familiar to anthropologists: the construction of status and the reproduction of reciprocal social ties through exchange relations (Appadurai 1986; Mauss [1925] 1967). Basic economic factors also deeply inform the meanings of radio. The local economic and material conditions of radio listening and ownership shape Zambians' experiences of radio, which differ dramatically from patterns of media use in more affluent societies. Radios and their batteries are expensive, and signals are sometimes weak. The functioning radio and radio station cannot be taken for granted. Moreover, radios are valuable property, and theft is common. And finally, a major aspect of radio's material reality in Zambia is its mobility: radios are portable machines, and their sounds drift through social spaces.

THE MATERIAL CONDITIONS OF LISTENING
AND MODES OF AUDIENCE ENGAGEMENT

Radio is the most widely consumed medium in Zambia, reaching 57 percent of all national households and 60 percent of the national population (Claypole and Daka 1993; Yoder, Hornik, and Chirwa 1996). Until 1994, state-run Radio Zambia—with its three different channels, Radio 1, Radio 2, and Radio 4—was the only domestic radio operation.[3] Since then, ten independent radio stations have joined the Zambian airwaves.

In Zambia, the price of a basic radio is far beyond the reach of most people unless great sacrifices are made. The simplest radio is an expensive commodity for an average middle-class family, even with a dual income. During my research in the late 1980s, a standard single-band radio cost the equivalent of twenty-six dollars (K249, in Zambian kwacha). This was roughly 30 percent of a primary teacher's gross monthly salary. A two-band radio cost twice that amount. Despite extremely high inflation over a ten-year period, the standard single-band radio still cost the equivalent of twenty-six dollars (K52,000) in 1998. But because salaries have not completely kept up with inflation, people's purchasing power has been reduced. In 1998 terms, a single-band radio cost 40 percent of a primary teacher's gross monthly salary. In comparison, a low-tech two-band radio cost less than 1 percent of a teacher's salary in the United States. In the 1990s, typical monthly battery costs—six dollars in 1998—remained just slightly below what a large household would spend for a one- to two-week supply of staple food (eight dollars in 1998).[4] In the current context of overstretched household budgets and decreasing spending power (Ferguson 1999), batteries are carefully conserved and dead batteries may not be replaced for some time.

Those who can purchase radios tend to be single, middle class, and able to draw from carefully accumulated savings. Significantly, most owners of radios bought them years ago. Broken radios frequently go unrepaired and unreplaced. Based on their 1991 national survey of radio and television use, Claypole and Daka estimate that 8 percent of households have a radio that is not working. Twelve percent of the nation's radio owners cannot tune in, either because the radio is broken (8 percent) or because it needs batteries (4 percent) (Claypole and Daka 1993: 63). Though the average radio repair cost (ten dollars) seems modest from a Western perspective, it is prohibitive for most Zambian families. In addition, repair shops often do not have the correct spare parts to do repairs, and when they do, they may decide to refuse service to owners of the simple one-band and two-band radios. For example, during field research in 1989, the owner of Chola Electron Service in Kasama reported suspending the repair of small radios because new spare parts reap more profits when put in more expensive machines. The economics of ownership for one listener are illustrated below:

> On weekends, Joseph Kabwe, a 26-year-old public sector office worker, sits on the stoop of his one-room home and listens to the radio.[5] Inside the tiny room, his prize possession—a 1960s model radiogram housed in a four-foot-long wooden cabinet—takes up an entire wall and one-quarter of the floor space. With twelve batteries it still runs as good as new, but he needs to replace them

every month. In January 1989, at the government-controlled price of K6.47 each (U.S. $.67 each), the cost of twelve batteries took up roughly 8 percent of Joseph's monthly salary. Being single, he could afford it, but for others those twelve batteries could be seen as a 50 kg bag of roller meal, enough to feed a large family for nearly a month.[6] He lives in Chiba, a nonelectrified, high-density, low-income neighborhood in Kasama, the capital city of Zambia's Northern Province. (Spitulnik, field notes)

In nonelectrified homes and in other places where people are listening to battery-operated radios (at markets, on porches, in transit), radio owners are very concerned about conserving battery energy. Claypole and Daka report that 65 percent of all radio owners use batteries, and of these, nearly one-third report that batteries are not always available (1993: 63), a circumstance that is felt in subtle but constant ways in everyday life, as this example reveals:

> It's Sunday at the Muzhamas' house. BanaDanny (mother of Danny) and I are chatting, and BashiDanny (father of Danny) is sorting beans. The portable radio is right next to him, but it's not on. After a bit, he looks at his watch. It's 18 hours—time for "News." He turns on the radio and it's already tuned to Radio 2, the English channel. BashiDanny doesn't listen very closely, and his wife doesn't listen at all because she doesn't know much English. When the "News" is over, BashiDanny turns off the radio; he's saving batteries. (Spitulnik, field notes)

Many radio users are compelled to innovate as they rig up their power sources. For example, old batteries can be minimally recharged by placing them in the sun or on the warm coals of a fire. A long string of nearly exhausted batteries can provide a charge that is strong enough to power a radio for a short time.

> We are sitting around the fire on a cool Sunday morning, cooking sweet potatoes for breakfast in the village of Ndona. Altogether there are seven of us. A man named Edwin comes by, carrying his portable radio in one hand and a bundle of six batteries in the other. The batteries don't fit into the case; he has taped them together and then wired them into the radio. It works just fine, but reception in the area is pretty weak. The *Kabuusha Taakolelwe Boowa* Bemba advice program is on, and periodically there are lulls in our conversation and we listen in. The two men who are sitting closest to the radio are paying more attention to the show, and as it ends, Edwin speaks in time with the two broadcasters, who call out the program's standard closing, "*Buleecha*" [It is dawning]. The 8 hours news follows, and after the opening theme song, the newsreader, as usual, says the national motto—Edwin, without missing a beat, joins in—"One Zambia, One Nation." (Spitulnik, field notes)

For those with electrified homes and radios with A/C power, energy conservation is less of an issue. Electricity costs are heavily subsidized by the government, and in many cases the monthly electricity bill is paid by the employer. Although this might imply that radio access is much more regular and inexpensive for people who live in electrified homes, this is not universally the case in Zambia. Economic class is the determining factor. Even though most urban middle-class households do have electricity, they cannot afford radios with A/C power capability. In addition, much radio use—especially by men—is outdoors, making a battery operated portable radio essential. The main owners of A/C-capable radios are upper-class families. Usually their models are high-end machines with stereo sound and one or two built-in cassette decks, as is the case with the Hamukoma family:

> The Hamukoma's radio is in the kitchen, and it's almost always on, even if no one is listening. The family spends most of the time in the living room, where the TV is. Chilufya tells me that she likes to have some lively music when she's cooking. She's an ob-gyn doctor, and her husband, Passmore, is a senior executive for the national mining company where they live in Lusaka. Their little 2½-year-old daughter, Lweendo, likes to sing the horn part of the "News" theme song when it comes on. She can also sing all the words to a popular radio song, "Daddy I love you . . . You are my hero." Passmore's cousin Judy wrote down all the lyrics from the radio and then taught them to Lweendo. (Spitulnik, field notes)

Taken together, what these economic factors mean in the contemporary Zambian context is that the typical household with a working radio is urban or peri-urban and has at least one member with a steady income. The prevalence of working radios in remote rural areas and among lower-income groups has diminished greatly over the past twenty years. Yoder, Hornik, and Chirwa (1996) report that nearly three-quarters of all urbanites listen to the radio, while only about half of all rural dwellers do. In addition, gender identity is a major factor in the manner and degree to which one engages with radio. Men are much more likely to own and control radios than women are. They also tune in more frequently. In their 1991 national survey of radio use, Yoder and his colleagues found that urban men were 1.3 times more likely to listen to radio than urban women, and rural men were 1.5 times more likely to listen to radio than rural women (ibid.). Consistent with these findings, Claypole and Daka report that rural women constitute the largest proportion of nonlisteners (1993: 64). Significantly, many of these "nonlistening" survey respondents describe themselves as being around and hearing radios, but as not ever listening in.

As illustrated in the vignettes above, people listen to the radio with varying degrees of attentiveness. BashiDanny listens to "News" with mixed attention, but his wife and children hardly listen at all. In group settings, radio listening usually alternates with conversation. Often, one or two members of the group (especially the radio owner) listen with more intensity than the others. Radio is also used to accompany other activities, as with Chilufya Hamukoma's preference for radio music while cooking. In this sense, radio is a kind of mood setter or pleasant background noise, and it is not listened to attentively.

These examples also demonstrate that people participate in radio broadcasting not only by listening but also by speaking with the radio and by speaking like the radio. For example, listeners often take pleasure in voicing a standard radio formula along with the announcer. Standard radio phrases and radio songs, especially those in English, are used for language learning and pronunciation practice, as in the case of 2½-year-old Lweendo and her cousin. And finally, one finds that children and young teens especially enjoy imitating radio voices, radio personalities, and radio program scenarios (Spitulnik 1996).

POSITIONING RADIOS AROUND THE HOME

In addition to the specific economic realities of radio ownership and access discussed in the previous section, another significant local factor that shapes reception practices in Zambia is the sociality of domestic space. The positioning of radios in and around the home changes frequently during the day, primarily because of the way that the social use of this arena changes over the course of the day. In circumstances where there are portable radios and batteries, people listen outside during daylight. Such listening may occur in an outdoor workspace, under a shade tree, on the stoop of the home, at the marketplace, or on the road. If one uses electricity, then the radio remains inside, at full volume, so that those outside can hear. Although it is extremely difficult to generalize across the whole nation, divergent social settings, and diverse socioeconomic groups, the tendency is for most daytime social activity and a great deal of domestic labor to take place outdoors, and thus the portable radio moves as people move. In most communities, and particularly among people at lower socioeconomic levels whose interior home is rarely a space for daytime visiting and entertaining, it is antisocial to remain inside during the day unless the weather is bad or one is doing indoor domestic work.

In the evenings, however, radios are taken inside, where it is cooler and safer and there are fewer mosquitoes. Especially in middle-class homes, the radio is placed at the center of the sitting or dining room, from about dinnertime onward, and becomes a focal point of the evening's activities unless there is a television. Finally, at the end of the evening the radio is moved once again. When the head of the household retires for the night, he or she secures the radio in the bedroom, where virtually all valuable household property is stored. Night break-ins are common in urban areas, and electronic goods are the first to go. The practice in Zambia is to secure these

Sidney Kambowe tunes the radio outside his home while younger brother Alex, cousin Enis, and sisters Caroline, Yvonne, and Beauty take a break from daily chores. New Town, Kasama, Zambia. (Photo: Debra Spitulnik)

goods (TVs, VCRs, radios, cameras) in the master bedroom, which becomes a kind of psychological, if not actual, fortress and hiding place if thieves come. The circulation of radios around the home is thus structured essentially by sociality and antisociality: sharing the radio and hiding the radio. The portability of the small radio works both in its favor—by being adaptable to different types of social spaces and listening situations—and to its disadvantage by being easy to steal.

CIRCULATING RADIOS BEYOND THE HOME

The impact and meaning of radio in Zambia is strongly linked to its existence as a small mobile machine. People carry radios to the office when presidential press conferences or football matches are to be broadcast and take them into the field to listen to while farming (Spitulnik, forthcoming). Radios are on in public spaces such as bus stops, minibuses, shops, foodstands, bars, and markets. In many of these public uses, the radio is a dual medium: some portable radios also contain cassette decks, which add to the machine's flexibility.

Radios are not only taken from home to work; sometimes they originate at work and are brought home. Some government offices issue radios to government workers; for example, the local Ministry of Agriculture office for listening to farming programs, and the Ministry of Education for listening to educational broadcasts. These radios are often appropriated by high-ranking employees, who view them as job perks and the sign of a good position. Their removal from the workplace is not perceived as pilferage, however; rather, it is an act of *theft prevention*. A radio that is left overnight in the office may not be there in the morning. The responsible employee thus takes the radio home at night; and this shuttling of the radio ends up as a temporary or permanent relocation of the radio to the employee's home.

Radios are sometimes carried on long-distance trips (for example, 400 miles from the capital city to the grandparents' village) and circulated in a community where they have been scarce for some time. Usually these two situations are linked. In Zambian villages, radios are extremely rare, and their presence is nearly always a result of the relocation or visit of an urban wage laborer. A radio owner who travels to another town or village invariably takes the radio along. As many people explained to me during field research, empty homes are targets for house thefts; moreover, it is easier to bring the radio than to worry about entrusting it to relatives who remain at home.[7] In addition, it provides some entertainment on the long trip and at one's destination.

Once one has arrived in a rural community, the radio tends to circulate freely among relatives. Thus, in great contrast to the lack of trust in urban areas that motivates the long-distance hauling of a radio as *personal possession*, when it arrives in a smaller community the radio to some extent becomes a *community possession*. An example of this occurred in the medium-sized village of Chitimukulu when a young relative from the Copperbelt showed up for a brief visit:

For weeks there had been no radio sounds coming from the homes of the Chitimukulu village residents, only from the homes of the government employees who work at the local clinic, post office, school, court, or police station. One day while I pass through kwaTompwe (one of the two villages that constitute Chitimukulu), I hear a radio blaring; it's coming from banakulu-Lesa's home.[8] It's the morning newscast and I wander over. Her youngest son, who works as a miner in Ndola, has just arrived; she's cooking him a big breakfast, and several neighbors are gathered around to hear the radio and see the new visitor. The news is in English, and most people don't seem to be really listening. In a short time the meal is brought out, and the educational broadcasts come on. The young man turns it off; the schools broadcasts are of no interest. Another young man seated next to me wants to look at the radio, and it is passed over to him. I look on and notice a long red plastic strip taped along the top of the radio above the frequency band. It is a punch-typed label that reads: EMISS MULENGA. This is how I learn the name of the radio's owner, the young miner. And this is how I come to track the radio's circulation around Chitimukulu over the next few days. I first see it the following day as I walk by the well at kwaKoni (the other main village of Chitimukulu).

A group of young girls are walking up to the well to fetch water; one is carrying a radio, which surprises me not only because of the scarcity of radios, but because I have never seen a girl carry one. As they get closer I notice the red label EMISS MULENGA. Turns out the girl is a young niece of banakuluLesa. The next day, as I am walking through the most distant edge of kwaTompwe village, I see a group of men listening to a radio: music in Bemba. While I greet them and walk by, I look down to the radio on the ground, it's the same three-band Panasonic with the name: EMISS MULENGA. Emiss Mulenga is nowhere to be seen, but his radio is now at his uncle's home. Finally, a few days later, on Sunday, I see Emiss with the radio. He and his friend are walking down the path through the government homes carrying it; they have just returned from a long day of visiting among some of the outlying villages. They come over and start telling me about how they wish they were in the urban areas so that they could hear the pop music channel, Radio 4. The English-language Radio 2 has a few good music programs on Friday night and during the weekend, but otherwise there has been nothing to listen to out here. Anyway the batteries are finished. (Spitulnik, field notes)

This portrayal of a few days in the life of a radio illustrates the extent of radio's portability and mutability across social contexts in a rural area. Emiss Mulenga's radio temporarily became a collective asset within his wider kin and friendship networks, but in each instance as it circulated it retained his personal mark: the typed red label EMISS MULENGA. In essence, the circulation of the radio was also Emiss's circulation through the village. Moreover, he did not mind passing it around; away from his favorite urban station, there was hardly anything he wanted to listen to anyway. A sign of a salaried worker, the radio brought him a degree of status among the rural relatives, which in turn passed on to them when they subsequently used the radio in their cohort groups. Significantly, Emiss took the radio (with dying batteries) as he went visiting in the outlying villages. Everyone within the immediate Chitimukulu area had known of his possession within two or three days of his arrival, and he had little to do with it after the first day. But it was important to be seen with it in the other villages.

The radio as a mobile machine and a "mobile term" thus has the potential to shape contexts and social relations in manifold ways. The actual portability of radios allows for this circulation in a way unachievable by most other mass media.[9] Radios do, however, circulate much as other material possessions do, such as sunglasses among young men, bracelets among young girls, and cooking utensils among neighboring women. In all these cases, the circulating material good is part of a more general relation of exchange and reciprocity that exists and is constantly renewed between those involved (Appadurai 1986; Mauss [1925] 1967). Culture, in the broad sense I am emphasizing here, is crucial for understanding these kinds of radio reception practices: sharing radios fits into other local patterns of creating status and reproducing social ties through exchange relations.

Finally, consider the circumstance of a radio-cassette recorder being carried by one young man through the stages of a day-long wedding ceremony that spanned two villages:[10]

We were in Edward village, just outside Mporokoso, one of the small district capitals in the Northern Province. Peter Mutale was getting married, and we had been up half the night participating in the evening preparations, going back and forth between Peter's village and the village of the bride. As we sat around in the morning, waiting for Peter's uncles to prepare him, some of the young revelers from the night before started up again with their *kalindula* music. This morning I had come with my tape recorder and got up enough nerve to ask them if I could run the tape. They were a three-piece band, with five or so cameo vocalists such as "DJ Jere" and "Abena D. Kacasu" (lit., "person of the grain alcohol"). Identifying themselves into the mike, they debated the name of the group: they were either the "Mporokoso jive band" or the "Edward village jazzy band" (or both).

In any case, one young man suddenly came by with a large stereo radio-cassette deck. I was surprised to see such a large machine so far out in the bush, but later noticed the deeply etched owner's name on the bottom of the box: "GRZ—Ministry of Agriculture."[11] Peter was the Mporokoso district rural agricultural outreach officer. The carrier of the radio, Bwalya, a young cousin of Peter's, asked for a blank cassette tape and started recording along with me. For the next ten hours Bwalya did not let the radio out of his sight. In fact he seemed to carry it under his right arm, perched on his hip, for nearly the whole time. As far as I know, he recorded nothing more than what I recorded: several wild jamming *kalindula* songs by the Edward village jazzy band (or the Mporokoso jive band!) and the more traditional wedding songs sung later on. The *kalindula* songs told of urban adventures and rural sweethearts, unfaithful husbands and the love of beer; Bwalya played them over and over again during the day as we accompanied Peter through the various phases of his wedding ceremony.

Bwalya's first big move occurred as we set off for the bride's village. After Peter and his uncles emerged from the home where he had been prepared for the ceremony, we assembled for the procession. Looking elegant but tired in his black suit, red shirt, and white tie, Peter stood waiting with his head bowed. The three uncles, all wearing suit jackets, one with a tie, lined up on both sides of Peter, and everyone else assembled behind them. Bwalya—technically out of order, but carrying the prestigious radio-cassette deck—squeezed into the front line between the rightmost uncle and the tall dry grass on the edge of the path. We were ready to walk out of Edward village to bring Peter down the road to his bride, Charity. As we entered into the main path leaving Edward village, Bwalya turned on the tape player. It was one of the *kalindula* songs. After about two minutes, the elder uncle asked him to turn it off. It was time to start singing the wedding songs. Realizing that his musical selection was not so appropriate, Bwalya started to record the wedding processional, a loud and wavering chorus of voices singing of the lucky groom and his happy family.

As we approached the bride's village, the singing subsided. We entered the village's main path in silence, but Bwalya soon turned on the machine, this time playing the loud wedding processional that we had just been singing. Again Bwalya's ritual intervention was tolerated for only a few minutes—no doubt it served to display the recording technology of the groom as we approached— but again the elder uncle requested that the machine be turned off. Charity, in full-length wedding gown with white veil, gloves, and heels, was then brought to meet Peter and his escorts, and together they were marched up a small path to meet her senior relatives. By now a self-designated attendant, Bwalya again squeezed into the front line of the wedding party, this time between the maid of honor (also in a formal white wedding gown) and the tall dry grass on the edge of the path. All the uncles were now on Peter's left side; Charity stood to his right, next to her attendant and Bwalya with the silent radio-cassette deck. Within moments this arrangement was broken up. After walking up the aisle to the doorstep of the bride's family's house, the bride, her bridesmaid, and Bwalya the musical escort stepped aside so that the groom could stand alone with his closest kin. For the first time, a female relative stood with Peter, along with the three uncles. They were then addressed by Charity's father's sister and her three most senior male relatives. (Spitulnik, field notes)

This is only half the story, but it provides yet another view of the mobility of the radio machine. Bwalya continued to stay on the periphery, waiting for further chances to play the tape, and later ended up socializing with the younger people, who were excluded from the indoor rites. In this case what was valued was not the radio as such, but the cassette recorder, or just the box itself—a prestige commodity in a remote rural area. The mobile machine circulated throughout the wedding ceremony, but it was always held by one individual. Like Emiss Mulenga's radio, however, it circulated as both *communal* and *individual* property. Displayed prominently in the arms of Bwalya, who marched in the front line with the groom, the machine represented the groom's wedding party, the groom (who had been issued the machine as part of his prestigious government job), and of course Bwalya himself.

During much of the procession the machine was actually silent and thus occupied the position of "carried ritual object," somewhat analogous to the family staff carried by Peter or the flowers carried by Peter's senior aunt. Of course, as a tape recorder the machine came to also occupy a whole new role, namely, the voice (or revoicing) of the groom's wedding party. The radio-cassette deck was incorporated into the ritual not only as a commodity but as an active participant—at least for those few brief moments when Bwalya was allowed to play it. In this mixed-media village wedding, with a bride and groom employed as civil servants in the small town nearby, the active use of the radio was met by a certain level of toleration, amusement, and tension. The senior relatives still had ultimate control and dominion over the proceedings, but Bwalya was able to interject and adopt his musical contributions within limits.

As an example not only of the mobility of the radio machine, but of its *mobilization,* we can now revisit Grossberg's observation that the force of a mass medium changes with the context and the accompanying activities. Rather than ascribing this potential strictly to the flexibility of the medium "taking shape as it situates itself" (1987: 34), however, we also need to interject a sense of the agency and interconnections of the particular radio users. These extended ethnographic examples indicate that the individual and group mobilization (use, placement, circulation) of the radio machine is an essential part of radio culture. Radio users, sharers, carriers, and deniers play off the significance of the radio as a prestige commodity within a wider set of social relations involving kinship obligations, gender relations, generational differences, socioeconomic status, urban-rural tensions, and so on. Whether one is "studying, dating, driving somewhere else, partying" (ibid.: 34), going to the well, or accompanying a cousin in a wedding procession, the mobilized radio enters into these social relations, and indexes the person who has actively chosen to carry or share it.

CONCLUSION

In this essay I have located my analytical center of gravity away from the more conventional location of *media as cultural spectacle/product/process/text.* I have focused instead on media's "inscription with the routines of everyday life" (Morley and Silverstone 1990: 33) and have argued that the practical and economic conditions of radio listening and radio ownership are part of the broader problem of the sociocultural meanings of radio. The consequence of this view for questions of "audience" and "reception" is that the consumption and use of a mass medium such as radio does not strictly revolve around people's interactions with media content. The notions of "audience" and "reception"—if limited to the sender/receiver dyad and the individual interpretive moment of decoding messages—neither exhaust nor encompass the range of relations that people have with radio. This does not mean that these notions should be discarded, but rather that they should be expanded or supplemented by the study of other activities and domains of experience that structure media meanings and use. In Zambia the consumption of radio includes the culturally specific ways that people attune themselves to (or attenuate themselves from) the radio machine, its technology, its portability, its commodity status, and the fact that it produces unique sounds that can travel through communities.

These facts are dramatic illustrations that radio technology in Zambia *only occasionally* has a "relative invisibility in use," in contrast to its claimed status within Western societies (Morley and Silverstone 1990: 36), where the functioning media apparatus is taken for granted and is generally part of the background in a social situation. Although there are instances in Zambia where media technology has been absorbed and naturalized in everyday life, there are infinitely more situations in which radios are not at all invisible—where the radio as machine, as commodity, as urban transplant, and as portable or borrowed object is foregrounded and even more important than the sounds emanating from it. In Zambia people are acutely conscious of radio's physicality and its commodity status—that is, its vulnerability to theft, the weakness of batteries, and its potential for display in a social situation. Related to this, a smaller point needs to be made about radio and the construction of social space. In contrast again with what has been claimed for radio and television in Western societies, radio in Zambia is not strictly, or even primarily, a "domestic" technology (Morley and Silverstone 1990). Radios circulate far beyond the home and enter into a variety of social relations and social situations *beyond* the same-residence family.

Most Zambians have not experienced that same kind of increased interiorization of social life and location of leisure time within the home that has occurred in Western cultures since the advent of broadcasting (Morley and Silverstone 1990; Spigel 1992). With dramatic rates of urbanization and the emergence of a highly economically stratified society in Zambia, interior social life has increased for middle- and upper-class sectors of the population. But there are two crucial differences. First, these "interior families" are fairly fluid extended families, not nuclear families. Second, leisurely moments at home rarely constitute a moment where *all* family members are relaxing together around the radio. Quite often, the male head of the household is absent from the scene; his leisure time is frequently spent outside the home. And in many cases the female head of the household is also not present, or only partly present; instead she is busy working in the home or conversing with other adult women such as neighbors or visitors.

In fact, even the claim about radio's domesticity is overstated for the Western case. Car radios and portable boom boxes are the best examples of the mobile machine in U.S. culture, and it may be that these are now the primary modes of radio listening in the United States. Scenes analogous to Emiss's circulating radio and Bwalya's maneuvering for attention and "airplay" can be found in a wide range of contexts—including the American use of blaring car radios and boom boxes during urban commutes, street cruising, and picnics—to achieve prestige and attract attention. At least three things are the same in these vastly different social contexts. First, the radio is portable. Second, it has a commodity status that is correlated with the prestige of the owner or user. And third, it has a presence and an ability to create social spaces; that is, it has the exact opposite of "invisibility in use." The culturally specific differences between the Zambian and U.S. cases outstrip the similarities, however, because they involve different sets of variables such as: the social identities of users and listeners (kin networks vs. youth networks) and of those whose attention is being attracted (members of the community vs. peer groups and potential sexual partners). There are additional cultural differences in the specific ways that prestige is created in ongoing practices. For example, is status signaled simply by indicating ownership or possession of a radio? Or does it also require demonstrating the volume capabilities of the radio machine or one's conversance with the latest music? Along these lines, more comparative research needs to be done to determine, on the one hand, the extent to which culture matters in the integration of media in daily life and, on the other hand, the extent to which certain media technologies have inherent properties that predispose them to certain kinds of uses and interpretations regardless of culture. And it may be that in some instances it is not possible to make an absolute determination one way or the other.

In widening the frame of reception studies to include the whole of culture—understood as the habitual practices, institutions, maps of meanings, and modes of meaning-making through which reality and lives themselves are made intelligible and compelling—documenting media as lived experience becomes all the more challenging. The idealized picture of the single interpreting subject and the nostalgic "radio or TV as hearth" (with the attentive family audience clustered around it) may exist in the minds of many media producers and public policy planners. But in Zambia there is more often a complex nexus of social relations and activities where numerous things are happening simultaneously: other media, other sounds, children, visitors, activities like baking buns and pounding maize, and so on. To de-essentialize the audience does not mean that one ceases to consider the positioning of people, by both themselves and by media producers, as groups who collectively participate in the consumption of the same media form. It also does not mean that everything is up for grabs; that there are myriad possibilities for media interpretation and media use within the flux of everyday life. To the extent that culture and place still matter, there are important regularities and cross-cultural differences in what people do with media and media technologies. In Zambia, radio culture is integrated within the textures of daily life; as such it is shaped by local constraints and preoccupations, particularly economic ones. From an anthropological perspective, to determine precisely where radio culture ends and where the rest of daily life takes over may be beside the point; it is their meaningful integration that merits the bulk of our attention. It may be more a matter of accepting, in Hebdige's terms, that "we are in a field without fences" (1988: 81). The effort to document media culture at this early point should wander in this field—beyond the living room—and welcome the unboundedness of its subject.

NOTES

This essay is a revised version of "Documenting Radio Culture as Lived Experience: Reception Studies and the Mobile Machine in Zambia," in *African Broadcast Cultures: Radio in Transition,* edited by R. Fardon and G. Furniss (2000), and is published with permission of Praegar Publishers, an imprint of Greenwood Publishing Group, Inc., Westport, CT.

This essay is part of a larger project that examines radio culture and the national public in Zambia (Spitulnik, forthcoming). Research was supported by Fulbright-Hays, National Science Foundation, and Spencer Foundation fellowships and facilitated by the Institute for African Studies at the University of Zambia during 1988–90. I would like to extend my sincere thanks to these institutions and to the many Zambians who shared their days, homes, and lives with me during that time. Special thanks goes to my research assistants, Simon Bwalya and Brian Mfula, for assistance in documenting radio use and radio sales in the Kasama area. I am also greatly indebted to Mansur Abdulkadir, Jean Comaroff, Christopher Davis, Richard Fardon, Graham Furniss, Mark Hobart, Bruce Knauft, and the editors of this volume for their helpful comments on earlier versions of this essay.

1. See for example: Abu-Lughod 1997; Ang 1996; Curran 1996; Moores 1993; Morley 1996; Radway 1988; Spitulnik 1993.

2. See Manuel 1993; Silverstone and Hirsch 1992; Tacchi 1998; Turkle 1995.

3. For more information on Radio Zambia and an overview of broadcasting in the country, see Claypole and Daka 1993 and Spitulnik 1996, 1998, and forthcoming.

4. The staple food in Zambia is *nshima,* a dense starchy dough made from mealie meal, a type of maize flour. In a typical household, a twenty-five kilogram bag lasts roughly one to two weeks. In 1989 a twenty-five kilogram bag of the coarsely ground roller meal cost $4; in 1998 it cost $8.

5. Indented paragraphs are vignettes of radio use, based on ethnographic field notes. They are a combination of direct observational notes and contextualizing remarks about real people in real situations. I use the present tense to convey the sense of habituality (such as typical behaviors and scenes) as well as the senses of immediacy and unfolding ethnographic discovery. In accord with people's wishes, I use real names instead of pseudonyms.

6. Joseph's salary was K1,000/month ($104). At that time (January 1989), the price of twelve batteries (K6.47 each) was K77.64 total ($8), and the cost of a fifty-kilogram bag of roller meal was K82. Joseph's case is exceptional because most radios are portable and use only four batteries. With such radios, the monthly battery expenditure for regular users at this time was K25.88 ($2.68). The significant point is that even for such uses, the proportion of monthly income going for radio batteries (1–3 percent) is dramatically higher than among comparable income brackets in the United States (0.3–0.5 percent).

7. This nervousness on the part of household heads about entrusting relatives with the security of the home is real and not paranoia. During my research I heard of several instances in which heads of households returned from short trips to find that valuable items had been stolen; in one, a relative was suspected of being complicit and sharing the resale profits with the robbers.

8. Chitimukulu is the home of the paramount chief of the Bemba people. Besides the palace grounds, there are two distinct villages (kwaKoni and kwaTompwe),

between which is an area of government houses for civil servants assigned to the area.

9. Newspapers and magazines are also portable and circulate from person to person, but their consumption is usually more individual.

10. I use the past tense in this ethnographic excerpt because it is an in-depth narrative recounting of a series of events that occurred over several hours.

11. GRZ stands for "Government of Zambia."

REFERENCES

Abu-Lughod, Lila. 1997. The Interpretation of Culture(s) after Television. *Representations* 59: 109–34.

Ang, Ien. 1996. *Living Room Wars: Rethinking Media Audiences for a Postmodern World.* London: Routledge.

Appadurai, Arjun. 1986. Introduction: Commodities and the Politics of Value. In *The Social Life of Things: Commodities in Cultural Perspective,* edited by Arjun Appadurai, pp. 3–63. Cambridge, England: Cambridge University Press.

Claypole, Andrew, and Given Daka. 1993. Zambia. In *Global Audiences: Research in Worldwide Broadcasting 1993,* edited by Graham Mytton, pp. 59–70. London: John Libbey.

Corner, John. 1991. Meaning, Genre and Context: The Problematics of "Public Knowledge" in the New Audience Studies. *Mass Media and Society,* edited by James Curran and Michael Gurevitch, pp. 267–84. London: Edward Arnold.

Curran, James. [1990] 1996. The New Revisionism in Communication Research. In *Cultural Studies and Communications,* edited by James Curran, David Morley and Valerie Walkerdine, pp. 256–78. London: Arnold.

Dickey, Sarah. 1993. *Cinema and the Urban Poor in South India.* Cambridge, England: Cambridge University Press.

Evans, W. A. 1990. The Interpretive Turn in Media Research: Innovation, Iteration, or Illusion? *Critical Studies in Mass Communication* 7 (2):147–68.

Ferguson, James. 1999. *Expectations of Modernity: Myths and Meanings of Urban Life on the Zambian Copperbelt.* Berkeley: University of California Press.

Ginsburg, Faye. 1999. Shooting Back: From Ethnographic Film to Ethnography of Media. In *A Companion to Film Theory,* edited by Toby Miller and Robert Stam, pp. 295–322. Malden, Mass.: Blackwell.

Grossberg, Lawrence. 1987. The In-Difference of Television. *Screen* 28 (2): 28–45.

Hebdige, Dick. 1988. *Hiding in the Light: On Images and Things.* London: Comedia.

Larkin, Brian. 1999. Introduction to Media Technologies and the Design for Modern Living. *Visual Anthropology Review* 14 (2): 11–13.

Mankekar, Purnima. 1999. *Screening Culture, Viewing Politics: An Ethnography of Television, Womanhood, and Nation in Postcolonial India.* Durham, N.C.: Duke University Press.

Manuel, Peter. 1993. *Cassette Culture: Popular Music and Technology in North India.* Chicago: University of Chicago Press.

Mauss, Marcel. [1925] 1967. *The Gift: Forms and Functions of Exchange in Archaic Societies*. New York: Norton.

Miller, Daniel 1998. *Material Cultures: Why Some Things Matter*. Chicago: University of Chicago Press.

Moores, Shaun. 1993. *Interpreting Audiences: The Ethnography of Media Consumption*. London: Sage.

Morley, David. [1992] 1996. Populism, Revisionism and the "New" Audience Research. In *Cultural Studies and Communications*, edited by James Curran, David Morley, and Valerie Walkerdine, pp. 279–93. London: Arnold.

———. 1997. Theoretical Orthodoxies: Textualism, Constructivism and the "New Ethnography" in Cultural Studies. *Cultural Studies in Question*, edited by Marjorie Ferguson and Peter Golding, pp. 121–37. London: Sage.

Morley, David, and Roger Silverstone. 1990. Domestic Communication: Technologies and Meanings. *Media, Culture, and Society* 12 (1): 31–55.

Radway, Janice. 1988. Reception Study: Ethnography and the Problems of Dispersed Audiences and Nomadic Subjects. *Cultural Studies* 2 (3): 359–76.

Silverstone, Roger, and Eric Hirsch, eds. 1992. *Consuming Technologies: Media and Information in Domestic Spaces*. London: Routledge.

Spigel, Lynn. 1992. *Make Room for TV: Television and the Family Ideal in Postwar America*. Chicago: University of Chicago Press.

Spitulnik, Debra. 1993. Anthropology and Mass Media. *Annual Review of Anthropology* 22: 293–315.

———. 1996. The Social Circulation of Media Discourse and the Mediation of Communities. *Journal of Linguistic Anthropology* 6 (2): 161–87.

———. 1998. Mediating Unity and Diversity: The Production of Language Ideologies in Zambian Broadcasting. In *Language Ideologies: Practice and Theory*, edited by Bambi Schieffelin, Kathryn Woolard, and Paul Kroskrity, pp. 163–88. Oxford, England: Oxford University Press.

———. 1998/99. Mediated Modernities: Encounters with the Electronic in Zambia. *Visual Anthropology Review* 14 (2): 63–84.

———. Forthcoming. *Media Connections and Disconnections: Radio Culture and the Public Sphere in Zambia*. Durham, N.C.: Duke University Press.

Tacchi, Jo. 1998. Radio Texture: Between Self and Others. In *Material Cultures: Why Some Things Matter*, edited by Daniel Miller, pp. 25–45. Chicago: University of Chicago Press.

Turkle, Sherry. 1995. *Life on the Screen: Identity in the Age of the Internet*. New York: Simon and Schuster.

Yoder, P. Stanley, Robert Hornik, and Ben C. Chirwa. 1996. Evaluating the Program Effects of a Radio Drama about AIDS in Zambia. *Studies in Family Planning* 27 (4): 188–203.

18

The Indian Work of Art in the Age of Mechanical Reproduction

Or, What Happens When Peasants "Get Hold" of Images

Christopher Pinney

[Silent film] has to achieve its effect visually, without the aid of the spoken word. The result is an exaggeration of physical expression and suggestive action. Every device is employed in order to intensify the visual impression, such as the well-known device of the "close-up," and thus a peculiarly direct and vivid impression is produced upon the mind of the spectator.
REPORT OF THE INDIAN CINEMATOGRAPH COMMITTEE, *1927–28*

It hit the spectator like a bullet, it happened to him, thus acquiring a tactile quality.
WALTER BENJAMIN, *Illuminations*

One of the achievements of Michael Taussig's *Mimesis and Alterity* is to rescue— through a creatively idiosyncratic reading—Walter Benjamin's 1936 "Work of Art" essay from a utopian hypothesis about the consequences of mechanical reproduction (which all known evidence contradicts), in favor of a complex set of insights about the sensory procedures involved in "getting hold" of images. The stress on the new mimetic technologies' creation of "an object-implicated enterprise" and on the eye as an organ of tactility (Taussig 1993: 24, 21) is a productive starting point for theorizing the impact of the first Indian-made films in the second decade of the twentieth century, which reconstituted the cinema as a zone of sensory mutuality in which the "space of contemplation" had been abolished.

In this paper I argue that this zone of mutuality, which is so evident in much popular early cinema, is equally apparent in film's interocular bedfellow, popular chromolithography. The consumption of these images by central Indian peasants in the village of Bhatisuda in Madhya Pradesh forms the central focus of my discussion. The detail and nuance of the later material make evident the complex specificity of popular Hindu discourses about the mutuality and tactility of vision. My intention, however, is not simply to map out a local media practice that stands apart from other better-known ones, but to explore the parallels across a range of visual practices that the close study of one case helps to bring into a better focus.

The popular Indian practices discussed here may appear on the face of it to be radically different from dominant authorized "Western" practices, but it is my claim that the distance between diverse popular practices is, in fact, surprisingly small. My strategy parallels the use made of anthropological analyses of Melanesian personhood to destabilize the mythic authorized modes of Western personhood. Thus in developing my argument with reference to Merleau-Ponty and Heidegger among others, my desire is not to overscript the ethnographic material in terms of a sovereign Western reason but—in explicit opposition to this—to sketch out a countertheory of Western visuality that can meet, halfway, a different tradition with which it shares much in common. This confrontation is the ground on which a "provincialization" of Euro-American discourses can be explored (Chakrabarty 1992: 20–22).

Rather than attempting to reinscribe an opposition of cultural alterity, what I hope to demonstrate is the existence of hostile continua within societies in which there are strikingly similar oppositions between popular practices of corporeal visuality and elite "decarnalized" practices (Bryson 1983: 95). The anthropological study of media practices in this way draws our attention to the differences *within* and the similarities *between* "cultures."

Read as utopian fantasy, Benjamin's essay forecasts the decay of a reactionary, hierarchical "aura" as mechanical reproduction floods the world with copies whose "originals" cease to have any significance. Dissolving the originals' "unique existence at the place where it happens to be," mechanical reproduction "emancipates the work of art from its parasitical dependence on ritual" (Benjamin 1992: 214, 218). Taken at face value, Benjamin's thesis seems easily—indeed inevitably—refutable: its central argument can find little support from ethnographic and historical enquiry. Authors who have subsequently addressed these themes in diverse cultural contexts have acknowledged Benjamin's provocations but reached opposed conclusions about the relationship between art objects and their reproductions. John Berger, for instance, wonderfully elaborates Benjamin's propositions, noting the effect of transposing images from the places for which they were made into public realms of the ephemeral and ubiquitous (Berger 1972: 32). But while Berger can claim programmatically and in the true spirit of Benjamin that reproduction has destroyed "the authority of art," his case studies suggest an entirely contrary effect. Here, as in the case of the Leonardo cartoon in London's National Gallery, the mass dissemination of postcard reproductions serves to reinvest originals with a new aura. The original artwork now comes to embody what the reproduction lacks and must be enclosed in shrinelike security structures to protect them from the admiring, and sometimes hateful, gestures of their devotees:

"The bogus religiosity which now surrounds original works of art, and which is ultimately dependent upon their market value, has become the substitute for what paintings lost when the camera made them reproducible" (Berger 1972: 230). While Berger does indeed echo Benjamin in a complex way, this re-auraticized object is difficult to reconcile with Benjamin's central narrative. I might also mention here Mary Beard's study of the most popular postcards in various London galleries and museums whose function she suggests are relics of visitors' pilgrimage to the great temples of art and culture and affirmations of a canon of great objects and whose postcard dissemination underwrites further future pilgrimages (Beard 1992).

Stephen Sprague's (1978) work on the role of photography in Yoruba *ibeji* cults records a similar underwriting (rather than dissolution) of cultic behavior. Mechanical reproduction in the form of photography has largely taken the place of wooden sculptural forms in this cultic veneration of twins. An appeal might be made to Benjamin's stress on the manner in which "cult value does not give way without resistance" and finds its "ultimate retrenchment" in the "human countenance." *Ibeji* photography would, by this reckoning be merely an affirmation of Benjamin's concession that "the cult of remembrance of loved ones, absent or dead, offers a last refuge for the cult value of the picture" (Benjamin 1992: 219). A skeptic, reading Benjamin without the benefit of Taussig, however, might detect a striking neutrality of technology as carving is replaced by mass-produced plastic dolls and then by the mimetic magic of the photograph. It is not that one needs the human face as an escape clause—as Benjamin suggests—so much as a wholesale revision of the argument, for there is no sign at all of mechanical reproduction enabling an emancipation from the parasitical dependence on ritual.

Benjamin's observation that "every day the urge grows stronger to get hold of an object at very close range by way of its likeness, its reproduction" (Benjamin 1992: 217) has generally been read as a sign of the ineluctability of encroaching media practices that have increasingly virtualized the world. Taussig, however, suggests another approach that reconstitutes Benjamin's work as centrally relevant for anthropological work on media. Taussig chooses to see Benjamin's notion of the "optical unconscious" not as "ebullient Enlightenment faith in a secular world of technological reason" in which "magic" is replaced by "science," but rather as a visceral domain in which objects become sensorily emboldened in a "magical technology of embodied knowing" (Taussig 1993: 24).

Reading Benjamin through a Taussigian lens allows us to retain many of the "Work of Art" essay's crucial insights without having to discard it as simply a flawed hypothesis. Recall that the simplistic reading of Benjamin might focus on his privileging of film as the ultimately cathartic mimetic technology with an unrivaled power to detach "the reproduced object from the domain of tradition" resulting in a "tremendous shattering." For example, without Taussig's lens it is difficult to reconcile the intention of and Indian audience responses to D. G. Phalke's early mythological movies with film's "destructive, cathartic aspect, that is, the liquidation of the traditional value of the cultural heritage" (Benjamin 1992: 215). In 1917, following his earlier successes, including *Raja Harishchandra* (1913), Phalke released *Lanka Dahan (The Burning of Lanka)* at the West End Cinema at Girgaum, Bombay, where it was shown every hour from 7 A.M. until midnight (Dharap 1985). This was Phalke's greatest success and was a triumph for the actor A. Salunke, who played both the goddess Sita and the god Rama. Barnouw and Krishnaswamy record that when Rama appeared, the audience prostrated itself before the screen (Barnouw and Krishnaswamy 1963: 15). It has been claimed that when it was shown in Pune the crowds almost broke down the door and that in Madras the film's takings had to be transported in a bullock cart with police protection (Dharap 1985: 43). An account of its Bombay opening by the filmmaker J. B. H. Wadia provides some sense of its huge impact upon the audience: "I remember that devout villagers from nearby Bombay had come in large numbers in their bullock carts to have *darshan* of their beloved God, the Lord Rama. The roadside was blocked with the caravan of bullock carts. Many of the villagers had stayed overnight in their improvised dwellings just to see the film again the next day" (Wadia 1985: 24). (*Darshan* is a practice of Hindu visuality predicated on the mutuality of "seeing and being seen" by the images of the deities one worships [Eck 1981].)

One year later, in 1918, Phalke released *Shree Krishna Janma*, of which a portion survives in the National Film Archive in Pune. The greater resources of the Hindustan Film Company enabled Phalke to present a greatly more sophisticated product, which as Suresh Chabria notes, "contains sequences of amazing virtuosity" that suggest comparison with Méliès. From the very start, as Chabria further observes in his stimulating analysis, Phalke "dazzles his audience with magical transformations appropriate to the subject of Vishnu's *avatars*" (Chabria 1994: 105, 106). Chabria's sensitive description of the remarkable opening sequences deserves to be cited at length:

> The plain Hindi calligraphy of the film's title transforms to letters written with flowers. . . . Superimposed on this floral design appears a circle rotating in a metaphor of ceaseless time and representing the *sudarshana-chakra* or flaming discus which is one of the attributes of Vishnu and Krishna. Within this design a close up of the child Krishna is now seen in full frontality giving a prologue *darshan* to his devotees. It is as if the temple and the cinema hall are merged. (Chabria 1994: 106)

The opening sequences of *Shree Krishna Janma* also conflate spectators and supplicants, filmic apparition and divine incarnation. After the initial shot of Krishna set against the swirling *sudarshana-chakra,* the cinema audience sees a foregrounded group of devotees with their backs to the camera beseeching the gods. A title appears: "All human efforts having turned out futile, the Almighty God is never at a great distance when prayed for sincerely and wholeheartedly" (cited by Rajadhyaksha 1987: 69). And then Vishnu rises magically from the waters revealing himself before the supplicants just as the film itself appears in front of the audience. There is then a series of shots in which the supplicants' and Krishna's gaze are interposed. As Rajadhyaksha notes, "Every shot is along the perpendicular axis of the gaze, emphasizing it, and reciprocating from within the frame" (1987: 70).

This "locking in" is a recurrent feature of Hindu devotional practice. There are many later filmic examples (some of which are discussed below), and it emerges as the key trope in chromolithograph consumers' articulations of their relationships to images. It is also clearly expressive of *darshan*. However, I would suggest that this practice exceeds its discursive accompaniments. Local understandings of *darshan* must certainly nuance and finesse our understanding of popular Indian visuality, but underlying this there is a much more widespread practice of what I term "corpothetics" (sensory, corporeal aesthetics). This local Indian practice is certainly on the face of it dissimilar to dominant-class Western practices that privilege a disembodied, unidirectional, and disinterested vision. However, they are not strikingly unlike a whole range of culturally diverse popular practices that stress mutuality and corporeality in spaces as varied as those of religious devotion and cinematic pleasure. So while the power and specificity of local discourses is clearly crucial, I wish to resist a wholesale reduction of meaning to such discourses. Rather than create an anthropologized enclave of *darshan*-related practices, I am interested in the continuities and resonances with an emerging counterhistory of visuality that is in the process of destabilizing and provincializing (and in the process revealing as historically and sociologically fallacious) authorized dominant-class visualities in Europe, America, and elsewhere. The choice here should not be seen as simply one between a universalism and a cultural specificity (as is implied by Davis 1997: 265 n. 5), for there are also rhizomatic pathways (simultaneously implying similitude and difference) that establish a field which is less than universal and more than local.

Phalke's "locked-in" and "reciprocated" gazes are expressions of an affective intensity that abolishes the "space of contemplation" conceptualized as a disembodied cerebral construction of the world as picture. Heidegger's superb "The Age of the World Picture" was produced in 1935—one year before Benjamin's "Work of Art" essay, and there are certain intriguing parallels between them. Both essays develop extraordinarily broad and ambitious evolutionary narratives, and both are surely key reference points for an anthropology of media. In Benjamin's optimistic history, the decay of an earlier situated aura is presaged by new technologies of picturing. In Heidegger's pessimistic history, a positively valorized premodern dwelling is ruptured by what Martin Jay has termed "Cartesian perspectivalism" in which the world comes to be seen as picture—a zone of representation established as something exterior to existence. Picturing becomes inseparable from modernity: "The fact that the world becomes a picture at all is what distinguishes the modern age" (Heidegger 1977: 130).

Whereas for Parmenides, Heidegger argues, "man is the one who is looked upon by that which is" in the modern age, "that which is . . . come[s] into being . . . through the fact that man first looks upon it." Looking upon the world and constructing the world as picture entails man placing himself against and before nature as something separate: the world is "placed in the realm of man's knowing and of his having disposal" (Heidegger 1977: 131, 130).

Heidegger does not discuss the role of the body explicitly, but the world as picture clearly implies a separation between that picture and the look that addresses it "for the purposes of gaining mastery" (Heidegger 1977: 132). The Parmenidean paradigm invokes something akin to a Levy-Bruhlian mystical participation in which bodies are not detachable from the world. This sense of immersion and mutuality, which Heidegger locates in a premodernity, resonates with Elizabeth Grosz's exploration of what Merleau-Ponty termed the "double sensation" of touching and being touched: "My right hand is capable of touching my left hand as if the latter were an object. But in this case, unlike any object, my left hand feels the right hand touching it. My left hand has the double sensation of being both the object and the subject of touch" (Grosz 1994: 100).

Both Heidegger and Merleau-Ponty can be seen as historiographers of a counterhistory of modernity that is of pressing relevance to anthropologists of visuality. The fragile counterhistory they gesture at suggests pathways toward a corporeal visuality—explicitly marked in some local practices (such as that in the central Indian village I will shortly describe) and though present, more difficult to recuperate in others.

In addition to the early filmic examples outlined above, there are vivid examples of the "double sensation" in more recent Hindi films. The celebrated *Jai Santoshi Ma* (1975) included several sequences in which the desperate heroine Satyavadi implores the assistance of Santoshi Ma. In these sequences— one of which has been discussed by Lawrence Babb (1981)—the goddess's vision is shown as a physical extrusive force (a beam of scorching fire), and intercut shots of the Satyavadi's and Santoshi's faces are used repetitively to inscribe the mutuality of vision that binds the devotee to the goddess.

In *Amar Akbar Anthony*, released two years later in 1977, the process of *darshan* is literally vision-enhancing: being seen becomes the ground from which one's own vision is possible. Chased by ruffians, the elderly blind mother of the three central characters is attracted by the noise of an ecstatic song in praise of Sai Baba conducted—in keeping with the ecumenical spirit of the film—by her son Akbar (for recondite reasons the three sons have been raised in different religions). While the congregation praises the visibility of god in the Shirdhi Sai Baba and his ability to relight lamps and to turn dark nights of sorrows into brightness, the blind mother is ineluctably drawn by some mutual corporeal attraction toward the image in the temple. Though blind, she is compulsively drawn to the face and body of Sai Baba who—as the song proclaims the relighting of lamps—reciprocates her devotion with his own brightness in the form of two flames that migrate from his eyes to hers, liberating her from blindness. Touching Sai Baba's feet, she proclaims her ability to see and to have *darshan* of the god and tells Akbar that it is thanks to his devotion and the Baba's "magic" *(chamatkar)*.

ACROSS GENRES AND MEDIA

Phalke's work emerges from a wider popular visual culture in which mass-produced chromolithographs played a large part, and his films in turn influenced the production of later chromolithographic images. In addition to working as a photographer and a magician, Phalke had worked as a lithographic block maker at the Ravi Varma Press—the leading popular picture publisher of its day.

Phalke's motivation in producing the "first Indian-made films" was explicitly nationalistic. He wanted to make films for Indian audiences, and *Raja Harishchandra* was advertised as "an entirely Indian production by Indians" (Chabria 1994: 9).[1] The reclaiming of the technological means of control also involved the reappropriation of a space of perception. Within film, chromolithography, and studio photography one can trace parallel movements that involved the abolition of the space of contemplation and the intensification of an erotic tactility. Contemplation was integral to the disembodied, disinterested—what Susan Buck-Morss would call "anaesthetized"—aesthetics that indigenized Indian practice reacted against (Buck-Morss 1992). Contemplation—which was promulgated in India through colonial art schools from the mid-1850s onward—might be seen as concerned with "hermeneutics" in Sontag's terms, its abolition allowing the emergence of a new "erotics" (Sontag 1986).

This new space was not simply visual. Ashis Nandy has written about the aural zone of mutuality that emerged during two hijackings of Indian Airlines jets by Sikh militants in 1984. In Nandy's romanticized yet provocative reading, the claustrophobic technological space of the aircraft soon becomes configured by "the limits imposed by another moral order" (Nandy 1995: 22). Here Nandy gestures toward coterminous "vestigial dialects" that resonate with Heidegger's idealized premodernity.

A significant element in the articulation of this new morality was the meeting ground afforded by popular Hindi film music. A young hijacker sang "melancholy songs of separation and love from Hindi films," and the passengers asked him to sing more. For Nandy (and here I identify very closely with his project) this is evidence of a Ginzburgian subaltern resourcefulness—the ability to conjure up "vestigial traces of a dialect which everyone had half-forgotten" and that were likely to jar the sensitivities of the Indian haute bourgeoisie.

Parallel, though differently historically located strategies, can be seen at play in the privileging of "frontality" in early Indian film (Rajadhyaksha 1987; Kapur 1987) and of the "surface" in early chromolithography. Elsewhere I have argued that this increasing preoccupation with the surface can be seen in part as a rejection of a Cartesian perspectivalism associated with an ethically dubious colonial rationality (see Pinney 1999). Many of the earliest Indian-produced chromolithographs incarnate a series of colonial concerns with the utility of single-point perspective and the necessity of defusing the magical power of images through such technical procedures. Concomitant to this, ritually efficacious images became "representationally" efficacious inasmuch as they came to be judged as successful or otherwise implementations of colonially authorized strategies ("realism," "perspectivalism," etc). In the early twentieth century there was a growing sense that these strategies were themselves ethically and politically problematic and required rejection or revision in favor of another figural zone. This rejection is marked in various ways, including the "dressing" and adornment of images in such a way that accreted surfaces occlude depth, through an energizing of antiperspectival neotraditional and neofolk forms that stylistically renounce the colonial, and through the emergence of a magical realist aesthetic that—like Carpentier's notion of the Baroque—"flees from all geometrical arrangements" (Carpentier 1995: 93).

It is against this historical background that the current rural somatic and "corpothetic" consumption of Hindu chromolithographs must be understood. These chromolithographs are produced throughout India by many different companies and may be divided into "framing pictures" and "calendar pictures." The former (which in this local context constitute the overwhelming majority) used to refer to those images printed with a white border that purchasers would frequently have framed, although it now includes large, laminated, bled-to-the-edge images that are almost never framed. Calendar images (the majority of which are printed in Sivakasi in southern India) all have a distinct size and format and are printed with a section beneath the main image that is left blank for local overprinting. Within the national economy the vast majority of calendar images are distributed free by commercial concerns to their clients, but in the Indian village in central India that I am concerned with, most calendars have been purchased from local stalls and may or may not have overprinting on them.

The village of Bhatisuda—where I have investigated this and other issues intermittently since the early 1980s—is located in Madhya Pradesh, about halfway between Bombay and Delhi. It is near the main railway line linking those two cities and lies six kilometers from Nagda, a major industrial town in whose industrial plants a significant number of villagers either work or have recently worked.

Although it is undoubtedly true that in certain key respects popular Hinduism mobilizes a recuperative idiom within a decaying universe, it is fundamentally constructed by what the playwright Brian Friel (in a very different context) once described as a "syntax opulent with tomorrows" (Friel 1981: 42). Mass reproduction gives formerly excluded classes access to all the high gods they can approach directly, in search of their tomorrows, without the intercession of priests. Chromolithographs are popular across all castes and religious groups. Jains and Muslims own images as well as Hindus, and Scheduled Caste Chamars and (warrior) Rajputs or (priestly) Brahmans own similar numbers of images. Across the village as a whole there is an average of 6.9 images per household. These are usually displayed (tacked to the mud wall or propped up in frames) above a thin wooden shelf on which there are various *puja* accoutrements (incense stick holders, small bells, and various offerings, together with small three-dimensional clay and metal statues of deities).

The "syntax opulent with tomorrows" that emerges in Bhatisuda practice is one that springs from a corpothetic practice (that is, an embodied sensory aesthetics) in which it is the devotee's visual and bodily performances that contribute crucially to the potential power—one might say *completion*— of the image.

Some sense of the mechanism here can be gleaned from this fragment with a taped interview with Lila—a village "sweeper"—in which the gradual transformation that overtakes an image following its purchase is discussed:[2]

> [CP:] When the picture is [for sale in the market] is there any *shakti* [energy] in the picture?]
>
> [Lila:] It's just paper. That's all? Yes, paper. It's just paper, it hasn't been "seated" *[baithana]*. You see those pictures that are "seated"? [Lila pointed to the images on the wall.] Those are paper, but by placing them before our eyes [*ankh rakhna* = to love, to entertain friendship, to admire], *shakti* [energy] has come into them. . . . We take [the pictures] inside and do *puja*. We place *agarbatti* [incense sticks] against his name, against the god's name. Yes, it's a paper photo but we recite, we recite while the *agarbatti* burns. OK, so it's a paper photo but [that makes no difference]. We entreat the god and the god comes out because the god is saluted. That's how it is.

The image is installed through "seating" it, and the alienable commodity becomes an inalienable embodiment of the divine, which generates a performative praxis grounded in affective intensity.

The other sense in which Bhatisuda images are opulent with tomorrows lies in the stress on their capacity to give *barkat*—plenitude. Samvaliyaji, a local incarnation of Krishna, is an example par excellence of a deity who gives *barkat.* Whereas orthodox deities such as Shiva are considered essential to *alaukik labh* (disinterested profit—that is, transcendental concerns), Samvaliyaji can produce *bhautik labh* (material or physical profit). Under the general label of *bhautik,* various predicaments are subsumed: uncertainties relating to wealth and bodily health and illness, and matters relating to employment and agricultural productivity.

The consumption of images by Bhatisuda villagers needs to be understood in terms of the processes of bodily empowerment that transform pieces of paper into powerful deities through the devotee's gaze, the proximity of his or her heart, and a whole repertoire of bodily performances in front of the image (breaking coconuts, lighting incense sticks, folding hands, shaking small bells, the utterance of mantras).

In Bhatisuda I once asked Pukhraj Bohra whether blind people could have *darshan* of a *murti* (statue). His response helps elucidate both the sequence in the film *Amar Akbar Anthony* discussed above and the general question of the relationship between visual and broader corporeal perceptions. "Oh yes," he replied, "you get *darshan* through *divyajyotish* [lit. divine radiance, related to *divyachaksu* and *divya drishti* (divine vision)]. If your disposition is truthful an internal vision will let you know that the image is in front of you."

The most fundamental mark of the images' sensory quality—their predisposition to this corpothetic regime—is their ocular directness. The vast majority of images behold their owners directly, engaging and returning their vision. As Diane Eck observes, the primacy of sight as the idiom of articulation between deity and devotee is lexically marked so that devotees will usually stress that they are going to the temple for darshan, to see and be seen by the deity: it is this "exchange of vision [that] lies at the heart of Hindu worship" (Eck 1981: 6).

The desire to see and be seen by deities is also evidenced in the prevalence of mirrored images within the village. Frequently these are mass-produced paper prints that have been carefully mounted behind partially mirrored glass. The central image of the deity remains visible, surrounded by a complex tracery of tain in which the devotee sees his or her own face in proximity to the deity. These images are usually associated with pilgrimage. *Darshan* can be thought of as a physical relationship of visual intermingling. The value of images is related to the visual access they give to the deity. Mirrored images allow the devotee to (literally) see himself looking at the deity (in this case there is a double corpothetics—of the devotee's movement through space on the pilgrimage where he bought the image, and of the devotee's visual elision with the deity when he places himself in front of the image).[3]

Underlying all the overlapping oppositions that have been outlined above is a distinction between a disinterested anaesthetics that proposes a disembodied unidirectional vision and an aesthetics that stresses the mutuality of seeing and being seen. This mutuality of perception is also expressed in stories concerning the *akarshan* (allurement) that images can produce. Pukhraj Bohra related how the *murti* of the Jain tirthankara Nageshvar Pareshavar near Alod (in Madhya Pradesh) had exerted its hold over him. He first went there fifteen years ago and made a *man* (wish). He asked that his business should go well and that the crops should prosper, and then he returned to the village. But there was some psychic *(mansik)* effect from this, some allurement *(akarshan)* born in the *murti*. When he was away he felt that he had to go back and see the image, had to see it again and again.

In the village, the overlaying of a purely visual perception with tactile extensions that feed into a broader haptic field is apparent in other modes of image customization. The application of glitter or *zari* (brocade) or the adhesion of paper surrounds or plastic flowers moves the image closer to the devotee. It transforms the ostensible representation or window into a figurative surface deeply inscribed by the presence of the deity and the work of the devotee and links the image with the wider field of what Bourdieu terms the postural schemes within which it is embedded.

Arati is a procedure in image worship in which a flame is moved in a circle around an image. In Bhatisuda, villagers then cup their hands over the flame and wash the blessing from the deity onto their face. *Ramdevji ki arati*, painted by B. G. Sharma in the mid-1950s (and still in print), exists in several copies in the village and in this artist's characteristically semiotically dense manner inserts the narrative of the deity Ramdev into the very act of worship. The process of *darshan* and the transmission of the "content" of the picture onto the devotee's face becomes itself the subject and dictates the form of the picture.

Finally we may note that the whole process of the progressive empowerment of images through daily worship involves a continual burdening of the surface with traces of this devotion. Although some households replace all their images every year at Divali, most have a number of old images that continue to accrue potency as they become accreted with the marks of repeated devotion—vermilion tilaks placed on the foreheads of deities, the ash from incense sticks, smoke stains from burning camphor.

Even at the end of its life, a picture's trajectory is determined by corpothetic requirements, in this case the necessity of ensuring that the image never comes into contact with human feet. Again a fragment from a conversation with Lila:

> [The images] are paper, and when they have gone *kharab* [bad] we take them from the house and put them in the river. That way we don't get any *pap* [sin]. [CP: You don't throw them away?] No. no. we don't throw them away. You take them out of the house and put them in the river or in a well, and place them under the water. This way they won't come under anyone's feet. You mustn't throw them away or they will get lost. That's the *tamizdar* [proper; decorous] way to do it—in the river or well. In our *jat* we say *thanda kardo*—make cold. That way they won't come under [anyone's] feet.

Bihari, a Bhatisuda resident, holds a mirrored version of a B. G. Sharma chromolithograph depicting Ramdevji. The framed print was purchased by Bihari at Ramdevra, the main Ramdevji pilgrimage center. (Photo: Christopher Pinney)

I asked Pannalal whether he threw his old pictures away: "No no, no. It's become just like a small temple *[madhi]*. We put them in water, we break a coconut and give them *paraba*⁴ in the water. If you throw them in the street they will come under someone's feet." In Hindi the phrase *pair ankh se lagana* literally means to look at the feet; idiomatically, "to respect, venerate" and to touch someone's feet is to physically express one's obeisance. Certain images in Bhatisuda encode this hierarchical relationship in which the devotee submits his body—through his eyes—to the feet of the deity.⁵ It is fundamentally important to Bhatisuda villagers that the bodies of the deities that they have so carefully brought to life should not suffer the dangerous indignity of having this relationship reversed.

DISTANCING ART

Several dozen of the images in Bhatisuda village are the work of Bhanwarlal Girdharilal Sharma, known as "B. G. Sharma." Sharma, founder of Sharma Picture Publications, has profoundly influenced the nature of contemporary mass-picture production in postcolonial India. After an abortive period of study at the J. J. School of Art in Bombay just before independence, he published images of Hindu deities and political leaders with Har Narayan of Jodhpur, S. S. Brijbasi, and other outlets before founding his own company in 1951. His distinctive application of a brash palette to the aesthetics inculcated through an upbringing in a traditional Brahman painting tradition in the Rajasthani pilgrimage town of Nathdvara gained him an enormous pan-Indian market, and all other companies and artists had subsequently to adjust to this style to maintain a toehold in the market. Sharma's images remain extremely popular and have a wide currency throughout rural India, where many millions of peasants worship deities made visible in Sharma Picture Publications chromolithographs.

B. G. Sharma now lives in a large personal museum in Udaipur. Hanging on the marble walls are signs of the global recognition that have come to him since the 1970s—including a framed letter from Nancy Reagan and a photograph of Sharma with Roger Moore taken while the James Bond movie *Octopussy* was filmed at Udaipur.

In the early 1990s, when I met with him several times, he was keen to distance himself from his earlier work, having found a new idiom through which to express his talent. His earlier populism is a source of unease, and he refers to his 1950s work as the sort of thing one might encounter on the "footpath" (sidewalk). "Nowadays I do very little work in this style, I do most in Mughal style . . . large cloth paintings, on ivory, or watercolors on paper." Whereas he says his earlier "commercial work" was "rough" and "ordinary," his present "classical" work requires great patience and skill. His testimonial books are crammed with comments from the famous and the worthy: Rajiv Gandhi wrote, "I'm delighted that the ancient Indian artistic spirit has once again come alive."

B. G. Sharma's unease draws our attention to the simultaneous existence within India of what Hans Belting (1994) referred to as "an era of art" and an "era before art" or what Walter Benjamin referred to as the regimes of the "exhibitional" and the "cultic." Sharma's predicament results from the realization that his art discourses are not reciprocated by his consumers, who desire objects of ritual utility that they can "get hold of." In the local "export of meaning" (Liebes and Katz 1990) a cultic domain of popular consumption emerges whose preferences and expectations are very different from those of the images' producers. Taussig's rereading of Benjamin permits us to rethink the ways in which local consumers "get hold" of mechanically produced images and to at last recognize the significance of Valery's claim (with which Benjamin prefaced "The Work of Art" essay): "In all the arts there is a physical component which can no longer be considered or treated as it used to be" (cited by Benjamin 1992: 211).

NOTES

1. The quoted phrase appears in a contemporary ad reproduced by Chabria.

2. Members of 117 households in the village were interviewed in 1995–96, and Lila's testimony is consistent with all but one of the others.

3. This corpothetics is often reinscribed as the owner traces the journey either with his eyes or his fingers in recalling the journey. Bhavaralal Ravidas pointed out various parts of his Pavagadh image as he traversed a mountainous pathway depicted in the image with his finger: "There is a temple here that you can't visit because there is a tiger living near the path."

4. The Hindi equivalent of this Malwi term is *visarjan*, meaning "ritual cooling."

5. These include, for instance, photographic images of a Surat-based guru, Shri Paramhansji (illustrated in Pinney 1997: 166) and some Jain images of the (literal) footprints of *acharyas*.

REFERENCES

Babb, Lawrence A. 1981. Glancing: Visual Interaction in Hinduism. *Journal of Anthropological Research* 37: 387–401.

Barnouw, Erik, and S. Krishnaswamy. 1980. *Indian Film.* New York: Oxford University Press.

Beard, Mary. 1992. Souvenirs of Culture: Deciphering (in) the Museum. *Art History* 15 (4).

Belting, Hans. 1994. *Likeness and Presence: A History of the Image before the Era of Art.* Translated by E. Jephcott. Chicago: University of Chicago Press.

Benjamin, Walter. 1992. The Work of Art in the Age of Mechanical Reproduction. In *Illuminations,* pp. 211–35. London: Fontana.

Berger, John. 1972. *Ways of Seeing.* Harmondsworth, England: Penguin Books.

Bryson, Norman. 1983. *Vision and Painting: The Logic of the Gaze.* New Haven, Conn.: Yale University Press.

Buck-Morss, Susan. 1992. Aesthetics and Anaesthetics: Walter Benjamin's Artwork Essay Reconsidered. *October* 62: 3–41.

Carpentier, Alejo. 1995. Baroque and the Marvelous Real. In *Magical Realism: Theory, History, Community,* edited by Lois Parkinson Zamora and Wendy B. Faris. Durham N.C.: Duke University Press.

Chabria, Suresh. 1994. D. G. Phalke and the Méliès Tradition in Early Indian Cinema. In *Light of Asia: Indian Silent Cinema,* edited by Suresh Chabria. New Delhi: Wiley Eastern.

Chakrabarty, Dipesh. 1992. Postcoloniality and the Artifice of History: Who Speaks for "Indian" Pasts? *Representations* 37: 1–26.

Davis, Richard H. 1997. *Lives of Indian Images.* Princeton, N.J.: Princeton University Press.

Dharap, B. V. 1985. Dadasaheb Phalke: Father of Indian Cinema. In *70 Years of Indian Cinema (1913–1983),* edited by T. M. Ramachandran, pp. 17–31. Bombay: CINEMA India-International.

Eck, Diane L. 1981. *Darsan: Seeing the Divine Image in India.* Chambersburg, Penn.: Anima Books.

Friel, Brian. 1981. *Translations.* London: Faber and Faber.

Grosz, Elizabeth. 1994. *Volatile Bodies: Towards a Corporeal Feminism.* Bloomington: Indiana University Press.

Heidegger, Martin. 1977. The Age of the World Picture. In *The Question Concerning Technology and Other Essays.* New York: Harper.

Kapur, Geeta. 1987. Mythic Material in Indian Cinema. *Journal of Arts and Ideas* 14/15: 79–107.

Liebes, Tamar, and Elihu Katz. 1990. *The Export of Meaning: Cross-Cultural Readings of Dallas.* New York: Oxford University Press.

Nandy, Ashis. 1995. The Discreet Charms of Indian Terrorism. In *The Savage Freud and Other Essays on Possible and Retrievable Selves,* pp. 1–31. Delhi: Oxford University Press.

Pinney, Christopher. 1997. *Camera Indica: The Social Life of Indian Photographs.* Chicago: University of Chicago Press.

———. 1999. Indian Magical Realism: Notes on Popular Visual Culture. In *Subaltern Studies X,* edited by Gautam Bhadra, Gyan Prakash, and Susie Tharu, pp. 201–33. Delhi: Oxford University Press.

Rajadhyaksha, Ashish. 1987. The Phalke Effect: Conflict of Traditional Form and Modern Technology. *Journal of Arts and Ideas* 14/15: 47–78.

Sontag, Susan. 1986. *Against Interpretation.* New York: Farrar Straus and Giroux.

Sprague, Stephen. 1978. Yoruba Photography: How the Yoruba See Themselves. *African Arts* 3 (1): 52–60.

Taussig, Michael. 1993. *Mimesis and Alterity: A Particular History of the Senses.* New York: Routledge.

Wadia, J. B. H. 1985. The Indian Silent Film. In *70 Years of Indian Cinema (1913–1983),* edited by T. M. Ramachandran, pp. 17–31. Bombay: CINEMA India-International.

19

Live or Dead?

Televising Theater in Bali

Mark Hobart

Television has come to attract vast mass audiences in many Asian countries in the 1990s. Among the issues this popularity raises are what happens when "traditional" media, such as theater, are broadcast on television. Drawing on ethnography from Bali, in Indonesia, I consider some of the questions involved. Bali is a particularly good case study because few societies are as famous for their popular theater and also have been catapulted so abruptly into the world of electronic mass media.

At first glance, the issue is fairly straightforward: how does a change of medium affect the performance, whether understood as the message, the text, or its effects upon the audience? However, this question presumes that there is a content, notionally separate from, and transcending, the form, the medium, and the circumstances of communication. Are we justified in applying this dichotomy to the practices of peoples in other parts of the world or, perhaps especially, to electronic media at all? The difficulties are compounded when electronic mediation, such as television, becomes a common mode of disseminating performances. How adequate is our existing language in dealing with new media? How appropriate is it to analyze television as something to be read, as a form of text, without stretching the notion of textuality to absurdity? To what extent should the task of anthropologists be to challenge the intellectual hegemony of textuality and demand critical inquiry into all the new kinds of practice that electronic media have brought about?[1]

THEATER AND TELEVISION IN BALI

Television has come to occupy an important place in Bali. The New Order regime of former President Suharto relied heavily on television to put across the priorities of economic and social development and to promote "culture" as a commodity and as the acceptable face of differentiation according to religion and ethnicity. Although state television is highly centralized, regional stations, most notably in Bali, have wrested free a significant number of slots, especially in evening prime time, for "cultural" broadcasts, often on minuscule budgets (see Hughes-Freeland 1992). How exactly programs get approved, financed, filmed, promoted, and broadcast—in other words, production practices—remains to be studied.

Other issues are clearer, however. Balinese actors are explicit that they much prefer performing before live audiences than in recording studios. In this essay I examine some of the differences discernible in the same plays as acted in front of village audiences and as broadcast on Indonesian state television. Such a study suggests that far more is at stake than actors' unfamiliarity with the exigencies of performing for television, with the inevitable differences between acting on stage and in television studios. Balinese theater, especially in the genres I consider, is largely extemporized around a minimal plot. So the circumstances under which the play takes place and the performance of the audience are crucial to what happens. Theater involves not just ad libbing the exchanges between actors, but also a less obvious, but overlapping, dialogue between actors and audience. In a different and little remarked upon way, the audience also performs.

In Bali, plays are not productions that are finalized before their performance, even though the minimal parameters of the plot have, of course, to be set for there to be a play at all. There seems to be no requirement to suspend disbelief comparable to that in European theater. Each performance, especially ones before live local audiences, is unfinalizable—and unrepeatable. The whole theatrical event hinges upon different sets of relationships working well simultaneously, notably those between audience and actors and among the actors themselves. Balinese theater depends on others to make it happen. The question "What are the differences between live and televised theater?" is therefore partly misplaced. Different performances depend upon different audiences and the relationship between actors and audiences. There is no essential, unsituated performance to measure.

Acting to the camera changes what is going on in complex ways. It is not just recording or broadcasting a theatrical event. For a start, it invites us to consider what is involved in dialogic models of social action and in communication itself. An inquiry into what happens with theater once performances start to be reproduced in different ways raises wider questions. From the moment that people become familiar with reading stories in newspapers, books, or as cartoons, with hearing them on radio, or with seeing them on television, the idea of theater itself is transformed. The possibility is born of discriminating nostalgically between authentic "live" performances and their mechanical or electronic reproduction. In fact, however, it is the contrast itself that creates the conditions of possibility of a privileged, essential, originary form, against which divergent versions may be compared. Once theater is reproduced electronically, live performance itself changes, because it is always framed against what it is not.

RESEARCH ON TELEVISION

The impact of television on theater can be judged by the fact that, according to the best estimate, over 80 percent of theater troupes in Bali disappeared during the 1980s, when audiences became bent on watching only "the best." With theater becoming a mainstay of local television peak-hour scheduling, I found myself caught up in frequent conversations between actors, whether as performers or viewers, who complained about the rigidity of the medium. Television had in fact become sufficiently important as to merit a research project in its own right.[2] A central part of the project was recording broadcasts of Balinese theater, and a way of testing and fleshing out the actors' appreciations was to commission performances of the plays previously recorded from television. We chose the occasion of local temple festivals in Tengahpadang, a pseudonym for the village where I have done research since 1970, because that is when Balinese themselves put on theater plays. The selection was made in collaboration with local aficionados of theater who chose which plays they had enjoyed the most and which they also considered to be good examples of their respective genres.

Villagers from Tengahpadang are enthusiastic and often knowledgeable theatergoers. If they found a play interesting, they talked about it, sometimes for days afterward.[3] Three of my Balinese colleagues were themselves actors. The oldest was a well-known Arja teacher and dancer, then in his early nineties. Another key figure was a former village head, who happened to be a skilled player of ministers and servants in the theater genre called Derama Gong. There was also a wealthy farmer and devotee of shadow theater; a very clever, but poor, flower-seller; and a tenant farmer who knew a great deal about theater but assumed a guise of naïve stupidity in company. His granddaughter, who was training as a actress-dancer, also took an active part. Various other friends and relatives who had watched the plays dropped in and out of the discussions of the plays. This essay draws on their conversations.

The play I analyze here was called *Gusti Ayu Ratih,* after the main character. It belongs to the Derama Gong genre (hereafter simply Derama), which sprang up in the late 1960s, not coincidentally after the abortive coup d'état in 1965. For nearly thirty years Derama was the rage. The plots are "modern" in the sense that the characters draw upon new fashions, such as the hero and heroine holding hands, and may allude to contemporary themes and interests, although they are still set in the unspecific precolonial past. Unlike much other theater that draws on adaptations of written stories, Derama is in effect set in a never-never land, where the good win and the bad get their just deserts. It bears little relationship to any contemporary social, political, or economic realm of lived experience.

The play was first serialized on Balinese television between March and April 1991; it was performed by the Bhara Budaya troupe, one of the best known on the island. The live performance was filmed as part of the television research project in August 1992 during temple festivals in Tengah-padang. Both the live and the televised performances lasted some seven hours, the latter having been broadcast in weekly hour-long episodes. The dialogue was extemporized. The bare outlines of the plots were set, but the order of scenes changed somewhat. I am not concerned here with the structure of the plots but with the relationships between the various parties involved in the occasion as a whole.

WARMING UP THE AUDIENCE

Balinese audiences require wooing to becoming engaged. A favorite topic among actors, and a corollary of interactive theater, is the difficulty of getting the play started. Even an experienced actor or dancer does not know who constitutes the audience each night, or their mood. (It is usual for the hosts to serve a meal backstage before the performance, with local dignitaries present. This gives the actors a chance to get a sense of the venue, local concerns, and so forth.) In Derama, it is commonly actors playing servants, either male or female, in comic roles, whose job it is to warm up the audience. Television performers, in contrast, know little about their audience and do not have any means of gauging its receptiveness.

Let us compare how the same pair of male actors worked a television audience and a local live show. The play was about Gusti Ayu Ratih, the sheltered and beautiful daughter of a minister to the court of Daha to whom the heir to the throne becomes attracted. He seduces and impregnates her, but, ensorcelled by a princess from another kingdom (who lusts after him), he abandons her. Ayu Ratih goes mad and runs wild in the forest before a wise hermit realizes what has happened and reconciles the two lovers. The opening half-hour or so has virtually nothing to do with the plot other than setting the scene.

THE TELEVISED VERSION

Two close servants of the prince, Gangsar and Gingsir, entered and began talking about the state of affairs in the kingdom of Daha. The scene was set, the television audience knew where they were narratively. They started in a low-key manner with two jokes about there being many food-sellers around the theater, trying out various routines to establish what would make this particular audience laugh. They moved to listing the kinds of cakes on sale in the stalls around the open theater stage, laying the foundations of a banter that would lead them to a popular Javanese song on television via a pun on a kind of cake, ketuk lèndri, which is close to the title of a song, "Getuk Lèndri."

The song made the spectators laugh, not because of the words, which were Javanese and these Balinese did not know, but at Gingsir's dancing a Javanese pop song and movements in the style of Jogèd Bungbung, a genre in which a female dancer invites and dances flirtatiously serially with male members of the audience. In the middle, Gingsir wove idiosyncratic noises into the song: Kaing! Kaing! which is the Balinese verbalization of a dog barking (Woof! Woof!). Gangsar told him to shut up (Cèk! Cèk!), the rebuke used to silence a dog. They switched to a takeoff on the sort of pop group that performs "Getuk Lèndri." Gingsir swung his arms and hands out to his sides ever more wildly in a parody of disco dancing, until he finally grabbed Gangsar—who looked suitably mortified—by the genitals.

At several points what the spectators are to make of what happens on stage is not clearly determined. It is not obvious to what extent the song is about broadening Balinese horizons or about domesticating, or making fun of, Javanese popular culture, which Balinese sometimes fear is becoming dominant in Indonesia. It would be satisfying to be able to interpret what happened as a commentary by peripheralized Balinese on their place within the Javanese-dominated Indonesian state. However I have little evidence that such a message was intended by the actors or appreciated by the audience. Analysts may speculate on what it is all *really* about, but the interpretive possibilities at many points in the play are carefully left open.[4] Many of the people I spoke to refused interpretation at all and said they simply enjoyed the event. On what grounds are we to claim to know better?

For the audience members in Tengahpadang who viewed a video of the televised play, the scene was an occasion for talking about a range of issues: from the cast's performance—what they enjoyed or found funny, sad, or moving—to cryptic sections of dialogue. Those who had been actors commented on technique, timing, and so on. At suitable junctures I asked the group direct questions. Did they find the exchange funny? Not particularly. Gangsar and Gingsir were often much better, but they had to be careful what they said in front of television cameras. More important, the television audience (from Tohpati, near Denpasar) was "raw"—their appreciation of theater was limited and they did little to help the actors. Why then did the television audience laugh? Because they were taken by surprise by the unexpectedly topical reference. Did anyone have an idea why they used that particular song? The group often gives live shows around Bali in addition to their televised appearances. So they have begun to run out of fresh jokes and have chosen a song that they know is likely to appeal to the young, while the older spectators enjoyed watching the send-up of the song. The overriding aim in any event is to make the audience like them, appreciate their performance, and want to pay to see them again. Here live theater has a great advantage over television. It is *ramé*, crowded, with the busy atmosphere that Balinese cherish. However lively Balinese may make watching television, it has become mostly domestic entertainment.

THE PLAY

The live performance of the play took place in front of the temple, Pura Dalem Kauhm, in Tengahpadang during the temple festival there. The seating for several hundred was sold out, and there was a further large crowd floating among the play, temple, stalls, and gambling groups. The play started conventionally, with a deep voice through the microphone offering an apology for any mistakes or faults on the part of the actors, a request to Divinity that the audience enjoy the performance and to bring peace of mind.

The same servants, Gangsar and Gingsir, were the first on stage. After some local references, they complained that they were poor servants who received only leftovers to eat and one checkered sarong each to wear. How much better the audience was turned out than they! Obviously the audience appreciated what is fitting according to Hindu religion and were dressed suitably for a temple festival.

Gingsir protested that he was ashamed to go to court in old clothes. But how was he to get new ones? He had no money. They despaired, until they suddenly came up with the idea that they could get money if one of them pretended to be dead. Ni Wayan Suci (a woman who was running a stall at the side of the show) would give Rp. 1,000 (then about U.S.$0.50) when she heard her relative, I. Gangsar, was dead (a further play on local knowledge). With some splendid mathematics, they worked out that, if they could manage to persuade two people to give Rp. 1,000 each, they would have 2 million rupiah and be rich! After some persuasion Gangsar agreed to mimic being dead. Gingsir whipped out a length of white cloth and put it over Gangsar, who promptly leapt up and ran in fear off stage (fearing that witches would think he really was a corpse and come and eat him). Gingsir had to go off and entice him back.

No sooner had the white cloth been put over him again than Gangsar had to get up to have a very public pee in the shrubbery that made up the back of the set. The two then sat down for a moment and gloated over what they could buy with all the money they would get. They would buy a car! Gangsar lay down again and promptly got an enormous erection. Gingsir asked him, "What dead person stands up like that?" and detumesced Gangsar hard with his foot, to a bar from the orchestra. Gingsir then threw himself into a wild fit of mourning, lifting his sarong to expose a vast pair of red underpants (not the sort of thing you do in a televised performance) and hurled himself about the stage howling in grief. Gangsar ran off again in fear and had

to be dragged back by Gingsir, who explained that he, Gingsir, had to cry re-
alistically if they were to get people to believe them and pay up.

Balinese are noted for their restraint in mourning. So once again how the
audience is to take this exchange is left open. There is no final interpretation.[5] It could be a commentary on, or caricature of, the difficulty or impossibility of ordinary people so rigorously repressing their feelings. It could
be a play on what the actors have seen on television and so frame Balinese
practice. By this stage, it should be evident that the task of theater is to encompass quite different points of view, a double- or multiple-voiced commentary. It is a singular form of commentary because the commentators do
not set themselves above what they comment on. On the contrary, they exemplify and embody it. In other words, we are dealing with the coexistence
of different points of view, even epistemologies, where the actors, who are
at once their own authors, refuse to allow themselves that "surplus of vision"
that distinguishes the authoritative author. The complex authors of the play,
the actors with the help of the audience, have no superior point of view; neither do they predetermine, except in the minimal terms set by the plot, how
the roles shall develop.

To return to the scene, Gingsir then went into a sort of comic dance to
show his misery. At this point the king of Kuripan entered and asked why he
was crying. The following is an edited version of their conversation:

Gingsir: Because Gangsar is dead.

Prince: But I was chatting to him only this morning.

Gingsir: He died all of a sudden. He said his stomach hurt, he got hiccups and
died.

Prince: (Obviously moved) Remember the words of wise priests, you should not
cry near to a corpse.

Gingsir: Yes.

Prince: It makes the passage harder for the soul of the deceased.

Gingsir: That's why I'm crying over here![6]

SOME LOCAL COMMENTS

The evening after the play I invited a group of people round and asked them
what they thought of the two versions of the play. The flower-seller said that
he liked the version in Tengahpadang much better than the televised version (which I had showed them on video some weeks earlier). The farmer
said that he did not really like either, because he did not like Derama on
principle, but he confessed that the live performance had made him laugh
and that the broadcast had not. The old actor disagreed sharply with them,
although he did admit the jokes were far funnier in the live version. He

specified in detail the differences and his reasons for preferring the televised version: the dancing was better, the actors' expressions were more developed, their movements were more appropriate to dance, and they followed the plot, with the correct stages of its introduction, which he listed and defined.

The ex-headman arbitrated. He opined that because the old actor was a professional, only he fully realized all the faults. The scene of playing dead was very clever because it hit several targets at the same time. The development of the jokes was much better in the live performance because the audience helped the actors much more than the theater audience in the televised version, who were stiff and unresponsive.

LIVE OR DEAD?

The contrasts between performances for television and for live local audiences were probably greater in the early 1990s than a decade later. Local audiences increasingly expected plays to be as-seen-on-TV and actors to replicate favorite routines from television performances. Casts became more adept at coping without audiences and so on. Certain broad differences remain discernible in the examples discussed. In televised performances there was greater restraint and formality in the style of dancing, and the structure of scenes and speech was more thought through. There were fewer attempts to improvise whole sections, although the dialogue was still extemporized. The jokes were more restrained. The actors did not set out to surprise the audience or one another as they might have done in live performances.

Most people agree now that actors on television are serious and feel weighed down by the occasion. Partly, of course, this is because of the draconian censorship imposed under Suharto, which takes the edge off the social criticism expected of theater. Obviously, actors have a far freer rein to engage in criticism before a live audience, when they are not being recorded. Johannes Fabian has made the point that such socially critical theater is quite common and that when academics capture such live moments of intellectual guerrilla warfare, as it were, in writing, they may imperil the people they work with (1991). The actors themselves, though, stress that they suffer the constraints of broadcasting to a large, heterogeneous, and unknown audience.

When actors complain of performances on television being dead (the word they often used was, literally, dead, *mati*), they are pointing to the absence of dialogue with the audience. To the actors, the television studio makes their performances closer to monologue. The dialogic world of Balinese theater enables us to see better how Europeans and Americans tend to fetishize texts and presume the naturalness of producer-centered models. A Balinese theater play is the complex product of the organizers of the occasion, the managers and actors of the troupe, and the audience. Because audiences are relatively silent in comparison with the actors does not mean that they are not agents. There are many kinds of quiet, including reflection, judgment, and waiting. Balinese actors know only too well that they have to convince and seduce each new audience.

The older villagers often complain that television, in combination with other aspects of development in Indonesia, is having deleterious effects. They say they fear a generation is emerging that is largely ignorant of the vast repertoire of previous practices, from medicinal cures to command of rhetorical skills. It was ever thus. It may or may not be true that fewer young people appreciate the subtleties of theater than did in the past. There is no way to measure the issue. What is true is that the best troupes and new genres take up much of the broadcasting time devoted to Balinese "culture" (one to two hours a night). Most of the local theater troupes have died out and with them much of the regional and local variation in style, which was so striking a feature of Bali. Balinese themselves widely attribute this change to televised theater. The move to increasing standardization and homogenization is not just due to television, but also to a broader aspect of the New Order's vision of culture as a commodity and means of ideological domination.

SOME IMPLICATIONS

The scenes of the play discussed earlier make little sense until they are treated as an engagement with the circumstances and the context of that particular performance. Significantly, then, the quality of the play is dependent upon, and so defined by, what is outside it. In other words, one cannot extract the essence of a performance from the contingent circumstances of the occasion. That is what Bakhtin called "theoretism," insisting on understanding events in terms of rules or structures and failing to appreciate how particular, open, and unfinished they are: "We cannot break out into the world of events from *within* the theoretical world. One must start with the act itself, and not with its theoretical transcription" (Bakhtin 1984–85: 91). Anthropologists often claim that, unlike their intellectual colleagues, they have long appreciated the dialogic and open nature of social life and are unfettered by the theoretism that blinkers other, more ethnocentric, disciplines. Ethnography starts with the act. That, at least, is the claim. The theoretical problems of imagining a theory-light description or translation of performance suggest we need to look more critically at works purporting to be "dialogic."

Mark Poster, one of the more thoughtful critics in media studies, has criticized transmission models of communication for reifying and fetishizing information at the expense of appreciating mediation as involving different kinds of social practice, which necessarily constitute knowledge, language, and its subjects or objects differently (1990: 43–68). Television itself, he argues, following Baudrillard, belongs to a broadcast model of communication, in a media age that is increasingly superseded by a new age of interactive media (1995), which requires us radically to rethink of our presuppositions about communication, its subjects, and its objects. Poster takes interactivity to be a function of new technologies. Yet as the scene outlined above shows, interactivity has likely always been around.

Poster, however, retains the language of message, referent, and sender/receiver, which a more radical version of Baudrillard would undermine. The object-subject duality also remains, with the audience being at once subject, object, and referent. A strength of Poster's analysis, however, is that it recognizes the extent to which the objects of analysis are not static but are produced and changed by social practices. This process notably includes the act of inquiry itself. A good example is the important controversy surrounding the nature of the audience. Is it the product of sociologically identifiable processes? Or is it inevitably a textual construction? The debate is haunted by the vestiges of representationism: how best to treat the relationship between text and fact?

Poster points to the problem: "When an individual watches a TV ad he or she is watched by a discourse calling itself science but in fact disciplining the consuming subject to the ends of rationality and profit" (1990: 49). Theoretical formulations of audiences are underdetermined by biomass, whether distributed on theater seats, on couches watching a cathode ray tube, or in statistical columns. Insofar as we can talk about them, audiences are the product of social practices that include both textualizing and naturalizing them, and much more besides. For the commentators in Tengahpadang, the televised play's audience in Tohpati was a moment of response, or rather lack of it, which they contrasted with other occasions. For actors performing on stage, the audience is closer to something disparate and unformed that they reach out to and try to seduce into a malleable interlocutor. For actors in television studios, it seems to be closer to something they have to imagine in its absence. In short, the point is that audiences are indeterminate. They are not reducible to subjects, objects, or textual constructs, ineffable or definite. Because audiences are the necessary (even if only imaginary) condition for a play, the congeries of practices that make up the media event in turn constitute audiences themselves.

SOME BROADER CONSIDERATIONS

These briefly examined extracts of Balinese theater shed light on critical dialogic analyses and received ideas about communication, particularly through the work of Bakhtin and Volosinov (1973). In almost any reading, dialogue is central to the work of Bakhtin, who used the term in at least three rather different senses in different contexts. Dialogue emerges as the mode of all utterance, in the sense that it is an extralinguistic element opposed to logic. In dialogue there is always an addressee, that is, the persons to whom the speech as a whole is addressed.[7] In Bali this is the theater audience. Television inhibits this dialogue but does not eradicate it: the addressee is still there but under different discursive conditions. There is also a super-addressee: the audience in yet another form. That audience comprises the imagined but immediate interlocutors who, in the last resort, the speaker is most concerned should understand him or her, be they Divinity, an ideal colleague, or the informed and appreciative spectator. Then there is dialogue in the sense of complex utterances, which contain within themselves the recognition of polyphony. Last there is dialogue as a global notion, with truth itself as dialogic (Bakhtin 1984a: 293). Dialogue shatters the monolithic nature of ideology by pointing out that it is an articulation made by agents to which there always have been, and in due course will be, counterarticulations.

Bakhtin provided different sketches of what he had in mind by polyphony, and they seem to be linked closely in some respects to what Balinese actors are engaged in. Polyphony suggests the coexistence of different historical consciousnesses. It presupposes beings who are situated, partly autonomous and irreducible to any single consciousness. A truly polyphonic work would consist of a "plurality of independent and unmerged voices and consciousnesses, a genuine polyphony of fully valid voices" (1984b: 6). This stands in contrast to the surplus of vision that authors of monologic works (whether novels, plays, or ethnographies) have over their characters and by means of which they finalize and close the narrative. In one sense Balinese theater exemplifies a significant degree of polyphony insofar as the actors develop their characters as beings in their own right and do not just go through the motions of patching together bits and pieces from past performances. However, the singular nature of extemporized multiauthored theater in Bali invites us to reconsider and develop the notion of polyphony to see where it leads.

The result is to swing attention toward the circumstances under which different representations are made, how assertions about structures, knowledge, and truth came to be articulated in the first place. Articulation then emerges as a crucial notion (Slack 1996). The point of articulation is that it brings together how ideas are related with the social and political practices through which they are mediated on specific occasions, placing attention firmly on the circumstances, purposes, and consequences of mediation, and so on how television works. Theater is one of a number of recognized and powerful modes of articulation by which Balinese set about understanding and commenting on the world into which they find themselves thrown. They do so using distinctive intellectual practices, which the participants themselves usually understand rather better than academics appreciate.

Though one might think that the shift from live to televised performance would be significant (and its apparent effect on numbers of theater troupes suggests that), it might be better to consider how Balinese theater, whether presented live or on television, consists of different degrees and kinds of dialogic performances. These occur simultaneously among actors; among scriptwriters, actors, and producers; between actors and audiences; between the producers (however conceived) and their targets; among viewers themselves; between one performance and its predecessors and successors; among ways of imagining the world. Although some recent work in anthropology has shown recognition of the complexity of representing the object of study of performance, I wonder how useful it is to try to address the problem by tinkering with modes of academic writing, which are pretty unremittingly monologic. While representing, by definition, transforms what it represents, what kinds and degrees of mediation are we dealing with, and to what effect?

I am suggesting that we consider not just unrecorded theater performances, but all the occasions on which performances are reproduced and enjoyed, as congeries of practices that require new kinds of engagement with Balinese theater and its audiences. The study of Balinese television should then arguably be the inquiry into all the new kinds of practice that electronic media have brought about, not least the authenticizing of unrecorded performances. Such a study would involve a degree of openness not common in anthropological and other academic analyses. A problem of studying audiences, and viewers' commentaries, is the precarious sense of contingency that hovers over the endeavor. As Balinese actors will tell you, to presume to anticipate how the next audience will respond is foolish. And the next commentary you hear may shatter the pattern you imagined to be emerging neatly through your inquiries. In the anthropological study of media, the usual criteria of closure, comprehensiveness, and certainty may well be the hallmark of the death of critical inquiry. Need openness, uncertainty, and indeterminacy be the prerogative of audiences?

NOTES

1. One of the more interesting spin-offs of the academic practice of textualizing is the textualizing and authenticizing of unrecorded performances as somehow original. Treating electronic mediation as derivative is not recognizing a fact of nature but imposing a set of—highly elitist—presuppositions.

2. The first aim of the project was to document and study important theater performances. The second was to study the impact of television on performance, and vice versa. In the absence of television archives or available materials on television, it was first necessary to record and document the range of broadcast materials on Balinese television. The resulting Balinese Television Project was a joint endeavor involving the School of Oriental and African Studies in London and STSI (the Indonesian Academy of Performing Arts) in Denpasar, Bali. A brief account of the project can be found in Hobart 1999. The recordings discussed below are part of an archive of over 1,500 hours of cultural materials broadcast by state television since September 1990, a selection of 150 hours of which have been encoded in MPEG and are available on CD for the use of scholars. The cameraperson for the live performances was Dr. Felicia Hughes-Freeland, who has extensive experience in ethnographic film

and who collaborated on the television project during its first three years (see Hughes-Freeland 1992).

3. I spoke at length with several of the actors, but my translation and analysis of the performances also relies heavily on the comments of villagers. I mention only the immediately relevant figures with whom I worked as a group, the setting in which Balinese commonly discuss theater.

4. If interpretive closure of the text hinges in some way on the original intention of the playwright, then it is often impossible in practice to know what this might be and how we would decide upon it. In what sense then is it useful even to try to determine intentionality in these quicksilver, ad-libbed, unrepeatable exchanges that depend so much upon the moment?

5. The analysis is mine but draws upon the commentators' disagreement over what, if any, significance Gingsir's crying had.

6. Gingsir engages in a play on textual authority by taking the terms of the text quite literally. It is also therefore rather a nice play on the conditions of referentiality.

7. Bakhtin's senses of dialogue are not therefore to be confused with the commonsense English usage, which is often not dialogic, as when an author farms out a single monologic idea between different speaker-functions.

REFERENCES

Bakhtin, M. M. 1984a. *Problems of Dostoevsky's Poetics*. Translated by C. Emerson. Minneapolis: University of Minnesota Press.

————. 1984b. Towards a Reworking of the Dostoevsky Book. Appendix 2 to *Problems of Dostoevsky's Poetics*. Translated by C. Emerson. Minneapolis: University of Minnesota Press.

————. 1984–85. Towards a Philosophy of the Act (K filosofii postupka.). In *Filosofiia i sotsiologiia nauki i tekhniki, a Yearbook of the Soviet Academy of Sciences,* translated by G. S. Morson and C. Emerson. Moscow: Nauka.

Fabian, J. 1991. Dilemmas of Critical Anthropology. In *Constructing Knowledge: Authority and Critique in Social Science,* edited by L. Nencel and P. Pels. London: Sage.

Hobart, Mark. 1999. The End of the World News: Articulating Television in Bali. In *Staying Local in the Global Village: Bali in the Twentieth Century,* edited by L. Connor and R. Rubinstein. Honolulu: University of Hawaii Press.

Hughes-Freeland, F. 1992. Representation by the Other: Indonesian Cultural Documentation. In *Film as Ethnography,* edited by P. Crawford and D. Turton. Manchester, England: Manchester University Press.

Poster, M. 1990. *The Mode of Information.* Cambridge, England: Polity Press.

————. 1995. *The Second Media Age.* Cambridge, England: Polity Press.

Slack, J. D. 1996. The Theory and Method of Articulation in Cultural Studies. In *Stuart Hall: Critical Dialogues in Cultural Studies,* edited D. Morley and K-H. Chen. London: Routledge.

Volosinov, V. N. 1973. *Marxism and the Philosophy of Language.* Translated by L. Matejka and I. R. Titunik. Cambridge, Mass.: Harvard University Press.

20

A Room with a Voice

Mediation and Mediumship
in Thailand's Information Age

Rosalind C. Morris

Somewhere, in Central Thailand, there is a spirit *(phii)* of such extraordinary power that it need not incarnate itself in order to be heard.[1] It speaks in a language that does not require any human to lend its voice.[2] It emanates from a room where mortals may go to be addressed, but it has no bodily location. And it leaves no trace. Or so the spirit mediums of Chiang Mai say. In the early 1990s they conveyed to me this fabulous rumor of a room with a voice, speaking with awe, and implicitly marking the limits of their own regionally marked practices in the process.[3]

It is probably safe to say that this story of a disembodied voice constituted the imaginary rendition of an ideal that would, by definition, forever elude the women and (less often) men of Northern Thailand in whom spirits may otherwise manifest themselves. Indeed, the story envisions the absolute effacement of mediation, the withholding of the sign in the moment of signification. As such, it is an ambivalent fantasy of modern possession performance, a fantasy in which mediums are themselves surpassed. My purpose here is to inquire about the conditions in which practitioners in a tradition of magical transmission come to embrace this fantasy of their own surpassing. In this essay, which asks to be read as a speculation as much as an argument, I want to suggest that this dream of a transmission so pure that it requires no medium is precisely the dream of mass mediation in the age of electronification. In their thrall to this dream, spirit mediums in Northern Thailand betray their own submission to a new modality of communication—electronic information—and the era of its emergent hegemony.

What can it mean to say that urban spirit mediumship in Northern Thailand has become modern, and even a symptom of a massified and electronified modernity? The answers to these questions are twofold. They address matters of both geopolitical history and technological modernity, and they open onto a complex dialectical story in which the Thai state's efforts to deploy media technology in the interest of an abstract, homogeneous space-time of national belonging have generated ironic apparitional after-effects. These aftereffects, which appear first in the mode of anachronism— as ritual "revival" and the belief in spirits who are always arriving from else-where—and then as the absolute untranslatability of the spiritual Real, testify to the impossibility of that smooth and silent space that is the fantasy of modern national cultural ideology. At the same time, they evidence the emergence of an utterly unprecedented signifying logic. These aftereffects appear as noise in the system even as they emanate the luminous image of a perfect transmission, an informational connection to a putatively pure presence beyond history and difference.

THE MEDIA, THE NATION, AND THE HISTORIES OF MASS MEDIATION

In the early 1990s, when spirit mediums described this disembodied voice to me, two issues seemed to beg special attention. The first issue concerned the strange form of locality that was attributed to the voice. The voice resided, or was said to manifest, in a room whose only specificity derived from its geopolitical situation, in Central Thailand *(phaak klaang)*. The location was significant, for Central Thailand is the ideologically unmarked center of national cultural discourse and the locus of state power, that blind spot of national vision from which local difference is seen and indeed rendered as the visible. It is also associated with the "standard" form of the Thai language, the bureaucratically official medium of the state and the instrument of national integration for more than a century (Diller 1991). Compared to Central Thailand's "standard" language, all other speech is notable for its departures (as regional accent or, in some cases, dialect variation).

In this context, then, the particular location of the rumored voice provokes questions about the relationships between Northern mediumship and national-cultural history. By remarking on the invisibility (bodilessness) of the voice, mediums parodied the state's discourse of standardization, repudiating the very possibility that language could ever be utterly dissociated from the accented body of sending. Not incidentally, the words for medium, *rang song* or *khon song cao*, can be translated literally as "the body of sending" or "the one who receives the prince." An improbable correspondence between the languages of magic and technology thus reveals the rapprochement between magic and mundane mediation and thereby points out that technological histories are also geopolitical ones.

One of the most remarkable features of this "story" is that, beyond location and the fact of transmission, it has no discernible message. No one ever told me what the voice had said. Neither could anyone answer my questions about the language or referent of its speech. The spirit spoke. It was, in fact, a speaking. And yet the spirit did not say anything. Every attempt at a description of the spirit's message was thwarted by this fundamental *aporia* in the rumor, for the communication had no content that anyone could relate. No reference to the world nor to moral orders had been conveyed, no lessons imparted. To the contrary, the speaking seemed to take place beyond the very question of meaning. Information theorists would perhaps describe this stumbling as the result of mediums' incapacity to address analytically what is, in fact, a radically new order of signification. For, in the idiom of information theory, the mediums were describing a transmission whose only "message" was the fact of that transmission. All that could be said was that a saying was "taking place." The speech was, as it were, on or off.

In this context it is tempting to say, simply, that the rumor thematizes the arrival of the electronic age, an arrival from without, masquerading as a story about Thailand's uneven entry into the future. In this case, we could say that mediums in urban Northern Thailand articulate a sense of belatedness in relation to technology, which they associate with Bangkokian modernity and to which they respond with a mirror dance of atavistic dimensions. But this rumor is not a response so much as an effect. In other words, the rumor partakes precisely of what McLuhan described as the mass media's logic. It contains that which went before and makes of the medium its own message. We will therefore want to consider not only the overt use of media technologies by spirit mediums and the "revival" of mediumship in general, but also the tendency for mediums to stage the dislocation of voice and language, body and truth, in the performance itself. As we shall see, such a staging is achieved in the noisy insistence on untranslatability as much as in the rumors of perfect transmission. However, after a century in which the values of arch-nationalism have been structured into the very organization of schools, the military, and official public culture, mediums have also come to espouse the tenets of its self-representation, including monarchism, Buddhism, and anticommunism. The result is that, in mediumship, difference speaks in a Northern Thai accent, and universal speech resides in Central Thailand.

REPRESENTING MEDIUMSHIP: PAST AND FUTURE HISTORIES OF TRANSMISSION

In Friedrich Kittler's analysis, it is the perception of the relation of writing to orality as one of loss and irremediable absence that summons the invention of new media, including both phonography and cinema (1999). It is, moreover, the displacement of writing by new media that finally nullifies the sense of belatedness that accrues to writing and makes of communication a matter of information or noise. In the meantime, there is nostalgia, a period of forgiveness in which the past becomes not merely that which is irrevocably outside of writing, not merely that which needs representation (in both political and aesthetic senses), but indeed, that which is desired, that which wants to be "restored."

Such a nostalgia has transformed the perception of both Northern Thailand and spirit mediumship over the past half-century. For as long as ritualism could be perceived as the meaningless repetition of gesture, and for as long as the belief in magic was deemed to be a misrecognition of linguistic power—a mistaking of representational capacity for transformative effect—Northern Thai religiosity, and especially spirit possession, would remain the objects of disavowal for the Buddhist orthodoxy centered in Bangkok. Popular sentiment was mainly allied with official opinion in this regard, and mediumship began to decline in the urban areas of Northern Thailand. When, however, the absence in writing could be thematized under the rubric of authenticity, Northern Thailand's status as the metonymic sign of ritualism and orality could make it an object of longing (Morris 2000).

The kind of mediumship that functions in this way as an object of nostalgic investment is one in which magical practice has been neutralized as such and converted into a mere sign of pastness. Indeed, it is from this assemblage of mutely signifying performances that the bodiless speech of the spirit described at the beginning of this paper departs, and it is worth considering this ethnographically more familiar kind of mediumship before returning to phantasms of mass-mediated transmission. In general, possession performances in Northern Thailand are overtly bodily affairs in which the fact of reincarnation by powerful beings is explained in terms of *kammic* debt.[4] Normally, spirits are said by mediums and their acolytes to return to this world in order to make merit *(bun)* because they failed, somehow, to compensate for the demerit *(bap)* that the violent founding of a law-bound polity necessarily entails. Mediums themselves come from a variety of class positions, though at present most are at least of lower-middle-class standing (a minimal amount of disposable income being necessary to purchase the accoutrements of possession performance).[5] They are bound by affliction but not by kin, and after the long apprenticeship in which they accommodate themselves to the demands of daily possession, they tend to assume private professional practices, recognizing each other only on formal occasions of tributary dancing, when the spirits of a single tutelary overlord gather together to express their fealty in the mode of bodily grace.[6] The possessing personae of mediums often take the form of generic types—princes, Buddhist saints, and hermits *(rysii)*—but the most famous and the most powerful are named figures associated with the births of cities, states, or new, and especially Buddhist, eras: Prince Saeng Muang Ma, Queen Chamadevi, Kings Naresuan, Chulalongkhorn, and Ramkhamhaeng.

In the typified discourse of Northern Thai mediums, the birth of rule (in the sense of both regulation and regularity that are proper to the French term *règle*) produces an unexpiable stain on the soul of even the most righteous ruler. So the ruler who founds a city, an empire, or a new era of moral being must return and cancel his failure, which is also his debt, by inculcating a knowledge of the *dhamma* in the subject who will attend his words. Official Buddhism, and especially the scripturalist orthodoxy of the dominant Thammayut sect, frowns upon mediumship as an indulgence in false ontology and accuses its practitioners of both ignorance and dissimulation. However, mediums are emphatic in their claims to membership in Buddhism's community, and they are outspoken advocates of what they take to be the truth and law of *dhamma*. This is why contemporary spirit mediums are overtaken by the spirits of rulers, and this is why spirits speak to lesser individuals. In possession, the spirit *gives* the law that, before, when he was a ruler, he *required by force*.[7]

Now, after a century of reform in religious, jural, and political domains, the medium transmits in speech and corporeal form the sense of an originary utterance that once worked magically. What is communicated is a distilled and indeed clichéd rationale for ethical action in the world. Mediums replay, again and again, the inheritance of law, as such, which the Buddha gave to his students and which they communicated in oral teachings and then wrote down. In this, they ironically reenact their own encompassment by both centrist reform Buddhism, inaugurated in the mid-nineteenth century during a period of nation-building, and the statist bureaucracy that was associated with it. They communicate other messages, of course: about the auspicious dates for planting rice fields, taking college exams, or selling stock; about the causes of illness and the procedures for effecting a cure; and about the sources of familial tension. But all of these messages are inserted into another meta-discourse on the nature of the moral universe. There is a calculus of action whose axes are those of filial piety, social hierarchy (including both gendered and generational hierarchy), devotion to the nation, and adherence to the principle of monarchical authority. Illness is invariably explained as the result of a transgression of the law. And catastrophe is almost always the sign of a universe's displeasure at impertinence, greed, lust, or simple self-indulgence.

Although marginal, spirit mediumship in Northern Thailand has rarely been politically oppositional, save in defense of northern aristocracy against southern or central aspiration. By the 1970s, mediums sounded every bit like the politically conservative monks who were espousing the assassination of communists, and their discourses had become obsessed, as Walter Irvine has remarked, with phantasms of communist infection and border penetration (Irvine 1982). But something else was also happening. The very orality of possession performance, the dramaturgy of an inspired speech, was beginning to function as a sign of authenticity itself, of that primal relation to origins that, it was said, had been lost in and by modernity. Like the shamans so beloved by media theorists like Walter Ong, Northern Thailand's mediums came to represent oral culture. Indeed, this is the source of their status as *representatives* of "popular Buddhism" in public, state-sponsored ceremonies celebrating a now-commodified ethnic diversity in Thailand. More than this, though, mediums began to embrace those technologies that previously threatened their own auratic value: photography, and later, film. Photographs began to appear in the shrines of mediums, and self-documentation became a signal part of the fame game in which mediums competed with each other for renown. As this happened, noise entered the system, and the voluptuous rites of pastness were interrupted by sounds without meaning, speech without content. Untranslatability began to proliferate in new communities of mediums wherein new techniques of ecstasy and bodily transcendence have begun to assume prominence.

In the past decade or so, Chiang Mai's relatively sedate community of mediums has been augmented by the arrival of other mediums, who, coming from the South and being of mainly Sinothai descent, are adherents of more flamboyant, Saivite-influenced traditions. These traditions entail feats of physical endurance and ecstatic trance—including fire-walking, body-piercing, and the like—which are otherwise rare in the North (though quite common in the South and Southeast of the country). Patronized by wealthy military henchmen, entrepreneurs, mafia bosses, and other gamblers of the late capitalist world, this new tradition has, as one of its most salient features, the theatricalization of unintelligible speech. Other kinds of possession have always been marked by a speech that is said by adherents to manifest the dialect or the accent of antiquity, mainly in the form of a bluntly pronounced Thai Yuan (Northern Thai). The new kinds of mediumship, however, inhabit the cusp of a more radical illegibility.

In some rare instances, contemporary possession may be marked by what linguists would formally term glossolalia.[8] But more frequent than this kind of unredeemably nonsensical speech is that whose untranslatability is performed as a function of mediation itself. This latter untranslatability is marked, rather ironically, by the presence of teams of translators, who accompany the medium during possession and act as interlocutors for those seeking divination or therapy. They often remark on the difficulty of their task, describing their first encounters with the spirit's speech as ones of terror in the face of a meaning that they were inadequate to apprehend but knew they needed. But they also describe the gift that the spirit bestowed upon them as a miraculous ability to discern meaning in the guttural, atonal grunts and moaning near-words that emit from the medium during possession. Sometimes they consult with each other to clarify particulars when, for example, the persona of Siva screams instructions for herbal treatments or demands that an ascetic regimen be undertaken by the client. As though the labor of translation itself were something mitigated by being rendered a communal task, they collaborate to undertake a heroic hermeneutics. Occasionally, they admit their limits and say, simply, that they do not understand, that Siva has not made himself available to them, and that, unfortunately, they are too feeble to traverse the space between humanity and divinity.

The more visible and the more alienated the process of translation, the more heroic is its accomplishment, of course. But heroism itself opens a chasm between the spirit and the recipient of the spirit's instructions and makes of speech a blunt and inadequate medium for the transmission of power or meaning. It is in this context that one recognizes how significant is the fact that the mediums themselves often claim to have received instructions in dreams, having had the image *(ruup)* of a shrine or a gesture implanted in their unconscious by the spirit—the image itself being a trace of the spirit's communicating presence.

The story of a room with a voice has exceeded even this suspicion of language's incapacity to transmit anything other than itself, of course. For it gives off no image whatsoever. But in the dramas of untranslatability and in the privileging of the immediacy of dream-images, mediums also submit to a new regime in which the failure of communication is attributed to the inadequacy of the medium, either language or the body itself. In these instances, it is clear that the aspiration of mediation is the disclosure of the Real, which otherwise cannot be contained in or by language. Like phonography and cinema, the newly "revived" mediumship theatricalizes the body—as the Real—by making that body, its sounds and textures, the very stuff of transmission. The untranslatability of the utterance is then the excess of the body. Its gutteral sounds, convulsive exclamations, and sound without shape or tone constitute sensuality at the point of senselessness. Strangely enough, this new sense of the medium as a body of sending then demands to be recorded, giving back, in a twice alienated fashion, what was lost, in so many ways, to writing and especially the writing of prose.

The medium most renowned for his fire-walking and the untranslatability of his speech is also the master of what can only be called media-technological auto-archiving. His sprawling compound includes a media room in which are kept catalogued videotapes of his possession performances and the preparation that precedes them. These are professionally edited, overlaid with music tracks from Indian cinema, and subtitled with dates and credits. Such an elaborately self-aestheticizing practice is perhaps more extreme than that of most mediums in Chiang Mai today, but it is certainly not unique. On major ritual occasions, such as praise ceremonies *(phithii yok khru),* one is apt to encounter several videographers. They arrive early to light the space of shooting and to check out camera angles and then move freely during the proceedings, seemingly unconcerned about their effect on the ceremony. These are not tourists (though foreign television cameras are not infrequent at the more prominent public events) but commissioned archivists whose job is to produce a record, to store the performance for future consumption and recall by the medium and her or his clients. If a certain humor afflicts the conversations about filming and the seeming hubris of a medium imagining herself "as a movie star" (as it often does), it is tempered by pathos. For the video will probably only be seen by the medium, and perhaps her most immediate kin and assistants. The archiving is primarily a private affair, the archive a personal memory bank—albeit in the form of infinite publicizability. Ultimately, it only redoubles the alienation that the medium experiences from herself and from the spirit during possession, for, in Northern Thai possession, the rupture of subjectivity during possession is absolute, its mark being a total forgetfulness of what transpired during possession.

Beyond the fact that everyone in Thailand is now, as it were, possessed by photography, compelled by the technology of future remembrance to imagine every event as a potential souvenir, one wonders about this archiving. What failures within more "traditional" forms of mediumship account for the alacrity with which mediums now submit themselves to media-technological archiving practices, producing video libraries of their performances, and photo albums in which newspaper stories of their public appearances are documented? What failure is transcended by the voice without medium? One imagines, for a moment, that the videos will supplement memory, acting as prostheses for the medium who has been so evacuated as to be without memory of her body's experience. The video would, one surmises, capture or re-present the spirit for the viewer, making the occasion of possession endlessly repeatable as a spectatorial experience—even for the one who served as the vehicle for this presencing. There is no doubt that the tapes generate visual pleasure, that they are consumed with the languor that accompanies soap opera viewing—if only by a small circle of intimates. But what they present to their viewers, and especially those viewers who, as mediums, are featured in them, is not the spirit but the medium. One sees the body possessed, its vomiting and convulsions, its mechanical assumption of princely attire, its tributary dancing, its speaking, and its laying of hands upon the bodies of afflicted clients. But one does not "see" the spirit, any more than one sees a life essence or, in Buddhist idiom, those thirty-two life essences that are said to constitute the living soul of the human. The body appears in the video as a material signifier, the evidence of possession, but the video does not give access to the presence of the spirit. It defers that presence, endlessly. One wants to say that it makes the medium the message.

McLuhan has already said it, of course: every medium has as its content another medium. But it is one thing to say that film had photography and audiotape within it, or that "the fact that the minimal unevenness between stroke and paper can store neither a voice nor an image of a body presupposes in its exclusion the invention of phonography and cinema" (Kittler 1999: 9). It is quite another to suggest that mediumship partakes of this structure. The disjuncture between the person of the medium and the person of the spirit, which is always remarked upon in possession performances and in the conversations that surround them, is accentuated in the video. The medium watches and is split in watching. She is there, in her home, watching the screen when her image appears, and in this moment of uncanny doubling she observes herself as one who is possessed, acting like a stranger. Sometimes, she will remark—with shame or shy delight—that the spirit is unlike her: impolite, regal, powerful, obscene, lecherous, drunken, loud, violent. She will see someone who is not not herself but who nonetheless resembles her, smoking when she is a nonsmoker. He will see someone who is not not himself but who resembles him, as a physically strong man when he is frail. She will see herself desire a woman. He will see himself abuse a woman. The medium appears, as they so often say, "like a stranger" *(baep farang)*. She "does not know herself" *(mai ryy tua)*. Something, namely the body of the medium, is experienced as an interruption that obstructs the flow of information and introduces, if not feedback, then at least a question. In the era of electronic media, this complex mirror stage of mediumship offers less an ideal image than an image of radical difference, one that is unrecuperable even within the myths of origins that continue to infuse the practice in the age of national theme parks and transnational tourism. This does not prevent Japanese news stations from sending cameramen to document and store the disappearing world of Northern Thai mediumship. But disappearance is not the risk now. What threatens Northern Thai mediums now is simply the extravagant florescence of communication, the possibility that the noise of movement across the channels of transmission will obliterate all sense.

MORE HISTORIES OF THE FUTURE

Kittler remarks both that cinema and phonography are motivated by the desire to *restore* the presence that writing could not store in itself, and that these media are "engulfed by the noise of the real" (Kittler 1999: 14). It is, for him, the hissing of the phonograph and the fuzziness of the cinematic image that marks the Real's intrusion into, and interruption of, the hallucinatory homogeneity of meaning that is associated with writing and thence with the symbolic. Cinema and phonography do not, then, merely complete or supplement writing. They do not store what writing could not, but something entirely other: not the symbolic but the Real. And in the wake of the split between these dimensions, whose analysis in the form of psychoanalysis Kittler reads as mere symptom (ibid: 15), it became possible for the Real to overwhelm everything else. It is, in fact, this domination by the Real— and the concomitant belief in indexicality—that makes the media's domination of writing possible.

One then discerns two stages in the recent history of mediumship's revival in Chiang Mai. That revival, beginning in the 1960s, must be placed in relation to the prior moment of near disappearance and seen as a function of mediumship's capacity to represent orality in the face of confluent factors that, together, facilitated the apparent homogenization of the Thai polity. Among these were: the rendering of nontextualist Buddhism in the idiom of the "popular";[9] the consolidation of state authority and the integration of regional populations through the policies of cultural Siamification (see Barmé 1993; Reynolds 1991); and the imagination of alterity as an extranational entity whose most dangerous form was Chinese and Vietnamese communism. In this milieu, mediumship could and did appear to be the return of the body, that practice which communicates the magicality of utterance, the full presence and force of a voice that appeared to be lost by the asceticism of writing and textualist Buddhism. It could seem like the restoration of the dead as presence because it was the performance of an orality liberated from its entombment by the forces of Buddhist scripturalism. But this was only possible because it also was inhabited by the force of that scripturalism, because it took on the form of a codified and rationalized morality. This is the significance of the discourse of *kam* that is imparted in the exchanges between mediums and clients. And more than any other, the codification of the moral law is the act whose repetition marks the history of Buddhism in modern Thailand.[10] Mediumship partook of both textuality and orality, only, however, because writing itself was on the wane. Its revival was in fact a symptom of that development.

One might say, then, that mediumship of the 1960s and 1970s was to the *sangha* (Buddhist clergy and institutions) what phonography was to writing. Certainly this was the age of radio's hegemony, the period in which sound recording had made possible the integration of the nation as a listening and not merely a reading community. The point of phonography, in Kittler's reading of its effect on European thought, is that it was associated with a radical break, a movement from the belief that language was communication of something divine, to the merely oppositional distinction between noise and information. Says Kittler, speaking of Edison, "articulateness becomes a second-order exception in a spectrum of noise" (1999: 23). The phonograph inaugurated a new era of inscription in which writing would no longer necessarily have a subject, when signs would appear and signify nothing other than themselves or the fact of signification (ibid: 44). Kittler reminds us that the phonograph does not hear itself and that the difference between the medium and the subject is precisely that the former does not hear itself. This is as true of the possession vehicle as it is of the phonograph, of course. And when the spirit medium views herself on video, she does not hear the voice of herself any more than does the tape itself, for what is heard there is simply the instrument of speaking, disarticulated from meaning (the spirit). Possession, always described in the language of inspiration despite its formalization, is now, in Northern Thailand, a matter of accidental convergences.

The spirit borrows what is at hand. Language appropriates a voice, but there is no necessary relationship between the medium and the message, only the message of a medium in whom articulateness is "an exception" and whose very body generates noise. The dramaturgy of untranslatability alienates this fact and thereby emphasizes it, in a Brechtian fashion. Noise enters the system, a function of transmission itself. Meaning is not transparent and, in the end, becomes secondary to the fact that transmission is possible. What needs to be understood here is that the new theatricalization of mediumship (one wants to say mediation) takes place not in the age of phonographic storage but in the age of full digitization. And this is as true of orthodox Buddhism as it is of spirit mediumship.

Consider, for example, the rise of organizations like Dhammakaya, the massively popular and highly technologized Buddhist movement whose abbot came under scrutiny in the late 1990s by the Supreme Patriarchy of the *sangha*. Dhammakaya is a form of Buddhism that is perhaps best compared to the kind of Christianity manifested by Pat Robertson's "700 Club." Now at the center of a scandal by virtue of the ordination status of its leader, the organization boasts millions of members, many of whom come from the financial bourgeoisie. Its infamous mass gatherings attract hundreds of thousands of longing devotees, but more than these colossal meetings it is the mass-mediatization of Buddhism that is associated, in local press accounts, with Dhammakaya. With television stations, newspapers, web-based information sites, and digitally integrated information systems, Dhammakaya is religion for the twenty-first century, its hallmark being the promise of an accelerated access to the next level of existence, and ultimately, to *nibbana*. Devotees anticipate the completion of a facility that can accommodate a million people, and some attend services in the massive outdoor temple complex where more than 40,000 individuals can receive amplified sermons, but in the meantime, all can link up to the organization via the World Wide Web [www.dhammakaya.th.org]. They may do this from home or from the myriad cyber-cafes or information system offices that have opened in many major cities in the past decade. A homepage site with voluptuous graphics and sound-byte representations of the movement's pop-psychology-influenced philosophy permits a simultaneous and dispersed community of readers far more extensive than Benedict Anderson's account of print-based nationalism could ever have imagined (Anderson 1983). The website does not, of course, mention that the organization operates more than a hundred shell companies, that some of its real estate transactions have been deemed illegitimate by the state, and that its ordination practices violate the standards set by the Supreme Patriarchy. But it reveals what must surely be evident in the minds of adherents, namely that the charges brought by the Patriarchy, which rely upon traditionalist readings of scripture, cannot mitigate the force of electronification upon the very conception of the world that modern Thai subjects inhabit. That world is one dominated not by writing but by the media. It is a world in which noise dominates precisely because, quantitatively, a maniacally accelerating transmission of information must cross an almost infinite number of channels, and each crossing produces a sound as spasmodic as that generated in the translation between computer systems and telephonic codes.

Everywhere that one looks in the cities of Thailand one sees the evidence of this intensifying and involuting web of transmission. During the democracy protests of 1992, for example, when rallying opponents of the military regime massed at Sanam Luang, more than 200,000 telephone calls were made from the protest site each day. Journalists remarked on this fact and saw it as testimony to the bourgeois quality of the democracy movement. This was a correct apprehension. But it was more than this. It was the breaking open of a new era.

Apparent in the fantasies of a room with a voice and in dramas of untranslatability, the new era is marked by new thresholds of the thinkable and new kinds of miracles. Outside of Siva's possession shrine (in whose interior recesses translators are agonizing over the interruption of information that the medium's body has introduced), a client is having a cellular telephone conversation with his stockbroker. He is instructing the broker to sell, and to bring land title deeds, whose sale he is also orchestrating, to him for signature. The signature, last residue of a belief in the irreducibility of the author, does not attenuate the fact that, from this phone call, an informational signal will be sent into the unreal world of cyberspace. There it will effect the transfer of title between parties who have no relation and never will have any relation to each other. In an instant: on and off. The message will fly around the globe as miraculously as the spirit who descends from another time. Perhaps, on some future occasion, the telephone line will become the repository of radio signals that were sent long ago, or which are being sent elsewhere but are overheard nonetheless. Uncanny doublings that make mediumship return again and again, to restore what comes from without, these fantasies still have the power to move people. On the periphery of a nation that is on the periphery of global order, people respond to the calls of technology as though they had summoned it themselves. And often, it is hard to know the difference.

NOTES

1. Central Thailand *(phaak klaang)* is the name of a region, distinguished from Northern Thailand *(phaak nüa)*, Northeast Thailand *(Isaan)* and Southern Thailand *(phaak tai)*. With Bangkok as its capital, Central Thailand is the most politically powerful and populous of the regions. From the perspective of many northerners, it is inextricably associated with the cultural politics of Siamese ethnic hegemony, hav-

ing been the seat of monarchical and bureaucratic power during the period of national identity formation. For discussions of the history in which the enforcement of Siamese cultural, linguistic, and political domination was achieved (through military and legislative means) in the North, readers may wish to consult Ratanaporn Sethakul 1989 and Ramsey 1971.

2. I owe this understanding of mediumship, as a process in which humans lend their voice to language, to James Siegel's discussion of possession and dreaming in Atjeh (Siegel 1978).

3. This research was conducted between 1991 and 1993 with funding from the Social Science Research Council, the University of Chicago, York University, and the John D. and Catherine T. MacArthur Foundation. In Thailand, I benefited enormously from the assistance of Anan Ganjanapan, Ruthaya Abukorn, and Kruamas Woodtikarn.

4. The locus classicus for studies of Northern Thai spirit mediumship is Shalardchai Ramitanondh's *Phii Cao Naai (Spirits of the Lords and Masters)* (1984). In English, see Cohen and Wijeyewardene 1984. Also see Wijeyewardene 1986 and Tanabe 1991.

5. Records from the nineteenth century indicate that, though not exclusive to the aristocratic classes, princely families had mediums attached to themselves. In some cases, these mediums exercised considerable influence over political decision-making. A particularly famous account is provided in Carl Bock's travelogue *Temples and Elephants*.

6. These occasions take place during the season of Buddhist lent and are referred to as *phitthii yok khruu*, or the "rites of praising the teacher." As the number of mediums has grown in Chiang Mai, the season itself has extended and now lasts for more than two months. Mediums travel from their homes to the sites of other spirits (whether these be private dwellings or public locations, such as the City Pillar of the Northeast Corner of the City) and are possessed en masse. The events themselves are orchestrated by acolytes and assistants and are scheduled well in advance. Printed invitations are sent forth among the mediums of a particular "lineage" of spirits according to the astrologically determined time of devotion. It should be noted, however, that the "lineage" is not a kin-based entity so much as it is a group of mutually obliged but hierarchically ordered individuals. For a fuller discussion of the new economy of mediumship and the politics of nostalgia that have transformed it into a sign of history, see Morris 2000.

7. My understanding of the aporetic structure of law's founding is, in many regards, indebted to Jacques Derrida's seminal essay "Force of Law" (1990).

8. Marjorie Muecke, personal communication.

9. The idea of "popular Buddhism" is generally attributed, in Thailand, to Phya Anuman Rajadhon, the "father of Thai folklore." The venerable monk's interests in ethnological renderings of unorthodox practices owed much to his friendship with Prince Damrong, the monumentally talented and productive younger brother of King Rama V, who oversaw judicial reform and bureaucratic modernization and who is treated as the primary historiographer of modern Thailand. Damrong's virtuosity aside, the force of ethnology in Thailand was significantly determined by the discourses of modernity that were circulating more widely in the world. For an account of the force of social typification in Thailand and its relationship to the problem of mediumship and popular Buddhism, see Morris 2000. Anuman's work itself has been

translated into English under the iconic title of *Popular Buddhism and Other Essays on Thai Studies* (1986).

10. David Wyatt has gone so far as to suggest that the first "subtle" revolution of the modern took place with the decision, on the part of Rama I, to codify and categorize the corpus of Buddhist texts. But other historians have devoted more attention to the systematic efforts at codification undertaken by Rama IV. In most cases, however, such codification is inextricably bound up with the eschewing of ritualism and the claiming of Buddhism's modernity (see Wyatt 1995; Reynolds 1976).

REFERENCES

Anderson, Benedict. 1983. *Imagined Communities: Reflections on the Origin and Spread of Nationalism.* London: Verso.

Phya Anuman Rajadhon. 1986. *Popular Buddhism and Other Essays on Thai Studies.* Bangkok: Thai Inter-Religious Commission for Development and Sathirakoses Nagapradipa Foundation.

Barmé, Scot. 1993. *Luang Wichit Wathakan and the Creation of a Thai Identity.* Singapore: Institute of Southeast Asia Studies.

Bock, Carl. [1885] 1985. *Temples and Elephants.* Bangkok: White Orchid.

Cohen, Paul T., and Gehan Wijeyewarden. 1984. Introduction. *Mankind,* special issue no. 3: Spirit Cult and the Position of Women in Northern Thailand, 14 (4): 249–62.

Derrida, Jacques. 1990. Force of Law: The Mystical Foundation of Authority. In *Deconstruction and the Possibility of Justice,* edited by Drucilla Cornell, Michael Rosenfeld, and David Gray Carlson, pp. 3–67. New York: Routledge.

Diller, Anthony. 1991. What Makes Thai a National Language? In *National Identity and Its Defenders: Thailand 1939–89,* edited by Craig J. Reynolds, pp. 87–132. Chang Mai: Silkworm.

Irvine, Walter. 1982. The Thai-Yuan "Madman," and the Modernizing, Developing Thai Nation as Bounded Entities under Threat: A Study in the Replication of a Single Image. Ph.D. diss., University of London.

Kittler, Friedrich. 1999. *Gramophone, Film, Typewriter.* Translated by Geoffrey Winthrop-Young and Michael Wutz. Stanford, Calif.: Stanford University Press.

Morris, Rosalind. 2000. *In the Place of Origins: Modernity and Its Mediums in Northern Thailand.* Durham, N.C.: Duke University Press.

Ramsey, James Ansil. 1971. The Development of a Bureaucratic Polity: The Case of Northern Siam. Ph.D. diss., Cornell University.

Ratanaporn Sethakul. 1989. Political, Social, and Economic Changes in the Northern States of Thailand Resulting from the Chiang Mai Treaties of 1874 and 1883. Ph.D. diss., University of Illinois.

Reynolds, Craig J. 1976. Buddhist Cosmography in Thai History, with Special Reference to Nineteenth Century Cultural Change. *Journal of Asian Studies* 35 (2): 203–20.

————. 1991. *National Identity and Its Defenders: Thailand 1939–89.* Chiang Mai: Silkworm.

Shalardchai Ramitanondh. 1984. *Phii Cao Naai (Spirits of the Lords and Masters).* Chiang Mai: Faculty of Social Sciences, Chiang Mai Unversity.

Siegel, James. 1978. Curing Rights, Dreams, and Domestic Politics in a Sumatran Society. *Glyph* 3: 18–31.

Tanabe, Shigeharu. 1991. Spirits, Power and the Discourse of Female Gender: The Phi Meng Cult in Northern Thailand. In *Thai Constructions of Knowledge,* edited by Manas Chitrakasem and Andrew Turton, pp. 183–212. London: SOAS.

Wijeyewardene, Gehan. 1984. Northern Thai Succession and the Search for Matriliny. *Mankind* 14 (1): 286–92.

————. 1986. *Place and Emotion in Northern Thai Ritual Behaviour.* Bangkok: Pandora.

Wyatt, David. 1995. The Subtle Revolution of Rama I of Siam. In *Studies in Thai History,* pp. 131–72. Chiang Mai: Silkworm.

CONTRIBUTORS

LILA ABU-LUGHOD is professor of anthropology and women's studies at Columbia University. She has written on gender, expressive culture, and sentiment in the Middle East, as well as on the politics of representations. Her books include *Veiled Sentiments: Honor and Poetry in a Bedouin Society*, *Writing Women's Worlds*, and *Remaking Women: Feminism and Modernity in the Middle East*. She is currently writing a book on the cultural politics of Egyptian television drama.

ARLENE DÁVILA is associate professor of anthropology and American studies at New York University. She is the author of *Sponsored Identities: Cultural Politics in Puerto Rico* and *Latinos, Inc.: The Marketing and Making of a People*, about the Hispanic advertising industry. Her previous work and research interests concern issues of identity and representation as manifested in popular and expressive culture.

BARRY DORNFELD is an ethnographer of communication, a documentary filmmaker, and the director of the Communication Program at the University of the Arts in Philadelphia. He is the author of *Producing Public Television, Producing Public Culture* and the coproducer of documentary films including *Powerhouse of God* (1988), *Gandy Dancers* (1994), and *Plenty of Good Women Dancers: African-American Women Hoofers in Philadelphia* (1997).

TEJASWINI GANTI is a postdoctoral fellow in the Department of Anthropology at Haverford College and the Center for Visual Culture at Bryn Mawr College. She received her Ph.D. in anthropology from New York University, as well as a certificate from the Anthropology Department's Program in Culture and Media. She has published a number of articles based on fieldwork in Bombay in 1996 and is working on a book based on her dissertation on the Hindi film industry, "Casting Culture: The Social Life of Hindi Film Production in Bombay." Her documentary *Gimme Somethin' to Dance To!* (1995) explores bhangra music in New York City and its relationship to South Asian diasporic youth identity.

FAYE D. GINSBURG is director of the Center for Media, Culture, and History at New York University, where she is also the David Kriser Professor of Anthropology. Her work addresses cultural activism and movements for social transformation, from her work on abortion activism *(Contested Lives: The Abortion Debate in an American Community)* and reproduction more generally *(Conceiving the New World Order: The Global Politics of Reproduction,* with Rayna Rapp), to her longstanding interest in ethnographic and indigenous media. She is currently completing a book on that topic entitled *Mediating Culture.*

ANNETTE HAMILTON is dean of arts and social sciences, University of New South Wales, Sydney, Australia. Inspired by the kinds of questions raised in Australia among Aboriginal people, she began research on media and culture in Thailand in 1985 and was particularly interested in the existence of a Thai media environment with very little foreign programming. More recently she has worked on tourism and on media, culture, and identity in the Southern Thai border zones and has written on everyday life in Bangkok, broadcasting on the border, and tribal minorities and internal colonialism. She is currently completing a book on culture, media, and modernity in Thailand.

JEFF D. HIMPELE is an anthropologist and ethnographic filmmaker who has taught most recently at New York University and Princeton. His most recent films include *Taypi Kala: Six Visions in Tiwanaku* (1994) and *Incidents of Travel in Chichen Itza* (1997). He has written on film distribution as a form of power/knowledge and social mediation in Bolivia. Other current research in Bolivia includes work on the indigenous middle class and capitalism, and on the history of cinema, video, and modernity. He is currently writing a book on television, popular politics, and the indigenous public sphere in La Paz, Bolivia.

MARK HOBART is senior lecturer in anthropology at the School of Oriental and African Studies in London, where he mainly teaches on non-Western media. He specializes in Southeast Asia and has done extensive research in Indonesia, on Bali in particular. He works on culture and media, philosophical issues and eurocentrism in the human sciences, and theater and mass media in Indonesia, themes explored in his recent book *After Culture: Anthropology as Radical Metaphysical Critique.* He is currently completing a monograph for Comedia, *Why Does Anthropology Matter to Media Studies?*

BRIAN LARKIN teaches anthropology at Barnard College, Columbia University. He conducts research on media and transnational flows of culture and religion in Nigeria. He has published on cinema and urban space, on the popularity of Indian films in Nigeria, and on Nigerian videos and the privatization of media. He is finishing a book on media and urbanization in Northern Nigeria. Currently he is Pionier Fellow at the Amsterdam School of Social Science Research.

RUTH MANDEL is a lecturer in social anthropology at University College London. She has published numerous articles based on her research on Turks in Germany, focusing on ethnicity, Islam, diaspora, and migration. Her current research interests include media, development, and nationalism in Central Asia, particularly in Kazakhstan, and the migration to Germany of Central Asia's deported Volga German population.

PURNIMA MANKEKAR is associate professor of anthropology at Stanford University. She is the author of several articles and a book, *Screening Culture, Viewing Politics: An Ethnography of Television, Womanhood, and Nation in Postcolonial India*. She is currently working on a project that examines South Asian public cultures from a transnational perspective.

MEG MCLAGAN is assistant professor of anthropology at New York University, where she teaches in the Program in Culture and Media. She has published several articles and completed a manuscript on the transnational Tibet Movement. She is currently developing a project on the relationship among globalization, media, and the emergence of new political formations. She is also a filmmaker and has worked on a range of independent film and video pieces in New York City since 1985.

ROSALIND C. MORRIS is associate professor in the Department of Anthropology at Columbia University, where she is also director of the Institute for Research on Women and Gender. She is the author of *New Worlds from Fragments: Film, Ethnography, and the Representation of Northwest Coast Cultures* and *In the Place of Origins: Modernity and Its Mediums in Northern Thailand*. Her articles on photography, sexuality, and the intellectual history of anthropology have appeared in the journals *Social Text, Public Culture, positions,* and *differences*. Her current work concerns the relationships between value and accident, and the mass mediation of disaster.

CHRISTOPHER PINNEY teaches material culture in the Department of Anthropology, University College London. For many years he taught South Asian anthropology at the School of Oriental and African Studies and has held visiting positions at the Australian National University, the University of Chicago, and the University of Capetown. He is the author of *Camera Indica* and coeditor (with Rachel Dwyer) of *Pleasure and the Nation*. His recent articles on popular Hindi chromolithography have appeared in *Critical Inquiry* and *Subaltern Studies X*.

HARALD E. L. PRINS is professor of anthropology at Kansas State University and visual anthropology editor for the *American Anthropologist*. Hailing from the Netherlands, he was trained in anthropology, history, and filmmaking. He has conducted extensive research among tribal peoples in North and South America and has been active in cultural survival and native rights advocacy issues. He has also written many articles on Algonquian ethnohistory and visual anthropology and is author of *The Mi'Kmaq: Resistance, Accommodation, and Cultural Survival*, coeditor of *American Beginnings: Exploration, Culture, and Cartography in the Land of Norumbega*, and coproducer of the documentary film *Our Lives in Our Hands*. He has also been a consultant for several other documentaries, including *Wabanaki: A New Dawn*. He is currently involved in an Apache tribal film project and has joined the land claims team of the Miawpukek First Nation in Newfoundland.

LOUISA SCHEIN is associate professor of anthropology at Rutgers University and writes on post-Mao China's cultural politics. She is the author of many articles on gender, ethnicity, and representation, and a book, *Minority Rules: The Miao and the Feminine in China's Cultural Politics*. She is currently working on a book about Hmong/Miao diasporic identities, transnationalism, and media.

DEBRA SPITULNIK is associate professor of anthropology at Emory University. Her research interests include media culture and media discourse, nationalism and national identity, code-switching and hybrid language use, and the experiences of modernity in Africa. She is the author of *Media Connections and Disconnections: Radio Culture and the Public Sphere in Zambia*. She is currently working on a book manuscript entitled "Voicing the Nation: Verbal Art and the Public in Zambian Talk Radio," which is about the thirty-year legacy of the most popular talk show in Zambian history.

TERENCE TURNER is professor of anthropology at Cornell University. He has conducted field research among the Kayapo of Central Brazil since 1962. His numerous writings on them cover social organization, myth, ritual, history, politics, interethnic contact, and aspects of cultural, social, political, and ideological change. He has also made ethnographic films about the Kayapo with the British Broadcasting Company and Granada Television; since 1991 he has directed the Kayapo Video Project, which has enabled the Kayapo to shoot and edit videos about their own culture and encounters with the Brazilians. He served on the American Anthropological Association's Ethics Committee (1969–72) and Committee for Human Rights (1992–97) and was head of the AAA Special Commission to Investigate the Situation for Brazilian Yanomami in 1991. In 1998 he received the Solon T. Kimball Award for outstanding contributions to the application of anthropology to human rights and development issues from the American Anthropological Association.

RICHARD R. WILK is professor of anthropology at Indiana University and chair of the department. He has worked in Belize since 1973 on a wide variety of issues, including consumerism, development, ecotourism, and indigenous land rights. His most recent books include a collection of essays about beauty pageants around the world, *Beauty on the Global Stage* (coedited with Colleen Cohen and Beverly Stoeltje); *Anthropology and the Environment* (edited with Nora Haenn); and a monograph called *Economics and Cultures*. He is currently working on issues connecting consumption, gender, and globalization, as well as on sustainability and energy consumption.

MAYFAIR MEI-HUI YANG teaches anthropology at the University of California at Santa Barbara. She is the author of *Gifts, Favors, and Banquets: The Art of Social Relationships in China*, the editor of *Spaces of Their Own: Women's Public Sphere in Transnational China*, and the director/producer of the documentaries *Through Chinese Women's Eyes* and *Public and Private Realms in Rural Wenzhou China*. At Princeton University's Institute for Advanced Study, she has been working on a book on civil society and popular religion and lineage revival in rural southeastern China, which includes work on a pilgrimage from Taiwan to China of worshippers of the maritime goddess Mazu and the coverage by satellite television.

INDEX

Note: Page numbers in italics indicate illustrations.

Text:	10/12 Baskerville
Display:	Baskerville
Compositor:	Integrated Composition Systems
Printer and binder:	Malloy
Indexer:	Ruth Elwell